Reader's Digest
GREAT
BIOGRAPHIES

*Reader's
Digest*

GREAT BIOGRAPHIES

*selected
and
condensed by
the editors
of
Reader's
Digest*

The Reader's Digest Association, Inc.
Pleasantville, New York
Cape Town, Hong Kong, London, Montreal, Sydney

READER'S DIGEST CONDENSED BOOKS

Editor-in-Chief: Barbara J. Morgan
Executive Editor: Tanis H. Erdmann
Senior Managing Editor: Marjorie Palmer
Managing Editors: Jean E. Aptakin, Thomas Froncek, Herbert H. Lieberman
Senior Staff Editors: Anne H. Atwater, Joseph P. McGrath, James J. Menick,
Angela H. Plowden-Wardlaw, Virginia Rice (Rights), Ray Sipherd
Senior Editors: Dana Adkins, M. Tracy Brigden, Catherine T. Brown,
Linn Carl, Thomas S. Clemmons, Maureen A. Mackey, John R. Roberson
Senior Associate Editor: Catharine L. Edmonds
Associate Editors: Christopher W. Davis, Ainslie Gilligan,
Alice Jones-Miller, Julie E. Sanders
Senior Copy Editors: Maxine Bartow, Claire A. Bedolis,
Jeane Garment, Jane F. Neighbors
Senior Associate Copy Editors: Rosalind H. Campbell, Jean S. Friedman
Associate Copy Editors: Jeanette Gingold, Daphne Hougham, Tatiana Ivanow,
Marilyn J. Knowlton, Charles Pendergast, Joan R. Wilkinson
Editorial Administrator: Ann M. Dougher
Art Director: Angelo Perrone
Executive Art Editors: William Gregory, Soren Noring
Associate Art Editors: George Calas, Jr., Katherine Kelleher

CB INTERNATIONAL EDITIONS
Managing Editor: Gary Q. Arpin
Associate Editors: Bonnie Grande, Eva C. Jaunzems, Antonius L. Koster

The credits and acknowledgments that appear on pages 606–608
are hereby made part of this copyright page.
Copyright © 1989 by The Reader's Digest Association, Inc.
Copyright © 1989 by The Reader's Digest Association (Canada) Ltd.
Copyright © 1989 by Reader's Digest (Australia) Pty. Limited
Copyright © 1989 by The Reader's Digest Association South Africa (Pty.) Limited
Copyright © 1989 by Reader's Digest Association Far East Limited
Philippines copyright 1989 by Reader's Digest Association Far East Limited
Reader's Digest, The Digest and the Pegasus logo
are registered trademarks of The Reader's Digest Association, Inc.

FIRST EDITION

All rights reserved. Unauthorized reproduction, in any manner, is prohibited.
Library of Congress Cataloging-in-Publication Data
(Revised for vol. 5-12)
Reader's digest great biographies.
Contents: v. 1. The Spirit of Saint Louis/by Charles A. Lindbergh. Florence
Nightingale/by Cecil Woodham-Smith. Edison/by Matthew Josephson. Hans Christian
Andersen/by Rumer Godden—[etc.]—v. 11. Captain Bligh and Mr. Christian/by
Richard Hough. The agony and the ecstasy/by Irving Stone. The life and work of
Sigmund Freud/by Ernest Jones. Good night, sweet prince/by Gene Fowler—
v. 12. St. Francis of Assisi/by E. M. Almedingen. Napoleon/by Emil Ludwig.
Act one/by Moss Hart. My early life/by Winston S. Churchill.
1. Biography—Collected works. I. Reader's Digest Association.
II. Reader's digest. III. Great biographies.
CT101.R42   1987   920'.02   86-29816
ISBN 0-89577-259-0 (v.1)   ISBN 0-89577-300-7 (v.8)
Printed in the United States of America

Contents

A CONDENSATION OF

The
Autobiography of
BENJAMIN
FRANKLIN

Introduction

by Bruce Bliven

OF THE FAMOUS HEROES of America's past, most seem to inspire awe. Washington was so severely perfect that even those close to him were a little afraid of him. Those who came in contact with Jefferson were taken aback by his intellect. Lincoln had the common touch, yet his image is tinged with a majestic sadness. But there is one famous person of whom no one can think without a glow of personal warmth. Benjamin Franklin, printer and author, philosopher and statesman, scientist and inventor, was in some respects the greatest man this continent has produced. In any age he would have been extraordinary. Mirabeau, the French revolutionary leader, called him the philosopher who did most to extend the rights of man over the whole earth. "Antiquity would have raised altars to this mighty genius," he declared.

Franklin's appearance commanded instant liking and respect. His glance was steady and kindly. He had big gray eyes set in a large face, a wide and humorous mouth and, as a young man, ample blond hair and the build and energy of an athlete.

Born in Boston in 1706, the fifteenth of seventeen children of a poor candlemaker, Franklin was to become the first self-made

American, breaking the rigid class bonds inherited from England. He had little more than a year of formal schooling, and almost everything he knew—in science, philosophy and languages—he taught himself; yet by the age of forty-two he had made a modest fortune and retired from business—only to spend forty years more in the service of his country.

IN HIS TIME Franklin was perhaps the best-known writer of the English-speaking world. The first great publishing success in America was *Poor Richard's Almanack*, started by Franklin when he was twenty-six. His *Autobiography*, though he never found time to finish it, is still one of the most widely read books of its kind.* He wrote the first part of it in two weeks, in England and from memory, recording correctly names and dates of forty and fifty years earlier.

Historians of science bracket Franklin with Newton as the first two important scientific figures of the modern age. Everyone has heard how Franklin drew electricity from a cloud on a kite string, but few are aware that he was the first to identify positive and negative electricity; we owe to him the words and concepts for battery, electric charge, condenser, conductor.

In 1744 Franklin organized the American Philosophical Society, the first scientific association of the country— "Philosophy" in those days embraced natural science. For its first fifty years the Society was in practice a national academy of science, as well as the first national library and museum and the first patent office.

His inventiveness was displayed in more practical ways as well. Franklin's mechanical hand for lifting objects from a high shelf and his kitchen stool that unfolds into a stepladder are still in use to this day. At seventy-eight he invented that blessing of the elderly: bifocal spectacles. Mozart and Beethoven com-

---

*EDITORS' NOTE: The *Autobiography* covers Franklin's life only until 1757. Part I was composed in 1771 as a letter to his son; later parts, written after the Revolutionary War, are more formal in tone, as if for a larger audience; for Franklin became estranged from his son when the latter sided with the British during the Revolution. Parts I, II and II^r are here given. Part IV, which is very brief and concerns the details of an embassy to London, has been omitted.

posed music for his "glass harmonica"—a series of glass hemispheres mounted on a rod and touched by the finger while revolving, to make music. He was a skilled performer on the harp, guitar and violin. Franklin also charted the Gulf Stream, and discovered that storms rotate while traveling forward. His influence in scientific matters was so strong that thirty years after his death the Franklin Institute was created in Philadelphia to interpret science and technology to the layman.

AS STATESMAN, Franklin was the first to think in terms of the nation rather than of separate colonies. Two decades before the Revolutionary War he invented the dual system of state governments united under a federal authority. During his years in London he presented the American case unceasingly. On a famous occasion he stood all day in the House of Commons, skillfully answering members' questions about American opposition to the hated Stamp Act. As a result Parliament repealed the Act, and war was thereby postponed for a decade. Sent to France in 1776, he persuaded the reluctant monarchy to send supplies secretly to General Washington, and finally to enter the war openly as an ally.

After the British were beaten, Franklin prevented collapse of the Constitutional Convention. The small states wanted equal representation in Congress, the big ones wanted delegations based on population. Franklin engineered the compromise under which the Senate is based on the first plan and the House on the second. When the Constitution was finally written, Benjamin Franklin more than any other man was responsible for getting it ratified by the states.

FRANKLIN'S LONG LIFE was at least partly due to his intelligence about health, and for half a century he poured out advice for successful living. Since he stuck to basic truths, nearly everything he said is valid today.

Throughout his long life Franklin had the deep humility of greatness. When in his old age he wrote the inscription for a new cornerstone of the library he had established, the first in Pennsylvania, he struck his name off the list to be carved on it.

Benjamin Franklin left his beloved France for the last time in 1785, at the age of seventy-nine. The people of Passy, where he had been living, clustered around the sedan chair in which illness forced him to travel, many of them weeping and imploring him to stay. Though he was suffering from a stone in the bladder, his spirit was unshakable. He afterward served as president of the Pennsylvania executive council, and as delegate to the Federal Constitutional Convention of 1787.

At eighty-two, he retired from public life. A few months later he received this letter: "If the united wishes of a free people, joined with the earnest prayers of every friend to science and humanity, could relieve the body from pain and infirmities, you could claim an exemption on this score. As long as I retain my memory you will be thought of with respect, veneration and affection by, dear Sir, your sincere friend and obedient humble servant, G. Washington."

The following year, 1790, Franklin died at eighty-four, the most famous private citizen and the best-loved public figure in the world. His funeral was the largest ever seen, up to that time, for any person not in office. The entire French government went into mourning for three days, and Jefferson wanted the American government to do the same. Washington regretfully said no, not wishing to set a precedent that might later prove embarrassing.

One of the best-known epitaphs ever written is the one Franklin composed for himself when still a young man: "The Body of B. Franklin, Printer, Like the Cover of an old Book, its Contents torn out, and stript of its Lettering and Gilding, lies here, Food for Worms. But the work shall not be wholly lost: for it will, as he believed, appear once more in a new & more perfect Edition, corrected and amended by the Author."

Dear Son,

I have ever had a Pleasure in obtaining any little Anecdotes of my Ancestors. You may remember the Enquiries I made among the Remains of my Relations when you were with me in England, and the Notes one of my Uncles (who had the same kind of Curiosity in collecting Family Anecdotes) once put into my Hands, furnish'd me with several Particulars relating to our Ancestors. From these Notes I learnt that the Family had liv'd in the same Village, Ecton in Northamptonshire, for 300 Years, and how much longer he knew not, (perhaps from the Time when the Name of Franklin that before was the Name of an Order of People was assumed by them as a Surname, when others took Surnames all over the Kingdom) on a Freehold of about 30 Acres, aided by the Smith's Business which had continued in the Family till his Time, the eldest Son being always bred to that Business. — When I search'd the Registers at Ecton, I found an Account of their Births, Marriages and Burials, from the Year 1555 only, there being no Register kept in that Parish at any time preceding. By that Register I perceiv'd that I was the youngest Son of the youngest Son for 5 Generations back. My Grandfather Thomas, who was born in 1598, lived at Ecton till he grew too old to follow Business longer, when he went to live with his Son John, a Dyer at Banbury in Oxfordshire, with whom my Father served an Apprenticeship. There my Grandfather died

and the Journey I took for that purpose.
7 Now imagining it may be equally agreeable to you to know the Circumstances of my Life, many of which you are yet unacquainted with; and expecting a Weeks uninterrupted Leisure in my present Country Retirement, I sit down to write them for you. To which I have besides some other Inducements. Having emerg'd from the Poverty & Obscurity in which I was born & bred, to a State of Affluence & some Degree of Reputation in the World, the Means I made use of that conduced to that and having gone so far thro' Life with a considerable Share of Felicity, the conducing Means I made use of, which with the Blessing of God so well succeeded, my Posterity may like to know, as they may find some of them suitable to their own Situations, & therefore fit to be imitated. — That Felicity, when I reflected on it, has induced me sometimes to say, that were it offer'd to my Choice, I should have no Objection to a Repetition of the same Life from its Beginning, only asking the Advantages Authors have in a second Edition to correct some Faults of the first. So would I if I might besides correcting the Faults change some sinister Accidents & Events of it for others more favourable. But tho' this were deny'd, I should still accept the Offer. Since such a Repetition is not to be expected, the next Thing most like living one's Life.

PART ONE

Twyford, at the Bishop of St. Asaph's 1771.

Dear Son,

I have ever had a pleasure in obtaining any little anecdotes of my ancestors. You may remember the enquiries I made among the remains of my relations when you were with me in England; and the journey I took for that purpose. Now imagining it may be equally agreeable to you to know the circumstances of *my* life, many of which you are yet unacquainted with; and expecting a week's uninterrupted leisure in my present country retirement, I sit down to write them for you. To which I have besides some other inducements. Having with the blessing of God emerged from the poverty and obscurity in which I was born and bred, to a state of affluence and some degree of reputation in the world, and having gone so far through life with a considerable share of felicity, my posterity may like to know the means I made use of, as they may find some of them suitable to their own situations, and therefore fit to be imitated. That felicity, when I reflected on it, has induced me sometimes to say, that were it offered to my choice, I should have no objection to a repetition of the same life from its beginning, only asking the advantage authors have in a second edition to correct some

The first handwritten page of Benjamin Franklin's "Autobiography."

faults of the first. However, since such a repetition is not to be expected, the next thing most like living one's life over again, seems to be a *recollection* of that life; and to make that recollection as durable as possible, the putting it down in writing. Hereby, too, I shall indulge the inclination so natural in old men, to be talking of themselves and their own past actions, and I shall indulge it, without being troublesome to others who through respect to age might think themselves obliged to give me a hearing, since this may be read or not as anyone pleases.

And now I speak of thanking God. I desire to acknowledge, that I owe the happiness of my past life to his kind Providence, which led me to the means I used and gave them success.

The notes one of my uncles (who had the same kind of curiosity in collecting family anecdotes) once put into my hands, furnished me with several particulars relating to our ancestors. From these notes I learnt that the family had lived in the same village, Ecton in Northamptonshire, for three hundred years, and how much longer he knew not, on a freehold of about thirty acres, aided by the smith's business which had continued in the family till his time, the eldest son being always bred to that business. When I searched the register at Ecton, I found an account of their births, marriages and burials, from the year 1555 only, there being no register kept in that parish at any time preceding. By that register I perceived that I was the youngest son of the youngest son for five generations back.

My grandfather Thomas, who was born in 1598, lived at Ecton till he grew too old to follow business longer, when he went to live with his son John, a dyer at Banbury in Oxfordshire, with whom my father served an apprenticeship. There my grandfather died and lies buried. We saw his gravestone in 1758. His eldest son Thomas lived in the house at Ecton, and left it with the land to his only child, a daughter, who with her husband, one Fisher of Wellingborough sold it to Mr. Isted, now lord of the manor there. My grandfather had four sons that grew up, viz. Thomas, John, Benjamin and Josiah. Thomas was bred a smith under his father, but being ingenious, and encouraged in learning by a gentleman in his parish, he qualified for the business of scrivener, and became a considerable man in county affairs, and a chief mover of public-spirited undertakings. The account we received of his life and character from some old people at Ecton, I remember struck you, as something extraordinary from its similarity to what you knew of mine. Had he died on the same day I was born, you said one might have supposed a transmigration.

This obscure family of ours was early in the Reformation, and continued Protestants through the reign of Queen Mary, when they were sometimes in danger of trouble on account of their zeal against Popery. They had got an English Bible, and to conceal it, it was fastened open with tapes under and within the frame of a stool. When my great-great-grandfather read in it to his family, he turned up the stool upon his knees, turning over the leaves then under the tapes. One of the children stood at the door to give notice if he saw the apparitor coming, who was an officer of the spiritual court. In that case the stool was turned down again upon its feet, when the Bible remained concealed under it as before.

Josiah, my father, married young, and about 1682 carried his wife with three children unto New England, where they expected to enjoy their mode of religion with freedom. By the same wife he had four children more born there, and by a second wife, my mother, ten more, in all seventeen, of which I remember thirteen sitting at one time at his table, who all grew up to be men and women, and married. I was born in Boston, New England. My mother was Abiah Folger, a daughter of Peter Folger, one of the first settlers of New England.

I was the youngest son and the youngest child but two. My elder brothers were all put apprentices to different trades. I was put to the grammar school at eight years of age, my father intending to devote me as the tithe of his sons to the service of the Church. My early readiness in learning to read (which must have been very early, as I do not remember when I could not read) and the opinion of all his friends that I should certainly make a scholar, encouraged him in his purpose. I continued however at the grammar school not quite one year, tho' in that time I had risen gradually to be the head of the class, and was removed into the next class above it. But my father in the meantime, from a view of the expense of a college education which he could not well afford, and the mean living many so educated were afterwards able to obtain, reasons he gave to his friends in my hearing, altered his first intention, and taking me from the grammar school, he sent me to a school for writing and arithmetic. There I acquired fair writing pretty soon, but I failed in the arithmetic, and made no progress in it.

At ten years old, I was taken home to assist my father in his business, which was that of a tallow chandler and soap boiler. Accordingly I was employed in cutting wick for the candles, filling the dipping mold, and the molds for cast candles, attending the shop, going errands, &c. I disliked the trade and had a strong inclination for the sea; but my father declared against it; however, living near the water, I was much in and about it.

I learnt early to swim well,* and to manage boats, and when in a boat with other boys I was commonly allowed to govern, especially in any case of difficulty. Sometimes I led them into scrapes, of which I will mention one instance, as it shows an early public spirit, tho' not then justly conducted. There was a salt marsh that bounded part of the mill pond, on the edge of which at high water, we used to fish for minnows. By much trampling, we had made it a mere quagmire. My proposal was to build a wharf there fit for us to stand upon, and I showed my comrades a large heap of stones which were intended for a new house near the marsh, and which would very well suit our purpose. Accordingly in the evening when the workmen were gone, I assembled my playfellows, and working with them diligently like so many emmets [ants], sometimes two or three to a stone, we brought them all away and built our little wharf. The

---

From an undated letter to Barbeu Dubourg: When I was a boy, I made two oval palettes, each about ten inches long and six broad, with a hole for the thumb, in order to retain it fast in the palm of my hand. They much resembled a painter's palettes. In swimming I pushed the edges of these forward, and I struck the water with their flat surfaces as I drew them back. I remember I swam faster by means of these palettes, but they fatigued my wrists . . . I also amused myself one day with flying a paper kite; and approaching the bank of a pond, which was near a mile broad, I tied the string to a stake, and the kite ascended to a very considerable height above the pond while I was swimming. In a little time, being desirous of amusing myself with my kite and at the same time

next morning the workmen, missing the stones, found them in our wharf; we were complained of; several of us were corrected by our fathers; and tho' I pleaded the usefulness of the work, mine convinced me that nothing was useful which was not honest.

I think you may like to know something of his person and character. He had an excellent constitution of body, was of middle stature, but well set and very strong. He was ingenious, could draw prettily, was skilled a little in music and had a clear pleasing voice, so that when he played psalm tunes on his violin and sung withal as he sometimes did in an evening, it was extremely agreeable to hear.

He had a mechanical genius too, and on occasion was very handy in the use of other tradesmen's tools. But his great excellence lay in a sound understanding, and solid judgment in prudential matters, both in private and public affairs. In the latter indeed he was never employed, the straitness of his circumstances keeping him close to his trade. But I remember well his being frequently visited by leading people, who consulted him for his opinion in affairs of the town or of the church he belonged to. He was also much consulted by private persons about their affairs, and frequently chosen an arbitrator between contending parties.

At his table he liked to have some sensible friend to converse with, and always took care to start some useful topic for discourse, which might improve the minds of his children. By this means he turned our attention to what was good, just, and prudent in the conduct of life; and little or no notice was ever taken of the victuals on the table, whether in or out of season,

---

of swimming, I returned. Loosing from the stake the string with the little stick which was fastened to it, I went again into the water, where I found that, lying on my back and holding the stick in my hands, I was drawn along the surface of the water in a very agreeable manner. Having then engaged another boy to carry my clothes round the pond to a place on the other side, I began to cross the pond with my kite, which carried me quite over without the least fatigue and with the greatest pleasure imaginable. I was only obliged occasionally to halt a little in my course, and resist its progress, when it appeared that by following too quick I lowered the kite too much; by doing which occasionally I made it rise again. I have never since that time practiced this singular mode of swimming, though I think it not impossible to cross in this manner from Dover to Calais. The packet boat, however, is still preferable.

of good or bad flavor. So that I was brought up in such a perfect inattention to those matters as to be quite indifferent what kind of food was set before me; and so unobservant of it, that to this day, if I am asked I can scarce tell, a few hours after dinner, what I dined upon. This has been a convenience to me in

BEN FRANKLIN'S BIRTHPLACE

Thomas Franklin

| Thomas | Benjamin |

John   Josiah and Ann Franklin *(first wife)*

| Elizabeth | Hannah | Ann | Joseph |
| *1677(?)-1759* | *1683-1723* | *1687-1729* | *1689-1689* |

| Samuel | Josiah | Joseph |
| *1681-1720* | *1685-c.1715* | *1688-1688* |

Josiah and Abiah Franklin *(second wife)*

| John | Mary | Sarah | Thomas | Lydia |
| *1690-1756* | *1694-1731* | *1699-1731* | *1703-1706* | *1708-1758* |

| Peter | James | Ebenezer | Benjamin | Jane |
| *1692-1766* | *1696(?)-1735* | *1701-1703* | *1706-1790* | *1712-1794* |

traveling, where my companions have been sometimes very unhappy for want of a suitable gratification of their more delicate because better instructed tastes and appetites.

My mother had likewise an excellent constitution. She suckled all her ten children. I never knew either my father or mother to have any sickness but that of which they died, he at eighty-nine and she at eighty-five years of age. They lie buried together at Boston, where I years since placed a marble stone over their grave with this inscription

Josiah Franklin
And Abiah his Wife
Lie here interred.
They lived lovingly together in Wedlock
Fifty-five Years.
By constant labour and Industry,
With God's Blessing,
They maintained a large Family
Comfortably;
And brought up thirteen Children,
And seven Grand Children
Reputably.
From this Instance, Reader,
Be encouraged to Diligence in thy Calling,
And distrust not Providence.
He was a pious & prudent Man,
She a discreet and virtuous Woman.
Their youngest Son,
In filial Regard to their Memory,
Places this Stone.
J.F. born 1655—died 1744. Ætat 89
A.F. born 1667—died 1752——85

By my rambling digressions I perceive myself to be grown
old. But one does not dress for private company as for a public
ball. 'Tis perhaps only negligence.

To return. I continued employed in my father's business for
two years, that is till I was twelve years old; and my brother
John, who was bred to that business having left my father, married and set up for himself at Rhode Island, there was all appearance that I was destined to supply his place and be a tallow
chandler. But my dislike to the trade continuing, my father was
under apprehensions that if he did not find one for me more
agreeable, I should break away and get to sea, as his son Josiah
had done to his great vexation. He therefore sometimes took
me to walk with him, and see joiners, bricklayers, turners,
braziers, &c. at their work, that he might observe my inclination, and endeavor to fix it on some trade on land. It has ever

since been a pleasure to me to see good workmen handle their tools; and it has been useful to me, having learnt so much by it, as to be able to do little jobs myself in my house, and to construct machines for my experiments.

From a child I was fond of reading, and all the little money that came into my hands was ever laid out in books. Pleased with *The Pilgrim's Progress*, my first collection was of John Bunyan's works, in separate little volumes. I afterwards sold them to enable me to buy R. Burton's historical collections. My father's library consisted chiefly of books in polemic divinity, most of which I read, and have since often regretted, that at a time when I had such a thirst for knowledge, more proper books had not fallen in my way. Plutarch's *Lives* there was, in which I read abundantly, and I still think that time spent to great advantage. There was also a book of Dr. Cotton Mather's, called *Essays to do Good* which perhaps gave me a turn of thinking that had an influence on some of the principal events of my life.

"I was to serve as an apprentice till I was twenty-one."

This bookish inclination at length determined my father to make me a printer, tho' he had already one son, (James) of that profession, with his business in Boston. I liked it much better than that of my father, but still had a hankering for the sea. To prevent the effect of such an inclination, my father was impatient to have me bound to my brother. I stood out some time, but at last was persuaded and signed the indentures, when I was yet but twelve years old. I was to serve as an apprentice till I was twenty-one, only I was to be allowed journeyman's wages during the last year. In a little time I made great proficiency in the business, and became a useful hand to my brother.

I now had access to better books. An acquaintance with the apprentices of booksellers, enabled me sometimes to borrow a small one, which I was careful to return soon and clean. Often I sat up in my room reading the greatest part of the night, when the book was borrowed in the evening and to be returned early in the morning lest it should be missed.

After some time an ingenious tradesman Mr. Matthew Adams who frequented our printing house, took notice of me, invited me to his library, and kindly lent me such books as I chose to read. I now took a fancy to poetry, and made some little pieces. My brother, thinking it might turn to account encouraged me, and put me on composing two occasional ballads. One was called the *Light House Tragedy*, and contained an account of the drowning of Captain Worthylake with his two daughters; the other was a sailor song on the taking of Teach or Blackbeard the pirate.

They were wretched stuff, in the Grub Street ballad style, but my brother printed them and sent me about the town to sell them. The first sold wonderfully, the event having recently made a great noise. This flattered my vanity. But my father discouraged me, by ridiculing my performances, and telling me verse-makers were generally beggars; so I escaped being a poet, most probably a very bad one. But as prose writing has been of great use to me in the course of my life, and was a principal means of my advancement, I shall tell you how I acquired what little ability I have in that way.

There was another bookish lad in the town, John Collins by name, with whom I was intimately acquainted. Very fond we were of argument, and very desirous of confuting one another. Which disputatious turn, by the way, is apt to become a bad habit, making people often extremely disagreeable in company, and thence, besides souring and spoiling the conversation, is productive of disgusts and perhaps enmities. I had caught it by reading my father's books of dispute about religion. Persons of good sense, I have since observed, seldom fall into it.

A question was once somehow or other started between Collins and me, of the propriety of educating the female sex in learning. He was of opinion that it was improper; and that they were naturally unequal to it. I took the contrary side, perhaps a little for dispute's sake.* I put my arguments in writing, which I copied fair and sent to him. He answered. Three or four letters had passed, when my father happened to find my papers, and read them. He observed that tho' I had the advantage of my antagonist in correct spelling and punctuation (which I owed to the printing house) I fell far short in elegance of expression, in method and in perspicuity. I saw the justice of his remarks and thence determined to endeavor at improvement in the manner of writing.

About this time I met with an odd volume of the *Spectator*.** I bought it, read it over and over, and was much delighted with it. I thought the writing excellent, and wished if possible to imitate it. With that view, I took some of the papers, and making short hints of the sentiment in each sentence, laid them by a few days, and then without looking at the book, tried to complete the papers again, by expressing each hinted sentiment in any suitable words that should come to hand.

Then I compared my *Spectator* with the original, discovered some of my faults and corrected them. But I found I wanted a stock of words, which I thought I should have acquired before that time, if I had gone on making verses, since the continual occasion for words to suit the measure, or for the rhyme, would have laid me under a constant necessity of searching for variety, and made me master of it. Therefore I took some of the tales and turned them into verse; and when I had pretty well forgotten the prose, turned them back again.

I also sometimes jumbled my collections of hints into confusion, and after some weeks, endeavored to reduce them into the best order. This was to teach me method in the arrangement of thoughts. I had the pleasure of fancying that in certain particulars of small import, I had been lucky enough to improve

---

*Later on Franklin saw to it that his daughter Sally learned French and music as well as such "useful" subjects as arithmetic and bookkeeping, and in England he helped his landlady's daughter, Polly Stevenson, to acquire some understanding of science.
**A paper issued daily between March 1, 1711, and December 6, 1712, containing essays by Joseph Addison and Richard Steele.

the method or the language of the original and this encouraged me to think I might possibly in time come to be a tolerable English writer, of which I was extremely ambitious.

My time for these exercises was at night, or before work in the morning; or on Sundays, when I contrived to be in the printing house alone, evading as much as I could the common attendance on public worship, which my father used to exact of me when I was under his care; and which indeed I still thought a duty; tho' I could not, as it seemed to me, afford the time to practice it.

When about sixteen years of age, I happened to meet with a book, written by one Thomas Tryon, recommending a vegetable diet. I determined to go into it. My brother being yet unmarried, boarded himself and his apprentices in another family. My refusing to eat flesh occasioned an inconveniency, and I was frequently chid for my singularity. I made myself acquainted with Tryon's manner of boiling potatoes or rice, making hasty pudding, and a few others, and then proposed to my brother, that if he would give me weekly half the money he paid for my board I would board myself. My brother instantly agreed, and I presently found that I could save half what he paid me. This was an additional fund for buying books. But I had another advantage in it. My brother and the rest going from the printing house to their meals, I remained there alone, and dispatching my light repast, (which often was no more than a biscuit or a slice of bread, a handful of raisins or a tart from the pastry cook's, and a glass of water) had the rest of the time till their return, for study, in which I made the greater progress from that greater clearness of head and quicker apprehension which usually attend temperance in eating and drinking.

Now it was that being on some occasion made ashamed of my ignorance in figures, I took Cocker's book of arithmetic, and went through the whole by myself with great ease. I also read Seller's and Sturmy's books of navigation, and became acquainted with the little geometry they contain. And I read Locke's *Essay Concerning Human Understanding*, and *Logic: or the Art of Thinking* by Messrs. du Port Royal, and an English grammar at the end of which there were two little sketches of the arts of rhetoric and logic, the latter finishing with a specimen of a dispute in the Socratic method.

I was charmed with this method, adopted it, dropped my abrupt contradiction, and positive argumentation, and put on the humble role of enquirer and doubter. And being then become a real doubter in many points of our religious doctrine, I found this method safest for myself and very embarrassing to those against whom I used it. Therefore I took a delight in it, practiced it and grew very artful in drawing people even of superior knowledge into concessions the consequences of which they did not foresee, so obtaining victories that neither myself nor my cause always deserved.

I continued this method some years, but gradually left it, retaining only the habit of expressing myself in terms of modest diffidence, never using when I advance anything that may possibly be disputed, the words, *certainly*, *undoubtedly*, or any others that give the air of positiveness to an opinion; but rather say, I conceive, or I apprehend a thing to be so or so, It appears to me, or I should think it so for such and such reasons, or I imagine it to be so, or it is so if I am not mistaken. This habit I believe has been of great advantage to me, when I have had occasion to persuade men into measures that I have been from time to time engaged in promoting.

And as the chief ends of conversation are to *inform*, or to be *informed*, to *please* or to *persuade*, I wish well-meaning sensible men would not lessen their power of doing good by a positive assuming manner that seldom fails to disgust, tends to create opposition, and to defeat every one of those purposes for which speech was given us, to wit, giving or receiving information, or pleasure.

My brother had in 1720 or '21, begun to print a newspaper. It was the second that appeared in America, and was called *The New England Courant*.* The only one before it, was the *Boston News Letter*. I remember his being dissuaded by some of his

---

*Franklin was in error here. *The Boston Gazette*, December 21, 1719, was the second; *The American Weekly Mercury*, December 22, 1719, was the third; and James's *New England Courant*, August 7, 1721, was the fourth.

From SATURDAY November 27. to SATURDAY December 4. 1 7 2 5.

The Life of Jonathan Wild *continu'd.*

E muſt remark here, that tho' *Jonathan* in the main us'd to talk up the Gentlemen of his Game, to be generally bright clever Fellows, yet when he was angry with ſome of them, he would own there were *Scoundrels of the Profeſſion.*

Notwithſtanding this Bounce of *Jonathan's,* the Priſoner underſtood how to ſoften this *Machiavel's* Temper, and thereupon whiſper'd him to go up to his Lodging, and look behind the Head of the Bed, which *Jonathan* did, telling the People of the Houſe, he muſt go up for the Fellow's Cloaths; which he brought down along with him, and in a Hole where the Thief directed him to, he found a Gold Watch, two Silver ones, Rings, and other Things of Value, which he put into his own Pocket, for any Body elſe would not have known what to have done with them; and the Priſoner being carry'd before the Juſtice, was committed on Suſpicion of Felony, and the next Seſſions no Body appearing againſt him, he was diſcharg'd.

The Succeſs that attent on with in his Buſineſs, rendent nous all over *London*, and he made uſe of ſeveral little Arts to make himſelf appear conſiderable to diſtant Parts of the Kingdom; particularly by ſome Printers of News Papers and Dying-Speeches, whom he prevail'd give him a Character therein, in which generally ſtiled, THIEF CATCHER-GENERAL OF GREAT BRITAIN.

His Houſe every where furniſh'd, and ſet out with Plate, Pictures, &c. and when his Wife appear'd abroad it was generally with a Footman in a fine lac'd Livery. He kept a Country Houſe, dreſs'd well, and in Company affected an Air of Grandeur. A little before his Cataſtrophe he promis'd me a Haunch or Side of Veniſon whenever I pleaſed, to ſend to him, ſaying, he had two Parks at his Command, well ſtock'd with Deer.

The Wealth that he was ſuppoſed to have amaſs'd by this Buſineſs, made ſeveral Perſons look upon him with Envy; and ſome well enough acquainted in the Rogueſh Arts, attempted to ſet up againſt him a few Years ago: The Principal were, one *Fe———n,* a ſuperannuated Thief, *Riddleſ———n* an Attorney and Thief, whoſe chief Merit for the Support of his Pretenſions to this Practice, was, his having ſacrilegiouſly and feloniouſly broke open the Royal-Chapel at *Whitehall,* and ſtole thence the Communion Plate, and Mr. *Li———n,* City Mar———l. This laſt, and *Jonathan,* wrote Pamphlets againſt each other, as it was the Cuſtom then between great Men; but *Jonathan* laying himſelf too open, *H———n* dropt the Pen, and took up the Cudgels of the Law, with which he bang'd *Jonathan,* ſo that he thought fit to buy his Peace at the Price of a Sum of Money.

However, none of them all was able to give *Jonathan* any notable Diſturbance in his Office; on the contrary, he found means ſoon after to get *Riddle———n* tranſported for not complying with the Conditions of his Pardon, to make *Felt———n* run mad, and *H———n* entirely to quit his Pretenſions.

Wherefore he turn'd himſelf again to his Buſineſs: And as we were enumerating how many Species of Thieves he had under his Command, we ſhall reſume that Part of our Story.

There were another ſort of Gentry under his Command, whoſe Buſineſs it was to loiter about the Streets in the Day-time; and as Servants who go of ſhort Errants to a Chandler's Shop, or Bakers, are apt to leave the Door a jar, (as they call it) they were to whip in, and ſeize upon the next Thing that was portable, and bring it off. They generally peep'd in, to ſee that no Body was in the Fore Parlours, and if by chance any Body ſhould ſurprize them, they were ready to enquire if ſome Perſon with a ſtrange Name did not live there; tho' it ſeldom falls out ſo, becauſe they generally do their Buſineſs in a Minute.

Theſe ſort of People ſometimes go in Liveries, and ſometimes dreſs'd like Ticket Porters, with Silver Badges either upon their Coats, or about their Necks; one of them ſome time ſince whip'd into a Houſe in *King-Street,* near *Long-acre,* which is divided into Tenements, the People furniſhing their own Lodgings, and going directly up two Pair of Stairs; from whence he ſaw a Woman who inhabited it, come down, he eaſily put back the Lock, and finding nothing in the Room of any Value, except the Bedding, he tied it all up, and was carrying it off, when the Owner happen'd to meet him at the lower end of the Stairs, and aſking him where he was carrying that Bedding, he anſwers

SIR,

IT may not be improper in the first Place to inform your Readers, that I intend once a Fortnight to present them, by the Help of this Paper, with a short Epistle, which I presume will add somewhat to their Entertainment.

And since it is observed, that the Generality of People, now a days, are unwilling either to commend or dispraise what they read, until they are in some measure informed who or what the Author of it is, whether he be *poor* or *rich*, *old* or *young*, a *Schollar* or a *Leather Apron Man*, &c. and give their Opinion of the Performance, according to the Knowledge which they have of the Author's Circumstances, it may not be amiss to begin with a short Account of my past Life and present Condition, that the Reader may not be at a Loss to judge whether or no my Lucubrations are worth his reading.

At the time of my Birth, my Parents were on Ship-board in their Way from *London* to *N England*. My Entrance into this troublesome World was attended with the Death of my Father, a Misfortune, which tho' I was not then capable of knowing, I shall never be able to forget; for as he, poor Man, stood upon the Deck rejoicing at my Birth, a merciless Wave entred the Ship, and in one Moment carry'd him beyond Reprieve. Thus was the *first* Day which I saw, the *last* that was seen by my Father; and thus was my disconsolate Mother at once made both a *Parent* and a *Widow*.

When we arrived at *Boston* (which was not long after) I was put to Nurse in a Country Place, at a small Distance from the Town, where I went to School, and past my Infancy and Childhood in Vanity and Idleness, until I was bound out Apprentice, that I might no longer be a Charge to my Indigent Mother, who was put to hard Shifts for a Living.

My Master was a Country Minister, a pious good-natur'd young Man, & a Batchelor: He labour'd with all his Might to instill vertuous and godly Principles into my tender Soul, well knowing that it was the most suitable Time to make deep and lasting Impressions on the Mind, while it was yet untainted with Vice, free and unbiass'd. He endeavour'd that I might be instructed in all that Knowledge and Learning which is necessary for our Sex, and deny'd me no Accomplishment that could possibly be attained in a Country Place; such as all Sorts of Needle-Work, Writing, Arithmetick, &c. and observing that I took a more than ordinary Delight in reading ingenious Books, he gave me the free Use of his Library, which tho' it was but small, yet it was well chose, to inform the Understanding rightly, and enable the Mind to frame great and noble Ideas.

Before I had liv'd quite two Years with this Reverend Gentleman, my Indulgent Mother departed this Life, leaving me as it were by my self, having no Relation on Earth within my Knowledge.

I will not abuse your Patience with a tedious Recital of all the frivolous Accidents of my Life, that happened from this Time until I arrived to Years of Discretion, only inform you that I liv'd a chearful Country Life, spending my leisure Time either in some innocent Diversion with the neighbouring Females, or in some shady Retirement, with the best of Company, *Books*. Thus I past away the Time with a Mixture of Profit and Pleasure, having no Affliction but what was imaginary, and created in my own Fancy; as nothing is more common with us Women, than to be grieving for nothing, when we have nothing else to grieve for.

As I would not engross too much of your Paper at once, I will defer the Remainder of my Story until my next Letter; in the mean time desiring your Readers to exercise their Patience, and bear with my Humours now and then, because I shall trouble them but seldom. I am not insensible of the Impossibility of pleasing all, but I would not willingly displease any; and for those who will take Offence where none is intended, they are beneath the Notice of

Your Humble Servant,
SILENCE DOGOOD.

friends from the undertaking, as not likely to succeed, one newspaper being in their judgment enough for America. At this time 1771 there are not less than five-and-twenty. He went on however with the undertaking, and after having worked in composing the types and printing off the sheets I was employed to carry the papers through the streets to the customers.

He had some ingenious men among his friends who amused themselves by writing little pieces for this paper, which made it more in demand; and these gentlemen often visited us. Hearing their accounts of the approbation their papers were received with, I was excited to try my hand among them. But being still a boy, and suspecting that my brother would object to printing anything of mine in his paper if he knew it to be mine, I contrived to disguise my hand, and writing an anonymous paper I put it in at night under the door of the printing house. It was found in the morning and communicated to his writing friends when they called in. They read it, commented on it in my hearing, and I had the exquisite pleasure, of finding it met with their approbation, and that in their different guesses at the author none were named but men of some character among us for learning and ingenuity.

I suppose now that I was rather lucky in my judges; and that perhaps they were not really so very good ones as I then esteemed them. Encouraged however by this, I wrote and conveyed in the same way to the press several more papers, which were equally approved,* and I kept my secret till my small fund of sense for such performances was pretty well exhausted, and when I revealed my secret I began to be considered a little more by my brother's acquaintance, and in a manner that did not quite please him, as he thought, probably with reason, that it tended to make me vain. And perhaps this might be one occasion of the differences that we frequently had about this time. Tho' a brother, he considered himself as my master, and me as his apprentice; and accordingly expected the same ser-

*Franklin wrote in the guise of Silence Dogood, the widow of a country minister. She commented on manners and morals, satirized the students of Harvard College, scoffed at fashions in women's clothes, and attacked hypocrisy in religion. The essays were remarkable compositions for a boy of sixteen.

vices from me as he would from another; I thought he demeaned me too much in some services he required of me, who expected more indulgence from a brother.

Our disputes were often brought before our father, and I fancy I was either generally in the right, or else a better pleader, because the judgment was generally in my favor. But my brother was passionate and often beat me, which I took extremely amiss; and thinking my apprenticeship very tedious, I was continually wishing for some opportunity of shortening it, which at length offered in a manner unexpected. (I fancy his harsh and tyrannical treatment of me, might be a means of impressing me with that aversion to arbitrary power that has stuck to me through my whole life.)

One of the pieces in our newspaper, on some political point, gave offense to the Assembly. My brother was taken up, censured and imprisoned for a month by the speaker's warrant, I suppose because he would not reveal his author. I too was taken up and examined before the council; but tho' I did not give them any satisfaction, they contented themselves with admonishing me, and dismissed me; considering me perhaps as an apprentice who was bound to keep his master's secrets.

During my brother's confinement, which I resented a good deal, notwithstanding our differences, I had the management of the paper, and I made bold to give our rulers some rubs in it, which my brother took very kindly, while others began to consider me in an unfavorable light, as a young genius that had a turn for libeling and satire. My brother's discharge was accompanied with an order of the House, (a very odd one) *that James Franklin should no longer print the paper called The New England Courant.* There was a consultation held in our printing house among his friends what he should do. Some proposed to evade the order by changing the name of the paper; but it was finally concluded on as a better way, to let it be printed for the future under the name of *Benjamin Franklin.* And to avoid the censure of the Assembly that might fall on him, as still printing it by his apprentice, the contrivance was, that my old indenture should be returned to me with a full discharge on the back of it, to be shown on occasion; but to secure to him the benefit of my service I was to sign new indentures for the remainder of the term, which were to be kept private.

A very flimsy scheme it was, but it was executed, and the paper went on under my name for several months. At length a fresh difference arising between my brother and me, I took upon me to assert my freedom, presuming that he would not venture to produce the new indentures. It was not fair in me to take this advantage, and this I therefore reckon one of the first errata of my life; but the unfairness of it weighed little with me against my resentment for the blows he too often bestowed upon me. Tho' he was otherwise not an ill-natured man; perhaps I was too saucy and provoking.

When he found I would leave him, he took care to prevent my getting employment in any other printing house of the town, going round and speaking to every master, who accordingly refused to give me work. I then thought of going to New York as the nearest place where there was a printer; and I was the more inclined to leave Boston, when I reflected that I had already made myself a little obnoxious to the governing party; and it was likely I might if I stayed soon bring myself into scrapes; and farther that my indiscreet disputations about religion began to make me pointed at with horror by good people, as an infidel or atheist.

I determined on the point; but my father now siding with my brother, I was sensible that if I attempted to go openly, means would be used to prevent me. My friend Collins therefore undertook to manage for me. He agreed with the captain of a New York sloop for my passage, under the notion of my being a young acquaintance of his that had got a naughty girl with child, whose friends would compel me to marry her, and therefore I could not appear or come away publicly. So I sold some of my books to raise a little money, was taken on board privately, and as we had a fair wind in three days I found myself in New York near three hundred miles from home, a boy of but seventeen, without the least recommendation to or knowledge of any person in the place, and with very little money in my pocket.

My inclinations for the sea, were by this time worn out, or I might now have gratified them. But having a trade, and supposing myself a pretty good workman, I offered my service to the printer of the place, old Mr. William Bradford. He could give me no employment, having help enough already; but, says he, my son at Philadelphia has lately lost his principal hand, Aquila Rose, by death. If you go thither I believe he may employ you.

Philadelphia was one hundred miles farther. I set out in a boat for Amboy, leaving my chest to follow me round by sea. In crossing the bay we met with a squall that tore our rotten sails to pieces, and drove us upon Long Island. A drunken Dutchman, who was a passenger, fell overboard; when he was sinking I reached through the water to his shock pate and drew him up so that we got him in again.

His ducking sobered him a little, and he went to sleep, taking first out of his pocket a book which he desired I would dry for him. It proved to be my old favorite author Bunyan's *Pilgrim's Progress* in Dutch, finely printed on good paper with copper cuts, a dress better than I had ever seen it wear. Honest John was the first that I know of who mixed narration and dialogue, a method of writing very engaging to the reader, who in the most interesting parts finds himself as it were brought into the company, and present at the discourse. Defoe in his *Cruso* [*Robinson Crusoe*] and other pieces, has imitated it with success, and Richardson has done the same in his *Pamela*.*

When we drew near the island we found there could be no landing, there being a great surf on the stony beach. So we dropped anchor and swung round towards the shore. Some people came down to the water edge and halloed to us, as we did to them. But the wind was so high and the surf so loud, that we could not understand each other. There were canoes on the shore, and we made signs and halloed that they should fetch us, but they went away, and night coming on, we had no remedy but to wait till the wind should abate. The boatman and I concluded to sleep if we could, and so crowded into the scuttle with the Dutchman who was still wet, and the spray

---

*Franklin's reprint of *Pamela* in 1774 was the first novel published in America.

beating over the head of our boat, leaked through to us, so that we were soon almost as wet as he. In this manner we lay all night with very little rest. But the wind abating the next day, we made a shift to reach Amboy before night, having been thirty hours on the water without victuals, or any drink but a bottle of filthy rum.

In the evening I found myself very feverish, and went in to bed. But having read that cold water drunk plentifully was good for a fever, I followed the prescription, sweat plentifully most of the night, my fever left me, and in the morning crossing the ferry, I proceeded on my journey, on foot, having fifty miles to Burlington, where I was told I should find boats that would carry me the rest of the way to Philadelphia.

It rained very hard all the day, I was thoroughly soaked and by noon a good deal tired, so I stopped at a poor inn, where I stayed all night, beginning now to wish I had never left home. I cut so miserable a figure too, that I found by the questions asked me I was suspected to be some runaway servant, and in danger of being taken up on that suspicion. However I proceeded the next day, and got in the evening to an inn within eight or ten miles of Burlington, kept by one Dr. Browne.

He conversed with me while I took some refreshment, and finding I had read a little, became very sociable. Our acquaintance continued as long as he lived. He had been, I imagine, an itinerant doctor, for there was no town in England, or country in Europe, of which he could not give a very particular account. He had some letters, but was much of an unbeliever, and wickedly undertook some years after to travesty the Bible in doggerel verse. By this means he set many of the facts in a very ridiculous light, and might have hurt weak minds if his work had been published; but it never was.

The next morning I reached Burlington; but had the mortification to find that the regular boats were gone, a little before my coming, and no other expected to go till Tuesday, this being Saturday. Wherefore I returned to an old woman in the town of whom I had bought gingerbread to eat on the water, and asked her advice; she invited me to lodge at her house till a passage should offer, and I accepted the invitation.

She gave me a dinner of oxcheek with a great goodwill, accepting only of a pot of ale in return. And I thought myself fixed till Tuesday should come. However walking in the evening by the side of the river a boat came by, which I found was going towards Philadelphia, with several people in her. They took me in, and as there was no wind, we rowed all the way; and about midnight not having yet seen the city, some of the company were confident we must have passed it, and would row no farther, the others knew not where we were, so we put towards the shore, got into a creek, landed near an old fence with the rails of which we made a fire, the night being cold, in October, and there we remained till daylight. Then one of the company knew the place to be Cooper's Creek a little above Philadelphia, which we saw as soon as we got out of the creek, and arrived there about eight or nine o'clock, on the Sunday morning, and landed at the Market Street wharf.

I have been the more particular in this description of my journey, and shall be so of my first entry into that city, that you may in your mind compare such unlikely beginnings with the figure I have since made there. I was in my working dress, my best clothes being to come round by sea. I was dirty from my journey; my pockets were stuffed out with shirts and stockings; I knew no soul, nor where to look for lodging. I was fatigued with rowing and want of rest. I was very hungry, and my whole stock of cash consisted of a Dutch dollar and about a shilling in copper. The latter I gave the people of the boat for my passage, who at first refused it on account of my rowing; but I insisted on their taking it, a man being sometimes more generous when he has but a little money than when he has plenty, perhaps through fear of being thought to have but little.

Then I walked up the street, gazing about, till near the market house I met a boy with bread. Inquiring where he got it, I went immediately to the baker's he directed me to in Second Street; and asked for biscuit, intending such as we had in Boston, but they it seems were not made in Philadelphia. Then I asked for a threepenny loaf, and was told he had none such: so not knowing the names of his bread, I bade him give me threepennyworth of any sort. He gave me accordingly three great puffy rolls. I was surprised at the quantity, but took it, and having no room in my pockets, walked off, with a roll under each arm, and eating the other.

Thus I went up Market Street as far as Fourth Street, passing by the door of Mr. Read, my future wife's father, when she standing at the door saw me, and thought I made as I certainly did a most awkward ridiculous appearance. Then I turned and went down Chestnut Street and part of Walnut Street, eating my roll all the way, and coming round found myself again at Market Street wharf, near the boat I came in, to which I went for a draught of the river water, and being filled with one of my rolls, gave the other two to a woman and her child that came in the boat with us and were waiting to go farther. Thus refreshed I walked again up the street, which by this time had many clean-dressed people in it who were all walking the same way. I joined them, and thereby was led into the great meetinghouse of the Quakers near the market. I sat down among them, and after looking round awhile and hearing nothing said, being very drowsy through want of rest, I fell fast asleep, and continued so till the meeting broke up, when one was kind enough to rouse me. This was therefore the first house I was in or slept in, in Philadelphia.

"I walked off, with a roll under each arm."

Walking again down towards the river, and looking in the faces of people, I met a young Quaker man whose countenance I liked, and requested he would tell me where a stranger could get lodging. We were then near the sign of the Three Mariners. Here, says he, is one place that entertains strangers, but it is not a reputable house; if thee wilt walk with me, I'll show thee a better. He brought me to the Crooked Billet in Water

Street. Here I got a dinner. And while I was eating it, several sly questions were asked me, as it seemed to be suspected from my youth and appearance, that I might be some runaway.

After dinner my sleepiness returned: and being shown to a bed, I lay down without undressing, and slept till six in the evening; was called to supper; went to bed again early and slept soundly till the next morning. Then I made myself as tidy as I could, and went to Andrew Bradford the printer's. I found in the shop his father, whom I had seen at New York, and who traveling on horseback had got to Philadelphia before me. He introduced me to his son, who received me civilly, but told me he did not at present want a hand, being newly supplied with one. But there was another printer in town lately set up, one Keimer, who perhaps might employ me; if not, I should be welcome to lodge at his house, and he would give me a little work to do now and then till fuller business should offer.

The old gentleman said, he would go with me to the new printer; and when we found him, Neighbor, says Bradford, I have brought to see you a young man of your business, perhaps you may want such a one. Keimer asked me a few questions, put a composing stick in my hand to see how I worked, and then said he would employ me soon, tho' he had just then nothing for me to do. And taking old Bradford, whom he had never seen before, to be one of the townspeople, entered into a conversation on his prospects; saying he expected soon to get the greatest part of the business into his own hands. Bradford drew him on by artful questions, to explain all his views, and in what manner he intended to proceed. I who stood by and heard all, saw immediately that one of them was a crafty old sophister, and the other a mere novice. Bradford left me with Keimer, who was greatly surprised when I told him who the old man was.

Keimer's printing house I found, consisted of an old shattered press, and one small worn-out font of English, which he was then using himself, composing in it an elegy on Aquila Rose before mentioned, a young man much respected, clerk of the Assembly. I endeavored to put his press (which he had not yet used, and of which he understood nothing) into order fit to be worked with; and promising to come and print off his elegy as soon as he should have got it ready, I returned to Bradford's who gave me a little job to do, and there I lodged. And a few days after Keimer sent for me and set me to work.

These two printers I found poorly qualified for their business. Bradford had not been bred to it, and was very illiterate; and Keimer tho' something of a scholar, was a mere compositor, knowing nothing of presswork. He had been one of the French

"*A few days after Keimer sent for me and set me to work.*"

Prophets* and could act their enthusiastic agitations. At this time he did not profess any particular religion, and had, as I afterwards found, a good deal of the knave in his composition. He did not like my lodging at Bradford's while I worked with him. He had a house indeed, but without furniture, so he could not lodge me; but he got me a lodging at Mr. Read's before mentioned, who was the owner of his house. And my chest and clothes being come by this time, I made rather a more respectable appearance in the eyes of Miss Read, than I had done when she first happened to see me eating my roll in the street.

I began now to have some acquaintance among the young people of the town, that were lovers of reading with whom I spent my evenings very pleasantly. Gaining money by my industry and frugality, I lived very agreeably, forgetting Boston as much as I could, and not desiring that any there should know where I resided, except my friend Collins who kept my secret when I wrote to him. But at length an incident happened that sent me back again much sooner than I had intended.

I had a brother-in-law, Robert Homes, master of a sloop, that

*A group of French Protestants given to trances and revelations.

traded between Boston and Delaware. He being at Newcastle forty miles below Philadelphia, heard there of me, and wrote me a letter, mentioning the concern of my friends in Boston at my abrupt departure, assuring me of their goodwill to me, and exhorting me earnestly to return to them. I wrote an answer to his letter, thanked him for his advice, but stated my reasons for quitting Boston, and in such a light as to convince him I was not so wrong as he had apprehended.

Sir William Keith governor of the province, was then at Newcastle, and Captain Homes happening to be in company with him when my letter came to hand, spoke of me, and showed him my letter. The governor read it, and seemed surprised when he was told of my age. He said I appeared a young man of promising parts, and therefore should be encouraged; the printers at Philadelphia were wretched; and if I would set up there, he made no doubt I should succeed; for his part, he would procure me the public business, and do me every other service in his power. This my brother-in-law told me afterwards in Boston. But I knew as yet nothing of it.

One day Keimer and I being at work together near the window, we saw the governor and another gentleman (which proved to be Colonel French, of Newcastle) come directly across the street to our house, and heard them at the door. Keimer ran down, thinking it a visit to him. But the governor enquired for me, and with a condescension and politeness I had been quite unused to, made me many compliments, desired to be acquainted with me, and would have me away with him to the tavern where he was going with Colonel French to taste as he said some excellent Madeira.

"My friend agreed with the captain of a New York sloop for my passage."

I was not a little surprised, and Keimer stared like a pig poisoned. I went however with the governor and Colonel

French, to a tavern at the corner of Third Street, and over the Madeira the governor proposed my setting up my business, laid before me the probabilities of success, and both he and Colonel French assured me I should have their interest and influence in procuring the public business of both governments. On my doubting whether my father would assist me in it, Sir William said he would give me a letter to him, in which he would state the advantages, and he did not doubt of prevailing with him. So it was concluded I should return to Boston in the first vessel. In the meantime the intention was to be kept secret. I went on working with Keimer as usual, the governor sending for me now and then to dine with him, a very great honor I thought it, and conversing with me in the most affable and friendly manner imaginable.

About the end of April 1724, a little vessel offered for Boston. I took leave of Keimer as going to see my friends. The governor gave me an ample letter, saying many flattering things of me to my father, and strongly recommending the project of my setting up at Philadelphia. We struck on a shoal in going down the bay and sprung a leak, we had a blustering time at sea, and were obliged to pump almost continually, at which I took my turn. We arrived safe however at Boston in about a fortnight.

I had been absent seven months and my friends had heard nothing of me. My unexpected appearance surprised the family; all were however very glad to see me and made me welcome, except my brother. I went to see him at his printing house. I was better dressed than ever while in his service, having a genteel new suit from head to foot, a watch, and my pockets lined with near five pounds sterling in silver.

He received me not very frankly, looked me all over, and turned to his work again. The journeymen were inquisitive where I had been, what sort of a country it was, and how I liked it? I praised it much, and the happy life I led; expressing strongly my intention of returning to it; and one of them asking what kind of money we had there, I produced a handful of silver and spread it before them, which was a kind of raree-show they had not been used to, paper being the money of Boston. Then I took an opportunity of letting them see my watch; and lastly, I gave them a piece of eight for drink and took my leave. This visit of mine offended my brother extremely. For when my mother some time after spoke to him of a reconciliation, and of her wishes to see us on good terms together, and that we might live for the future as brothers, he said, I had insulted him in such a manner before his people that he could never forget or forgive it. In this however he was mistaken.

My father received the governor's letter with some apparent surprise. Captain Homes returning, he asked what kind of a man Keith was; adding his opinion that he must be of small discretion, to think of setting a boy up in business who wanted yet three years of being at man's estate. Homes said what he could in favor of the project; but my father was clear in the impropriety of it; and at last gave a flat denial to it. Then he wrote a civil letter to Sir William thanking him for the patronage he had so kindly offered me, but declining to assist me as yet in setting up, I being in his opinion too young to be trusted with the management of a business, for which the preparation must be so expensive.

My friend Collins, who was a clerk at the post office, pleased with the account I gave of my new country, determined to go thither also. He set out before me by land to Rhode Island, leaving his books to come with me to New York where he proposed to wait for me. My father, tho' he did not approve Sir William's proposition was yet pleased that I had been able to obtain so advantageous a character from a person of such note where I had resided, and that I had been so industrious; therefore, he gave his consent to my returning to Philadelphia, advised me to behave respectfully to the people there, and avoid lampooning and libeling to which he thought I had too much inclination. He told me, that by steady industry and a prudent parsimony, I might save enough by the time I was one-and-twenty to set me up, and that if I came near the matter he would help me out with the rest. This was all I could obtain, except some small gifts as tokens of his and my mother's love, when I embarked again for New York, now with their approbation and their blessing.

The sloop putting in at Newport, Rhode Island, I visited my

brother John, who had been settled there some years. He received me very affectionately, for he always loved me. A friend of his, one Vernon, having some money due to him in Pennsylvania, about thirty-five pounds, desired I would receive it for him, and keep it till I had his directions what to remit it in. Accordingly he gave me an order. This afterwards occasioned me a good deal of uneasiness.

At Newport we took in a number of passengers for New York, among which were two young women, companions, and a grave, sensible matronlike Quaker woman with her attendants. I had shown an obliging readiness to do her some little services which impressed her I suppose with a degree of goodwill towards me. Therefore when she saw a daily growing familiarity between me and the two young women, which they appeared to encourage, she took me aside and said, Young man, I am concerned for thee, as thou has no friend with thee, and seems not to know much of the world, or of the snares youth is exposed to; depend upon it those are very bad women, I can see it in all their actions, and if thee art not upon thy guard, they will draw thee into some danger. I advise thee in a friendly concern for thy welfare, to have no acquaintance with them.

As I seemed at first not to think so ill of them as she did, she mentioned some things she had observed and heard; and now convinced me she was right. I thanked her for her advice, and promised to follow it. When we arrived at New York, they told me where they lived, and invited me to come and see them; but I avoided it. And it was well I did; for the next day, the captain missed a silver spoon and some other things from his cabin, and knowing that these were a couple of strumpets, he got a warrant to search their lodgings, found the stolen goods, and had the thieves punished. So tho' we had escaped a sunken rock which we scraped upon in the passage, I thought this escape of rather more importance to me.

At New York I found my friend Collins. We had been intimate from children, and had read the same books together. While I lived in Boston most of my hours of leisure for conversation were spent with him, and he had continued a sober as well as an industrious lad, much respected for his learning, and seeming to promise making a good figure in life. But during my absence he had acquired a habit of sotting with brandy; and I found by his own account and from others, that he had been drunk every day since his arrival at New York, and behaved very oddly. He had gamed too and lost his money, so that I was obliged to discharge his lodgings, and defray his expenses to and at Philadelphia, which proved extremely inconvenient to me.

The then governor of New York, William Burnet, hearing from the captain that one of his passengers had a great many books, desired he would bring me to see him. I waited upon him accordingly, and should have taken Collins with me but that he was not sober. The governor treated me with great civility, showed me his library, and we had a good deal of conversation about books. This was the second governor who had done me the honor to take notice of me, which to a poor boy like me was very pleasing.

We proceeded to Philadelphia. I received on the way Vernon's money, without which we could hardly have finished our journey. Collins wished to be employed in some countinghouse; but whether they discovered his dramming by his breath, or by his behavior, he met with no success, and continued lodging at the same house with me and at my expense. Knowing I had that money of Vernon's he was continually borrowing of me, promising repayment as soon as he should be in business. At length he had got so much of it, that I was distressed to think what I should do, in case of being called on to remit it.

When a little intoxicated he was very fractious. Once in a boat on the Delaware with some other young men, he refused to row in his turn. I will be rowed home, says he. We will not row you, says I. You must or stay all night on the water, says he, just as you please. The others said, Let us row; what signifies it? But my mind being soured with his other conduct, I continued to refuse. So he swore he would make me row, or throw me overboard; and stepping on the thwarts towards me, when he struck at me I clapped my hand under his crutch, and rising pitched him headforemost into the river.

I knew he was a good swimmer, and so was under little concern about him; but before he could get round to lay hold of the boat, we had with a few strokes pulled her out of his reach. And ever when he drew near the boat, we asked if he would row, striking a few strokes to slide her away from him. He was ready to die with vexation, and obstinately would not promise to row; however seeing him at last beginning to tire, we lifted him in; and brought him home dripping wet in the evening.

"We proceeded to Philadelphia."

We hardly exchanged a civil word afterwards. He left me then, promising to remit me the first money he should receive in order to discharge the debt. But I never heard of him after.

The breaking into this money of Vernon's was one of the great errata of my life. And this affair showed that my father was not much out in his judgment when he supposed me too young to manage business of importance. But Sir William, on reading his letter, said he was too prudent. There was great difference in persons, and discretion did not always accompany years, nor was youth always without it. And since he will not set you up, says he, I will do it myself. Give me an inventory of the things necessary to be had from England, and I will send for them. You shall repay me when you are able; I am resolved to have a good printer here, and I am sure you must succeed.

This was spoken with such an appearance of cordiality, that I had not the least doubt of his meaning what he said. I had hitherto kept the proposition of my setting up a secret in Philadelphia, and I still kept it. Had it been known that I depended on the governor, probably some friend that knew him better would have advised me not to rely on him, as I afterwards heard that he was known to be liberal of promises which he never meant to keep. Yet unsolicited as he was by me, how could I think his generous offers insincere? I believed him one of the best men in the world.

I presented him an inventory of a little printing house, amounting by my computation to about one hundred pounds sterling. He liked it, and asked me if my being on the spot in England to choose the types and see that everything was good, might not be of some advantage. Then, says he, when there, you may establish correspondences in the bookselling and stationery way. I agreed that this might be advantageous.

Then says he, get yourself ready to go with Annis. Captain Annis was master of the annual ship, and the only one at that time passing between London and Philadelphia. But it would be some months before Annis sailed, so I continued working with Keimer, in daily apprehension of being called upon by Vernon for his money, which however did not happen for some years after.

I believe I have omitted mentioning that in my first voyage from Boston, being becalmed off Block Island, our people set about catching cod and hauled up a great many. Hitherto I had stuck to my resolution of not eating animal food; and on this occasion, I considered the taking of every fish as a kind of unprovoked murder, since none of them had or ever could do us any injury that might justify the slaughter. But I had formerly been a great lover of fish, and when this came hot out of the frying pan, it smelt admirably well. I balanced some time between principle and inclination, till I recollected, that when the fish were opened, I saw smaller fish taken out of their stomachs; then thought I, if you eat one another, I don't see why we mayn't eat you. So I dined upon cod very heartily and continued to eat with other people, returning only now and then to a vegetable diet. So convenient a thing it is to be a *reasonable creature*, since it enables one to find or make a reason for everything one has a mind to do.

Keimer and I lived on a familiar footing. He loved argumentation, and we therefore had many disputations. I used to work him so with my Socratic method, and had trepanned him so often by questions apparently distant from any point we had in hand, and yet by degrees led to the point, that at last he grew ridiculously cautious, and would hardly answer me the most common question without asking first, *What do you intend to infer from that?* However, it gave him so high an opinion of my abilities, that he seriously proposed my being his colleague in setting up a new sect. He was to preach the doctrines, and I was to confound all opponents.

When he came to explain with me upon the doctrines, I found several conundrums which I objected to unless I might have my way a little too, and introduce some of mine. Keimer wore his beard at full length, because somewhere in the Mosaic law it is said, *thou shalt not mar the corners of thy beard*. He likewise kept the seventh day Sabbath. I disliked both these points, but agreed to admit them upon condition of his adopting the doctrine of using no animal food.

I doubt, says he, my constitution will not bear that. I assured him that he would be the better for it. He was a great glutton, and I promised myself some diversion in half starving him. He agreed to try the practice if I would keep him company. I did so and we held it for three months.

We had our victuals dressed and brought to us regularly by a woman in the neighborhood, who had from me a list of forty dishes, in all which there was neither fish flesh nor fowl, and the whim suited me the better at this time from the cheapness of it. I went on pleasantly, but poor Keimer suffered grievously, longed for the fleshpots of Egypt, and at last ordered a roast pig. He invited me and two women friends to dine with him, but it being brought too soon upon table, he could not resist the temptation, and ate it all up before we came.

I had made some courtship during this time to Miss Read. I had a great respect and affection for her, and had some reason to believe she had the same for me. But as I was about to take a long voyage, and we were both very young, only a little above eighteen, it was thought most prudent by her mother to prevent our going too far at present. A marriage if it was to take place would be more convenient after my return, when I should be as I expected set up in my business. Perhaps too she thought my expectations not so well founded as I imagined them to be.

"We had a sociable company."

My chief acquaintances at this time were, Charles Osborne, Joseph Watson, and James Ralph; all lovers of reading. The two first were clerks to an eminent scrivener in the town, the other was clerk to a merchant. Joseph Watson was a pious sensible young man, of great integrity. The others rather more lax in their principles of religion, particularly James Ralph, who as well as Collins had been unsettled by me. Charles Osborne was sensible, candid, sincere, and affectionate to his friends; but in literary matters too fond of criticizing. Ralph was genteel in his manners, and extremely eloquent; I think I never knew a prettier talker. Both of them were great admirers of poetry, and began to try their hands in little pieces. Many pleasant walks we four had on Sundays into the woods near Schuylkill, where we read to one another and conferred on what we read.

Ralph was inclined to pursue the study of poetry, not doubting but he might make his fortune by it. Osborne dissuaded him, assured him he had no genius for poetry, and advised him to think of nothing beyond the mercantile business he was bred to. I approved the amusing one's self with poetry now and then, so far as to improve one's language, but no farther. On this it was proposed that we should each of us at our next meeting produce a piece of our own composing. As language and expression were what we had in view, we agreed that the task should be a version of the Eighteenth Psalm, which describes the descent of a Deity.

When the time of our meeting drew nigh, Ralph called on me first, and showed me his piece; and it appeared to me to have great merit. Now, says he, Osborne never will allow the least merit in anything of mine, but will make a thousand criticisms out of mere envy. He is not so jealous of you. I wish therefore you would produce this piece as yours. I will pretend not to have had time.

It was agreed, and we met. Watson's performance was read; there were some beauties in it, but many defects. Osborne's was read; it was much better. I was backward; but produce I must. It was read and repeated; Watson and Osborne gave up the contest, and joined in applauding it immoderately.

Ralph made some criticisms, and Osborne told him he was no better a critic than poet. As they two went home together, Osborne expressed himself still more strongly. Who would have imagined, says he, that Franklin had been capable of such a performance; such painting, such force! such fire! he has even improved the original! In his common conversation, he hesitates and blunders; and yet, good God, how he writes!

When we next met, Ralph revealed the trick, we had played, and Osborne was a little laughed at. This transaction fixed Ralph in his resolution of becoming a poet. More of him hereafter.

But as I may not have occasion again to mention the other two, I shall just remark here, that Watson died in my arms a few years after, much lamented, being the best of our set. Osborne went to the West Indies, where he became an eminent lawyer and made money, but died young. He and I had made a serious agreement, that the one who happened first to die, should if possible make a friendly visit to the other, and acquaint him how he found things in that separate state. But he never fulfilled his promise.

The governor had me frequently to his house; and his setting me up was always mentioned as a fixed thing. I was to take with me letters recommendatory to a number of his friends, besides the letter of credit to furnish me with the money for purchasing press and types, paper, &c. I was appointed to call at different times, when these letters were to be ready, but a future time was still named. Thus we went on till the ship was on the point of sailing. Then when I called to take my leave and receive the letters, his secretary, Dr. Baird, came out to me and said the governor was extremely busy, but would be down at Newcastle before the ship, and there the letters would be delivered to me.

My friend James Ralph, tho' married and having one child, had determined to accompany me in this voyage. It was thought he intended to obtain goods to sell on commission. But I found afterwards, that through some discontent with his wife's relations, he purposed to leave her on their hands, and never return again. Having taken leave of my friends, and exchanged some promises with Miss Read, I left Philadelphia in the ship, which anchored at Newcastle. The governor was there. But when I went to his lodging, the secretary came to me from him with the civilest message in the world, that he could not then see me, being engaged in business of the utmost importance; but should send the letters to me on board, and wished me heartily a good voyage and a speedy return. I returned on board, a little puzzled, but still not doubting.

Mr. Andrew Hamilton, a famous lawyer of Philadelphia, had taken passage in the same ship for himself and son; and with Mr. Denham a Quaker merchant, and Messrs. Onion and Russell masters of an iron work in Maryland, had engaged the great cabin; so that Ralph and I were forced to take up with a berth in the steerage; and none on board knowing us, were considered as ordinary persons. But Mr. Hamilton being recalled by a great fee to Philadelphia to plead for a seized ship, and just before we sailed Colonel French coming on board, and showing me great respect, I was more taken notice of, and with my friend Ralph invited by the other gentlemen to come into the cabin, there being now room.

Understanding that Colonel French had brought on board the governor's dispatches, I asked the captain for those letters that were to be under my care. He said all were put into the bag together; and he could not then come at them; but before we landed in England, I should have an opportunity of picking them out. So I was satisfied for the present.

We had a sociable company in the cabin, and lived uncommonly well, having the addition of Mr. Hamilton's stores, who had laid in plentifully. In this passage Mr. Denham contracted a friendship for me that continued during his life. The voyage was otherwise not a pleasant one, as we had a great deal of bad weather.

When we came into the Channel, the captain kept his word with me, and gave me an opportunity of examining the bag for the governor's letters. I found none upon which my name was put, as under my care; I picked out six or seven that by the handwriting I thought might be the promised letters, especially as one of them was directed to Basket the king's printer, and another to some stationer. We arrived in London the 24th of December, 1724. I waited upon the stationer first, delivering the letter as from Governor Keith. I don't know such a person, says he; but opening the letter, O, this is from Riddlesden, and turned on his heel.

Beginning to doubt the governor's sincerity, I found my friend Denham, and opened the whole affair to him. He let me into Keith's character, told me there was not the least probability that he had written any letters for me, that no one who knew him had the smallest dependence on him, and he laughed at the notion of the governor's giving me a letter of credit, having as he said no credit to give. On my expressing some concern about what I should do, he advised me to endeavor getting some employment in the way of my business. Among the printers here, says he, you will improve yourself; and when you return to America, you will set up to greater advantage.

But what shall we think of a governor's playing such pitiful tricks, and imposing so grossly on a poor ignorant boy! It was a habit he had acquired. He wished to please everybody; and having little to give, he gave expectations. He was otherwise an ingenious sensible man, and a good governor for the people. Several of our best laws were of his planning, and passed during his administration.

Ralph and I were inseparable companions. We took lodgings together in Little Britain Street at three shillings and sixpence per week. He now let me know that he never meant to return to Philadelphia. He had brought no money with him, the whole he could muster having been expended in paying his passage. I had fifteen pistoles; so he borrowed occasionally of me, to subsist while he was looking out for business. He first endeavored to get into the playhouse, believing himself qualified for an actor; but Wilkes, to whom he applied, advised him candidly that it was impossible he should succeed in that employment. Then he proposed to a publisher in Paternoster Row to write for him a weekly paper like the *Spectator*, on certain conditions, which the publisher did not approve. Then he endeavored to get employment as a hackney writer to copy for the lawyers about the Temple, but could find no vacancy.

I immediately got into work at Palmer's a famous printing house in Bartholomew Close; and here I continued near a year. I was pretty diligent; but spent with Ralph a good deal of my earnings in going to plays and other places of amusement. We had together consumed all my pistoles, and now just rubbed on from hand to mouth. He seemed quite to forget his wife and child, and I by degrees my engagements with Miss Read, to whom I never wrote more than one letter, and that was to let her know I was not likely soon to return. This was another of the great errata of my life, which I should wish to correct if I were to live it over again.

At Palmer's I was employed in composing for the second edition of Wollaston's *Religion of Nature*. Some of his reasonings not appearing to me well founded, I wrote a little metaphysical piece, in which I made remarks on them. It was entitled, *A Dissertation on Liberty and Necessity, Pleasure and Pain*. I printed a small number. Mr. Palmer expostulated with me upon the principles of my pamphlet which to him appeared abominable.

While I lodged in Little Britain Street I made an acquaintance with one Wilcox a bookseller, whose shop was next door. He had an immense collection of secondhand books. Circulating libraries were not then in use; but we agreed that on certain reasonable terms, I might take, read and return any of his books.

"Thus I spent about eighteen months in London."

My pamphlet by some means falling into the hands of one Lyons, a surgeon, he called on me often, to converse, and introduced me, to Dr. Pemberton, at Batson's Coffeehouse, who promised to give me an opportunity some time or other of seeing Sir Isaac Newton, of which I was extremely desirous; but this never happened.

I had brought over a few curiosities among which the principal was a purse made of the asbestos, which purifies by fire. Sir Hans Sloane heard of it, came to see me, and invited me to his house in Bloomsbury Square, where he showed me all his curiosities, and persuaded me to let him add that to the number, for which he paid me handsomely.

In our house there lodged a young woman; a milliner, who had a shop in the Cloisters. She had been genteelly bred, was sensible and lively, and of most pleasing conversation. Ralph read plays to her in the evenings, they grew intimate, she took another lodging, and he followed her. They lived together some time, but he being still out of business, and her income not sufficient to maintain them with her child, he took a resolution of going from London, to try for a position in a country school. This however he deemed a business below him, and confident of future better fortune when he should be unwilling to have it known that he once was so meanly employed, he changed his name, and did me the honor to assume mine. For I soon after had a letter from him, acquainting me, that he was settled in a village in Berkshire, where he taught reading and writing to ten or a dozen boys at sixpence each per week, recommending Mrs. T. to my care, and desiring me to write to him directing for Mr. Franklin schoolmaster at such a place.

He continued to write frequently, sending me large specimens of an epic poem, which he was then composing, and desiring my remarks and corrections. I endeavored rather to discourage his proceeding. One of Young's Satires was then just published, which set in a strong light the folly of pursuing the Muses with any hope of advancement. I copied and sent him a great part of it. All was in vain. Sheets of the poem continued to come by every post.

In the meantime Mrs. T. having on his account lost her friends and business, was often in distresses, and used to send for me, and borrow what I could spare. I grew fond of her company, and being at this time under no religious restraints, I attempted familiarities, (another erratum) which she repulsed with a proper resentment, and acquainted him with my behavior. This made a breach between us, and when he returned again to London, he let me know he thought I had canceled all the obligations he had been under to me. So I found I was never to expect his repaying me what I lent to him. This was not then of much consequence, as he was totally unable. And in the loss of his friendship I found myself relieved from a burthen.

I now began to think of getting a little money beforehand; and I left Palmer's to work at Watts's, near Lincoln's Inn Fields, a still greater printing house. Here I took to working at press, imagining I felt a want of the bodily exercise I had been used to in America, where presswork is mixed with composing. I drank only water; the other workmen, near fifty in number, were great guzzlers of beer. On occasion I carried up and down stairs a large form of types in each hand, when others carried but one in both hands. They wondered to see from this and several instances that the Water-American as they called me was *stronger* than themselves who drank *strong* beer.

We had an alehouse boy to supply the workmen. My companion at the press, drank every day a pint before breakfast, a

"I drank only water; the other workmen were great guzzlers of beer."

pint at breakfast with his bread and cheese; a pint between breakfast and dinner; a pint at dinner; a pint in the afternoon about six o'clock, and another when he had done his day's work. It was necessary, he supposed, to drink *strong* beer that he might be *strong* to labor. I endeavored to convince him that the bodily strength afforded by beer could only be in proportion to the grain or flour of the barley dissolved in the water of which it was made; that there was more flour in a pennyworth of bread, and therefore if he would eat that with a pint of water, it would give him more strength than a quart of beer. He drank on however, and had four or five shillings to pay out of his wages every Saturday night for that muddling liquor. And thus these poor devils keep themselves always under.

Watts after some weeks desiring to have me in the composing room, I left the pressmen. A new sum for drink, five shillings, was demanded of me by the compositors. I thought it an imposition, as I had paid below. The master thought so too, and forbad my paying it. I stood out two or three weeks, and had so many little pieces of private mischief done me, by mixing my sorts,* transposing my pages, breaking my matter, if I were ever so little out of the room, and all ascribed to the chapel [printing house] ghost, which they said ever haunted those not regularly admitted, that I found myself obliged to pay the money; convinced of the folly of being on ill terms with those one lives with.

I was now on a fair footing with them. From my example a great part of them left their muddling breakfast, finding they could with me be supplied from a neighboring house with a large porringer of hot gruel, sprinkled with pepper, crumbed with bread, and a bit of butter in it, for the price of a pint of beer. This was a more comfortable as well as cheaper breakfast, and kept their heads clearer. Those who continued sotting with beer all day, were often out of credit at the alehouse, and used to make interest with me to get beer, *their light*, as they phrased it, *being out*. I watched the pay table on Saturday night, and collected what I stood engaged for them, sometimes paying near thirty shillings a week on their accounts. This, and my being esteemed a pretty good riggite, that is a jocular verbal satirist, supported my consequence in the society. My constant attendance, I never making a St. Monday [being absent on Monday because of weekend dissipation], recommended me to the master; as did my uncommon quickness at composing. So I went on now very agreeably.

My lodging being too remote, I found another in Duke Street opposite to the Romish Chapel. It was two pair of stairs backwards at an Italian warehouse. An elderly widow lady kept the house; a Protestant clergyman's daughter, converted to the Catholic religion by her husband, whose memory she much

---

*Sort: a letter or character in a font of type. A printer who is "out of sorts" tends to become angry; hence the familiar expression.

revered. She had lived much among people of distinction, and knew a thousand anecdotes of them as far back as the times of Charles the Second. She was lame in her knees with gout, and seldom stirred out of her room, so sometimes wanted company; and hers was so highly amusing to me; that I was sure to spend an evening with her whenever she desired it. Our supper was only half an anchovy each, on a very little strip of bread and butter, and half a pint of ale between us. But the entertainment was in her conversation. My always keeping good hours, and giving little trouble, made her unwilling to part with me; so that when I talked of a lodging I had heard of, nearer my business, for two shillings a week, she bid me not think of it, for she would abate me two shillings a week for the future. So I remained with her at one shilling and sixpence as long as I stayed in London.

In a garret of her house there lived a maiden lady of seventy in the most retired manner. She was a Roman Catholic, had been sent abroad when young and lodged in a nunnery with an intent of becoming a nun; but the country not agreeing with her, she returned to England, where there being no nunnery, she had vowed to lead the life of a nun as near as might be done in those circumstances. Accordingly she had given all her estate to charitable uses, reserving only twelve pounds a year to live on, and out of this sum she still gave a great deal in charity, living herself on gruel only, and using no fire but to boil it. A priest visited her, to confess her every day. I have asked her, says my landlady, how she, as she lived, could possibly find so much employment for a confessor? O, says she, it is impossible to avoid *vain thoughts*.

I was permitted once to visit her. The room had no other furniture than a mattress, a table with a crucifix and book, a stool, which she gave me to sit on, and a picture over the chimney of Saint Veronica, displaying her handkerchief with the miraculous figure of Christ's bleeding face on it, which she explained to me with great seriousness. She looked pale, but was never sick, and I give it as another instance on how small an income life and health may be supported.

At Watts's printing house I contracted an acquaintance with

an ingenious young man, one Wygate, who, better educated than most printers, was a tolerable Latinist, spoke French, and loved reading. I taught him, and a friend of his, to swim, going twice into the river. They introduced me to some gentlemen from the country. We went to Chelsea by water and at the request of the company, whose curiosity Wygate had excited, I stript and leapt into the river, and swam from near Chelsea to Blackfriar's [about three and a half miles], performing on the way many feats that surprised and pleased them. I was much flattered by their admiration. Wygate at length proposed to me traveling all over Europe together, supporting ourselves everywhere by working at printing. I was inclined to it. But mentioning it to my good friend Mr. Denham, with whom I often spent an hour, when I had leisure, he dissuaded me from it, advising me to think only of returning to Pennsylvania.

This good man had formerly been in business at Bristol, but failed in debt to a number of people, compounded and went to America. There, by a close application to business as a merchant, he acquired a fortune in a few years. Returning to England in the ship with me, he invited his old creditors to an entertainment, at which he thanked them for the easy composition they had favored him with, and when they expected nothing but the treat, every man at the first remove, found under his plate an order on a banker for the full amount of the unpaid remainder with interest.

He now told me he was about to return to Philadelphia, and should carry over a quantity of goods in order to open a store there. He proposed to take me over as his clerk, to keep his books (in which he would instruct me) copy his letters, and attend the store. He added, that as soon as I should be acquainted with mercantile business he would send me with a cargo of flour and bread, &c. to the West Indies, and procure me commissions from others; which would be profitable, and would establish me handsomely. The thing pleased me, for I was grown tired of London, and wished again to see Pennsylvania. Therefore I immediately agreed, on the terms of fifty pounds a year, Pennsylvania money; less indeed than my present gettings as a compositor, but affording a better prospect.

I now took leave of printing, as I thought forever, and was daily employed in my new business; going about with Mr. Denham, to purchase various articles, see them packed up, do errands, &c. One day I was to my surprise sent for by a great man I knew only by name, a Sir William Wyndham. He had heard of my swimming, and of my teaching Wygate and the other young man to swim. He had two sons about to set out on their travels; he wished to have them first taught swimming; and proposed to gratify me handsomely if I would teach them. They were not yet come to town and my stay was uncertain, so I could not undertake it. But from this incident I thought it likely, that if I were to remain in England and open a swimming school, I might get a good deal of money. And it struck me so strongly, that had the overture been sooner made me, probably I should not so soon have returned to America. After many years, you and I had something of more importance to do with one of these sons of Sir William Wyndham, become Earl of Egremont.

Thus I spent about eighteen months in London. Most part of the time, I worked hard at my business, and spent but little upon myself except in seeing plays and in books. But tho' I had by no means improved my fortune, I had picked up some very ingenious acquaintance whose conversation was of great advantage to me.

We sailed from Gravesend on the 23d of July 1726. At sea I formed a *Plan** for regulating my future conduct in life. It is the more remarkable, as being formed when I was so young, and yet being pretty faithfully adhered to quite through to old age.

We landed in Philadelphia the 11th of October. Keith was no longer governor: I met him walking the streets as a common citizen. He seemed a little ashamed at seeing me, but passed without saying anything. I should have been as much ashamed at seeing Miss Read, had not her friends, despairing with reason of my return, persuaded her to marry another, one Rogers, a potter. With him however she was never happy, and soon parted from him, refusing to cohabit with him, or to bear his

---

*Only the preamble and heads of it survive. The *Plan* itself is lost.

name it being now said that he had another wife. He was a worthless fellow tho' an excellent workman which was the temptation to her friends. He got into debt, ran away to the West Indies, and died there. Keimer had got a better house, a shop well supplied with stationery, new types, a number of hands tho' none good, and seemed to have a great deal of business.

Mr. Denham took a store in Water Street, where we opened our goods. I attended the business diligently, and grew in a little time expert at selling. We lodged and boarded together, he counseled me as a father, and I respected and loved him. We might have gone on together very happily; but in the beginning of February 1727 when I had just passed my twenty-first year, we both were taken ill. My distemper was a pleurisy, which very nearly carried me off: I suffered a good deal, gave up the point in my own mind, and was rather disappointed when I found myself recovering; regretting in some degree that I must now some time or other have all that disagreeable work to do over again. I forget what his distemper was. It held him a long time, and at length carried him off.

He left me a small legacy, as a token of his kindness for me, and he left me once more to the wide world. For the store was taken into the care of his executors, and my employment under him ended. Keimer tempted me with an offer of large wages by the year to take the management of his printing house. I was not fond of having any more to do with him. I tried for farther employment as a merchant's clerk; but not readily meeting with any, I closed again with Keimer.

I found in *his* house these hands; Hugh Meredith a Welsh Pennsylvanian, thirty years of age, bred to country work: honest, sensible, something of a reader, but given to drink. Stephen Potts, a young countryman of uncommon natural parts, and great wit, but a little idle. These he had agreed with at extreme low wages, to be raised as they would improve in their business. Meredith was to work at press, Potts at bookbinding. John ____ a wild Irishman brought up to no business, whose service for four years Keimer had purchased from the captain of a ship. He too was to be made a pressman. George Webb, an

Oxford scholar, whose time for four years he had likewise bought, intending him for a compositor. And David Harry, a country boy, whom he had taken as apprentice.

It was an odd thing to find an Oxford scholar in the situation of a bought servant. Webb was not more than eighteen years of age, and gave me this account of himself; that he was born in Gloucester, educated at a grammar school, belonged to the Witty Club there, and had written some pieces in prose and

"We landed in Philadelphia the 11th of October."

verse which were printed in the Gloucester newspapers. Thence he was sent to Oxford; there he continued about a year, but not well satisfied, wishing of all things to see London and become a player. At length receiving his quarterly allowance of fifteen guineas, he walked out of town, hid his gown in a furze bush, and footed it to London, where he fell into bad company, soon spent his guineas, found no means of being introduced among the players, grew necessitous, pawned his clothes and wanted bread. Walking the street very hungry, a crimp's bill was put into his hand, offering immediate encouragement to such as would bind themselves to serve in America. He went directly, signed the indentures, was put into the ship and came over; never writing a line to acquaint his friends what was become of him. He was lively, witty, good-natured, and a pleasant companion, but idle, thoughtless and imprudent to the last degree.

I soon perceived that Keimer's intention of engaging me at wages so much higher than he had been used to give, was to have these raw cheap hands formed through me, and as soon as I had instructed them, then, they being all articled to him, he should be able to do without me. I went on however, very cheerfully; put his printing house in order, which had been in great confusion, and brought his hands by degrees to mind their business and to do it better.

John the Irishman soon ran away. With the rest I began to live very agreeably; for they all respected me, the more as they found Keimer incapable of instructing them, and that from me they learnt something daily. We never worked on a Saturday, that being Keimer's Sabbath. So I had two days for reading. My acquaintance with ingenious people in the town, increased. Keimer treated me with great civility; and nothing now made me uneasy but my debt to Vernon, which I was unable to pay being hitherto but a poor economist. He however kindly made no demand of it.

Our printing house often wanted sorts, and there was no letter founder in America. However I now contrived a mold, made use of the letters we had, as puncheons, struck the matrices in lead, and thus supplied in a pretty tolerable way all deficiencies.

I also engraved several things on occasion. I made the

"*I . . . made use of the letters we had.*"

ink, I was warehouseman and everything, in short quite a factotum.

But I found that my services became every day of less importance, as the other hands improved. And when Keimer paid my second quarter's wages, he let me know that he felt them too heavy. He grew less civil, frequently found fault, was captious and seemed ready for an outbreaking.

At length a trifle snapt our connection. For a great noise happening near the courthouse, I put my head out of the window to see what was the matter. Keimer being in the street looked up and called out to me in an angry tone to mind my business, adding some reproachful words, that nettled me the more for their publicity, all the neighbors who were looking out being witnesses. He came up into the printing house, continued the quarrel, high words passed on both sides, he gave me the quarter's warning we had stipulated, expressing a wish that he had not been obliged to so long a warning. I told him his wish was unnecessary for I would leave that instant; and so taking my hat walked out; desiring Meredith whom I saw below to take care of some things I left, and bring them to my lodging.

Meredith came accordingly in the evening, when we talked my affair over. He had conceived a great regard for me, and dissuaded me from returning to my native Boston which I began to think of. He reminded me that Keimer was in debt for all he possessed, that his creditors began to be uneasy, and that he kept his shop miserably. That he must therefore fail; which would make a vacancy I might profit of.

I objected my want of money. He then let me know, that his father had a high opinion of me, and from some discourse that had passed between them, he was sure would advance money to set us up, if I would enter into partnership with him. My time, says he, will be out with Keimer in the spring. By that time we may have our press and types in from London. I am sensible I am no workman. If you like it, your skill in the business shall be set against the stock I furnish; and we will share the profits equally.

The proposal was agreeable, and I consented. His father approved of it, the more as he saw I had great influence with his son, had prevailed on him to abstain long from dram drinking, and he hoped might break him of that wretched habit entirely, when we came to be closely connected. I gave an inventory to the father, who carried it to a merchant; the things were sent for; and in the meantime I was to get work if I could at the other printing house.

I found no vacancy there, and so remained idle a few days, when Keimer, on a prospect of being employed to print some paper money, in New Jersey, which would require cuts and types that I only could supply, sent me a very civil message, that old friends should not part for a few words, and wishing me to return. Meredith persuaded me to comply; it would give opportunity for his improvement under my instructions. I returned, and we went on more smoothly. The New Jersey job was obtained. I contrived a copperplate press for it, the first that had been seen in the country. We went together to Burlington, where I executed the whole to satisfaction.

At Burlington I made an acquaintance with many principal people of the province. Several of them had been appointed by the Assembly a committee to attend the press, and take care that no more bills were printed than the law directed. Generally he who attended brought with him a friend or two for company. My mind having been much more improved by reading than Keimer's, I suppose it was for that reason my conversation seemed to be more valued. They had me to their houses, introduced me to their friends and showed me much civility, while Keimer, tho' the master, was a little neglected. In truth he was an odd fish, ignorant, fond of rudely opposing others' opinions, slovenly to extreme dirtiness, and a little knavish withal.

We continued there near three months, and by that time I could reckon among my acquired friends, Judge John Allen, Samuel Bustill, the secretary of the province, members of the Assembly, and Isaac Decow the surveyor general. The latter was a shrewd sagacious old man, who told me that he began for himself when young by wheeling clay for brickmakers, and learnt to write after he was of age. He had now by his industry acquired a good estate; and says he, I foresee, that you will soon work this man out of his business and make a fortune in it at Philadelphia. These friends were afterwards of great use to me, as I occasionally was to some of them. They all continued their regard for me as long as they lived.

Before I enter upon my public appearance in business it may

be well to let you know the then state of my mind, with regard to my principles and morals, that you may see how far those influenced the future events of my life. My parents had early given me religious impressions, and brought me through my childhood piously in the Dissenting way. But I was scarce fifteen when, after doubting by turns of several points as I found them disputed in the different books I read, I began to doubt of Revelation itself. Some books against Deism fell into my hands. It happened that they wrought an effect on me quite contrary to what was intended by them; for the arguments of the Deists which were quoted to be refuted, appeared to me much stronger than the refutations. In short I soon became a thorough Deist.

My arguments perverted some others, particularly Collins and Ralph; but each of them having afterwards wronged me greatly without the least compunction and recollecting my own conduct towards Vernon and Miss Read which at times gave me great trouble, I began to suspect that this doctrine tho' it might be true, was not very useful. That vice and virtue were empty distinctions appeared now not so clever a performance as I once thought it.

So at last I grew convinced that *truth, sincerity and integrity* in dealings between man and man, were of the utmost importance to the felicity of life, and I formed written resolutions, to practice them ever while I lived. And this persuasion, with the kind hand of Providence, or some guardian angel, preserved me (through this dangerous time of youth and the hazardous situations I was sometimes in, remote from the eye and advice of my father) without any *willful* gross immorality or injustice that might have been expected from my want of religion. I had therefore a tolerable character to begin the world with, and determined to preserve it.

We had not been long returned to Philadelphia, before the new types arrived from London. Meredith and I settled with Keimer, and left him. We found a house to hire near the market. To lessen the rent, we took in Thomas Godfrey a glazer and his family, who were to pay a considerable part of it, and we to board with them. We had scarce put our press in order, before an acquaintance of mine brought a countryman to us; whom he had met in the street enquiring for a printer. All our cash was now expended and this countryman's five shillings being our first fruits, gave me more pleasure than any crown I have since earned; and from the gratitude I felt, has made me often more ready than perhaps I should otherwise have been to assist young beginners.

There are croakers in every country always boding its ruin. Such a one then lived in Philadelphia, a person of note, an elderly man, with a wise look. His name was Samuel Mickle. This gentleman stopt one day at my door, and asked me if I was the young man who had lately opened a new printing house. Being answered in the affirmative; he said he was sorry for me, because it was an expensive undertaking and the expense would be lost; for Philadelphia was a sinking place, the people already half bankrupts. He left me melancholy. Had I known him before I engaged in this business, I never should have done it. This man continued to live in this decaying place; refusing for many years to buy a house there, because all was going to destruction, and at last I had the pleasure of seeing him give five times as much for one as he might have bought it for when he first began his croaking.

I SHOULD HAVE MENTIONED before, that in the autumn of the preceding year I had formed most of my ingenious acquaintance into a club for mutual improvement, which we called the Junto. We met on Friday evenings. The rules I drew up required that every member in his turn should produce one or more queries on any point of morals, politics or natural philosophy, to be discussed by the company, and once in three months produce and read an essay of his own writing on any subject he pleased. Our debates were conducted in the sincere spirit of enquiry, without fondness for dispute, or desire of victory; and to prevent warmth all expressions of positiveness were after some time prohibited under small pecuniary penalties. The first members were:

Joseph Brientnall, a copier of deeds for the scriveners; a good-natured middle-aged man, and a great lover of poetry; very ingenious in many little nicknackeries, and of sensible conversation.

Thomas Godfrey, a self-taught mathematician, afterwards inventor of what is now called Hadley's quadrant.

Nicholas Scull, a surveyor, afterwards surveyor general, who sometimes made a few verses.

William Parsons, bred a shoemaker, but loving reading, had acquired a considerable share of mathematics, which he first studied with a view to astrology that he afterwards laughed at. He also became surveyor general.

William Maugridge, a joiner, a most exquisite mechanic.

Hugh Meredith, Stephen Potts, and George Webb, I have characterized before.

Robert Grace, a young gentleman of some fortune, generous, witty, and a lover of punning.

William Coleman, then a merchant's clerk, who had the coolest head, and the best heart, of almost any man I ever met with. He became afterwards a merchant of great note, and one of our provincial judges.

The club continued almost forty years and was the best school of philosophy, morals and politics that then existed in the province. Every one of the members also exerted themselves in recommending business to us. Brientnall procured us from the Quakers, the printing of forty sheets of their history, and upon this we worked exceeding hard. I composed of it a sheet a day, and Meredith worked it off at press. What with the little jobs sent in by our other friends it was often eleven at night and sometimes later, before I had finished my distribution for the next days work.

This industry visible to our neighbors began to give us character and credit; although the general opinion was that the new printing office must fail, there being already two printers in the place. But Dr. Baird gave a contrary opinion. For the industry of that Franklin, says he, is superior to anything I ever saw of the kind: I see him still at work when I go home from club; and he is at work again before his neighbors are out of bed.

George Webb, who had found a female friend that lent him wherewith to purchase his time of Keimer, now came to offer himself as a journeyman to us. We could not then employ him, but I foolishly let him know, as a secret, that I soon intended to begin a newspaper, and might have work for him. The then only newspaper, printed by Bradford was a paltry thing, in no way entertaining; and yet it was profitable. I therefore thought a good paper could scarcely fail of good encouragement.

I requested Webb not to mention it, but he told it to Keimer, who immediately published proposals for printing one himself, on which Webb was to be employed. I resented this, and to counteract them, as I could not yet begin our paper, I wrote several pieces of entertainment for Bradford's paper, under the title of the Busy Body. By this means the attention of the public was fixed on that paper, and Keimer's proposals which we burlesqued and ridiculed, were disregarded. He began his paper however, and after carrying it on three quarters of a year, with at most ninety subscribers, he offered it to me for a trifle, and I took it in hand directly, and it [*The Pennsylvania Gazette*] proved in a few years extremely profitable to me.*

I perceive that I am apt to speak in the singular number, though our partnership still continued. The reason may be, that the whole management of the business lay upon me. Meredith was no compositor, a poor pressman, and seldom sober.

Our first papers made a quite different appearance from any before in the province, a better type and better printed. Some spirited remarks of my writing on the dispute then going on between Governor Burnet and the Massachusetts Assembly, struck the principal people, and in a few weeks brought them all to be our subscribers. Their example was followed by many, and our number went on growing. This was one of the first good effects of my having learnt a little to scribble. Another was, that the leading men, seeing a newspaper in the hands of one who could also handle a pen, thought it convenient to

---

*After Franklin and Meredith took over *The Pennsylvania Gazette* in 1729, it soon became perhaps the liveliest and most readable newspaper in all the colonies. Franklin's connection with it ceased entirely in 1766, though it continued until 1815. Its relationship to the modern *Saturday Evening Post* is extremely remote; certainly the assertion formerly made that Franklin founded the *Post* in 1728 is historically incorrect.

The Pennſylvania Gazette.

Containing the freſheſt Advices Foreign and Domeſtick.

From Tueſday, January 5. to Tueſday, January 12. 1730-31.

The S P E E C H *of the Honourable* Patrick Gordon, *Eſq; Governor of the Province of* Pennſylvania, *and Counties of* New-Caſtle, Kent *and* Suſſex *upon* Delaware.

To the Repreſentatives of the Freemen of the ſaid Province, met at *Philadelphia*, Jan. 6. 1730-31.

G E N T L E M E N,

THE Tranquility which this Province at preſent enjoys, and the growing Unanimity amongſt us which has happily prevailed over the paſt Feuds and Diſſenſions, are now ſo viſible, that I cannot but Congratulate the Repreſentative Body of this good People, on a Proſpect, ſo delightful in itſelf, ſo deſireable by every good Man who has a real and hearty Love for his Country, and which as it muſt give the higheſt Satisfaction to a Governor, cannot fail of being equally agreeable to the Governed.

Amongſt the many valuable Privileges derived to this Colony from our late honourable Proprietor, that of annual Elections is none of the leaſt, whereby frequent Opportunities are given to the Legiſlature of inſpecting and regulating our publick Affairs; and as the Perſons choſen to that important Truſt are ſuppoſed to be Men of Virtue, Wiſdom and Ability, ſo likewiſe from the Opportunities they have in their reſpective Counties, of knowing the State and Condition of their Country, they cannot but, when convened together and ſeriouſly diſpoſed to promote the publick Intereſt, be very good Judges of thoſe Means, by which our Happineſs and Proſperity may be promoted: And from hence it is, Gentlemen, that I think it unneceſſary at this Time to mention to you ſeveral Things, which as they naturally fall under your Conſideration in the Courſe of your Proceedings, will no doubt be as ſeriouſly attended to, as if they had come particularly recommended from me.

I muſt neverthelſs obſerve, that as it hath pleaſed God this laſt Year to bleſs not only theſe Parts of *America* with a very plentiful Harveſt, but alſo as we hear moſt of the Countries in *Europe*, which of Courſe has put a Stop to their Demand for our Produce; it therefore naturally follows that our own Proviſion muſt be low: We ought however, as Plenty of the Fruits of the Earth has ever been held one of the greateſt Bleſſings of Heaven, not only to acquieſce but be humbly thankful for our preſent Affluence; yet as many may by this Means be pinched by a Stagnation of the Currency, which ever enſues in all Countries where their Produce is not in demand, it may at this Time be incumbent on us to think of all poſſible Meaſures to recommend our Manufactures to a greater Degree abroad, that when at Market they may find a readier Sale.

I have underſtood that when this Colony was young, and had but little Experience, it exceeded all its Neighbours in the Fineneſs of its Flour and Bread, and Goodneſs of its Beer, which are the only Produce of our Grain; the Regulations which have already been made in the two Firſt, have greatly contributed to their Improvement, as well as the Reputation of the Province, and it will ſtill become the Legiſlature to continue their Care and Concern in a Point of ſuch Conſequence to the whole Country: But the Abuſes in the laſt are ſo groſs, that you cannot but be all ſenſible of the Reproach brought on us, when you hear how we have of late been ſupplied by a neighbouring Colony; and therefore I need ſay little to excite your moſt vigorous Reſolutions to apply a proper Remedy, which in my Opinion may very eaſily be found.

And if beſides ſuch Meaſures as may render the Produce of our Grain more valuable, and conſequently bring it more into demand, Encouragement were given to raiſe ſome other Commodities that might have a conſtant and ready vent in *Britain*, and thereby help to make Returns, it would certainly be of vaſt Advantage to the Publick.

In my Speech to the firſt Aſſembly choſen after my Arrival, I mentioned Iron, Hemp and Silk; in the firſt of theſe divers proceeded with Vigour, till the vaſt Quantities unexpectedly imported into *Britain*, from the new Works in *Ruſſia*, where the poor People labour almoſt for nothing, has given ſome damp to that Manufacture: But as Silk comes from Countries long ſettled and accuſtomed to the Buſineſs, where their Prices cannot much alter; and as no Climate in the World is found to agree better with the Silkworm than this; ſince it is impoſſible, that as the Inhabitants increaſe, the raiſing of Grain ſhould always turn to Account for Exportation, nothing in my Judgment can be more worthy of your Application, than to excite the People to the Planting of Mulberry Trees, and furniſhing themſelves with Silkworms, ſince it is a Work of which the pooreſt and feebleſt Families are capable, and Children who can be of little other Service, may here find an Employment ſuitable to their Years; as the Buſineſs is new, People will naturally be backward in falling into the Practice; but if we conſider that all Manufactures were ſo at firſt, that the *Weſt-Indies* were for ſome time ſettled, before they thought of raiſing Sugars, from whence they now make vaſt Eſtates; we ſhould not be diſcouraged: For all Things of this Kind require only Reſolution in the Beginning, at which moſt Things appear difficult, that afterwards become eaſy and familiar. I therefore recommend it to you, *Gentlemen*, to think of ſome ſuitable Encouragement that may prompt the Inhabitants to proper Endeavours on their Parts, and I ſhall uſe mine to procure Perſons of Skill, to lead them into a Way of finiſhing their Labours to Advantage. The raiſing of Hemp, and dreſſing it by Water-rotting, the only Method we find for rendring it truly uſeful, has already its Encouragement; and it is hoped in Time, this alſo may be applied to make Returns.

Theſe are the Points I ſhall now recommend to you, in which, as I have nothing in View but the true Intereſt and Honour of the Province, and of every Subject under my Care, I cannot doubt your ready Concurrence. This Diſpoſition will naturally lead you to Unanimity and Diſpatch, the only Means of giving Succeſs to all our Counſels, and of a happy and ſpeedy Iſſue to the Seſſion; which that we may attain, with ſincere Expreſſions, and real Proofs of Loyalty to his Majeſty, Fidelity to our honourable Proprietors, and with the Increaſe of Love and Good-will amongſt all our Inhabitants, is the higheſt of my preſent Wiſhes.

P. G O R D O N.

To the Honourable PATRICK GORDON, *Eſq; Lieut. Governor of the Province of* Pennſylvania, *&c.*

The *A D D R E S S* of the Repreſentatives of the Freemen of the ſaid Province in General Aſſembly met.

May it pleaſe the GOVERNOR,

" AS we are very ſenſible of the great Bleſſings of
" Peace and Unanimity which at this Time ſeem to
" ſubſiſt amongſt all Sorts of People in this Province; ſo
" we do aſſure the Governor, nothing can give us more
" real Satisfaction, than to ſee the juſt Senſe the People in
" general

On POVERTY. By STEPHEN DUCK, Ætat. 25.

THERE is no Ill on Earth which Mortals fly
With so much Dread, as abject POVERTY.
O despicable Name! We Thee to shun,
On every other Evil blindly run.
For fear of Thee, distrustful Niggards go
In tatter'd Rags, and starve their Bodies too;
And still are poor, for Fear of being so.
For Fear of Thee, the Trader swears and vows
His Wares are good, altho' his Conscience knows
That he hath us'd his utmost Art and Skill,
Their Faults and Imperfections to conceal.
The Sailor terrify'd with Thoughts of Thee,
Boldly attempts the Dangers of the Sea:
From East to West, o'er Rocks and Quicksands steers,
'Tis POVERTY, 'tis that alone he fears.
The Soldier too, whom nought but Thee can scare,
In hopes of Plunder, bravely meets the War:
To fly from POVERTY, he runs on Death,
And shews he prizes Riches more than Breath.
Strange Terror of Mankind! by Thee misled,
Not Conscience, Quick-sands, Rocks, or Death they dread:
And yet thou art no formidable Foe,
Except to little Souls, who think Thee so.
'Tis only the Imagination, that
The blunted Edge of POVERTY can whet.
'Tis servile Fear that does affright us most;
'Tis that transforms a Shadow to a Ghost.
Thus when a tim'rous Man, in Fears grown old,
Reminds the Fairy Tales his Nurse has told;
In the dark Night he oft will sideways squint,
And see a Goblin when there's nothing in't.
Contented POVERTY's no dismal Thing,
Free from the Cares unweildy Riches bring:
At distance both alike deceive our View,
Nearer approach'd, they take another Hue.
The poor Man's Labour relishes his Meat;
His Morsel's pleasant, and his Rest is sweet.
The little, Nature craves, we find with ease;
Too much but surfeits into a Disease:
And what we have, more than we can enjoy,
Instead of satisfying, does but cloy.
But should we in another Prospect take it;
Was Poverty so hideous as they make it;
That steady Man is worthy of our Praise,
Who in Distress, or pinch'd with Hunger, says,
Let Poverty, or Want, be what it will,
It does proceed from God, therefore's no Ill.
How much his great heroic Soul aspire
Above that sordid Wealth the rest admire!
His noble Thoughts are fix'd on Things above,
Where by true Faith, he sees the God of Love
Hold forth th' attractive Prize, which makes him run
His mortal Race, to gain th' immortal Crown.
Not all the Snares a crafty Dev'l can lay,
Can intercept', or stop him in his Way;
His God-like Soul pursues the Thing that's good,
And soars above the common Multitude.
Not all the scornful Insults of the Proud,
Nor Censures of the base and groveling Croud:
Not POVERTY, in all her Terrors drest,
Can shake the solid Quiet of his Breast.
Unmov'd he stands, against his worst of Foes,
And mocks the Darts which adverse Fortune throws;
Calm and compos'd amidst or Ease or Pain,
Enjoys that true Content, which others seek in vain.
So stands a fixed Rock, lofty and steep,
Within the Confines of the briny Deep:
Lash'd by the foaming Surges on each Side,
Yet can't be shaken by th' indignant Tide.
Then why should Fantoms discompose the Mind,
Or Woes, so far from real, fright Mankind?
Since Wealth is but imaginary Fame,
Since POVERTY is nothing but a Name;
Since both from GOD's unerring Hand are sent.
Lord, give me neither, give me but CONTENT.

PHILADELPHIA, Feb. 2.
Custom-House, Philadelphia, Entries None. Our River's is Fast and full of Ice.

*** The agreeable Letter signed Parthenope is come to Hand, and shall be taken Notice of in due Time. ***

Buried in the several Burying-Grounds of this City in a Week past
Church - - - - 3. Baptists - - - - - - - - 0.
Quakers - - - - 1. Strangers Whites - - 0.
Presbyterians - - 1. Blacks - - - 4.

Advertisements.

PHILADELPHIA: Printed by B. Franklin and H. Meredith, at the New Printing-Office near the Market, where Advertisements are taken in, and all Persons may be supplied with this Paper, at Ten Shillings a Year.

encourage me. Bradford still printed the votes and laws and other public business. He had printed an address of the House to the governor in a coarse blundering manner; we reprinted it elegantly and correctly, and sent one to every member. They voted us their printers for the year ensuing.

Mr. Vernon about this time put me in mind of the debt I owed him. I craved his forbearance a little longer, and as soon as I was able I paid the principal with interest and many thanks. So that erratum was in some degree corrected.

But now another difficulty came upon me, which I had never the least reason to expect. Mr. Meredith's father, who was to have paid for our printing house, was able to advance only one hundred pounds, which had been paid. A hundred more was due to the merchant, who grew impatient and sued us. We gave bail, but saw that if the money could not be raised in time, the suit must come to a judgment, and our hopeful prospects must be ruined, as the press and letters must be sold for payment.

In this distress two true friends whose kindness I never shall forget while I can remember anything, came to me separately unknown to each other, and without any application from me, offered each of them to advance me all the money necessary to enable me to take the whole business upon myself. They did not like my continuing the partnership with Meredith, who as they said was often seen drunk in the streets, much to our discredit. These two friends were members of the Junto, Coleman and Grace. I told them I could not propose a separation while any prospect remained of the Merediths fulfilling their part of our agreement, because I thought myself under great obligations to them. But if they finally failed in their performance, and our partnership must be dissolved, I should then think myself at liberty to accept the assistance of my friends.

Thus the matter rested for some time, when I said to my partner, Perhaps your father is dissatisfied at the part you have undertaken in this affair of ours, and is unwilling to advance for you and me what he would do for you alone. If that is the

"Our first papers made a quite different appearance from any before in the province."

case, I will resign the whole to you and go about my business. No says he, my father has been disappointed and is really unable; and I am unwilling to distress him farther. I see this is a business I am not fit for. I was bred a farmer, and it was a folly in me to come to town and put myself at thirty years of age an apprentice to learn a new trade. Many of our Welsh people are going to settle in North Carolina where land is cheap. I am inclined to go with them, and follow my old employment. You may find friends to assist you. If you will

Three-pence note printed by Franklin.

take the debts of the company upon you, return to my father the hundred pounds he has advanced, pay my little personal debts, and give me thirty pounds and a new saddle, I will relinquish the partnership and leave the whole in your hands.

I agreed to this proposal. It was drawn up in writing, signed and sealed immediately. I recurred to my two friends; I took half what each had offered, paid off the company debts, and went on with the business in my own name. I think this was about the year 1729. Meredith went soon after to Carolina; from whence he sent me next year two long letters, containing the best account that had been given of that country, the climate, soil, husbandry, &c. for in those matters he was very judicious. I printed them in the papers, and they gave great satisfaction to the public.

About this time there was a cry among the people for more

paper money, only fifteen thousand pounds being extant in the province and that soon to be sunk. The wealthy inhabitants opposed any addition, being against all paper currency, from an apprehension that it would depreciate as it had done in New England. We had discussed this point in our Junto, where I was on the side of an addition, being persuaded that the first small sum struck in 1723 had done much good, by increasing the trade employment, and number of inhabitants in the province, since I now saw all the old houses inhabited, and many new ones building. I remembered well, that when I first walked about the streets of Philadelphia, eating my roll, I saw most of the houses in Walnut Street between Second and Front streets and many likewise in Chestnut Street, with bills on their doors, to be let; which made me then think the inhabitants of the city were one after another deserting it.

I wrote and printed an anonymous pamphlet, entitled, *The Nature and Necessity of a Paper Currency*. It was well received by the common people; but the rich men disliked it; for it increased the clamor for more money; and they happening to have no writers among them that were able to answer it, the point was carried by a majority in the House. My friends there thought fit to reward me, by employing me in printing the money, a very profitable job, and a great help to me. This was another advantage gained by my being able to write.

The utility of this currency became by time and experience so evident, as never afterwards to be much disputed, so that it grew in 1739 to eighty thousand pounds since which it arose during war to upwards of three hundred fifty thousand pounds, trade, building and inhabitants all the while increasing; tho' I now think there are limits beyond which the quantity may be hurtful.

I soon after obtained, through my friend Andrew Hamilton,* the printing of the Newcastle paper money, another profitable job, as I then thought it; small things appearing great to those in small circumstances. He procured me also the printing of the laws and votes of that government.

---

*Andrew Hamilton was speaker of both the Delaware and the Pennsylvania assemblies.

I now opened a little stationer's shop. I had in it blanks of all sorts the correctest that ever appeared among us. I had also paper, parchment, chapmen's books, &c. One Whitmarsh a compositor I had known in London, now came to me and worked with me, and I took an apprentice the son of Aquila Rose.

I began gradually to pay off the debt I was under for the printing house. In order to secure my credit and character as a tradesman, I took care to be industrious and frugal. I drest plainly; I never went out a-fishing or shooting; a book, indeed, sometimes debauched me from my work; but that was seldom, and gave no scandal; and to show that I was not above my business, I sometimes brought home the paper I purchased at the stores, through the streets

"I sometimes brought home the paper I purchased, on a wheelbarrow."

on a wheelbarrow. Thus being esteemed an industrious thriving young man, paying duly for what I bought, the merchants who imported stationery solicited my custom, others proposed supplying me with books, and I went on swimmingly. In the meantime Keimer's credit and business declining daily, he was at last forced to sell his printing house to satisfy his creditors. He went to live in Barbados.

There remained now no competitor with me at Philadelphia, but the old one, Bradford, who was rich and easy, did a little printing now and then, but was not very anxious about the business. However, as he kept the post office, it was imagined he had better opportunities of obtaining news, his paper was thought a better distributer of advertisements than mine, and therefore had many more, which was a disadvantage to me.

I HAD CONTINUED TO BOARD with Godfrey who lived in part of my house with his wife and children, and had one side of the shop for his glazier's business. Mrs. Godfrey projected a match for me with a relation's daughter, and took opportunities of bringing us often together, till a serious courtship on my part ensued, the girl being in herself very deserving. The old folks encouraged me by continual invitations, and by leaving us together, till at length it was time to explain.

Mrs. Godfrey managed our little treaty. I let her know that I expected as much money with their daughter as would pay off my remaining debt for the printing house, which was not then above a hundred pounds.* She brought me word they had no such sum to spare. I said they might mortgage their house in the loan office. The answer to this after some days was, that they did not approve the match; that on enquiry of Bradford they had been informed the printing business was not a profitable one, the types would soon be worn out and more wanted, that S. Keimer had failed, and I should probably soon follow him. Therefore I was forbidden the house, and the daughter shut up.

Whether this was a real change of sentiment, or only artifice, on a supposition of our being too far engaged in affection to retract, and therefore that we should steal a marriage, which would leave them at liberty to give or withhold what they pleased, I know not. But I suspected the latter, resented it, and went no more. This was resented by the Godfreys, we differed, and they removed, leaving me the whole house, and I resolved to take no more inmates.

This affair having turned my thoughts to marriage, I made overtures of acquaintance in other places; but found that the business of a printer being generally thought a poor one, I was not to expect money with a wife unless with such a one, as I should not otherwise think agreeable. In the meantime, that hard-to-be-governed passion of youth, had hurried me into intrigues with low women that fell in my way, which were attended with some expense and great inconvenience, besides a continual risk to my health.

---

*According to the customs of the day, marriages were often arranged in which financial considerations were more important than romantic affection, if the parties seemed to each other and their families adequately "deserving." Franklin's expectation of a monetary settlement as part of the proposed "treaty" was by no means unusual.

A friendly correspondence as neighbors, had continued between me and Mrs. Read's family, who all had a regard for me from the time of my first lodging in their house. I was often invited there and consulted in their affairs, wherein I sometimes was of service. I pitied poor Miss Read's unfortunate situation, for she was generally dejected, seldom cheerful, and avoided company. I considered my giddiness and inconstancy when in London as in a great degree the cause of her unhappiness; tho' the mother was good enough to think the fault more her own than mine, as she had prevented our marrying before I went thither, and persuaded the other match in my absence.

Our mutual affection was revived, but there were now great objections to our union. The other match was indeed looked upon as invalid, a preceding wife being said to be living in England; but this could not easily be proved, because of the distance. And tho' there was a report of his death, it was not certain. Then tho' it should be true, he had left many debts which his successor might be called on to pay. We ventured however, over all these difficulties, and I [took] her to wife September 1, 1730. None of the inconveniences happened that we had apprehended, she proved a good and faithful helpmate, assisted me much by attending the shop, we throve together, and have ever mutually endeavored to make each other happy. Thus I corrected that great erratum as well as I could.*

MEMO.

Thus far was written with the intention expressed in the beginning and therefore contains several little family anecdotes of no importance to others. What follows was written many years after. The affairs of the Revolution occasioned the interruption.

---

*In the absence of full proof that John Rogers had a "preceding wife" in England, Deborah Read could not get her marriage to him annulled, and Pennsylvania had no law under which she could divorce him. If she and Franklin had gone through the marriage ceremony prescribed by Pennsylvania law and Rogers had later reappeared, both Deborah and Benjamin could have been convicted of bigamy and punished by whipping with thirty-nine lashes and imprisonment at hard labor for life. Deborah's family and all their friends thereafter accepted this informal "common-law" marriage as adequate, and the two children she is known to have borne him were regarded as legitimate.

PART TWO

Continuation of the Account of my Life.
Begun at Passy 1784.*

NOT HAVING ANY COPY here of what is already written, I know not whether an account is given of the means I used to establish the Philadelphia public library, though I remember to have come down to near the time of that transaction, 1730. I will therefore begin here, with an account of it, which may be struck out if found to have been already given.

At the time I established myself in Pennsylvania, there was not a good bookseller's shop in any of the colonies southward of Boston. Those who loved reading were obliged to send for their books from England. The members of the Junto had each a few. We had left the alehouse where we first met, and hired a room to hold our club in. I proposed that we should all of us bring our books to that room, where they would not only be ready to consult in our conferences, but become a common benefit, each of us being at liberty to borrow such as he wished to read at home; and we filled one end of the room.

Finding the advantage of this little collection, I proposed to render the benefit from books more common by commencing a public subscription library. Each subscriber engaged to pay a certain sum down for the purchase of books and an annual contribution for increasing them. So few were the readers at this time in Philadelphia, and the majority of us so poor, I was not able with great industry to find more than fifty persons, mostly young tradesmen, willing to pay down for this purpose forty shillings each, and ten shillings per annum. On this little fund we began.

This was the mother of all the North American subscription libraries. The books were imported [from England]. The library was open one day in the week for lending them to the subscribers, on their promissory notes to pay double the value if

---

*Franklin was in France at this time as minister.

not duly returned. The institution soon manifested its utility and was imitated by other towns. Reading became fashionable; our people having no public amusements to divert their attention became better acquainted with books, and in a few years the common tradesmen and farmers were observed by strangers to be better instructed and more intelligent than people of the same rank generally are in other countries. These libraries perhaps have contributed to the stand so generally made throughout the colonies in defense of their privileges.

The objections I met with in soliciting the subscriptions, made me soon feel the impropriety of presenting one's self as the proposer of any useful project that might be supposed to raise one's reputation in the smallest degree above that of one's neighbors, when one has need of their assistance. I therefore put myself as much as I could out of sight, and

"I established the Philadelphia public library."

stated it as a scheme of a *number of friends*, who had requested me to propose it to such as they thought lovers of reading. In this way my affair went on more smoothly, and I ever after practiced it on such occasions; and from my frequent successes, can heartily recommend it. The present little sacrifice of your vanity will afterwards be amply repaid. If it remains a while uncertain to whom the merit belongs, someone more vain than yourself will be encouraged to claim it, and then even envy will be disposed to do you justice, by plucking those assumed feathers, and restoring them to their right owner.

This library afforded me the means of improvement by constant study, for which I set apart an hour or two each day; and thus repaired in some degree the loss of the learned education my father once intended for me. Reading was the only amusement I allowed myself. I spent no time in taverns, games, or frolics of any kind. And my industry in my business continued as indefatigable as it was necessary. I was in debt for my printing house, I had a young family coming on to be educated,* and I had to contend with for business two printers who were established in the place before me. My circumstances however grew daily easier: my original habits of frugality continuing. And my father having among his instructions to me when a boy, frequently repeated a proverb of Solomon, *"Seest thou a man diligent in his calling, he shall stand before kings, he shall not stand before mean men,"* I from thence considered industry as a means of obtaining wealth and distinction, which encouraged me, tho' I did not think that I should ever literally stand before kings, which however has since happened—for I have stood before five, and even had the honor of sitting down with one, the King of Denmark, to dinner.

We have an English proverb that says,

> He that would thrive
> Must ask his wife;

it was lucky for me that I had one as much disposed to industry and frugality as myself. She assisted me cheerfully in my business, folding and stitching pamphlets, purchasing old linen rags for the papermakers, &c. &c. We kept no idle servants, our table was plain and simple, our furniture of the cheapest. For instance my breakfast was a long time bread and milk, (no tea) and I ate it out of a twopenny earthen porringer with a pewter spoon. But mark how luxury will enter families, and make a progress, in spite of principle. Being called one morning to breakfast, I found it in a china bowl with a spoon of silver. They had been bought for me by my wife, and had cost her the enormous sum of three-and-twenty shillings, for she thought *her* husband de-

---

*Franklin's children were: William, called by his family and close friends "Billy," born about 1731, an illegitimate son; Francis Folger, called "Frankie," born 1732, died 1736; and Sarah, called "Sally," born 1743. There are no direct descendants with the surname Franklin today. There are many in the United States with other surnames, descended through Sarah, who married Richard Bache in 1767. Direct descendants in England trace through William's granddaughter Ellen Franklin, who married Capel Hanbury in 1818.

Project and my Studies; Resolution once
become habitual, would keep me firm in my
Endeavours to obtain all the subsequent Virtues;
Frugality & Industry, by freeing me from Debt &
necessity, producing Affluence & Independance
would make more easy the Practice of Sincerity
and Justice, &c. &c... Conceiving then that
agreable to the Advice of Pythagoras in his
Golden Verses, daily Examination would be
necessary, I contriv'd the following Method
for conducting that Examination.

    I made a little Book in which I allotted
a Page for each of the Virtues. I rul'd each
Page with red Ink so as to have seven Columns,
one for each Day of the Week, marking each
Column with a Letter for the Day. I cross'd
these Columns with thirteen red Lines,
marking the Beginning of each Line with the
first Letter of one of the Virtues, on which
Line & in its proper Column I might mark by a little
black Spot every Fault I found upon Examination to have
committed respecting that Virtue upon that Day.

        Form of the Pages

^ my remaining

* Insert these Lines that direct it
in a Note

	S	M	T	W	T	F	S
Temperance. *Eat not to Dulness. Drink not to Elevation.*							
T							
S	•	•		•		•	
O	•	•	•		•	•	•
R				•		•	
F			•		•		
I		•					
S							
J							
M							
C							
T							
C							
H							

served a silver spoon and china bowl as well as any of his neighbors. This was the first appearance of plate and china in our house, which as our wealth increased augmented gradually to several hundred pounds in value.

I had been religiously educated as a Presbyterian; and tho' some of the dogmas of that persuasion appeared to me doubtful, and I early absented myself from the public assemblies of the sect, I never was without some religious principles. I never doubted, for instance, the existence of the Deity, or that our souls are immortal; I avoided all discourse that might tend to lessen the good opinion another might have of his religion; and as our province increased in people and new places of worship were continually wanted, and generally erected by voluntary contribution, my mite for such purpose, whatever might be the sect, was never refused.

Tho' I seldom attended any public worship, I had still an opinion of its propriety, and its utility, and I regularly paid my annual subscription for the support of the only Presbyterian minister or meeting we had in Philadelphia. He used to visit me sometimes as a friend, and admonish me to attend his administrations, and I was now and then prevailed on to do so, once for five Sundays successively. Had he been, *in my opinion*, a good preacher perhaps I might have continued, notwithstanding the occasion I had for the Sunday's leisure in my course of study; but his discourses were all to me very dry and unedifying, since not a single moral principle was inculcated, their aim seeming to be rather to make us Presbyterians than good citizens. At length I was disgusted, and attended his preaching no more. I had some years before composed a little liturgy for my own private use, viz, in 1728, entitled, *Articles of Belief and Acts of Religion*. I returned to this, and went no more to the public assemblies.

It was about this time [he was twenty-two] that I had conceived the bold and arduous project of arriving at moral perfection. I wished to live without committing any fault at any time; I would conquer all that either natural inclination, custom, or company might lead me into. As I knew, or thought I knew, what was right and wrong, I did not see why I might not *always* do the one and avoid the other.

I soon found I had undertaken a task of more difficulty than I had imagined. While my *attention was taken up* in guarding against one fault, I was often surprised by another. Habit took the advantage of inattention. Inclination was sometimes too strong for reason. I concluded at length, that the mere conviction that it was our interest to be completely virtuous, was not sufficient; contrary habits must be broken and good ones acquired and established, before we can have a steady uniform rectitude of conduct.

For this purpose I therefore contrived the following method. I proposed to myself, for the sake of clearness, to enumerate names of all the virtues that occurred to me as necessary or desirable. These totaled thirteen, and I annexed to each a short precept, which fully expressed the extent I gave to its meaning. These names of virtues with their precepts were

1. TEMPERANCE.

Eat not to dulness.
Drink not to elevation.

2. SILENCE.

Speak not but what may benefit others or yourself. Avoid trifling conversation.

3. ORDER.

Let all your things have their places. Let each part of your business have its time.

4. RESOLUTION.

Resolve to perform what you ought. Perform without fail what you resolve.

5. FRUGALITY.

Make no expense but to do good to others or yourself: i.e. waste nothing.

6. INDUSTRY.

Lose no time. Be always employed in something useful. Cut off all unnecessary actions.

7. SINCERITY.

Use no hurtful deceit.
Think innocently and justly; and, if you speak, speak accordingly.

8. JUSTICE.

Wrong none, by doing injuries or omitting the benefits that are your duty.

9. MODERATION.

Avoid extremes. Forbear resenting injuries so much as you think they deserve.

10. CLEANLINESS.

Tolerate no uncleanness in body, clothes or habitation.

11. TRANQUILITY.

Be not disturbed at trifles, or at accidents common or unavoidable.

12. CHASTITY.

Rarely use venery but for health or offspring; never to dulness, weakness, or the injury of your own or another's peace or reputation.

13. HUMILITY.

Imitate Jesus and Socrates.

My intention being to acquire the *habitude* of all these virtues, I judged it would be well not to distract my attention by attempting the whole at once, but to fix it on one of them at a time, and when I should be master of that, then to proceed to another, and so on till I should have gone through the thirteen. And as the previous acquisition of some might facilitate the acquisition of certain others, I arranged them with that view as they stand above.

Temperance first, as it tends to procure that coolness and clearness of head, which is so necessary where constant vigilance was to be kept up, and guard maintained, against ancient habits, and the force of perpetual temptations. This being established, *Silence* would be more easy, and my desire being to gain knowledge at the same time that I improved in virtue, and considering that in conversation it was obtained rather by the use of the ears than of the tongue, and therefore wishing to break a habit I was getting into of prattling, punning and joking, I gave *Silence* the second place.

This, and the next, *Order*, I expected would allow me more time for attending to my project and my studies; *Resolution*, once become habitual, would keep me firm in my endeavors to obtain all the subsequent virtues; *Frugality* and *Industry*, by freeing me from my remaining debt, and producing affluence and independence, would make more easy the practice of *Sincerity* and *Justice*, &c. &c.

Conceiving then that daily examination concerning these virtues would be necessary, I contrived the following method for conducting that examination.

I made a little book in which I allotted a page for each of the virtues. I ruled each page with red ink, so as to have seven columns, one for each day of the week. I crossed these columns with thirteen red lines, marking the beginning of each line with the first letter of one of the virtues, on which line and in its proper column I might mark by a little black spot every fault I found upon examination to have been committed respecting that virtue upon that day.

I determined to give a week's strict attention to each of the virtues successively. Thus in the first week my great guard was to avoid the least offense against *Temperance*, leaving the other virtues to their ordinary chance, only marking every evening the faults of the day. If in the first week I could keep my first line marked T clear of spots, I supposed the habit of that virtue so much strengthened that I might venture extending my attention to include the next, and for the following week keep both lines clear of spots.

Proceeding thus to the last, I could go through a course complete in thirteen weeks, and four courses in a year, and have the encouraging pleasure of seeing on my pages the progress I made in virtue.

This my little book had for its motto these lines from Addison's *Cato;*

> *Here will I hold: If there is a Pow'r above us,*
> *(And that there is, all nature cries aloud*
> *Thro' all her works) He must delight in virtue,*
> *And that which he delights in must be happy.*

And conceiving God to be the fountain of wisdom, I thought it necessary to solicit His assistance; to this end I formed the following little prayer, which was prefixed to my tables of examination; for daily use.

O powerful Goodness! bountiful Father! merciful Guide! Increase in me that wisdom which discovers my truest interests; strengthen my resolutions to perform what that wisdom dictates. Accept my kind offices to Thy other children, as the only return in my power for Thy continual favors to me.

The precept of *Order* requiring that *every part of my business should have its allotted time,* one page in my little book contained the following scheme of employment for the twenty-four hours of a natural day,

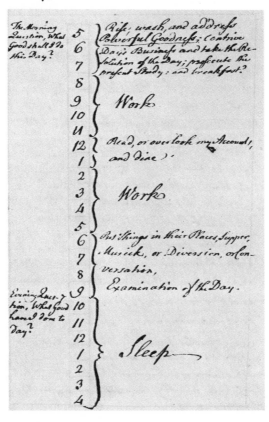

I entered upon the execution of this plan for self-examination, and was surprised to find myself so much fuller of faults than I had imagined, but I had the satisfaction of seeing them diminish. To avoid the trouble of renewing my little book, I transferred my tables to the ivory leaves of a memorandum book, on which the lines were drawn with red ink that made a durable stain, and on those lines I marked my faults with a black lead pencil, which marks I could easily wipe out with a sponge. After a while I went through one course only in a year, and afterwards only one in several years, till at length I omitted them entirely, being employed in voyages and business abroad, but I always carried my little book with me.

My scheme of *Order*, gave me the most trouble, with regard to places for things and papers. I made so little progress, and had such frequent relapses, that I was almost ready to give up, and content myself with a faulty character in that respect. Like the man who in buying an axe of a smith my neighbor, desired to have the whole of its surface as bright as the edge; the smith consented to grind it bright for him if he would turn the wheel. He turned while the smith pressed the broad face of the axe hard and heavily on the stone, which made the turning of it very fatiguing. The man at length would take his axe as it was without farther grinding. "No," says the smith, "turn on, turn on; we shall have it bright by and by; as yet 'tis only speckled." "Yes," says the man; "but—*I think I like a speckled axe best.*" For something that pretended to be reason was every now and then suggesting to me, that such extreme nicety as I exacted of myself might be a kind of foppery in morals, that a perfect character might be attended with the inconvenience of being envied and hated; and that a benevolent man should allow a few faults in himself, to keep his friends in countenance.

But on the whole, tho' I never arrived at the perfection I had been so ambitious of obtaining, but fell far short of it, yet I was by the endeavor a better and a happier man. And it may be well my posterity should be informed, that to this little artifice, with the blessing of God, their ancestor owed the constant felicity of his life down to his seventy-ninth year in which this is written. To *Temperance* he ascribes his long-continued health. To *Industry* and *Frugality* the early easiness of his circumstances, and acquisition of his fortune, with all that knowledge which enabled him to be a useful citizen. To *Sincerity* and *Justice* the confidence of his country, and the honorable employs it conferred upon him.

My list of virtues contained at first but twelve. But a Quaker friend having kindly informed me that I was generally thought proud; that my pride showed itself frequently in conversation; I determined to cure myself if I could of this vice or folly among the rest, and I added *Humility* to my list, giving an extensive meaning to the word. I cannot boast of much success in acquiring the *reality* of this virtue; but I had a good deal with regard to the *appearance* of it.

But there is perhaps no one of our natural passions so hard to subdue as *Pride*. Disguise it, struggle with it, beat it down, stifle it as much as one pleases, it is still alive, and will every now and then peep out. You will see it perhaps often in this history. For even if I could conceive that I had completely overcome it, I should probably be proud of my humility.

Thus far written at Passy 1784.

PART THREE

I AM NOW ABOUT TO WRITE at home, August 1788, but cannot have the help expected from my papers, many of them being lost in the war. I have however found the following.

Having mentioned *a great and extensive project* which I had conceived, it seems proper that some account should be here given of that project and its object. Its first rise in my mind appears in the following little paper, accidentally preserved, viz

OBSERVATIONS on my reading history in library, May 9, 1731.

. . . .

That few in public affairs act from a mere view of the good of their country, whatever they may pretend; and tho' their actings bring real good to their country, yet men primarily considered

Poor Richard, 1733.

AN

Almanack

For the Year of Chrift

1 7 3 3,

Being the Firft after LEAP YEAR:

And makes fince the Creation	Years
By the Account of the Eaftern *Greeks*	7241
By the Latin Church, when ☉ ent. ♈	6932
By the Computation of *W.W.*	5742
By the *Roman* Chronology	5682
By the *Jewifh* Rabbies	5494

Wherein is contained

The Lunations, Eclipfes, Judgment of the Weather, Spring Tides, Planets Motions & mutual Afpects, Sun and Moon's Rifing and Setting, Length of Days, Time of High Water, Fairs, Courts, and obfervable Days.

Fitted to the Latitude of Forty Degrees, and a Meridian of Five Hours Weft from *London*, but may without fenfible Error, ferve all the adjacent Places, even from *Newfoundland* to *South-Carolina.*

By RICHARD SAUNDERS, Philom.

PHILADELPHIA:
Printed and fold by *B. FRANKLIN*, at the New Printing-Office near the Market.

that their own and their country's interest was united, and did not act from a principle of benevolence.

That fewer still in public affairs act with a view to the good of mankind.

There seems to me at present to be great occasion for raising an united party for virtue, by forming the virtuous and good men of all nations into a regular body, to be governed by suitable good and wise rules, which good and wise men may probably be more unanimous in their obedience to, than common people are to common laws.

I at present think, that whoever attempts this aright, and is well qualified, cannot fail of pleasing God, and of meeting with success.   B. F.

My ideas at that time were, that a sect should be begun and spread at first among young and single men only; that each person to be initiated should have exercised himself with the thirteen weeks' examination and practice of the virtues as in the before-mentioned model; that the existence of such a society should be kept a secret till it was become considerable; that the members should engage to afford their advice assistance and support to each other in promoting one another's interest, business and advancement in life.

I communicated this project to two young men, who adopted it with some enthusiasm. But the necessity I was then under of sticking close to my business, occasioned my postponing the farther prosecution of it at that time, and my multifarious occupations public and private induced me to continue postponing, so that it has been omitted till I have no longer strength or activity left sufficient for such an enterprise, tho' I am still of opinion that it was a practicable scheme. I have always thought that one man of tolerable abilities may work great changes, if he first forms a good plan, and makes the execution of that same plan his sole study and business.

In 1732 I first published my Almanack, under the name of *Richard Saunders*; it was continued by me about twenty-five years, commonly called *Poor Richard's* Almanack. I endeavored to make it both entertaining and useful, and it accordingly came to be in such demand that I reaped considerable profit from it, vending annually near ten thousand. And observing scarce any neighborhood in the province being without it, I considered it as a proper vehicle for conveying instruction among the common people, who bought scarce any other books. I therefore filled all the little spaces that occurred between the remarkable days in the calendar, with proverbial sentences, chiefly such as

An illustration from "Poor Richard's Almanack."

inculcated industry and frugality, as the means of procuring wealth and thereby securing virtue, it being more difficult for a man in want to act always honestly, as (to use here one of those proverbs) *it is hard for an empty sack to stand upright.* These proverbs, which contained the wisdom of many ages and nations, I assembled into a connected discourse prefixed to the Almanack of 1757. It was presented as the harangue of a wise old man to the people attending an auction. The piece was copied in all the newspapers of the Continent, and great numbers bought by the clergy and gentry to distribute gratis among their poor parishioners and tenants.

I considered my newspaper also as another means of communicating instruction, and in that view frequently reprinted in it extracts from moral writers, and sometimes published little pieces of my own which had been first composed for reading in our Junto. In the conduct of my newspaper I carefully excluded all libeling and personal abuse, which is of late become so disgraceful to our country. Whenever I was solicited to insert anything of that kind, and the writers pleaded the liberty of the press, and that a newspaper was like a stagecoach in which anyone who would pay had a right to a place, my answer was, that I would print the piece separately if desired, and the author might have as many copies as he pleased to distribute himself, but that having contracted with my subscribers to furnish them with what might be either useful or entertaining, I could not fill their papers with private altercation in which they had no concern. Now many of our printers make no scruple of augmenting animosity even to the producing of duels.

In 1733, I sent one of my journeymen to Charleston South Carolina where a printer was wanting. I furnished him with a press and letters, on an agreement of partnership. On his decease, the business was continued by his widow, who being born and bred in Holland, where as I have been informed the knowledge of accounts makes a part of female education, she not only sent me a clear state of the transactions past, but also managed the business with such success that she brought up reputably a family of children, and at the expiration of the term was able to purchase of me the printing house and establish her son in it. I mention this affair chiefly for the sake of recommending that branch of education for our young females, as likely to be of more use to them and their children in case of widowhood than either music or dancing.

In 1733 I also began to study languages. I soon made myself a master of the French, and I then undertook the Italian. An acquaintance who was also learning it, used often to tempt me to play chess with him. Finding this took up too much of the time I had to spare for study, I at length refused to play anymore, unless on this condition, that the victor in every game, should have a right to impose a task, in Italian grammar or in translation, &c. which tasks the vanquished was to perform upon honor before our next meeting. As we played pretty equally we thus beat one another into that language. I afterwards with a little painstaking acquired as much of the Spanish as to read their books also.

After ten years' absence from Boston, I made a journey thither to visit my relations. In returning I called at Newport, to see my brother then settled there with his printing house. Our former differences were forgotten, and our meeting was cordial and affectionate. He was fast declining in health, and requested of me that in case of his death which he apprehended not far distant, I would take home his son, then but ten years of age, and bring him up to the printing business. This I accordingly performed, sending him a few years to school before I took him into the office. His mother carried on the business till he was grown up, when I assisted him with an assortment of new types, those of his father being worn out. Thus it was that I made my brother ample amends for the service I had deprived him of by leaving him so early.

In 1736 I lost one of my sons, [Frankie] a fine boy of four years old, by the smallpox. I long regretted bitterly and still regret that I had not given it to him by inoculation. This I mention for the sake of parents, who omit that operation on the supposition that they should never forgive themselves if a child died under it; my example shows that the regret may be the same either way, and that therefore the safer should be chosen.

Our club, the Junto, was found so useful, and afforded such satisfaction to the members, that several were desirous of introducing their friends, which could not well be done without exceeding what we had settled as a convenient number, twelve. We had from the beginning made it a rule to keep our institution a secret, to avoid applications of improper persons for admittance. I was against any addition to our number, but instead made a proposal, that every member separately should endeavor to form a subordinate club, with the same rules, and without informing them of the connection with the Junto. The advantages proposed were the promotion of our interests in business by more extensive recommendations; and the increase of our

"*I endeavored to make my Almanack both entertaining and useful.*"
Illustration from "Poor Richard's Almanack."

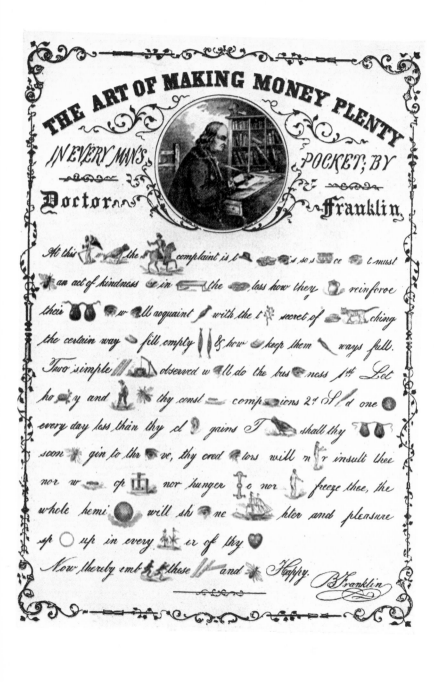

influence in public affairs by spreading through the several clubs the sentiments of the Junto. The project was approved, and every member undertook to form his club. Five or six only were completed, which were called by different names, as the Vine, the Union, the Band, &c. They were useful in influencing the public opinion on particular occasions, of which I shall give some instances in course of time as they happened.

My first promotion was my being chosen in 1736 clerk of the General Assembly. But the year following when I was again proposed a new member made a long speech against me, in order to favor some other candidate. I was however chosen; which was the more agreeable to me, as besides the pay for immediate service as clerk, the place gave me opportunity to secure the business of printing the votes, laws, paper money, and other occasional jobs for the public. I therefore did not like the opposition of this new member, who was a gentleman of fortune, and education, with talents that were likely to give him in time great influence in the House. I did not however aim at gaining his favor by paying any servile respect to him, but after some time took this other method. Having heard that he had in his library a certain very scarce and curious book, I wrote a note to him requesting he would do me the favor of lending it to me. He sent it immediately; and I returned it in about a week, with another note expressing my sense of the favor. When we next met in the House he spoke to me with great civility. Afterwards we became great friends. This is another instance of the truth of an old maxim I had learnt, which says, *He that has once done you a kindness will be more ready to do you another, than he whom you yourself have obliged.* And it shows how much more profitable it is prudently to remove, than to resent, return and continue inimical proceedings.

In 1737, Colonel Spotswood, late governor of Virginia, and then postmaster general, being dissatisfied with the conduct of his deputy at Philadelphia, respecting some negligence in his rendering of accounts, took from him the commission and offered it to me. I found it of great advantage; tho' the salary was small, it facilitated the correspondence that improved my newspaper, and increased the number demanded, as well as the advertisements, so that it came to afford me a very considerable income. Thus my old competitor Bradford suffered greatly. I mention it as a lesson to those young men who may be employed in managing affairs for others that they should always render accounts and make remittances with great clearness and punctuality.

I BEGAN NOW TO TURN my thoughts a little to public affairs. The city watch was one of the first things that I conceived to want regulation. It was managed by the constables of the respective wards in turn. The constable warned a number of housekeepers to attend him for the night. Those who chose never to attend paid him six shillings a year for hiring substitutes. This in reality was much more than was necessary, and the constable for a little drink often got ragamuffins about him as a watch, so that walking the rounds was often neglected, and most of the night spent in tippling. I thereupon wrote a paper to be read in Junto, representing these irregularities, and proposing a watch of proper men to serve constantly in that business. This idea being approved by the Junto, was communicated to the other clubs, but as arising in each of them. It paved the way for the law obtained a few years after, when the members of our clubs were grown into more influence.

About this time I wrote a paper, (first to be read in Junto but it was afterwards published) on the different accidents by which houses were set on fire. This gave rise to a project of forming a company for the more ready extinguishing of fires, and mutual assistance in removing and securing of goods when in danger. Associates in this scheme presently amounted to thirty. Our articles of agreement obliged every member to keep always fit for use, a certain number of leather buckets, with strong baskets (for packing and transporting of goods) which were to be brought to every fire; and we agreed to meet once a month and spend an evening together, for communicating useful ideas upon the subject of fires.

The utility of this institution soon appeared, and others formed companies, till they became so numerous as to include most of the inhabitants who were men of property. The small fines paid by members for absence at the monthly meetings, were applied to the purchase of fire engines, ladders, and other implements for each company, so that I question now whether there is a city in the world better provided with the means of putting a stop to beginning conflagrations.

In 1739 arrived among us from England the Reverend Mr. Whitefield, who had made himself remarkable there as an itinerant preacher. He was at first permitted to preach in some of our churches; but the clergy taking a dislike to him, soon refused him their pulpits and he was obliged to preach in the fields. Multitudes of all sects and denominations attended his sermons, and greatly admired him, notwithstanding his com-

The Court House, Second Street north from Market Street, Philadelphia.

mon abuse of them. He assured them they were naturally *half beasts and half devils,* and it was wonderful to see the change this soon made in the manners of our inhabitants. From being thoughtless about religion, it seemed as if all the world were growing religious; so that one could not walk through the town in an evening without hearing psalms sung in different families of every street.

Mr. Whitefield, in leaving us, went preaching all the way

through the colonies to Georgia. The settlement of that province had lately been begun; but instead of being made with industrious husbandmen accustomed to labor, it was with families of broken shopkeepers and other insolvent debtors, taken out of the gaols. Being set down in the woods, unqualified for clearing land, and unable to endure the hardships of a new settlement, they perished in numbers, leaving many helpless children unprovided for. The sight of their miserable situation inspired Mr. Whitefield with the idea of building an orphan house there, in which they might be supported. Returning northward he preached up this charity, and made large collections.

In time I became intimately acquainted with him, (being employed in printing his sermons, &c.) and we became sincere friends, though we had no religious connection. He used indeed sometimes to pray for my conversion, but never had the satisfaction of believing that his prayers were heard. He once wrote to me from Boston that he should come soon to Philadelphia, but knew not where he could lodge when there. My answer was, You know my house, if you can make shift with its scanty accommodations you will be most heartily welcome. He replied, that if I made that kind offer for Christ's sake, I should not miss of a reward. And I returned, *Don't let me be mistaken; it was not for Christ's sake, but for your sake.*

Mr. Whitefield had a loud and clear voice, and articulated his words so perfectly that he might be understood at a great distance, especially as his auditories, however numerous, observed the most exact silence. He preached one evening from the top of the Court House steps, which are in the middle of Market Street, and on the west side of Second Street which crosses it at right angles. Both streets were filled with his hearers to a considerable distance. Being among the hindmost in Market Street, I had the curiosity to learn how far he could be heard, by retiring backwards down the street towards the river. I found his voice distinct till I came near Front Street,* when some noise in that street, obscured it. Imagining then a semi-

---

*About 500 feet from the Court House steps. Whitefield attracted crowds estimated at 6,000 to 8,000, remarkable in a city of about 10,000 people.

circle, of which my distance should be the radius, and that it were filled with auditors, to each of whom I allowed two square feet, I computed that he might well be heard by more than thirty thousand. This reconciled me to the newspaper accounts of his having preached to twenty-five thousand people in the fields, and to the ancient histories of generals haranguing whole armies, of which I had sometimes doubted.

MY BUSINESS WAS NOW continually augmenting, and my circumstances growing daily easier, my newspaper having become very profitable, being for a time almost the only one in this and neighboring provinces. I experienced too the truth of the observation, that *after getting the first hundred pound, it is more easy to get the second,* money itself being of a prolific nature.

The partnership at Carolina having succeeded, I was encouraged to engage in others, and to establish several of my workmen with printing houses in different colonies. Most of them did well, being enabled at the end of our term, six years, to purchase the types of me; and go on working for themselves, by which means several families were raised. Partnerships often finish in quarrels, but I was happy in this, that mine were all carried on and ended amicably; owing I think to the precaution of having very explicitly settled in our articles everything to be done by or expected from each partner, so that there was nothing to dispute, which precaution I would therefore recommend to all who enter into partnerships.

I had on the whole abundant reason to be satisfied with my being established in Pennsylvania. There were however two things I regretted: there being no provision for defense, nor for a complete education of youth; no militia nor any college.

With respect to defense, Spain had been several years at war against Britain, being at length joined by France, which brought us into greater danger.* The long-continued endeavors of our

---

*Great Britain declared war on Spain in 1739 (the War of Jenkins' Ear), and on France in 1744 (the War of the Austrian Succession, or, in America, King George's War). French and Spanish privateers in Delaware Bay during the spring and summer of 1747 caused the immediate alarm, which ended when news of the Peace of Aix-la-Chapelle reached Philadelphia in August 1748.

governor George Thomas to prevail with our Quaker Assembly to pass a militia law having proved abortive, I determined to try what might be done by a voluntary association of the people. To promote this I first wrote and published a pamphlet, entitled, *Plain Truth*. In it I stated our defenseless situation in strong lights, and promised to propose in a few days an association for our defense.

The pamphlet had a sudden and surprising effect. I was called upon for the instrument of association. Having settled the draft of it with a few friends, I appointed a meeting of the citizens in a large building. The house was pretty full. I had prepared a number of printed copies, and provided pens and ink dispersed all over the room. I harangued them a little on the subject, read the paper and explained it, and then distributed the copies, which were eagerly signed.

When the papers were collected we found above twelve hundred hands; and other copies being dispersed in the country the subscribers amounted at length to upwards of ten thousand. These all furnished themselves as soon as they could with arms; formed themselves into companies, and regiments, chose their own officers, and met every week to be instructed in military discipline. The women, by subscriptions among themselves, provided silk colors, which they presented to the companies, painted with different mottos which I supplied.

I then proposed a lottery to defray the expense of building a battery below the town, and furnishing it with cannon. It filled expeditiously and the battery was soon erected, the merlons being framed of logs and filled with earth. We bought some old cannon from Boston, but these not being sufficient, we wrote to England for more; and we solicited at the same time our proprietaries, [hereditary governors] for some assistance, tho' without much expectation of obtaining it.

Meanwhile Colonel Lawrence, William Allen, Abraham Taylor, Esquires, and myself were sent to New York by the associators, commissioned to borrow some cannon of Governor Clinton. He at first refused us peremptorily: but at a dinner with his council where there was great drinking of Madeira wine, as the custom at that place then was, he softened by

degrees, and said he would lend us six. After a few more bump-
ers he advanced to ten. And at length he very good-naturedly
conceded eighteen. They were fine cannon, eighteen-pounders,
with their carriages, which we soon transported and mounted
on our battery, where the associators kept a nightly guard while
the war lasted. And among the rest I regularly took my turn of
duty there as a common soldier.

It was thought by some of my friends that by my activity
in these affairs, I should offend the Quakers, and thereby lose
my interest in the Assembly where they were a great majority.
A young gentleman who had likewise some friends in the House,
and wished to succeed me as their clerk, acquainted me that it
was decided to displace me at the next election. He therefore
in good will advised me to resign, as more consistent with my
honor than being turned out. My answer to him was, that I had
read or heard of some public man, who made it a rule never to
ask for an office, and never to refuse one when offered to him.
"I approve," says I, "of his rule, and will practice it with a small
addition; I shall never *ask*, never *refuse*, nor ever *resign* an office."
I was chosen again, unanimously as usual, at the next election.

Indeed I had some cause to believe, that the defense of the
country was not disagreeable to any of the Quaker sect, provided they were not required to assist in it. And I found that a
much greater number of them than I could have imagined, tho'
against offensive war, were clearly for the defensive. One
honorable and learned Quaker, Mr. Logan, told me the following anecdote of his old master William Penn, respecting defense. Mr. Logan had come over from England, when a young
man, with that proprietary, and as his secretary. It was war-
time, and their ship was chased by an armed vessel supposed to
be an enemy. Their captain prepared for defense, but told William Penn and his company of Quakers, that he did not expect
their assistance, and they might retire into the cabin. They did,
except James Logan, who chose to stay upon deck, and was
quartered to a gun. The supposed enemy proved a friend; so
there was no fighting. But when the secretary went down to
communicate the intelligence, William Penn rebuked him
severely for staying upon deck to assist in defending the vessel,

contrary to the principles of *Friends*, especially as it had not been required by the captain. This reproof being before all the company, piqued the secretary, who answered, "I being thy servant, why did thee not order me to come down? But thee was willing enough that I should stay and help to fight the ship when thee thought there was danger."

My being many years in the Assembly, the majority of which were constantly Quakers, gave me frequent opportunities of seeing the embarrassment given them by their principle against war, whenever application was made to them by order of the Crown to grant aids for military purposes. The common mode at last adopted was to grant money under the phrase of its being *for the King's use*, and never to enquire how it was applied. But if the demand was not directly from the Crown, that phrase was found not so proper, and some other was to be invented. As when powder was wanting, (I think it was for the garrison at Louisbourg,) and the government of New England solicited a grant of some from Pennsylvania, which was much urged on the House by Governor Thomas, they could not grant money to buy powder, because that was an ingredient of war. Instead, they voted an aid to New England, of three thousand pounds, to be put into the hands of the governor, and appropriated it for the purchasing of bread, flour, wheat, *or other grain*. Some of the council desirous of giving the House still farther embarrassment, advised the governor not to accept provision, as not being the thing he had demanded. But he replied, "I shall take the money, for I understand very well their meaning; *other grain*, is gunpowder"; which he accordingly bought; and they never objected to it.

These embarrassments that the Quakers suffered from having established it as one of their principles, that no kind of war was lawful, and which being once published, they could not afterwards, however they might change their minds, easily get rid of, reminds me of what I think a more prudent conduct in another sect among us; that of the Dunkers. I was acquainted with one of its founders, Michael Wohlfahrt, who complained to me that they were grievously calumniated by the zealots of other persuasions, and charged with abominable principles to which they were utter strangers. I told him that to stop such abuse, it might be well to publish the articles of their belief. He said that it had been proposed among them, but not agreed to, for this reason; "From time to time God has been pleased to afford us farther light, and our principles have been improving, and our errors diminishing. We fear that if we should once print our confession of faith, we should feel ourselves as if bound and confined by it." This modesty in a sect is perhaps a singular

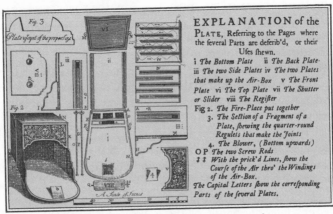

"I invented an open stove, for the better warming of rooms."

instance in the history of mankind, every other sect supposing itself in possession of all truth, and that those who differ are so far in the wrong.

In order of time I should have mentioned before, that having in 1742 invented an open stove, for the better warming of rooms and at the same time saving fuel, as the fresh air admitted was warmed in entering, I made a present of the model to Mr. Robert Grace, one of my early friends. He, having an iron furnace, found the casting of the plates for these stoves a profitable thing, as they were growing in demand. To promote that demand I wrote and published a pamphlet entitled, *An Account of the New-Invented* PENNSYLVANIA FIRE PLACES: *Wherein their Construction and manner of Operation is particularly explained; their Advantages above every other Method of warming Rooms demonstrated; and all Objections that have been raised against the Use of them answered.* Governor Thomas was so pleased with the stove, that he offered to give me a patent for the sole vending of them for a term of years; but I declined it from a principle which has ever weighed with me on such occasions, viz. *That as we enjoy great advantages from the inventions of others, we should be glad of an opportunity to serve others by any invention of ours, and this we should do freely and generously.* An ironmonger in London, however, after making some small changes in the machine, which rather hurt its operation, got a patent for it there, and made I was told a little fortune by it. And this is not the only instance of patents taken out for my inventions by others, which I never contested, hating disputes.

Peace being concluded, and the militia association business therefore at an end, I turned my thoughts again to education, to the affair of establishing an academy. The first step I took was to associate in the design a number of active friends, of whom the Junto furnished a good part; the next was to write and publish a pamphlet entitled, *Proposals relating to the Education of Youth in Pennsylvania.* This I distributed among the principal inhabitants gratis; and as soon as I could suppose their minds a little prepared by the perusal of it, I set on foot a subscription for opening an academy. It was to be paid in quotas yearly for five years; by so dividing it I judged the subscription might be larger, and I believe it was so, amounting to no less than five thousand pounds. In the introduction to these proposals, I stated their publication not as an act of mine, but of some *public-spirited gentlemen;* avoiding as much as I could, according to my usual rule, the presenting myself to the public as the author of any scheme for their benefit.

The subscribers, to carry the project into immediate execution chose out of their number twenty-four trustees, and appointed Mr. Francis, then attorney general, and myself, to draw up constitutions for the government of the academy, which being done and signed, a house was hired, masters engaged and the schools opened I think in 1749. The scholars increasing fast, the house was soon found too small, and we were looking out for a piece of ground, with intention to build, when Providence threw into our way a large house ready built, which with a few alterations might well serve our purpose.

It is to be noted, that the contributions to this building being made by people of different sects, care was taken in the nomination of trustees that one of each sect was appointed, viz. one Church-of-England man, one Presbyterian, one Baptist, one Moravian, &c. The Moravian happened not to please his colleagues, and on his death, they resolved to have no other of that sect. The difficulty then was, how to avoid having two of some other sect. At length one mentioned me, with the observation that I was merely an honest man, and of no sect at all; which prevailed with them to choose me.

"I turned my thoughts to the affair of establishing an academy."

The trustees of the academy were put in possession of the premises, and by dividing the great hall into stories and rooms, the whole was soon made fit for our purpose, and the scholars moved into the building. The trouble of agreeing with the workmen, purchasing materials, and superintending the work fell upon me. I went through it the more cheerfully, as it did not then interfere with my private business, having the year before taken a very able and honest partner, Mr. David Hall. He took off my hands all care of the printing office. This partnership continued eighteen years, successfully for us both.

The trustees of the academy after a while were incorporated by a charter from the governor; their funds were increased by contributions in Britain, and grants of land from the proprietaries, to which the Assembly has since made considerable addition, and thus was established the present University of Philadelphia.* I have been continued one of its trustees from the beginning, now near forty years, and have had the very great pleasure of seeing a number of the youth who have received their education in it, distinguished by their improved abilities, serviceable in public stations, and ornaments to their country.

WHEN I DISENGAGED myself as above mentioned from private business, I flattered myself that by the sufficient tho' moderate fortune I had acquired, I had secured leisure during the rest of my life, for philosophical studies and amusements. I purchased all Dr. Spencer's apparatus, who had come from Scotland to lecture here; and I proceeded in my electrical experiments with great alacrity. But the public now considering me as a man of leisure, laid hold of me for their purposes; every part of our civil government imposing some duty upon me. The governor put me into the commission of the peace; the corporation of the city chose me of the common council, and soon after an alderman; and the citizens at large chose me a burgess to represent them in Assembly. This latter station was the more agreeable to me, as I was at length tired with sitting in the House to hear debates in which as clerk I could take no part, and which were often so unentertaining, that I was induced to amuse myself with making magic squares, or circles, or anything to avoid weariness. And I conceived my becoming a member would enlarge my power of doing good. I would not however insinuate that my ambition was not flattered by all these promotions. It certainly was. For considering my low beginning they were great things to me.

The year following, a treaty was to be concluded with the Indians at Carlisle, and the governor sent a message to the House, proposing that they should nominate some of their members to be joined with some members of council as commissioners for that purpose. The House named the speaker (Mr. Isaac Norris) and myself; and being commissioned we went to Carlisle, and met the Indians accordingly. As those

*Now the University of Pennsylvania.

people are extremely apt to get drunk, and when so are very disorderly, we strictly forbad the selling any liquor to them; and when they complained of this restriction, we told them that if they would continue sober during the treaty, we would give them plenty of rum when business was over. They promised this; and kept their promise, and the treaty was conducted very orderly, and concluded to mutual satisfaction.

They then claimed and received the rum. This was in the afternoon. They were near one hundred men, women and children, and were lodged in cabins built in a square just without the town. In the evening, hearing a great noise among them, the commissioners walked out to see what was the matter. We found they had made a great bonfire in the middle of the square. They were all drunk men and women, quarreling and fighting. Their dark-colored bodies, half naked, seen only by the gloomy light of the bonfire, running after and beating one another with firebrands, accompanied by their horrid yellings, formed a scene the most resembling our ideas of hell that could well be imagined.

There was no appeasing the tumult, and we retired to our lodging. At midnight a number of them came thundering at our door, demanding more rum; of which we took no notice. The next day, sensible they had misbehaved, they sent three of their old counselors to make their apology. The orator laid the fault upon the rum; and then endeavored to excuse the rum, by saying, *"The great Spirit who made all things made everything for some use, and whatever use he designed anything for, that use it should always be put to; now, when he made rum, he said,* LET THIS BE FOR INDIANS TO GET DRUNK WITH. *And it must be so."* And indeed if it be the design of Providence to extirpate these savages in order to make room for cultivators of the earth, it seems not improbable that rum may be the appointed means.

In 1751, Dr. Thomas Bond, a particular friend of mine, conceived the idea of establishing a hospital in Philadelphia, for the cure of poor sick persons. He was zealous in endeavoring to procure subscriptions for it; but the proposal being a novelty in America, he met with small success. At length he came to me, with a compliment. "For," says he, "I am often asked by those to whom I propose subscribing, Have you consulted Franklin upon this business?"

I enquired into the probable utility of his scheme, and receiving from him a very satisfactory explanation, I not only subscribed to it myself, but engaged heartily in the design of procuring subscriptions from others. Previous however to the solicitation, I endeavored to prepare the minds of the people by writing on the subject in the newspapers, which was my usual custom in such cases, but which he had omitted.

The subscriptions afterwards were more free and generous, but beginning to flag, I saw they would be insufficient without some assistance from the Assembly, and therefore proposed to petition for it, which was done. The requisite sum at last being raised, a convenient and handsome building was soon erected, the institution has by constant experience been found useful, and flourishes to this day.

OUR CITY, THO' LAID OUT with a beautiful regularity, the streets large, straight, and crossing each other at right angles, had the disgrace of suffering those streets to remain long unpaved, and in wet weather the wheels of heavy carriages ploughed them into a quagmire. I had lived near the Jersey Market, and saw with pain the inhabitants wading in mud while purchasing their provisions. A strip of ground down the middle of that market was at length paved with brick, so that being once in the market they had firm footing, but were often over shoes in dirt to get there.

By talking and writing on the subject, I was at length instrumental in getting the street paved with stone between the market and the bricked foot-pavement that was on each side next the houses. This for some time gave an easy access to the market, dry-shod. But the rest of the street not being paved, whenever a carriage came out of the mud upon this pavement, it shook off and left its dirt upon it, and it was soon covered with mire, which was not removed, the city as yet having no scavengers.

After some enquiry I found a poor industrious man, who was willing to undertake keeping the pavement clean, by sweeping it twice a week and carrying off the dirt from before all the neighbors' doors, for the sum of sixpence per month, to be paid by each house. I then wrote and printed a paper, setting forth the advantages to the neighborhood that might be obtained by this small expense. I sent one of these papers to each house, and in a day or two went round to see who would subscribe an agreement to pay these sixpences. It was unanimously signed, all the inhabitants of the city were delighted with the cleanliness of the pavement that surrounded the market, and this raised a general desire to have all the streets paved; and made the people more willing to submit to a tax for that purpose.

After some time I drew a bill for paving the city, and brought it into the Assembly. It was just before I went to England in 1757, and did not pass till I was gone, and then with an additional provision for lighting as well as paving the streets, which was a great improvement.

It was a private person, the late Mr. John Clifton, who gave a sample of the utility of lamps by placing one at his door, and thus first impressed the people with the idea of enlighting all the city. The honor of this public benefit has also been ascribed to me, but I did but follow his example; and have only some merit to claim respecting the form of our lamps as differing from the globe lamps we at first were supplied with from London. Those admitted no air below, the smoke therefore did not readily go out above, but circulated in the globe, lodged on its inside, and soon obstructed the light. I therefore suggested composing the lamps of four flat panes, with a long funnel above to draw up the smoke, and crevices admitting air below, to facilitate the ascent of the smoke. By this means they were kept clean, and did not grow dark in a few hours as the London lamps do, but continued bright till morning.

Some may think these trifling matters not worth minding or relating. But human felicity is produced not so much by great pieces of good fortune that seldom happen, as by little advantages that occur every day. Thus if you teach a poor young man to shave himself and keep his razor in order, you may contribute more to the happiness of his life than in giving him a thousand guineas. The money may be soon spent, but in the other case he escapes the frequent vexation of waiting for barbers, and of their sometimes dirty fingers, offensive breaths and dull razors. With these sentiments I have hazarded the few preceding pages, hoping they may afford hints which may be useful perhaps to some of our towns in America.

Having been for some time employed by the postmaster general of America, as his comptroller, in regulating the several offices, and bringing the officers to account, I was upon his death in 1753 appointed jointly with Mr. William Hunter to succeed him, by a commission from the postmaster general in

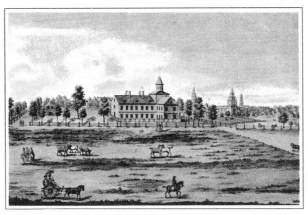

"In 1751, Dr. Thomas Bond, a friend of mine, conceived the idea of establishing a hospital in Philadelphia."

England. The American office had never hitherto paid anything to that of Britain. We were to have six hundred pounds a year between us if we could make that sum out of the profits of the office. To do this, a variety of improvements were necessary; some of these were inevitably at first expensive; so that in the first four years the office became above nine hundred pounds in debt to us. But it soon after began to repay us, and before I was displaced, by a freak of the minister's, we had brought it to yield *three times* as much clear revenue to the Crown as the post office of Ireland.

The business of the post office occasioned my taking a journey this year to New England, where the College of Cambridge presented me with the degree of Master of Arts. Yale College in Connecticut, had before made me a similar compliment. Thus without studying in any college I came to partake of their honors. They were conferred in consideration of my discoveries in the electric branch of natural philosophy.

In 1754, war with France being again apprehended, a congress of commissioners from the different colonies, was by an order of the Lords of Trade, to be assembled at Albany, there to confer with the chiefs of the Six Nations, concerning the means of defending both their country and ours. Governor James Hamilton, having received this order, acquainted the House with it, requesting they would furnish proper presents for the Indians, to be given on this occasion. He named the speaker (Mr. Norris) and myself, to join Mr. John Penn and Mr. Secretary Peters, as commissioners to act for Pennsylvania.

We met at Albany about the middle of June. In our way thither, I projected and drew up a plan for the union of all the colonies, under one government so far as might be necessary for defense, and other important general purposes. I ventured to lay it before the Congress. It then appeared that several of the commissioners had formed plans of the same kind.

A committee was then appointed one member from each colony, to consider the several plans and report. Mine happened to be preferred, and with a few amendments was accordingly reported. By this plan, the general government was to be administered by a president general appointed by the Crown, and a grand council to be chosen by the several colonies meeting in their respective assemblies.

The debates upon the plan in Congress went on daily hand in hand with the Indian business. At length the plan was unanimously agreed to, and copies ordered to be transmitted to the Board of Trade and to the assemblies of the several provinces. Its fate was singular. The assemblies did not adopt it as they all thought there was too much *prerogative* in it; and in England it was judged to have too much of the *democratic*. The Board of Trade therefore did not recommend it for the approbation of his Majesty; but another scheme was formed whereby the governors of the provinces with some members of their councils were to meet and order the raising of troops, building of forts, &c. &c. and to draw on the treasury of Great Britain for the expense, which was afterwards to be refunded by an act of Parliament laying a tax on America.

I am still of opinion it would have been happy for both sides the water if my plan had been adopted. The colonies so united would have been sufficiently strong to have defended them-

John Street in the eighteenth century.

selves; there would then have been no need of troops from England; and of course the subsequent pretense for taxing America, and the bloody contest it occasioned, would have been avoided. But history is full of the errors of states and princes.

> Look round the habitable world, how few
> Know their own good, or knowing it pursue.

Those who govern, having much on their hands, do not generally like to take the trouble of considering and carrying into execution new projects. The best measures are therefore seldom *adopted from previous wisdom,* but *forced by the occasion.*

The governor of Pennsylvania in sending it down to the Assembly, expressed his approbation of the plan "as appearing to him to be drawn up with great clearness and strength of judgment, and therefore recommended it as well worthy their closest and most serious attention." The House however, by the management of a certain member, took it up when I happened to be absent, and reprobated it without paying any attention to it at all, to my no small mortification.

In my journey to Boston this year I met at New York with our new governor, Mr. Robert Hunter Morris, just arrived from England, with whom I had been before intimately acquainted. He brought a commission to supersede Mr. Hamilton, who, tired with the disputes his proprietary instructions subjected him to, had resigned.

Mr. Morris asked me, if I thought he must expect as uncomfortable an administration. I said, "No; you may on the contrary have a very comfortable one, if you will only take care not to enter into any dispute with the Assembly." "My dear friend," says he, pleasantly, "how can you advise my avoiding disputes. You know I

Franklin's historic slogan ("It would have been happy for both sides if my plan had been adopted").

love disputing. However, to show the regard I have for your counsel, I promise you I will if possible avoid them."

He had some reason for loving to dispute, being eloquent, an acute sophister, and therefore generally successful in argumentative conversation. He had been brought up to it from a boy, his father (as I have heard) accustoming his children to dispute with one another for his diversion while sitting at table after dinner. But I think the practice was not wise, for in the course of my observation, these disputing, contradicting and confuting people are generally unfortunate in their affairs.

Notwithstanding his promise to me, it was a continual battle between him and the House, as long as he retained the government. I had my share of it; I was put on every committee for answering his speeches, and by the committees always desired to make the drafts. Our answers as well as his messages were often tart, and sometimes indecently abusive. And as he knew I wrote for the Assembly, one might have imagined that when we met we could hardly avoid cutting throats. But he was so good-natured a man, that no personal difference between him and me was occasioned by the contest, and we often dined together.

These public quarrels were all at bottom owing to the proprietaries, our hereditary governors; who when any expense was to be incurred for the defense of their province, with incredible meanness instructed their deputies to pass no act for levying the necessary taxes, unless their vast estates were in the same act expressly excused; and they had even taken bonds of these deputies to observe such instructions. The assemblies for three years held out against this injustice, tho' constrained to bend at last. At length Captain William Denny, who was Governor Morris's successor, ventured to disobey those instructions; how that was brought about I shall show hereafter.

But I am got forward too fast with my story; there are still some transactions to be mentioned that happened during the administration of Governor Morris.

War was by now, in a manner, commenced with France. Still the British government did not choose to permit the union of the colonies, as proposed at Albany, and to trust that union with their defense, lest they should thereby grow too military, and feel their own strength; so for the purpose of defense it sent over General Braddock with two regiments of regular English troops. He landed at Alexandria in Virginia, and thence marched to Frederic Town in Maryland, where he halted to wait for wagons.

Our Assembly apprehended, from some information, that he had conceived violent prejudices against them, believing them to be averse to his operations. They therefore wished me to wait upon him, not as from them, but as postmaster general, under the guise of proposing to settle with him the mode of conducting dispatches between him and the governors of the several provinces. My son accompanied me on this journey. We found the general at Frederic Town, waiting impatiently for the return of those he had sent through Maryland and Virginia to collect wagons. I stayed with him several days, dined with him daily, and had full opportunity of removing all his prejudices, by the information of what the Assembly had before his arrival actually done and were still willing to do to facilitate his operations.

When I was about to depart, the returns of wagons were brought in, by which it appeared that they amounted only to twenty-five, and not all of those were in serviceable condition. The general and all the officers were surprised, declared the expedition was then at an end, being impossible, and exclaimed against the ministers for ignorantly landing them in a country destitute of the means of conveying their stores, baggage, &c. not less than one hundred and fifty wagons being necessary.

I happened to say, I thought it was pity they had not been landed rather in Pennsylvania, as in that country almost every farmer had his wagon. The general eagerly laid hold of my words, and said, "Then you, sir, who are a man of interest there, can probably procure them for us; and I beg you will undertake it."

I asked what terms were to be offered the owners of the wagons; and I was desired to put on paper the terms that appeared to me necessary. This I did, and they were agreed to. As soon as I arrived at Lancaster, I published the terms in an advertisement, which I insert here, as follows.

ADVERTISEMENT
Lancaster, April 26, 1755.

Whereas 150 wagons, with 4 horses to each wagon, and 1500 saddle or packhorses are wanted for the service of his Majesty's forces; and his Excellency General Braddock hath been pleased to empower me to contract for the hire of the same; I hereby give notice, that I shall attend for that purpose at Lancaster from this time till next Wednesday evening; and at York from next Thursday morning till Friday evening; where I shall be ready to agree for wagons and teams, or single horses, on the following terms, viz.

That there shall be paid for each wagon with 4 good horses and a driver, fifteen shillings per *diem*. And for each able horse with a packsaddle or other saddle and furniture, two shillings per *diem*. And for each able horse without a saddle, eighteen pence per *diem*. And in case of the loss of any wagon, team or horse in the service, a price according to fair valuation, is to be allowed and paid.

Note. My son William Franklin, is empowered to enter into like contracts with any person in Cumberland County.

B. Franklin.

To the Inhabitants of the Counties of Lancaster, York, and Cumberland.

Friends and Countrymen,

Being occasionally at the camp at Frederic a few days since, I found the general and officers of the army extremely exasperated, on account of their not being supplied with horses and carriages, which had been expected from this province as most able to furnish them; and it was proposed to send an armed force immediately into these counties, to seize as many of the best carriages and horses as should be wanted.

If you are really, as I believe you are, good and loyal subjects to his Majesty, you may now do a most acceptable service, and make it easy to yourselves, by furnishing these necessary wagons, horses, and drivers. But if you do not this service to your king and country voluntarily, when such good pay and terms are offered you, your loyalty will be strongly suspected; so many brave troops, come so far for your defense, must not stand idle; wagons and horses must be had; and violent measures will probably be used.

I have no particular interest in this affair; as (except the satisfaction of endeavoring to do good and prevent mischief) I shall have only my labor for my pains. If this method of obtaining the wagons and horses is not like to succeed, I am obliged to send word to the general in fourteen days; and I suppose Sir John St. Clair the hussar, with a body of soldiers, will immediately enter the province, for the purpose aforesaid, of which I shall be sorry to hear, because I am, very sincerely and truly your friend and well-wisher,

B. Franklin.

In two weeks, the 150 wagons with 259 carrying horses were on their march for the camp. The advertisement promised payment according to the valuation, in case any wagon or horse should be lost. The owners however, alleging they did not know General Braddock, or what dependence might be had on his promise, insisted on my bond for the performance, which I accordingly gave them.

While I was at the camp, supping one evening with the officers of Colonel Dunbar's regiment, he represented to me his concern for the subalterns, who could ill afford in this dear country to lay in the stores that might be necessary in so long a march through a wilderness. I wrote the next morning to the committee of Assembly, who had the disposition of some public money, warmly recommending the case to their consideration, and proposing that a present should be sent these officers of necessaries and refreshments. My son, who had had some experience of a camp life, and of its wants, drew up a list for me, which I enclosed in my letter. The committee approved, and used such diligence, that conducted by my son, the stores arrived at the camp as soon as the wagons. They consisted of twenty parcels, each containing

> 6 lb loaf sugar
> 6 lb good Muscovado ditto
> 1 lb good green tea
> 1 lb good bohea ditto
> 6 lb good ground coffee
> 6 lb chocolate
> 1/2 cwt. best white biscuit
> 1/2 lb pepper
> 1 quart best white wine vinegar
> 1 Gloucester cheese
> 1 keg containing 20 lb good butter
> 2 doz. old Madeira wine
> 2 gallons Jamaica spirits
> 1 bottle flour of mustard
> 2 well-cured hams
> 1/2 doz. dried tongues
> 6 lb rice
> 6 lb raisins.

These twenty parcels well packed were placed on as many horses, each parcel with the horse, being intended as a present for one officer. They were very thankfully received. The general too thanked me repeatedly and requested my farther assistance in sending provisions after him. I undertook this also, and was busily employed in it till we heard of his defeat.

This general was I think a brave man, and might probably have made a figure as a good officer in some European war. But he had too much self-confidence, too high an opinion of the validity of regular troops, and too mean a one of both Americans and Indians. George Croghan, our Indian interpreter, joined him on his march with one hundred of those people, who might have been of great use to his army as guides and scouts, if he had treated them kindly; but he slighted them, and they gradually left him.

In conversation with him one day, he was giving me some account of his intended progress. "After taking Fort Duquesne," says he, "I am to proceed to Niagara; and having taken that, to Frontenac, if the season will allow time; and it will; for Duquesne can hardly detain me above three or four days; and then I see nothing that can obstruct my march to Niagara."

Having before revolved in my mind the long line his army must make in their march, by a very narrow road through the woods; and also what I had read of a former defeat of fifteen hundred French who invaded the Iroquois country, I had conceived some fears for the campaign. But I ventured only to say, "To be sure, sir, if you arrive well before Duquesne, with these fine troops so well provided with artillery, that place, not yet as we hear completely fortified, can probably make but a short resistance. The only danger I apprehend is from ambuscades of Indians, who by constant practice are dextrous in laying and executing them." He smiled at my ignorance, and replied, "These savages may indeed be a formidable enemy to your raw American militia; but upon the King's regular and disciplined troops, sir, it is impossible they should make any impression."

The enemy however did not take the advantage of his army which I apprehended its long line of march exposed it to, but let it advance without interruption till within nine miles of

Fort Duquesne. Then when more in a body, and in a more open part of the woods than any it had passed, they attacked its advanced guard, by a heavy fire from behind trees and bushes; which was the first intelligence the general had of an enemy's being near him.

This guard being disordered, the general hurried the troops up to their assistance, which was done in great confusion through wagons, baggage and cattle; and presently the fire came upon their flank; the officers being on horseback were more easily picked out as marks, and fell very fast; and the soldiers were crowded together in a huddle, having or hearing no orders, and standing to be shot at till two thirds of them were killed. Then being seized with a panic the whole fled with precipitation. The wagoners took each a horse out of his team, and scampered, so that all the wagons, artillery and stores were left to the enemy. The general being wounded was brought off with difficulty, and out of 86 officers 63 were killed or wounded, and 714 men killed out of 1100. These 1100 had been picked men, from the whole army, the rest had been left behind with Colonel Dunbar, who was to follow with the heavier part of the baggage.

The flyers, not being pursued, arrived at Dunbar's camp, and the panic they brought with them instantly seized him and all his people. And tho' he had now above one thousand men, and the enemy who had beaten Braddock did not exceed four hundred, Indians and French together; instead of proceeding and endeavoring to recover some of the lost honor, he ordered all the stores and ammunition to be destroyed, that he might have more horses to assist his flight towards the settlements. He was there met with requests from the governors of Virginia, Maryland and Pennsylvania, that he would post his troops on the frontiers so as to afford some protection to the inhabitants; but he continued his hasty march through all the country, not thinking himself safe till he arrived at Philadelphia, where the inhabitants could protect him. This whole transaction gave us Americans the first suspicion that our exalted ideas of the prowess of British regulars had not been well founded.

In their first march too, from their landing till they got

beyond the settlements, they had plundered and stript the inhabitants, totally ruining some poor families, besides abusing and confining people if they remonstrated. This was enough to put us out of conceit of such defenders if we had really wanted any. How different was the conduct of our French friends in 1781, who during a march through the most inhabited part of our country, from Rhode Island to Virginia, near seven hundred miles, occasioned not the smallest complaint, for the loss of a pig, a chicken, or even an apple!

Captain Orme, who was one of the general's aides-de-camp, and being grievously wounded was brought off with him, and continued with him to his death, which happened in a few days, told me, that Braddock was totally silent, all the first day, and at night only said, *Who'd have thought it?* That he was silent again the following days, only saying at last, *We shall better know how to deal with them another time;* and died a few minutes after.

As soon as the loss of the wagons and horses was generally known, all the owners came upon me for the valuation which I had given bond to pay; and some began to sue me. General Shirley at length relieved me from this terrible situation, by appointing commissioners to examine the claims and ordering payment. They amounted to near twenty thousand pounds, which to pay would have ruined me.

Governor Morris had continually worried the Assembly with message after message before the defeat of Braddock, to beat them into making acts to raise money for the defense of the province without taxing among others the proprietary estates, and had rejected all their bills for not having such an exempting clause. Now he redoubled his attacks, with more hope of success, the danger and necessity being greater. The Assembly however continued firm, believing they would be giving up an essential right. In one of the last bills, indeed, which was for granting fifty thousand pounds, the governor's proposed amendment was only of a single word. The bill expressed that all estates real and personal were to be taxed, those of the proprietaries *not* excepted. His amendment was: for *not* read *only.* A small but very material alteration!

However, when the news of this disaster reached England, our friends there raised a clamor against the proprietaries for their meanness and injustice in giving their governor such instructions, some going so far as to say that by obstructing the defense of their province, they forfeited their right to it. The proprietaries were intimidated by this, and sent orders to their receiver general to add five thousand pounds of their money to whatever sum might be given by the Assembly, for such purpose. This the House accepted in lieu of their share of a general tax, and a new bill was formed with an exempting clause which passed accordingly. By this act I was appointed one of the commissioners for disposing of the money, sixty thousand pounds. I had been active in modeling it, and procuring its passage.

I had at the same time drawn a bill for establishing and disciplining a voluntary militia, which I carried through the House.* To promote the association necessary to form the militia, I wrote a dialogue, stating and answering all the objections I could think of to such a militia, which was printed and had as I thought great effect. While the several companies in the city

Colonel Franklin escorted by his regiment.

and country were forming and learning their exercise, the governor prevailed with me to take charge of our northwestern frontier, which was infested by the enemy, and provide for the

*Franklin's militia bill provided for absolute exemption of Quakers and other conscientious objectors, voluntary enlistment, election of the company officers by the ranks, and practically no military discipline. Altogether it was a most unusual piece of legislation, which Governor Morris and his friends proclaimed a "Solemn Farce," yet it was the first act establishing a military force ever passed in Quaker-controlled Pennsylvania.

defense of the inhabitants by raising troops, and building a line of forts. I undertook this military business, tho' I did not conceive myself well qualified for it. He gave me a commission with full powers and a parcel of blank commissions for officers. I had but little difficulty in raising men, having soon five hundred sixty under my command. My son who had in the preceding war been an officer in the army raised against Canada, was my aide-de-camp, and of great use to me.

The Indians had burnt Gnadenhut,* a village settled by the Moravians, and massacred the inhabitants, but the place was thought a good situation for one of the forts. In order to march thither, I assembled the companies at Bethlehem, the chief establishment of those people. I was surprised to find it in a good posture of defense. The principal buildings were defended by a stockade. They had purchased arms and ammunition from New York, and had even placed quantities of small paving stones between the windows of their high stone houses, for their women to throw down upon the heads of any Indians that should attempt to force into them. The armed brethren too, kept watch, and relieved as methodically as in any garrison town. Knowing they had obtained an act of Parliament exempting them from military duties in the colonies, I had supposed they were conscientiously scrupulous of bearing arms. But common sense aided by present danger, will sometimes be too strong for whimsical opinions.

It was the beginning of January when we set out upon this business of building forts. I sent one detachment towards the Minisinks in the Delaware Valley region, with instructions to erect one fort there for the security of the upper part of the country; and another detachment to the lower part, with similar instructions. And I concluded to go myself with the rest of my force to Gnadenhut, where a fort was thought more immediately necessary.

The Moravians procured me five wagons for our tools, stores and baggage. Just before we left Bethlehem, eleven farmers who had been driven from their plantations by the Indians, came

---

*Gnadenhütten, now Lehighton and Weissport, Pennsylvania.

to me requesting firearms, that they might go back and fetch off their cattle. I gave them each a gun with ammunition.

We had not marched many miles before it began to rain, and it continued raining all day. There were no habitations on the road, to shelter us, till we arrived near night, at the house of a German, and in his barn we were all huddled together as wet as water could make us. It was well we were not attacked in our march, for our arms were of the most ordinary sort and our men could not keep their gunlocks dry. The Indians are dextrous in contrivances for that purpose, which we had not. They met that day the eleven poor farmers above mentioned and killed ten of them. The one who escaped informed us that his gun and his companions' guns would not go off, the priming being wet with the rain.

The next day being fair, we continued our march and arrived at the desolated Gnadenhut. There was a sawmill near, round which were left several piles of boards, with which we soon hutted ourselves. Our first work was to bury more effectually the dead we found there, who had been half interred by the country people.

The next morning our fort was planned and marked out, the circumference measuring four hundred fifty-five feet. Our axes, of which we had seventy were immediately set to work, to cut down trees. Seeing the trees fall so fast, I had the curiosity to look at my watch when two men began to cut at a pine. In six minutes they had it upon the ground; and I found it of fourteen inches diameter. Each pine made three palisades of eighteen feet long, pointed at one end.

While these were preparing, our other men, dug a trench all round of three feet deep in which the palisades were to be planted. When they were set up, our carpenters built a stage of boards all round within, about six feet high, for the men to stand on when firing through the loopholes. We had one swivel gun, which we mounted on one of the angles; and fired it as soon as fixed, to let the Indians know that we had such pieces; and thus our fort, (if such a magnificent name may be given to so miserable a stockade) was finished in a week, tho' it rained so hard every other day that the men could not work. This kind of fort, however contemptible, is a sufficient defense against Indians who have no cannon.

We now ventured out in parties to scour the adjacent country. We met with no Indians, but we found the places on the neighboring hills where they had lain to watch our proceedings. It being winter, a fire was necessary for them. But a common fire on the surface of the ground would by its light have revealed their position at a distance. They had therefore dug holes in the ground about three feet diameter, and somewhat deeper. We saw where they had with their hatchets cut off the charcoal from the sides of burnt logs lying in the woods. With these coals they had made small fires in the bottom of the holes, and we observed among the weeds and grass the prints of their bodies made by their laying all round with their legs hanging down in the holes to keep their feet warm, which with them is an essential point. This kind of fire, so managed, could not reveal them either by its light, flame, sparks or even smoke. It appeared that their number was not great, and they saw we were too many to be attacked by them with prospect of advantage.

We had for our chaplain a zealous Presbyterian minister, Mr. Beatty, who complained to me that the men did not generally attend his prayers and exhortations. When they enlisted, they were promised, besides pay and provisions, a gill of rum a day, which was served out to them half in the morning and the other half in the evening, and I observed they were punctual in attending to receive it. Upon which I said to Mr. Beatty, "It is perhaps below the dignity of your profession to act as steward of the rum. But if you were to deal it out, and only just after prayers, you would have them all about you." He undertook the office, and never were prayers more generally and more punctually attended.

My three intended forts being now completed, and the inhabitants contented to remain on their farms under that protection, I resolved to return. I was escorted as far as Bethlehem, where I rested a few days. The first night being in a good bed, I could hardly sleep, it was so different from my hard lodging on the floor of our hut at Gnaden, wrapt only in a blanket or two.

While at Bethlehem, I enquired a little into the practices of the Moravians. I found they worked for a common stock, ate at common tables, and slept in common dormitories. I enquired concerning Moravian marriages, whether the report was true that they were by lot? I was told that lots were used only in particular cases. That when a young man was disposed to marry, he informed the elders, who consulted the elder ladies that governed the young women. If it should happen that two or three young women were found to be *equally* proper for the young man, the lot was then recurred to. I objected, "If the matches are not made by the mutual choice of the parties, some of them may chance to be very unhappy." "And so they may," answered my informer, "if you let the parties choose for themselves"; which indeed I could not deny.

Being returned to Philadelphia, I found the association went on swimmingly; those who had come into it had formed themselves into companies, and chosen captains, lieutenants and ensigns. The officers' meeting chose me to be colonel of the regiment; which I accepted. I forget how many companies we had, but we paraded about twelve hundred well-looking men, with a company of artillery who had been furnished with six brass fieldpieces, which they had become so expert in the use of as to fire twelve times in a minute. The first time I reviewed my regiment, they accompanied me to my house, and would salute me with some rounds fired before my door, which shook down and broke several glasses of my electrical apparatus. And my new honor proved not much less brittle; for all our commissions were soon after broken by a repeal of the law in England.

During the short time of my colonelship, being about to set out on a journey to Virginia, the officers of my regiment took it into their heads that it would be proper for them to escort me out of town as far as the Lower Ferry. Just as I was getting on horseback, they came to my door, between thirty and forty, mounted, and all in their uniforms. Being naturally averse to the assuming of state on any occasion, I was a good deal chagrined when they appeared. Worse, as soon as we began to move, they drew their swords, and rode with them naked all the way. Somebody wrote an account of this to the proprietor, and it gave him great offense. No such honor had been paid him when in the province; and he said it was only proper to princes of the blood royal; which may be true for aught I know. This silly affair however greatly increased his rancor against me, which was before considerable, on account of my conduct in the Assembly, respecting the exemption of his estate from taxation.

IT MAY NOT BE AMISS here to give some account of the rise and progress of my philosophical reputation. In 1743 being at Boston, I met there with a Dr. Spencer, who was lately arrived from Scotland, and showed me some electric experiments. They were imperfectly performed, as he was not very expert; but being quite new to me, they equally surprised and pleased me.

Soon after my return to Philadelphia, our library company received from Mr. Peter Collinson, Fellow of the Royal Society of London a present of a glass tube, with some account of the use of it in making such experiments. I eagerly seized the opportunity of repeating what I had seen at Boston, and by much practice acquired great readiness in performing those also which we had an account of from England, adding a number of new ones.* I say much practice, for my house was continually full for some time, with people who came to see these new wonders. To divide a little this incumbrance among my friends, I caused a number of similar tubes to be blown at our glass-house, with which they furnished themselves, so that we had at length several performers. Among these the principal was Mr. Kinnersley, an ingenious neighbor. I drew up for him two lectures, in which the experiments were ranged in order and accompanied with explanations. His lectures were well attended and gave great satisfaction; and after some time he went through the colonies exhibiting in every capital town.

Obliged as we were to Mr. Collinson for his present of the tube, &c. I wrote him several letters containing accounts of our experiments, and he got them read in the Royal Society, where

---

*In the early period of electrical investigation static electricity was usually produced for experimental purpose by rubbing a glass tube or globe with the hand or a piece of cloth or leather.

they were not at first thought worth so much notice as to be printed in their transactions. One paper which I wrote on the sameness of lightning with electricity, I sent to Dr. Mitchell, an acquaintance of mine, and one of the members also of that society; who wrote me word that it had been read but was laught at by the connoisseurs. The papers however being shown to Dr. Fothergill, he thought them of too much value to be stifled. They were accordingly printed in a pamphlet, and Dr. Fothergill wrote the preface. By the additions that arrived afterwards they swelled to a quarto volume, which has had five editions. It was however some time before those papers were much taken notice of in England.

A copy of them happening to fall into the hands of Georges-Louis Leclerc, the Count de Buffon, a philosopher of great reputation in France, he prevailed with M. Thomas-François Dalibard to translate them into French, and they were printed at Paris. The publication offended the Abbé Jean-Antoine Nollet, preceptor in natural philosophy to the royal family, and an able experimenter, who had formed and published a theory of electricity, which then had the general vogue. The abbé could not at first believe that such a work came from America, and said it must have been fabricated by his enemies in Paris, to decry his system. Having been assured that there really existed such a person as Franklin of Philadelphia, he wrote and published a volume of letters, defending his theory, and denying the verity of my experiments.

I once purposed answering the abbé, and actually began the answer. But on consideration that my writings contained only a description of experiments, which anyone might repeat and verify; and reflecting that a dispute between two persons writing in different languages might be lengthened greatly by mistranslations, I concluded to let my papers shift for themselves. The event gave me no cause to repent my silence; for my friend M. Jean-Baptiste le Roy, of the Royal Academy of Sciences took up my cause and refuted him, my book was translated into Italian, German and Latin, and the doctrine it contained was by degrees universally adopted by the philosophers of Europe in preference to that of the abbé.

What gave my book the more sudden and general celebrity, was the success of one of its proposed experiments, made by Messrs. Dalibard and Delor, at Marly-la-Ville, for drawing lightning from the clouds. This engaged the public attention everywhere. M. Delor, who had an apparatus for experimental philosophy, and lectured in that branch of science, undertook to repeat what he called the *Philadelphia Experiments*, and after

Franklin flying his famous kite.

they were performed before the king and court, all the curious of Paris flocked to see them. I will not swell this narrative with an account of that capital experiment, nor of the infinite pleasure I received in the success of a similar one I made soon after with a kite at Philadelphia, as both are to be found in the histories of electricity.*

Dr. Wright, an English physician then at Paris, wrote to a friend who was of the Royal Society an account of the high

---

*Some of Franklin's electrical theories seem naïve and inadequate today, but in the words of Nobel Prize winner Robert A. Millikan, they "laid the real foundation on which the whole superstructure of electrical theory and interpretation has been erected." Millikan included him in 1941 among "the fourteen most influential scientists who have lived since Copernicus was born in 1473."

esteem my experiments were in among the learned abroad, and of their wonder that my writings had been so little noticed in England. The society on this resumed consideration of the letters that had been read to them, and some members of the society, having verified the experiment of procuring lightning from the clouds, soon made me more than amends for the slight with which they had before treated me. Without my having made any application for that honor, they chose me a member, and also presented me with the gold medal of Sir Godfrey Copley for the year 1753, the delivery of which was accompanied by a very handsome speech of the president Lord Macclesfield, wherein I was highly honored.

Our new governor, Captain Denny, brought over for me the before-mentioned medal from the Royal Society, which he presented to me at an entertainment given him by the city. After dinner, when the company as was customary at the time, were engaged in drinking, he took me aside into another room, and acquainted me that he had been advised by his friends in England to cultivate a friendship with me, as one who was capable of giving him the best advice, and of contributing most effectually to the making his administration easy. He said much to me of the proprietor's good dispositions towards the province, and of the advantage it might be to us all, and to me in particular, if the opposition that had been so long continued to his measures, were dropt, and harmony restored between him and the people, in effecting which it was thought no one could be more serviceable than myself, and I might depend on adequate acknowledgments and recompenses.

The drinkers finding we did not return immediately to the table, sent us a decanter of Madeira, which the governor made liberal use of, and in proportion became more profuse of his solicitations and promises. My answers were to this purpose, that my circumstances, thanks to God, were such as to make proprietary favors unnecessary to me; and that being a member of the Assembly I could not possibly accept of any. That I was much obliged to him (the governor) for his professions of regard to me, and that he might rely on everything in my power to make his administration as easy to him as possible. But that I hoped that he had not brought with him the same unfortunate instructions his predecessor had been hampered with.

On this he did not then explain himself. But when he afterwards came to do business with the Assembly the old instructions appeared again, the disputes were renewed, and I was active as ever in the opposition. But between us personally no enmity arose; we were often together, he was a man of letters, had seen much of the world, and was very entertaining in conversation.

The Assembly finally, finding the proprietaries obstinately persisted in manacling their deputies with instructions inconsistent not only with the privileges of the people, but with the service of the Crown, resolved to petition the king against them. They appointed me their agent to go over to England, to present and support the petition.

I agreed at New York for my passage, and my stores were put on board a packet.* There were at the time two packet boats in New York, remaining there in daily expectation of sailing. The time for the dispatching of these packet boats however was in the disposition of General Lord Loudoun, who was at that time in charge of his Majesty's army in America. I was not then so well acquainted with his lordship's character, of which *indecision* was one of the strongest features.

It was about the beginning of April that I came to New York, and it was near the end of June before we sailed, while the packets were detained for the general's letters, which were always to be ready tomorrow. Another packet arrived and she too was detained, till presently all three packets went down to Sandy Hook, to join the fleet there. The passengers thought it best to be on board, lest by a sudden order the ships should sail, and they be left behind. There we were about six weeks, consuming our sea stores, and obliged to procure more.

At length the fleet sailed, with General Lord Loudoun and all his army on board, bound to Louisbourg on Cape Breton Island with intent to besiege and take that fortress. All the packet boats in company were ordered to attend the general's

_____

*The packets were fast vessels operated for the British government to carry mail and dispatches across the Atlantic.

ship, ready to receive his dispatches when those should be ready. We were out five days before we got leave to part, and then our ship quitted the fleet and steered for England. The other two packets the general still detained, carried them with him to Halifax, where he stayed some time to exercise the men in sham attacks upon sham forts, then altered his mind as to besieging Louisbourg, and returned to New York with all his troops, together with the two packets above mentioned and all their passengers. During his absence the French and savages had taken Fort George on the frontier of that province, and the savages had massacred many of the garrison after capitulation.

On the whole I then wondered much, how such a man came to be entrusted with so important a business as the conduct of a great army; but having since seen more of the great world, and the means of obtaining and motives for giving places and employments, my wonder is diminished.

Our captain of the packet had boasted much before we sailed, of the swiftness of his ship. Unfortunately when we came to sea, she proved the dullest of ninety-six sail, to his no small mortification. After many conjectures respecting the cause, when we were near another ship almost as dull as ours, which however gained upon us, the captain ordered all hands to come aft and stand as near the ensign staff as possible.

We were, passengers included, about forty persons. While we stood there the ship mended her pace, and soon left our neighbor far behind, which proved clearly what our captain suspected, that she was loaded too much by the head. The casks of water it seems had been all placed forward. These he therefore ordered to be removed farther aft; on which the ship recovered her character, and proved the best sailer in the fleet.

The captain (whose name was Lutwidge) said the packet had once gone at the rate of thirteen knots, which is accounted thirteen miles per hour.* We had on board as a passenger Captain Kennedy of the navy, who contended that no ship ever sailed so fast, and that there must have been some mistake in heaving the log. A wager ensued between the two captains, to

---

*That is, thirteen nautical miles, or not quite fifteen land miles per hour.

be decided when there should be sufficient wind. Kennedy examined rigorously the log line and being satisfied, determined to throw the log himself. Accordingly some days after when the wind blew very fair and fresh, and the captain of the packet said he believed she then went at the rate of thirteen knots, Kennedy made the experiment, and owned his wager lost.

The above fact I give for the sake of the following observation. It has been remarked as an imperfection in the art of shipbuilding, that it can never be known till she is tried, whether a new ship will or will not be a good sailer; the model of a good sailing ship has been exactly followed in the new one, which has proved on the contrary remarkably dull. I apprehend this may be partly occasioned by the different opinions of seamen respecting the modes of lading, rigging and sailing of a ship. Each has his system. Even in the simple operation of sailing when at sea, I have often observed different judgments in the officers who commanded the successive watches. The wind being the same, one would have the sails trimmed sharper or flatter than another, so that they seemed to have no certain rule to govern by. Yet I think a set of experiments might be instituted, first to determine the most proper form of the hull for swift sailing; next the best dimensions and properest place for the masts; then the form and quantity of sails, and their position as the winds may be; and lastly the disposition of her lading. This is the age of experiments; and such a set accurately made would be of great use.

We were several times chased on our passage, but outsailed everything, and in thirty days had soundings. The captain judged himself so near our port, (Falmouth) that if we made a good run in the night we might be off the mouth of that harbor in the morning, and by running in the night might escape the notice of the enemy's privateers, who often cruised near the entrance of the channel. Accordingly all the sail was set that we could possibly make, and the wind being very fresh and fair, we went right before it, and made great way.

The captain shaped his course as he thought so as to pass wide of the Scilly Isles; but it seems there is sometimes a strong indraught setting up St. George's Channel which deceives seamen. This indraught was probably the cause of what happened to us.

We had a watchman placed in the bow to whom they often called, *Look well out before, there;* and he as often answered *Aye, Aye!* But perhaps he had his eyes shut, and was half asleep at the time; for he did not see a light just before us, which had been hid by the studding sails from the man at helm and from the rest of the watch. Then by an accidental yaw of the ship it was discovered, and occasioned a great alarm, we being very near it, the light appearing to me as big as a cartwheel.

It was midnight, and our captain [Lutwidge] fast asleep. But Captain Kennedy jumping upon deck, and seeing the danger, ordered the ship to wear round, all sails standing, an operation dangerous to the masts, but it carried us clear, and we escaped shipwreck, for we were running right upon the rocks on which the lighthouse was erected. This deliverance impressed me strongly with the utility of lighthouses, and made me resolve to encourage the building more of them in America, if I should live to return there.

In the morning it was found by the soundings, &c. that we were near our port, but a thick fog hid the land from our sight. About nine o'clock the fog began to rise, like the curtain at a playhouse, discovering underneath the town of Falmouth, the vessels in its harbor, and the fields that surrounded it. A most pleasing spectacle to those who had been so long without any other prospects, than the uniform view of a vacant ocean!

I set out immediately, with my son for London, and we only stopt a little by the way to view Stonehenge on Salisbury Plain, and Lord Pembroke's house and gardens, with his very curious antiquities at Wilton.

We arrived in London the 27th of July 1757.

EDITORS' NOTE: The fourth section of the *Autobiography*, omitted here, is devoted to Franklin's account of his negotiations with the proprietaries.

MARY
QUEEN
OF SCOTS

MARY
QUEEN OF
SCOTS

A CONDENSATION OF THE BOOK BY

Antonia Fraser

The great and tragic story of Mary Stuart has long intrigued romantic imaginations. As a beautiful young queen of only sixteen, she was married to the fragile dauphin, who would soon be crowned King of France. But within two years of the splendid coronation Mary had returned to Scotland a widow, to be confronted by the bitter struggles of her own corrupt courtiers. In this classic biography Antonia Fraser brilliantly re-creates the life and death struggles of the ill-fated Mary Queen of Scots, who is still revered as a symbol of Catholic martyrdom.

Part One: The Child Queen
1

THE WINTER OF 1542 was marked by tempestuous weather throughout the British Isles: in the north, on the borders of Scotland and England, there were heavy snowfalls in December and frost so savage that by January the ships were frozen into the harbor at Newcastle. These stark conditions found a bleak parallel in the political climate which then prevailed between the two countries. Scotland as a nation groaned under the humiliation of a recent defeat at English hands at the battle of Solway Moss. As a result of the battle, the Scottish nobility, which had barely recovered from the defeat of Flodden a generation before, were stricken yet again by the deaths of their leaders in their prime. Of those who survived, many prominent members were prisoners in English hands, while the rest met the experience of defeat by quarreling among themselves, loyal to their own ambitions rather than to the troubled land. Furthermore, the Scottish national Church, although still officially Catholic, was torn between those who wished to reform its manifold abuses from within, and those who wished to follow England's example by breaking away from Rome. And the king of this divided country, James V, having led his people to defeat, lay dying with his face to the wall, the victim as much of his own passionate nature as of the circumstances which had conspired against him.

The dynastic position of the Stewart monarchs of Scotland in the fifteenth and sixteenth centuries was peculiarly perilous for a number of reasons. In the first place, there had been no adult succession since the fourteenth century—a total of seven royal minorities had had the inevitable effect of weakening the power of the crown and increasing that of the nobility. Secondly, their own humble origins gave the Stewarts a special reason for needing to raise themselves above the nobility into a cohesive royal family. The Stewarts, as their name denotes, had formerly been stewards, or estate managers, first of all to the ruling family of Brittany, and later more splendidly, great stewards to the kings of Scotland. It was Walter, sixth great steward, who by marrying Marjorie Bruce, daughter of Robert I, and fathering Robert II, King of Scots, thus founded the Stewart royal line.

The ramifications of the Stewart family were henceforward focused on the throne. By the 1540s there were a number of rival Stewart families descended from younger sons or daughters of the kings—the Lennox Stewarts (who later came, like Mary Queen of Scots, to use the French spelling of Stuart), the Atholl Stewarts, and many more. Even those whose name was not actually Stewart often stood in close relationship to the crown through marriage or descent; throughout her reign Mary correctly addressed as "cousin" the earls of Arran, of Huntly and of Argyll, heads respectively of the families of Hamilton, Gordon and Campbell. Unfortunately such royal kinship was universally held to strengthen the position of the family concerned, rather than add to the resources of the monarch. Compared to the Stewarts, how fortunate then—or how prudent—were their Tudor relations who ruled in England. [See genealogical table that follows.] By the reign of Queen Elizabeth I, her forebears had seen to it that the crown was not surrounded by a host of ambitious relatives, through a policy of steadily eliminating possible rivals. The many Scottish minorities meant that the Stewart kings had never ruled for long enough to follow this same course.

James V had inherited a bankrupt kingdom, and anxious to find new sources of income, he had embarked on a prolonged search for a wealthy foreign bride. In view of the predatory attitude toward Scotland of his uncle, Henry VIII of England,

James decided upon the traditional Scottish alliance with France. On January 1, 1537, he finally brought about his marriage to Madeleine, daughter of the French King Francis I, head of the house of Valois. Her dowry was desirable and so was the support of her father; but her fragile beauty seems to have played on a genuine chord of romance in the nature of the Scottish king. Alas! The sixteen-year-old queen, who arrived in Scotland in May, was dead by July.

The woman on whom James's matrimonial negotiations now focused was Mary of Guise, the eldest daughter of the large and flourishing family of Claude, Duke of Guise, and his wife, Antoinette. Mary was tall and well-built, of the type calculated to appeal to a monarch in search of heirs. She was also tolerant, courageous, intelligent, but James sought her hand for strictly conventional reasons. Their marriage, in 1538, strengthened once again the important French alliance.

His foreign policy did nothing to endear James to England and neither did his refusal to join Henry VIII in plundering the Catholic Church. By the summer of 1542 the English forces were being mobilized with instructions from their king for bringing the Scots to heel. Queen Mary, having already lost two sons in early infancy, was once again expecting a child, and, as she awaited the birth of the longed-for heir, her husband rallied his army.

The Scottish forces encountered the English at Solway Moss on November 24, 1542. They were driven back in a disorderly rout. Twelve hundred Scots were captured, among them many of the leading nobles. The king, in a state of appalling mental anguish, retired to his palace at Falkland, where he underwent a complete nervous collapse. He lay on his bed, sometimes railing at the cruel fate which had led to his defeat, sometimes silent and melancholy. Into this sad sickroom came a messenger with the news that the queen had given birth to a daughter. The fact that he now had an heir did little to alleviate the king's sorrow, and six days later, at the age of thirty, he was dead.

The daughter and only surviving legitimate child of James V succeeded to the throne of Scotland. She had been born on December 8 at the palace of Linlithgow, West Lothian. This splendid palace was a traditional lying-in place of Scottish queens, and James V himself had been born there. His child was baptized Mary, by tradition in the Church of St. Michael, at the gates of the palace.

For the first ten days of her life, all the rumors which spread about little Mary were of an exceptionally frail baby. It certainly seems likely that she was born prematurely; a report by English observers stated that "the said Queen was delivered before her time of a daughter, a very weak child, and not likely to live as it is thought."

Perhaps with the English the wish was father to the thought, since the death of the infant queen would have increased the confusion of Scotland still further. The secret wishes of the Scots on the other hand are probably expressed by another rumor of the time that the child was actually a boy. In the sixteenth century, before the successful reign of Queen Elizabeth I, the position of a country with a child heiress at its head was widely regarded as disastrous. To the disadvantages of Mary Stuart's situation at birth was therefore added the disadvantage of being of the weaker sex.

Admittedly the English thought it unseemly for their commander to pursue an attack against the kingdom of a dead man, and thus, curiously enough, the premature death of King James had the beneficial, if short-term, effect of staying the avenging hand of the English army after Solway Moss. But as a result, the first year of Mary's existence, instead of being threatened by English armies, was dominated by two other questions—who was to govern the kingdom during her infancy, and whom she was destined to marry.

If Scotland was to survive as an independent nation, the office of governor had to be filled at once. Despite this urgency, a fierce controversy arose on the subject. It arose out of the clash between the hereditary claim of the Earl of Arran, a supporter of the reformed religion and head of the house of Hamilton, and the rival claim of Cardinal Beaton, which he based on a forged will purporting to have been made by the late king. The prize was a rich one: the importance of the governor, or regent, was equivalent to that of the king himself, and the political powers were interwoven with the material rewards of office. As well as being responsible for the administration of the crown revenues, it was traditional for the governor to take over the palaces, jewels and treasure of the late king during the minority of his successor.

As it happened, the man with the hereditary right to this important office, James, Earl of Arran, was a vacillating figure, singularly unfit to hold it. The dowager queen, Mary of Guise, described him succinctly as the most inconstant man in the world. Yet as head of the House of Hamilton, he was destined for the most prominent position among Scottish nobles.

Arran's grandfather, the first Lord Hamilton, had been married to Princess Mary Stewart, sister of James III and great aunt of James V. If the child queen Mary died, Arran could fairly claim the Scottish throne. It was true that there was a complication: there was some doubt whether Arran's father had ever been properly divorced from his second wife, so Arran, as the fruit of the third marriage, might be illegitimate. In that case, the Lennox Stewarts who descended perfectly correctly from Princess Mary and Lord Hamilton—but from a daughter not a son—were the true heirs to the throne. Despite this Lennox shadow across the Hamilton claim, which caused explosive relations between the two families during this period, the Hamiltons managed to retain their position as nearest heirs to the Scottish throne for almost one hundred years.

There was nothing indecisive about David Beaton, the Cardinal-Archbishop of St. Andrews, the man who now opposed Arran's claim. The evidence that Beaton actually forged the will made in his favor seems conclusive, but in view of the weakness of Scotland at the time, it may be argued that he was making a bid to give his country some sort of strong government. Yet despite Cardinal Beaton's strength of purpose, the deciding factor in the contest proved to be the return of those Scottish nobles captured at Solway Moss, who were dispatched north again by Henry VIII as emissaries of his policy. While in London, they had pledged to help Henry advance the cause of England in Scotland, in return for which they were given suitable pensions.

Under their influence the weak Arran was confirmed in his office of governor in January, and a few days later Cardinal Beaton was arrested. Thus it seemed certain that the rulers of Scotland during Queen Mary's minority were to be a Protestant pro-English faction. Equally, the matrimonial future of the young queen seemed to lie in the direction of England. Henry's son, Prince Edward, then aged five, seemed the ideal spouse to unite Scotland and England under English suzerainty, and Henry furthermore intended to bring up the Scottish queen at the English court. It must be recalled, in Arran's defense, that at this date Catherine de Medicis, wife of the heir to the French throne and descendant of the important merchant family, appeared to be barren. Thus there was no French prince whose merits could be weighed against those of Prince Edward.

On July 1, 1543, the Treaties of Greenwich were drawn up, providing for the marriage of Edward and Mary. These treaties respected Scotland's independence as a country and provided for the return of Mary as a childless widow if Edward died; the main point on which the Scots insisted and on which Henry disagreed was that the child should not actually leave Scotland until she was ten years old. But the point was never put to the test, since by that summer the internal situation in Scotland had changed radically. Opinion was no longer predominantly favorable to the Protestant and pro-English cause. Cardinal Beaton had eluded captivity and was once more in a position to galvanize Catholic pro-French opinion. Arran's vacillating wits were no match for the machinations of the cardinal. French subsidies began to enter Scotland to vie with the English ones, and the very day after the Treaties of Greenwich had been signed it was reported to Henry that French ships had been seen lying off the coast of Scotland.

Henry reacted to the news predictably, demanding that the queen be moved away from Linlithgow, which he thought altogether too accessible to the French if they landed. In point of fact, it was fear of abduction by the English, rather than by the French, which now prompted the Scots to move her. Mary's new home, Stirling Castle, was considered the strongest castle in Scotland by the lords who there incarcerated their queen for safety.

The time when Henry would have any say in Scotland's affairs was rapidly passing. The king made a series of frantic efforts to maintain his ascendancy over Arran, but his arrest of some Scottish merchant ships sailing to France aroused popular indignation. The temper of the country was turning against Henry. After torments of indecision, Arran finally decided to throw in his lot with Beaton and the pro-French party, his mind probably made up in the end by the promise of the little queen's hand for his own son. On September 8, in the church of the Franciscans at Stirling, Arran did penance for his apostasy and received the Catholic sacrament. The day after his change of faith, on September 9, 1543, Mary Stuart was solemnly crowned in Stirling Castle chapel at the age of nine months.

THE DEFECTION OF ARRAN marked the first turning point in the life of Mary Queen of Scots. It decided Henry, among other things, no longer to woo the Scots with gifts, but to attempt to constrain them by force, and it encouraged both the papacy and the French king to renew their support for Scotland. In December 1543 the "auld bands" between the Scots and the French were once more confirmed. A secondary effect of Arran's *volte-face* was that his rival Lennox was unable to endure the fact that Arran still retained his position as governor of Scotland. The classic policy of the Lennox Stewarts had been to ally themselves with the enemies of the Arran Hamiltons. Lennox now turned his eyes toward England, and offered himself as a bridegroom to Lady Margaret Douglas, daughter of Margaret Tudor, niece of Henry VIII, and, in time to come, the mother of Henry Stuart, Lord Darnley.

Thus by the time Mary Stuart was one year old, the pieces on the chessboard which lay between Scotland and England had been rearranged to form an altogether different pattern. In twelve months the possibility of a marriage between Mary and Edward had receded with amazing rapidity. With the renewal of the French alliance, and the birth of a son, Francis, to Catherine de Medicis and Henry II, heir to the French throne, in January 1544, the prospect of a very different education and marriage unfolded before the child queen.

Four and a half years were to elapse before the young Queen of Scots was finally dispatched to the safety of France. They were years in which the policy of Henry VIII toward Scotland did little to correct the impression he had already given of being a vindictive bully. In May 1544, Henry's commander, the Earl of Hertford, set out on a program of devastation of Scottish territory. Henry's instructions to him strike a note of ruthlessness

Linlithgow Palace, where Mary was born

*Enlarged miniature of Mary and
Francis II of France taken from
Catherine de Medicis' Book of Hours*

*Antoinette, Duchesse
de Guise, Mary's
grandmother and mentor*

The Child

Portrait of Mary by Clouet, probably painted at the time of her mourning

which chills the spirit, and the English records make it clear that their armies were remarkably successful in carrying out this "scorched-earth" policy.

That summer the weight of the dowager queen's counsels were felt for the first time in the shifting scales of Scottish national policy. It is safe to assume that Queen Mary's secret wishes were steadily in favor of a French marriage—France was the country of her able family, and the country with enough resources to quell the English if necessary. The climate of opinion in Scotland, however, was not yet ready for such a match. Mary of Guise had two specific hazards to overcome—Arran's desire for the marriage of her daughter and his own son, and Cardinal Beaton's steady opposition to the idea of a French marriage, as marked as had been his opposition to an English one, and for the same nationalistic reasons.

But Cardinal Beaton's days were numbered. Scotland's religious life was in a ferment. In a poor country such as Scotland, with a primitive economy, the Church presented a picture of disproportionate wealth. It was felt that while monks and friars idled and were supported by the community, the true deservers of social pity were being neglected. By 1543 the anticlerical movement was being continually fed by books, pamphlets and broadsides advocating the reformed religion. Many who were drawn to Protestantism were men of the most ascetic nature, who felt they could no longer worship under the corrupt Scottish Catholic Church; others were merely animated by a strong dislike of the Catholic clergy. In time past the Scottish nobles had often endowed the Church with land, in order that they might be prayed for in perpetuity; their reactions, once it was explained to them by the reformers that these prayers were not necessarily an assured passport to heaven, were predictably angry. In March 1546, George Wishart, a leading Protestant preacher of outstandingly gentle character, was burned to death in the forecourt of the castle of St. Andrews while Cardinal Beaton and his bishops watched from cushioned seats on the castle walls. Three months later a band of nobles broke into St. Andrews, seized the cardinal, and after asking him to repent the shedding of Wishart's blood, did him to death.

Within a year, the death of the French king, Francis I, and the accession of his son Henry II to the throne had made French opinion newly favorable to aid for Scotland: Henry II was anxious to conciliate his powerful Guise subjects, whose close relatives were evidently in such a dangerous situation there. In England, on the other hand, the death of Henry VIII in January 1547 had no effect in reducing the savagery of the English attitude toward the Scots.* In late August of that year, the former Earl of Hertford, now Protector Somerset, mounted an expedition against Scotland which was to rival in ferocity anything the late king had commissioned.

The decisive English victory at Pinkie Cleugh on September 10 made it clear to the Scots that a closer alliance with France, even at the price of a French marriage for their little queen, was their best hope. A council was held in November 1547 at which the queen's removal to France was discussed, as well as the necessity of placing Scottish strongholds in French hands.

By the end of December French troops had begun to arrive in Scotland, and on January 27 a contract was signed by which Arran bound himself to give consent to the marriage of the queen with Henry and Catherine's infant son, and her deliverance to France. In return Arran was to receive a French duchy.

The Scottish Parliament finally gave its assent to the marriage of Mary to Francis in July 1548. At the end of the month, after a tearful farewell to her mother, who was to remain in Scotland, the five-year-old girl set sail for France. With her went her guardian, Lord Erskine; her governess, Lady Fleming; and a train of noblemen's sons and daughters, all about Mary's age.

2

F ROM THE MOMENT of her arrival in France, and indeed for the next twelve years, Mary Stuart was the focus of excited happy interest. Duchess Antoinette of Guise was in ecstasies at the appearance of her granddaughter, and wrote immediately to Mary of Guise in Scotland to express her approval.

---

*Henry VIII was succeeded by his frail nine-year-old son, Edward VI. When the young king died in 1553, his half-sister Mary Tudor assumed the throne.—THE EDITORS.

MARY QUEEN OF SCOTS
*Her relationships to the Scottish,
English and French Crowns*

*Portrait of
Mary as a young
woman by an
unknown artist*

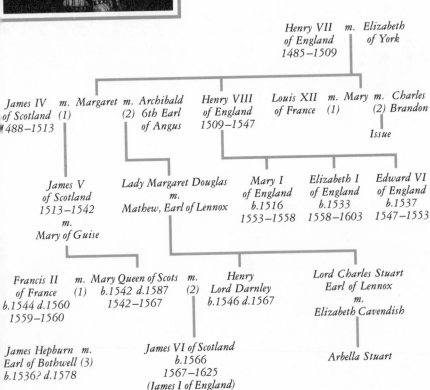

Henry VII *m.* Elizabeth
of England   of York
1485–1509

James IV *m.* Margaret *m.* Archibald   Henry VIII   Louis XII *m.* Mary *m.* Charles
of Scotland *(1)*   *(2)* 6th Earl   of England   of France *(1)*   *(2)* Brandon
1488–1513   of Angus   1509–1547

                                                            Issue

James V   Lady Margaret Douglas   Mary I   Elizabeth I   Edward VI
of Scotland   *m.*   of England   of England   of England
1513–1542   Mathew, Earl of Lennox   b.1516   b.1533   b.1537
m.   1553–1558   1558–1603   1547–1553
Mary of Guise

Francis II *m.* Mary Queen of Scots *m.*   Henry   Lord Charles Stuart
of France *(1)*   b.1542 d.1587   *(2)*   Lord Darnley   Earl of Lennox
b.1544 d.1560   1542–1567   b.1546 d.1567   *m.*
1559–1560   Elizabeth Cavendish

James Hepburn *m.*   James VI of Scotland
Earl of Bothwell *(3)*   b.1566   Arbella Stuart
b.1536? d.1578   1567–1625
(James I of England)
1603–1625

The duchess was, however, a great deal less enthusiastic over Mary's Scottish train, whom she described as thoroughly ill-looking and *farouche*. She clearly shared the general desire of the French to organize the education of this child and thoroughly expunge from her all traces of her Scottish past, which it was felt would ill equip her for her glorious role as queen of France. No qualms were felt at the prospect of cutting the little Scottish queen off immediately from her Scottish attendants. Mary of Guise, however, with superior foresight, had sent instructions that Lady Fleming was to continue as her governess.

Mary was now propelled into the French royal nursery. It is difficult to believe that any prince or princess in the history of Europe could have been so lavished with care and attention as were the children of Henry II and Catherine de Medicis. Following the birth of an heir, the once-barren Catherine produced six more children in quick and satisfying succession. The devotion lavished upon them was fully shared during childhood by Mary, who received in addition the extra care of her Guise relations. And so concerned were they over her welfare that her uncle, the Cardinal of Lorraine, appeared as worried about her toothache as about matters of national policy. Her grandmother, dedicated to the cause of the child's moral welfare, combined with the King of France himself to make Mary's upbringing one of rigorous supervision. Henry, now a man of thirty, swarthy and melancholy of visage, took a genuine tender delight in children. Of Mary, he wrote quite simply that she was the most perfect child he had ever seen.

Another crucial encounter for Mary at the French court was with her intended husband, the dauphin, Francis of Valois. It is to be presumed that if these two children, aged nearly six and nearly five respectively, had heartily disliked each other on sight, marriage would still have proceeded. Nevertheless, the French courtiers hung over the meeting of the two royal children like so many sentimental cupids. Whatever the contrast between the bouncing, healthy little girl and the timid, sickly boy a year her junior, the meeting was pronounced to be a great success.

Mary Stuart, with the facility of childhood, had evidently picked up enough French in the short interval since her arrival to communicate with a fellow child. Later, she was to be described as speaking French with perfect grace and elegance, and French became the language which Mary naturally wrote and spoke for the rest of her life. It thus happened that the most intimate female friend of Mary Stuart's childhood and adolescence was Princess Elisabeth of France, younger by two and a quarter years. With Elisabeth, Mary had in common the elevating but separating gift of royal blood; she became the woman of whom Mary felt herself afterward to be most fond, and of whom she retained the most nostalgic memories in later life.

It is often said that a secure childhood makes the best foundation for a happy life. In marked contrast to her cousin Elizabeth Tudor, Mary Stuart enjoyed an exceptionally cosseted youth. It is left to the judgment of history to decide whether it did, in fact, adequately prepare her for the extreme stresses of her later life. What is certain is that her next six years had a dreamlike quality, in which she was surrounded by servants whose only duty was to nurture the royal nurslings in as great a state of luxury as possible. Her life divided into two parts—at court with the princes and princesses, and with her Guise relations. The ambitious Guises were, however, fully aware of the value of maintaining their little cuckoo in the royal nest, and made no difficulties over having her brought up for so much of the time at court.

At this period the household of the royal children was by no means fixed. It was essential that an establishment of such dimensions be moved every few months in order that the castle which it had inhabited might be literally spring-cleaned. Mary's life consisted largely of a series of glamorous journeyings from one sumptuous royal palace to another. With the royal children went a mountain of luggage, in part accounted for by the extensive royal wardrobes.

It was thought right that Mary should be more richly attired than the princesses, to mark her future position as their brother's bride. Her accounts reveal both the abundance and the formality of a royal child's wardrobe: dresses of gold damask, dresses of black edged with silver, white Florentine serge stockings, a farthingale to hold out the dresses, shot-taffeta petticoats and orange taffeta petticoats lined with red serge. Her accessories were equally elaborate: there is mention of bonnets of silver thread and black silk, shoes of every color, and furs to trim her clothes. There are bills for exquisite embroideries, and bills for leather gloves of dogskin and deerskin. Three brass chests were needed to hold her jewels.

Education was taken seriously. Although Mary Stuart never had a brain of the caliber of Elizabeth Tudor, she was by nature bright and eager to learn. In true Renaissance fashion, she was given an all-around education: she learned not only Latin, but Italian, Spanish and some Greek; she learned to draw; she learned to dance, an art at which she excelled; she learned to sing and to play the lute. Graceful, athletic, she was above all anxious to please those around her.

Mary Stuart's letters to Mary of Guise bear witness to the enormous interest which the mother took in the smallest details of her daughter's upbringing. The sphere in which she appears to have exerted the strongest influence of all is that of her daughter's religious education. Mary of Guise laid down that her daughter was to hear daily Mass, and as well as retaining her Scottish chaplain, she was given a French one of her own. Happily, Duchess Antoinette was able to report to Mary of Guise that her daughter was extremely devout. When the duchess and the Cardinal of Lorraine felt that it was time for the child to make her first Holy Communion, Mary wrote to her mother eagerly of her desire to do so, signing herself, "Your very humble and obedient daughter, Marie."

In 1550 Mary of Guise went to France to judge the progress of her very humble and obedient daughter. The visit represented the central point of Mary's childhood; evidently she had conceived a sort of hero worship for her mother, an image of strength, reliability and comfort, and she wished to do her best to impress her. Mary was overjoyed at the prospect of the visit.

Mary of Guise arrived in September. Her household had made detailed preparations for the journey to fashionable France—although the recent death of her father, Duke Claude of Guise, meant that her clothes were all of black. Throughout the winter the dowager queen of Scotland enjoyed the plentiful pageantry of the court ceremonies, and enjoyed also the company of her daughter. Nothing seems to have marred the affection which existed between mother and daughter. When Mary of Guise sailed back to Scotland a year later, having had what turned out to be the last sight of her daughter, she left behind such strongly growing roots of love in her daughter's heart that the young Mary had a virtual nervous breakdown with grief at the news of her death in 1560, even though she had not seen her for nine years.

The atmosphere of the visit was marred, however, by the flagrant affair which had sprung up between Henry II and Mary's governess, Lady Fleming. The liaison resulted in Lady Fleming giving birth to a son, Henry, later known as the Bastard of Angoulême. Lady Fleming was punished for her indiscretion by being sent home to Scotland, and Mary was given a new governess, a Mme. de Parois.

The substitution of Mme. de Parois for Lady Fleming marked a further step in the obliteration of Mary's Scottish personality. Mary liked to dress up in Scottish national costume, but by now Scottish clothes were for her a form of fancy dress. Nothing could alter the fact that with the passing of every year, the progress of Mary toward becoming a Frenchwoman—a child of the smooth land of France rather than of the rugged land of Scotland—became still more marked.

BY THE END of 1553, when she entered her twelfth year, Mary Stuart's charmed childhood was drawing to a close. The time had now come for her to have her own household. On January 1, 1554, Mary entered into her new estate, and to celebrate the occasion she invited her uncle, the Cardinal of Lorraine, to supper that evening.

The choice was significant. Previously the Guises had been content to let their nursling spend much of her time in the royal household. But from now on it was important that she should receive her early lessons in statecraft from the people who stood to gain so much from her future high position in France—the Guises.

Every letter to her mother at this time bears witness to the detailed supervision which the cardinal was giving to her upbringing. Under his careful tutelage, Mary was encouraged to take an interest in Scottish affairs, which were the more vivid to her now that her mother had succeeded the ineffective Arran as regent.

After a robust childhood, Mary Stuart's general health began to show cause for concern. When she was thirteen, her uncle thought it necessary to write to her mother in order to contradict reports that Mary was ailing. He stated that the verdict of the doctors was that she would outlive all her relations, although she sometimes got indigestion due to a hearty appetite. The truth was that throughout her life Mary Stuart was to suffer from gastric troubles of which these were only the first ominous symptoms. In the summer and autumn of the following year, 1556, she fell ill with a series of fevers, possibly the precursor of the convulsive fevers which haunted her the rest of her days, and for all his angry denials to outsiders, the cardinal's letters to Mary of Guise showed that he felt extreme concern.

THE HISTORY OF Europe in the early part of the 1550s was dominated by the rivalry between France and the Hapsburg Empire, which included Spain in its vast dominions. In 1556 peace was temporarily established by the Truce of Vaucelles. However, the Cardinal of Lorraine persuaded the pope to enter into an alliance with France against the Spanish imperialists, and war was resumed once more. Eventually Philip of Spain convinced his wife, Queen Mary Tudor of England, to bring England into the war on the side of Spain. In 1557 Philip captured Saint-Quentin, in northern France, and seemed set to march on Paris. It was Francis, second Duke of Guise and brother of the cardinal, who came to the rescue of the French people. By turning the tables of the war and recapturing Calais after its 220 years in English hands, Francis of Guise elevated the prestige of his family to new heights.

The victory at Calais had an important effect on the fortunes of Mary. She was now, in the spring of 1558, over fifteen, and the dauphin, Francis, was just fourteen. By the standards of the age, Mary was marriageable; Francis only marginally so. But Henry II had two strong motives for the finalization of this marriage: the gratification of the Guises and the strengthening of the Scottish alliance against England. Henry sent to Scotland to remind the Scottish Parliament that the time had come to implement their promises. Commissioners were duly appointed in Scotland to come to France in order to carry out the marriage negotiations.

As a result, the betrothal of the young pair took place on April 19, 1558, in the great hall of the new Louvre, with the Cardinal of Lorraine joining their hands together. A magnificent ball followed. By the terms of the betrothal contract, the dauphin declared that of "his own free will and with the fullest consent of the King and Queen his father and mother" he promised to espouse the Queen of Scotland on the following Sunday, April 24.

Sickly in childhood, the dauphin had become difficult and sullen in adolescence. He suffered from a chronic respiratory infection; his height was stunted; and there is considerable doubt whether he actually reached puberty before his death, when he was not quite seventeen. He showed little aptitude for learning, although his enthusiasm for the chase astonished the courtiers, considering his frail physique. Obviously, for better or for worse, he had become conscious of his high position, and in 1552 he was described unappealingly as having a considerable sense of his own importance.

However, despite the political considerations which had prompted his elders to hurry toward the match, this rather unattractive and stubborn invalid evidently exhibited real signs of love toward his future bride. Capello, the Venetian ambassador, wrote that the dauphin adored "*la Reginata de Scozia*" who was destined to be his wife, and whom Capello called an exceptionally pretty child. He paints a touching picture of the pair of them drawing apart into a corner of the court, in order to exchange kisses and secrets. Mary was young, romantic and beautiful. It would have been odd indeed if the dauphin had not loved and admired this exquisite and radiant bride who was in addition a comforting friend from his childhood.

What were Mary's own feelings for her bridegroom? First of all it must be said that it is not difficult for the young to be fond of those who are fond of them. Furthermore, Mary responded exceptionally easily to love all her life. She was used to being loved in the widest sense since her childhood; where she saw love, or thought she saw it, she found it easy to bestow her own generous affections in return. To those who have never known romantic love, companionship is an agreeable substitute. Mary felt that she "loved" her bridegroom in a most worthy manner, although his infantile physique and immaturity make it unlikely that he actually aroused in her any of the feelings with which most adults endow the word.

While the two protagonists of the match were thus perfectly content to be united, there were certain political arrangements to be made. The marriage treaty provided terms with which the Scottish delegates were satisfied: the young queen bound herself to preserve the ancient freedoms and privileges of Scotland; so long as she was out of the country, it was to be governed by the regency of the queen mother, and the French king and the dauphin both bound themselves, in case of Mary's death without children, to support the succession to the Scottish throne of the nearest heir by blood. It was further agreed that the dauphin should bear the title of King of Scotland and that, on his accession to the French throne, the two kingdoms should be united under one crown. Up until the death of Henry, Francis and Mary were to be known as the king-dauphin and the queen-dauphiness. In the case of the death of her husband, Mary was to be allowed to choose whether to remain in France or to return to her kingdom. As a widowed queen, Mary was to receive a fortune of 600,000 *livres*; should there be issue, the eldest surviving male child would inherit both crowns, whereas if the couple bore only daughters, owing to the workings of the Salic law in France, the eldest daughter would inherit the Scottish crown alone. The Scottish Parliament agreed that the dauphin should be granted the crown matrimonial, and that the state documents of Scotland were henceforth to be signed by both Francis and Mary jointly.

All these terms were nothing more than those the standards of the time dictated. But Mary Stuart could scarcely have been blamed for thinking more of her forthcoming wedding than of these political arrangements.

THE FRENCH COURT, in true Renaissance fashion, desired its principals to shine out against a background of endless pageantry; never were its wishes more splendidly gratified than in the marriage ceremonies of Francis, Dauphin of France, and Mary Queen of Scots. The wedding itself took place on Sunday, April 24, at the cathedral of Notre Dame. Notre Dame was embellished with a special structure outside to make a kind of open-air theater, and an arch twelve feet high inside. The royal fleur-de-lis was embroidered everywhere, and positively studded the canopy in front of the church.

The first sight to meet the eyes of the eagerly waiting crowds was the Swiss guards, resplendent in their liveries, who entered the theater to the sound of tambourines and fifes. Then came Francis, Duke of Guise, hero of France and uncle of the bride. Next came a procession, headed by musicians dressed in yellow and red, with trumpets, flageolets and violins. Then followed a hundred gentlemen-in-waiting of the king, and then the princes of the blood, gorgeously appareled, to the wonder of the onlookers. Then came abbots and bishops bearing rich crosses and wearing jeweled miters, and after them the princes of the Church, even more magnificently dressed, including the cardinals of Bourbon, Lorraine and Guise.

Now entered King-Dauphin Francis, led by King Antoine of Navarre, and finally Mary, the centerpiece of the occasion, led by Henry II and the Duke of Lorraine. Mary Stuart, on this the first of her three wedding days, was dressed in a robe as white as lilies. Since white was traditionally the mourning color of the queens of France, Mary had defied tradition to wear it on her wedding day; it certainly remained a favorite shade with her throughout her youth, and even in later years. Tall and elegant, she must have glittered like the goddess of a pageant, with diamonds round her neck, and on her head a golden crown garnished with pearls, rubies, sapphires and other precious stones.

The young queen was followed by Catherine de Medicis, Mme. Marguerite, the king's sister, and other princesses and ladies dressed with sumptuous grandeur. At a given moment, the king drew a ring off his finger and gave it to the Cardinal of Bourbon, who espoused the pair.

Afterward the nobility entered the church itself, where the

Bishop of Paris said Mass; during the offertory, gold and silver coins were distributed to the crowd outside. When Mass was over, the fine display of aristocrats paraded all over again, with Henry taking the greatest care to show himself to his people.

A long banquet followed and then a ball. This was only the beginning: when the ball was over at four or five in the afternoon, the entire court moved to the palace of the Parliament. The crowds who rushed to watch them pass, almost blocking their progress, were rewarded by a sight of the new queen-dauphiness in a golden litter, and the king-dauphin following on horseback with his gentlemen, their horses adorned with crimson velvet trappings.

The president, counselors and officers of the Parliament were all present at the supper which ensued, their scarlet robes mingling with glittering robes of the court. After supper, a second celebratory ball was held, even more splendid than the first. It was punctuated by a series of masques and mummeries—theatrical entertainments—in which the royal family themselves took part. Twelve life-size horses made of gold and silver cloth were brought into the ballroom. The dauphin's brother, the Guise children and other princelings then mounted the horses, and proceeded to pull along a series of coaches with them. After this spectacle, six ships were drawn into the ballroom, their silver sails so ingeniously made that they seemed to be billowing in an imaginary wind. Each of these magic barques had room for two voyagers, and after touring the ballroom, the noble gentlemen at the helm selected the ladies of their choice, and helped them into their boats. It was difficult to decide which was lighting up the ballroom more brightly, the *flambeaux* or the flash of the royal jewels.

Throughout the elaborate ceremonies, Mary fulfilled to perfection the role for which she had been trained since childhood. Her new husband loved her and she thoroughly enjoyed her elevated rank as queen-dauphiness, for which she felt herself to be eminently fitted. When she needed advice, her uncles were at hand, anxious to supply it. She relished the feminine friendship of her sister-in-law Elisabeth, and various Guise relations. She was young. She was beautiful. She was admired. An ecstatic letter to her mother in Scotland, written on her actual wedding day, is almost incoherent with happiness.

The beauty of Mary Stuart is legendary. Whether she was a beauty by our standards or not, she was certainly rated a beauty by the standards of her own time. When she was twenty-three, the Venetian ambassador wrote of her being a princess who was "personally the most beautiful in Europe." Her effect on the men around her was certainly that of a beautiful woman. Back in Scotland after the untimely death of Francis, Mary's beauty is said to have captured the hearts of the dashing Sir John Gordon and the handsome George Douglas. Even the venomous Calvinist John Knox, never inclined to pass compliments to those with whose convictions he disagreed, described her as "pleasing," and recorded that the people of Edinburgh called out "Heaven bless that sweet face" as she passed.

Her most marked physical characteristic must have been her height. At her French wedding she is said to have stood shoulder to shoulder with her Guise uncles: she was about five feet eleven inches tall. Her height and slenderness gave her a graceful appearance. She was also an excellent dancer and a good athlete, who could hunt, hawk and even dazzle the public eye riding at the head of an army.

Portraits of Mary Stuart show that she had a small, well-turned head, beautiful long hands, bright golden-red hair, amber-colored eyes and an incomparable complexion. Nor must it be forgotten that to these physical attributes she added the powerful human ingredient of charm. It was the charm of Mary Stuart, that charm which is at once the most dangerous and the most desirable of all human qualities, which put the finishing touches to her beauty.

TOWARD THE END OF 1558 an event occurred of profound importance to Mary. On November 17 Mary Tudor, Queen of England, died leaving no children. Her throne was inherited by her twenty-five-year-old half sister Elizabeth. Until Elizabeth herself should marry and have heirs, Mary Stuart, by virtue of her descent from her great-grandfather Henry VII of England [see genealogical table], was next in line to the English throne. But the situation was in fact more complicated. By strict Catholic standards Elizabeth was illegitimate, and Mary Stuart should rightly have inherited the throne of Mary Tudor. Elizabeth was the daughter of Henry VIII and his second wife Anne Boleyn; as Henry's divorce from his first wife had never been recognized by the Catholic Church, his marriage to Anne was considered void, and Elizabeth herself was thus incapable of inheriting the English throne.

Therefore, immediately on the death of Mary Tudor, Henry II of France formally caused his daughter-in-law Mary Stuart to be proclaimed Queen of England, Ireland and Scotland. Up until then England had been firmly allied with Spain through Mary Tudor's marriage to the Spanish king; Henry now hoped to redress the situation by making a French claim to English dominion. It seems certain that Mary, trained in obedience since childhood, had little say in this matter. "They have made the Queen-Dauphiness go into mourning for the late Queen of England," commented the Venetian ambassador, who was in no doubt as to where the initiative for these moves came from. All the same, this political action on the part of the French king was to be flung in Mary's face for the rest of her life.

THE YEAR 1559 SEEMED destined at its outset to be a year of royal weddings. Mme. Marguerite, the long unmarried sister of Henry II, was to wed the Duke of Savoy; the Princess Elisabeth, Mary Stuart's beloved companion, faced the prospect of marriage at the age of fourteen to Philip of Spain, widower of Mary Tudor.

But the year suddenly became one of royal death. King Henry was mortally wounded in a joust: splinters from his opponent's lance pierced the king's right eye and throat and he lay unconscious for nine days. At one a.m. on July 10 he died with grossly swollen hands and feet, all showing signs of a virulent infection.

Francis II was now king at the age of fifteen and a half, and Mary Stuart queen at the age of sixteen. In one blow of a lance, the fortunes of the Guises had changed. Their niece was now in the very seat of power. Mary Stuart had fulfilled the ultimate expectations of her family.

3

O N SEPTEMBER 18, 1559, the puny young Francis was solemnly crowned king at Rheims. But although the ancient crown of St. Denis had been placed on his head, the real power of France was very far from his grasp. The state was in fact jointly governed by the Cardinal of Lorraine and the Duke of Guise.

France was suffering from cruel inflation; at the same time the kingdom was endangered by the presence of two rival religions, Catholicism and French Calvinism. Even if the country had not had such grave problems, some sort of regency would have been necessary for the young Francis. His mind, without being actually feeble, had never really developed to the point where the possibilities of power excited him. As a king he lacked the necessary restraint to attend to the business of government when pleasure offered, his tutors in youth having concentrated more on the importance of his future role than on the duties which were attached to it. The enemies of the Guises accused them of encouraging their nephew in his pursuit of pleasure in order to have the government of the realm to themselves. But their work had already been done for them by Catherine de Medicis, who with all her loving care had not developed self-discipline in her son.

The Guises, however, did have a plan to uphold their influence on the throne of France in the persons of the children of Francis and Mary who, with their share of Guise blood, would one day rule after them. The only flaw in this plan was that there was as yet no clutch of Valois-Guise children to lay up security for the future—only an adolescent boy and girl.

The question of the consummation of the marriage of Francis and Mary is a delicate subject. Yet in tracing the development of Mary's character, not only in France but later in Scotland in the course of her confrontation with Darnley, it is useful to consider whether she had any sort of physical relationship with her first husband. From contemporary evidence it seems quite probable that Francis suffered from the condition known medically as undescended testicles, and descriptions of his physical deformity suggest that there was no real hope of fertility.

This does not rule out the possibility that the marriage was in some fashion consummated. There is evidence that, despite the cynicism of the court, Mary herself believed that her marriage was a complete one. A month after the death of Henry II, the general rumor was that the queen was pregnant. Mary assumed the floating tunic, the conventional garb at the time for pregnant women, and the court went to Saint-Germain for the sake of better air for her health. However, by the end of September, these interesting rumors perished for lack of further support.

To what then do we attribute these summer vapors of the young queen? The general hope of the court, and the passionate desire of the Guises, was that Mary should conceive a child. This desire must have been communicated to her most strongly, and it seems likely that Mary transformed in her mind the feeble passion of the king into a true consummation of her marriage. In the same way, probably, she transformed in her mind the symptoms of ill-health into the symptoms of pregnancy. Whether or not Mary was technically a virgin when she returned to Scotland, her physical relations with Francis can hardly have given her any real idea of the meaning of physical love.

TROUBLESOME AS WAS the internal situation in France, the situation in Scotland was not much better—and here again religious differences mingled with those of civil policy. French troops had been sent in increasing numbers to the assistance of the queen regent, Mary of Guise. In their turn the Scottish insurgents, being Protestant lords of the congregation, had received aid from Protestant England. When in October 1559 the Duke of Châtelherault (previously Earl of Arran) joined the party of congregation, he presented them with a titular leader who had a claim to the Scottish throne. Then, on August 11, 1560, the Scottish Parliament promulgated a Protestant confession of faith, and five days later abolished the pope's jurisdiction and prohibited the celebration of Mass. Only a few weeks before this settlement, Mary's mother, a gallant woman who had always attempted to do the best she could for peaceful administration, was severely stricken with dropsy and had died, horribly swollen and in great pain.

The Scottish Reformation was a strictly parliamentary affair.

Although, constitutionally speaking, the enactment which produced the Reformation needed the queen's assent, in fact it never received it. Yet, at one manifestation of the parliamentary will, the whole image of the Scottish monarchy had been altered in the minds of the Scottish people.

At the time, however, this long-term effect was certainly not visible to Mary. From the distance of the French court, it was difficult to realize that in the future the Protestant Scots would logically turn to England rather than to France for help. Still more difficult was it to envisage that if Mary ever returned to Scotland, her French Catholic connections would inevitably be held against her; a country which had newly reformed its religion by act of Parliament without the assent of the sovereign would regard her monarchical power, religious convictions and French upbringing as threatening to its status quo.

Mary Stuart's grief when she received the news of her mother's death was heartrending, and she underwent one of the physical collapses which inordinate sorrow was apt to induce in her. The Venetian ambassador reported: "The death of the Queen Regent of Scotland was concealed from the most Christian Queen till the day before yesterday, when it was at length told her, for which her Majesty showed and still shows such signs of grief, that during the greater part of yesterday she passed from one agony to another."

Mary's love for her mother spurred her forward in her knowledge of Scottish politics; her appreciation of French and English politics was spurred on by her position as Queen of France and heiress to—or even, some said, the rightful possessor of—the English throne. Life was uncertain, and Elizabeth was childless and unmarried; if Mary did not actually acquire the English throne by force, she might easily do so by inheritance. Sir Nicholas Throckmorton, the English ambassador to France, was particularly interested in keeping a watchful eye on the nature and qualities of this young girl, whom fate might one day establish as his own mistress.

The Cardinal of Lorraine had been the instructor of her youth, but as Queen of France, Mary had a new mentor—her mother-in-law Catherine de Medicis. The records show that during the seventeen months in which Francis II reigned as king, the Dowager Queen Catherine and Queen Mary were constantly in each other's company. A great deal has been made of the story that Mary openly despised Catherine for her lowly birth, and described her contemptuously as nothing but the daughter of a merchant. Whether or not Mary, with the imprudence of youth, made this unwise remark, and whatever her mother-in-law's private feelings, outwardly Catherine exhibited positively maternal kindness toward Mary. Moreover, Mary did not fail to be influenced by the personality of her mother-in-law. From Catherine she learned two thoroughly feminine lessons—that the considerations of a child or unborn child, the continuance of the dynasty, should be placed above all others, and that the most effective weapons in a queen's hands were those of diplomatic intrigue. Mary was not by nature an adept intriguer, yet she was to become an enthusiastic one, and the effect of Catherine's early lessons can certainly be discerned in Mary's later career.

As the Guises' fortunes had been transformed by the sudden death of Henry II, so just seventeen months later the fragility of ambitious hopes founded on the life of a solitary human being was demonstrated once more. On Saturday, November 16, Francis returned from a day's hunting in the country complaining of a violent earache, and on Sunday he fell down in a faint while at vespers. A large swelling now appeared behind his left ear, probably caused by an inflammation of the middle ear, a chronic condition he'd had since childhood.

Mary spent the last weeks of her husband's life patiently nursing him in his darkened chamber. Unlike their niece, the Guises bore the king's affliction with little patience; in their frenzy, they attacked the doctors for not doing more for the king than they would have done for a common beggar. But neither Mary's patient nursing, nor the rages of the Guises, affected the progress of the king's illness. The inflammation spread upward into the brain, and on December 5, 1560, a month before his seventeenth birthday, Francis II died.

Mary's position was transformed by her husband's death; at the age of just eighteen she was no longer Queen but Queen Dowager of France. Her entire position in Scotland, which had been founded on the protection which the French crown had extended, was likely to be in jeopardy. But it is doubtful whether these political considerations were uppermost in the young queen's mind during the days of mourning. On the contrary, the evidence shows that, almost alone at the French court, Mary abandoned herself to passionate grief at the death of the king, a grief founded on the deep affection she had felt for him.

By tradition the mourning period of a queen of France lasted for forty days. However, once Mary's storm of sorrow had abated, it was inevitable that she should consider her future in the world. There were two cornerstones on which this could be founded: a second marriage, and/or her return to Scotland.

One historian has accused Mary herself of speculating on her next choice of husband before her first husband's body was cold. In fact the marriage of a queen was unavoidably a political issue in the sixteenth century. The subject obsessed ambassadors and courtiers, to say nothing of her Guise relations, quite regardless of her personal feelings. A whole week before Francis's death, Sir Nicholas Throckmorton reported gossip about a second marriage, and he cited several names. And by the time Mary emerged from her forty days of mourning, possible candidates could have been said to include almost any currently unmarried male of roughly suitable age, whose own position could be held to benefit in any way that of the Queen of Scots.

The torrent of speculation made it inevitable that Mary herself, once she returned to the ways of ordinary life, would have to express some sort of personal view on the two subjects of remarriage and Scotland—unless, of course, she was content to leave her affairs in the hands of her uncles as she had done in the past. This, however, she did not seem inclined to do. It has been suggested that the Guises lost interest in their niece once she no longer occupied the throne, but the evidence of Mary's widowhood in France shows, on the contrary, that it was she who was making the first efforts to think for herself, and in a way which impressed all those around her. Throckmorton reported to England that since her husband's death she had shown that she had "both a great wisdom for her years, modesty, and also great judgment in the wise handling of herself, which cannot but turn greatly to her commendation and reputation."

A Spanish marriage was Mary's first choice for her future after Francis's death, and she was certainly a willing participant in marriage negotiations with Don Carlos of Spain, the son of King Philip. Marriage to Don Carlos, a Catholic and heir to the great throne of the Spanish empire, was an infinitely more glorious prospect than a highly speculative return to a distant kingdom.

Fortunately or unfortunately, Mary Stuart was not destined to become a Spanish bride. The hostility of Catherine de Medicis toward the match—though hidden from Mary by a delusive mask of friendship—proved an implacable obstacle in the way of the negotiations. Catherine feared that the position of her own daughter Elisabeth might be threatened by Mary's marriage to Don Carlos if Elisabeth's husband, Philip of Spain, should die. So, while Catherine gave Elisabeth precise instructions on how to frustrate the match from the Spanish end, she herself complicated the issue by suggesting another royal bride for Don Carlos—her own younger daughter, Marguerite.

France was not the only country where Mary's Spanish match was looked on with concern. In England the prospect of Mary Stuart's marriage to a foreign prince, especially a Spanish one, was regarded as threatening to the maintenance of English power also. To Philip, confronted with the firm hostility of Catherine and of Elizabeth of England, the prospect of Mary as a future daughter-in-law no longer seemed alluring. By the end of April the negotiations had foundered.

Meantime, in the middle of March, Mary had decided to leave the French court for a prolonged round of visits to her Guise relations. Apart from her natural desire to visit her family, it seems likely that Mary was also anxious to discuss her future with them. It so happened that while she was on the journey she received an envoy from the self-constituted Scottish Protestant government which, at the moment when the Spanish negotiations were foundering, opened up new possibilities. The emissary was her half brother Lord James Stewart, James V's illegitimate son by the highborn Margaret Erskine, and now part of the ruling Protestant parliamentary regime.* Some twelve years older than

---

*James V had nine known illegitimate children, and a number of them would occupy positions at Mary's court.—THE EDITORS.

his half sister, Lord James was a man of solemn manner and appearance; yet although more politically gifted than his contemporaries, Lord James was far from immune from that avarice so characteristic of the Scottish nobility of this period—nor did he lack hypocrisy. But his temperament, and above all the quality of his religious views, meant that he was always able to deal easily with the English politicians of the period.

His interview with Mary was not unsatisfactory to either of them, despite their widely differing points of view. As well as asking her to return to Scotland, Lord James had been instructed to ask the queen to embrace the Scottish Protestant faith. This she steadily refused to do. But she did state with some courage that she was prepared to come home, provided she could practice her own religion in private. This Lord James himself had already expressed publicly to the Scots as being an acceptable demand, and he convinced her that it was politically wise to give the Protestant party its head for the time being in Scotland. As a result of this meeting Mary must have been impressed with the notion that Lord James would constitute her natural adviser in Scotland by virtue of their blood connections, as the Guises had done in France.

James's advice to his sister accorded well with Mary's own temperament. In religious matters, her leaning was toward the tolerance of her mother, rather than the fanaticism of a Cardinal of Lorraine. As a born Catholic who had known no other creed, her faith was something which she took for granted, and yet which was essential to her; it was, however, in no sense a fierce faith which demanded the sacrifice of all others. Mary's innate clemency in matters of religion has sometimes been mistaken for lukewarm conviction. The truth was that she drew a distinction between private faith and public policy. Although the English ambassador to Scotland, Thomas Randolph, later wrote: "She wishes that all men should live as they please," such permissiveness did not mean that Mary's personal Catholicism was not total.

By the time she returned to court from visiting her Guise relations, Mary had evidently made up her mind to return to Scotland, though it was not the only alternative open to her. Mary's rank in France entitled her to an honorable position at the French court; her dowry had given her widespread and lucrative estates; if she remained on the Continent, it was not likely to be long before some royal suitor other than Don Carlos emerged. Mary must be given the credit for having settled on a bold course of adventure rather than the less demanding existence which it would still have been possible for her to lead in France.

As it happened, at the same moment the Scots themselves were beginning to feel more warmly about their absent queen. They realized that a malleable young ruler, with a strong claim to succeed to the throne of England—and apparently prepared to behave reasonably over religion—was certainly not to be discarded in a hurry. Lord James wrote her a letter on June 10 which constituted a virtual invitation on behalf of the Protestant lords to return. Scotland for Mary, therefore, was a hopeful venture.

Naturally Lord James was not put out by the fact that Mary had consistently declined to recognize Elizabeth as Queen of England. Elizabeth, however, regarded the matter somewhat differently. When Mary applied to Elizabeth for safe-conduct on her route back to Scotland, she received a point-blank refusal.

This refusal gave Mary Stuart her first public opportunity of rising to a crisis; she now displayed magnificently that quality of cool courage which was to be a feature of her later career. She began by expressing in polite terms her regrets that she should have bothered Elizabeth by demanding a passport which she did not in fact require. She had reached France in safety thirteen years before, she pointed out proudly, in spite of English efforts to intercept her. Now she would surely once more reach her own country with the help of her own people. She then prepared to set forth across the North Sea, unblessed by any safe-conduct from the English queen, on the six-hundred-mile journey to her kingdom.

Taking her leave of the king, the court and her Guise relations, Mary embarked with her retinue at Calais in the middle of August. Now that the ships were actually ready to take her away from all she had known and loved for what seemed to her like her whole life, Mary's steadfast spirit temporarily deserted her.

As the galleys surged forward toward the unknown coast of Scotland, Mary gazed pathetically on the fast-receding coast of France. Mingling with the sound of the wind and the roar of the sea, a voice broken with tears could be heard, uttering a melancholy and prophetically final farewell: *"Adieu France! Adieu donc, ma chère France. . . . Je pense ne vous revoir jamais plus."*

Part Two: The Personal Rule
4

THE JOURNEY turned out to be uneventful, and on Tuesday, August 19, 1561, after an absence of thirteen years, Mary Queen of Scots set foot once more on her native soil at the port of Leith. Her arrival, though unexpectedly early, was greeted with enthusiasm and joy. The common people were excited by the spectacle before their eyes: Mary at the age of eighteen, tall, graceful, commanding, was everything in appearance that the popular imagination could have conjured up for its newly arrived queen. Mary was delighted with her reception and what was more, she was able to express her pleasure to her subjects in their own language, for she had not lost her Scots despite the years spent in France.

Mary was installed in the magnificent towered and turreted palace at Holyrood. Lying on the outskirts of the city of Edinburgh, outside the actual town walls, Holyrood enjoyed the amenities of wild country just beyond its very windows as well as the convenience of having the capital city close at hand. Queen Mary now took possession of the magnificent royal apartments in the northwest corner of the palace.

On her very first Sabbath in Scotland, Mary was to discover how different her new kingdom was from her old one. On Sunday Mary, who had been assured by Lord James of the private practice of her religion, ordered Mass to be said in the chapel royal at Holyrood. The preparations for the service were all too familiar in a country which had been officially Protestant for only one year. An angry crowd gathered outside the chapel, while inside the queen attended a Mass which was understandably fraught with tension—the English ambassador reported that the priest seemed in a state of mortal fear.

If the queen received a rude shock from the incident, she did not allow it to affect her determinedly tolerant religious policy. The next day she issued a proclamation in which she announced that she intended with the aid of her Estates (the Scottish Parliament) to pacify the differences in religion. In the meantime, she commanded the whole world to make no attempt against the form of public worship which she had found commonly practiced on her arrival in Scotland—under pain of death. She further commanded that no one molest any of her domestic servants or those who had come with her out of France in the practice of their own religion.

This proclamation may seem, from a modern standpoint, comparatively wise, and certainly free from Catholic bigotry. It aroused, however, the venomous ire of many of the extremist Protestants, and especially that of their leading evangelist, John Knox. The next Sunday, Knox took the opportunity of preaching a great denunciation of the Mass from the pulpit. While still in France, Mary had already formed the most unfavorable impression of Knox. Now she determined to grasp the nettle; she sent for Knox to come to Holyrood.

Knox was now a man of forty-seven; having been rescued from "the puddle of papistry," as he put it, he had become a potent disciple of Calvin. The strength of his character and the force of his convictions enabled him to win over many men to Protestantism, and made him a force on the Scottish scene. It was unlucky for Mary Stuart that he happened to be in Edinburgh during the first year of her residence there, to present all her actions in the most malevolent light.

Mary's very sex was against her in Knox's opinion. In the sixteenth century it was theoretically considered to be against natural law for women to rule men. Nevertheless, most people were content to regard an actual woman ruler as a necessary evil which might have to be endured from time to time. Knox, however, in his *First Blast of the Trumpet against the Monstrous Regiment of Women*, published in 1558, declared roundly that to promote any woman—those "weak, frail, impatient, feeble and foolish creatures"—to any form of rule was contrary to God and repugnant to nature. Now he was confronted in a personal interview with one of these feeble and foolish creatures sitting on the throne of Scotland.

Mary began by attacking Knox for raising her subjects against her and also for writing *The Monstrous Regiment*. Knox conceded that if she behaved well and the realm was not brought to disaster, he would not disallow her rule on the grounds of her sex alone. When Mary struggled with him over the religious issue, however, she found him much less accommodating. Finally Knox agreed to tolerate her for the time being—his unflattering phrase was "to be as well content to live under your Grace as Paul was to live under Nero." But he still asserted the rights of the subject to rise up against the unworthy ruler who opposed God's word.

Knox has been accused of speaking churlishly to the queen. He certainly spoke to her in a manner to which she was scarcely accustomed, but she on the other hand seems to have been stimulated rather than otherwise by his abruptness. It is true that she lapsed into tears at one moment, but all her life Mary Stuart had a feminine ability to give herself suddenly up to tears when her sensibilities were affronted, and it never prevented her actions from being extremely hardheaded once she had recovered her composure. Knox himself quickly realized that Mary was far from being a feeble puppet. He told his friends: "If there be not in her a proud mind, a crafty wit and an indurent heart against God and his truth, my judgment faileth me."

Mary was still being enthusiastically greeted by her subjects. She had been received with elaborate rejoicings on her ceremonial entry into Edinburgh, and, after three weeks at Holyrood, when she set out for a short progress around her kingdom, she was met with the same kind of enthusiasm.

The sights she saw during her journey confirmed her conviction that it was in the best interests of peace and stability in Scotland to preserve the Protestant status quo. Curiously, the right of the Scottish monarch to grant livings and benefices had remained unaffected by the edict which officially changed the religion of Scotland, and this right became a powerful system of royal patronage. Wisely, although under no obligation to do so, Mary made financial provision for the ministers of the new

Church, showing once again that she drew a sharp distinction between the private Mass in her chapel and the public weal in Scotland. Her tactful behavior brought the reward of considerable personal popularity.

THE CONCILIATION OF her Scottish subjects was only one half of Mary's plan: reconciliation with Elizabeth was the other. The English queen had ultimately relented and had granted Mary safe-conduct—after she had set sail from France. Once she was assured, however, that Elizabeth had actually dispatched a letter of safe-conduct, Mary's mood toward her cousin was purposely friendly. Only thirteen days after her arrival in Scotland, she commissioned William Maitland, the most experienced diplomat out of the rather limited selection offered by the Scottish nobility, to go to England and try to treat with the English queen on the subject of succession.

The Scottish point of view had already been put to Elizabeth in a letter from Lord James: Mary would surrender her present claim to the English throne in exchange for Elizabeth's acknowledgment that Mary stood next in line to the throne after herself and her lawful issue. In reply, Elizabeth showed herself nothing if not friendly toward the Queen of Scots. She even went so far as to say that she knew of no better right than Mary's. At the same time she positively declined to give Mary the acknowledgment she desired. With this Maitland had to be content.

Mary was extremely unpopular in England at this period, being considered a Frenchwoman as well as a Catholic, and she was especially disliked by the English Parliament which was strongly Puritan in tone. There were other claimants whom the English as a body might be thought to prefer: Margaret, Countess of Lennox, a granddaughter of Henry VII; or Lady Catherine Grey, the younger sister of the ill-fated Lady Jane Grey and granddaughter of Henry VIII's sister Mary. Under these circumstances it is easy to understand why Mary believed that the personal favor of Elizabeth constituted her best hope of being recognized.

Throughout the autumn Mary devoted all her efforts to bringing about a meeting with Elizabeth, by which she felt certain she could win the all-important affections of the English queen. With friendly letters, gifts and even verse she wooed her, and Elizabeth rose to the bait. The Scottish Council had agreed to the meeting in principle, although they were worried about Mary's safety in view of the fact that it was less than a year since the English queen had been threatening to imprison her if she landed on English soil. Furthermore, the Scottish Protestants feared that if Elizabeth were seduced by Mary's charm she might cease to keep them under her protective wing, while the Scottish Catholics were concerned that their queen might be corrupted by a meeting with the Protestant Elizabeth.

At the last moment, however, with that element of unhappy fatality which never seems far absent from the story of Mary Stuart, the meeting had to be put off—through no lack of keenness on the part of Elizabeth, but owing to the explosive situation in the rest of Europe. In March 1562 civil war broke out in France between Catholic and Huguenot. Elizabeth was forced to turn her attentions across the Channel, for at any moment England might be called upon to intervene on behalf of the Protestant cause.

On hearing of the sudden debacle of her plans, Mary allowed herself to be comforted by the news that Elizabeth was willing to plan the interview for the following year. Little did she know that the meeting between Elizabeth and Mary, which has been so often fabled by poets and dramatists, and of which the possible consequences are incalculable, was destined never to take place.

WHILE MARY NEGOTIATED for the throne of distant England, the volatile and unruly Scottish nobles presented her with very different problems at home, involving not only the public peace but also her own physical safety.

The might of the Gordons, under their magnificent but unpredictable head, George, fourth Earl of Huntly, had long loomed over the Highland territories in northern Scotland. As the leading Catholic magnate, Huntly might have been a powerful ally to Mary. But instead he now incurred her displeasure by making no secret of his disapproval of her tolerant policy toward the Scottish Protestants. Thus, when one of his sons, Sir John Gordon, imprisoned in the south for his part in a street brawl, escaped and fled northward, Mary set out on a royal progress with the dual purpose of rallying the Highlanders to her side and of pursuing Sir John. Encouraged by her half brother Lord James, she intended to demonstrate once and for all that the Gordons could not behave as they pleased with impunity.

As Mary traveled north, Sir John gathered a force of a thousand horse and proceeded to harry the queen's train with the deliberate intention of abducting her. When Mary reached Inverness, the keeper of the royal castle, Alexander Gordon, another of Huntly's numerous offspring, refused her entrance. This was not so much insolence as actual treason, and after Mary finally gained entry, the keeper was hanged over the battlements. Huntly and John Gordon were outlawed. Not content to retire to the wilds, Huntly gathered his forces and marched against the queen at Aberdeen. In the ensuing clash the Gordons were hacked down by Lord James's forces, and at this dramatic moment Huntly fell dead from his horse in front of his captors, either from heart failure or apoplexy. His sons were executed or imprisoned and his wealth and property confiscated. The tumbling of Huntly's power in the north left a vacuum which Lord James was able to fill, and he received the earldom of Moray and various sheriffdoms previously held by Huntly.

This episode reveals just how closely Mary's lot was joined with that of the new Earl of Moray. At this point she was making no attempt to rule the Scottish nobles by balancing them against each other, but was clearly backing Moray in whatever he chose to do. This policy would be satisfactory so long as the interests of Queen Mary and her half brother coincided: should they ever diverge, the queen might find that she would need the support of other strong nobles in the kingdom.

The crown had two great weaknesses. First, it had no standing army; should it be involved in war, the crown had to depend on the locally raised hosts of loyal nobles. Secondly, the financial resources of the Scottish crown were cripplingly restricted. Although Mary Stuart received an annual income of 40,000 livres as Queen Dowager of France, the lands and properties of her Scottish father had been largely squandered during her minority or apportioned to the nobles. Since she did not have a right to reclaim these until her twenty-fifth birthday, the royal income was dependent on export dues derived from duties on trade and ecclesiastical revenues. The total royal revenue in 1560 was around £10,000 sterling. Compared to this, that of Queen Elizabeth was £200,000.

Despite these gloomy considerations, Mary Stuart made a fair attempt to re-create the conditions of the French court and to enjoy the native resources of Scotland. Fortunately she was blessed with youthful high spirits and enthusiasm; in particular, she had a positive mania for outdoor pursuits—her physical constitution demanding a daily ration of fresh air and exercise. Although later in her life this caused her to suffer cruelly from the conditions of close confinement, it meant that now she was well suited to life in Scotland, where she was destined to spend nearly half her time in the saddle, progressing about her dominions. In the Scottish countryside she also had endless opportunities for the hawking and hunting which she loved. Archery appealed to her as well, and she had butts set up in her private gardens at Holyrood. She played golf and croquet and loved to walk in the gardens surrounding her palaces.

Mary Stuart had her resplendent side, but she had another, touchingly domestic, side to her character in marked contrast to her dazzling public persona. She loved to embroider, and is described as sitting at her Council placidly plying her needle. Her life was also marked, in its early no less than in its later stages, by close attachments to her servants, with whom she felt she could share her joys and woes without fear either of their presumption or their disloyalty.

Mary's court therefore had an agreeably intimate character. There were certainly indoor pleasures enough to be enjoyed. The queen loved to dance and play cards, and she enjoyed billiards, chess and backgammon. She was a considerable linguist, and her library contained books in Italian, Spanish and Greek as well as French and Latin. For music Mary would seem to have had a profound feeling which, like her love of poetry, appealed to the romantic side of her nature. She herself played both the lute and the virginals and had a charming singing voice which won much admiration.

In her dress at least Mary Stuart was able to give the femininity of her nature full rein, because to be magnificently attired was expected of a sixteenth century queen. She dressed herself elegantly, with innate good taste, lacking her cousin Elizabeth's inclination to ostentation. As a dramatic foil for her red-gold hair and amber eyes, white appears and reappears throughout the list of dresses in her wardrobe. This list of robes, with their descriptions and colors, fully explains why she came to be known as "*la reine blanche*" in France.

Ordinarily, Mary wore dresses of damask or serge, stiffened in the neck and mounted with lace and ribbons. Her riding skirts and cloaks were of Florentine serge, often edged with black velvet or fur. Beneath her gowns were *vasquines*, stiffened petticoats to hold out her skirts, expanded with hoops of whalebone to give a crinoline effect. Her hats and caps were of black velvet and taffeta, her veils of white.

On state and ceremonial occasions, the queen's clothes were glittering. The inventory of her dresses made at Holyrood in February 1562 lists 131 entries, including sixty gowns of cloth of gold, cloth of silver, velvet, satin and silk: the embroidery was so rich and detailed that it was often passed from dress to dress, and was listed separately among the jewelry.

Mary's jewels were of enormous importance to her. They of course represented something more than adornment, since as solid financial assets they could be given as presents, held for security, or sold to pay troops, if necessary. The inventory of her jewelry, made also in 1562, contains 180 entries. As she loved white, so the queen seems to have had an especial affection for pearls. But rubies she also seems to have admired, as she loved to wear crimson velvet; and among her profusion of rings, necklaces and earrings, there is mention of enamel, cornelian and turquoise, as well as gold and diamonds.

The Queen of Scots had a childish love of dressing up which she preserved throughout her life. With a romantic love of the Highlands, Mary adopted the custom of wearing the so-called "Highland mantles"—loose cloaks reaching to the ground and generally embroidered. She also loved to adopt male costume and wander about the streets, incognito, among her subjects.

Mary's simple sense of fun fitted in well with the boisterous sense of humor of her Scottish subjects at this time. The reformation of their religion did not necessarily lead the sixteenth century Scots to end those hearty, bucolic games and sports which they had long enjoyed: they loved the favorite May game of Robin Hood, with its Abbot of Unreason and its Queen of the May. The people who enjoyed this sort of entertainment naturally loved the pageantry brought to the country by Mary and her court.

To the argument that Mary was extravagant, it may be answered that she was considerably less extravagant than her cousin Elizabeth. In any case, such display on the part of the sovereign was an essential part of personal and monarchical government. The result, as even her harshest critics admitted, was that this pretty, high-spirited creature, with her hunting, her hawking, her clothes, her jewels, was able to charm the Scots nation.

5

MARY STUART was young and beautiful. She was also a queen and could offer an independent kingdom as a dowry. In theory she had a wide choice of possible husbands, but in practice so many considerations had to be taken into account that it was impossible to find a candidate meeting all the necessary requirements. The only point on which everyone agreed was that the choice was an important one, because whomever Mary Stuart married would inevitably expect to be granted the crown matrimonial of Scotland.

The first consideration was that of religion. Was Mary to marry a Catholic like herself or should she attempt the more daring policy of binding together her subjects by wedding someone of their own religion? A Catholic marriage, by emphasizing that she was very much a Catholic at heart, would inevitably upset the balance she was so carefully maintaining between her private religion and the public religion of her country. A Protestant marriage, on the other hand, would be difficult to explain to her Catholic relations and allies on the Continent, on whom she still depended.

Then there was the question of status. Was she to marry an independent prince with a kingdom of his own? Or choose a subject within a kingdom: an Englishman, a Scot or a Frenchman such as the Duke of Nemours. There were obvious disadvantages to both courses. An independent ruler with a kingdom of his own could not fail to treat Scotland as a satellite, and could scarcely be expected to put Scottish interests above those of his own country; the raising-up of a mere subject to royal rank, on the other hand, would certainly arouse jealousy among the Scottish nobles.

Then there was the matter of the views of Queen Elizabeth; Mary's foreign policy had been directed toward getting herself recognized as Elizabeth's successor, and in this endeavor Mary's putative husband was obviously a trump card. Yet how was Mary to marry to Elizabeth's satisfaction, if Elizabeth did not express any definite choice? In the autumn of 1563 Elizabeth began to drop broad hints. The only trouble was that Elizabeth's candidate, her own favorite, Robert Dudley, Earl of Leicester, was sufficiently eccentric to arouse serious doubts as to whether it was a genuine suggestion, or whether on the contrary Elizabeth was merely trying to prevent Mary from making any marriage at all. Leicester was generally considered to be Queen Elizabeth's lover, and whatever the truth of their relationship, her familiarity with him had certainly caused scandal throughout Europe, as had the death, in the most suspicious circumstances, of his first wife, Amy Robsart. The disadvantages of Leicester as a husband for Mary notwithstanding, a lengthy round of negotiations was eventually entered into.

Throughout the autumn courtiers noted that the queen frequently succumbed to fits of weeping and depression, alternating with bursts of merriment. Her French physician attempted to cure her by putting her on a diet. But the death of her uncle, the Duke of Guise, further problems with the uncharmable Knox, and her own loneliness—these were enough to produce a pattern of nervous ill health. In December she took to her bed with an unidentifiable pain in her right side—which was to recur for the rest of her life. Randolph suggested that her collapse might have been due to exhaustion after dancing too long on her twenty-first birthday, and she herself put it down to praying too long in an icy chapel after Mass. By mid-January she had recovered. The whole attack may well have been exacerbated by Mary's tension at the lack of conclusion over her marriage plans.

In fact, Don Carlos of Spain was still the object of her desire, but in August, Philip II, having procrastinated for eighteen months, closed the negotiations. The Leicester negotiations wound on without, however, anything definite being promised to Mary. By the beginning of 1565 she was no nearer getting either a husband or the succession to the English throne. Then, in February, the young Lord Darnley arrived in Scotland, ostensibly to visit his father, the Earl of Lennox.

It is intriguing that Henry Darnley, young, eligible and handsome, the great-grandson of Henry VII, a Catholic with the royal blood of England and Scotland in his veins, should be allowed to travel to Scotland at this very moment with the express consent of Queen Elizabeth. At the time the Scots believed that Elizabeth herself had launched Darnley, in order to lure Mary into a demeaning marriage, but it seems to have been Leicester and Sir William Cecil, Elizabeth's chief adviser, who combined together to get the boy his license to come north. Elizabeth's part seems to have been a passive one. Having an extraordinary inability to make up her mind on matters of emotion, she probably did not know herself whether she desired the marriage of the beloved Leicester and Mary. This inability nearly always turned out fortunately for her, since it allowed others to take the action, and in doing so, it was they who made the mistakes. In this particular case, it is likely that Leicester and Cecil, encouraged by the indecisive passivity of Elizabeth, launched Darnley as a sort of Trojan horse into the Scottish queen's kingdom.

Queen Mary could not fail to be interested in such an obvious candidate for marriage. The young man whom she saw before her was eminently handsome, and well over six feet one inch tall. In contemporary portraits, Darnley at the age of eighteen appears like a young god, with his golden hair, his perfectly shaped face and above all the magnificent legs in their black hose. His height could hardly fail to commend itself to Mary; beautiful as she was, Mary was nevertheless tall enough to tower over most of her previous companions. For once she could feel herself not only overtopped at dancing, but also physically protected by her admirer if she so wished, a novel and pleasant sensation.

The handsome youth had been well trained in all the arts

considered suitable for a gentleman of the period; he could ride, hunt, dance gracefully and play the lute. The aim of his ambitious mother, Margaret Lennox, had been to make his courtly ways as winning as his outward appearance; to his interior qualities she had unfortunately paid less regard. The truth was that Darnley was thoroughly spoiled. The outward manifestations of power appealed to him: the realities of its practice were alien to his indolent and pleasure-loving temperament. Vanity was by far his strongest characteristic, and vanity brought out his touchy temper and fatally boastful nature, making him incapable of assessing any person or situation at its true worth.

None of this was apparent to Mary at her first meeting with her cousin in Scotland. Her reaction was instantaneously romantic. She told her adviser Sir James Melville that "he was the properest and best proportioned long man that ever she had seen. . . ." Although the long man went on to see his father Lennox, he was back with the Queen in a week. From then on he was scarcely allowed to be away from her side.

Yet, however much Mary enjoyed the company of Darnley, she did not show any evidence of passion for him. In March she still seems to have regarded Darnley as one possible candidate among many. But in April the situation dramatically changed. Darnley fell ill. The illness itself was of no great consequence; it began with a cold and then turned to measles. Incarcerated in his sickroom in Stirling Castle, Darnley was visited with increasing frequency by the young queen. She became his nurse, and when measles was succeeded by an ague, she redoubled her care. Under the influence of the tenderness brought forth by the care of the weak and the suffering—and the handsome—Mary had fallen violently, recklessly and totally in love.

There can be no doubt that, whether Mary herself realized it or not, her feelings for Darnley were overwhelmingly physical. The demanding nature of her passion can easily be explained by pent-up longings which were the result of an inadequate first marriage. In the years since Francis's death she had led a life of celibacy, and her thoughts about marriage had been concentrated on the power it would bring her. Now at one touch of Darnley's hand, the discretion and wisdom which all had praised in her during her four years as Queen of Scotland—all were swept away in a tide of tumultuous feelings Mary Stuart can scarcely have known she possessed.

Mary's adviser William Maitland was promptly dispatched to London to acquaint Elizabeth with the news and win her approval of the marriage—this sanction being doubly necessary because Darnley was a member of the English royal family through his Tudor descent. And now the honeyed trap—as Darnley turned out to be—was sprung. Mary to marry Darnley! No indeed; Elizabeth, made newly aware of the disapproval of the Scottish Protestants for a Catholic bridegroom and anxious to dissociate herself from the project, took the line that the whole idea was preposterous, and that it represented a renewed attempt on Mary's part to acquire the English throne for herself. Regardless of the fact that Darnley had gone north with her express permission, Elizabeth exploded with anger and demanded his instant return.

At this point Mary would have been wise to take serious thought. It was true that the approval of Philip of Spain and Charles IX of France had been sought and won, but these were nothing compared to the approval of Elizabeth, for after all Elizabeth could offer Mary what no other potentate had the power to extend—the reversion of her own throne. Only the rashest of women would have proceeded now without taking heed of Elizabeth's declared disapproval—but this was what love had apparently made of Mary Stuart.

She was in no state to listen to the advice of even the sagest counselor. For the first time she could hear no other voice except the dictates of her own passionate feelings. The English ambassador Randolph wrote in anguish of the "poor Queen whom ever before I esteemed so worthy, so wise, so honourable in all her doings," now so altered by love that she had "all care of common wealth set apart, to the utter contempt of her best subjects."

Darnley himself reacted predictably. Randolph bewailed the queen's infatuation, and in the same breath reported that Darnley was now grown so proud that he was intolerable even to his friends. The ambassador went on to make a gloomy but singularly accurate prophecy: "I know not, but it is greatly to be feared that he can have no long life among these people."

The truth was that even if Darnley had spoken with the

tongues of men and of angels, Mary Stuart would have had problems in persuading her court to accept him as her bridegroom. Her brother Moray had viewed the match with gloom from the start, since he had little desire to see the rival Lennoxes rise in position; and he withdrew from court at the beginning of April. Thus the benefit of his advice, which Mary had enjoyed for so long, was removed from her. Also, quite apart from Moray, there were other Scottish nobles who had feudal or hereditary reasons for disliking and fearing the Lennoxes.

All the while Mary was caught fast in the tangled bonds of passion. On July 29 the heralds proclaimed that Darnley should henceforth be styled "King of this our Kingdom." On that same day, between five and six o'clock in the morning, a radiant Mary was conveyed to the chapel royal at Holyrood on the arm of her future father-in-law, the Earl of Lennox, there to await her chosen consort.

For this wedding, however, there was to be no dazzling white marriage robe for Mary Stuart. Whatever the romantic passion which inspired her, she wore a great mourning gown of black, with a wide mourning hood attached to it. This was to indicate that she came to her new husband as a widow, a Queen Dowager of France. They exchanged the vows of marriage according to the Catholic rite and three rings were put on Mary's finger, the middle one a gleaming diamond. Then, with the marriage completed, Mary went to her chamber and cast off her mourning garments to signify that she was about to embark upon "a pleasanter life."

The festivities of a nuptial celebration then followed. There was a banquet for the full court of nobles, the sound of trumpets, and largesse scattered among the crowd. After the dinner there was dancing, and a brief respite for recovery before the magnificent supper. Finally, as Randolph reported, "and so they go to bed." It is to be hoped that Mary Stuart found this part of the ceremony also to her satisfaction.

SIR WILLIAM CECIL, Elizabeth's principal adviser, once commented on the ill-fated marriage of Leicester and Amy Robsart that carnal marriages begin with happiness and end in strife. Mary was allowed little enough time to enjoy the happiness of her own "carnal marriage" before the first presages of strife were made apparent. Even before her wedding, Moray's behavior had been plainly rebellious; he declined to attend a convention of the nobility and then solicited a subsidy of £3000 from Elizabeth. Rumors circulated that he intended to kidnap Lennox and Darnley and ship them back to England, but the existence of this plot has never been concretely proved. In any event, furious with Mary for her choice of Darnley, Moray's intention was to show that she was endangering the Protestant religion. But in her desire to win support for her marriage, Mary had taken the trouble to court the favor of the reformers. Darnley himself, although a professed Catholic, had happily listened to the sermons of John Knox in St. Giles' Church. His faith appeared to have had a chameleon-like quality which enabled it to assume whatever color seemed convenient at the time. Mary's conciliatory attitude on the subject of religion showed up Moray's rebellion for what it was—jealous disaffection springing from feudally inspired hatred of the Lennoxes rather than a genuine revolt of conscience.

In August Moray was outlawed for refusing to put in an appearance before his sister to explain his treasonable behavior. His two most powerful allies, Châtelherault and Argyll, were informed that they would be outlawed in their turn if they gave him any further assistance. Mary now mustered troops to march against the rebels, and on August 26 she rode out of Edinburgh with Darnley at her side in gilt armor. The vivid emotion brought such a sparkle into her spirits that in the course of the campaign even Knox's narrative expressed admiration of her as she rode at the head of her troops: "Albeit the most part waxed weary, yet the Queen's courage increased manlike, so much that she was ever with the foremost."

In the course of Mary's four years in Scotland the ordinary people had seen no evidence that she intended to deprive them of the practice of their new religion, and they positively enjoyed the acquisition of a young and beautiful queen. Therefore, with no sign that help was to be forthcoming from Elizabeth, Moray realized his cause was hopeless and fled across the border into England.

The Chaseabout Raid, as Moray's abortive rebellion was

called, marked a significant change in Mary's attitude to her Scottish nobles. Already during her short reign, two major subjects, Huntly and Moray, had both revolted against her in the interests of their own power. She had defeated them both, but these experiences had taught her never to trust her own nobility at any point where her interest might conflict with theirs. She therefore took the natural step of relying more and more on those who had no mighty clans to back them up, no family feuds to sway them, and who did not belong to the spider's web of Scottish family relationships. Mary began to make use of a sort of middle-class secretariat. It was a move which was passionately resented by the nobles who saw themselves about to be edged out of the center of a stage they had occupied for so long.

Of these men, Davy or David Riccio, an Italian who was appointed Mary's secretary in 1564, was the most interesting character. He came of a good but impoverished Savoyard family and was a Catholic. Also, although he was extremely ugly—a fact which appears in every contemporary record whether written by a friend or foe—his face being considered "ill-favored" and his stature small and hunched, Riccio was a fine musician and an amusing conversationalist. His loyalty, furthermore, was beyond question.

Mary had a horror of disloyalty, especially when it accompanied ingratitude. By nature frank and open, she was also passionate, quick to love, quick to hate, easy to weep, easy to laugh. This meant inevitably that she had a love of being committed; she preferred action, whatever the cost, to inaction, whatever the gain. But this in turn meant that she felt bitterly betrayed when those around her seemed to neglect her interests. Her fiercest hatreds were reserved for those whom she had elevated in life and who now let her down—Moray came into this category and Darnley was shortly to enter into it.

UNFORTUNATELY THIS JULY marriage, begun in the high summer of love, did not preserve its warmth into autumn and winter. At first Mary was so delighted with Darnley that she did him great honor herself, and willed everyone who desired her favor to do the like. But after the honeymoon was over—a honeymoon spent, as it happened, virtually on the field of battle defending Darnley as a choice of husband—Mary was ready to return to the more serious business of ruling Scotland. In her work she was only too happy to have Darnley beside her—yet Darnley was obviously not much interested in the process of government. He spent his time hunting, hawking and in the pursuit of pleasure, and governmental measures were often held up by his absence, since they demanded a joint signature. Eventually an iron stamp or seal was made of his signature to prevent delays.

At the beginning of December, Mary went to the palace of Linlithgow to convalesce after a serious bout with the recurring pain in her side. This time, her illness may have been exacerbated by other symptoms; she was by then about two and a half months pregnant. The birth of an heir was of vital importance to Mary's plans; if she gave birth to a son, she would automatically be placed in a much stronger position with regard to the English succession than a mere childless queen.

The prospect of motherhood, much as she must have desired it for dynastic reasons, did not increase Mary's affection for Darnley. In fact, her infatuation for him did not survive the onset of pregnancy. It was, however, one thing for Mary to get on badly with her husband, and quite another for this disagreement to be put to savage use by Mary's enemies. Darnley by himself was powerless, whatever his posturings. But Darnley as the tool of Mary's opponents could have a cutting edge. For it was a regrettable fact that by the beginning of 1566 quite a number of Scottish nobles were the queen's enemies. The combination of two forces of disaffection was capable of proving very dangerous for Mary—and fatal for her servant David Riccio.

6

IN JANUARY 1566 Queen Mary was in her own estimation riding high, with her courage unimpaired after the recent ordeal through which she had passed with such success. The future, bringing with it the prospect of the birth of an heir, looked bright. But there was no denying that the opposition which was building up against her both within and without Scotland had an ugly aspect to it: if she had appreciated its real extent, even Mary in her most buoyant mood might have experienced some unquiet moments.

First of all, set steadily against her were those Protestant lords temporarily in exile, such as Moray; their primary desire was to return to Scotland, but their hostility to Mary was given a new edge when she threatened, in addition to banishment, to attaint them and to declare their properties forfeited at the forthcoming session of Parliament to be held in the spring.

Then there were Knox and his followers, who feared to see Mary take advantage of her new strength to advance the claims of the Catholic Church; this they also suspected she might try to accomplish at the coming parliamentary session.

Added to these two groups were other Protestant nobles within the confines of Scotland, such as the Earl of Morton and William Maitland, who hated to see Mary's "base-born" advisers advanced to the detriment of their own position. Riccio was the natural scapegoat for their hostility. He was also the obvious suspect on whom Darnley could pour his rage and jealousy against his wife. It was now the work of Mary's opponents at court to incite the foolish, excitable Darnley into such a frenzy that he might be persuaded to join their own more serious enterprises. In order to do so it was necessary to convince Darnley that in the opinion of many Scottish nobles he, not Mary, would make the most suitable ruler of Scotland.

With extreme cynicism, the Scottish nobles, including Moray, were now proposing a scheme which involved the coronation of the very man against whose elevation they had rebelled in August. Darnley's Catholicism was apparently no longer of account to the Protestant lords once their persons and properties were threatened.

It was now plainly suggested to Darnley that his wife was Riccio's mistress, and that the waning of his own power was due to the machinations of the Italian. Mary added fuel to the flames by openly finding pleasure in Riccio's company. Could there have been any truth in the story? Neither Riccio's height nor his ugliness would have been any certain bar against a woman finding him desirable. Yet all we know of Mary's relations with

Riccio seems to fit into the pattern of ruler and confidant, rather than mistress and lover. And what really militates against the possibility of Mary having had a love affair with Riccio is the timing of it. Later the reproach was to be flung in the face of James VI that he was actually "Davy's son." But by the time her obvious infatuation with Darnley was over she was already several months pregnant. Thus it seems that the worst that Mary can be accused of is a certain lack of prudence, which was very much part of her character, rather than some more positive indiscretion.

Meanwhile, Darnley indulged in a series of debauched and roistering parties, which caused considerable scandal in Edinburgh. His drinking was beginning to constitute a public problem. And when Mary tried to restrain him, he insulted her. Nor was drunkenness his only weakness. On the one hand there were rumors of love affairs with court ladies; on the other, there were hints at something which had taken place at a festivity, something so disgraceful that Mary now slept apart from her husband.

Despite the anxiety caused by Darnley's behavior, Mary persisted in her plan to hold a Parliament in March at which the Protestant lords who had rebelled would be attainted and their properties forfeited. Under these circumstances the conspiracy to restore these lords and give Darnley the crown went forward. In a letter to Leicester, Ambassador Randolph hinted at "things intended against her own [Mary's] person." Let us not forget what was surely ever-present in the minds of the Earl of Lennox and his son, Darnley—that if Mary vanished from the scene and her unborn child never saw the light of day, Darnley had an excellent chance of becoming King of Scotland in his own right.

A bond was now drawn up and signed by the conspirators, who included James Douglas, Earl of Morton, and his illegitimate half brother George Douglas; Patrick Lord Ruthven; Lord Patrick Lindsay and the Earl of Argyll, as well as Moray. The declared intentions of the signatories were the acquisition of the crown for Darnley, the upholding of the Protestant religion and the return of the exiles. The lords were careful to obtain Darnley's signature in order that he be as thoroughly implicated as themselves; but in all the clauses of the bond there was no mention of any sort of violence. Only one item had a faintly menacing ring: "So shall they not spare life or limb in setting forward all that may bend to the advancement of his [Darnley's] honour."

In the meantime Mary brushed aside her adviser Sir James Melville's warnings of rumors and "dark speeches" that he had heard, and on Thursday, March 7, Parliament assembled. The following Tuesday was fixed as the day on which the bill of attainder against Moray would be passed. The fixing of this date automatically induced the climax of the conspirators' plans. On the evening of Saturday, March 9, the queen, advanced in pregnancy, was holding a small supper party in her apartments at the palace of Holyrood. Those present were her half brother Lord Robert Stewart, her half sister and confidante Jean, Countess of Argyll, her equerry Arthur Erskine, her page Anthony Standen, and of course David Riccio. Perhaps there was to be music later, or perhaps this was to be one of those evenings, which Darnley so much resented, when the queen and Riccio played cards until one or two in the morning. At any rate the atmosphere was innocuous and domestic.

Mary's apartments in Holyrood lay in the northwest corner of the palace, on the second floor; there was a large presence chamber at the head of the main staircase, a bedchamber lying directly off it, and off that again two small rooms in each corner, one a type of dressing room, the other a supper room. Beneath these apartments, on the first floor of the palace, lay Darnley's rooms. The two sets of apartments were connected by a narrow privy staircase which came out in the queen's bedroom, close to the entrance to the supper chamber.

As supper was being served, to the great surprise of those present, the figure of Darnley suddenly appeared up the privy staircase; although he was by now a comparative stranger to these domestic occasions, he was still welcomed as the king. But a few minutes later there was a far more astonishing apparition on the staircase—Patrick Lord Ruthven. "Let it please your Majesty," he said, "that yonder man David come forth of your privy-chamber where he hath been overlong." Mary replied with amazement that Riccio was there at her own royal wish and asked Ruthven whether he had taken leave of his senses. To this

Ruthven merely answered that Riccio had offended against the queen's honor. On hearing these words, the queen turned quickly and angrily to her husband, and asked him if this was his doing. Ruthven then launched into a long and rambling denunciation of Mary's relations with Riccio, reproaching her for her favor to him, and for her banishment of the Protestant lords.

Riccio had shrunk back into the large window at the end of the little room, and when Ruthven made a lunge toward him, Mary's attendants, who seem to have been stunned into inaction, at last made some sort of protest. "Lay not hands on me, for I will not be handled," cried Ruthven. This was the signal for his followers to rush into the room from the privy staircase, pistols and daggers at the ready. In the ensuing confusion the table was knocked over, and Lady Argyll was just able to save the last candle from being extinguished by snatching it up as it fell. Riccio was dragged, screaming and kicking, from the room, through the presence chamber to the head of the main staircase where he was done to death, the dagger wounds variously estimated at between fifty-three and sixty—a savage butchery for a small body. His pathetic voice could be heard calling as he died: *"Sauvez ma vie, madame, sauvez ma vie!"*

The fact that the murder was deliberately planned to take place in the presence of the queen when she was nearly six months pregnant points to some malevolent intentions toward her own person as well as the elimination of a presumptuous servant. And indeed, for the rest of her life Mary Stuart was to believe that her own life had been threatened in the course of the tumult in the supper room, and that Darnley had intended her own destruction and that of her unborn child. It is indeed impossible to understand her later attitude to Darnley without taking into account this steadfast conviction. But the quality of Mary's spirit, her courage and daring, was proof even against such an appalling experience.

When Ruthven, Darnley and the others had departed, Mary sent one of her ladies for news of Riccio's fate. When she was told that he was dead, she wept for a moment, but then she dried her tears and exclaimed, "No more tears now; I will think upon revenge."

So far the conspirators seemed to be in complete command of

the situation. This very night, when their triumph seemed certain, was crucial in the history of Mary Stuart. At one point in the course of it she must have taken the bold decision to choke down her feelings of revulsion for Darnley and win him over to her side, reasoning that his character was the weakness in the conspirators' cause. Therefore, when Darnley went to her chamber next morning, he found his wife calm rather than reproachful, and during that day she won him back by convincing him that under the new regime his own prospects would be as bleak as hers. It was a triumph of a stronger character over a weaker one.

Mary was able to greet the conspirators on Monday with composure and even charm. She promised that she would overlook recent hideous events. Moray, apprised of what was about to take place, had arrived back in Edinburgh, and Mary, unaware at this point of his complicity in the plot, flung herself into his arms, crying: "Oh my brother, if you had been here, they had not used me thus."

In the evening Mary privately sent for the captain of the royal guard, Erskine her equerry, and Standen her page; she begged them in the name of chivalry to assist her not only as a defenseless woman, but also as the mother of the future King of Scotland. These gallant gentlemen promised to stand by her escape, in the manner she now outlined.

At midnight the queen and Darnley made their way down the privy staircase, up which the assassins had filed only fifty-two hours before, and out through the servants' quarters. Erskine, Standen and two or three loyal soldiers with horses were outside to meet the royal couple. Mary mounted pillion behind Erskine and in a short while, under cover of darkness, they were clear of the town.

The plan was to go to Dunbar Castle. Darnley, in a panic of fear at being hunted down by the men he had so recently betrayed, kept spurring his own horse and flogging that of the queen, shouting: "Come on! Come on! By God's blood, they will murder both you and me if they can catch us." Mary pleaded with him to have regard for her condition, at which Darnley only flew into a rage. By the time they reached Dunbar Castle, twenty-five miles from Edinburgh as the crow flies, the long night was almost over. For a woman in an advanced state of pregnancy, a five-hour marathon of this nature must have been a grueling ordeal. Even now, the queen's formidable courage did not desert her, and she set about consolidating the advantage which her liberty had given her.

James Hepburn, Earl of Bothwell, the Earls Atholl, Fleming, Seton and the young Earl of Huntly, whom Mary had pardoned and restored to his father's title, came to her at Dunbar, and, stirred up by these royal agents, others began to flock to the queen's side. On March 18 she was able to reenter Edinburgh victoriously at the head of 8,000 men, only nine days after the murder which had caused her to flee the city so precipitately.

Darnley rode beside her like a sulky page. At the news of his defection his fellow plotters had fled from Edinburgh, realizing that their rebellion no longer had any focal point. Moray alone remained in Edinburgh, since he had cunningly arrived in the city too late to seem to be implicated in the bloody events.

IT WAS EASY ENOUGH, once Mary was back in Edinburgh, to rescue the body of Riccio from its common grave and have it reburied according to the Catholic rite in her own royal chapel. Yet the murder of the Italian had marked a turning point in Mary's affairs; it was not easily forgotten.

The most obvious result was Mary's abiding hatred of Darnley. The conspirators had taken the understandable if vindictive step of sending the bond to the queen, so that she should see for herself the full extent of her husband's complicity. Yet once more Mary was obliged to put a good public face upon the situation for the time being, and issue a statement of his innocence. It was clearly not her thought to take any action against her husband before the baby was born, since Darnley was quite capable of casting doubts upon the child's legitimacy, if it suited his purpose.

As Mary's relations with Darnley settled down into an uneasy truce, it was natural that she should come to rely increasingly for political advice on those nobles who had proved loyal to her throughout the crises she had faced in the past year.

Into this category fell notably James Hepburn, Earl of Bothwell, who seemed to display that combination of resourcefulness, loyalty and strength which Mary had so persistently sought among her Scottish nobles. Recently allied by marriage to Huntly, he now emerged in Mary's estimation as a useful loyal member of the Scottish polity. Yet Bothwell in his turbulent, contentious character summed up those very paradoxical contrasts which made it difficult for anyone not brought up among them to understand the nature and behavior of the Scottish nobles. Once again Queen Mary was to make a mistake of judgment, and come to see in Bothwell the mirage of a strong, wise protector.

Bothwell was not a stupid man; he had been well educated and was well traveled. He came of the great border family of Hepburns, and, as a feudal baron and primarily a soldier, he was apt to choose the quick, if bloody, solution to any problem. It was true that he showed signs of administrative ability, but his personal qualities made him the last person to unite successfully that essentially disunited and suspicious body, the Scottish nobility. Violent and boastful, he was certainly not a man who was prepared to try using charm to gain his objectives.

In appearance Bothwell lacked the beauty of Darnley; he was but of moderate stature, and the only known portrait said to be of him shows a face which is certainly not conventionally handsome, yet which might well prove attractive to women because it is strong and vital. His name was, in fact, linked to a number of women; and he was later accused of having an adulterous liaison with Mary. It is important to note that there is no uncontested evidence in letters or reports—whether French, English or Scottish—written *before* Darnley's death in February 1567, to show that Mary was involved in an affair with Bothwell while her husband was still alive. Not one observer made any attempt during this period to connect the queen's growing scorn for Darnley with growing affection for Bothwell, although the point would have been one which the ever watchful ambassadors would have been delighted to make if they had felt it to be true. Mary was wracked in health, and Bothwell steadily bent on his own personal advancement. It is questionable whether the one had the energy, and the other the inclination, for an adulterous love affair when there were so many important matters at hand.

At the beginning of June Mary began to make preparations

for the birth of her child. At the wish of her Council, she had been lodged in Edinburgh Castle since early April. The great castle frowning on its rock over the town below was evidently a safer locality for this important event than Holyrood, so recently demonstrated to have the flimsiest defenses. On June 3 the queen took to her lying-in chamber ceremoniously, according to the custom of the time, to await the confinement, and on Wednesday, June 19, after a long, painful and difficult labor, the baby Prince James was born; despite the length of the labor, he was an impressively healthy child.

The birth of a male heir was signaled with immense rejoicings in Edinburgh, and five hundred bonfires illuminated the city and the surrounding hills with their festive flames. The whole artillery of the castle was discharged, and lords, nobles and people gathered together in St. Giles' Church to thank God for the honor of having an heir to their kingdom. Sir James Melville rode off to London to break the news to Queen Elizabeth. The English queen reacted with her famous outcry, the primitive complaint of the childless woman for a more favored sister: "Alack, the Queen of Scots is lighter of a bonny son, and I am but of barren stock."

The birth of James duly enhanced Mary's merits as a candidate for the English throne, but it also inevitably moved the child's own father, Darnley, farther down the line of succession. Queen Mary took care to display the baby publicly and announce, "My Lord, God has given you and me a son, begotten by none but you." She went on, uncovering the child's face, "Here I protest to God as I shall answer to him at the great day of Judgment, that this is your son and no other man's son. I am desirous that all here bear witness." Having thus, as she hoped, preserved her child from the stigma of illegitimacy, Mary devoted the rest of her time in Edinburgh Castle to his care, having the baby sleep in her own room, and frequently watching over him at night.

Since her return to Edinburgh after the murder of Riccio, Mary had taken the trouble to reconcile her subjects to each other and to her. In September Du Croc, the French ambassador, reported to Catherine de Medicis the newly excellent relations which existed between Queen Mary and her subjects.

Darnley, on the other hand, was equally ill-regarded by both parties.

The birth of James had had two dramatic effects upon Mary Stuart: she no longer had any pressing motive for a public reconciliation with Darnley, and at the same time her own precarious health was almost destroyed. There is no evidence that she ever really recovered it before her extremely serious illness four months later. In view of the state of her health and her conviction that Darnley had conspired toward her death and that of her child, Mary's refusal to grant him his conjugal rights would be easy to understand, but his humiliation as a husband was later to be one of Darnley's main points of complaint.

In early October Mary traveled to Jedburgh, in the Scottish border country, to hold a court of justice. While there she received news that Bothwell, now her lieutenant on the borders, had been badly wounded in a foray and was lying in danger of death at Hermitage Castle. The queen decided to pay Bothwell a visit, not so much to express her sympathy as for the practical reason that he was one of her chief advisers, and she needed to consult with him. On October 16, the queen rode over to the Hermitage accompanied by Moray and a large number of her court and, since this border fortress was not prepared to receive the burden of a royal stay, returned to Jedburgh that same day. The day's journey meant a ride of a little over fifty miles, not an outstanding hardship to a queen accustomed to riding hard in the saddle all her life.

However, on her return to Jedburgh, Queen Mary fell violently ill. She had evidently been heading for some sort of breakdown for weeks, and physical and mental stress now apparently combined to produce an attack of illness so severe that many of those who observed Mary in the throes of it formed the opinion that she was unlikely to recover. First the queen was seized by a prolonged fit of vomiting—so long and severe that she several times fell into unconsciousness; two days later, she could neither speak nor see, and had frequent convulsions. There was a temporary recovery, but by October 25 she had become so ill again—"all her limbs were so contracted, her face was so distorted, her eyes closed, her mouth fast and her feet and arms stiff and cold"—that she was once more considered to be on the verge of death. The situation was saved by the queen's physician, who bandaged her very tightly, and then having her mouth opened by force, poured wine down her throat. The queen vomited blood, and subsequently began to recover.

The exact medical causes of Mary's undoubted ill health have been the subject of several modern investigations. It used to be suggested that her symptoms indicated a gastric ulcer. But recent studies of a disease known as porphyria have identified the recurrent illness of George III as belonging to it, and similar symptoms have been traced back to his ancestors James VI and Mary Queen of Scots. The symptoms of porphyria are severe attacks of abdominal pain, with vomiting, extreme distress and even transient mental breakdown. The attacks may occur frequently or at long intervals; and despite the severity of the attack, the patient recovers quickly afterward. It certainly seems far easier to relate these symptoms than those of a gastric ulcer to Mary; it is clear also that she underwent genuine sufferings, which at times amounted to a complete breakdown indistinguishable from madness.

Darnley was in the west of Scotland and scarcely showed himself the devoted husband throughout this period of illness. He paid the queen a brief visit eleven days after she first fell ill, and then returned to Glasgow. The breach in their relationship was complete.

The next episode in the mounting tragedy of Darnley took place at the castle of Craigmillar, an enormous baronial edifice on the outskirts of Edinburgh. Mary, still in the hands of her physicians, was apparently in a state of deep depression. Du Croc commented that no future understanding could be expected between the queen and her husband for the two reasons of his arrogance and her suspicion. And Mary's chief nobles, lodged with her at Craigmillar, were equally resolute in their hatred of Darnley.

At the end of November Moray and Maitland broached the subject of a divorce to the queen. Maitland opened up the argument by saying that means would be found for Mary to divorce Darnley if she would only pardon Morton and the other Riccio assassins still in exile. The queen promised her consent, but said that the divorce must be legally obtained without prejudice to her son. Maitland then suggested "other means," and in a famous phrase told the queen that "Moray would look through his fingers." At this the queen quickly asked them to do nothing against her honor, and Maitland replied, "Let us guide the matter among us, and your Grace shall see nothing but good, and approved by Parliament." This was to be the case of Mary's supporters in later years, to prove her innocence over the death of Darnley. They maintained that the queen, although anxious to rid herself of Darnley, could not have known that the nobles actually intended to kill him, since Maitland had assured her that whatever happened would have parliamentary approval.

It seems virtually certain that a bond was then drawn up and signed at Craigmillar by those nobles who intended to get rid of Darnley, including Maitland, Bothwell, Argyll, Huntly and Sir James Balfour, with Morton signing later on his return to Scotland, much as a bond was signed before the murder of Riccio. The actual document does not survive for inspection, but following the parallel with the Riccio bond, it is unlikely that the murder was specifically mentioned.

In December the queen was able to turn her mind to the happier matter of her son's baptism. Shortly after the birth, messages had been sent to the King of France, the Duke of Savoy and the Queen of England to act as godparents. Darnley objected to the inclusion of Elizabeth, because she had never officially countenanced his marriage, but his objections were overruled by Mary, who visualized a golden future for her son, James, if Elizabeth's goodwill could be secured. On December 17 the ceremony took place, according to the Catholic rite, in the chapel royal of Stirling Castle. The little prince, now just six months old, was carried in the arms of the Count of Brienne, proxy for the King of France, from the royal apartments to the chapel between two rows of courtiers, the whole scene lit by flaring torches. Queen Elizabeth had sent a magnificent gold font as a present for her godson, and Jean, Countess of Argyll, acted as proxy godmother for Elizabeth and held James in her arms.

The accomplishment of the ceremony was celebrated with all the magnificence which Mary could command. She clothed the nobility in gold and silver at her own expense for the occasion, and afterward there were fireworks and special entertainments called masques.

In all these rejoicings, there was only one mysteriously absent figure, that of the baby's father, although he was actually present in the castle at the time. It seems likely that Darnley hated the idea of the English, from whose ranks he sprang, seeing how far he had fallen in prestige at the Scottish court. It would certainly be in his character to avoid any occasion of public humiliation, real or imaginary. At the end of December, Darnley left Stirling abruptly and went to Glasgow, the traditional center of Lennox Stewart power, where he hoped to be more royally treated.

7

IN OCTOBER AT JEDBURGH Mary Queen of Scots had nearly died. At Glasgow in the New Year Darnley in his turn fell extremely ill. At the time it was announced that he had smallpox, but it seems more likely that he was actually suffering from syphilis. The queen did not immediately visit her husband, but she sent him her doctor.

Despite this kindness, she continued to ponder legal ways of ridding herself of this degenerate husband. For Darnley was still in some respects dangerous, even though he was threatened from so many quarters. He was clever enough to see that he had a possible line of attack against Mary in her determinedly laissez-faire policy toward the Scottish Church, and he was unscrupulous enough to contemplate blackening her reputation in the eyes of the Catholic powers abroad with the aim of elevating himself as the champion of the faith. His ambitions were strong enough still to picture himself ruling Scotland as guardian of his infant son—with his wife of course overthrown. It will never be known exactly how much reality there was behind the rumors of this "Catholic" plot. But certainly at the turn of the year there were whispers loud enough to reach the queen's ears that Darnley was once more intriguing against her.

On January 20 Mary set off for Glasgow to bring back her sick husband on a litter to Edinburgh, to finish his convalescence in her own company. In view of the contempt which she quite openly held for him, it is necessary to consider exactly what prompted her to make the journey. Some more compelling argument than sheer humanity must be advanced to explain her actions—and also to explain why Darnley so readily agreed to follow her back.

In January some sort of conference took place at Whittingham, one of the Douglas castles, between Bothwell, Morton—newly returned to Scotland, Morton's cousin Archibald Douglas, and Maitland. It is clear that a plan was beginning to take shape, although it is important to notice that none of the conspirators ever suggested that the queen had any foreknowledge of it. But their plan demanded that Darnley should be in Edinburgh, rather than Glasgow, where he was surrounded by his own Lennox Stewart adherents. It is possible that Maitland indicated to Mary that it was unwise to allow Darnley to remain in Glasgow where he might be either plotting or breeding dissension with his wild schemes.

The question still arises exactly how Mary induced her husband to accompany her back to Edinburgh, for it is clear that once Mary arrived in Glasgow, Darnley freely consented to the move, despite the fact that he had heard some rumor of what had transpired at Craigmillar. The promise which Mary seems most likely to have held out to Darnley was the resumption of full marital relations on his return to health. Mary's coldness as a wife had wounded his vanity as a man and also, he felt, threatened his status as a king. This promise would have been enough to bring him willingly out of his own feudal domain of influence into hers.

As to the place where Darnley should spend the rest of his convalescence, Mary had intended to bring him to the castle of Craigmillar, a little way outside Edinburgh, but Darnley declined to enter the stronghold. Perhaps he was afraid to do so. He chose instead a house of moderate size on the outskirts of Edinburgh, in a quadrangle known as Kirk o'Field.

The house in which Darnley now settled was ideally suited for convalescence. It lay on a slight hill and the site was open and healthy compared to the low-lying Holyrood; the air was thought by doctors to be most salubrious. It was far enough from Holyrood for the king's illness not to be an embarrassment to him, yet it had the security of lying just within the town wall.

Darnley took up residence on Saturday, February 1. The next week of his life was pleasant and almost domestic. Queen Mary felt confident that her husband had for the time being no opportunity to weave any plot against her. She settled into a routine of visiting Darnley with her retinue and returning to Holyrood for the ceremonies of court life. Relations at this point between Darnley and his wife were perfectly amicable. On that Wednesday the queen spent the night at Kirk o'Field.

Meanwhile, Bothwell and his fellow conspirators were hard at work. Darnley could not be expected to stay in the lodging forever, and Holyrood with its guards would obviously present more of a problem from the point of view of assassination than Kirk o'Field.

Sunday, February 9, was to be the last day of Darnley's convalescence. It was announced that he would move to Holyrood early on Monday. It was also the last Sunday before the beginning of Lent, and, as such, a day of carnival and rejoicing. In the morning Mary's favorite valet, Bastian Pages, was married, and after a formal dinner the queen and her court rode down to Kirk o'Field to spend the evening with Darnley. The queen planned to sleep Sunday night at Kirk o'Field, at the end of her day of revelry.

The royal entourage crowded into the king's chamber. The nobles played dice while the queen chatted pleasantly to the king. There was probably some music, a song in the background with the sound of the lute or the guitar. It was the sort of evening the queen much enjoyed; but at ten or eleven o'clock someone reminded her that it was the hour of Bastian's wedding masque, which she had promised to attend. Queen Mary was unable by nature to resist this sort of obligation. Since Darnley was coming back to Holyrood early the next morning, it now seemed unnecessarily inconvenient for her to return once more to his lodging after the masque. Darnley was sulky at the change of plan, but the queen lightly gave him a ring as a pledge of her goodwill. Then she bade him goodbye and went down the staircase and out the door. As she stood to mount her horse, she paused for a moment, puzzled. In front of her she saw her own page, French Paris, a former servant of

Bothwell's. "Jesu, Paris," said the queen, "how begrimed you are!"

Little did the queen know that her innocent observation touched at the core of secret happenings. For at some point during the day which she had spent in formal court ritual, Bothwell's henchmen, including Paris, had placed enough gunpowder in the vaults of the cellar of Darnley's house to reduce it to a heap of rubble. The figure who handled the practical details of the crime seems to have been Bothwell's then close associate, Sir James Balfour. The earl himself had a full schedule that day in official attendance on the queen.

Mary, in happy ignorance that the house in which she had just spent a relaxed evening was in fact heavily mined, now returned to Holyrood. Here she attended Bastian's masque and at about midnight retired peacefully to sleep in her apartments. It was a cold night; there was a new moon and a little snow powdered the streets.

It was now time for Bothwell to join his underlings at the scene of the crime to supervise the lighting of the fuses. He was not the only nobleman present. From a nearby house came Archibald Douglas and some of his men; although the Douglases were kinsmen to Darnley, they were under the leadership of Morton, and were sworn to the destruction of the man who had betrayed them over Riccio.

Meanwhile, within the doomed house, Darnley retired for the night, with his valet sleeping in the same room and three other servants in the adjoining gallery. All was calm over Kirk o'Field.

At two o'clock in the morning or thereabouts, the silent air was rent by an explosion of remarkable proportions. Paris said afterward that the air was rent by the "crack" and that every hair of his head stood on end. People in nearby houses came rushing out into the streets in fear, to find the house in which their king was lodged reduced to a pile of rubble. And in its garden lay the dead bodies of the king and his valet. The king was still in his nightgown, and beside him was a furred cloak, a chair, a dagger and some rope. There was no sign of the work of the blast on them. The king and his servant had been strangled.

The almost ludicrous element in the whole situation was that

Bothwell had not actually killed Darnley by his mighty explosion. For something had frightened Darnley so badly as he lay in the mined house that he escaped out of the lodging in only a nightgown. The most likely explanation of Darnley's precipitate departure would be that he was wakened by some noise and looked out his window to see the gathering of Bothwell's men and the Douglas faction in the garden. The sight would certainly have suggested some imminent danger.

But for Darnley, once outside the house, there was no escape. He and his servant had one dagger between them. The chair and rope indicate the improvised method of their escape—a chair let down by a rope out a window. And then the fleeing figures in their white nightgowns were spotted by some of the Douglas men and efficiently strangled, even as the house itself exploded in a roar of flames.

Some women living in the nearby houses said afterward that they overheard Darnley's wretched last plea for mercy to the Douglas men, who after all were his relations: "Pity me, kinsmen, for the sake of Jesus Christ, who pitied all the world. . . ." The plea went unanswered. Darnley, a boy of not yet twenty-one, died as pathetically and unheroically as he had lived.

8

AT THE PALACE of Holyrood Queen Mary was woken from her sleep by a noise like twenty or thirty cannon. Shortly afterward messengers brought her the news that the house at Kirk o'Field had been totally destroyed, and her husband's dead body found lying nearby. Her first reactions were horror and shock—horror at what had happened and shock at the feeling that she herself had had such a narrow escape. She wrote the same day to her ambassador James Beaton in Paris, pouring forth her amazement and distress. "The matter is so horrible and strange," wrote the queen, "as we believe the like was never heard of in any country." The queen did not yet know who was responsible, but was certain that with "the diligence our Council has begun already to use . . . the same being discovered . . . we hope to punish the same with such rigour as shall serve for example of this cruelty to all ages to come."

It is evident that at the moment she wrote this letter, it had not yet struck the queen that any of her chief nobies were involved; nervously convinced that she herself had only escaped death by a miracle, Mary was at first inclined to ponder more on her own enemies than on Darnley's. The official letter sent to France by the lords of the Council on the same day also emphasized the danger to the queen. So far, then, Bothwell's strategy had succeeded.

The royal widow behaved with perfect correctness. Darnley's body was brought to Holyrood and laid formally in state for several days before being buried in the vaults of the chapel royal. The queen also embarked on the traditional forty days' mourning for her husband. Her spirits had never recovered properly from her Jedburgh illness; now her nervous health became so critically weakened by the shock of the crime that she was earnestly exhorted by her doctors to get away from the tragic and gloom-laden atmosphere of Edinburgh. So the queen went to Seton, one of her favorite haunts close to Edinburgh, a week after the murder, and spent three recuperative days there. Although Mary's enemies subsequently accused her of dallying at Seton with Bothwell, it was the task of Bothwell and Huntly, as chief nobles of the kingdom, to remain at Holyrood to guard the person of Prince James.

Once the true nature of the two murders became known, it could not fail to occur to Mary that this was no hideous outrage by unknown assassins, but a deliberately planned coup on the part of those nobles who had hated Darnley, and who had openly discussed his removal with her. Rumors were already spreading rapidly around Edinburgh. A quantity of people, many of them servants, had been involved; it was hardly likely that the outrage would remain a total mystery for very long. Placards began to appear in the streets, the most virulent of which showed Queen Mary as a mermaid, naked to the waist, with a crown on her head, and Bothwell as a hare—the crest of the Hepburns—crouching in a circle of swords. The implication of the mermaid was insulting, since the word was commonly used in the sixteenth and seventeenth centuries to denote a prostitute.

This was the supreme moment for Mary to show herself the prudent and ruthless sovereign, and benefit from the actions of others to make her own position thoroughly secure. Her Achilles' heel in Scotland—her husband Darnley—had been eliminated from her path by her own nobility. She had not known of the crime beforehand, and was not implicated in the details. Now her best course—urged on her by both Catherine de Medicis and Elizabeth—was to pursue the murderers with public vengeance, in order to establish once and for all her own innocence.

As it was, however, her conduct bordered on madness. The Privy Council had, immediately after the deed, announced a reward of £2,000 for the capture of the criminals; but beyond that no further steps were taken to secure any arrests. Neither the placards, the rumors, nor Lennox's furious denunciations of his son's murderers seemed to have had the power of penetrating Mary's passive state of despair and melancholy. Since ill health and shock had clearly robbed Mary of any shred of political judgment, she was exceptionally dependent upon her advisers. But they were all for one reason or another unwilling to point out the true facts of the situation. Never was Mary Stuart's pathetic lack of loyal, disinterested consultants more disastrous to her than in the period immediately after Kirk o'Field.

Moray's first concern was to clear himself of any possible guilt in the eyes of his English friends. He left for London at the beginning of April, anxious to put as much distance as possible between himself and the Scottish court. Of the queen's other possible advisers, Maitland had been involved in the plot, and could therefore scarcely advise her to pursue its punishment, and Bothwell too was hardly likely to counsel such a course. There was thus no force to conjure the queen out of her mood of lassitude and melancholia. The Scotland of her early happiness now seemed to her a cruel and barbarous country: her secretary and now her husband had been done to death within a year. In her despair, she leaned increasingly on the one man close to her who still showed strength of purpose, energy and determination—and was also only too anxious to direct the affairs of state. Unfortunately for Mary, that man was Bothwell, the chief suspect in her husband's murder.

ON MARCH 25, THE FORTIETH DAY after Darnley's death, the queen's period of mourning officially came to an end. By then the vociferous demands of Lennox for justice had reached such a pitch that even Mary felt herself unable to ignore them. In a letter of March 24 she agreed to allow Lennox to bring a private proceeding in front of Parliament against Bothwell as the slayer of his son. On the day appointed for the trial, Bothwell rode magnificently down the Canongate, with Morton and Maitland flanking him. Although the due processes of justice were observed, the absence of the accuser Lennox—understandably afraid to appear in Edinburgh in view of the fact that the city was swarming with Bothwell's adherents—meant that Bothwell was inevitably acquitted.

Bothwell's next move was predictable: if he was to make his power even more effective by occupying the position of king, he needed the support of at least some of his fellow nobles. The expedient of a bond was once more called into play. In order to secure adherents for this new bond, on Saturday, April 19, Bothwell duly entertained many of the nobles and prelates then in the capital at a lavish feast. At the end of this momentous party, Bothwell produced a long document, the main point of which, apart from his own innocence in the murder of Darnley, was that the queen was now "destitute of a husband." If the "good qualities" of the earl might move her to select him for that role, then the signatories were to promise themselves to promote the marriage by counsel, vote and assistance. To this remarkable manifesto, known as the Ainslie bond after the name of the tavern where the supper party took place, those present, including Morton, Maitland, Argyll, Atholl and Huntly, now put their signatures. Although the motives of some of the signatories must be considered highly suspect, nevertheless Bothwell now had in his pocket the document he needed for his next bold move forward.

The queen having gone to her favorite palace of Seton again, Bothwell followed her there. According to Queen Mary's own story, it was here that he first paid suit to her, suggesting both that she needed a husband and that he was the best man to fill the role, since he had been selected to do so by her nobles. This direct approach threw the queen into a state of confusion. She always asserted afterward that she refused Bothwell's proposals at this point, on the grounds that there were too many scandals about her husband's death.

With this refusal uppermost in her thoughts, the queen proceeded to Stirling Castle to pay a visit to her baby, who, as custom demanded, had now been handed over into the care of his hereditary governors, the Erskines. Mary arrived on Monday, April 21, and spent all of Tuesday enjoying the company of her child. The queen played with him happily, unaware that this was the last meeting she was ever to have with her son.

Mary started back to Edinburgh with only Maitland, Huntly, James Melville and about thirty horsemen to accompany her. As the queen and her little troop reached the Bridges of Almond, about six miles from Edinburgh, Bothwell suddenly appeared with a force of about eight hundred men. He rode forward, put his hand on the queen's bridle, and told her that since danger was threatening her in Edinburgh, he proposed to take her to the castle of Dunbar, out of harm's way. Some of Mary's followers reacted disagreeably, but the queen said gently that she would go with the Earl of Bothwell rather than be the cause of bloodshed. Docilely she allowed herself to be conducted about forty miles across the heart of Scotland, and by midnight she was within Dunbar Castle, surrounded by a force of Bothwell's men, with the gates of the castle firmly shut behind her.

This abduction represents a typical example of Bothwell's thinking. He clearly considered that a sufficiently public outrage would cover in some curious way a multitude of private sins, and confidently believed that an abduction would put an end to all further argument about the marriage. Was Queen Mary enlightened in advance as to her fate? The intended abduction was certainly widely known about beforehand among the nobles, and contemporary evidence points strongly to the fact that the scheme had been outlined also to the queen, who had agreed to it weakly, still envisaging Bothwell as her help and support among the nobles.

Once within the castle of Dunbar, Bothwell made his second planned move. He decided to complete his formal abduction of the queen's person by the physical possession of her body. His intentions in this aggressive act were, as before, perfectly straightforward: he intended to place the queen in a situation from which she could not possibly escape marrying him. Bothwell was certainly not in love with Mary, but in the course of the gratification of his ambitions, he was not likely to shrink from rape. It is interesting to note that Mary's contemporaries believed that the abduction had been rigged and intended to save the queen's face. But it was also widely believed that Bothwell had completed his scheme by making love to the queen, and that this was probably against her will.

It is sometimes suggested that Mary found a sexual satisfaction with Bothwell which she had not experienced with either of her previous husbands. Yet to the end of her life the queen always firmly attributed her marriage to Bothwell to reasons of state rather than of the heart. In fact, the events leading up to her marriage to Darnley point far more clearly to the workings of physical infatuation than those leading up to the Bothwell marriage. In the spring of 1565 Mary Stuart was a young and beautiful woman, healthy and energetic, long-widowed, eager to be married; in the spring of 1567 she was broken in health, distraught, nervously concerned about the future of her government. It also seems extremely doubtful whether she and Bothwell were the sort of couple who would have been drawn to each other if political considerations had not been involved: this elegant, literary-minded woman was not the type to appeal to Bothwell, who in the past had always shown an inclination toward more earthy women. The important fact in Bothwell's eyes was that she was Queen of Scotland, with the power to make her husband king consort and effective ruler of the country.

And as for Mary, whatever her inner feelings for Bothwell may have been, she had three pressing reasons for giving her consent to the marriage. In the first place, he must have succeeded in convincing her that he would provide her with an able and masterful consort, one with whom she might share the strains of government. He had subjugated her by the undoubted strength of his personality at a time when broken health had induced in her a fatally indecisive state of mind.

Second, Bothwell was able to show her the Ainslie bond, which proved to her satisfaction that the majority of her nobility were prepared to accept him as their overlord. Mary had married Darnley defiantly, against the advice of most of her nobles; she did not intend to make the same mistake again. Third, Bothwell had effectively ensured that the queen would not be able to go back on her word by the act of physical rape. The union had already been consummated; it remained to transform it into a legal marriage.

Having secured the queen's acquiescence, Bothwell quickly obtained a divorce from his wisely unprotesting first wife, and on May 6 he brought the queen back to Edinburgh. A contemporary diary records that Earl Bothwell led the queen's majesty by the bridle of her horse, as though she were a captive.

As Mary moved in a trance toward her public union with Bothwell, the nobles were already reacting against his meteoric rise. Furious at the realization that Bothwell—one of their own—had made himself a virtual dictator, on May 1 a party of dissidents gathered at Stirling. In yet another communal bond they vowed to set their queen at liberty and defend her son, Prince James. It is significant that the key figures at this meeting were Morton, Argyll and Atholl—all three of whom only ten days before had signed the Ainslie bond promising to forward Bothwell's suit of the queen. The conspirators sent a message to Mary offering her their support against the Lord Bothwell. But the queen could scarcely credit that he had already lost the support of the fickle Scottish lords, and ignored them.

The days passed with horrible speed toward her wedding day. On Thursday, May 15, just over three months after the death of Darnley, Mary married Bothwell in the great hall of Holyrood. A greater contrast to the two previous weddings of the queen could hardly be imagined. The very fact that the ceremony took place according to the Protestant rite showed how much the queen had lost control of her destiny. Afterward there were no masques or "pleasures and pastimes" as there had been before, but merely a wedding dinner at which the people were allowed to watch Mary eating her meal at the head of the table, with Bothwell at the foot. There were no rich presents for Bothwell as groom, and no lavish replenishment of the queen's wardrobe. Her preparations were confined to having an old yellow dress relined with white taffeta, and an old black gown done up with gold braid.

Judging from the comments of observers, Mary's marriage

with Bothwell brought her absolutely no personal happiness. The French ambassador, Du Croc, commented on the strange formality between the queen and her husband on their wedding day, and later she confessed to a confidante, in floods of tears, how much she already repented of what she had done. The day after the wedding, Sir James Melville heard her actually ask for a knife to kill herself. The hysterical nature of Mary's reaction shows not only how far she was from feeling any kind of personal love for Bothwell, but also how far her self-control had vanished. As it began to dawn on her that she might have betrayed her whole reputation in order to marry a man who was no more suited than Darnley to advise her or govern Scotland, the future began to look very black indeed.

Subsequently, the lords claimed that Bothwell kept Mary a virtual prisoner. From the day of the marriage none of them was able to speak to her without Bothwell being present. So suspicious had Bothwell become that he kept the queen's chamber door perpetually guarded by his own men of war. The queen's distress was the talk of the court. Never, it seemed, had a woman changed so much in appearance in so short a space of time. The mermaid and the hare were evidently as ill-suited to live together as might be expected of a half-fairy sea creature and a wild animal of the earth.

FAST AS EVENTS HAD MOVED before Mary's wedding, the speed only increased after the ceremony. By the end of May many enemies were gathering against Bothwell, among them Maitland and Morton. In order to give a dimension of morality to their quarrel it was necessary to emphasize that Bothwell, as the king's murderer, must be brought to justice. The treachery of Sir James Balfour surpassed that of anyone else, for he, who had been closely involved in the murder of Darnley, and who had been granted the custody of Edinburgh Castle as a reward, now secretly agreed to support the conspirators' cause on condition that his custody of the castle be confirmed.

On June 6 Bothwell took Mary from Holyrood to the castle of Borthwick, a stark, twin-towered, fifteenth-century fortress twelve miles south of Edinburgh. The Lord of Borthwick was an ally of Bothwell's, but the castle was soon surrounded by the insurgents, and Bothwell realized that it was ill-situated to withstand a siege. He therefore slipped away through a postern gate, with only one companion, leaving Mary to hold the castle. The besiegers called up to the queen to abandon her husband and accompany them back to Edinburgh. When she refused they shouted insults to her. She had not, however, lost all her old spirit, and she disguised herself as a man and escaped out of the castle by night to the nearby Black Castle at Cakemuir. Here she met up with Bothwell and together they made their way to Dunbar.

It was at Dunbar that the ultimate treachery of Balfour revealed itself, for it was his message to the queen that she would do better to return to Edinburgh, where the guns of the castle would support her, which brought her and Bothwell out of this comparatively safe place before the royal forces had mustered to anything like a secure strength. The queen's reputation no longer had its pristine purity in the minds of her ordinary subjects, and they did not join the royal cortège as had been expected. By the time the queen reached Haddington she had only about six hundred horsemen. Mary and Bothwell passed the night—their last together—at the palace of Seton, the house which Mary had loved so well in her six years in Scotland.

On Sunday, June 15, 1567, at two in the morning, the confederate lords marched out of Edinburgh. In the van of their procession was borne a white banner showing a green tree with the corpse of Darnley lying underneath it, his infant son kneeling before him, and the legend: "Judge and avenge my cause, O Lord." A few hours later the royal army under Bothwell also moved out and took up a commanding position on Carberry Hill. The nobles then established their position on a hill opposite. Between the two armies, neither of them exactly certain as to how they should proceed, there appeared the figure of Du Croc, the French ambassador, who had panted out from Edinburgh after the insurgents.

Du Croc was now deputed by the rebels to beg Mary to abandon Bothwell, in which case they would continue to be her loyal subjects. This Mary absolutely declined to do. She pointed out in a passion of indignation to Du Croc that these same lords had signed a bond recommending the marriage with the very man they were now opposing so vehemently—"It was by them that Bothwell had been promoted," she kept repeating.

By her own account Mary had no inkling at this point that the lords intended to charge Bothwell with the murder of Darnley, and she certainly felt no temptation to desert Bothwell. In the first place, she felt no confidence about the behavior of men of the caliber of Morton, Lindsay and Ruthven. Second, the queen must by now have realized herself to be pregnant by Bothwell, which in her mind sealed their union.

As Mary refused to relinquish Bothwell, both sides now gave themselves up to a series of chivalric parleys, in which challenges to personal combat were given but no actual battles took place. Bothwell, according to Du Croc, was in high spirits—"a great Captain, speaking with undaunted confidence, and leading his army gaily and skilfully. . . ." But even as these parleys were proceeding, the royal troops were melting away.

At evening the rebels decided to press their advantage with a new parley, and a negotiator rode forward. Aware that the royal party was suffering from a striking lack of troops, Bothwell suggested to Mary that they should retreat to Dunbar, where there was a possibility of rallying much more support to the queen's side. But Mary could not believe that the situation was so desperate. She considered that the wisest course to pursue in the interests of peace was to accept a safe-conduct for Bothwell, and to trust herself to the confederate lords. Bothwell, it was agreed, would go to Dunbar to await developments in the capital. Mary and the man for whom she had sacrificed so much embraced in full view of both armies. At sunset Bothwell mounted his charger and, after five weeks of power, galloped away down the road to Dunbar. It was the last sight Mary was ever to have of him.

The Queen of Scots was now thoroughly alone. And her entry into the camp of the rebels immediately and rudely jolted her confidence in the love which she still believed her subjects bore her. Here was no enthusiastic reception, no cheers, no protestations of devotion. On the contrary, the soldiers shouted crude insults at her. She, who all her life had been greeted publicly with adulation and enthusiasm, now heard the soldiers shout, "Burn her, burn the whore, she is not worthy to live!" as they conveyed her along the road into Edinburgh. Amazed, the queen allowed tears of shock and humiliation to pour down her cheeks. For the first time she began to realize what the effect had been on the ordinary people of Scotland—the people who had once loved her—of her reckless action in marrying the man they believed to be her husband's assassin. To them she was now no longer their young and beautiful queen, but an adulteress—and an adulteress who had subsequently become the willing bride of a murderer.

In Edinburgh the queen was taken to the house of the provost. The nobles sat down to a hearty supper, but the queen retreated in a daze of horror to her bedroom. Even here, however, she could not find peace, since the guards insisted on remaining with her inside the room so that she could not even undress. Mary now lay down on the bed and gave herself up to despair. There seemed no hope, and certainly no honor in Scotland, since the nobles, to whom she had freely surrendered, now held her a humiliated and unconsidered captive.

By the next day Mary's self-control had utterly collapsed. She came to the window and cried out to the people that she was being kept in prison by her subjects who had betrayed her. The sight of her brought rioting outside and more insults. The lords pulled her back but before they did so, many of her subjects had seen the distraught woman at the open window—her hair hanging down around her face, her clothes torn open, her beauty ravaged, her courage gone. Where now was the exquisite princess who had fascinated half of Europe? The people of Edinburgh were shocked at the sight of this wretched, near-demented creature hanging out the window of an Edinburgh prison, shrieking that she had been betrayed. It was four weeks since Mary's marriage to Bothwell, and not quite two years since her boldly triumphant marriage to Darnley. This was the nadir of Mary Stuart.

9

THE CONFEDERATE LORDS were aware that they were on extremely delicate ground with regard to the queen's imprisonment, since this imprisonment had followed her own voluntary surrender in the interest of civil peace. Mary herself had genuinely expected a parliamentary investigation into the murder of Darnley to follow her surrender, but it was just this inquiry which Morton, Maitland and Balfour in particular had good reason to fear. Under these circumstances, the lords decided that it would be too dangerous to keep the queen in custody in Edinburgh itself. The people of the city regarded the queen's wretched state with sad astonishment. It would certainly be easier to keep their moral disapproval of her behavior at fever pitch during her absence, when rumors of her depravity could be spread without fear of contradiction.

On Monday evening, therefore, the queen was escorted hurriedly north. She was not allowed to take any of her ladies-in-waiting with her, nor was she allowed to take any clothes, not even a nightdress or linen. Late that night Mary reached the vast waters of Lochleven. Here, on one of the four islands in the middle of the loch, lay the dour castle of Sir William Douglas. Douglas was a most trustworthy jailer from the point of view of the lords; he was the half brother of Moray, and he was cousin to Morton. The lords could certainly rely on his interests being bonded to theirs.

The queen was now rowed across the bleak waters of the loch. On arrival in the castle she was conducted unceremoniously to the laird's room, which had in no way been prepared for her visit. Mary sank once more into a stupor in which sickness, pregnancy, despair and exhaustion all played a part. She remained in this semicoma for a fortnight, neither speaking to anyone nor eating, until many of those within the house actually thought she would die.

Mary had visited the castle of Lochleven before under happier auspices, using it as a center from which to hunt in Kinrosshire. But Lochleven was in fact more suited to be a prison than a pleasure haunt. The island on which this fortress stood was so small that it hardly extended beyond the walls, and the dominating, square main tower stuck up out of the lake like a symbol of inviolability. The castle also possessed another tower, built in the corner of the courtyard, and here the queen was eventually incarcerated. The loch itself, more than twelve miles across, was a bleak place even in summer, with the Lomond hills lowering over it; during the winter, the winds and rain would sweep across the lake and make it a desolate place indeed. It was a prison from which escape would prove virtually impossible without connivance from the inside.

On June 16 the warrant for the queen's imprisonment was signed by nine lords, including Morton. In view of the fact that the previous bond of the rebel lords had expressly referred to their intention of releasing Mary from the thralldom of Bothwell, and restoring her in liberty to rule as before, it was small wonder that the queen now felt totally and grievously betrayed.

Meanwhile, Bothwell himself was still at liberty. From Carberry Hill he had gone to Dunbar, but on hearing of the queen's imprisonment, he attempted with great energy and singlemindedness to raise support for her. At first he enjoyed a certain success, but having ignored the summons to appear in Edinburgh to answer charges of murdering Darnley and kidnapping the queen, he was formally declared an outlaw and his followers melted away. Even so, he managed to elude capture and make his way to the Orkney Islands, northeast of Scotland, where he hoped to rally support once more. Unlike Mary, the lords now took care to pursue with relentless ferocity those of Bothwell's underlings who had been involved in the murder of Darnley. The series of executions, which continued throughout the rest of the year, was intended to distract public attention from the complicity in the crime of the new governors of Scotland— Morton, Balfour and Maitland.

Mary's incarceration was an agonizing experience for her, for reasons beyond that of her wretched health. Queen Elizabeth's emissary, Throckmorton, who had been sent north to parley with the lords, heard that the queen was kept "very straightly"; the lords did not intend that there should be any dramatic moonlight flittings from Lochleven.

The queen still absolutely refused to hear of divorcing Bothwell, for fear of compromising the legitimacy of her unborn child. Moreover, her extreme suspicion of the lords had only been deepened by their behavior since Carberry Hill. Although Maitland told her that if she agreed to a divorce she would be restored to liberty and freedom, Mary must have doubted whether the lords would have carried out their part of the bargain. Had the lords wished to reestablish her, they had had an excellent opportunity after Carberry Hill, instead of which they locked her up in Lochleven. The existence of the infant Prince James, which had once seemed to promise so much for Mary's future, now told strongly against her. A long royal minority, with a series of noble regents, was traditionally regarded by the Scottish aristocracy as a time for self-advancement. It should be borne in mind that in early December 1567 Mary would be approaching her twenty-fifth birthday, on which date it was possible for a sovereign to reclaim properties given out during his or her own minority. To the Scottish nobility, the rule of the thirteen-month-old James was infinitely preferable to that of his mother, whether she divorced Bothwell or not.

It is noticeable that Throckmorton was deeply shocked by the brutal attitude of the Scots toward their sovereign. The lords were adamant that Throckmorton should not visit the queen personally, despite his many requests to do so. He was thus compelled to depend on their own bulletins as to her state of mind. They assured him that Mary was still madly infatuated with Bothwell, and said in addition that she would be willing to abandon her kingdom for him (a statement for which there is no other confirmation and on which Mary's subsequent career casts considerable doubt). More importance can be attached to her first communication to Throckmorton, which he reported on July 18, when she sent word that she would in no way consent to a divorce from Bothwell, "giving this reason, that taking herself to be seven weeks gone with child, by renouncing him, she should acknowledge herself to be with child of a bastard."

It was now some eight weeks since the queen's marriage to Bothwell: in her letter she therefore suggests that the baby had been conceived subsequent to the marriage. Then, at some date before July 24, no doubt as a result of privations and stress, she miscarried, and according to her secretary, found herself to have been bearing "*deux enfants*." If the twins had been conceived at Dunbar, on or about April 24, they were about three months grown at the moment of miscarriage, and recognition of the double fetus would have been perfectly possible.

What is virtually impossible is the suggestion, sometimes made since by historians, that the queen could have conceived by Bothwell in January, before Darnley's death. There is no reference of any sort through March, April and May to a royal pregnancy, which would had been becoming rapidly more apparent as the queen's figure changed; and this was an age in which such facts were speedily known by the accurate news service of servants' gossip. In the spring months following the Kirk o'Field tragedy, Mary's every word and action were reported; an event of such moment as her growing pregnancy outside the bonds of marriage could never have passed unnoticed.

It was while the queen was lying in bed after her miscarriage, by her own account "in a state of great weakness" and scarcely able to move, that Lord Patrick Lindsay came to her and told her that he had been instructed to make her sign certain letters for the resignation of her crown. Mary now believed herself to be in great danger on this tiny island in the middle of an enormous loch, whose waters could claim any victim silently without the circumstances of their death being ever properly known. Despite her fears, the queen was outraged at the monstrousness of the request, and continued to demand the parliamentary inquiry which she had been promised. Lindsay's rough words on the subject, that she had better sign or they would simply cut her throat, only convinced her further of her own personal danger.

Not everyone in the castle was hostile to Mary, however. The Laird of Lochleven's brother, for example, George Douglas, a handsome, debonair young man, was already showing himself susceptible to the charms of the beautiful prisoner. But from the actual signing of the letter of resignation there was no escape. Mary told her secretary later that Throckmorton had managed to smuggle her a note in the scabbard of a sword, telling her to sign to save her own life, as something so clearly signed under duress could never afterward be held against her. Thus Mary, on a lonely island, without any advisers, signed away the crown in favor of her own infant son and the regency of her half brother, Moray. Shortly afterward, Mary fell seriously ill again; her skin turned yellow, and she began to believe she might have been poisoned. This disease, which seems to have had something to do with the liver, was relieved by bleeding and by a potion which was said to strengthen the heart.

On July 29 James was crowned King of Scotland at the Protestant church just outside the gates of Stirling Castle, at the tender age of thirteen months. The circumstances strongly recalled those of Queen Mary's own coronation twenty-four years before. Once more the Scottish crown belonged to a puny child, hedged round by a grasping nobility. On the day of the coronation, the gloomy peace of Lochleven was disturbed by all the artillery of the house being discharged; the queen, sending to find out what the matter was, discovered that bonfires had been lit in the garden, and that the laird was celebrating riotously at the news. He asked her mockingly why she too was not making merry at the coronation of her own son, at which Mary started to weep.

On August 22, James Stewart, Earl of Moray, recently returned to Scotland, was proclaimed regent. This announcement, coupled with the disappearance of Bothwell, led to a period of comparative calm. Bothwell had been pursued to the Orkneys by his inveterate enemy Sir William Kirkcaldy, and had escaped to Norway, where King Frederick, joint sovereign of Denmark and Norway, quickly perceived in his uninvited guest a useful pawn in international politics. Bothwell was taken prisoner and, although Moray pressed for his extradition, he was destined to remain in a series of Danish prisons, of increasing squalor, for the rest of his life.

Gradually, on the little island of Lochleven, the queen's health returned, since the enforced seclusion, however odious, did at least ensure her the rest which she so grievously needed. With health returned also resolution and calm, positive thinking. By the beginning of September, she was able to write to one of her servants in her old vein of practical decisiveness, asking for materials, silks to embroider, and clothes for her ladies, who had recently been allowed to join her. Much of her gilded wardrobe was gone forever, seized by the confederates, and not a great deal of attention seems to have been paid to her luggageless state. To a queen accustomed to the lavish grandeur of royal state since childhood, this was the painful diet of captivity. But, as captivities go, it was not particularly stringent, and on Lochleven the queen gradually began to develop those agreeable but petty activities with which royal prisoners while away their time—an unwitting rehearsal for the long years of imprisonment which lay ahead. She began to dance once more, and played cards. She embroidered. She walked in the garden. She also looked out the window toward the distant edge of the loch and, fed by the prisoners' fare of hope, pictured the moment when she too would be standing at liberty on that windblown shore.

Mary had by now completely gained the sympathy of George Douglas, the Laird of Lochleven's brother. This young man, personable and gallant, saw in his sovereign a fragile and beautiful woman, the victim of a cruel fate. The queen drew his sympathies by the exertion of her famous personal charm and gentleness, and she was also able to promise more than her own affections. As Bothwell had now disappeared, there was in theory no reason why George Douglas should not aspire to her hand. But Mary's aim in this relationship was quite clearly to escape from the castle of Lochleven; she now hoped to have found in her admirer the weak link in the Douglas chain.

Throckmorton returned to England at the beginning of September, having made it clear that Queen Elizabeth did not acknowledge Queen Mary's abdication from the throne of Scotland; nor did she acknowledge the regency of Moray. But regardless of this disapproval from across the border, the Marian party in Scotland seemed temporarily in abeyance, and by the middle of October the country was quiet.

THE AUTUMN OF 1567 was remarkable for an unpleasant development in Mary's affairs. The governing lords changed the official reasons for her imprisonment; for, having procured her abdication, they needed to provide some further public justification for their behavior toward her. Now, in December 1567— nearly a year after the event—Mary was herself publicly blamed for the death of Darnley.

Certain documents which implicated Mary in the crime were mentioned for the first time in front of the Privy Council on December 4. The actual documents were never produced, but their existence was used to justify a new act of Council which stated that the official cause of Mary's detention was her involvement in her husband's death. She was said to have encouraged the outrage "in so far as by divers her privy letters written and subscribed with her own hand and sent by her to James Earl Bothwell, chief executioner of the horrible murder." At the Parliament convened by Moray on December 15, Mary's abdication of the government was said to be "lawful and perfect"; Moray's appointment as regent was confirmed, and the lords who had taken up arms at Carberry Hill were formally vindicated. Thus for the first time the subject of Mary's guilt was introduced: a change of emphasis which boded no good for her future.

The news that Moray was summoning a Parliament had cast Mary into a state of agitation. She addressed a long letter to him, asking that she be allowed to vindicate herself before it, as previously arranged; she touched on the favors she had shown him, his promises to support her, and earnestly suggested that she would even lay aside her queenly rank, if only she could be allowed a hearing; she also pointed out pathetically her past virtues as a ruler—how she had never been extravagant or embezzled her subjects' money. To this cri de coeur, in which can be heard the desperation of the captive, Moray sent only a few lines of acknowledgment.

Yet by midwinter the graph of Scottish loyalties was rising once more in Mary's favor. For one thing, the Hamiltons were annoyed that Moray had assumed the regency, which they thought belonged rightfully to their family. Kirkaldy and Maitland were both concerned lest Mary's abdication under duress might be considered illegal in the future. The Scots people, who had been told that their queen had been removed for complicity in Darnley's murder, could see for themselves that many nobles, far more involved than she, were not only at liberty, but forming part of the government.

As spring came to Lochleven, Mary was able to smuggle out a few letters to France and England, describing her plight and appealing for aid. But it was inside rather than outside assistance which proved effective. George Douglas quarreled with his brother the laird (they both seem to have had their share of the peppery Douglas temper) and was ordered out of the house and off the island. This gave him the opportunity to alert on the queen's behalf lords such as the faithful Seton, on whose loyalty she knew she could rely. Not only had George Douglas incurred his brother's wrath, but his rumored plans to marry the queen had also brought down the anger of Moray on his head, so that he was in a mood of fair rebellion by the spring, and Queen Mary was able to turn this to full advantage.

There was by now another spy within the castle dedicated to the queen's cause—young Willy Douglas, an orphaned cousin of the house, who was also won over by her charm and kindness. The date fixed for the escape attempt was May 2, 1568. On that day Mary received word from George Douglas that all was ready and, while the laird was at supper, Willy Douglas dexterously removed his keys. The queen, dressed in a red kirtle and a hood like those worn by countrywomen, boldly crossed the courtyard, although it was full of servants passing to and fro, and went out the main gate. With the gate relocked behind them, the queen and Willy Douglas made their way down to a boat on the shore and, hidden beneath the boatman's seat, the queen was carried safely across the loch.

Mary was welcomed ashore by George Douglas and John Beaton, one of her servants. By a piece of ironic justice, Beaton had with him the best horses belonging to the Laird of Lochleven, stolen out of the stables which were located on the mainland. Mary mounted and set off to meet Lord Seton and his followers. The country people, who recognized the queen, cheered as she passed. The music of popular acclaim must have sounded sweetly in her ears.

Queen Mary was once more at liberty after two and a half months of captivity on a tiny island. The Laird of Lochleven fell into such a passion of distress at the news that he tried to stab himself with his own dagger. But it is pleasant to record that those two other Douglases, George and Willy, who had placed devotion to their queen above family interest, were duly rewarded by her continual gratitude in later life and remained in her service during her English captivity.

Part Three: The Captivity
10

REGENT MORAY WAS in Glasgow when he learned the amazing news that his sister had escaped from her prison. By now Mary had reached nearby Hamilton, and the regent's first instinct was to desert the unhealthy area of western Scotland, where such loyal Marian lords as Herries and Maxwell held sway. But Moray decided to stand firm, rather than let the whole west unite for the queen; as it turned out, he was amply repaid for this decision.

Supporters had flocked to the queen as a result of the series of proclamations in which she had once more sought her subjects' allegiance. The Marian party had by now reached impressive proportions. Estimates vary from 6,000 royalists to Moray's 4,000, to 5,000 and 3,000 respectively, but all agree that Mary's party had considerable numerical superiority.

This preponderance had the fatal effect of encouraging the queen's army to skirt Glasgow in the hopes of drawing the regent into a fight and annihilating him. For, despite being greater in number, the Marians were poorly led, and when they clashed with Moray's forces at the small village of Langside, their lines broke before the enemy. The queen watched this gloomy contest from a nearby hill. At one point she mounted her horse and rode into the battle to encourage her troops to advance; she would have led them to the charge in person, but she found them all quarreling among themselves, more inclined to exchange blows with each other than to attack the rebel host.

Once the battle was clearly decided in favor of Moray, the queen had no choice but to ride like a fugitive away from the scene of her defeat. Guided by Lord Herries, she decided to flee into the southwestern territories of Scotland which were still loyal to her as well as extremely Catholic in feeling. A rough and wild journey brought Mary to the Maxwell castle of Terregles.

It was here at Terregles that the critical decision was made to flee farther on into England. The decision was the queen's alone, even though her supporters cautioned her piteously not to trust Queen Elizabeth. The general view was that she should either stay in Scotland—where Herries guaranteed that she could hold out for at least another forty days—or go to France and rally some support there. In retrospect, either course would seem to have been more sensible than seeking an English refuge. We cannot tell what considerations weighed with Mary Stuart, what dreams of alliance with Elizabeth still possessed her; yet the mirage of Elizabeth's friendship and the English succession were still strong enough to blot out the stable image of the proven friendship of France, the shores of which could be reached so easily from western Scotland. In France Mary had the estates and incomes of a queen dowager; as a Catholic queen fleeing from a Protestant country, she had every reason to expect the support of her brother-in-law, Charles IX, to say nothing of her Guise relations. The French would always have a vested interest in helping the Scottish queen against her Protestant insurgents.

In place of friendly France, Mary Stuart chose to fling herself upon the mercy of unknown England, a land where she had no money, no estates, no relatives except her former mother-in-law Lady Lennox, who hated her, and Queen Elizabeth herself, whose permission she had not even obtained to enter the country. As decisions go, it was a brave one, a romantic one even, but certainly not a wise one. Perhaps ten months in prison had served to bring out in Mary's nature that romantic streak which leads the subject fatally to prefer hope and high adventure to the known quantity. From now on, like most captives, Mary Stuart was to live far more in the world of dreams than in that of reality. The queen herself described her fatal decision in a letter written toward the end of her life, in a sentence as sad as any she ever wrote: "But I commanded my best friends to permit me to have my own way . . ."

The decision made, Herries wrote to Richard Lowther, the Deputy Governor of Carlisle, asking permission for the Scottish queen to take refuge in England. But Mary did not even wait for the return of the messenger. In disguise she made her way west from Terregles to the abbey of Dundrennan, and on the afternoon of Sunday, May 16, she went down to the little port at the mouth of the abbey burn. From this undistinguished seashore she could actually see the coast of England across the Solway Firth, and at three o'clock in the afternoon the queen embarked in a small fishing boat, with only a tiny party of loyal followers. In this humble fashion, Mary Stuart, a princess of Scotland, left her native country, never to return.

ACCORDING TO ONE tradition, during her four-hour journey the queen had a sudden premonition of the fate which awaited her in England, and ordered the boatmen to take her after all to

France; but the winds and tide were against her, and the boat went remorselessly on toward England. Yet when Queen Mary arrived at the small Cumberland port of Workington at seven in the evening, she seemed as elated as ever. The next morning Deputy Governor Lowther arrived with a force of four hundred horsemen, and by May 18 Mary was installed in semicaptivity at Carlisle Castle.

Lowther reported that the attire of the Scottish queen was "very mean." Once more in Mary's history a hurried escape from danger, in disguise, had left her with nothing in the way of a change of clothes. Noting that the Scottish queen had so little money with her that it would scarcely cover the costs of clothing she so sadly needed, Lowther gallantly ordered her expenses to be defrayed. He was evidently puzzled as to exactly how he should treat this strange bird which had so confidently flown into the English aviary.

Lowther's bewilderment was as nothing compared to the perturbation of Elizabeth's advisers in London. How was Queen Elizabeth to treat the royal fugitive? Queen Mary had arrived of her own free will, expressly seeking English assistance, as her own letters immediately before and after her arrival testified—a point which was to be raised again and again by Mary during her years as an English prisoner. Yet Mary's request to be restored to her own throne posed Elizabeth a whole series of problems. It was unthinkable for the Protestant English queen to take arms against Scotland on behalf of her Catholic cousin; on the other hand if Elizabeth did not do so, there was nothing to stop Mary making the same request to the French, who might seize the opportunity for entry onto the British mainland. That the Scottish queen should be received at the English court was an equally obnoxious prospect: Mary Stuart at liberty might prove an unpleasant focus for the loyalties of the English Catholics. Elizabeth's principal adviser, William Cecil, had not forgotten that ten years before, as dauphiness of France, Mary had claimed to be the rightful queen of England.

Taken all in all, the most politic course from the English point of view was to temporize. In the long run, it would probably be wisest to dispatch Mary back to her difficult subjects, rather than let her loose in either England or France, but of course

Embroidery done by Mary in prison

The Captive Queen

Medieval Tutbury Castle, the prison Mary hated most

Sir Francis Walsingham, Secretary of State to Elizabeth, who was responsible for placing spies among those close to Mary

Thomas Howard, Duke of Norfolk and suitor to Mary, who was executed for treason

there was no question of restoring Mary by the force of an English army; the terms on which the Scots would accept Mary back would have to be discovered by cautious inquiries. In the meantime it would be best to keep Mary in the north—not exactly a prisoner, but not exactly free either. The only course which was emphatically to be debarred her was that of seeking French help: Mary was to be told plainly that Elizabeth intended to assist her herself. The old scandal of Darnley's death now provided a convenient excuse for putting Mary off until she should be cleared of all guilt.

Queen Elizabeth's next move was to send her trusted counselor, Sir Francis Knollys, to negotiate with her guest-captive along these delicate lines. Knollys, now about fifty-five, was a man of the highest honor and a leading Puritan. Despite their religious differences, Mary made an immediately favorable impression upon this experienced courtier. He discovered in her an intelligent woman, blessed with an eloquent tongue and practical good sense; to these qualities, she also joined considerable personal courage. Knollys wondered what on earth was to be done with such a spirited creature, and he questioned his correspondents in London whether it was "wise to dissemble with such a lady."

The answer came back from the south that it was indeed wise to dissemble. Knollys was instructed to tell Queen Mary that she could not be received at the English court until she had been purged of the stain of her husband's murder, and this could only be achieved if she submitted herself to the judgment of Elizabeth.

Mary's state within Carlisle Castle was on Knollys's own admission far from luxurious. There were heavy iron gratings across her windows, and a series of three antechambers packed with soldiers led to her own chamber. Whenever she walked or rode she was attended by a guard of a hundred men. Her chief lack was of waiting women: she who had been surrounded all her life by ladies of the highest rank now had only two or three to attend her. The arrival of Mary Seton, one of Mary's most devoted ladies, provided a welcome relief, more especially as she was an expert hairdresser. Such feminine skills were all the more necessary since the queen had chopped off her beautiful red-gold hair during her flight to avoid recognition; it never grew again to its old abundance, and it seems that for the rest of her life Mary was dependent on wigs and hairpieces. Clothing still remained a problem. Queen Elizabeth, appealed to for help, responded with gifts of such mean quality that the embarrassed Knollys tried to explain them away by saying that they had been intended for Mary's maids. Moray dispatched three coffers of his sister's clothes from Scotland, but the queen noted angrily that there was but one taffeta dress among them, the rest merely cloaks and "coverage for saddles"—ironically useless to a captive.

To Mary the conditions of her confinement were secondary to her grand design to reach the presence of Queen Elizabeth. After her arrival at Workington, Queen Mary wrote over twenty letters to Queen Elizabeth, most of them extremely long, intelligent pieces of pleading, all elaborations on the same theme of Mary's need for succor to regain her Scottish throne, and her trust in Elizabeth to provide it. To such beguilements, Elizabeth was deaf. Mary would have to agree to a formal inquiry.

In Scotland, Moray and his supporters had quite independently reached the same conclusion. Mary's guilt over Darnley's death and her subsequent marriage to Bothwell were the points to be stressed if Mary were to be kept where Moray would most like to see her—in an English prison. The difference between Elizabeth and Moray was that Elizabeth at this point intended ultimately to restore Mary to Scotland and only wished to delay the process. Moray on the other hand was determined to make the mud already thrown at Mary stick so hard that there could be no question of her returning to reign on any terms whatsoever.

It was significant that Cecil himself, in a private memorandum, could find Mary's alleged moral turpitude the only excuse for keeping her off the Scottish throne and in an English prison. In favor of setting Mary at liberty were the following arguments: that she had come of her own accord to England, trusting in Elizabeth's frequent promises of assistance; that she herself, as a queen subject to none, had been illegally condemned for the murder of Darnley without ever being allowed to answer for her crimes; and lastly, there were her own frequent offers to justify her behavior personally in front of Queen Elizabeth. It was indeed a hard case to answer; it was certainly not answered by Mary's opponents at the time, nor has the unrolling of history revealed anything to justify England's subsequent behavior.

It was under these circumstances that, shortly after Mary's flight to England, a new campaign to blacken her reputation was begun by the men who now occupied her throne. The queen's "privy letters," which had first been heard of in the Parliament of the previous December, now made a new appearance on the political scene. Moray's secretary was dispatched to London with copies of the letters and instructions to show them secretly to the English establishment, in order to hint at what Moray might be able to bring against his sister if only the English would encourage him to do so. At this critical juncture, it seems likely that Cecil did in fact send some private written assurances to Moray: whatever Elizabeth might say in order to lure the Scottish queen into accepting her arbitration, she did not in fact intend to restore Mary to Scotland if she were found to be guilty. At all events, at the end of June Moray began to endorse the plan of an English "trial" with enthusiasm.

While Mary's emissary in London, Lord Herries, discussed with Elizabeth the possibility of Mary agreeing to such a "trial," Mary herself suffered a change of prison. It was decided to remove her to Bolton Castle in Yorkshire, as Carlisle was dangerously near the Scottish border. The move was complicated by the fact that Mary was still not officially a prisoner. When the suggestion of a change was first broached to Mary, she quickly asked whether she was to go as a captive. She was told diplomatically that Elizabeth merely wished to have Mary stationed nearer to herself. To which Mary replied with equal diplomacy that since she was in Elizabeth's hands, she might dispose of her as she willed. But when the moment came to leave Carlisle, Mary—whose temper was rapidly quickening with the frustrations of imprisonment—began to weep and rage, and Knollys had to exercise all his patience to get her to agree to proceed.

In spite of her incarceration, Mary had some inkling of the intrigues which were now being spun between Edinburgh and London, and her knowledge of Scotland led her to guess more. The news that some of her own letters were to be used against her reduced her to a state of nervous collapse, and her move proved a severe handicap, for Bolton was an isolated castle in a remote corner of Yorkshire. Mary was from now on placed physically outside the mainstream of political life, and for the next nineteen years she was deprived of any sort of worldly contact by which to judge the situations reported to her. Her own counselors, although loyal, were no match for the English politicians with whom they had to deal.

Herries came to Bolton from London at the end of July and put the English proposals to his queen; it is easy to understand how Mary, lit up by false hopes of restoration, agreed to the prospect of an English "trial." The fact that the English had no right to try her seemed now less important than the fact that Elizabeth had promised to restore her, whatever the outcome. On September 20 Elizabeth in fact wrote privately to Moray promising him what Cecil had already divulged in secret: no matter what impression Elizabeth might have given Mary, the Scottish queen would not be restored to her throne if she were found guilty. Moray now had every impetus to prepare the blackest possible case against his sister.

The Conference of York opened in October 1568. It had been decided that the "trial" should take the form of examination of the evidence by an English panel, headed by Thomas Howard, Duke of Norfolk. Both Mary and Moray were allowed commissioners. The conference was remarkable from the first for the confusion of aims among its participants. Of those present, only Moray was able to show true singleness of purpose, in that he intended to prove the Queen of Scotland's guilt up to the hilt; with this object in view he took with him to York the debatable "privy letters" in their famous silver casket. (The casket, and the documents it contained, had apparently come to light when one of Bothwell's henchmen was apprehended for his part in the Kirk o'Field plot.) The incriminating documents were described as "missive letters, contracts or obligations for marriage, sonnets or love ballads, and all other letters contained therein." In addition Moray had also commissioned a *Book of Articles* to denounce Mary, and this was also to be presented to the conference.

Moray's supporters were much less singleminded than their chief in their aims. Maitland, in particular, dangled after a scheme for Anglo-Scottish union, in which a restored Mary could play her part. Nor were Mary's own commissioners, including John Leslie and Lord Herries, as resolute in their determination to prove her innocence as was the queen herself; having lived through the troubled times of the queen's marriage to Bothwell, they conceived their role as rather to secure some sort of compromise. As for the English "judges," it soon transpired that they too were not immune to private considerations. Norfolk, England's leading noble, had been recently widowed; the Queen of Scots was now generally regarded as once more marriageable, despite the fact that divorce from Bothwell was not yet secured, and Norfolk's name had been mentioned in this context, even before the opening of the conference. Under these circumstances it was hardly surprising that the proceedings at York achieved little, and Elizabeth reacted by arranging for the whole conference to start again at Westminster.

On November 29 Moray presented his "eik," or list of accusations, before the commission at Westminster. Mary protested strongly at not being allowed the right to attend personally on the same footing as Moray. An English commissioner summed up the alternatives this way: If Mary appeared before the tribunal she would obviously deny the authenticity of the casket letters in toto, as a result of which she could never be convicted on their evidence. On the other hand, if Mary were not allowed to appear, the whole matter could probably be "huddled up" without exposing the Scottish lords as forgers and Mary could still be kept in prison. It was a shrewd summary and a prophetic one. Elizabeth refused Mary's request on the ingenious grounds that no proof had as yet been shown against her (the casket letters had not yet been produced in court); there was thus no point in her appearing at this juncture, when as far as Elizabeth knew, Mary might be declared innocent in absentia.

Moray was now asked to produce additional proofs of his eik, and he exhibited the December 1567 Act of Parliament claiming her abdication to be lawful in view of her involvement in Darnley's murder, and the *Book of Articles*. Finally he produced the casket. Mary's commissioners were not even admitted to the proceedings while the tribunal examined copies of the letters.

In the meantime Elizabeth had given Mary three choices: she could answer the accusations either through her own commissioners, in writing herself, or personally to some English nobles sent to Bolton expressly for the purpose. To all these alternatives Mary returned an indignant negative. She could hardly be expected to answer accusations based on evidence neither she nor her commissioners were allowed to see, or surrender the traditional right of the prisoner to face her accusers. But Elizabeth said that if Mary refused these three alternatives, "it will be thought as much as she were culpable."

At last Mary was beginning to have some inkling of the treacherous quagmire into which she had so unwarily walked. On December 19 she belatedly drew up her own eik for the accusation of Moray. Not surprisingly, she waxed especially furious over Moray's accusation that she had planned the death of her own child to follow that of his father, and beyond that she dwelt on the murder of Riccio and the manifest illegality of Moray's regency.

Despite Mary's counteraccusations, the conference at Westminster was officially ended by Elizabeth on January 11, 1569, without either Mary or her commissioners being allowed to glimpse the debatable documents which were said to arraign her. The verdict of the tribunal was ambivalent; it was decided that neither party had had anything sufficiently proved against them. Mary had not proved that her nobles had rebelled against her—but, on the other hand, the casket letters apparently had not convinced the tribunal of her guilt. In short, neither side was adjudged guilty at the end of the "trial," the only difference between them being that whereas Moray was now allowed to depart for Scotland—incidentally with a £5,000 subsidy in his pocket—Mary was still held at Bolton.

11

As the last farcical acts of the Conference of Westminster were taking place, preparations were already afoot in faraway Yorkshire to move Queen Mary to an even more secure prison at Tutbury in Staffordshire. And this time, since hearing the news that Moray had been allowed to return to Scotland unscathed, Mary could hardly persuade herself that she was no longer a prisoner, or that restoration to her throne was imminent.

The medieval castle of Tutbury was of all her many prisons

the one Mary hated most. She always maintained afterward that she had begun her true imprisonment there, and this in itself was sufficient reason to prejudice her against it; but Tutbury quickly added evil associations of its own. The castle, large enough to be more like a fortified town than a fortress, was in many parts ruined and extremely damp. Much of the ancient structure was mere wood and plaster, through which the wind whistled into every corner of Mary's chamber. Its magnificent view of the Midlands included a large marsh from which malevolent fumes rose, especially unpleasant for a woman of Mary Stuart's delicate health.

Mary was now in the hands of a new jailer, George Talbot, Earl of Shrewsbury, and his wife, known to history as Bess of Hardwick. A man of about forty, Shrewsbury was to act as the queen's jailer for the next fifteen and a half years. He was a Protestant and immensely rich, possessing an enormous range of properties across the center of England. Shrewsbury had long proved his loyalty to Elizabeth, and his character, fussy and constantly nervous about the reactions of the central government to his behavior or that of his prisoner, made him in many ways an ideal jailer. Moreover, Mary could be contained in safety in his string of dwellings across the Midlands, equally distant from the London of her desire and from the dangerously Catholic northern counties.

The queen and her new captors got on agreeably enough. Mary was allowed to set up her cloth of state, a sign of royalty to which she attached much importance, and a certain John Morton was introduced into her ménage. He was a Catholic priest, a fact of which Shrewsbury was either ignorant or agreed to turn a blind eye. The queen and Bess were described by Shrewsbury as sitting long hours together embroidering in Bess's chamber, where they delighted in "devising" fresh works to carry out.

Embroidery was to prove the great solace of Queen Mary's long years of captivity. It was a taste she had already acquired as a young queen and now, with all too ample leisure at her command, the taste was to become almost a mania. Pieces of embroidery were the gifts which Queen Mary sent to Elizabeth, lovingly and hopefully done with her own hand, as though the needle could pierce the stony heart where the pen could not.

Into her embroidery the queen put much of herself, including her love of literary devices and allusions, which she had first acquired at the French court. The now famous motto of Mary Stuart, "*En ma fin est mon commencement*" (In my end is my beginning"), was embroidered on her cloth of state.

In captivity Mary's health was her most obvious problem, apart from her desire for freedom. It was often the old pain in her side which put an end to a day's embroidering. Her health was only worsened by the discomfort of Tutbury. In March Shrewsbury noted that she was severely ill from what he termed "grief of the spleen" and which her doctor told him was the result of "windy matter ascending to the head," strong enough to make her faint. Even a move from the odious Tutbury to the more salubrious Shrewsbury dwelling of Wingfield Manor did not effect the desired cure. Queen Mary's health now became a chronic problem for her and her jailers, and there are few of her letters in the ensuing years which do not refer in some manner to the physical pain she had to endure.

The secret moves to marry Mary to Norfolk, and then presumably restore her to the throne of Scotland, now proceeded apace. Mary's captivity in England had after all no legal basis, and her abdication had been made under duress, which robbed it of its validity; in the meantime her blood relationship to Queen Elizabeth, and her possible succession to the English throne, made her a rich prize. Elizabeth's disapproval was by no means a foregone conclusion: in fact, she herself had suggested Norfolk as a possible bridegroom for Mary before her marriage to Darnley. Many Scots were said to look on the scheme with favor, and even Moray himself appeared to play along with the idea of the marriage for the time being. Many of the English nobles, who disliked the dominance of Cecil within the English Privy Council, saw in the elevation of Norfolk as Mary's bridegroom a convenient way of dealing with Cecil's rising influence.

The actual part played by Queen Mary herself in the cobwebs of intrigue and counterintrigue which followed was negligible. There was no one more anxious to end her captivity than Mary herself, and in all the first attempts or conspiracies to procure her release, she adopted exactly the same attitude: since her imprisonment was illegal, she would consider herself free to try to achieve her liberty by any means in her power. Her part in the marriage negotiations, however, was confined to writing a series of affectionate and even loving letters to Norfolk; yet since she never met their object, these letters must have belonged very much to the world of dreams rather than to that of reality. He was now to Mary "my Norfolk," to whom she emphasized her unhappiness and the desire for liberty. "My Norfolk," she wrote charmingly on one occasion, "you bid me command you, that would be beside my duty many ways, but pray you I will, that you counsel me not to take patiently my griefs. . . ."

It is clear that, despite these affectionate demonstrations, Mary was very much following the line of conduct presented to her by her advisers. When she finally gave her consent to the Norfolk match, it was on the strict understanding that Elizabeth's approval would be secured. It is evident that she was seeking an honorable exit from her cage approved by Elizabeth rather than involvement in a life-and-death conspiracy.

In the summer of 1569 Elizabeth had shown encouraging signs of favor to Mary by sounding out the Scots on the subject of restoration again. But the series of proposals, to which Elizabeth herself seems to have been genuinely well disposed, were turned down by the Scots. Six weeks later Elizabeth discovered the Norfolk marriage plot. Her rage was extreme. Mary found herself moved back to the hated Tutbury. Her rooms were roughly searched by men with pistols, and Elizabeth angrily ordered that Mary should neither give nor receive messages to the outside world. Norfolk was imprisoned in the Tower.

In the meantime events in troubled Scotland were about to take another dramatic turn: on January 11, 1570, Regent Moray was struck down by an assassin—a member of a rival family—in the main street of Linlithgow. Scotland was by now a hotbed of warring factions, and continued so throughout the minority of James. Lennox, Mary's bitterest enemy, now became regent, largely as a result of the favor of Elizabeth, who supported him as being a likely tool of English policy.

Back in England, a papal bull formally excommunicating Elizabeth, which had been promulgated by Pope Pius V, reached London in May. It was to have an enormous effect on Mary's future, since it declared that Elizabeth's Catholic subjects were released from their loyalty to her. In the summer of 1570 an ill-conceived plot to rescue Mary from Chatsworth, where she was now held, was hatched by some local squires. Mary responded unenthusiastically; she was by now nearly thirty, on the verge of middle age by the standards of the time, and the old impetuosity of her youth was gone. She was chronically sick and alone in a country she did not know. Under these circumstances she preferred more substantial hopes.

In August 1570 Norfolk was released from the Tower. He became involved during the next year in a further conspiracy, inspired by an Italian banker based in London named Roberto Ridolfi. Ridolfi's aim was apparently to secure an invasion of England from the Netherlands, led by Philip II's general there, the Duke of Alva; it was to be supplemented by a rising of native Catholics within England. This combination of invaders and internal rebels would free Mary and, having seized Elizabeth, place Mary on the throne of England, side by side with her consort Norfolk.

Mary's personal involvement in Ridolfi's schemes is open to question. It is possible that, after three years' onerous English captivity, she did allow herself to be persuaded to write the incriminating letters to Ridolfi quoted against her at Norfolk's trial. Yet she had not despaired of Elizabeth's assistance, and in October she wrote to the English queen, stating her desire to have her succession rights discussed in the English Parliament. Subsequently Mary did admit to having given some sort of financial commission to Ridolfi, but she always denied that it had been anything so dangerous to England as was suggested.

News of what was afoot began to trickle through to the English government in the late spring, and by September the conspirators had been rounded up. Norfolk was arrested once more and in January 1572 was tried for treason. He was condemned and finally executed the following June. When Queen Mary heard of the execution of "her Norfolk" she cried bitterly and kept to her room.

At this point Mary's character underwent a dramatic change in the eyes of the English nobility and Parliament. The circumstances of her arrival, now four years away, were quite forgotten in the tide of popular hatred which spread against her—this "monstrous dragon," as one member of Parliament termed her. Mary was now seen as a Catholic spider, spinning her webs in order to depose the English Protestant queen; the fact that she was an isolated prisoner with very little money was ignored. But although Elizabeth did reluctantly agree to the execution of Norfolk, she refused to consider the execution of Mary. She personally prevented the Commons from passing a bill of attainder on the Scottish queen; instead a bill was passed merely depriving Mary of her right to succeed to the English throne, and declaring her liable to a trial by peers of the English realm should she be discovered plotting again.

Elizabeth's preservation of Mary's life in 1572 by personal intervention must be allowed to be to her credit. Elizabeth, like Mary, had a dislike of spilling blood. She was also conscious that Mary was by now her closest adult relation. Mary's son was still a child, and Elizabeth may have been afraid of leaving her kingdom to the care of a minor (which had proved so fatal in Scotland) if an assassin should find her as he had found Moray. Most of all, however, she was aware that Mary, like herself, was a sovereign princess. The death of one princess might strike at them all.

Little is known of Elizabeth's inner feelings for Mary, since the English queen had learned in childhood to hide all emotions. That closeness which two queens and near cousins should feel for each other, so often chanted by Mary, may have found more echoes in Elizabeth's heart than she ever admitted. In the meantime a certain affection could not fail to be noticed by Elizabeth's advisers. The point was made that if ever the execution of Mary Stuart was to be secured, Elizabeth would have to be thoroughly convinced that her good sister had repaid her clemency with flagrant ingratitude.

BY THE SUMMER of 1572 the public cause of Mary Stuart seemed lost indeed, and this outward decline in her circumstances was completed by the turn of events in Scotland. Morton became regent in October 1572, following the death of Lennox; he was no friend of Mary's and also an Anglophile. Moreover, the Marian party was by now sadly depleted; leading supporters like

Argyll, in despair of her cause, had abandoned it, and Kirkcaldy was dead. Under Morton, the country enjoyed a period of comparative calm. Its quondam queen, Mary Stuart, also entered a phase of enforced tranquillity, in which the minor pains or pleasures of her prison routine became temporarily more important than European or Scottish politics.

The actual conditions of her captivity were not in themselves particularly rigorous during the 1570s. Mary was officially allowed a staff of thirty, which was enough to make her adequately comfortable. At the time of her first committal to Shrewsbury this thirty included Lord and Lady Livingston; Mary Seton; three ladies of the chamber and Jane Kennedy, Mary's favorite bedchamber woman; John Beaton, her master of the house, her cupbearer and her physician; then there were her grooms of the chamber; Gilbert Curle, her secretary; and Willy Douglas, now described as her usher. In time Sir John Morton, the secret priest, died and was succeeded by another chaplain, de Préau. Beyond the official figure of thirty crept in others, however, bringing the total to forty-one. This proliferation was tolerated by Shrewsbury out of kindness.

But as the royal retinue grew, its increase in numbers inevitably reached the ears of the government in London, who took a much less generous view. At times there would be demands from London that numbers should be cut; this would result in tears and protests from Mary, coupled with guilty denials from Shrewsbury that he had ever allowed the number to rise.

Although Shrewsbury never failed to protest his extreme loyalty to Elizabeth and his eternal vigilance as a jailer, there is no doubt that he did not always interpret the rules in the harshest possible light. The reason is not hard to find: if Elizabeth died suddenly, Mary might be transformed overnight into the queen, and if Mary were to ascend the throne, then Shrewsbury could expect much from his former charge if he had shown himself a sympathetic host to her in her times of distress. This possibility died away in the 1580s after James grew to manhood, but it was very much present in the minds of English statesmen in the 1570s—not only Shrewsbury, but also Cecil and Leicester.

From Mary's own point of view she was, of course, anxious to be allowed to receive as many local people and enjoy as much local life as possible. Such visits helped to while away the tedium of her imprisonment: the great families of Staffordshire and Derbyshire, the Manners and the Pagets, shared her particular enjoyment of musical festivities. Their visits also provided an excellent cover for messengers and messages to slip by secretly.

Mary's little household found the locality of their prison changing from time to time, owing to the sanitary arrangements of the era. The contemporary method of cleansing large houses was to transfer all its inhabitants to another house, and then clean the dwelling from top to bottom. Not all Mary's prisons were as uncomfortable as Tutbury. Wingfield was a great Derbyshire manor house of considerable style and grandeur, and even Mary approvingly called it a palace. Sheffield Castle and Sheffield Manor lay close together, and the propinquity of the two houses made cleaning easier. At Chatsworth Mary could enjoy the beauty of its park and of the wild country in which it was set.

Within the pattern of these moves, the queen's household had its own tiny excitements and dramas. Mary was allowed to ride when governmental suspicions were not too keen, and even went hawking with Shrewsbury. She was allowed the pleasure of archery, and the little delights of small dogs and caged birds. Nor did the queen lose all her interest in fashion and dress, being prepared to send off for patterns of dresses such as were then worn at the London court, and cuttings of suitable gold and silver cloth.

Mary's access to the baths at Buxton, which lay comparatively close to Chatsworth, was the subject of a long-drawn-out skirmish between Elizabeth and Mary. Buxton was endowed with a well, whose healing waters had been known even to the Romans. The baths enjoyed a considerable vogue with Elizabeth's courtiers, and to visit these baths became Mary's dearest wish; again and again she pleaded the near breakdown of her health in an effort to secure permission. But every time Elizabeth appeared to be on the point of agreeing, she seemed to hear of some fresh plot to rescue the prisoner. Eventually permission was reluctantly granted, and Mary paid her first visit to Buxton at the end of August 1573, staying for five weeks. Thereafter it was the outing to which she most keenly looked forward, not only for the effects of the waters, but for the opportunity to mix with court people.

A household event of some significance was the appointment of Claude Nau as her secretary in the summer of 1574. Mary's accounts were in chaos and causing her great concern; she needed a secretary with a good business brain. Nau was clever and quick-witted, although less engaging than her other secretary, the melancholy but charming Gilbert Curle. It was to Nau that Mary now related the important memorials to her personal rule in Scotland.

Mary's day-to-day life during the 1570s and early 1580s was not particularly arduous in itself; but there was one factor which made the whole era intolerably burdensome—her appalling health, made worse by the fact that she was confined. Few seasons passed without her being subjected to some really violent bout of illness. The eternal nagging pain in her side prevented her sleeping, and reduced her at times to real throes of agony. Norfolk's death brought on a passion of sickness. In 1581 she had another dangerous attack, which began as gastric influenza, and in November 1582 the same symptoms led the royal physicians to believe that she was actually dying. Her legs were also extremely painful, and by the date of her death she was almost permanently lame.

Mary had to endure two additional ordeals with regard to her health. In the first place, her captors were extremely reluctant to believe that she was genuinely ill, suspecting that she merely invented her symptoms in order to secure further freedom or privileges. Second, Mary was also unfortunate in that all her life she had shown a mania for physical exercise, but now she found herself severely deprived of it. Her very muscles seemed to seize up with lack of use, and Mary herself attributed her increasing sickness to her deprivation of sufficient exercise and fresh air. Time and captivity had in turn altered the "sweet face" which the good people of Edinburgh had blessed nearly twenty years ago. Portraits dating from the later years of her life show a woman with a drawn face, a beaky prominent nose, and a small, rather pinched mouth; the smallness of the whole face is in contrast to the fullness of the body, now matronly in its proportions. The years of imprisonment had taken their toll on Bothwell, too. He died in April 1578, driven mad by the intolerable conditions in his Danish prison, at last freeing Mary from the bonds of matrimony.

The outward changes in the appearance of Mary Queen of Scots were paralleled by the inward changes in her character. Up to then Mary's religious beliefs had never truly been tested. In France there had been nothing to try and much to encourage them, and in Scotland it had not been difficult to insist on the practice of her own religion. But now she was living in a country where Catholics were not only not tolerated, but often persecuted, and to exercise her religion needed cunning and tenacity. Moreover to Mary, as to many others in whom the hectic blood of youth fades, her religion had become much more important. It was not only that the Catholic powers abroad represented her best hope of escape from captivity; it was also that she herself had undergone a profound change of attitude to her faith, and indeed to life itself. With age, her whole character deepened. Having been above all things a woman of action, she now became, under the influence of the imprisonment which she so much detested, far more philosophical and contemplative. Mary's utterances in her forties show an infinitely nobler and deeper spirit, an internal repose quite out of keeping with her previous behavior.

Mary achieved this serenity at the cost of much soul-searching and suffering. She, who had never lacked an adviser, was compelled in the last years of her life to exist without any sort of reliable advice or support from outside. She was now the shoulder on whom her servants leaned, and to whom her envoys looked for direction; she might secretly write to the outside world for advice, and receive it, but when it came to taking action there was Mary and only Mary to make the decisions. The pretty puppet-queen of France, the spirited but in some ways heedless young ruler of Scotland, could never have carried through the remarkable self-control which Mary Stuart was to display in her last years. Adversity was to teach her a strength of character which was to enable her to outwit Elizabeth at the last by the heroic quality of her ending.

12

WHILE MARY LANGUISHED in captivity, the child whom she had last seen as a ten-month-old baby at Stirling Castle in 1567 had grown to a precocious adulthood. Mary still pined for the infant she had lost, and prompted by the dictates of natural affection which she believed must always exist between a child and its mother, she genuinely imagined that James also longed for her. The reality was very different.

Mary had made frantic efforts to maintain some sort of maternal contact with her son during his childhood. Just before Moray's death, she had sent James a small pony, with a pathetic little note to accompany it: "Dear Son, I send three bearers to see you and bring me word how ye do, and to remember you that ye have in me a loving mother that wishes you to learn in time to love, know and fear God." Mary wrote in vain, for none of her letters or presents were allowed by Elizabeth to pass to Scotland, to the son who could not remember his mother. James himself, far from being taught his duty to his mother, was being instructed to regard her as the murderess of his father, an adulteress who had deserted him for her lover, and the protagonist of a wicked and heretical religion.

It is true that James subsequently turned on Regent Moray and called him that "bastard who unnaturally procured the ruin of his own sovereign and sister." But the point remained that enough had been done in early childhood to rob James of any natural feeling at all, let alone the love of a son for his mother, since this newly lighted flame had been extinguished so shortly after his birth by Mary's enemies.

James had been brought up to believe himself to be a ruling monarch, despite the fact that his mother was still alive, and therefore Mary's position as Queen of Scots threatened his as King. During her few days of liberty in May 1568 Mary had revoked the abdication she made under duress at Lochleven; in her own mind, therefore, and in those of her supporters, she was still the true queen of the country, James a usurper. This was Mary's real connection with her son in 1580, rather than the natural ties of affection, and it was under these circumstances that, early in 1581, Mary outlined to France and Spain her own plan for "Association"—or the joint rule of mother and fourteen-year-old son—through a Guise emissary, a scheme which naturally involved the restoration of Mary to Scotland.

Mary once more envisaged the prison gates opening and, to promote the idea of the Association, she now enlisted Patrick, Master of Gray, into her service. Gray, a young man of Lucifer-like beauty, had all the talent and treachery of the former archangel. Although entrusted by Mary to represent her at the Scottish court, Gray quickly appreciated that it would be far more profitable personally to ally himself with the son, a king on a throne, than with the mother, a prisoner without a kingdom. Yet Mary continued to trust him to work for her, as she continued to believe in the affections of James.

The key to the Association in James's mind was of course the attitude of Elizabeth; English approval was still very much a factor of Scottish politics. On reflection, it was only too easy for James to see that the return of Mary to Scotland would be a serious nuisance to having his own kingship recognized; how much better to secure the benefit of the Association, in the shape of Elizabeth's favor and foreign approval, without the release of Mary. In the summer of 1584 it was Gray who was sent down to London to conduct these delicate negotiations on behalf of the king. Meanwhile Mary was specifically assured of James's welcoming attitude toward her proposals by a letter in very friendly terms from James himself.

In a series of letters to Gray, Mary showed herself highly conscious that her only hope of escaping her prison was if James made her release one of his conditions of negotiating with Elizabeth. She gave Gray very explicit instructions, stressing the importance of her release and begging Gray to make Elizabeth realize that by liberating Mary, she would be meriting the approval of James. But even as Mary wrote, it was being made clear to Elizabeth that in fact this was the very last thing that would merit James's approval.

In November, Mary's secretary, Nau, drew up twenty-eight proposals on the subject of the Association. Mary announced herself prepared to stay in England, to forgive all wrongs she had suffered at the hands of the English, to renounce the pope's bull of excommunication, and to abandon forever her own pretensions to the English crown. In Scotland she was prepared to allow an amnesty, to agree that there should be no upset of the present religion of the country; the only demand she made was for the immediate softening of her present harsh captivity. Such sweeping concessions made it clear that after sixteen years' imprisonment, Mary had one aim in view, and one aim only— her freedom, by any means at all.

By January 1585 Gray had successfully concluded his mission in London on James's behalf. He had indicated to Elizabeth that the release of Mary was not necessary to win James's friendship, and he had learned from Elizabeth that her friendship could be won without taking into account the desires of the imprisoned Queen of Scots. The Association was now doomed; it became stamped merely as the unrealistic scheme of a tiresome middle-aged woman in prison.

It was in March that the horrifying truth could no longer be kept from Mary. James formally announced that the "Association desired by his mother should neither be granted nor spoken of hereafter." At first Mary, in her pathetic desire to protect the image of her son in her own mind, tried to persuade herself that the betrayal was all the work of Gray. But her letters reveal the depth of her agitation: "I am so grievously offended at my heart at the impiety and ingratitude that my child has been constrained to commit against me." In letters to Elizabeth, James is referred to as "this badly brought up child," and she bewails the mischief which had been made recently between herself and James by sinister counsels.

But it was not a few months' troublemaking by Gray which had led to the breach between mother and son. In the delicate game of Anglo-Scottish relations, James had discovered that whereas he held some of the cards and Elizabeth held some others, Mary held none at all. There was nothing Mary could do within the walls of her prison except rage and weep at the perfidy of her son.

THE EFFECTS OF THE 1570 papal bull of excommunication against Elizabeth had now begun to be felt in earnest. The appearance of Jesuit missionaries from abroad made the English

Catholics themselves more sanguine and zealous; in turn, the English government tightened up the laws against the recusants (those who refused to attend the official Protestant services) and, using the double-edged weapon of the papal excommunication, began to blur the distinction between recusant and rebel. In view of the delicate situation of England, perpetually facing the prospect of a Spanish invasion, it was a natural act of public relations on the part of the government to seek to present the Catholics as dangerous aliens within the state. Similarly, the personal danger to Queen Elizabeth was underlined in order to boost her popularity with her subjects, as a symbol of national solidarity. Both moves augured extremely ill for the future of the Queen of Scots, who was both a Catholic and a rival queen to Elizabeth.

In the forefront of this campaign was the leading secretary of state, Sir Francis Walsingham. Walsingham, a prominent Puritan, had a remarkably modern conception of the uses of a spy system within the state: he understood to perfection the art of infiltrating his enemies' organizations with his own men. Mary had a counselor in Paris, Archbishop James Beaton. Walsingham now managed to place a certain Thomas Morgan as chief cipher clerk to the archbishop. This put Walsingham in virtual control of the French correspondence with Mary. It was not surprising that Mary's reputation became increasingly besmirched in Elizabeth's mind, as certain plots against the English queen were uncovered.

The first of these, the Throckmorton plot, was apparently Guise-inspired, although right at the center of it lay one of Walsingham's most successful agents. Uncovered in November 1583, it led to the arrest of Francis Throckmorton, a Catholic cousin of Sir Nicholas, on suspicion of carrying letters to and from Mary. The details of the plot involved the invasion of England by Spain, and the release of Mary. Throckmorton made a full confession before his execution in which he thoroughly implicated the Queen of Scots. The discovery of the plot gave Walsingham an excellent opportunity to excite a wave of popular indignation against the Catholics and their figurehead, Mary.

One of the cruelest aspects of Mary's last years was that while Walsingham was engaged in building up her image as a dangerous conspirator with agents at every foreign Catholic court, Mary was in fact no longer in complete sympathy with her Guise relations or indeed with her ambassador of so many years, James Beaton. She began to be convinced that the Guises were only intending to seize England in order to hand it over to Spain and had no interest in her release. The risk of losing touch with reality is one which every long-term prisoner has to face. In Mary's case, at the exact moment when her need to concentrate on the aid of Spain and the Guises grew more acute, she became the prey of false notions and grew to rely more on private schemes than on Beaton.

From June 1584 onward there had been murmurings in Parliament of a new pledge of allegiance to the crown. But it was a pledge with a difference. The signatories of this new pledge or bond did not only swear to bring about the death of all those who might plot against Elizabeth; in addition they swore—and the inspiration was Walsingham's—to bring about the death of *all those in whose favor such plots might be instigated*, whether they had connived at them or not. In other words, if it could be proved that a particular conspiracy had been aimed at the elimination of Elizabeth and the placing of Mary on the throne, Mary herself was as much eligible for execution as any of the plotters, even if she had been in complete ignorance of what was afoot. This bond was formally enacted into a statute in the spring of 1585. Mary, ever conscious of the need for Elizabeth's favor, actually offered to sign the bond herself. But her pathetic offer could not gloss over the fact that the bond amounted to her own death warrant; it was hardly likely that many years would pass before some conspiracy or other in Mary's favor would be brought to book by Walsingham.

By the spring of 1585 there was very little that was encouraging in the situation of the Queen of Scots. Her son had repudiated and betrayed her; her French organization was in chaos, penetrated by Walsingham's spies; Mary herself no longer felt complete trust in her erstwhile allies abroad; and her position in England was like being tied down over a powder keg which may at any moment be accidentally exploded by a match held by an overenthusiastic friend. To add to Mary's distress, in early January 1585 she was once more incarcerated in the loathsome fortress of Tutbury. Not only that, but at the same time the care of her person was handed over to a new and infinitely more severe jailer, Sir Amyas Paulet, who became in time as odious to her as the masonry of Tutbury itself. Under these doleful circumstances, Mary Stuart entered on the last and most burdensome phase of her captivity.

THE HARSH CHARACTER OF Sir Amyas Paulet was apparent from his very first action as Mary's jailer. This was to take down from above her head and chair that royal cloth of state by which she set such store, since it constituted a proof of her queenship. Paulet believed profoundly in the letter of the law. He had been specially selected by Walsingham because he was not only a prominent Puritan but also a mortal enemy of the Queen of Scots and all she stood for. Walsingham understood his man; Paulet was quite immune to the charms of the queen. Since honor and loyalty were his gods, and these Mary Stuart seemed to offend with her every action, Paulet's Puritan conscience had allowed him to hate her in advance. When they actually met, Paulet disliked his captive all the more for her possible attractions.

Paulet's instructions from London were clear: Mary's imprisonment was to be transformed into the strictest possible confinement. She was not even to be allowed to take the air, that terrible deprivation which she dreaded. In particular her private letters and messages were to be stopped once and for all. At no point in her captivity so far had Mary been cut off so completely. Her correspondence with Beaton and her other foreign agents had depended on a secret pipeline of letters. During the whole of 1585, under the orders of the Elizabethan government, Mary was totally deprived of the news she wanted so much.

Paulet achieved this isolation by the most rigorous supervision of domestic arrangements. There were naturally to be no more visits to the baths at Buxton. Not only was Mary herself not allowed to ride abroad, but her coachman was not allowed to ride out without permission, and then he had to be accompanied. Paulet also prohibited all Mary's servants from walking on the thick walls of Tutbury (where they could signal, it was thought, to passersby).

Her renewed sojourn at damp and drafty Tutbury thoroughly broke down Queen Mary's health, and her pleas for a change of air grew pitiful. Yet it is clear from Paulet's letter books that he felt no sympathy with her sickness, and seems to have regarded it as just retribution for her sins.

However, in the autumn of 1585 the protests of the French court to Elizabeth led to a search for a new prison for Mary. Various Staffordshire residences were proposed, but in the end the lot fell upon Chartley Hall, an Elizabethan manor house belonging to the young Earl of Essex, with a large moat around it, which made it suitable from the point of security. On arrival at Chartley Mary fell severely ill, and even Paulet found himself "for charity's sake" bound to report her complaints. On this occasion Mary was obliged to keep to her bed for more than four weeks, and it was toward the end of March, eight or nine weeks later, before she felt any real improvement from the "painful deluxions" which plagued her.

Walsingham meanwhile took the opportunity of the move from Tutbury to mount a new stage in his campaign to incriminate the Queen of Scots. His aim was, of course, to prove once and for all that it was too dangerous to keep Mary alive. To any plot to rescue the Scottish queen from captivity, foreign aid in the shape of an invasion of England was absolutely essential for success: the English Catholics could not carry through such a revolution alone. It was therefore one of Walsingham's more subtle moves to make his agents among the English conspirators exaggerate the possibility of this foreign aid, generally supposed to be Spanish, and thus encourage them dangerously in their plans.

One false agent in a chain of correspondence can cast a completely different slant on a whole subject. The preliminaries of the Babington plot, for example, involved a new Walsingham agent—Gilbert Gifford—at their very heart. He presented himself at the French embassy in London, where the secret letters which could no longer be smuggled to the Scottish queen had been piling up, and offered to get packets of them to Mary. On January 16, 1586, to her joy, Mary Stuart received the first secret communication she had had for over a year. Not only that, but she was informed that the same strange pipeline by which the packet had come—the local brewer—could be used to smuggle out her own notes.

In fact, the letters smuggled out of Chartley by the brewer in one of his casks were passed via Gifford to Walsingham, who having deciphered and noted the contents, returned them to Gifford for delivery to the French. Thus the method by which Mary believed she would be contacting the outside world in fact merely signaled her private thoughts and schemes directly to her worst enemy. In the spring of 1586, therefore, while Mary was intoxicated by the pleasure of renewed communications, Paulet had the grim satisfaction of watching this woman he had never trusted reveal herself to be every bit as deceitful as he had suspected.

It was at this point that the conspiracy of a number of English Catholic gentlemen under the leadership of Anthony Babington emerged. These young men showed a very different attitude to the imprisoned Queen of Scots from that of the previous generation; indeed, the Babington plot may perhaps be regarded as the first manifestation of that romantic approach to the beleaguered Stuart dynasty which was afterward to play such a part in British history. In recent years Mary had come to symbolize the martyrdom of the Catholic faith in England. Gone were the days when she had represented the spirit of religious compromise in Scotland. A whole generation had grown up in England since the shameful, hasty Bothwell marriage. To these young men Mary was a Catholic princess in an English tower and Elizabeth was the monstrous dragon who held her in thrall.

Spurred on by Gifford with lavish promises of foreign aid, Babington concocted a plan to rescue the Queen of Scots. In early July he composed a letter to Mary outlining the main points of the conspiracy. This missive was duly delivered by the brewer—by which time, of course, it had been thoroughly scrutinized by Walsingham. It was Mary's reaction which was crucial, for although she was already doomed by the terms of the bond, it would have been far more difficult for Walsingham to turn Elizabeth against her if Mary had given the Babington plot a cool reception. While Mary pondered, the English gloatingly awaited her reply. Finally, on July 17, she wrote back to Babington an extremely long letter approving his schemes in principle. There was no wonder that Walsingham's chief agent drew a gallows mark on the outside of this letter when he passed it on to him. Mary had fallen plumb into the trap which had been laid for her.

It is important to judge Mary's acceptance of the Babington conspiracy against the background of her own mood in the course of the summer of 1586. Her mental state was by now very different from what it had once been; the old notion of establishing her on the throne of England, however much it appealed to her youthful champions, was not uppermost in her own mind. Mary herself was weary of the prolonged battle for some sort of decent existence in which she had now been involved for eighteen years, and she began to speak of liberty in terms of retirement rather than government. In July, only a few days before Mary's vital answer to Babington, her exhausted mind received a terrible shock from the news that James and Elizabeth had actually signed a treaty of alliance, totally excluding Mary and her interests. The maternal heartbreak Mary had suffered in the spring of 1585 was now spiked with fearful bitterness.

There was no doubt that the publication of the treaty put her temporarily off her balance, and robbed her of the powers of reason which might have led her to act more cautiously. Even the fact that her health was now somewhat restored by the better conditions of Chartley contributed toward her downfall, for with renewed health came greater energy to escape. It was against this background that Mary tacitly acceded to—her words came to no more than that—a plot involving Elizabeth's assassination.

With the gallows letter in his hands, Walsingham now rounded up the conspirators; Babington confessed every detail of the conspiracy and all his fellow conspirators, as well as the Queen of Scots, were fatally incriminated.

Mary herself had absolutely no inkling of the dramatic turn which events had taken. Her spirits were high at the beginning of August: she felt she might even hope again. On August 11, when the dour Paulet suggested that she might like a ride out of Chartley in the direction of Tixall, a neighboring mansion, in order to enjoy a buck hunt, this seemed yet another favorable omen of future happiness, since such manifestations of goodwill from her jailer were rare. Under the impression that she might be meeting some of the local gentry at the hunt, Mary took particular trouble with her costume. Her secretaries Nau and Curle, and Bourgoing, her personal physician, accompanied her. It was a fine day. The queen's mood was so gay and so gentle that when she noticed Paulet lagging behind, she remembered that he had recently been ill, and stopped her horse to let him catch up.

As the little procession wound its way across the moors, the queen suddenly spied some horsemen coming fast toward her. They were strangers. For one wild moment her heart leaped and she actually believed that they were the Babington plotters coming to rescue her. Their leader speedily undeceived her. This was Sir Thomas Gorges, Queen Elizabeth's emissary, who dismounted from his horse and strode over toward Mary. "Madame," said Gorges in a ringing voice, "the Queen my mistress finds it very strange that you, contrary to the pact and engagement made between you, should have conspired against her and her State, a thing which she could not have believed had she not seen proofs of it with her own eyes and known it for certain."

As Mary, taken off her guard and flustered, protested that she had always shown herself a good sister and friend of Elizabeth, Gorges told her that her own servants were immediately to be taken away from her, since it was known that they too were guilty. From Gorges's tone, Mary even imagined that she might be now taken summarily to execution. She turned to Nau and Curle and begged them not to allow her to be snatched away without some defense. But there was little the wretched secretaries could do. They were dragged from her side—in fact she never saw either of them again—and taken to prison in London. Mary herself, with her physician, was conducted directly to Tixall.

Tixall was an exquisite Elizabethan house built about thirty years earlier, but its beauties were lost on the woman now imprisoned there. Mary did not leave her chambers once during the time she spent in the house. She begged to be allowed to write Queen Elizabeth, but Paulet refused to bring her paper.

Meanwhile her apartments at Chartley were thoroughly searched, her letters and ciphers taken away to London. After a fortnight at Tixall, in which anguish for the past mingled with apprehension for the future, Mary was conducted back to Chartley.

Walsingham, meanwhile, was able to convince Elizabeth of the abominable perfidy of her sister Mary. Elizabeth was plunged into a panic of acute physical fear, unaware how much of the assassination plot had in fact been elaborated by Walsingham's own agents. In a letter to Paulet, the English queen described Mary as "your wicked murderess" and any future fate, however rigorous, no more than "her vile deserts." It was understandable that Elizabeth should feel a mixture of fear and horror at the danger to her personal safety; the confessions of the Babington conspirators, arrested and examined in turn, did nothing to reassure her. In mid-September they were tried, condemned and then executed.

There was now little left for Mary to hope for. But there was one terrible thing left for her to dread: the secret death, the drip of poison, the assassin's knife, which would deprive her of the public martyrdom by which she now hoped to proclaim the Catholic faith at her death. Her hope was to triumph at the moment of her death, her fear was to be extinguished meaninglessly without an opportunity of bearing witness to the truths in which she believed. In September she managed to write to this effect to her cousin, Henry, Duke of Guise: "For myself, I am resolute to die for my religion. . . . With God's help, I shall die in the Catholic faith. . . . My heart does not fail me. . . . *Adieu, mon bon cousin.*"

It was in this heroic frame of mind that Queen Mary allowed herself to be taken without protest out of Chartley on September 21 to begin her last journey, toward Fotheringhay. Mary's triumph was that by her behavior in the last months of her existence, she managed to convert a life story which had hitherto shown all the elements of a tragedy into something which ended instead in the classic Christian triumph through death. This transfiguration in the last months of her life, which has the effect of altering the whole balance of her story, was no accident. The design was hers.

Contemporary Dutch watercolor
showing the beheading of
Mary at Fotheringhay

The Martyred Queen

James VI
of Scotland, Mary's
son, in 1595, at the age of
twenty-nine. Eight years later
he became James I of England

13

ON SEPTEMBER 25 Mary Stuart first sighted the ancient towers of Fotheringhay Castle. Fotheringhay had been built in the time of William the Conqueror and rebuilt in the reign of Edward III; here, in 1452, Richard III had been born. It was now used entirely as a state prison, and was of sufficiently bleak reputation for the wretched Catherine of Aragon to have refused to go there unless, as she said, she were dragged thither. The front of the castle and the gateway faced north, the mighty keep rose to the northwest; a large courtyard filled the interior. There was a double moat system along three sides, and the River Nene winding along the very edge of the castle made up the fourth side of the defenses. Around its grim towers stretched the flat Northamptonshire countryside.

Despite the size of Fotheringhay, Mary found herself incarcerated in comparatively mean apartments. From this Mary drew the correct conclusion that she was about to be tried, and at this evidence her physician Bourgoing reported: "Her heart beat faster and she was more cheerful and in better health than ever before."

In London, commissioners were appointed to judge the Scottish queen under the bond enacted in 1585. This Act had been especially framed in order to be able to try to execute the Queen of Scots; now it was coming into its own. The provisions of the Act were so heavily weighted against Mary that she stood absolutely no chance of acquittal. At the forthcoming trial she was to be allowed no witnesses in her defense; she was not even to be allowed a secretary to help her prepare her own case. She was left quite alone, a woman who knew nothing of English laws, to conduct her own defense against the best legal brains in the country.

Yet, curiously enough, the true injustice of the trial of Mary Stuart lay primarily in the fact that the trial took place at all. How, by the standards of the sixteenth century, could it ever have been legal for Mary as sovereign, the queen of a foreign country, to be tried for treason, when she was in no sense one of Elizabeth's subjects? In 1586 the sovereignty of a ruler was taken extremely seriously. If Mary had taken part in treasonable activities in England where in any case she was a prisoner, the correct remedy was surely to expel her from the country. It was the foundation-stone of English justice that every man had a right to be tried by his peers, or equals; Mary being a queen had no peers in England except Elizabeth herself. Thus the mere judicial proceedings for trying a sovereign by English common law presented enormous difficulties. The only possible justification was the Act, which by stating that the commission was to try *anyone* found coming within its terms, cut through all the laws, both national and international, of the time.

On Saturday, October 11, the commissioners began to arrive at Fotheringhay. Mary was given a copy of the commission which had summoned them, and the next day a deputation of lords waited on her. The object of this mission was to get Mary to consent to appear in person at the trial and thus acknowledge its legality. To this Mary replied in fine style:

"I am myself a Queen, the daughter of a King, a stranger, and the true Kinswoman of the Queen of England. I came to England on my cousin's promise of assistance against my enemies and rebel subjects and was at once imprisoned. . . . As an absolute Queen, I cannot submit to orders, nor can I submit to the laws of the land without injury to myself, the King my son and all other sovereign princes. . . . For myself I do not recognize the laws of England nor do I know or understand them as I have often asserted. I am alone, without counsel, or anyone to speak on my behalf. My papers and notes have been taken from me, so that I am destitute of all aid." On the subject of her actual guilt, Mary admitted that she had thrown herself under the protection of Catholic kings and princes, but denied any knowledge of an actual attempt against Elizabeth.

The next morning Mary received another less courteous deputation. She was told that whatever she might protest, she was subject to the laws of England, and that if she did not appear in person at her trial she would merely be condemned in absentia. Mary shed a few tears and exclaimed that she was no subject, and she would rather die a thousand deaths than acknowledge herself one. After prolonged discussions she finally succumbed on October 14 and agreed to appear in order to answer the single charge that she had plotted the assassination of Elizabeth.

Mary has been criticized for faltering in her determination never to appear before this illegal court; but there can be no doubt that her noble bearing at this trial, and the magnificent speeches she made there, did much to enhance her image as the martyr queen. Furthermore, the full publicity she was able to give at it to her wrongs also distracted attention from her vulnerable points, such as the letter she had written to Babington.

The trial of Mary Queen of Scots began on Wednesday, October 15, in a room directly above the great hall of Fotheringhay Castle. Queen Mary entered at nine o'clock, with an escort of soldiers. She wore a dress and mantle of flowing black velvet, her traditional white headdress with its widow's peak, and a long white gauzy veil. She was now so lame with rheumatism that she could scarcely walk to the chair allotted to her.

The trial was opened by a speech from the Lord Chancellor, Sir Thomas Bromley, in which he explained how Queen Elizabeth had been informed that the Queen of Scots had planned her fall and was therefore bound to convoke a public assembly to examine the accusation. He ended by stating that Queen Mary would have every opportunity of declaring her own innocence. To all this Mary replied by again denying the jurisdiction of the court over a queen, laying great stress on the conditions under which she had first arrived in England. In answer the Lord Chancellor utterly denied that Mary had arrived in England under promise of assistance from Elizabeth, adding that her protests against the jurisdiction of the court over her were futile.

Letters said to have been dictated by Babington before his death were then read aloud, and copies of the correspondence between Mary and him were passed around, together with the confessions of the other conspirators. Mary strongly protested against this secondhand evidence, suggesting that her own ciphers could all too easily have been tampered with. Despite her lonely position without counsel, Mary never for a moment lost her head. She continued to draw a sharp distinction between the actions which she as a prisoner had taken to try to secure her own rescue ("I do not deny that I have earnestly wished for liberty and done my utmost to procure it for myself. In this I acted from a very natural wish") and actual connivance at the death of Elizabeth, which she strongly denied.

Mary was now reproached with her pretensions to the English throne. She responded with a long and closely argued speech which made two main points: first, she had never at any time wished to usurp the English throne while Elizabeth lived; second, and in no way contradicting her previous point, she had "no scruple of conscience in desiring the second rank as being the legitimate and nearest heir."

The queen now went on to declare that, although she knew her enemies wished to obtain her death by unlawful means, yet with God's help she would still meet her end publicly as a witness to her faith. In a moving passage, which marked her as far more tolerant than the age in which she lived, Mary gave her own philosophy of life: "I do not desire vengeance. I leave it to Him who is the just Avenger of the innocent and of those who suffer for His Name under whose power I will take shelter."

According to the physician Bourgoing's account, the whole trial now broke down into a bedlam of accusations. Mary's judges attacked her like furies, all shouting that she was guilty. When Mary returned to her own apartments, she was utterly exhausted.

As she entered the room on the second morning of her ordeal, the queen was extremely pale. But she immediately made it known that she wished to address the assembly. Mary's first point was to protest strongly and movingly against the manner in which she had been treated on the previous day. Weak and ill as she was, she was alone among them, with no papers, no notes and no secretary, taken by surprise by a commission which had long been preparing such charges against her. Under such circumstances she concluded, "there is not one among you, let him be the cleverest man you will, but would be incapable of resisting or defending himself were he in my place."

Accusations were now piled on Mary's head—from the intended murder of the queen, to the prayers said in Rome for Mary as the true Queen of England. Throughout all these speeches, Mary adhered steadfastly to the statement that she had neither planned nor known of any lethal enterprise. She appealed to her own reputation for mercy and tolerance, and freely admitted that she had always desired her own deliverance and the support of the Catholic cause in England. Beyond these aims, she no longer wished for anything, neither honors nor kingdoms; and in defense of the last aim she was prepared to die. The queen's last demand was to be granted a full hearing in front of Parliament, and to be permitted to confer personally with Queen Elizabeth. Mary then rose. As she proceeded from her chair, she regarded the assembly, and most regally declared that she pardoned them for what they had done: "My lords and gentlemen, I place my cause in the hands of God."

In answer to the express wish of Elizabeth, who wanted no sentence pronounced before she herself had considered the proceedings, the court was now postponed and the noblemen rode away from Fotheringhay.

The next few weeks represented a strangely serene interlude, the Indian summer of Mary's captivity, when she was able to add to the self-discipline of the long-held prisoner the peace of mind of one who knew her confinement was rapidly moving toward its finish. Bourgoing noted that "I had not seen her so joyous, nor so constantly at her ease for the last seven years."

On October 25 the commissioners met again in London and found Mary guilty of "compassing and imagining . . . matters tending to the death and destruction of the Queen of England." The two Houses of Parliament now presented an address to Elizabeth in which they prayed fervently for the execution of the Scottish queen for the sake of Elizabeth's own safety. Elizabeth replied in a long and ambivalent speech, stating that the execution was one thing for the Commons to demand, quite another for a fellow queen to confirm.

In the meantime Paulet was instructed on Elizabeth's express orders to secure a full confession from Mary. On the evening of November 19 Paulet and Lord Buckhurst visited Mary, who afterward described the whole interview in a letter to James Beaton in Paris. "I thanked God and them for the honor they did me in considering me to be such a necessary instrument of the re-establishing of religion in this island . . . I offered willingly to shed my blood in the quarrel of the Catholic Church." This was of course the very last answer which Paulet and Buckhurst wanted; they told Mary roughly that as she was to die for the intended murder of Elizabeth, she would certainly not be regarded as either a saint or a martyr. But Mary was quite intelligent enough to see that, despite Paulet's protests, matters were going in the direction she hoped.

It was now the end of November. Mary believed that her days were truly numbered. She spent two days writing farewell letters to her friends on the Continent. Religious rather than dynastic interests now swayed Mary in the dispositions she laid down for the English throne after her death. In a letter to the pope she begged him to let the Catholic King of Spain secure her rights to the crown of England in place of James, if he remained a Protestant.

As she wrote, Mary could hear the banging of workmen in the great hall of the castle. She imagined quite genuinely that she was listening to the sound of her own scaffold being erected. But Elizabeth hesitated to confirm the sentence of death. The English people might rejoice and ring their bells at the news, but their queen was still very far from resolving her own dilemma. Quite apart from the fact that Mary was an anointed queen and her own cousin, there were foreign relations to consider. How would France, where Mary had once been queen, react to the news of her execution—still more Scotland, where she had actually reigned? As the prospect of war with Spain loomed nearer, the goodwill of France and the continuance of the alliance with Scotland became more important. Were such benefits really worth sacrificing for the death of an elderly and sick woman?

14

WHEN KING JAMES first heard the news of his mother's arrest at Chartley, he contented himself with observing that she should "drink the ale she had brewed" and in future be allowed to meddle with nothing except prayer. It was not until after the trial and death sentence that it was made clear to James that he might shortly have to choose between his mother's life and the continuation of the newly formed Anglo-Scottish alliance, which involved his hopes of inheriting the English throne.

But James's dilemma did not cause him the human anguish which Elizabeth was undergoing. She told the French ambassador at the beginning of December that she had never shed so many tears over anything as this "unfortunate affair," and there is no reason to doubt the genuineness of her emotion.

Public opinion in Scotland was reacting most strongly to the idea that its former sovereign might be executed in a foreign country. In fact James would find it hard to keep the peace if her life were touched. James himself pointed out his invidious position to Elizabeth, in language which made clear that it was fear of a national outcry which animated him, rather than some more personal emotion: "Guess ye in what strait my honour will be, this disaster being perfected," he wrote, "since I already scarce dare go abroad, for crying out of the whole people."

Despite these fears, the one sanction which James had it in his power to invoke to save his mother's life was never made. At no point did he say that he would break the Anglo-Scottish alliance if his mother's death were brought about by England. His threats were meaningless, intended simply to save his face in Scotland, and once this became apparent to the English, the date of the Scottish queen's death drew appreciably nearer.

The protests made by the French were more authentically passionate, but proved in the end equally ineffective. A special ambassador was sent by King Henry III to plead with Elizabeth, and the resident French ambassador, Guillaume de Châteauneuf, made valiant efforts to save Mary, but in January his attempts were curtailed by the discovery by Walsingham of yet another plot against Elizabeth's life. This led to Châteauneuf's house arrest, and rendered him impotent during Mary's last crucial weeks.

In mid-December Mary sent a farewell letter to Elizabeth, in which she requested that after her death her servants be allowed to convey her body to France, rather than Scotland, where by her standards the Protestant burial rites would constitute a profanation. She also asked to be allowed to send a jewel and last farewell to her son James. She concluded on a magisterial note of warning to Elizabeth: "Do not accuse me of presumption if, on the eve of leaving this world and preparing myself for a better one, I remind you that one day you will have to answer for your charge, as well as those that are sent before. . . ." Mary signed the letter, "Your sister and cousin, wrongfully imprisoned."

Slowly the autumn days passed by. Three months after the trial there was still no news from London that the end was near. Then, in the middle of January, Paulet informed Sir James Melville, the queen's steward, and her chaplain de Préau that, although they were to continue in residence in Fotheringhay, henceforth they were to be parted from their mistress. The removal of these loyal servants lowered Mary's spirits; her old fears of a secret death were revived. When Mary expressed these fears to Paulet through her physician, he fell into a rage and said that "he was a man of honor and a gentleman, and he would not so dishonor himself as to wish to exercise such cruelty." Man of honor as he professed himself—and time was to prove the truth of his claim—Paulet had no objections to imposing a series of further petty humiliations on his prisoner. Her butler was forbidden to carry the rod before her meat dishes, a service usually performed by Melville. In answer to her protest Mary received a chilling reply from Paulet that her rod had been taken from her, because she was no longer a queen but "an attainted, convicted and condemned woman."

Attainted, convicted, and condemned Mary might be, yet there was still no official word concerning her execution. But it was said afterward that on Sunday, January 29, between midnight and one o'clock in the morning, the heavens gave their own portent that the end was not far off; a great flame of fire illuminated the windows of the queen's room. If this was a supernatural warning, it was certainly borne out by events. Three days later, at her court at Greenwich, Queen Elizabeth at last sent for the secretary of the Council to bring the warrant for the execution, which for so long had lacked her signature. He discreetly placed the warrant in the middle of a pile of other papers the queen was due to sign. The ruse—for Elizabeth had made it clear to her ministers that she must be the subject of a ruse—was successful. It was thus, in the midst of an innocuous conversation about the weather, that Elizabeth finally signed the warrant with all her other papers, and threw them idly down on the table.

Elizabeth did, however, stipulate that she personally was to be told no more on the subject of the execution until it was successfully completed. And she murmured wistfully that if a loyal subject were to save her from embarrassment by dealing the blow before the execution, the resentment of France and Scotland might be disarmed. The obvious loyal subject to assume this helpful role was Paulet, and a letter was duly sent to him.

Now the issue was squarely placed before her jailer, and it is one of the ironies of history that Mary was saved from the private extinction which she dreaded by the Puritan who had done so much to make her last months uncomfortable and humiliating. Paulet seized his pen and wrote back to his royal mistress in the most trenchant language refusing the odious commission: "God forbid that I should make so foul a shipwreck of my conscience, or leave so great a blot on my poor posterity, to shed blood without law or warrant."

It was left to Elizabeth, on whom the action reflects no credit, to exclaim furiously at the "niceness" of those "precise fellows" who professed great zeal for her safety but would perform nothing.

Elizabeth's Council, with the warrant in their possession, set proceedings in hand immediately. The warrant was handed to Beale, the Clerk of the Council, who set forth immediately for Fotheringhay, accompanied by the earls of Shrewsbury and Kent.

The sadly depleted royal household at Fotheringhay had no inkling of what was afoot. On Saturday, February 4, Bourgoing asked Paulet if he might visit the neighboring villages and search for certain herbal remedies which might help the queen against her rheumatism. Paulet was evasive. On Sunday, however, Mary learned that Beale had arrived at Fotheringhay and, interpreting the significance of his arrival correctly, told Bourgoing he might cease searching for a cure since she would now have no need of it. But it was not until after dinner on Tuesday that a deputation of Paulet, Beale and the two earls asked to see the queen. Shrewsbury told Mary that she had been found guilty and condemned to death, and Beale read aloud the warrant. Mary received the news with absolute calm. When Beale had finished, she replied with great dignity and no show of emotion, "I thank you for such welcome news. You will do me great good in withdrawing me from this world out of which I am very glad to go." She said that she was overjoyed to have the opportunity at the end to shed her blood for the Catholic Church; she then placed her hand on the New Testament and solemnly protested herself to be innocent of all the crimes imputed to her.

Mary's captors then offered her the services of a Protestant minister but she refused to consider it. When she asked instead for her own chaplain to be readmitted to her presence, in order to make ready her soul, she was denied. This was a serious blow to Mary, who had not anticipated this final inhumanity. However, when Kent exclaimed, "Your life would be the death of our religion, your death would be its life," her face lit up. At least his words revealed that already in the opinion of the world her death was linked with the survival of the Catholic Church in England.

When the queen asked at what hour she was to die, Shrewsbury replied in a faltering voice, "Tomorrow morning, at eight o'clock." Mary once more begged vainly for her chaplain; finally she asked that her body might be interred in France, only to be told that Elizabeth had ruled against it. Mary's servants tried to get some sort of stay of execution, weeping and protesting that the time was too short, to no avail. There was to be no delay.

The Queen of Scots was left alone to spend the last evening of her life with her servants, some of whom, like Jane Kennedy, had spent a whole generation in her service. She tried to rally them. "Well, Jane Kennedy," said the queen. "Did I not tell you this would happen? . . . I knew they would never allow me to live, I was too great an obstacle to their religion." Mary then asked for her supper to be served as speedily as possible in order that she might have time to put her affairs in order. It was a heartbreaking meal, the servants outdoing themselves in assiduousness as though there was some comfort to be had in making each little gesture as perfect as possible. Bourgoing presented the dishes to his mistress and, as he did so, he could not prevent the tears from pouring down his cheeks. The queen ate little. She sat in a sort of dream, from time to time referring to Kent's outburst on the subject of her death and her religion.

"Oh how happy these words make me," she murmured. "Here at last is the truth."

Mary now went through her belongings in detail, dividing off certain mementoes for royalties and her relations abroad. From the rest she bestowed numerous little personal objects on all her servants. Bourgoing received her music book bound in velvet to remind him of the many musical evenings of the captivity, as well as rings and silver boxes. Melville received a little tablet of gold set with a portrait of James. Having disposed of those possessions which remained to her, the queen drew up an elaborate testament. She asked for Requiem Masses to be held in France, and made detailed financial arrangements for the benefit of her servants.

Deprived of the presence of her chaplain de Préau, Mary wrote a farewell letter to be handed to him as a general confession of her sins, in which she asked him to spend the night in prayer for her. Mary's last letter of all was to her brother-in-law, King Henry III of France; she related the abrupt circumstance in which the sentence had been broken to her, and her conviction that it was her religion which was the true cause of her death. She begged him to listen to the personal testimony concerning her execution which her physician should give to him as soon as he could reach France, and her last thoughts were for the faithful servants who had served her so long—she asked that pensions might be paid throughout their lives, and in particular that de Préau, her chaplain, might be awarded some little benefice in France from which he could spend the rest of his days in prayer for his dead mistress. When these elaborate dispositions were finally completed, it was two o'clock in the morning. Mary's letter to the King of France was thus dated Wednesday, February 8, 1587, the day of her execution.

The queen now lay down on her bed without undressing. She did not try to sleep. Her women gathered around her already wearing their black garments of mourning, and Mary asked Jane Kennedy to read aloud the life of some great sinner. The life of the good thief was chosen, and as the story reached its climax on the Cross, Mary observed aloud, "In truth he was a great sinner, but not so great as I have been." She then closed her eyes and said nothing further. Throughout the night the sound of hammering came from the great hall where the scaffold was in truth at last being erected. Soldiers' boots could be heard ceaselessly tramping up and down outside the queen's room, for Paulet had ordered them to watch with special vigilance, lest their victim escape at the last. The queen lay on her bed without sleeping, eyes closed and a half-smile on her face.

So the night passed. At six o'clock, long before light, the queen rose, handed over the will, and gave her women a farewell embrace. Her menservants were given her hand to kiss. Then she went into her little oratory and prayed alone. She was extremely pale but quite composed. Bourgoing handed her a little bread and wine to sustain her. The day now dawned fine and sunny; it was one of those unexpected early February days when it suddenly seems possible that spring will come. Between eight and nine a loud knocking was heard at the door, and a messenger shouted through it that the lords were waiting for the queen. Mary asked for a moment to finish her prayers, at which the lords entered, fearing some sort of last-minute resistance might be planned. But they found Mary kneeling quietly in prayer in front of the crucifix which hung above her altar.

Her groom now bore this crucifix before her as she was escorted to the great hall. The queen was totally calm, and showed no sign of fear. Her bearing was regal, and some observers even described her afterward as cheerful and smiling. The last moment of agony came in the entry chamber to the hall, when her servants were held back and the queen was told that she was to die quite alone, by the orders of Elizabeth. Melville, distracted at this unlooked-for blow, fell on his knees in tears. The queen said gently, "You ought to rejoice and not to weep for that the end of Mary Stuart's troubles is now done. Carry this message from me and tell my friends that I died a true woman to my religion, and like a true Scottish woman and a true French woman . . ." And commending Melville to go to her son, and tell him that her dearest wish had always been to see England and Scotland united, that she had never done anything to prejudice the welfare of the kingdom of Scotland, she embraced him and bade him farewell.

Mary now turned to Paulet and the lords and pleaded with them to allow at least some of her servants to be with her so that they could later report the manner of her death in other countries. Kent replied that her wish could not well be granted, for before the execution her servants were sure to cry out and disquiet the company, while afterward they might easily attempt to dip their napkins in her blood for relics which, said Kent grimly, "were not convenient."

"My Lord," replied Mary, "I will give my word and promise for them that they shall not do any such thing as your Lordship hath named. Alas poor souls, it would do them good to bid me farewell." After hurried whispered consultations, the lords relented and Melville, Bourgoing, Jane Kennedy and three others were allowed to go forward with the queen.

Mary now entered the great hall in silence. The spectators gathered there—about three hundred of them by one account—gazed with awe at this legendary figure. They saw a tall and gracious woman, dressed in black, save for the long white lace-edged veil which flowed down her back to the ground like a bride's, and the white stiffened and peaked headdress. Her satin dress was embroidered with black velvet; through the slashed sleeves could be seen inner sleeves of purple. She held a crucifix and a prayer book in her hand, and two rosaries hung down from her waist. Despite the fact that Mary's shoulders were now bowed with illness, and her figure grown full with the years, she walked with immense dignity. Time and suffering had long ago worn away the youthful charm of her face, but to many of the spectators her extraordinary composure had its own beauty. Above all, her courage was matchless, and this alone in many people's minds still gave her the right to be called a queen.

In the center of the great hall was set a wooden stage, all hung with black. On it were two stools for Shrewsbury and Kent and beside them, also draped in black, the block, and a little cushioned stool on which it was intended the queen should sit while she was disrobed. The great ax was already lying there.

Once led up the three steps to the stage, the queen listened patiently while the commission for her execution was read aloud. Her expression never changed. The first sign of emotion was wrung from her when the Protestant Dean of Peterborough stepped forward. "Mr. Dean," said the queen firmly, "I am settled in the ancient Catholic Roman religion, and mind to spend my blood in defence of it." Shrewsbury and Kent both exhorted her to listen to him, and even offered to pray with the queen. "If you will pray with me, my lords," Mary said to the two earls, "I will thank you, but to join in prayer I will not, for that you and I are not of one religion." And when the dean finally knelt down on the scaffold steps and started to pray out loud, Mary still paid no attention but turned away, and started to pray out of her own book in Latin. When the dean was at last finished, the queen began to pray in English for the afflicted English Catholic Church, for her son, and for Elizabeth, that she might serve God in the years to come. Kent remonstrated with her, but the queen prayed on, calling on the saints to intercede for her; and so she kissed the crucifix she held, and crossing herself, ended, "Even as Thy arms, O Jesus, were spread here upon the Cross, so receive me into Thy arms of mercy, and forgive me all my sins."

When the queen's prayers were finished, the executioners asked her, as was customary, to forgive them in advance for bringing about her death. Mary answered immediately: "I forgive you with all my heart, for now I hope you shall make an end of all my troubles." Then the executioners, helped by Jane Kennedy, assisted the queen to undress, until, stripped of her black, she stood in a red velvet petticoat and red satin bodice, trimmed with lace; one of her women handed her a pair of red sleeves, and it was thus wearing all red, the color of martyrdom, that the Queen of Scots died. All the time her clothes were being stripped from her, it was notable that the queen neither wept nor changed her calm and almost happy expression; she even retained her composure sufficiently to remark wryly of the executioners that she had never before had such grooms of the chamber to make her ready. It was the queen's women who could not contain their lamentations. Finally Mary had to turn to them and admonish them softly; once more she bade them not mourn but rejoice, for they were soon to see the end of all her troubles.

The time had come for Jane Kennedy to bind the queen's eyes with the white cloth embroidered in gold which Mary had herself chosen for the purpose the night before. Jane first kissed the cloth and then wrapped it gently over her mistress's eyes.

The women then withdrew from the stage. The queen, without even now the faintest sign of fear, knelt down on the cushion in front of the block. She recited aloud in Latin the psalm *In you Lord is my trust, let me never be confounded*—and then feeling for the block, she laid her head down upon it, placing her chin carefully with both hands. The queen stretched out her arms and legs and cried: *"In manus tuas, Domine, confide spiritum meum"*—"Into your hands, O Lord, I commend my spirit"— three or four times. When the queen was quite motionless, the executioner's assistant put his hand on her body to steady it. Even so, the first blow missed the neck and cut into the back of the head. The second blow severed the neck. It was about ten o'clock in the morning of February 8, the Queen of Scots being then forty-four years old and in the nineteenth year of her English captivity.

In the great hall of Fotheringhay, before the eyes of the crowd, the executioner now held aloft the dead woman's head, crying out as he did so, "God save the Queen." But at this moment the auburn tresses in his hand came apart from the skull and the head itself fell to the ground. It was seen that Mary Stuart's own hair had in fact been quite gray and very short, and for her execution she had chosen to wear a wig. The spectators were moved by the unexpected sight and re- mained silent. It was left to the Dean of Peterborough to call out strongly, "So perish all the Queen's enemies," and for Kent to echo, "Such be the end of all the Queen's, and all the Gospel's enemies." But Shrewsbury could not speak, and his face was wet with tears.

It was now time for the executioners to strip the body of its remaining adornments before handing it over to the embalmers. But at this point Mary's little lap dog, a Skye terrier which had managed to accompany her into the hall under her long skirts, crept out from beneath her petticoat, and in its distress sta- tioned itself piteously beside the body. Nor would this poor animal be coaxed away, even though the sad corpse lying on the floor of the stage, with its face now sunken to that of an old woman in the harsh disguise of death, bore little resemblance to Mary Queen of Scots. The spirit had fled the body. The chain was loosed to let the captive go.

At Fotheringhay now it was as if a murder had taken place. The weeping women in the hall were pushed away and locked in their rooms. The body was lain unceremoniously in the presence chamber, wrapped in a coarse woolen covering. The bloodstained block was burned. Every particle of clothing or object associated with the Queen of Scots was burned, scoured or washed, so that not a trace of her blood might remain to create a holy relic in years to come. The little dog was washed and washed again. It subsequently refused to eat and so pined away. At about four o'clock in the afternoon the organs of the body were removed and buried in a secret spot deep within the castle; the body was then wrapped in a waxed winding sheet and incarcerated in a heavy lead coffin.

Only one messenger was allowed to gallop forth from the castle, and he toward London, to break the news to Elizabeth. He reached the capital the next morning. When Elizabeth was told the news, she received it at first with great indignation, and then with terrible distress: "Her countenance changed, her words faltered, and she gave herself over to grief, putting herself into mourning weeds and shedding an abundance of tears." Before grief could overcome her altogether, however, she turned like an angry snake on her secretary, and had him thrown into prison for daring to use the warrant which she herself had signed. She now maintained that she had only signed it for "safety's sake," to be kept, not to be used. Unlike the queen, London itself suffered from no such doubts. The bells were rung, fires were lighted in the streets and there was much merrymaking and banqueting to celebrate the death of her whom they had been trained to regard as a public enemy.

But at Fotheringhay, cut off from the rest of the world, Mary's attendants were still kept in prison, and none of them was allowed to return to their native lands as Mary had stipulated. Spring turned to summer. The snowdrops which had scattered the green meadows on the day of her death gave place to purple thistles, sometimes romantically called Queen Mary's Tears. Still the body of the dead queen, embalmed in its lead coffin, was given no burial, but remained walled up within the precincts of the castle where she had died.

Epilogue

IMMEDIATELY AFTER THE death of the Queen of Scots, the English ports were closed. It was three weeks before the French ambassador Châteauneuf, released now from house arrest, could write to Paris with tidings of the calamity. The news of the death of Mary Stuart, their own queen dowager, was received in France with national mourning. Mary's wish to be buried in France was never fulfilled, but on March 12 a Requiem Mass was held in the black-draped cathedral of Notre Dame, where nearly thirty years before she had married Francis amid so much magnificence.

In other ways, however, Mary's last wishes were being met, for, despite all the English precautions, news of her bravery leaked out, and by March 7 Mendoza, the former Spanish ambassador to London, was able to spread the tale of her heroic death to Spain. Not only her courage but even her sanctity were discussed in sermons that virtually canonized Mary as one who had died in the cause of the Catholic faith.

James's grief is more difficult to estimate, and contemporary accounts differ radically in their reports of how he received the news of his mother's execution. According to one story, he shammed sorrow in public, but observed to his courtiers gleefully in secret: "Now I am sole King." Other reports spoke of his evident grief, how he became very sad and went to bed without eating. Whatever James's outward show of lamentation, it is difficult to believe that news of his mother's death had aroused at long last the filial passion which had been in so little evidence during her life. His subsequent conduct showed that so long as the English crown still dangled within his reach, he was prepared to swallow the insult to his family and his nation.

The Scottish people as a whole showed more spirit. When James ordered the Scottish court into mourning as a formal gesture, according to one tradition the Earl of Sinclair appeared before him dressed in steel armor in place of black. When James asked him whether he had not seen the general order for mourning, Sinclair replied sternly, "This *is* the proper mourning for the Queen of Scotland." There was a general clamor for war, and James did make the gesture of breaking off formal communications with England for a time, but he finally accepted Elizabeth's explanation of her own "unspotted" part in the execution and the Anglo-Scottish alliance remained unsevered.

It was, however, in deference to James that the subject of burial of the Queen of Scots was raised again in the summer after her death. The coffin had remained unburied; now it was planned to give it an honorable burial in Peterborough Cathedral. The line adopted seemed to be that Mary had been a revered dowager queen of Scotland who happened to die in England of natural causes. Heralds, nobles and mourners were imported from London to give the occasion the right degree of solemnity, but no Scots were present, apart from the late queen's servants, who had been allowed out of their seclusion at Fotheringhay to attend the service. The coffin had been transported from Fotheringhay to Peterborough at dead of night for fear of demonstrations. The whole ceremony was, of course, Protestant and thus sung in English.

The coffin was placed in a vault of the cathedral and when the service was completed, the courtiers and the ecclesiastics adjourned to the Bishop's Palace for a funeral banquet of considerable festivity. While the English caroused, Mary's servants gathered in another room and wept bitter tears for their beloved mistress.

There was a further delay of two months before these poor people were allowed to depart from their melancholy prison. In October, Bourgoing went to King Henry III as he had been instructed, and told his tale of the uplifting last months and hours of the late Queen of Scots. The farewell letters written nearly a year before reached their destinations at last, and King Philip of Spain, moved by this reminder from beyond the grave, honored Mary's last requests for payments of her servants' wages, and her debts in France. He also pursued the subject of what he believed to be Mary's last gift to him in her will—the reversion of the English crown. It was in the next year, 1588, that Philip took the momentous decision to pursue his supposed English inheritance with the great force of the Spanish Armada. Ironically enough, the mighty Spanish fleet of rescue, for which Mary had waited so long and so hopefully, only sailed toward England after her death.

Even after the burial at Peterborough, the earthly journeys of the Queen of Scots were not at an end. When James ascended the English throne in 1603, it was felt that something should be done for his mother's memory. Thus it was, in 1612, that the Queen of Scots's body found its final resting place in Westminster Abbey. The tomb, commissioned by James, is magnificent, a monument to his taste, if not to his filial piety. By the white marble of which it is composed, Mary Stuart becomes once more "*la reine blanche*" of her first widowhood. It shows her lying full-length beneath a great ornamental canopy, her face serene, her long fingers stretched out in an attitude of prayer. She wears the simple peaked headdress in which she died, but a royal cloak edged with ermine stretches around her body, and at her feet rests the lion of Scotland.

So the Queen of Scots found peace at last. There can be little doubt that Mary, who cared so much for the English succession, would have been satisfied at the last with her burial place among the kings and queens of England. Her rights as a queen, to which she attached such importance, had thus been respected. She who never reigned in England, who was born a queen of Scotland, and who died at the orders of an English queen, lies now in Westminster Abbey, where every sovereign of Britain since her death has been crowned, down to the present queen. As Mary herself had embroidered so long ago on the royal cloth of state which was destined to hang over the head of a captive queen: *In my end is my Beginning.*

WILL
ROGERS

His
Life
and
Times

WILL ROGERS
His Life and Times

A condensation of the book by
RICHARD M. KETCHUM

Cowboy, Wild West show trouper, trick roper without peer, Will Rogers was one of the pioneer stars of vaudeville, movies, and radio. But more than that, he was a perceptive, tongue-in-cheek social commentator who could reduce complex issues to their essentials, humble the mighty, puncture the pompous. For an entire generation he was the witty and beloved spokesman for sanity, common sense, and steady faith in the American dream. That is why at his death a friend aptly said, "A smile has disappeared from the face of America." And that is why, in an even more complex and unsmiling time, Will Rogers deserves to be remembered.

1

"My ancestors didn't come on the Mayflower but they met the boat."

LIKE SO MANY Americans, Will Rogers was a composite of many worlds. He happened to be born in Indian Territory—in what is now the state of Oklahoma—in 1879, when nearly everyone there bore the scar of that shameful episode in United States history known as the great removal. This was the eviction in the 1830s of the so-called Five Civilized Tribes (Choctaw, Chickasaw, Creek, Seminole, and Cherokee) from their ancestral lands in the southeast, and their forced migration to lands beyond the Mississippi River.

To this day no one knows with certainty the origins of the Cherokees. When encountered by Hernando de Soto in 1540, the tribe had been living, for as long as archaeological evidence can determine, in a vast region in the southern Appalachians. There were probably about twenty-five thousand Cherokees then—farmers and hunters who ranged from the Carolinas and Georgia into northern Alabama, the Cumberland Plateau in Tennessee, and along the Ohio River.

To the white settlers Cherokees were "warlike"—a term frequently used to justify killing or removing Indians; but it might be more accurate to say that the Cherokees had an abiding unwillingness to be pushed around. And they were as proud as they were determined: as an English officer remarked, "They are like the Devil's pigg; they will neither lead nor drive."

Continually fighting with their neighbors, they boasted that they could, on short notice, put six thousand braves on the warpath.

From 1730 on, English, Scottish, German, and Irish entrepreneurs were actively moving about the Cherokee lands, trading with the Indians, marrying Cherokee women, siring children of mixed blood, and slowly turning members of the tribe toward white ways. Will Rogers' paternal great-grandfather, Robert Rogers, married a half-blooded Cherokee woman; his maternal great-grandfather, John Gunter, married a full-blooded Cherokee. By the end of the eighteenth century a great deal of such interbreeding had occurred.

Meanwhile other whites were pushing in the perimeters of the hunting grounds. During the American Revolution the Cherokees remained loyal to the king, for His Majesty's representatives in America usually respected treaty obligations, whereas the colonial frontiersmen tended to ignore them.

Will Rogers on Indians: *"They sent the Indians to Oklahoma. They had a treaty that said, 'You shall have this land as long as grass grows and water flows.' It was not only a good rhyme but looked like a good treaty, and it was till they struck oil. Then the government took it away from us again."*

The Cherokees fought the rebels long after Cornwallis surrendered—which did nothing to endear them to citizens of the new republic.

In 1791 the tribe negotiated a treaty with George Washington affirming "Perpetual peace" between the United States and the Cherokees and forbidding Americans to hunt on Cherokee lands; but never again did they know a President whose policy was to defend the rights of Indians. Presidents Adams, Jefferson, Madison, and Monroe were no friends of the Cherokees, while Jackson proved to be the worst enemy of all.

After the 1791 treaty the United States government forced the Cherokees into a number of others involving land cessions, and as their ancestral lands diminished in size, the Cherokees came to a truly remarkable decision—considering their independent spirit. They concluded that they would adopt the white man's ways, accept his missionaries and religion, and pattern their government on that of the new United States. This meant almost total abandonment of an ancient culture and its replacement with that of the educated Christian white, all in hopes of convincing the American that they were entitled to his respect and friendship. As a consequence, they came to be known, along with other tribes of the southeast, as "civilized" Indians. But they continued to be treated as savages.

Early in the nineteenth century the Cherokees added one more accomplishment to their list: they became literate almost overnight. Some credit for this must go the presence of missionaries and to the continuing practice of intermarriage with educated whites; but the giant step was taken in 1821 when the Cherokee council approved a highly successful system of phonetics by which an intelligent Cherokee could learn to read or write his native tongue within a matter of days; a Cherokee named Sequoya had worked for about ten years to devise the system. By 1828 the newly organized Cherokee Nation had, in addition to its own written language and a newspaper called the *Cherokee Phoenix,* a republic, a constitution, a principal chief or president, a bicameral legislature, a supreme court, and a codified body of laws. It was a society, one might have thought, worthy of acceptance by white Americans. But no one who believed so reckoned with the cupidity the Cherokees were about to encounter.

IN 1828 THE Georgia legislature suddenly declared that it had jurisdiction over all Cherokee holdings within the state's boundaries and conducted a statewide lottery for distributing the Indians' land and homes to white residents. That same year gold was discovered in Cherokee territory. Those whites who poured into the region and who were disappointed in their search for the precious metal were consoled by their first glimpse of the magnificent deep woods covered with enormous stands of hickory, oak, chestnut, mountain laurel, magnolia, and azalea; broad, sunlit savannas where corn, cotton, and orchards bloomed; mountain pastures where cattle and horses grazed. Some of the Cherokee houses, on the scale of small plantations, were equally tempting. The whites took one look and began moving in.

The Georgians were abetted by President Andrew Jackson, who in his first message to Congress announced plans to remove all the southeast Indians to lands west of the Mississippi River. In May 1830 the Indian Removal Bill passed by a slim margin, and on May 23, 1836, the U.S. Senate ratified a treaty setting a date for the final removal of the Cherokees two years later. During that period about two thousand Cherokees—deciding to leave while they could still take their belongings with them—made their way to the lands bordering the Arkansas River, leaving about fifteen thousand fellow tribesmen behind.

The major exodus began on May 23, 1838, according to schedule, supervised by army regulars who treated the Indians with kindliness and respect, and by Georgia volunteers, who urged on the laggards at bayonet point. As one regular recalled years afterward, "I fought through the Civil War and have seen men shot to pieces and slaughtered by thousands, but the Cherokee removal was the cruelest work I ever knew."

The summer of 1838 saw the worst heat and drought men could remember, and the Cherokees obtained permission from the army to conduct their own removal in October, after the drought abated. Then about fourteen thousand of them set out on the thousand-mile trip toward an unknown land.

In camps along the way most of them had only tents and blankets to protect them from the severe early winter; at tollgates they were charged outrageous prices; merchants and farmers gouged them mercilessly when they tried to buy food; their wagons bogged down in the November rains. Their number included old people, newborn babies, pregnant women, the halt, the lame, the blind, many of them suffering from disease. Along the line of march they left the shallow graves of four thousand—nearly one-fourth of the entire Cherokee Nation. Ever afterward the Indians called it the Trail of Tears.

When at last this caravan of heartbreak and misery arrived in Indian Territory, it was to find that its predecessors in the removal—those who had gone to Arkansas and beyond—were now firmly entrenched. They had their own farms, mills, and stores, none of which they were eager to share with the new arrrivals. For a time the two groups came close to civil war, and not until 1846, when the Cherokees were given land in what is now eastern Oklahoma and were reimbursed to some extent for their losses in the southeast, did anything like harmony prevail in the relocated nation.

AMONG THE HUNDREDS of Cherokees who had moved west in anticipation of the removal were Robert Rogers and his wife, Sallie Vann. Robert Rogers' father—also named Robert—was a white man, his mother was part Indian; Sallie was one-fourth Cherokee and three-quarters Irish. They settled in 1835 or 1836 in the Going Snake district in what is now Oklahoma, where Rogers established a ranch. When a child was born to the couple in 1839, Robert Rogers had only one more year to live. It is with this son, Clement Vann, that the story of Will Rogers properly begins.

Clem grew up on his father's ranch. He hated school and did not get along with his stepfather, William Musgrove, whom his mother married when Clem was five. At the age of seventeen he left home to find a new life in what was called the Cooweescoowee country, bordering the Verdigris River. His mother and his long-suffering stepfather gave him twenty-five longhorns, a bull, four horses, supplies for the ranch and trading post he intended to start, and two slaves, brothers named Rabb and Huse.

In 1856 the Cooweescoowee district was virgin land, held in common by the Cherokee Nation for use by any of its members. Wild turkeys, quail, and prairie chickens were as "thick as blackbirds." In the Verdigris bottomland were wild geese, flocks of green parakeets, deer, wolves, and panthers. While his two slaves planted corn for feed, young Clem turned his cattle out on the bluestem grass that stretched unbroken for miles. His trading post flourished, and several years later he married a tall, dark-haired girl named Mary America Schrimsher, whom he had met in Tahlequah. One quarter Cherokee, Mary had attended a Cherokee school in Arkansas and may have gone to the Cherokee-run Female Seminary near Tahlequah.

When she moved to Clem's ranch the only neighbors were a few scattered settlers, itinerant fur traders, and Osage Indians who came to trade or steal. Life was not easy, but both the ranch and trading post were successful, and for three years Clem's future looked secure. Then, as so often in the past, the shadow of the white man fell across the Cherokee land.

IT WAS 1861, and the Rogers ranch was only thirty miles from the Kansas border, where Union and Confederate sympathizers were turning the prairies into a dark and bloody ground. The Indians were as divided on the conflict between North and South as they had been over the question of the removal (even the Negro brothers Rabb and Huse, Clem's slaves, fought on opposite sides during the war). John Ross, the principal chief of the Cherokee Nation, hoped to preserve neutrality, but Southerners were quick to see that the Indian Territory provided bases for raids into Kansas, a highway to Texas, and a source of supplies.

David L. Hubbard, the Confederacy's commissioner of Indian affairs, appealed to the Cherokees to support the South. "Go North among the once powerful tribes," he told them, "and see if you can find Indians living, and enjoying power and property & Liberty, as do your people. . . . If you can, then say I am a liar and the Northern States have been better to the Indian than the Southern States." Few could deny the logic of his message, and on October 7, 1861, the Cherokee Nation made an alliance with the Confederate States of America.

After sending Mary to his mother's home (where she remained for a time before finally fleeing to Texas with her parents and sisters), Clem Rogers enlisted in the Cherokee Mounted Rifles. He served as captain under Stand Watie, a leader of the mixed-bloods, who became a Confederate brigadier general in 1864. When the war ended, the federal government contended that the Five Civilized Tribes had forfeited their lands by supporting the Confederacy, but it took only the western portion of their territory, as a future home for other Indian tribes. It was hoped that the tribes would unite in a territorial government that would one day become a state. A treaty referred to this potential commonwealth as Oklahoma, from the Chocktaw *okla homma*—red people.

Returning after four years of war, Clem Rogers found the

Both Will's mother, Mary, and his father, Clement Vann Rogers, a big rancher in what is now Oklahoma, were part Cherokee Indian.

entire Cherokee Nation devastated. His own ranch had been overrun by troops and had grown up to brush; his cattle and horses had been confiscated and his slaves freed; there was no money with which to begin again. After joining Mary and their baby, Sallie, in Texas, he made his way back toward the old homestead by degrees, stopping for a year with his mother and stepfather in the Chocktaw Nation. He then spent two hard years driving a six-mule freight wagon from Kansas City to Fort Gibson, saving enough money, finally, to buy some cattle.

In 1868 he chose a location for his second ranch, about seven miles east of the original one. This land, according to the traditional practice of the Cherokees, was free to anyone who would occupy and improve it. The region Clem Rogers picked out was a rancher's paradise. Rich grazing land abounded; the bottomland along the Verdigris River was fertile, and the river itself provided abundant water for livestock. The nearest towns of any consequence were Coffeyville, Kansas, forty-odd miles to the north, and Fort Gibson, sixty miles south in Indian Territory.

In the fall of 1870 Clem brought Mary to the new ranch, where he had constructed a log house, and three years later they began building what was to be their permanent home—a two-story structure of hewn logs, plastered on the inside and weatherboarded on the outside, with seven large rooms. Downstairs was the big, square parlor, with an open fireplace, the only piano in the Cooweescoowee district, and curtains hung with lace. Across the entrance hall was the family bedroom, where their children would be born; and in the rear were the dining room, kitchen, and a bunkroom for cowboys working on the ranch. On the second floor were two large bedrooms, eventually used by the Rogers daughters. When the house was completed in 1875, it was considered one of the finest homes in the territory.

Mary Rogers possessed a quality that made the ranch a warm, inviting place that everyone liked to visit. She was a gay, lighthearted soul with a fine sense of humor and a love of music and dancing; she was always asking entire families to spend the night and enjoy an evening of square dancing and songs. She and Clem were also known for their willingness to help anyone in trouble; friends remembered how Mary would travel on horseback or in a buggy, day or night, to take food to the sick. By 1878 seven children had been born to Mary and Clem—five girls and two boys—but three died in infancy, leaving only Sallie, Robert, Maud, and Mary. On November 4, 1879, the eighth and last child was born, a boy who was christened William Penn Adair Rogers for a Civil War comrade-in-arms of his father's.

At the time Will was born Clem Rogers was one of the most successful men in the territory. His range included about sixty thousand acres, forming an enormous V or wedge between the Caney River on the west and the Verdigris on the east.

Clem Rogers bought steers in Texas, drove them to his ranch for a year's fattening on bluestem grass, then trailed them to St. Louis, the closest market. He handled as many as five thousand head a year this way. After assembling a herd in Texas, it took him two or three months to drive it to the Verdigris valley, covering twelve or fifteen miles daily.

At dawn the cowboys would get the cattle to drifting along, grazing as they went; by midmorning they would push them closer together, prodding the lead steers to move faster. At noon the cattle grazed while the cowboys ate at the chuck wagon; then the process began all over again, with the herd moving northward until twilight. With the coming of darkness the men rode slowly around the herd in ever-tightening circles, moving the longhorns into a compact mass until they lay down for the night. All through the night the cowboys took turns on watch, circling the herd, softly singing to quiet the animals, always on the alert for the sudden noise—a clap of thunder, even the snapping of a stick—that would startle the cattle into a stampede.

A cowboy had to be as skilled at his trade as any craftsman, and the horse he rode almost human in its understanding of what was required of it. Clem Rogers loved fine horses, and he purchased or raised some of the best in the territory. On the trail they knew how to move quietly and slowly; they could swim rivers and avoid potholes at night; and they were absolutely essential in every aspect of the cattle business—cutting out steers, tying, branding, penning, and shipping them.

By the time Will Rogers was old enough to know what was going on around him, the pattern of life at the ranch was well established, and it was a good one indeed. In 1890 there were three dwellings, seven other structures, three farms, three hundred enclosed acres, three hundred acres under cultivation. Improvements were valued at $15,000, and the ranch was producing three thousand bushels of corn and a thousand bushels of wheat, along with oats, apples, mules, goats, domestic fowl, and—of course—cattle and horses.

As Will's wife wrote years later, many people thought—because he was careless about his speech and dress and manners—that he was "a poor, uneducated cowboy who struggled to the heights from obscure beginnings." True, he had no college education, she said, but that was because he would not go to school. And as for his being poor, "the truth is that, as the only surviving son of an indulgent father"—his older brother Robert died when he was two—"Will had everything he wanted. He had spending money and the best string of cow ponies in the country. No boy in the Indian Territory had more than Clem's boy."

"Three years in McGuffey's Fourth Reader, and I knew more about it than McGuffey did."

IN NEARLY every respect Will Rogers' growing up was close to the nostalgic ideal of a nineteenth-century boyhood. The hard, lean years of the frontier were passing—for the Rogers family, certainly—and life was full of the joys of a childhood in rural America. From the time he could walk, Willie—as everyone called him—was riding a horse or working a rope in his hand. He was given his first pony at the age of five. His mother worried about him; watching the little sorrel mare rear up on her hind legs when Willie tried to pull himself into the saddle, she would cover her face and call to his father, "Clem, you're going to get my boy killed." But Willie was determined, fearless, and he had the advantage of all Oklahoma youngsters, he said later: "I was born bowlegged so I could sit on a horse."

Will spent the long, golden days of youth galloping hell-bent across the prairie, or riding to the swimming hole, hollering to his companions, "Come on, fellers, the last one in is a Ring Tail Hoss!" There were always plenty of friends to play with—white, Negro, and Indian children—and usually something exciting was going on at the ranch. Neighbors stopped by for a visit or a picnic; it was even an outing to go for *The New York Times,* which had to be picked up at the nearest post office, twelve miles away.

More than anything else, Will liked roping, and he spent hours learning to throw a rope under the guidance of Uncle Dan Walker, a Negro cowboy who worked for Clem. When he was older there were days at a stretch when instead of riding the range as he was supposed to do, he would find a shady place and practice "cutting curliques" or lassoing prairie dogs.

When he was six his oldest sister, Sallie, married a man named Tom McSpadden, and later that year Willie embarked on his first experience with education. He went to live with the McSpaddens, whose farm was near a schoolhouse, and every morning Sallie would help him tie his dinner pail to the saddle horn and make certain he headed for the classroom. The schoolhouse was a small, one-room log cabin, and all the students—

most of them Indians—rode horseback or walked for miles to get there. Will hated the routine and the endless drills, and he spent most of his time racing with the Cherokee children, on foot or on horseback.

When it was apparent that this school was not going to take, Will was sent off to Harrell International Institute in Muskogee, a girls' boarding school which his sister Mary attended. The Reverend T. F. Brewer, president of the school, had an eight-year-old son and decided that the two boys could attend classes with all the young ladies, but Will said he felt just as Custer did when he was surrounded by Indians. The experiment was not successful, and before long Mr. Brewer was writing to Clem: "I regret to inform you that your son is not doing well in school and would suggest you remove him."

On education: *"There is nothing as stupid as an educated man if you get him off the thing he was educated in."*

About this time Will's mother fell ill with amebic dysentery. Everything that could be done for her was done; but on May 28, 1890, Mary America Rogers died and was buried in a family cemetery on the ranch, beside her son Robert and the three infants. Will and his mother were alike in many ways: her gentle manner, sense of humor, love of music, and her easy way with people were some of the traits the boy inherited. Will's wife said later that he never got over his mother's death; he cried when he told her about it years afterward, and he once wrote, "Mamas name was Mary and if your Mother was an old-fashioned Woman and named Mary you dont need to say much for her, everybody knows already."

That fall Will was hustled off to yet another school, this time in Tahlequah, and he liked it no better than its predecessors. Next his father sent him to Willie Halsell College (roughly the equivalent of a junior high school) at Vinita, about forty miles from the ranch. Most of the pupils were boys and girls with whom Will had grown up, and he spent four happy years there.

Now his father insisted that he attend Scarritt Collegiate Institute in Neosho, Missouri, but at the end of the first term

Will unexpectedly appeared at the ranch. He had been expelled. Clem was not pleased, and announced to his son that he was sending him to Kemper Military School in Boonville, Missouri.

WHEN Will showed up to begin what would now be called sophomore year in high school, he cut quite a figure; he had on a cowboy hat, a flannel shirt with a fiery-red bandanna at his throat, a brightly colored vest, and high-heeled boots with red tops and spurs.

Along with his luggage were lariats of various sizes, for all the cadets to see. Will had had his eyes opened to another side of the roping art at the Chicago World's Fair in 1893. He and his father had seen all the wondrous sights at the exposition, including Buffalo Bill's *Wild West Show*. The high point of the visit for Will was the performance given by one Vincent Oropeza, billed as "the greatest roper in the world."

Oropeza, gloriously attired in an embroidered jacket and buckskin trousers with brass buttons, went through dozens of spectacular rope tricks, concluding with one in which he wrote his name with his lasso, one letter at a time, in the air. Will was hooked.

At Kemper, as at all the other schools, Will was bright enough, but his academic interest waxed and waned. In elocution class the students were taught to speak the classic orations—Marc Antony's "Friends, Romans, countrymen, lend me your ears," Patrick Henry's "liberty or death" speech, and others— all with textbook gestures; but Will never could resist an opportunity to get a laugh out of his audience, and his gift for timing and for misplaced emphasis often broke up the class.

He played football and baseball, but mostly it was the lariat that kept him occupied. Exasperated teachers were always taking ropes away from him, but inevitably he managed to lay hands on another. Between his fascination with the lasso and his distaste for cleaning his rifle, Will accumulated one hundred and fifty demerits, which had to be worked off by an equal number of hours of solitary marching. He would arrange for his penance to be paid off near the kitchen and then ask the cook "if he wouldn't do something for the vanishing American."

In the spring of Will's second year at Kemper the old wanderlust overtook him, and he decided to "quit the entire school

Will (left) never cared much for school. One of his two years at Kemper Military School in Missouri, he said jokingly, was spent "in the guardhouse."

business for life." Which he did, at the age of eighteen.

The first his father knew about it was when he received a letter from his friend W. P. Ewing in Higgins, Texas, saying that Will was there and what should he do with him?

Clem suggested that Ewing try to get any work he could out of the young man, and for several months Will stayed on the ranch before striking out for what looked like greener pastures in Amarillo, Texas. There, hearing of a trail boss who needed a hand, he arrived in time to listen to another cowboy applying for the position. "And right there," he said, "I saw a fellow talk himself out of a job." The other boy told the trail boss in glowing terms what a good cowhand he was, and by the time he had finished, the man told him, "I'm in need of a hand, all right, but I think you'd suit me too well." Will, having learned the lesson, said to the boss, "Maybe I could do the work." He was told to get on his horse and come out to the boss's camp. To Rogers, "Them was the happiest words I ever heard in my life." He rode seven days a week, rounding up cattle, roping and branding calves, as happy as a teenage boy could be.

On his first visit home he shipped his saddle by express and traveled himself by freight train. Clem and Will's friend Jim O'Donnell were riding through a pasture at the Rogers ranch when they saw Will galloping toward them. It was obvious, O'Donnell remembered, that Will was not certain what his father was going to say about his running away from school. "He started right in tellin' us all about workin' for the big cow outfit in the Panhandle. He didn't get very far, when Uncle Clem says, 'Son, go back to the house and wash your neck and ears and put on a clean shirt.'"

Later Will drifted out to New Mexico, where he worked on other ranches, until he was sent to California with a trainload of cattle for the Hearst ranch. After they had been delivered, he and another cowboy went to San Francisco and put up at a small hotel. The next morning when they didn't appear, someone went to their room and discovered they had nearly been asphyxiated. The boys were used to kerosene lamps back in Indian Territory, and before going to bed one of them had simply blown out the gas jets. His father sent Will to Hot Springs, Arkansas, to recuperate, and when he returned to the ranch after another stay in Texas, Clem decided it was time for him to settle down.

THE FOURTEEN YEARS between Will Rogers' birth and his visit to the Chicago World's Fair of 1893 had brought immense changes to the old Indian Territory—changes that altered forever the life of the Cherokee Nation, and of the big ranchers like Clem Rogers. The final subjugation of the Plains Indians was going on, feverish railroad building was interlacing all but the most remote places in the West, and millions of acres of land were opening up for settlement.

In 1862 Congress had passed the Homestead Act, providing that any adult citizen, or alien who had filed his first papers, could, after paying a ten-dollar fee, claim 160 acres of the public domain, and—if he stayed there five years—obtain title to it.

Thousands upon thousands of small farmers and stockmen moved west, gobbling up acreage, building sod huts, and erecting fences, applying the same relentless pressure on cattlemen that the cattlemen had exerted on Indians. Railroad owners whose lines crossed Indian Territory discovered that some of the five Civilized Tribes—by their participation on the Confederate side—had forfeited nearly two million acres to the government after the Civil War, and that these "unassigned" lands had not yet been allocated to other tribes. Lobbyists pressed for legal seizure of this enormous domain, and finally the government capitulated, paid the Indians $1.25 an acre for the land in what is now central Oklahoma, and surveyed it into 160-acre parcels for settlement. It was opened for claims at noon on April 22, 1889.

On Congress: *"Never blame a legislative body for not doing something. When they do nothing, that don't hurt anybody. When they do something is when they become dangerous."*

That morning some twenty thousand people—on horseback, on foot, driving wagons, wheelbarrows, and every imaginable conveyance—lined up at different entry points on three sides of the area and awaited the pistol shot that would signal the opening of the verdant prairies to settlement. When the gun was fired bedlam broke loose. Within a few hours nearly all of the two million acres had been claimed; tents, shacks, and other structures were being erected all over the once empty prairie; and by dark the new settlement of Oklahoma City had ten thousand people, Guthrie nearly fifteen.

Clem Rogers realized that it was only a matter of time until settlers would be swarming into the Verdigris valley. The little town of Oologah had come into existence as a whistle-stop on the Missouri Pacific in 1887, a few miles southwest of Clem's ranch, and from then on the area was destined to be farm country instead of cattle country. Clem, seeing what lay ahead, began to alter his operation from grazing longhorns on the open range to feeding shorthorn cattle in fenced pastures.

In 1891 he built the first barbed-wire fence in the Verdigris country. For some time he had been upgrading his herd, pur-

In 1893 the Cherokees sold the Cherokee Strip to the United States, and the ensuing rush of white settlers (above) signaled the end of Clem Rogers' vast cattle empire. Years later Will wrote, "We spoiled the best Territory in the World to make a State."

chasing the first purebred shorthorn bulls in the territory, adding Herefords later. He was also breeding hogs and poultry, and was the first man in the region to introduce wheat on a large scale. In 1895 the Claremore *Progress* observed proudly that "Clem Rogers, the Oologah wheat king," had harvested thirteen thousand bushels.

West of the Cherokee Nation lay the tribe's most extensive and richest cattle ranges—some six and a half million acres of grassland south of the Kansas border, known as the Cherokee Strip. After unremitting pressure by white farmers on Congress, the Cherokee Strip was sold to the United States government for $8,500,000, and in 1893 the most spectacular land rush of all followed, with a hundred thousand people stampeding across the waving grasslands to stake out claims. The following year the Cherokees received the first of five annual payments for the sale, each Indian getting $367.50 in cash.

But it was the passage of the Curtis Act in 1898 that finally put an end to Clem's cattle empire. That law forced allotment to individuals of all land held in common by the Cherokee Nation, abolished tribal law, and substituted a new code of U.S. laws for the Indian Territory. Between them, Clem and Will received allotments of 148.77 acres—all that remained to them of the sixty-thousand-acre ranch. It was clear that thousands more settlers would come in the wake of the Cherokee Run, and Clem Rogers, now almost sixty, once again saw opportunity in the offing. He and several friends concluded that Claremore—a rail junction about twenty-four miles northeast of Tulsa—was the most promising town in the area for a bank, and in 1898 Clem sold his cattle, rented his farmland, and moved into town.

A curious dichotomy pervaded the lives of people like Clem and, to a lesser extent, Will Rogers—a kind of dual personality forced upon them by the circumstance of an Indian heritage and the relentless encroachment of white civilization. One can only speculate about Clem's feelings on the subject, but, as Will's son Bill suggested, Clem and Will were both "upwardly mobile, ambitious men, and I am sure they saw nothing wrong in trying to adopt the ways and attitudes that led to success, i.e., the white man's way. Today we might say that they should have paid more attention to the ancient Cherokee culture. But I think that was a concept that did not occur to them."

WHEN Will returned to the ranch after a year in Texas, he discovered that his father was living in Claremore and was expecting him to run what was left of the old operation. In January 1899 Clem restocked it with cattle, gave Will some animals of his own, and sent Will's friend Spi Trent to help manage the place. For about a year and a half they lived there, operating the ranch, but with Will always on the lookout for other forms of amusement. He sang tenor in a local quartet, attended every dance within riding distance, played baseball on the Oologah team, and participated in some of the roping contests then coming into vogue.

For a while Will and his buddy, Spi Trent (second from right), ran the Rogers ranch, but they found the time—and the company—to attend every outing within riding range.

Will was almost as determined to own every good roping horse he saw as he was to master the art of roping. Throughout his life he owned so many it was impossible to keep track of them all. But his all-time favorite was one he owned at this time, a little yellow pony named Comanche. As Jim O'Donnell, who rode the horse in a number of roping contests and followed rodeos for forty years, said long afterward, "I have seen some wonderful horses, but none like Comanche." He went on to tell about the time a cowboy, riding Comanche, roped his steer and threw it, but when he jumped off the horse to tie the animal, the steer got to its feet and charged him. Without a moment's hesitation Comanche turned, pulled the rope tight, and flipped the steer by himself. The high point of these days—and the beginning of Will's show-business career—was his trip to St. Louis in 1899 for the annual fair, where he participated in a roping-and-riding contest run by "Colonel" Zack Mulhall.

After the fair, Mulhall, who was the general stock agent for the Atlantic and Pacific Railroad (later the Frisco), organized a "cowboy" band of about sixty musicians and made a tour of state fairs throughout the Middle West. Since most of them, as Will said, "could not ride in a wagon unless their shirttails was nailed to the floor," Mulhall decided he should take along a few real cowboys for authenticity. During a performance Mulhall would offer to pick out boys from the band who could ride an outlaw horse or rope and tie a steer in less time than any man in the audience could, and Will and his friend Jim O'Donnell were employed for that purpose. The rest of the time Will sat with the band, pretending to play a trombone.

In San Antonio, after the steer-roping contest was over, the local people invited the band members to a barbecue, and someone asked Will to speak. It was the first of many after-dinner speeches he was to give and surely one of the shortest. He got to his feet, blinked, scratched his head, and stammered, "Well, folks, this is a mighty fine dinner, what there is of it." Laughter greeted that remark, so he said, trying to cover up, "Well, there is plenty of it, such as it is." The speech was a success.

3

"Nobody but an Indian can pronounce Oologah."

IN THE fall of 1899 a nineteen-year-old girl named Betty Blake arrived from Arkansas to visit her sister and her brother-in-law, who was the Oologah railroad station agent. She was recovering from typhoid fever, and her mother thought the change would do her good, even though the social life in Oologah might not be as lively as it was at home. "The only young people in town," Betty's sister warned, "are the daughters of the hotelkeeper, and there is one boy, Will Rogers, who lives out on a ranch."

Betty was born in the Ozarks in a town named Monte Ne. When she was three her father died, and her mother supported her brood of six daughters and two sons as a dressmaker in the nearby town of Rogers. For all the family's financial worries, the household was a gay, lively one, full of music and fun. As soon as the children were old enough they went to work, and for a time Betty was a railroad clerk.

By all accounts she was pretty, good company, and much sought after by young men. One of her admirers recalled that he used to call for her in a handcar while she was working for the railroad, and that they would travel on it to see plays in Fort Smith.

After such excitement Oologah must have been something of a letdown. The town consisted of a handful of frame houses and plank sidewalks on either side of the main—and only—street. Beyond were the rolling prairies. Twice a day passenger trains stopped at the station where Betty's sister and brother-in-law lived and worked, and the Arkansas girl would sit at the window of the depot watching the townspeople turn out to meet them.

One evening a young man stepped off the train from Kansas City and came up to the ticket window. Betty went over to see what he wanted. "I looked at him and he looked at me," she wrote later, "and before I could even ask his business, he turned on his heel and was gone." When her brother-in-law came in with the express packages, one of which was a banjo addressed to Will Rogers, she realized who the boy must have been, and that he had been too shy to ask for his parcel.

A few days later she met him; one of the hotelkeeper's daughters invited Betty for dinner because Will was coming over. During dinner he was awkward and silent, but afterward in the sitting room he gradually thawed out and began to sing without accompaniment all the new songs he had heard in Kansas City, including "Hello, Ma Baby." Afterward they popped corn and pulled taffy, and Will gave Betty the music for the new songs so that she could learn to play them on the piano.

The two met often that fall. There were visits to farms and ranches all over the neighborhood (the Vinita *Indian Chieftain* noted that "nutting parties, gypsy teas and possum hunts were all the go" that season), and many more evenings of music, with Betty playing the piano or banjo while Will sang. She left for Arkansas just before Christmas, and shortly after the first of the new year, 1900, she received her first letter from him, headed "My Dear Friend." He asked her to return soon, and concluded, "Hoping you will take pity on this poor heart broken Cow pealer."

In the middle of March another letter came, this time to "My

Will's future bride, Betty Blake, came from a large, fun-loving Arkansas family. "Sometimes," a friend recalled, "they'd overflow out into the yard, there was so many of them." Betty is third from bottom.

Dear Betty." It was unmistakably a love letter, which he asked her to burn. She didn't burn it, but neither did she reply. They saw each other again in the fall, at an Arkansas fair, and Will—lonely and shy—avoided her. That night there was a dance, and Betty kept looking for Will, but she had only a glimpse of him standing alone outside the hall, watching her dance by.

It was the last time she saw him for almost four years, for Will had the wanderlust again. There was a lot of talk circulating though the West about ranching in Argentina; down there, it was said, were endless pampas in a country free of farmers and barbed wire, where a man could ride all day and never see a plowed field or a fence.

Late in 1901 Will announced to his father his decision to leave for Argentina. Apparently the two had some sharp words. Clem wanted his son to stay on the ranch, but Will was determined to go his own way. Clem bought back for three thousand dollars the herd he had given Will. Will sold off his other steers and said good-by. As he headed out into the world he took with him the most enduring influences on his life: his Indian heritage, all the Oklahoma roots that ran so deep, and a warm spot in his heart for Betty Blake, the girl from Arkansas.

WILL had no difficulty persuading a kindred soul named Dick Parris to accompany him to Argentina. Neither had the slightest idea how to get there. They went to New York to find a ship going south, but there were none sailing for the Argentine.

They heard that ships from Liverpool, England, occasionally sailed for Buenos Aires, so in March 1902 the two embarked on the SS *Philadelphia,* bound for England. It was the first of many ocean voyages for Will, on each of which he would be deathly seasick. Once back on land, however, he was full of good humor again. He wrote his sisters that he and Dick were in a hotel room "almost papered with pictures of Queen Victoria, who certainly had a stand in with the photographer."

The time the two young men spent in London coincided with the preparations for Edward VII's coronation. The entire city was in a state of confusion, but the two Americans found their way to Parliament, London Bridge, the Tower, and to Westminster Abbey, to gaze at the monuments to the great. "I knew very few of the men personally," Will said. Then, in company with two hundred Spanish and Portuguese emigrants ("I can't understand a soul on this boat but Dick"), they set sail by slow freighter for Buenos Aires, arriving during the first week in May.

Argentina was a huge disappointment. Will wrote his father that he had been into the interior and had discovered that, while it was marvelous cattle and farm country, "it's no place to make money unless you have $10,000 to invest." There were hundreds of men competing for every job. Because of the language barrier, his unfamiliarity with the country, his distaste for the local food, and the wages offered (five to eight dollars a month), Will soon concluded that Argentina was not for him. Dick was so homesick that, on the theory that Clem might be sending him some money, Will bought his buddy a ticket home and spent most of what he had left on presents for his father and sisters.

No money was forthcoming, however, and by mid-June, Will was sleeping in the park. When he heard about a job tending cattle on a boat sailing for South Africa, he decided to take it.

During the twenty-five agonizing days it took the *Kelvinside* to run from Buenos Aires to Durban, Will served as night watchman on the cattle deck. As he said, he was too sick to do anything else, and there was no way they could fire him. In South Africa he worked for two months on the estate of an Englishman who raised and raced thoroughbred horses; the stables were "veritable palaces," Will said, "heated by steam and lighted by electricity." His job was to feed and exercise the horses, and help the veterinarian and the blacksmith.

By November's end Will was on the move again, driving some mules two hundred and fifty miles from Durban to Ladysmith. There, an import from America, Texas Jack's *Wild West Show,* was playing in the town, and for the young man it was like a breath of fresh air from home.

THE American cowboy and frontiersman were legends in their own time—at home and abroad—and the so-called Wild West shows were bringing riding and shooting exhibitions, roping demonstrations, and mock battles between cowboys and Indians to thrilled audiences throughout the United States, Europe, Australia, and to towns like Ladysmith in South Africa. The most famous troupe was Buffalo Bill's *Wild West Show and Congress of Rough Riders of the World,* featuring "Colonel" William Cody himself—former army scout and buffalo hunter.

Texas Jack's show was a long way down the line, but in 1902 it looked good to Will. He went to see Texas Jack, who immediately wanted to know how good he was at roping and riding. Will said he could do a few rope tricks, and proceeded to perform the Big Crinoline, a classic and surefire crowd pleaser. Starting with a small loop, the roper twirls the line around his body, gradually letting out more and more rope until the entire length—as much as thirty to sixty feet—forms a huge circle spinning around him. Jack gave Will a job then and there.

Will was billed as "The Cherokee Kid—the Man Who Can Lasso the Tail off a Blowfly," and he was getting to be quite a fancy roper indeed. At matinees, always crowded with children, Texas Jack gave a medal to the boy who could throw a lasso best, and Will was constantly trailed by youngsters who wanted him to show them what to do so they could win a medal.

He was homesick, he admitted in a letter to the folks in Indian Territory, but he had been raised from twenty to twenty-five dollars a week, and he was continuing to learn from Texas Jack, whom he later called "one of the smartest showmen I ever met." It was from Jack, Will said, that he "learned the great secret of the show business—learned when to get off. It's the fellow that knows when to quit that the audience wants more of." It was an immensely valuable experience, but by the fall of 1903 Will had had his fill of South Africa.

He thought he might as well head for the United States by first completing a trip around the world. Texas Jack hated to see him go, but he gave Will a glowing recommendation. It read:

I have the very great pleasure of recommending Mr. W. P. Rogers (The Cherokee Kid) to circus proprietors. . . . I consider him to be the champion trick rough rider and lasso thrower of the world. He is sober, industrious, hard working at all times and is always to be relied upon. I shall be very pleased to give him an engagement at any time should he wish to return.

Will renewed his acquaintance with the miseries of sea travel, crossing the Indian Ocean to New Zealand and then to Australia.

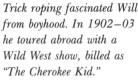

Trick roping fascinated Will from boyhood. In 1902–03 he toured abroad with a Wild West show, billed as "The Cherokee Kid."

He planned to be home not later than December 1, but decided he would just see a little of Australia as long as he was there. As usual, he was intrigued by all the sights: the greatest sheepraising country in the world; aborigines who could throw a boomerang so that "it will shave your hat off going and your head off coming back"; kangaroos as common as jackrabbits.

His tour of Australia consumed all the money he had earned with Texas Jack, so he took a job with the Wirth Brothers circus in New Zealand, performing a roping and trick-riding act which the Auckland *Herald* complimented as a "highly original exhibition" which "fairly dazzled the crowd."

For the second year in a row Will spent Christmas thousands of miles from home, but he vowed it would be the last one. He had heard that St. Louis was planning a world's fair in the summer of 1904, and he would be there for the opening, he assured the family.

BY THE time the prodigal returned in April, he had seen a lot of the world and had acquired, according to his friend Spi Trent, "a kind of sure-footedness . . . which comes to a feller who has learned to paddle his own canoe."

In Claremore business was booming. Clem Rogers was busy, as usual, in the affairs of the Cherokee Nation, which, as he had already foreseen, was about to vanish forever. Clem was looking to the future, and would now devote his great energy, strong opinions, and ability to the movement for Oklahoma statehood. (He was one of fifty-five delegates elected from Indian Territory to the constitutional convention that assembled in 1906, and that year the district he represented was named Rogers County in his honor. This work culminated in statehood for Oklahoma, proclaimed by President Theodore Roosevelt on November 16, 1907.)

But to Clem's son, Will, none of these developments was half as exciting as the exposition that would open in St. Louis on May 1, 1904, celebrating (one year late) the one-hundreth anniversary of the Louisiana Purchase. It would be the largest world's fair ever held, covering fourteen hundred acres. There were to be fifteen new buildings, laid out in the shape of a fan, including the Palace of Electricity and the Palace of Machinery. There would be extensive foreign exhibits, including grass-thatched huts from America's newest territorial acquisition, the Philippine Islands. Sculpture and statuary by Augustus Saint-Gaudens and Daniel Chester French were to be set off by a six-acre rose garden, a colossal floral clock, and numerous waterfalls and miniature lagoons.

Beyond the fair's array of exhibits stretched a long, wide midway called the Pike, where vendors swarmed (it was claimed that the ice-cream cone, the hot dog, and iced tea were introduced for the first time on the Pike that summer), and where the amusement concessions were also clustered. These included a 265-foot Ferris wheel, the Temple of Mirth, the Jungle of Mirrors, Hagenbeck's *Wild Animal Show,* and, predictably, a Wild West show.

ALMOST AS SOON AS he returned from his global junket, Will was summoned to Guthrie by his old employer, Colonel Zack Mulhall, who was assembling a group of riders for the Wild West show. The cowboys Mulhall had sent for were drifting in to his ranch every day; one of them was a young man named Tom Mix. Will stayed with them for nearly a week, working away at his rope tricks.

When they arrived at the fair the Mulhall cowboy troupe was combined with a troupe of Indians in a spectacular show involving some six or seven hundred horsemen. They had been performing for only about a month when Mulhall and the head stableman got into a fight; after an evening performance they met on the Pike, and Mulhall pulled a gun and started shooting. The colonel's shots only grazed his opponent but seriously wounded a young boy who was watching the battle, and Mulhall was hustled off to jail. In the aftermath of the shooting some of the cowboys pulled out and went home, but Will joined the Indian troupe on the midway and at some point performed in a small Wild West show Charles Tompkins was running inside the fairground.

BETTY BLAKE, unaware that Will was even back in the States, had come to St. Louis to visit one of her sisters and take in the fair. As she was walking through one of the exhibits on a Sunday morning, she overheard a girl remark that Will Rogers was performing in the Wild West show. Betty sent him a note, and back came a reply, to "Dear Old Pal," asking her to come to the afternoon performance and afterward they would have dinner and spend the evening together. Her sister and a friend gave her the usual hard time over her cowboy acquaintance, and since she "was not particularly thrilled about Will's profession" anyway, as she later confessed, she approached the arena with some misgiving.

When Will appeared her worst fears were realized. He was wearing a skintight red velvet suit trimmed with gold braid, and Betty was so embarrassed she didn't even hear the applause for his act. After the performance there was a long wait for Will to join them—he was chasing the manager all over the fairground to collect his back pay. When he showed up, breathless and apologetic, he explained the spectacular suit. In Australia, where he had occasionally been billed as "The Mexican Rope

Artist," Mrs. Wirth, the circus owner's wife, had made him the velvet costume on the theory that a Mexican rope artist would wear a colorful getup (Will had never quite forgotten the sensational Vincente Oropeza, either). He never wore the red suit again after seeing Betty's reaction.

The couple had dinner, strolled along the Pike, went to the Irish Village, where a tenor named John McCormack was singing for the first time in America, and said good-night.

WHEN Betty next heard from him it was late October and he was in Chicago. During that summer in St. Louis, on free Saturday afternoons, Will had taken a job at the Standard Theatre—a roping turn on the stage. Someone in the audience liked it well enough to write to the owner of a theater chain in Chicago, and the next thing Will knew he was offered a week's vaudeville engagement there for thirty dollars. During one show he was going through the rope tricks he had perfected with Texas Jack when a dog from an animal act ran onto the stage. Without thinking, Will tossed a loop over the animal and hauled him in. The laughter and loud applause made him realize that people wanted to see him actually catch something. And what quickly evolved in Will's mind was something that had never been done before in a theater—roping a running horse on the stage. He was sure he could bring it off if he could obtain the right animal. The right one, he knew, was a beautiful little bay pony that Mrs. Mulhall had offered to sell him for a hundred dollars.

Will didn't like Chicago much, he wrote Betty, and he was going back to St. Louis to earn enough money to buy the horse he needed. Then he launched into a subject that was very much in his thoughts: he wanted to know if she was "contracted for" or if she had "a steady fellow." If not "then please file my application." According to form, he said, both of them "should have matrimonied long ago. It wouldent do for this young gang to look at our *teeth,* you know." He went on. "I could just love a girl about your caliber. You know I was always kinder headstrong about you anyway. But I always thought that a cowboy dident quite come up to your Ideal."

After winning a blue ribbon at a performance for visiting

Will (left) made his big-time debut at New York's
Madison Square Garden with Zack Mulhall's troupe in
1905. He became an instant hero by roping and tying
a steer that broke loose and charged into the crowd.

cattlemen during the final days of the fair, Will returned to
Claremore, and soon he was rehearsing with the pony, Teddy—
named for Theodore Roosevelt—which he had bought from
Mrs. Mulhall. He had staked out a plot of ground as big as a
stage and was going over and over his new routine until he had it
down pat. By spring he was ready to try it out in New York, and
once again Colonel Mulhall figured in his plans. He had been
acquitted in the St. Louis shooting case, and was taking his Wild
West show to New York.

ON APRIL 27, 1905, Will Rogers made his New York debut in
Madison Square Garden with a Mulhall troupe that included
Mulhall's daughter Lucille, who had made quite a name for
herself as a performing cowgirl, Tom Mix, and a number of

Will's cronies. Two weeks after they opened Will got one of the big breaks of his career.

According to a New York *Herald* clipping he sent his family, Lucille Mulhall was roping to the music of the Seventh Regiment band when a big eight-hundred-pound steer, with horns that spread five feet, ran into the ring and suddenly started for the stands. Lucille and some of the cowboys tried to head it off, but the steer leaped the bars into the seats and, while the crowd panicked, loped up the stairs to the balcony. Hot on its heels came the cowboys, and, as the *Herald* article described it, "The Indian Will Rogers . . . headed the steer off" and got his rope around its horns. "Alone and afoot, he was no match for the brute's strength, but he swerved it down the steps on the Twenty-seventh street side, where it jumped again into the ring" and was roped by the men in the arena and led away. According to the account under the subhead INDIAN COW-PUNCHER'S QUICKNESS PREVENTS HARM, occupants of seats on one whole side of the arena stampeded for cover, and Colonel Mulhall was heard yelling to Lucille to "follow that baby up the stairs and bring him back or else stay there" herself.

No man to miss an opportunity, Will set out to capitalize on the publicity with theatrical managers. He had concluded that the days of the big Wild West shows were numbered, and he had decided to break into what was then the most exciting and glamorous aspect of show business—vaudeville.

4

"All other performers think I have the greatest act in the business."

SOMETHING like what came to be called vaudeville had flourished for a good many years in England, where it was generally known as "variety" entertainment. In this country vaudeville was a coming together of some peculiarly American forms of entertainment, including "dime museums" and "store shows"—conducted tours of midgets, sword swallowers, and the like—the minstrel show, the medicine wagon with its hired entertainers, and "car parks"—amusement areas at the end of trolley-car lines, where a family on an outing might be exposed to anything from ballet and opera to animal acts and acrobats.

So vaudeville had many antecedents, but what put it on the tracks was the Gaiety Museum, which opened in a deserted candy store in Boston, Massachusetts, in 1883. Operated by a former circus performer named Benjamin Franklin Keith, it featured, among other attractions, a stuffed mermaid, a tattooed man, a chicken with a human face, and a pair of comedians, Joe Weber and Lew Fields. Before long Keith was giving the customers continuous performances, hiring talented artists of the day, and bringing good clean acts to the city of Boston. In 1885 Keith and Edward F. Albee presented the popular

On women: *"I'll bet you the time ain't far off when a woman won't know any more than a man."*

operettas by William Gilbert and Arthur Sullivan, and their success in this venture enabled them to acquire the real estate which became the Keith-Albee chain of theaters, the most extensive in the world, with houses in nearly every large American city.

By the time Will Rogers entered vaudeville, Keith and Albee had a virtual monopoly on the booking of acts for theaters. But if they dominated the business of vaudeville, a man named Willie Hammerstein ruled what has often been called its heart.

Hammerstein's father, Oscar, had come to America from Berlin, gone into cigar making, and had somehow become the nation's impresario of grand opera, in which role he built a dozen theaters. Grandest of them all was the Victoria Theatre at the corner of Broadway and Forty-second Street in New York. There, for the fifty-cent admission price, one could take advantage of the theater, music hall, billiard room, Oriental Café, and roof garden—the last being Willie Hammerstein's particular domain.

Willie's special contribution to vaudeville was the "freak" act, and he often had a bizarre celebrity waiting in the wings to surprise and titillate customers—it might be a woman who had shot her husband or lover, a champion bicycle rider, or a polar explorer. No one knew what to expect. Nor was Hammerstein above perpetrating an occasional hoax on the public. There was, for example, "Abdul Kadar, Court Artist of the Turkish Sultan," who appeared with his three veiled wives. In fact, Abdul was a German named Adolph Schneider and the "wives" were his wife, daughter, and sister-in-law, who avoided talking to inquisitive reporters by falling to their knees and repeating the name of Allah whenever they were asked a question.

When the Victoria opened its doors in 1899 big-time vaudeville was just coming into its own, and under Willie Hammerstein's talented management his theater grossed more than twenty million dollars before it finally shut down.

Hammerstein's Victoria was the big time, but by 1910 there were some two thousand theaters in the small towns of America, offering what was known as small-time vaudeville. The show people drifted in and out of railroad depots with worn trunks plastered with stickers from faraway places and gave the natives the chance to ogle their sporty traveling clothes, flashy jewelry, and exotic women. But the veneer of glamour concealed a life of very real hardship. The touring actor had to travel constantly, in all kinds of weather. Enduring long, dirty train rides and second-rate hotels, he also had to tolerate the whims of uncooperative stagehands, and above all, the tyranny of the theater manager, who often cared little about performers and everything about box-office receipts.

The story of how Will Rogers broke into his new trade has all the elements of the classic show-business saga: the stagestruck rube arrives in the big city, receives some publicity as a result of performing a heroic feat (in this case, roping a half-crazed steer in Madison Square Garden), but is turned down by unfeeling booking agents who can't imagine that his act is any good (and who certainly don't believe he can rope a horse onstage). Finally he overhears one of them telephoning Keith's Union Square Theatre and saying, "Put this nut and his pony on at one of your supper shows and just get rid of him."

The supper show for which Will was engaged during the week of June 11, 1905, was the toughest possible way to break into vaudeville. It was scheduled between six and eight in the evening, when, as Will wrote later, "nobody that had a home or somewhere to eat would be in a theatre." His first appearance was announced by a sign bearing the singularly unprovocative message EXTRA ACT. But whether the audience felt sorry for him or whether they took pity on his pony, as Will supposed, the fact was that they liked his act, and the following week he

Will and Betty Blake conducted a nine-year
courtship, mostly by mail. One Christmas
he sent her a fur-collared coat and muff,
in which she posed proudly.

moved up to the Hammerstein's Paradise Roof—"the swellest Vaudeville place in America," he told his sisters.

Will's routine was quite a novelty. "Will P. Rogers, the sensational lariat thrower, is making his first appearance at the Paradise Roof, and has proved a sensation in every way," the New York *Herald* observed. As the orchestra played a medley of tunes—inevitably, "Pony Boy" and some cowboy songs—Will made a spectacular entrance on Teddy, who wore specially made felt-bottomed boots to keep him from slipping on the stage. Will would slide off the pony, give him a slap on the rump to send him into the wings, and then begin his rope tricks, which he performed silently in rhythm to the soft orchestra music.

Will's roping act is virtually impossible to describe. In one of his early silent films, *The Ropin' Fool,* he did fifty-three different tricks, ranging from the simple to the nearly impossible. What comes across in this film, as it did to the vaudeville crowds, is a combination of almost unbelievable timing, grace, and amazing skill. He usually began with the simplest of the so-called small-loop routines—the flat spin—in which he twirled the rope in front or to the side, parallel to the stage. From this he might go into the merry-go-round, in which the rope, constantly spinning, is passed from the right hand, under one leg, to the other hand behind the body, where the right hand picks it up again.

One of Will's specialties was the juggle, or bounce, in which the spinning loop travels up and down like a jumping jack, high over the roper's head and down to his feet, and up again. He could jump in and out of two loops simultaneously, or do the Texas skip, dancing back and forth through a large loop spinning in a vertical plane. (This was his favorite conditioning exercise, and he performed it almost daily to keep in shape.) He often climaxed his act by having an usher take one end of a ninety-foot rope up the aisle as far as it would reach while Will, standing at the footlights, held on to the other end to show the audience how long it was. Then he would haul it in and, after mounting Teddy, would begin twirling a small loop, lifting it over his head as it increased in size until all ninety feet were out in the Big Crinoline (which had earned him the job with Texas Jack), the glistening white rope spinning in a huge, beautiful circle far out over the heads of the audience.

Betty later described another portion of the act, in which Buck McKee, who was working with Will, rode Teddy, and Will roped horse and rider simultaneously. "There were many catches—throwing two ropes at once, catching the man with one loop and the horse with the other; a three-rope catch, a nose catch, a figure eight, and a tail catch so difficult that Will never ceased practicing on it." What she mentions lightly as "a figure eight" was in reality one of the most difficult catches; in it the spinning loop made a figure eight, one half of which caught the rider while the other half went around the head of the moving horse.

After watching Will, an actor suggested that it might be more effective if he told the crowd what he was going to do before he did it. One night, with no advance preparation, Will stopped the orchestra and announced that he wanted to explain his "next little stunt . . . I am going to throw about two o' these ropes at once," he said, "catching the horse with one and the rider with the other." He paused, grinned, and said, "I don't have any idea I'll get it, but here goes." Will's Western accent, his delivery, and the way he underplayed the statement tickled the audience, and to his embarrassment they started laughing. He came off-stage angry and humiliated, and although other performers tried to persuade him that laughs were good for his act, he was too serious about his roping to accept the idea.

There were other occasions, however, when he learned that a little talk could be helpful. One evening when he was unable to get any of his tricks to work the way he wanted, he grew flustered, the audience became increasingly restless, and suddenly he began to talk. "Swinging a rope is all right," he said, "when your neck ain't in it. Then it's hell." There were a few chuckles. "Out West where I come from," he went on, "they won't let me play with this rope. They think I might hurt myself." By then he had the audience with him; they forgot the tricks he had missed and began enjoying Will himself. But it was some time before he did any talking other than to announce the tricks.

A little notebook Will began keeping in the summer of 1905 shows how much in demand he was. After a week each at Keith's and Hammerstein's in New York, he traveled to Philadelphia and Boston before returning to Manhattan for an engagement at Proctor's and five triumphal weeks at Hammerstein's roof garden. Will started at seventy-five dollars a week in New York on June 12, 1905, and by August he got two hundred and fifty dollars for a week in Brooklyn. Through the fall and winter he was on the road constantly, with no time off; not until March 1906 was there a break in the two-a-day routine. The notebook reads: "Sailed Mar 17 from N.Y. on S.S. *Philadelphia* for Paris and Berlin."

Early in April, less than a year after he had roped the steer in Madison Square Garden, Will Rogers was playing the most important theater in Europe—the Wintergarten in Berlin. From there he went on to London's leading music hall, the Palace, for five weeks at more money that he had ever earned.

In mid-July of 1906 Will was home in Indian Territory for the first time in over a year, and his family and friends were glad to see that theatrical success hadn't changed him. His sister Maud invited Betty Blake to join them, and her visit was almost a repetition of the one she had made in the fall of 1899—a steady round of parties, dinners, horseback rides, and evenings of singing around the piano. Although Betty enjoyed her visit, she found Will himself strangely elusive and distant. He paid no particular attention to her, never saw her alone, and she recalled that she was "a baffled young lady when I left for home."

What made it so mystifying was that he had been corresponding constantly with her for over a year. A flood of telegrams, postcards, and letters had descended on Rogers, Arkansas, from every part of the country (the salutations had changed from "Dear Old Pal" to "Dearest Betty" and then "My Own Sweetheart"), and nearly all contained the message that he was "the most persistent lover you ever saw," that he wanted her to marry him and "see the world as the *wife* of Rogers the Lariet Expert."

Betty had been back in Arkansas for a week when Will stopped by to see her. He was on his way to New York and had the idea "that we should get married at once." He was earning two hundred dollars a week, he was fully booked for the coming fall and winter, and as far as he was concerned, the future looked bright indeed. But Betty didn't regard show business as a steady or particularly worthy profession, and she didn't fancy herself trouping around the country with Will. He couldn't understand her attitude, and they seem to have had an unhappy parting.

For the next two years he followed the old routine: out on the circuit playing most of the principal cities in the United States and Canada, with interruptions only for a visit to Oklahoma when his father was ill. And the correspondence with Betty went on continuously, Will ever hopeful, Betty ever warm and friendly, but not ready to give in.

When Will went home to see his father he visited Betty in Arkansas and spoke several times of quitting show business and returning to the old ranch life. But the panic of 1907 hit ranching as well as the vaudeville business, and Will decided to stick to his present occupation. Nevertheless, Betty remarked, "I felt that at last he was coming around to my way of thinking."

Will's little notebook tells the story of his activities. He was in Wilkes-Barre, Pennsylvania, the week of October 26, 1908. The next week was open (a rarity for him), and on November 9 he was heading home. He stopped off in Rogers, Arkansas, and as Betty remembered, announced flatly "that he was going to take me back to New York." There followed a notebook entry in big block letters for the week of November 23: GETTING MARRIED.

THE wedding took place at midday on November 25, 1908, at Betty's home in Arkansas, with only the two families present. Afterward the whole town gathered on the station platform to send the newlyweds off to St. Louis.

They had only a few days to themselves there, since Will was to open the following week at Proctor's in Newark, New Jersey. They went to a football game, had Thanksgiving dinner and champagne served in their room at the Planters Hotel, and saw *What Every Woman Knows,* starring Maude Adams.

In Newark, Betty watched Will for the first time on a stage, and she was not especially impressed. She had seen most of his rope tricks many times over. But his working hours were ideal for honeymooners; he arrived at the theater just in time to go on, and since Buck McKee had his ropes laid out, all Will had to do was slip on a dark-blue flannel shirt and leather chaps and walk onto the stage, perform for fifteen or twenty minutes, and then make his exit. Even though he was doing two performances a day, he and Betty had time to sightsee, attend other theaters,

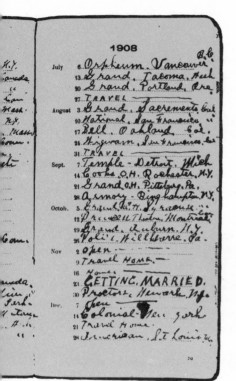

or visit with friends who were in town. To Will's disgust (since he had to wear his "Montgomery Ward" or wedding suit) they also went several times to the opera. Will later described one opera evening: "Caruso was the fellow who had played the part of a clown but I could not think of a funny thing that he did."

Their tour of the Orpheum circuit turned out to be a real honeymoon; Betty had seen little of the country before, and Will wanted to rediscover it all with her. Wandering about, taking in the sights, picnicking in the countryside, riding horseback in the city parks—it was a relaxed, carefree life. When the tour ended, an offer came for Will to play the Percy Williams theaters in the East at a much higher salary than he had been getting, and Betty agreed that he should accept. She was, she conceded, "growing reconciled to show business."

Will interrupted his vaudeville schedule in 1908 for a good reason. "The day I roped Betty," he said, "I did the star performance of my life."

After the Williams tour Will decided to put together an ambitious show of his own, featuring a variety of fancy ropers and trick riders. During this tour he made what was probably the most important decision in his theatrical career.

They were playing in Philadelphia and Will was onstage, watching the performances and making wry comments to the audience. Betty was in the wings, and the theater manager joined her. "Tell me, Mrs. Rogers," he said, "why does Will carry all those horses and people around with him? I would rather have Will Rogers alone than that whole bunch put together."

That decided it. Will would break up the troupe and go back to where he had started in vaudeville—just himself and his rope. The worst of the decision was saying good-by to Buck and Teddy, who had been an intimate part of Will's life for the past six years. But with their departure, theater audiences began seeing an entirely different Will Rogers. From an intense, serious lariat artist he had developed into a humorous talker who also spun a rope, and that was to be the pattern from now on.

His way of concentrating hard on the rope made any remark seem impromptu (as indeed it usually was) and fresh. The lariat would spin smoothly, a gleaming white circle above the footlights, and Will would remark, half to himself, "Worked that pretty good." Or, if he missed a throw, which he rarely did, he might comment, "I've only got jokes enough for one miss. I've either got to practice roping or learn more jokes." Once he missed a fairly easy trick in which he jumped with both feet inside a spinning loop. As he was gathering in the lasso to make another try, he drawled, "Well, got all my feet through but one." As Betty wrote, "Laughs didn't have to happen twice to Will," and he began missing that trick regularly in order to use the line.

The gum chewing, which became his trademark, was made part of the act by accident. Will was a great baseball fan and often would head for a ball park to shag flies with the local team. He picked up the habit of chewing gum from the ballplayers. One day he arrived at the theater barely in time for the matinee performance and was still chewing when he came onstage. When the audience began laughing, Will remembered the gum, walked back and stuck it onto the proscenium arch, and the crowd roared. From then on he often used the business of parking his chewing gum after he missed a rope trick; then he would do the trick perfectly, collect the gum, and resume chewing.

Another modification in the act came about as a result of his friendship with Fred Stone, the actor and dancer, whom Will had admired before they met. The two men often played the same city, and they formed the habit of practicing together in the morning, with Will teaching Stone rope tricks while Fred coached him on dance routines. ("Rogers is a surprise when he starts dancing," *Variety* commented, "and gets away with it big.") The two had a lot in common: both were outdoorsmen who had lived adventurous lives; both were wholly absorbed in their profession; and neither could tolerate idleness. The Rogers and Stone families spent much time together over the years.

Most of the Rogers' friends at this time were theater people, among them W.C. Fields. Fields, who had achieved billing as "the greatest juggler on earth" while still a young vaudeville performer, first met Will in a Cape Town saloon, and they ran into each other again after Will joined Texas Jack's *Wild West Show*. Will had the greatest affection for Fields—a feeling that Fields reciprocated, as his biographer Robert Lewis Taylor writes, "with his usual periodic reservations and suspicions."

Now that Will was doing a single again he was better off financially. Although he was making the same money as before, he had fewer expenses and fewer problems. Clem's pride in his son's achievements grew steadily, although for a long while he was baffled that Will could make so much money. "Two hundred and fifty dollars a week," he would say. "Looks like something is wrong somewhere." But the tune changed when he took his daughters, Sallie and Maud, to Washington, where Will was performing at Chase's Theatre. Clem attended every performance and late in the week looked out over the audience from his box seat and began counting the house. Age had not dimmed his business instinct. "I tell you, girls," he said, "that manager sure is making a lot of money off Willie."

Unhappily, just when Clem and his son were beginning to be close to each other, it turned out that there would be no more such occasions. On October 20, 1911, Betty gave birth to a son, named William Vann for Will and Clem, and about a week later a package arrived from Clem containing a pair of beaded Indian moccasins for the baby. On its heels came a telegram informing them that Will's father had died in his sleep.

Will never forgot that he was Clem Rogers' son. "I suspect that Will's modesty had its origin in a tremendous respect for his father," Betty wrote, "and a knowledge that, at least in early manhood, he was a disappointment to his family." There was a hint of this in the story Will liked to tell about several of his father's cronies who came to see him perform in New York. When they got back to Oklahoma another old-timer asked what

Will was doing. "Oh," said one, "just acting the fool like he used to do around here."

For several years after his father's death Will's career seemed to be stuck on a plateau. Show business generally was in the doldrums. In 1913 Betty gave birth to their second child, a daughter named Mary, while Will was playing vaudeville in Houston, Texas, and he was seriously concerned about his future. He sought Fred Stone's advice, and was urged to stay in New York. Will needed a part in a show and Stone felt he would never get one as long as he was off trouping in vaudeville. So the Rogers family rented a house for the summer in Amityville, Long Island, and Will played vaudeville houses around New York.

On taxes: *"The Income Tax has made more Liars out of the American people than Golf has."*

Their third child, James Blake, was born in the summer of 1915—a time that was also memorable for the arrival of a small, coal-black pony called Dopey. Will had spotted Dopey in Connecticut, liked him, and brought him home, where he became more family institution than pet. He entered the house, walked up and down stairs, and when the children started riding, Dopey, the little black horse, was the animal they rode. "He raised our children," according to Will.

The uncertainty surrounding Will's career was made no easier by his attitude toward money. He could *almost* never resist a salesman, he could *never* resist buying a horse he wanted, and he assumed that every man was honest unless proved otherwise. He liked to buy furs for Betty, and he purchased two diamond scarf pins and a huge diamond ring for himself—ready currency for a touring actor who might find himself stranded without funds. Will's ring was in and out of hockshops frequently.

Because he was so relaxed about money, Will was often overcharged, but his attitude toward this was typical: "I would rather be the one to pay too much," he would say, "than to be the man that charged too much." He carried his paychecks around in a pocket—often eight or ten of them at a time—until he needed money. Then he would cash them. He never kept accounts or business records. (Later, when he was making films, someone asked who his accountant was. "Haven't got any," Will replied. "We just put a check in the bank and draw on it until it's gone.")

Will spent most of the summer of 1915 at home with the family, and it was a nearly idyllic time. As far as vaudeville went, he had hit the top. He was the featured attraction for two weeks at the Palace on Broadway, the number one house in the country.

Late that fall Will was offered a two-week engagement in the *Midnight Frolic,* a late-night show on the roof of the New Amsterdam Theatre. This probably had more to do with determining his future than any date he ever played.

5

"He brought beauty into the entertainment world."

THE *Midnight Frolic* was the property of Florenz Ziegfeld, Jr., who also produced the most famous show in America—the *Ziegfeld Follies.* The idea of hiring Will came from Ziegfeld's right-hand man, Gene Buck, for Ziegfeld himself was virtually devoid of humor. He put up with comedians only because they filled in onstage while his girls were changing for their next number.

The *Frolic,* as Will described it, was "for folks with lots of money. And plenty of insomnia." It began on the stroke of twelve, and the cast included "the most beautiful girls of any show Ziegfeld ever put on." The loveliest ones, Will said, wouldn't work at a matinee—they never got up that early.

When he started out in the *Frolic,* Will did pretty much what he had been doing for the past several years—rope tricks punctuated with jokes about the show, Ziegfeld, and so on. The crowds took to him from the beginning, but Ziegfeld, sitting out front glum-faced, commented flatly, "I don't like him."

Gene Buck argued that the act was going over, so Ziegfeld agreed to watch it again another night. He did, and said, "Let him go. He doesn't fit in." For some days this byplay went on, Ziegfeld insisting each time that the roper be fired, and finally Buck went to give Will the bad news. But Will had an announcement to give him first.

"I want fifty dollars a week more," he blurted out. Besides, he added, he had a new idea for the act. "My wife says I'm always readin' the papers and I ought to talk about what I read."

*Rogers first went aloft at Atlantic City in 1915
in a Curtiss biplane piloted by E. K. Jaquith (right).
In later years flying became a passion with him.*

Reluctantly, Buck told him to try it, neglecting to say that Ziegfeld was going to let him go, since he knew that the producer would be out of town for a week. As it happened, Will's notion of commenting on the news coincided with the effort of the industrialist Henry Ford to stop World War I. Ford had chartered a ship, loaded it with pacifists, idealists, and feminists, and set sail for Norway, where he hoped to halt the fighting through neutral mediation. As Will came onstage one night, groping for something to warm up his audience, he remarked, "If Mr. Ford had taken this bunch of girls, in this show, and let 'em wear the same costumes they wear here, and marched them down between the trenches, believe me, the boys would have been out before Christmas." The outburst of laughter convinced him that all he needed was a new gag about Ford's peace ship for each show.

When Ziegfeld returned he asked Buck how his cowboy friend had reacted to the news that he was fired. "I haven't let him go," Buck admitted, and asked the producer to come that night.

Ziegfeld did, and had to concede that the customers loved the act. "We'll keep him another week," he said.

One more week led to another, and another; Will got his raise; and as Henry Ford vanished from the front pages he cast about for new material. "So I started to reading about Congress," said Will, "and I found they are funnier three hundred and sixty-five days a year than anything I ever heard of." He would devour the newspapers for hours at a time, trying to work out a humorous angle to the day's news. "A joke don't have to be near as funny if it's up-to-date," he observed. And he concluded, about this time, that he didn't really care for the jokes that got the biggest laughs. What he preferred was the sly, subtle line that prompted people in the audience to nudge their friends and say, "He's right about that, you know." Where audiences once had admired his roping and chuckled at his comments, now they were laughing with Will, who seemed more like an amiable friend than a performer.

WILL'S one-week engagement stretched out for months; he was still in the *Frolic* in the spring of 1916 when Ziegfeld—again as a result of Gene Buck's prodding—asked him to join the cast of the *Follies*. Will's refusal must have come as a surprise to the producer, but neither Will nor Betty thought the salary Ziegfeld offered was adequate, particularly since a *Follies* job meant that he would have to go on the road again. Will was enjoying a sane homelife for the first time in years; the family had a house in Forest Hills, Long Island, and kept horses in a nearby stable; he and Betty devoted a lot of time to the children and to riding.

They attended the opening of the 1916 *Follies*. The show was extravagant and spectacular; it was also deadly dull. Will's homespun act would have been a standout amid all that glitter. Through the long evening Will kept whispering to Betty, nudging her and saying, "See, Blake, what did I tell you? This was my one big chance." Or, "Boy, I wish I could have got my crack at it." They left the theater feeling that Will had lost an opportunity that might never come again.

Several days later Mr. Ziegfeld called (to Will he was always Mr. Ziegfeld) and admitted that the show lacked humor; he wanted Will to join it at once. By now Will was so eager to break into the *Follies* that he didn't even discuss salary.

"When Will went on the stage that night," Betty reported, "the audience broke into applause. Never had he gone over so well." He made a second appearance, spinning his rope and commenting on personalities and events, and immediately after the curtain rang down, he went upstairs to the roof to do his turn in the *Frolic*. As Betty wrote, "his magic stayed with him," and after the two shows they stayed up, eating sandwiches and drinking beer, waiting for the early editions of the morning papers. "All of them," she said, "gave Will excellent notices—the best, most important he had ever received."

Since the *Follies* and the *Frolic* were in the same theater and *Follies* patrons would drift up to the roof to eat, drink, and be entertained some more, Will now had to have an entirely different act twice every night, plus two matinees a week. He had acquired the habit of opening with the same phrase, "Well, all I know is just what I read in the papers," and going on from there. He pored over the noon editions of afternoon papers for his matinee performance; read stories from the final and home editions for the *Follies;* and for the midnight show extracted material from early editions of next morning's papers. "I buy more newspaper extras than any man in the world," he claimed. All his comments were brief—usually three or four lines; in the time that most monologuists told eight or ten stories, Will averaged forty or more.

He also formed the habit of introducing prominent personalities from the audience. Ushers would keep an eye out for celebrities and send notes to Will's dressing room indicating the location of their seats; or Ziegfeld would tell him when friends of his were in the house; or sometimes Will, peering over the footlights, would spot a friend or someone known to the audience. (The houselights were always kept on when he talked.) One night he swung his rope out over the crowd and lassoed Fred Stone, who was seated on the aisle near the front. Despite his protests, Will hauled him up onstage and made him perform

one of his own rope tricks, meantime leaning against the proscenium arch and visiting with him about Mrs. Stone and the children. It was the kind of unexpected treat that proved irresistible.

By the time Will joined Ziegfeld, the *Follies* was an established American institution. "A funny thing about the *Follies*,"
Will wrote, "people never spoke of it in comparison to any
other show. It was always 'It's better than the last year's, or it's
not as good as last year's.'" It was true: Ziegfeld was his own
greatest competition.

What had drawn people to the *Follies* ever since the first one
opened in 1907 was, of course, the combination of beautiful
showgirls, fantastic costumes and sets, and a sprinkling of high-
priced talent—W.C.Fields, Bert Williams, Fanny Brice, Ann
Pennington, Eddie Cantor, and dozens of other headliners.

In 1916 Will's roping-and-comedy routine became part of the Ziegfeld Follies, which featured "The Most Beautiful Girls in the World" (left and center). Soon he was among the headliners, like W.C. Fields (far left above) and Eddie Cantor (second from right above).

When rehearsals began in the winter, Will and Betty often sat together in the darkened house while Ziegfeld and his assistants worked out the various spectacular numbers. When it was Will's turn to rehearse he generally kidded amiably about the show, about the girls—most of whom worked hard, since every stage-struck hopeful dreamed of being picked for the *Follies*—or remarked on incidents that had occurred during the tryouts. But it was not, in fact, a rehearsal for him. His act was always as fresh to members of the cast as it was to the audience, and they usually collected in the wings to hear him every night.

When the time came for the show to go on tour, Will was determined not to leave New York unless he got a substantial raise. Ziegfeld overwhelmed him with an offer of a two-year contract at $600 a week the first year and $750 the second—far more than he had considered asking. Then the producer suggested that Will stop by his office the next day and sign the contract. Will said, "I don't like contracts. You can trust me and I know I can trust you." And that was to be their arrangement for ten years.

Ziegfeld looked after Will in numerous ways. The *Follies* cast traveled in a special train, and the producer arranged for two of Will's horses, with a cowboy friend in charge of them, to go along in the scenery car, so Will could ride each morning and practice roping on horseback.

Of all the road trips Will made he was proudest of the occasions on which he played for President Woodrow Wilson. The first time was a benefit performance in Baltimore in 1916, shortly before the United States entered the war. Just before the opening the cast heard that President and Mrs. Wilson were coming from Washington to see the show, and Will immediately developed a bad case of stage fright. He had planned to devote most of his act to the country's lack of preparedness and to the diplomatic notes then going back and forth between Wilson and various European powers. The closer it came to curtain time, the more nervous he grew. When the moment came Will had to be shoved out on the stage.

He stood there for a moment, grinning sheepishly, rubbing his head, and remarked to everyone's delight, "I am kinder nervous here tonight." Then he began easing into the material he had planned to use. "I shouldn't be nervous," he added, "for this is really my second Presidential appearance. The first time was when Bryan spoke in our town once, and I was to follow his speech and do my little Roping Act." Glancing at the presidential box and seeing Wilson laugh, he went on. "As I say, I was to follow him, but he spoke so long that it was so dark when he finished, they couldn't see my Roping." Then a pause: "I wonder what ever became of him."*

A few jokes about "Pancho" Villa, whom General John J. Pershing was chasing in Mexico, followed: "I see where they

---

*William Jennings Bryan, perennial Democratic presidential candidate, had helped obtain the nomination in 1912 for Wilson, who after he was elected appointed Bryan Secretary of State. Just the year before the benefit in Baltimore, Bryan had resigned in a disagreement over Wilson's foreign policy following the sinking of the *Lusitania*. Bryan and Will would meet again. [Editor's note.]

316

have captured Villa. Yes, they got him in the morning Editions and the Afternoon ones let him get away." Then he turned to the country's lack of preparedness—a subject on which Wilson was being criticized daily. "There is some talk of getting a Machine Gun if we can borrow one. The one we have now they are using to train our Army with in Plattsburg. If we go to war we will just about have to go to the trouble of getting another Gun." When Will saw that the President was leading the laughter, he added a pointed remark about the exchange of diplomatic notes with Germany, which Wilson afterward repeated to friends, saying it was the best joke told on him during the war. "President Wilson is getting along fine now to what he was a few months ago. Do you realize, People, that at one time in our negotiations with Germany that he was 5 Notes behind?"

Will later called this the proudest and most successful

On peace: *"Prominent men run out of Decoration Day speeches, but the world never runs out of wars. People talk peace, but men give their life's work to war. It won't stop till there is as much brains and scientific study put to aid peace as there is to promote war."*

night he had ever had—made more memorable by the fact that the President came backstage during intermission and shook hands with everyone in the cast.

UNITED STATES ENTRY into the war put no stop to Will's jokes about it. On the contrary, he found that Americans "laughed better during the war than any other time, if you happened to hit the right angle to it." At thirty-eight, with a wife and three children, he was exempt from the draft, but attempted to compensate for that by appearing at benefits and playing for returned veterans. To the president of the American Red Cross he wrote in May 1917, "While not a wealthy man, I earn a very good salary," and he pledged to donate ten percent of his next year's income—$5200.

He was telling *Follies* audiences that Germany couldn't understand how the United States could get trained men to Europe so quickly; what the enemy didn't comprehend, he said, was that "in our training manual there's nothing about retreating. When you only have to teach an army to go one way, you can do it in half the time." One of his most successful routines was his advice on how to obtain a commission and fight the war in Washington: all it required was a visit to your senator. But the hazards to be faced were legion: ten men had been wounded in one day getting in and out of taxicabs.

With the signing of the armistice, which read "like a second mortgage" while the peace terms read "like a foreclosure," Will commented that it had taken eighty thousand words to tell Germany what we thought of them. When veterans arrived back he remarked, "If they really wanted to honor the boys, why didn't they let them sit in the stands and have the people march by?"

By this time his jokes were being quoted so frequently that he collected a number of them into two books which achieved modest success. The first was *Rogers-isms: the Cowboy Philosopher on the Peace Conference,* on the dust jacket of which he explained, "I made this book short so you could finish it before the next war." That volume was followed quickly by *Rogers-isms: The Cowboy Philosopher on Prohibition.* "You wont find the Country any drier than this Book," the cover proclaimed, and inside was an assortment of gags about Prohibition which had enlivened his *Follies* and *Frolic* routines. It had already been "the cause of more road improvement between dry and wet towns than any other thing," he claimed, since "Bad roads have broke more bottles of booze than the authorities." The Volstead Act would remain one of his favorite targets.

These slim books marked Will's first venture onto the literary scene. But it was short-lived. During the summer of 1918 he had discovered another medium representing new opportunities.

6

"Anybody can open a Theatre. It's keeping it open that is the hard thing."

ALTHOUGH Will Rogers and thousands of his fellow countrymen had been exposed to the novelty known as moving pictures, they could not have guessed that this new medium would, during the next few decades, transform the entertainment world.

So far as the general public was aware, the excitement started at the Koster & Bial Music Hall, west of Broadway in New York City, one evening in April 1896 when Manhattan society turned out, dressed to the nines, to see a demonstration of "Thomas A. Edison's Latest Marvel, THE VITASCOPE." Following the usual vaudeville fare, a twenty-foot white screen descended in front of the stage, lights were extinguished, a curious mechanical object in the center of the balcony began to buzz and wheeze, and a brilliant light filled the screen. Suddenly the figures of two women appeared and were seen to smile, pirouette daintily around their parasols, and dance. They vanished, and in their place an angry, surging wave crashed toward the audience. Thomas Armat, operating the Vitascope, recalled afterward that the realism of the oncoming surf "started a panicky commotion" in the front seats. Later the spectators went wild when a showgirl named Annabelle performed "The Butterfly Dance" on the screen. In short, an audience of sophisticated New Yorkers was thrilled and delighted, and behaved like a flock of children.

In truth, the "invention" demonstrated that night was not Edison's own, but a projector developed by Armat and a man named Jenkins. Armat had turned it over to Edison to manufacture. Since the 1850s, when a shutter was added to the venerable magic lantern to make a series of drawings look like a figure in motion, various experimenters had produced workable motion-picture projectors. The principle—then and now—was based on the fact that the optic nerve "remembers" a still image for a fraction of a second. The trick was to flash a sequence of pictures on the screen at a speed of sixteen frames per second, so fast that the eye could not distinguish them as separate images.

Edison was only mildly interested in Armat's projector. He had begun marketing something called the Kinetoscope, which had been developed at his laboratory by an imaginative employee named William K.L. Dickson.

This was what came to be known as a peep show. These upright viewing machines were installed by the hundreds in "phonograph parlors" across the land, where customers were already congregating to listen to Edison's gramophone. By placing a coin in a slot, a person could activate a viewer and watch about fifty feet of film. When Edison's associates tried to interest him in a film projector, he replied, "We are selling a lot of these peep-show machines at a good profit. If we put out a screen machine, there will be use for maybe about ten of them in the whole United States. Let's not kill the goose that lays the golden egg."

Not surprisingly, the first institution to see the possibilities of the motion-picture projector was vaudeville, and from 1896 to 1900 many houses showed films to supplement their live stage entertainment. But the pictures were of movement for movement's sake—photographs of natural phenomena like Niagara Falls, of trains and fire engines in motion, and of occasional news scenes, William McKinley's 1896 presidential campaign being one of the first. These began to pall, however, and the novelty faded.

Yet while middle-class audiences in the vaudeville houses wearied of such fare, thousands of immigrants from Europe, eager for information about their adopted homeland and its customs, delighted in the garish penny arcades, where they could peer into a hand-cranked Kinetoscope and watch the bewitching pictures move. Arcade operators, sniffing the money that could be made by turning their establishments into picture theaters, began buying projectors and demanding new films to show on them. Before long these makeshift, back-room theaters became the most popular form of entertainment for America's lower class. While some saw all this as cheap claptrap, shrewder minds perceived in the growing popularity of films the makings of a new industry.

IN CHICAGO two entrepreneurs named Spoor and Aronson formed a company called Essanay and began to transfer elements of the Wild West show to the screen. Aronson (who changed his name and achieved fame as "Bronco Billy" Anderson) was soon grinding out horse operas at the rate of one a week. William Selig, another Chicagoan, got in touch with Will Rogers' old friend Tom Mix, hired him, and thereby gave the American boy one of his first screen idols.

The theater that provided a name for all the others was Pittsburgh's Nickelodeon, which opened in a converted store in

1905 with a showing of the first important Western, *The Great Train Robbery*. That film set the pattern for hundreds more to follow: beginning with a scene in which two badmen slug a stationmaster, it moves quickly to a murder in the baggage car of a train, the dynamiting of a strongbox, a horseback chase, and a gunfight between the good and bad guys. With the coming of a true narrative to the screen, the nickelodeon boom was on. By 1907 there were three thousand of them; by 1910, ten thousand—all with uncomfortable seats, the pungent odor of human sweat, Cracker Jack, and popcorn.

As the demand for films grew, so did the need for stories capable of being translated to

On lawyers: *"Every time a lawyer writes something, he is not writing for posterity, he is writing so that endless others of his craft can make a living out of trying to figure out what he said."*

film, for improved production and distribution facilities, and for actors, editors, cameramen, and directors. Inevitably there had been a good deal of pirating and copying of films by shrewd nickelodeon operators. But the movie business was soon big enough to have its own monopoly, the Motion Picture Patents Company. By 1909 no film could be photographed, processed, or exhibited without its consent.

The monopoly was a formidable antagonist for independent producers. Its spies raided unlicensed theaters and destroyed "illicit" projectors and films. By the time the monopoly was broken up under the Sherman Anti-Trust Act, the East Coast had become too hazardous for the independents. William Selig had taken his company to Los Angeles, which was near enough to the Mexican border to enable him to escape the monopoly's subpoenas and save his cameras from being smashed. Moreover he and other independent producers who followed him westward discovered that in southern California nature made it possible to produce movies in an entirely new manner. With sunshine almost the year around, interior scenes could be photographed outdoors without the need for electric lights. And California offered every type of landscape—mountains, deserts, fields, sea, lakes, islands—much of it unoccupied. These were the factors that brought to Los Angeles, in 1910, the man who was to initiate most of the changes that soon took place in the motion-picture industry.

In David Wark Griffith, a sensitive, intelligent Southerner who was the son of a Confederate officer, the industry found the director who made the American public take films seriously. Within a remarkably short period he turned out more than four hundred one- and two-reel pictures, filled with innovations. He made the camera a roving eye instead of a static piece of equipment. He originated such techniques as the long shot, the vignette, the close-up, the fade-in and fade-out, and the angle shot. He was the first to try night photography, and one of the first to insist that the public would accept pictures that ran longer than one reel, or fourteen minutes.

In the fall of 1914 Griffith began work independently on a film based on a novel called *The Clansman,* by Thomas Dixon, a melodrama about the Reconstruction period, depicting the Ku Klux Klan as chivalrous heroes. He visualized it in a dimension unheard-of in the industry—twelve reels, which would take six months to film, at a cost of a hundred thousand dollars. Released in February 1915 as *The Clansman*—the title was soon changed to *The Birth of a Nation*—the film aroused immediate and intense excitement. It was shown at the White House; it was hailed by the press, denounced in Boston, and became an overnight sensation wherever it played.

Meanwhile a former actor named Mack Sennett, who had worked with Griffith and absorbed many of his ideas, was directing one- and two-reelers which poked fun at the conventions of American society: the successful businessman suffered an ignominious pratfall or received a custard pie in the face; the innocent American girl was portrayed as a beautiful, dumb bathing beauty who had eyes only for a man's bankroll; the romantic lover was seen as cross-eyed Ben Turpin or Fatty Arbuckle; imbecilic Keystone Kops revealed the underlying contempt of the country for its law officers; and Sennett's cynical view of the almighty automobile took shape in the impossible adventures of the Model T, which inevitably came to an explosive demise.

The gifted comedians Buster Keaton, Harry Langdon, and

Charlie Chaplin (whom Sennett called the greatest artist who ever lived) all worked for Sennett, and millions of Americans began crowding into theaters to see their comedies.

ABOUT the time the Vitascope was unveiled at Koster & Bial's, a couple named Mr. and Mrs. H. H. Wilcox purchased one hundred and twenty acres of land northwest of Los Angeles, subdivided the property into lots, and named the development Hollywood. In 1910, when D. W. Griffith began filming a picture there, residents were dismayed by what happened to their town. Soon actors and actresses were everywhere; and as other companies followed Griffith, streets were roped off to stage parades or gun battles or automobile accidents; once-quiet hotels were filled with painted women, noisy cavalrymen, Indians, and cowboys; vacant land was gobbled up and turned into studios and movie lots.

In 1913 three partners arrived from the East, rented a barn near the corner of Sunset Boulevard and Vine Street, and began filming a motion-picture version of the stage play *The Squaw Man*. The three were Cecil B. DeMille, a former actor and playwright; Jesse L. Lasky, a vaudeville producer; and Lasky's brother-in-law, Samuel Goldfish, who had been born in the Warsaw ghetto and had made his way to the United States, later joining Lasky and DeMille.

In quick order DeMille made three successful movies, and the company was on its way. In those days everything about the making of a picture was highly informal. Scripts were rudimentary, not much more than a three- or four-page synopsis of a plot line which the actors and producers improvised on. While this casual approach was all very well for slapstick comedies, novels and plays that were translated into movies usually lost something in the process. The action tended to be static, and something clearly had to be done.

Samuel Goldfish, who was about to call himself Goldwyn, was a pioneer in the effort to improve the quality of scenario writing. Having formed his own company, he hired a group of novelists to whom he gave the resounding name of Eminent Authors. Among them were Mary Roberts Rinehart, Rupert Hughes, Gertrude Atherton, and Rex Beach. Beach's wife was the sister of Fred Stone's wife, and a friend of Will Rogers'.

Beach had sold Goldwyn one of his books, *Laughing Bill Hyde,* and his wife had the idea that Will was the ideal person to play the lead. Goldwyn came to New York to see Will and told him that the picture could be shot in a Fort Lee, New Jersey, studio during the summer, when the *Follies* was not playing. Will agreed to do it.

When *Laughing Bill Hyde* appeared, in September 1918, *The New York Times* greeted it enthusiastically: "Those inclined to believe that all of the magnetic Rogers personality is in his conversation will realize their mistake if they see this picture. The real Will Rogers is on the reels." Goldwyn was pleased with the box-office receipts and offered Will a two-year Hollywood contract. Will was drawing a good salary from Ziegfeld, but Goldwyn offered to double it for the first year and triple it for the second. There was a fourth child now—Freddie, named for Fred Stone—and according to Betty, they were attracted as much by the prospect of moving to California as by the generous salary terms. In the spring of 1919 Will headed alone for Los Angeles and located a house on Van Ness Avenue that would accommodate the family. When Betty and the children joined him he met them at the station in a big black Cadillac driven by a chauffeur.

His first picture under the contract with Goldwyn was *Almost a Husband,* in which he played opposite Peggy Wood. He was on location when the three boys, Bill, Jimmy, and Freddie, came down with diphtheria. No antitoxin was available in Hollywood, and Will drove all night to find some; Bill and Jimmy recovered, but the baby died.

That tragedy spoiled the house for them, and they bought another in Beverly Hills. They had decided to make California home, and the new property was spacious enough so that they could have a stable, a tanbark riding ring, a swimming pool, and two log cabins for the children.

Will was not only acting in his pictures, he also had a hand in the scripts and wrote the titles used as descriptive clues and as dialogue. He couldn't take himself very seriously as an actor and liked to tell about a letter he had received which said, "I understand you have never used a double in your

The primitive nature of early Hollywood cinematography is suggested by the shooting of this scene from Jubilo, *a Rogers silent movie, in 1919.*

pictures—now that I have seen you I wonder why you don't." He missed the presence of an audience, but he thoroughly enjoyed the work; he could go to bed early, arise early, and spend much of his time outdoors. All in all, it was "the grandest show business I know anything about, and the only place an actor can act and at the same time sit down in front and clap for himself."

By the time his contract expired, Will had made twelve pictures for Goldwyn, six in 1920 alone. In most of them he played romantic parts. The films were pleasant, amusing, and reasonably successful, but the expiration of Will's contract in 1921 came at a time when the industry was in the throes of reorganization. Goldwyn left the studio, and Will was suddenly on his own, without a contract.

Some of the leading actors and actresses in Hollywood had recently established their own independent companies; in 1919, when Griffith, Mary Pickford, Douglas Fairbanks, and Charlie Chaplin formed United Artists, word circulated through the movie colony that the lunatics had taken over the asylum. Will, following their lead, decided to go it alone and write, produce, and direct his own films—starring himself. He and Betty read innumerable books and scenarios, and they mortgaged the house to raise capital.

In this manner he produced three movies—*Fruits of Faith, The Ropin' Fool,* and *One Day in 365,* the story of a day at home with his wife and children. *The Ropin' Fool* was and is a delight, a highly amusing film for which Will wrote the titles and which showed him at his best, performing over fifty of his remarkable rope tricks. And *Fruits of Faith,* according to *The New York Times,* was a charming picture, unpretentious and with a slender story line, but made human and humorous by the skill of Will Rogers.

Everything Will owned—life insurance, Liberty bonds, savings, real estate—was tied up in those pictures. But none was a financial success, and soon the Rogers family was on the brink of bankruptcy. Finally he had to borrow money on the films themselves, depositing them at the bank as security. He was beginning to understand how Hollywood operated: "If the loan is made for a Moving Picture," he wrote, "the President of the bank wants to write the story for you. The Directors want to know who the Leading Lady is, and if they could, they would keep her as collateral."

Knowing there was work for him in New York, he went back to play in the *Follies.* What Betty remembered about that year were the countless train trips she made across the country to be with him. As for Will, she said he worked as hard "as he ever did in his life, and without a break or vacation of any kind." He missed his children and his favorite ponies. By the following summer, when he came home to accept a new movie contract, much of his indebtedness had been paid.

That was accomplished in large part because of his boundless energy. He had embarked on two new professions, in both of which he succeeded simply by being himself.

7

"Well, all I know is just what I read in the papers."

DURING a long, full career Will Rogers' best character part, as so many film reviewers pointed out, was playing himself. That is what he did to perfection in the two activities in which he now engaged: after-dinner speaking and writing a syndicated newspaper column.

Will had made after-dinner speeches before, mostly for theatrical friends at the Lambs and Friars clubs in New York. Now, to recoup the money lost in Hollywood, he began scheduling luncheon and dinner appearances at the rate of three or four a week all over Manhattan, usually for a fee of a thousand dollars. As a banquet speaker Will relied on the techniques that were so popular with *Follies* audiences. His act was completely personal, based on firsthand experience or observation. As he put it, his gags had to be based on facts. "Now rumor travels faster, but it don't stay put as long as truth."

Surprisingly, considering his years on the stage, he suffered from stage fright before every performance. "I never saw an audience that I ever faced with any confidence," he once admitted. The first few minutes in front of a crowd were agonizing for Will; he would fumble around nervously, half-muttering his lines, and he never did learn to hide his discomfort.

For a year, starting in 1922, he spoke at banquets of automobile dealers, hat- and dressmakers, leather and shoe men, corsetmakers, newspaper women, rug merchants, even New York City's Board of Aldermen. Each organization—to its delight—got the typical Will Rogers treatment.

Instead of opening with the usual formalities, he began by startling or insulting his audience. He told the automobile dealers they were "old time Horse-trading Gyps with white collars on." He addressed a group of advertising men as the "Robbing Hoods of America"; he advised the Association of Woolen Men to stay indoors in case of rain or there would be "about five hundred men choked to death by their own suits."

A roomful of astonished bankers heard that borrowing money on easy terms was a one-way ticket to the poorhouse. "If you think it ain't a sucker game," Will asked, "why is a banker the richest man in town?" He wished Congress would pass a bill forbidding any person to borrow from another, even if that put all bankers out of business. And as for their future: "Go to work, if there is any job any of you could earn a living at. Banking and after-dinner speaking are two of the most nonessential industries we have in this country. I am ready to reform if you are."

In April of 1923 Will was once again seeing Betty off to California—he wasn't sure, but he thought it was her eighth trip since the previous June. He remarked that every time she heard a locomotive whistle she stuffed a kimono into her suitcase and started running; and when they went out to dinner in New York, she would ask, "How many cars ahead is the diner?"

As much as he liked to make jokes about it, their life must have been almost unbelievably hectic. By mid-June of 1923, after a year and a half on the banquet circuit, he had had enough: "I have spoken at so many banquets that when I get home I will feel disappointed if my wife or one of the children don't get up at dinner and say, 'We have with us this evening a man who, I am sure, needs no introduction.' "

One talk Will gave during the frenetic period led to the offer to write a newspaper column. He appeared at a rally in New York's Town Hall on October 26, 1922, to speak in support of Ogden Mills's reelection to Congress. Had the candidate or his backers known what Will would say, it is doubtful they would have requested his assistance. Will told the audience that he didn't want his speech to go over; if it did he was afraid it might lead him into politics, and up to now he had tried to live honestly. He said he did not know his candidate's opponent, but assumed he must be a scoundrel and a tool of the special interests. Then he admitted that he hadn't met his *own* candidate: that was the reason he was "more apt to say something good of him than anyone else." Most people, he thought, took up politics through necessity or as a last resort, but Mills (whom he kept referring to as "this guy") was wealthy before he went into politics—"not as wealthy as now, but rich." Unfortunately, Will continued, Mills was handicapped by having been educated at Harvard, but he was the only candidate who owned his own

Will began writing a weekly commentary on events of the day for The New York Times *in 1922, and the column was quickly syndicated all over the nation.*

silk hat and the only politician other than Henry Cabot Lodge who could get past the front door of a Fifth Avenue residence without delivering something. Mills, Will recalled, sat through the talk without the suggestion of a smile, not knowing "whether I was for him or against him." He was reelected either because of or in spite of Will's support.

Will's speech was reported in *The New York Times,* where it was read by the founder of the McNaught Syndicate, a man named V.V. McNitt. With his partner, Charles V. McAdam, McNitt arranged to meet Will and suggested that the *Times* might be interested in his writing a weekly column.

BY NOW WILL HAD already done some writing for publication. His little books of jokes about the peace conference and Prohibition had appeared in 1919, and that same year, en route to California, he had written an amusing political commentary for the Kansas City *Star.* The *Star's* theater critic had sat up until three a.m., listening to Will tell story after story, and begged him to put them on paper.

Will agreed to write the column for the *Times,* and there never was a contract; McAdam and McNitt shook hands with Will and agreed to pay him five hundred dollars a week. Sometime later Will came into the McNaught offices and mentioned that a rival syndicate had offered him eight hundred dollars a week, to which McAdam replied that they would give him a thousand dollars. Will told McAdam he was nuts, but he loved him for it.

On American generosity: *"I have . . . heard lots of appeals, but I have yet to see one where the people knew the need . . . that they didn't come through. I don't know anything about 'America' being fundamentally sound and all that after dinner 'Hooey,' but I do know that America is 'Fundamentally Generous.' "*

Charles Driscoll, a McNaught editor, was responsible for coping with Will's spelling, punctuation, and grammar, and one of his first admonitions to the new columnist was to refrain from using the word ain't. That produced the response, "I know a lot of people who don't say ain't, ain't eating."

On December 24, 1922, the first column appeared in the *Times,* and a week later it was syndicated by McNaught—beginning a series that would continue for nearly thirteen years and become a familiar feature of America's Sunday newspapers.

The times were ripe for what Will Rogers had to say about the country and the world at large. Prohibition was turning out to be virtually impossible to enforce. The Ku Klux Klan, whose membership was said to be five million, was terrorizing minority groups in the North and Midwest as well as in the South.

There were also reports that President Harding, unlike his predecessor in the White House, did not care for Will Rogers' brand of humor—particularly the way Will poked fun at the nation's most sacred cow, Warren Gamaliel Harding himself. When Will was playing in the *Follies,* he heard that Harding wouldn't come to the show and concluded that it was "on account of the humorous relations between the White House and myself being rather strained."

In April 1923 those relations were strained further by a column Will wrote in the form of an open letter addressed to the President. In it Will applied for the job as ambassador to the Court of St. James's, citing his accomplishments as a speechmaker (which he said was ninety percent of the work), his motion-picture experience (he would never be caught in the background during the photographing of a big event), and his movie appearance in knee breeches ("we haven't had a decent looking leg over there in years"). While this was all bland enough, Harding may have been stung by the last line of the letter: "Now, as to Salary, I will do just the same as the rest of the Politicians—accept a small salary as pin Money, AND TAKE A CHANCE ON WHAT I CAN GET."

There were ugly, persistent rumors that things were not as they should be in the administration, but as yet few Americans were aware that Harding was a distraught and desperate man—betrayed by venal cronies he had put into positions of responsibility. Only after Harding's death, following a trip to Alaska, were the sordid scandals revealed.

On August 19, 1923, when Will wrote a tribute to the dead President, there was no way he could know that Harding's widow and a trusted assistant were at that very moment consigning case after case of the chief executive's papers to the flames—to "preserve his memory." Years later Will wrote that Harding was, in his opinion, the most human of any recent President. "If he had a weakness, it was in trusting his friends, and the man that don't do that, then there is something the matter with him. . . . Betrayed by friendship is not a bad memorial to leave."

WILL'S SYNDICATED COLUMN was a gently amusing, commonsense, down-to-earth approach to the problems, large and small, that bedeviled the American citizen and the people of the world. Initially it was Will's habit to turn from one subject to another in quick succession, but over the years the column became less staccato, with longer anecdotes and fewer punchy gags. Yet while the format changed, the tone of voice and the personality behind it did not.

Hardly a week went by without an entertaining story or joke about prominent men and women: kings and queens, presidents and prime ministers, congressmen, sports heroes, big businessmen, movie stars—no one escaped. But no matter how Will might disagree with their principles or their politics, he never resorted to malice. There was something about the way he could turn a phrase that removed the sting from his criticism.

What he said, or what he might say, was nevertheless a matter of continuing concern to Betty, who was often embarrassed by the informality of his approach to important people. She worried that he would go too far or that someone would take offense. Life with Will had, as she put it, an "explosive" quality, because neither she nor anyone else ever quite knew what he was going to say or do. The Rogers' two sons, long after their parents' death, remembered vividly the "civilizing" effect their mother had on their father. As Will, Jr., observed, his father came out of the world of Wild West shows, rodeos, the circus, and vaudeville— all "harum-scarum" activities that were not held in universal esteem—and it was Betty who "tamed him" and led him in a more respectable direction. Jim Rogers added, "And she was a censor. When Dad would come out with something a little raw, she would tell him, 'You just can't say that!' "

Fifty years later the weekly articles hold up astonishingly well. Topical as much of it is, the humor is still fresh, and contains nuggets of enduring wisdom and rare understanding. His comment about James Cox, the unsuccessful candidate for the presidency in 1920, is characteristic: "I don't know of any quicker way . . . to be forgotten in this Country than to be defeated for President. A man can leave the Country and people will always remember that he went some place. But if he is defeated for President they can't remember that he ever did anything."

Will formed the habit of opening his column with the line which began his *Follies* act: "Well, all I know is just what I read in the papers." All over the country Americans were turning every Sunday to those weekly asides on the news which were so distinctively Will Rogers. His exposure to the public was not only continuous, it was ubiquitous. He was appearing annually in the *Follies* and performing at frequent benefits: Americans were reading his weekly column and hearing him on the radio (he made his first broadcast over Pittsburgh's pioneer radio station, KDKA). And in 1923 he returned to Hollywood, at a salary of three thousand dollars a week, to make twelve comedies for producer Hal Roach. The films were successful enough as far as Roach was concerned, but they were not especially gratifying from Will's point of view. The problem, essentially, was that silent pictures lacked the dimension of conversation, the vital aspect of his stage act. So when the contract with Roach expired in 1924 Will headed east again.

IT WAS 1924, a presidential election year, and since Will had no set act in mind for the *Follies,* he informed his readers that he would stop off in Washington en route to New York to pick up some new jokes. "Congress," he explained, "has been writing my material for years."

Actually most of the politicking was going on outside the capital, and Will headed for Cleveland, where the Republicans were holding what he called the "Coolidge Follies—a one-star show." This was the first national political convention he attended, as a commentator for the McNaught Syndicate, and he was disappointed: it was altogether too tame. Coolidge, who had succeeded Harding upon the President's death, "could have been nominated by post card." As far as Will was concerned, the sole memorable moment was a lunch he had with William Jennings Bryan. The old Democratic war-horse was a correspondent covering the convention for the same syndicate, and when they first met in the press box Bryan said to Will, "You write a humorous column, don't you?"

Will admitted that he did.

"Well," Bryan remarked, "I write a serious article, and if I think of anything comical or funny I will give it to you."

"I thanked him," said Will later, "and told him, 'If I happen to think of anything of a serious nature, I will give it to you.' When he said he wrote seriously and I said I wrote humorously, I thought afterwards: 'We may both be wrong.' "

After seeing Coolidge nominated on the first ballot, Will left for the *Follies* rehearsals.The show opened on June 23, the same day the Democratic convention began at Madison Square Garden. Typically, Will was involved in both shows.

He had agreed to cover this convention for McNaught, too, and for a flat fee, which proved a costly mistake. The meeting lasted from June 24 to July 9, during which time the names of sixty candidates were placed in nomination for President.

As the convention dragged on endlessly, Will observed that the people in the hall heard the identical speech given by one man after another, each extolling the virtues of "the man I am going to name." Young Franklin D. Roosevelt had an opportunity, Will thought, to make a nominating speech that would have lived through the ages—if only he had had the sense to say, "Delegates, I put in nomination Alfred Smith; try and find out something against him."

On elections: *"Every time we have an election, we get in worse men and the country keeps right on going. Times have proven only one thing and that is you can't ruin this country ever, with politics."*

By July 2, the ninth tedious day of the convention, Will decided to place his own candidate in nomination, and wrote a speech in his behalf. The man he was about to name, he said, never saw Wall Street, was not a member of the Klan, and had no connection with oil. He was the only man who would win in 1924. His name, Will stated, was Calvin Coolidge.

On July 5, to his astonishment, two Arizona delegates, with half a vote each, cast them for Will Rogers. (He had never heard of the men before, he said, but he had heard of Arizona.) A few days later the by-line of thirteen-year-old Will Rogers, Jr., appeared on the column, which stated, "Papa called us all in last night and made his last will and testament. . . . He put in the will that I being the oldest was to take up his life's work, that of reporting the Democratic National Convention." Finally, on the 103rd ballot, John W. Davis was chosen as the nominee, and William Jennings Bryan's brother Charles was later nominated for Vice-President. Will could remind readers that he had predicted Davis' nomination. (A visit with Davis on July 1 had convinced him that he was "a political dark horse turning white.")

In one of his articles Will remarked that if Mrs. Davis got into the White House, no titled European visitor would ever embarrass her, since she knew all the rules of etiquette. "She will never tip her Soup plate even if she can't get it all," said Will.

When the results of the presidential election were in, Will wrote that they were "just as big a surprise as the announcement that Xmas was coming in December." Whatever he may have felt about Coolidge's victory, he could rejoice in the return of one of his favorite targets to the White House. The first time Will had mentioned Coolidge in his weekly column was a few weeks after Harding's death, when he discussed Coolidge's "failure" as the new President, enumerating all the problems Coolidge had failed to solve during his several weeks in office: he had not produced rain for the farmers, he had not come out against boll weevils, he had not raised the price of wheat, he had not made France pay its war debt, he had done nothing for capital or labor, and he had not taken a stand on what size baseball bat Babe Ruth should use.

During the next four years there were frequent mentions of Calvin Coolidge in Will's column—most of them sympathetic in tone. It was no accident that Will liked, admired, and was amused by the thirtieth President. Both men came from a plain, rural background, both had a simplicity of expression, a subtle, dry wit, and both frequently employed exaggeration or understatement to make their points.

THE 1924 edition of Ziegfeld's *Follies* was the last one for Will. After eight years he had had enough, and only when Ziegfeld promised that he could quit after the New York run did Will reluctantly agree to join the cast once again. As soon as the show went on the road, as it always did, Will was to leave; but this time Ziegfeld altered his traditional schedule. He kept the show in New York for over a year and held Will to his word, much to the latter's annoyance.

When the show closed he returned to California. Except for the period in 1928-29 when he filled in for his friend Fred Stone in *Three Cheers,* it was Will's last Broadway season.

During this period he made occasional radio appearances, but he was never entirely at ease behind a microphone, especially in a studio with no audience, for many of his best lines were spontaneous, impromptu reactions to the mood of the crowd.

"That little microphone that you are talking into," he wrote, "it's not going to laugh, so you don't know . . . whether to wait for your laugh, or just go right on."

Not long after he finished at the *Follies,* Will began playing to another kind of audience and, according to Betty, he got more satisfaction out of this experience than anything else he did in the 1920s. The idea of becoming a lecturer was proposed to him by Charles L. Wagner, probably the best-known lecture manager in this country at the time. Wagner offered to arrange a tour in which Will—backed up by a male quartet, the de Reszke Singers—would deliver sixty or more lectures between October 1 and November 30, 1925, for a fee of a thousand dollars each plus travel expenses. After December 1 he was to receive fifteen hundred dollars per appearance, which meant that it was possible for him to earn almost the same amount of money in eleven weeks as he had been making for twenty-six weeks' work in the *Follies.* (In 1924 his total earnings had been $157,428, of which $83,000 came from the *Follies;* the rest came from movies and his weekly articles. In 1925 he earned $235,000, of which the lecture tour accounted for $75,000.)

From October 1925 to mid-April of the following year, he gave a hundred and fifty-one lectures—speaking to women's clubs and social groups in theaters, school auditoriums, concert halls, lodge rooms, churches—in places he hadn't seen since the old vaudeville days. If the community had "a railroad and a Town Hall," he promised, "we will be there sooner or later."

Will was having the time of his life. On arrival in a town that was unfamiliar to him he would go to the newspaper office to collect what he called "the dope," material to work into the opening of his lecture. He inquired about traffic problems, the city council, the police force, the bond issue. "What about the mayor?" he would ask. "What's he doin' now?" He would write snippets of information on an old envelope, stuff it into his pocket, and just before going onstage read his notes to be sure he had the names right. Once on, he never looked at them again.

Notes and typewritten sheets, headed Lecture Routine, survive to indicate the type of material Will was using at this time. He had heard that we wanted to raise the guns on our battleships, but were prevented from doing so because of treaty

Will taught his children (from left, Bill, Jim,
and Mary) to ride soon after they learned to walk.
In 1925 he embarked on the first of several
lecture tours (below). Betty frequently went along.

commitments. All we asked, he said, was to be able to point the guns in the general direction of the enemy; the way they were pointing now, if the boat rocked we would shoot ourselves.

He would move on to discuss such topics as New York's subways, rumrunners, college football, and Coolidge. Often there was something of a personal nature to pass along. A congressman had read part of one of Will's articles into the *Congressional Record,* at which another legislator jumped to his feet and objected to the remarks of "a professional joke maker" being included in that august journal. As Will saw it, congressmen were the real comedians. "Every time they make a law it's a joke and every time they make a joke it's a law."

UNLIKE THE TRADITIONAL lecture fare, these performances were so informal and casual that it was virtually impossible for an audience not to warm to Will immediately, and he could play on his listeners the way a talented musician performs on an instrument. "You're doing fine," he would say when they roared with laughter. "We'll get out early tonight. It takes twice as long to get out when you have to explain the jokes." Frequently an audience kept him talking until he was exhausted and sat down on the edge of the stage with his feet hanging into the orchestra pit. He would grin at them and say, "I'm tired. Now, you folks go on out of here and go home—if you've got a home."

A nephew, Bruce Quisenberry, who managed Will's company for three seasons, remembered with a sense of awe his incredible energy. He never seemed to mind the killing pace of his schedule. He never worried, never asked to see the books or requested an accounting, and never disappointed an audience. Once a packed house of Texans kept him talking well past the appointed closing time, with the result that Will and his nephew missed the train they had planned to catch to Wichita, Kansas. He called the station agent to ask if he could hire a private train, and when told it would cost him eleven hundred dollars, said, "Tell 'em to saddle her up." And off they steamed, arriving in time to make the Kansas date. On another occasion he was driving through Arkansas, hurrying to a benefit performance, and came to a little town where twenty or thirty children were standing on the sidewalk holding a sign that read WELCOME

WILL ROGERS. Will told the driver to stop, explaining, "They may have been here all morning"; and although it made him late for the benefit, he got out one of his ropes, and did a few tricks for the children.

IN THE spring of 1926, at the conclusion of his first lecture tour, Will was asked by George Horace Lorimer, editor of the *Saturday Evening Post,* to go to Europe and write a series called "Letters of a Self-Made Diplomat to His President." Will agreed, and at the end of April he and Will, Jr., sailed on the *Leviathan.* In one open letter to Calvin Coolidge, published in the *Post,* Will explained that he had had some difficulty obtaining a passport—a little mixup

Before Will spoke to the Old Trail Drivers' Association in Texas in 1926, a smiling Mrs. R. R. Russell of the Ladies Auxiliary pinned a membership button on him. Her smile faded as Will remarked, tongue in cheek, "You Old Trail Drivers . . . did all right. You'd start out down here with nothing, and after stealing our cattle in the Indian Nation, you'd wind up in Abilene with two thousand head or more." By the time he sat down, Mrs. Russell was steaming. "My husband was no cattle thief," she told Will. "Don't insinuate that he was."

over the fact that he had no birth certificate: "You see, in the early days of the Indian Territory where I was born there was no such things as birth certificates. . . . We generally took it for granted if you were there you must have at some time been born. . . . Having a certificate of being born was like wearing a raincoat in the water over a bathing suit."

In England, as the self-appointed ambassador of the President, he managed to meet nearly everyone of any consequence— including the Prince of Wales, Lady Astor, Sir James M. Barrie, Sir Thomas Lipton, Sir Harry Lauder, and George Bernard Shaw. Then he and young Will were off to Paris by plane, and once he recovered from his initial nervousness about flying he realized that this was the way he wanted to get around from now on. Airplane travel precisely suited his passion to get from one place to another in the quickest possible way. Traveling around the Continent, he visited the preliminary conference on disarmament in Geneva; he met the king of Spain; he had an interview with Mussolini; and he went to Russia, hoping (but failing) to talk with Trotsky.

Perhaps nothing illustrates the man's sheer animal energy so well as his activities during the summer of 1926. Not only did Will take his wife and children on a rigorous sight-seeing trip through Europe (Betty, with Mary and Jim, joined Will and their older son in June), but he found time for a dizzying number of other projects. He was writing articles regularly for the *Post*—enough to make a fair-sized book when they were all complete. The material from his Russian trip became another book—*There's Not a Bathing Suit in Russia.* He returned to London and made a motion picture called *Tip Toes* with Dorothy Gish. He made twelve travelogues, for which he also wrote the humorous lines that appeared on the screen. He played in a musical review produced by Charles Cochran, whom Will called "the British Ziegfeld." He continued to write his regular weekly article for American newspapers. He made a radio appearance. He went to Dublin to play a benefit for the families of victims of a theater fire. And on July 29 he sent a cable to *The New York Times* which resulted in his writing a series of daily telegrams that would continue for the next nine years, making the name of Will Rogers a household word throughout the United States.

What prompted the cablegram was Lady Astor's imminent visit to New York. Will and Betty had lunched with her one day, and after she sailed for the States he wired Adolph Ochs, the publisher of the *Times:* NANCY ASTOR, WHICH IS THE NOM DE PLUME OF LADY ASTOR, IS ARRIVING ON YOUR SIDE ABOUT NOW. PLEASE ASK MY FRIEND JIMMY WALKER TO HAVE NEW YORK TAKE GOOD CARE OF HER. SHE IS THE ONLY ONE OVER HERE WHO DON'T THROW ROCKS AT AMERICAN TOURISTS. YOURS, WILL ROGERS.

Ochs printed the message in a box on the front page of the second section and wired Will, requesting more of the same. So for the rest of his stay in Europe, Will sent the short items to the *Times*. He had no particular thought of going on with the series, but when he returned to the States he discovered that readers were clamoring for more, and he decided to oblige.

The McNaught Syndicate dispatched the daily telegrams under the by-line "Will Rogers Says," and eventually they were featured in more than five hundred newspapers in the United States, reaching forty million readers.

From October 16, 1926, until the day of his death Will filed his telegram every day except Sunday, no matter where he was or what he was doing. Bruce Quisenberry described how they were produced while Will was on a lecture tour: "His newspaper dispatch . . . had to be filed by half past one. He would watch the time, then at the last possible moment, he would put his portable on his knees, stare into space for a few moments, then begin to peck. His hands—so amazingly skillful with a rope—were all thumbs when he tackled a typewriter. *Peck-peck-peck!* Sometimes he would stop, turn up the page and scowl at it for a minute. Then peck-peck-peck! When the telegram was finally ready, I would hop off the train at the first stop and file it. Sometimes I would have to run to catch the train. When I would finally get on he would say, 'I'll bet we lose you some day.'"

Written under every conceivable circumstance, while he was on location for a movie, in a hospital bed, or traveling about the world by steamship, airplane, automobile, or train, this concise expression of Will Rogers' philosophy cheered the American reading public. At the time he began it he was known as a popular comedian; now Americans began to realize that what he had to say was an authentic reflection of what most of them were thinking. Through this medium, more than any other, he emerged as a philosopher as well as a humorist. In the end he became a national institution.

THROUGHOUT THAT SUMMER of 1926, while the family toured Europe, Will gave Americans a view of it unlike anything they had read since Mark Twain's *Innocents Abroad* in 1869. England, he said, "has the best Statesmen and the Rottenest coffee of any Country in the world." In France, he learned, Nice is "pronounced neece. They have no word for nice in French." From Italy he reported that San Francisco bay would make the Bay of Naples look like the Chicago drainage canal. Until he got there he didn't know that "Rome had Senators. Now I know why it declined."

Interspersed with all the open leters to the President were special cablegrams, addressed to CALCOOL WHITEWASHHOUSE, and signed WILLROG, summarizing what Americans thought about Europe. The final cable to CALCOOL ended, BACK HOME AND BROKE. WILLROG. When he landed in New York, Will actually did send the President a telegram and was invited to the White House to make his "report." His summation of the summer's experience was that America "don't stand as good as a Horse Thief" in Europe. "The only way we would be worse with them was to help them out in another war."

When his collection of letters from the *Post* appeared in book form in October 1926, a *New York Times* reviewer commented, "There has rarely been an American humorist whose words produced less empty laughter or more sober thought." And Franklin D. Roosevelt remarked later that "the first time I fully realized Will Rogers' exceptional and deep understanding of political and social problems was when he came home from his European trip in 1926. . . . Will Rogers' analysis of affairs abroad was not only more interesting but proved to be more accurate than any other I had heard."

Will was now forty-seven years old and had entered upon the most productive and creative phase of his life. With the possible exception of films, he had succeeded magnificently at everything he had tried and was known not only in the United States but in most countries of the Western world. The man who used to sign his letters to Betty "Injun Cowboy" had come a long way.

8

"If your time is worth anything, travel by air. If not, you might just as well walk."

THE summer of 1926 was a fair sample of what Will Rogers' life was to be like from then on. As if driven by some inner demon, he was actively pursuing half a dozen careers simultaneously, without pause. Each day was a new adventure, launched with a spur-of-the-moment decision to go somewhere and see something he might otherwise miss. There were no vacations, in the usual sense of the word. "It's always a bird that never does anything that enjoys a vacation," he observed. "There's nothing in the world as hard as playing when you don't want to."

Although some of this bustle can be laid to that old restlessness that had been with him since he was a young boy, the continuous need for material for his newspaper articles also played a part. Never satisfied with secondhand information, he wanted to see things for himself, to talk with the people involved, and whenever the mood took him he hopped an airplane and was off. "I got one little old soft red grip," he said, "that if I just tell it when I am leaving it will pack itself. A few white shirts, a little batch of underwear and sox. All I take is my typewriter and the little red bag, one extra suit in it. It's always packed the same, no matter if I'm going to New York or to Singapore."

In a day when comedians and columnists rely on gag writers and researchers for much of their material, it is difficult to fathom how Will Rogers could have written everything himself, but that is precisely what he did. Much of it was composed hurriedly and carelessly, but it was all his own, and considering the circumstances under which it came to life, the overall quality is astonishingly high. Will's copy was enough to give an editor fits. He never retyped anything, never made a carbon, didn't bother to correct spelling, grammar, or punctuation. Frequently he didn't even read his articles over. "When I write 'em I am through with 'em," he admitted. "I am not being paid reading wages." Yet in the same way that his easy, relaxed manner took the bite out of certain remarks he made about people, the spelling, grammar, and construction of his written work had a curious softening effect.

If ever a man's office could be said to be in his hat, Will's was. Even when he finally did rent space in an office building in Beverly Hills, it was no more than a mail drop. Mrs. Daisy Tyler, a public stenographer hired to help with the daily accumulation of mail, recalled that during the eight years she worked for Will he probably never dictated more than eight replies. She would select the letters she thought would interest him, take them to his home, and on weekends he would type the answers himself, never making a carbon copy. As often as not he would fire off a telegram in response.

On American intervention: *"I don't care how little your country is, you got a right to run it like you want to. When the big nations quit meddling, then the world will have peace."*

WILL's frantic pace in 1926 is suggested by the fact that he set off on his second lecture tour the day after he visited Calvin Coolidge at the White House, following the frenetic summer in Europe. He was enlivening the talks now with fresh material from his travels on the Continent, and his lectures and his daily telegrams reflected an increasingly jaundiced view of the international situation. Wherever he looked, the United States seemed to be interfering in the affairs of other nations: "Our gunboats are all in the Chinese war, our marines have landed in Nicaragua. . . . If Nicaragua would just come out like a man and fight us, we wouldn't have to be hunting away off over in China for a war." He concocted slogans for the Central American adventure. One was "Stop Nicaragua while there is still time."

When he embarked on the lecture circuit Betty returned to California to enroll the two youngest children in school. Will, Jr., the oldest, was sent to Culver Military Academy; there, on his fifteenth birthday, he received a letter written by his father in Spartanburg, South Carolina. Will was planning to be home for Christmas, he said, and would see his son then. Meanwhile he was heading for Oklahoma, a new project in mind. He was going to buy some more land and "fix up the old ranch place."

On Will's part there was more sentiment than business sense involved in this decision. His roots—along with the family and friends he cared for deeply—were there and were never far from his thoughts. "I'm just an old country boy in a Big Town tryin' to get along," he said. "I been eatin' pretty regular, and the reason I have been is because I've stayed an old country boy."

In May 1925 he had made a sad journey to the town of Chelsea for the funeral of his sister Maud Lane, following which he wrote one of his few entirely serious weekly articles. "I am out in Oklahoma, among my People, my Cherokee people, who don't expect a laugh for everything I say. . . . I have just today witnessed a Funeral that for real sorrow and real affection I don't think will ever be surpassed anywhere. They came in every mode of conveyance, on foot, in Buggies, Horseback, Wagons, Cars, and Trains, and there wasn't a Soul that come that she hadn't helped or favored at one time or another. Some uninformed Newspapers printed: 'Mrs. C.L. Lane sister of the famous Comedian, Will Rogers.' . . . It's the other way around. I am the brother of Mrs. C.L. Lane, 'The Friend of Humanity.' And all the honors that I could ever in my wildest dreams hope to reach, would never equal the honor paid on a little western Prairie hilltop, among her people, to Maud Lane. If they will love me like that at the finish, my life will not have been in vain."

They were a close family, the old ties ran deep; and as Will's niece Paula McSpadden Love wrote, the greatest excitement in the lives of relatives in Oklahoma was to hear that Uncle Will was coming home, which he often did when crossing the country. If Betty was with him, she would play the piano after dinner while Will sang the latest musical hits in his high tenor voice. He impersonated other actors, told jokes and stories, and showed the home folks some of his new routines.

What Will liked to do best was to get on a pony and ride around the ranch or rope some goats, then have a plate of beans with ham hocks. He could always get good beans in Oklahoma. His nieces, wrote Irene McSpadden Milam, were taught "to cook navy beans as he liked them, with plenty of soup. Then there would be ham, hickory smoked, cured just the same as it was on the old ranch, and cream gravy with hot biscuits." And in the springtime there would be tiny wild onions, scrambled with eggs.

Yet as much as he loved Oklahoma, the homeplace, and the informality of life there, his commitments and interests simply would not permit him to return to the ranch near Oologah for any extended period. As a substitute for what he felt he was missing, he began turning over in his mind the possiblity of selling the Beverly Hills house and building on land he had acquired in the Santa Monica Mountains.

That was easier said than done. Just before Christmas of 1926 the daily telegram began to be signed Hon. Will Rogers. On December 21, when he returned home for the holidays, the residents of Beverly Hills turned out en masse—movie actors, a corps of motorcycle police, two brass bands, and people carrying banners—to see Will presented with a five-foot scroll honoring him as mayor. "They say I'll be a comedy mayor," he said in his acceptance speech. "Well, I never saw a mayor yet that wasn't comical. As to my administration, I won't say I'll be exactly honest, but I'll agree to split fifty-fifty with you and give the town an even break. I'm for the common people, and as Beverly Hills has no common people I won't have to pass out any favors."

Fortunately for Will's other interests, the mayoral term was brief. According to California law, in sixth-class cities like Beverly Hills the president of the board of trustees was constitutionally the mayor, so Mayor Rogers was deposed. "I ain't the first mayor that's been kicked out," he wrote. "If I'd knowed Beverly Hills was a sixth-class town I wouldn't made the race."

He began to concentrate with a vengeance on the Santa Monica place. He had purchased a hundred and fifty acres, which he eventually increased to three hundred—nothing to compare in size with the Oklahoma property, but he referred to it as a ranch. ("It sounds big and dont really do any harm.") There were no paved roads in the vicinity, the land was brushy and steep, laced with canyons, and the only open space in the sea of greasewood and sagebrush was a small clearing made by a truck gardener. This lay on a mesa that was accessible only by means of a virtually impassable road, but the view was worth all the trouble of reaching it—in those days before smog one could see off in the distance Santa Monica Bay, the Pacific Ocean, and Catalina Island.

After 1919 the family made California home. In 1926
his Beverly Hills neighbors appointed Will mayor, though
by law the head of the board of trustees automatically
held that office. Will "resigned" gracefully.

Things started to hum: Will hired men to clear away the brush
and build a corral and stables; then the ground was leveled for a
polo field. He had been introduced to polo years earlier, while
the family was living on Long Island. He taught all three children the game, and the four Rogerses made a family team until,
as Will said sadly, "Mary went social on us."

IN THE SPRING OF 1927, during his lecture tour, one of the worst
floods in history laid waste the Mississippi Valley. Hundreds
were dead, hundreds of thousands were homeless, the damage
ran into millions of dollars; but the federal government showed
a curious reluctance to do anything. The Coolidge administration was convinced that private relief agencies could handle the
immense task of feeding and clothing the destitute. Will
thought otherwise; the Red Cross was appealing for five million

dollars, but almost a million people had been victimized. "That would be only five dollars a head," Will said. "Five dollars ain't much good to you, even if the water's just up to your ankles."

In daily and weekly articles he plugged away at the need for assistance and donations. "Look at the thousands and thousands of Negroes that never did have much, but now its washed away," he wrote. "That water is just as high up on them as it is if they were white. The Lord so constituted everybody that no matter what color you are you require about the same amount of nourishment." He wired Florenz Ziegfeld to say that he would put on a benefit for flood victims if Ziegfeld would donate the theater, and Will and the tenor John McCormack raised nearly eighteen thousand dollars for the Red Cross. Another performance in New Orleans produced forty-eight thousand, and Will kept hammering away at his readers to open their pocketbooks.

ON MAY 21, 1927, the daily telegram expressed what was on the mind of every American. "No attempt at jokes today," it read. "An old slim, tall, bashful, smiling American boy is somewhere out over the middle of the Atlantic ocean, where no lone human being has ever ventured before." From that day on Will was one of Charles A. Lindbergh's most ardent fans. Almost half a century after the event, it is difficult to describe the worldwide outpouring of joy, excitement, and admiration that resulted from Lindbergh's twenty-seven-hour solo flight from New York to Paris in *The Spirit of St. Louis*. What somehow caught people's imagination was the American's exceptional integrity and courage, his indifference to the usual hallmarks of success. Lindbergh, Will Rogers said, was our biggest national asset and ought to be allowed to spend his time promoting aviation instead of making an "exhibition out of himself"—a message few Americans would heed. The flier not only fulfilled Will's concept of a hero, he was also a member of a fraternity Will had come to admire enormously: the barnstorming pilots of the twenties.

After World War I aviation had fallen on evil days in the United States. There was almost no demand for planes, military airfields were deactivated, and only a few adventurous young men and women would have any part of flying. They piloted surplus DH-4s and Curtiss Jennies, hopping from county fair to carnival to give exhibitions of wing walking, stunting, and parachute jumping. For a time they were very nearly the only non-military aviators around.

In Europe, by contrast, commercial aviation had prospered. One reason for this was that European governments were subsidizing commercial airlines, while the U.S. government avoided anything that smacked of federal control over private enterprise. What changed this attitude was the Post Office Department's disastrous experience in flying the mail.

After establishing airmail service from Washington to New York, it made plans for a route from New York to Chicago, but almost at once the hazards of crossing the Allegheny Mountains proved too much. Because of prevalent storms, the absence of navigational equipment, and the use of inferior, open-cockpit, rebuilt warplanes, thirty-two of the first forty pilots hired by the Post Office were killed before the operation was turned over to commercial fliers. Though in 1925 Congress finally passed legislation encouraging commercial aviation, there remained more profit in carrying mail, and few airlines were interested in attracting passengers. Only after 1926, when the landmark Air Commerce Act was passed, did the new Bureau of Aeronautics begin licensing American planes and pilots and setting up standards for aircraft, landing fields, and navigational aids. So it was little wonder that Will's was a lonely voice advocating public acceptance of flying.

IN 1927 WILL BEGAN TAKING planes whenever and wherever he could. Not that air travel was easy to arrange in those days. The only way he could fly to some out-of-the-way places was on a small commercial plane carrying the U.S. mail. His son Will, Jr., remembers that his father would come into his bedroom at the Beverly Hills house at two a.m. and shake him awake. "Come on, boy. Get up. I got to go to the airport," he would say, and they would drive through the darkness to a landing field on the edge of Los Angeles.

There Will would pull on a fleece-lined leather flying suit, a helmet, and goggles, and then get on the scales. "They didn't put stamps on him," Bill says, "but he paid for his own weight as if he were a package." As soon as Will climbed into the forward cockpit of the open plane, the ground crew would pile sacks of mail around him and on top of him. Usually it was still dark when the plane taxied onto the runway and warmed up at the end of the field; then it would roar down the strip, and young Bill, driving home, would see it climb into the dawn sky.

Will flew with most of the outstanding aviators of the time, and although he occasionally made a pretense of concern, it was clear that he had little, if any, fear of flying. Captain Frank Hawks said Will "never paid any attention to the weather or the flying procedure while he was in the air. He read most of the time. . . . He placed all his confidence in me, figured that I knew my business, and would always get him to his destination." Flying was simply one of his great enthusiasms, and he never lost his love for it.

HE WOULD be in several plane crashes; but in the early summer of 1927 Will had his first close brush with death, and it had nothing to do with airplanes. He was in Bluefield, West Virginia, lecturing, when he began to suffer intensely from what he said was nothing more than a bellyache. He had a recurrence of the symptoms a few weeks later, while visiting the ranch in Oklahoma, and when he arrived in Beverly Hills, Betty called in the family physician, Dr. Percy White, who diagnosed the problem as gallstones and advised that a specialist be consulted. As Will told the story, the doctor then "phoned for what seemed like a friend, but who afterwards turned out to be an accomplice." This man, a surgeon named Dr. Clarence Moore, advised an operation. ("Imagine asking a surgeon what he advises!" Will commented. "It would be like asking Coolidge, 'Do you advise economy?' ")

Although Will was seriously ill following the operation, he managed not to miss a single one of his daily columns (he wrote no weekly article, however, between June 19 and July 17); just before he was wheeled away to the operating room he dictated the daily wire: "I am in the California Hospital, where they are going to relieve me of surplus gall, much to the politicians' delight." On Sundays his wire did not appear, so he could skip

Saturday, but on the next day he dictated his Monday message, just six words long: "Relax—lie perfectly still, just relax."

While he was still hospitalized, hundreds of telegrams poured in from well-wishers, including Coolidge, and as Will remarked, "People couldn't have been any nicer to me if I had died."

With an uncanny ability to put experience to good use, Will not only wrote about the operation in his daily and weekly articles, but published several stories about it in the *Saturday Evening Post.* These were brought out later as a book, *Ether and Me: or, Just Relax.*

Back on his feet again, he began shooting what was to be his last silent film, *The Texas Steer,* in which he played the part of a Texas rancher who was elected to Congress. When the company arrived in Washington, D.C., to film some political scenes against the backdrop of the Capitol, the National Press Club gave him a reception and appointed him "congressman-at-large for the United States of America." Will was pleased, but said it was "the poorest appointment I ever got. I certainly regret the disgrace that's been thrust on me here tonight. I . . . have lived, or tried to live my life so that I would never become a Congressman."

While the Press Club's title was bestowed in fun, the next one Will received was intended seriously. He was invited to become the nation's "unofficial ambassador to Mexico."

9

"I'd rather be right than Republican."

RELATIONS between the United States and Mexico had never been serene. Following the war between the two countries in the 1840s, the United States had acquired from Mexico the territory that now comprises Arizona, Nevada, California, and Utah, parts of New Mexico, Colorado, and Wyoming, as well as its claims to Texas north of the Rio Grande. Mexicans had neither forgotten nor forgiven. In 1927 President Coolidge named his Amherst College classmate Dwight Morrow, a partner in J.P. Morgan & Co., as ambassador to Mexico. There were those—including Will Rogers and a good many Mexicans—who looked on the appointment as a mixed blessing.

Will had a genuine affection and sympathy for the Mexicans,

many of whom he had met in roping contests and rodeos, and he had decided views about the U.S. policy toward their country. "Up to now," he said, "our calling card to Mexico or Central America had been a gunboat or a bunch of Violets shaped like Marines." Mexico had her problems, he concluded, "and we are most of them."

Shortly after Ambassador Morrow arrived at his post he had an inspiration: to invite Will Rogers and Charles A. Lindbergh to visit the country on a goodwill mission. Already, Morrow had gotten off on the right foot with the Mexican man in the street by touring the country for several weeks with the popular President, Plutarco Calles. Will joined the two men aboard the heavily guarded presidential train.

On the second day of the trip he was late for dinner, and a member of Calles' party who found Will talking with the troops suggested that it was impolitic to keep Calles waiting. "You tell him," Will said, "that I've been in Mexico only a few days and I have found out that it's better down here to stand in right with the soldiers than with the President." Fortunately, Calles' interpreter was an American named Jim Smithers, who had a gift for reproducing Will's comments in Spanish. And Will's candor endeared him immediately to Calles, as did his love of close-harmony singing, which he and Morrow performed to the accompaniment of the president's guitar. He attended a bullfight, and to the amusement of the crowd buried his head in his arms to avoid seeing horses gored by the bull. He played polo, flew over the volcano Popocatepetl (he called it Popocatepillar), and was guest of honor at a banquet given by Morrow and attended by President Calles.

As a contribution to the goodwill mission, Lindbergh had agreed to fly nonstop from Washington to Mexico City, but lost his way somewhere over Mexico. Two hundred thousand people, including President Calles and his cabinet, waited patiently for eight hours and then gave him as tumultuous a welcome as he had received in Paris. As Will described it, "the streets were two inches thick with flowers." He and Morrow were resigning as ambassadors, he said; Lindbergh was taking over.

Seemingly the only person in the country who didn't care about seeing the aviator was Dwight Morrow's twenty-year-old daughter Anne, who had just arrived for the Christmas holidays and considered Lindbergh no more than a newspaper hero—of the baseball-player type. She was certainly not going to worship Lindy ("that *odious* name," she called it); but when she met him at the embassy she found him much more poised than she had expected, and quite unlike the grinning Lindy pictures she had seen. A year later she was writing to a friend to say, "Apparently I am going to marry Charles Lindbergh."

On bankers: *"{Bankers} are likeable rascals, and now that we are all wise to 'em, and it's been shown that they don't know any more about finances than the rest of us know about our businesses . . . why they are getting just as human as the groceryman, the druggist or the filling station man."*

Mrs. Morrow worried about the effect Lindbergh's arrival might have on Will Rogers' popularity, but speaking at a dinner that very evening, "he held the whole room in the hollow of his hand," she recalled. Like audiences everywhere, when the Mexicans were exposed to the typical Will Rogers performance they loved it. "I dident come here to tell you that we look on you as Brothers," he said. "We look on you as a lot of Bandits and you look on us as one Big Bandit."

He also offered some views on diplomacy: "A Diplomat is a man that tells you what he don't believe himself, and the man that he is telling it to don't believe it any more than he does. So Diplomacy . . . always balances." Morrow, he said, was different; he recognized that the only way for people to get along was to be honest with each other and get to understand one another. "He knows we don't hate you and that you don't hate us."

From the point of view of relations between Mexico and the United States, Will's visit was a triumph, and he carried away a lasting attachment for Ambassador Morrow, whom he described as "Wall Street's sole contribution to public life."

The meetings with Lindbergh in Mexico served only to whet Will's appetite for flying. Sometime before, he and Betty had flown with Lindbergh to California, with Will in the copilot's seat, asking innumerable questions. "How can you tell where to land when when you don't know which way the wind is blowing?"

Lindbergh pointed to a clothesline on which laundry was flapping in the breeze. "That tells me," he said.

"Suppose it ain't Monday?" Will asked.

"I just wait till it is," Lindbergh responded.

Will flew part of the way home from Mexico to be with his family for Christmas, and on December 29 he was in the air again, this time courtesy of the U.S. Navy, in a plane catapulted from the battleship *Pennsylvania*. "Just watch your head," he advised, "and see that you don't leave it behind you." And to President Coolidge he said, "Keep after this air stuff, Calvin. Let's get all the planes we can, do all the commercial aviation we can to keep the boys in training."

THE YEAR 1928 WAS ANOTHER presidential election year, and politics, naturally, was beginning to dominate the news. The Democrats' Jackson Day dinner in Washington, D.C., brought to Will's mind all that the Cherokees had suffered at Old Hickory's hands, and he remarked, "I am not so sweet on old Andy. He is the one that run us Cherokees out of Georgia and North Carolina. I ate the dinner on him, but I didn't enjoy it. I thought I was eating for Stonewall."

He began another lecture tour, and both his talks and his newspaper columns emphasized his growing concern about the nation's economic health. What he said came across in the good-humored Rogers style, but there was no mistaking his worry over the situation. His trips around the country had convinced him that the good times Americans were enjoying were only on the surface. The attitude of most people was, "We'll show the world we are prosperous, even if we have to go broke to do it."

Two weeks before the Republican National Convention, Will made his own debut as a presidential candidate. The popular magazine *Life* announced that it was sponsoring a new political movement, the Anti-Bunk Party, with Will Rogers as its nominee. In the same issue Will stated that his acceptance was based on one pledge: "If elected I absolutely and positively agree to resign [and] that's offering the Country more than any Candidate ever offered it in the history of its entire existence." From then until the election in November, the opening editorial pages of the magazine were devoted to Will's "campaign."

No Anti-Bunk candidate for the vice-presidency was chosen. As for a platform, the candidate promised that "whatever the other fellow don't do, we will." There were no commitments: "We want the wet vote, and we want the dry vote. We are honest about it." There would be no party leaders; no slogans ("slogans have been more harmful to the country than Luncheon Clubs, Sand Fleas, Detours and Conventions"); no "baby kissing, passing out of cigars, laying cornerstones, dodging issues."

While the voters were absorbing all this, Will was en route to Kansas City, where the Republicans were gathering. After Herbert Hoover was nominated for President, Will was tickled to see that Charles Curtis was picked for the second spot on the ticket. Curtis' mother had Kaw Indian blood, and thus he was "the only American that has ever run for that high office. Come on Injun," Will pleaded, "if you are elected let's run the white people out of this country."

Will was in Houston, Texas, at the end of June for the Democratic convention. He listened to Franklin Roosevelt, who at the 1924 convention had nominated Governor Alfred E. Smith of New York, "do his act from memory. Franklin Roosevelt could have gotten far in the Democratic party himself. But he has this act all perfected, and dont like to go to the trouble of learning something else. So he just seems satisfied going through life nominating Al Smith."

When it was all over, he considered that the party had nominated its best possible ticket: Governor Smith and Senator Joseph Robinson of Arkansas. One of the principal issues was Smith's Catholicism, and Will had something to say about that: "What do we care about a . . . Presidents religion. They dont do any business on Sunday anyway. Its week days we want to use him. Its one relief to find somebody mentioned for President who we do know what their religion is before they get in. There is not 2 out of 10 that can tell me what religion Coolidge is."

He liked and admired both presidential candidates, but he was disturbed during the campaign by the way the two parties tried to influence voters on the issue of prosperity. "How a speaker can convince a man that he is prosperous when he is broke, or that he is not prosperous when he is doing well, is beyond me. If a voter can't feel in his pockets and see if he is doing well without having some total stranger tell him, then his Government shouldn't be in the hands of the people."

As the campaign drew to a close, Will was disgusted with the whole thing. He predicted that Hoover was a shoo-in—had been, in fact, since the GOP convention in June. Smith's problem was that he was a Democrat.

The day after Hoover's election Will's daily telegram appeared in the form of a want ad. FOR SALE, it read, WOULD LIKE TO SELL, TRADE, DISPOSE OF OR GIVE AWAY FRANCHISE OF WHAT IS HUMOROUSLY KNOWN AS DEMOCRATIC PARTY. As the year came to a close he was depressed by the state of the Democratic Party, but more so by the state of the nation. In an unusually bittersweet column that is Will Rogers at his best, he told his readers why:

> The nation never looked like it was facing a worse Winter—birds, geese, Democrats and all perishable animals are already huddled up in three or four States down South. We are at peace with the world because the world is waiting to get another gun and get it loaded. Wall Street is in good shape, but Eighth Avenue never was as bad off. The farmers are going into the Winter with pretty good radios, but not much feed for their stock.
>
> Yours,
Will Rogers

IN THE summer of 1928 Will had come to the aid of an old friend in his typically generous way. The actor Fred Stone had learned to fly, and he was critically injured when his plane crashed. Stone was to open on Broadway that fall with his daughter, Dorothy, in a musical called *Three Cheers*. The show was already in rehearsal, the opening date was set, costumes and sets were made. When Will heard about the problem he immediately wired his friend to say that he would go into the show in Fred's place, "just to sort of plug along till you are able to rejoin, and I will do the best I can with the part." Will didn't even want any billing, though he would have to cancel his lecture tour at some financial sacrifice.

Will had only two weeks of rehearsals before the opening, but it didn't seem to matter. *Three Cheers* opened on October 25 and was an immediate smash hit. Will, of course, was playing himself—not the part written for Fred Stone. He simply used the part as a vehicle for the kind of routine he had done in the *Follies* for years—commenting on the news in the latest editions of the papers. One critic suggested that what was unique about Will was a public platform manner that made it possible for him to talk to an audience privately and confidentially. "Even before he opens his mouth to speak, the barrier of the footlights is down and we are in the same room with him."

This was to be Will's final Broadway performance. After a successful New York run, *Three Cheers* went on the road in April, 1929, and closed in Pittsburgh on June 1. The following day Will flew to California to launch another career: playing in talking pictures.

THOMAS EDISON had originally planned to combine his Kinetoscope with a phonograph to produce a moving picture with sound accompaniment. He lost interest in the scheme, but other inventors did not. Lee De Forest, originator of the triode or three-terminal tube that had made long-distance broadcasting feasible, synchronized sound and moving images on film, and his first "phonofilms" were shown in New York in 1923, but without causing much of a stir. Hollywood displayed no particular enthusiasm for talking pictures until 1926, when William Fox brought out something called a Movietone, and the nearly bankrupt Warner Brothers company agreed to take on the vitaphone produced by a subsidiary of the Western Electric Company.

The first sound films were shorts, but in 1927 the Warners produced the first feature with dialogue and music: *The Jazz Singer,* starring Al Jolson. It was an immediate and stunning success, and the rest of Hollywood realized that the old silent days were gone for good (only Charlie Chaplin held out into the thirties). Like all revolutions, this one left a cluster of pathetic derelicts in its wake—those once-popular stars who were not suited to the new medium. Pola Negri and Clara Bow, the "It" girl, disappeared, and John Gilbert, the great lover of the silent screen whose high-pitched voice was incongruous in the roles he played, was doomed to oblivion.

But to Will Rogers talkies were quite another matter. He had

Unlike many silent-movie stars, Will adapted easily to talkies, which he called "noisies." These are stills from his Hollywood years.

With Mickey Rooney in
The County Chairman

With Shirley Temple, another top box-office attraction

never been as successful in silent pictures as on the stage or the lecture platform, simply because his act was so dependent on what he had to say and the way he said it. When he went into talking pictures he had something else going for him, too—a personality already familiar to millions of Americans.

From the beginning, Will took a relaxed, amused view of what he called the "noisies." Yet when his first one, *They Had to See Paris,* opened in September 1929 he felt the old nervousness and lack of assurance that accompanied each new venture he attempted. As the time approached for the picture's preview, Will became increasingly apprehensive, and finally he announced to startled studio executives that he had to go to Oklahoma and would not attend. Not until a few days later was his mind set at ease; in Tulsa he received a telegram from Betty reporting that the picture had opened and he could come home.

The talkies he made ran to a pattern. He usually played a thinly disguised version of himself: a rustic, somewhat seedy

With Myrna Loy in
A Connecticut Yankee

On the set of
Down to Earth

common man, an underdog speaking out against wealthy, unscrupulous characters. He was the kindly, impractical philosopher, a sort of surrogate for the American conscience, reflecting the innate honesty and idealism of the plain folks of the land. To see any of Will's pictures—*A Connecticut Yankee, David Harum, The County Chairman, State Fair, Life Begins at Forty, Steamboat 'Round the Bend*—is to be transported suddenly into another world, a world that was gentle, kind, and thoroughly predictable, where the simple virtues and homely truths were opposed by easily discernible villainy, and where good would always triumph at the end. They were pictures that children wanted to see, and that their parents wanted them to see; in some towns school was dismissed so that students could attend special matinee performances of a Will Rogers film.

Will was a thoroughly untypical Hollywood star. Although a considerable portion of his income came from making movies, he never quite took it seriously, and it never became more than

359

a sideline as far as he was concerned. Yet every tourist who visited Hollywood wanted to see him, and he was continually badgered at the studio by people who dropped by to meet him.

Despite his growing fame, his dress remained as casual as his personality—as often as not he wore blue jeans and boots and a small cowboy Stetson or well-traveled felt hat. He drove his own car to the studio, the back seat filled with the paraphernalia of his trade: portable typewriter, a stack of newspapers, telegraph blanks, ropes, some old clothes, and an extra pair of boots. When he arrived, it was evident that he was the most popular person on the lot; everyone said good-morning to Will Rogers.

Will's approach to making a picture never failed to astound old hands in the business. The night before shooting was to begin he would take the script home and read it through, just to get the gist of it, and the next morning would appear on the set with no idea whatsoever of his lines. Oblivious to all the hectic activity around him, he would slouch in a canvas chair, eyeglasses down on his nose, reading the morning papers. When called to play a scene he would ask the script girl to read what he was supposed to say and that, as often as not, would remind him of a story which he would proceed to tell while the director and other players waited.

At last they would begin, and those actors who were unused to playing opposite Will Rogers suddenly realized what it meant. Most of them, Joel McCrea remembers, were scared to death, because no one knew for certain what he would say or how long he might talk. As one of Will's cameramen described an actor's dilemma, "He waits for a certain cue in a speech. The cue doesn't come. For Will ad-libs his lines. . . . It isn't because he's too lazy to learn them; it's because each time he rehearses a scene he thinks of a better way of delivering a speech."

At the end of the morning's shooting, Will would call out "Lunchee! Lunchee!" and head for the studio cafeteria trailed by the cast and crew, who knew they would be entertained by a running barrage of jokes throughout the meal. Afterward he would walk out to his car, climb in, and thumb through the newspapers again, marking items that interested him with the stub of an old pencil. When he had what he wanted, he would put the typewriter on his lap and sit with his feet on the running board, pecking away at the daily article. Frequently he read the finished copy to the studio crew, and if they didn't get what he was trying to say he would change it. Then he would send it by messenger to the telegraph office. Afterward, to the director's dismay, he might disappear to the car again for a nap.

Will seemed to have none of the usual professional jealousy about scene-stealing. In fact, he made a point of seeing that minor or bit players got more of a part than the director had planned for them. Bill Robinson, the great Negro dancer, recalled that Will "put me in fifteen or sixteen scenes in [a] picture that I wasn't written in for. . . . He wouldn't let them hide my face."

Romantic parts were not for Will. As he once told a scriptwriter, "Hollywood park benches are filled with ex-actors who didn't know they were too old to make love." But something else—an innate modesty and sense of propriety—kept him from playing love scenes. In one film the script called for him to kiss his wife, played by Irene Rich, but Will kept putting off the scene. Finally the director took Miss Rich aside and told her to give Will a kiss when the time came, and she did, taking him completely by surprise. Embarrassed, he grinned sheepishly, and said, "I feel as if I'd been unfaithful to my wife."

Although he was completely natural on the movie set, never using makeup, never seeming to act when he was before the camera, there was something about him that baffled those who thought they knew him well. Whenever people were around he was the Will Rogers of the stage—easygoing, wisecracking, friendly with everybody, seemingly a wholly uncomplicated person. But beneath the surface, one scriptwriter said, the private man was "vastly reserved; there was a wall that no one went beyond; and there were dark chambers and hidden recesses that he opened to no one." Spencer Tracy said Will was "at the same time one of the best-known, and one of the least-known, men in the world. By inclination, he is a grand mixer; by instinct, he is as retiring as a hermit."

Frank Borzage, a director who worked with Will on several movies, claimed that it was his ability to make audiences forget that he was a comedian from time to time that made him so

Though the Fox studio provided him with an ornate Spanish bungalow as a dressing room, Will preferred relaxing—or writing his column—in his car.

popular. He was capable of portraying simple, human emotions with sincerity and conviction, and people seeing his films realized that he was more than a comic who cracked jokes. He was basically a man of many causes, and the humor which came so naturally to him was the most effective means of getting a message across to people, whether he was putting ideas on paper or acting them out in motion pictures.

According to a chart of the top ten box-office stars compiled by *Motion Picture Herald,* Will was in ninth place in 1932. In 1933 he was second (behind Marie Dressler); in 1934 he reached the top of the ratings; and in 1935—the year of his death—he was in second place behind the sensationally popular child star, Shirley Temple. At the outset he received $110,000 for each picture he made, and he averaged three a year. In 1930 he signed a new contract with the Fox Film Corporation calling for payment of $1,125,000 for six pictures, or nearly $200,000 each.

He thoroughly enjoyed making a picture, and there were few dull moments when he was around. During the filming of *State Fair,* the plot of which centered around a prize boar, the film company bought Iowa's grand champion boar to use in the movie. Known as Blue Boy, it was a mountainous creature with huge tusks and a vile disposition, and when it arrived the director, Henry King, cautioned Will to keep away from it.

The first time a scene was to be shot with Blue Boy, King sent for Will, but he was nowhere to be seen. King and the other actors found him stretched out on the ground beside the sleeping Blue Boy, head pillowed on the hog's side and hat over his eyes, apparently sleeping. What Will knew and King did not was that as long as he didn't disturb the animal he was quite safe. As soon as he saw King's horrified reaction to the gag and had his laugh, he got to his feet and climbed out of the pen.

When the picture was finished, Will was asked if he would like to buy Blue Boy, as meat for the family. Will declined. "I wouldn't feel right eatin' a fellow actor."

10

"We are continually buying something that we never get, from a man that never had it."

In the fall of 1929 Will was invited to Detroit to speak at a celebration honoring the inventor Thomas Edison, who was nearing the end of his long, productive life. Henry Ford had built a museum devoted to the history of industry and invention—about a third of it memorializing Edison's achievements—and decided to combine the dedication of his Dearborn Village with a commemoration of the fiftieth anniversary of the lighting of Edison's first electric lamp. To this grand occasion he summoned the nation's most eminent figures, including President Hoover, a number of prominent businessmen and financiers, Orville Wright, and his friend Will Rogers.

Will had a good time at the Edison affair. The inventor, he remarked, "had no idea when he invented that all-day lantern that it would lead to so much glory and confusion. He just invented it because he needed it to work by," and Ford had honored him because another of Edison's inventions had enabled people to start a Model T car without breaking an arm cranking it. There were so many wealthy industrialists present, Will said, that every time he spilled some coffee out of his saucer, it landed on a millionaire—John D. Rockefeller, Jr., numerous railraod presidents and automobile executives, Julius Rosenwald, the head of Sears, Roebuck, and others.

Those big men had something rather more pressing than the good old days on their minds in the autumn of 1929, however, for the economic storm cloud was directly overhead now and threatening to burst. Since the armistice, unprecedented changes had shaken the nation's economic structure. Merger after merger had taken place, and the holding company, which Will described as "a thing where you hand an accomplice the goods while the policeman searches you," was now the accepted means of assembling a complex pyramid of stockholdings. By 1929 fifteen companies controlled ninety percent of all the power produced in the country; U.S. Steel owned more than half the nation's iron-ore deposits; the Aluminum Company of America was a virtual monopoly.

Yet statistics and statements by men in the know assured Americans that this was for the nation's good. Between 1923 and 1926 trading on the New York Stock Exchange had doubled, while the average price of twenty-five representative stocks was up fifty-four percent. There seemed no limit to the money that could be made in the right securities. The radio industry, for one, was clearly here to stay, and Radio Corporation of America rode the heady tide. The stock's low in 1928 was 85½; the next year it reached 549. Everyone in New York talked stock prices. Bootblacks and barbers, shoe clerks and cabbies—all had a tip to pass on. As Will put it, "There had never been a time in our history when as many fools are making money as now."

Inauguration Day—March 4, 1929—produced a confident message from the new President, Herbert Hoover: "I have no fears about the future of our country. It is bright with hope." Like Coolidge, he opposed government controls and meddling in the stock market, and the speculative spiral went on unabated. Despite temporary lapses, the listed value of stocks more than doubled during the six-month period between March 3 and September 3, 1929. But what no one at the time realized was that that final day, Tuesday, September 3, was the dying effort of the great bull market.

On September 5 came unwelcome news. The economist Roger Babson, speaking to the National Business Conference, stated flatly, "Sooner or later a crash is coming, and it may be terrific." This was the signal for the so-called Babson break in the market, and from then on the trend was down.

BABSON was by no means the only prophet of doom. According to a biographer of Calvin Coolidge, when someone pressed Grace Coolidge to explain her husband's reason for not "choosing" to run for reelection, she replied simply, "Poppa says there's a depression coming." Others saw portents in the continuing agricultural woes, with farm surpluses growing while prices went steadily down. There were waves of labor unrest, an increasing number of bank failures, exposures of cruelly low wages. (Congressional investigators heard in 1929 from a fourteen-year-old girl who received $4.95 a week for sixty hours' work in a Southern textile mill.) The thing was there, if anyone cared to heed the warning signs.

Yet on October 17, while the industrialists were on their way to Dearborn to honor Edison, there were some optimists. The political economist Irving Fisher of Yale asserted that the market was on a permanent high plateau. Less than a week later the president of New York's National City Bank said there was "nothing fundamentally wrong with the stock market or with the underlying business and credit structure" of the country. That remark preceded by just two days the landmark known forever after as Black Thursday, when the whole house of cards collapsed. Despite efforts of New York's most highly placed bankers to stem the tide, an angry, half-hysterical crowd of brokers on the floor of the exchange fought to unload their stocks before it was too late. On that day thirteen million shares were sold, and the ticker was four hours late at closing time. The following Monday was even worse: in a single day the value of stocks plummeted fourteen billion dollars, and no bottom was in sight.

Will was in New York City on Black Thursday, or "wailing day," as he called it, when "you had to stand in line to get a window to jump out of." The following Saturday he was in Oklahoma, musing about the contrast between the canyons of Wall Street and the lovely, pastoral countryside he had just flown over. "Why, an old sow and a litter of pigs make more people a living than all the steel and General Motors stock combined." A few days later, back in California, he was more rueful. What irked him was the talk about how Rockefeller and other financiers were "stabilizing" the market: "Sure must be a great consolation to the poor people who lost their stock in the late crash to know that it has fallen in the hands of Mr. Rockefeller, who will . . . see that it has a good home. . . . There is one rule that works in every calamity," he added: "Be it pestilence, war or famine, the rich get richer and the poor get poorer."

Toward the close of the year he tried to sum up what had gone wrong. People had been carried away by the fever of speculation, he wrote, and they had to get over the idea that they could live by gambling: "Somebody had to do some work."

What he neglected to say was that Wall Street was not so much a cause as a symptom of a far more serious and widespread disorder. And it is doubtful whether Will Rogers was fully aware just then how grave conditions in the country really were.

This is not to suggest that he was insensitive to the plight of most Americans—far from it, as his tireless efforts to help the unfortunate during the next few years were to demonstrate. But as 1929 drew to a close it must have been almost impossible for a man of his circumstances to comprehend the difficulties facing millions of his fellow countrymen. In 1929 the average family income was about $2300; three years later it would fall to $1600 or less. At the same period Will's annual income from movies, radio, and other appearances, and daily and weekly columns exceeded $500,000. He had never invested in the stock market. He had substantial capital in land, endowment policies totaling $200,000, nearly $500,000 in life insurance, plus annuities and U.S. bonds.

In 1930, when he signed a $72,000 contract for fourteen radio talks, there was criticism over the fact that he was being paid the unprecedented fee of $350 a minute to tell jokes. It was not generally known that he donated the money to charity.

IN 1930 THE Depression gnawed at the vitals of American society—on farms, in factories, small enterprises, and enormous industrial concerns. That year nearly four and a half million people were unemployed as compared with one and a half million in 1929. The figure would rise to eight million in 1931, twelve million in 1932, and thirteen million in 1933.

No one seemed to know what to do. The government in Washington did not fully comprehend the extent or the nature of the disaster. Hoover had no answers for the jobless, who were lining up outside soup kitchens waiting for something to eat; he approved an appropriation of forty-five million dollars to feed cattle affected by the 1930 drought while opposing the expenditure of twenty-five million to feed farm families. The latter, he believed, were the responsibilities of local governments or the Red Cross. He was convinced that the Depression was merely a passing interlude in the nation's life.

Drought seared the farm country. In a bountiful land breadlines were everywhere. During the second winter of the Depression, after five hundred farmers marched up to a country store in the little town of England, Arkansas, and demanded food for their wives and children, the Senate appropriated fifteen million dollars for food, but the House turned it down. A week later the same legislators voted the same amount of money to improve entrances to the national parks, and Will regarded it as a clear indication that "You can get a road anywhere you want to out of the government, but you can't get a sandwich." In two years, he supposed, there wouldn't be a poor farm that didn't have a concrete highway leading to it.

In January 1931 Will met with the President, exploring Mr. Hoover's proposal that the Red Cross should meet the crisis.

Dubious of that approach ("I don't think we have anybody in Washington that don't want to feed 'em, but they all want to feed 'em their way"), Will determined nevertheless to help raise funds for the Red Cross.

He set out on a trip across the country to see at first hand the farm communities most seriously affected by drought. "You don't know what hard times are till you go into some of these houses," he wrote. Later in the month he embarked on a charity tour for the benefit of the Red Cross, flying in a navy plane piloted by Frank Hawks, giving performances in several towns each day, paying all the expenses for himself and whatever additional talent he could scrape up, and adding his personal check to the contributions received. In eighteen days he visited fifty cities or small towns in Texas, Oklahoma, and Arkansas, raising $225,000 in cash, plus an additional amount in pledges.

On manners: *"Manners are nothing more than common sense, and a person has no more right to try and get every drop of soup out of his plate than he has to take a piece of bread and try and harvest all the Gravy in his plate. You must remember . . . that the question of the World today is, not how to eat soup, but how to get soup to eat."*

His only requests were that every cent of the proceeds go to the needy, to be divided equally between those in urban and rural areas, and that a portion of the $90,00 he had raised in Oklahoma be set aside specifically for the relief of Cherokee Indians.

The effects of Will's whirlwind tour went far beyond the money he raised. Suddenly people became aware that at least one prominent man in the nation cared deeply enough about them and their troubles to try to help. Their reaction was an outpouring of affection and love the likes of which few men are privileged to receive.

The most vivid record of it is in newsreel films from the time. On the edge of a desolate prairie landing strip outside a tiny Texas or Oklahoma town a crowd of people stands, looking off into the distance. Then the camera pans around to catch a small aircraft approaching, its wings wobbling in the wind as it comes in for the landing. Before the wheels touch the ground the crowd surges forward—men, women, and children running, overcoats flapping behind them. The camera picks up the blurred faces; they are laughing and cheering out of sheer joy, oblivious of everything but getting to that airplane as fast as they can. And then there is Will Rogers, climbing out of the plane, somewhat startled to see the size of the crowd, grinning, waving, shaking hands with hundreds of strangers who are his friends.

On Presidents: *"We shouldn't elect a President; we should elect a magician."*

When he had to return to California in February to make a picture, he read that the government had finally appropriated twenty million dollars for drought-stricken farmers. But the money was to be loaned against security put up by the farmers. "Now the man and his family that are hungry down there have no security," he explained. "If he had any security he wouldn't be hungry." Given the prevailing mood in Washington, there appeared to be no alternative to private assistance through the Red Cross, and in an unusually bitter column Will suggested that there were certain people the Red Cross couldn't reach—people so far back in the woods that the rest of the world had almost forgotten them: "I am speaking of the Senate and Congress of these United States."

Noting that the stock market had picked up a bit, he observed that U.S. Steel might go to a thousand, "but that don't bring one biscuit to a poor old Negro family of fifteen in Arkansas who haven't got a chance to get a single penny in money till their few little bales of cotton are sold away next fall." He was sick at heart over the attitude of the Republicans, who were claiming that business was getting better "because there is fewer apples being sold on the street. Lord that only means it's getting worse."

In the fall his active help was sought by the President— a remarkable request, all things considered, which indicated the extent of Will's hold on the American public. On October 31, 1931, in a nationwide hookup, Herbert Hoover and Will

Rogers spoke over the radio on the subject of unemployment.
Will's talk was basically an appeal for the type of public-spirited generosity and private support on which Hoover counted so heavily. What effect it had on the unemployment situation is difficult to ascertain—the situation having gone well beyond the thumb-in-the-dike measures Hoover was requesting. But it did cast Will Rogers in his most important role by far and produced the memorable line: "We are the first nation in the history of the world to go to the poorhouse in an automobile."

Meantime conditions were growing worse. In 1931 twenty-three hundred U.S. banks went under. In 1932 Detroit's unemployed auto workers, who had stood in line for days hoping for a few hours' work, confronted Henry Ford's factory guards in an ugly battle, leaving behind four dead and a number of wounded. And in May 1932 a band of World War veterans, determined to collect the bonus Congress had voted but had not appropriated, began moving eastward from the Pacific Northwest, picking up supporters in every city along the way.

These men were angry and desperate, but they were remarkably peaceable in their intentions. They were led by a veteran who had been out of a job for eighteen months, and who imposed on the Bonus Expeditionary Force the rules of "no panhandling, no drinking, no radicalism." When they arrived in Washington they were permitted to camp on the flats along the Anacostia River, where they waited patiently for Congress to deliver their bonus. The administration did little, a bill for immediate payment was voted down, and the thousands of increasingly restive men threatened to remain until they had seen Hoover and received their money. Toward the end of June the President called out the army. The chief of staff, General Douglas MacArthur, assisted by Major Dwight Eisenhower, Major George Patton, and other officers, led tanks, machine gunners, and a column of infantry with fixed bayonets along Pennsylvania Avenue to scatter the veterans and burn their camp in what was called the battle of Anacostia Flats.

While Will did not approve of the bonus march, he conceded that veterans had as much right to put pressure on Congress as any other lobbyists, particularly since they were acting only in their own behalf. He especially admired their conduct throughout the long, sordid mess. "They hold the record for being the best behaved of any 15,000 hungry men ever assembled anywhere in the world. They were hungry, and yet they remained fair and sensible. Would 15 thousand hungry bankers have done it? 15 thousand farmers? 15 thousand preachers? And just think what 15 thousand club women would have done to Washington even if they wasn't hungry. . . . It's easy to be a gentleman when you are well fed, but these boys did it on an empty stomach."

Further trouble was mounting in the farm belt. In the Plains states drought and erosion had turned thousands of acres to hardpan or dust, and the topsoil blew away on the summer winds or ran off in spring floods. In the early thirties the dust storms began—thick brown clouds, sometimes five miles high, that forced families to huddle indoors or tie handkerchiefs around their noses and mouths when they went outside. Thousands of debt-ridden tenant farmers packed up their pitiful belongings and drove away. In Iowa farmers armed with clubs and pitchforks blocked the roads, barring the movement of milk into the cities. (Dairymen were then receiving two cents a quart for their milk.) Violence broke out before the "strike" was called off, but nothing was accomplished; it only dramatized the critical situation in America's breadbasket.

Will sympathized with the farmers in Iowa, who were "stopping the trucks and eating what the other farmers send to town." It impressed him as a pretty good scheme; if farmers would eat all they raised, not only would they get fat but the price of farm products would undoubtedly rise. "Course," he added, "on account of this not being an economist's idea it might not work."

As often as Will criticized President Hoover and his method of dealing with the Depression, he had considerable sympathy for and understanding of the man. He once remarked, "Nobody ever asked Coolidge to fix a thing. We just let everything go, and everybody grabbed off what he could. . . . Now Mr. Hoover is elected and we want him to fix everything. Farm relief . . . Prohibition . . . Prosperity—millions of people never had it under nobody and never will have it under anybody, but they all want it under Mr. Hoover. If the weather is wrong, we blame it on Hoover."

Luck, he thought, had been against Hoover all the way. "He arrived at the picnic when the last hard-boiled egg had been consumed. Somebody slipped some limburger cheese into his pocket and he got credit for breaking up the dance."

11

"A Man that don't have a Horse, there is something the matter with him."

SOMETHING so untypical of Will Rogers' normal behavior occurred during 1931 that his wife Betty went out of her way to record it: after returning from a tour of Central America and the Caribbean he spent six months at home.

Home, by this time, was the Santa Monica ranch—and the move, Betty explained, had been prompted initially by their daughter Mary's lack of a bathroom. In the Beverly Hills house she shared a bath with her parents, who decided in 1928 that she ought to have one of her own. An architect was consulted, and remodeling began. Then termites were discovered, and Will, in disgust, finally had the workmen tear down the house. By then the Santa Monica place was finished and that, in any case, was where he wanted to live. He liked a lot of room to move around in, and he wanted more space for the horses.

The entrance to the ranch was off to the right of the road that eventually became Sunset Boulevard. A long curving drive— dotted with hundreds of eucalyptus trees set out by Will— wound up the hill. At the top was the long green sweep of a polo field. Beyond were the house, a garage and other outbuildings, a large horse barn, corrals, a cage for practicing polo, an oval-shaped roping ring, and a tennis court. At one side of the house were several golf holes for the use of his friends. Will never had cared for the game (he couldn't understand why anyone would walk when he could ride), and when visitors were playing he would ride around on a horse and with a polo mallet hit the balls back to the unnerved golfers.

The house, which Anne Morrow Lindbergh described after a visit as "so quiet and far away and protected" that she and her

Souvenirs of the Old West and of Will's career decorated the living room of his Santa Monica ranch house. The stuffed calf was for practicing roping. The large spread also had a horse barn, polo field, roping ring, tennis court, and a small golf course.

husband felt "completely private and free," looked as if it had always been lived in and loved—relaxed and comfortable, with a casual, unpretentious beauty. The original building included three small bedrooms, a large living room, and a patio built around two live oaks; later this structure was enlarged piecemeal—becoming, at last, a long, rambling house. There was no dining room, since Will hated formal dinners and preferred to eat or entertain on the patio, where he often did the cooking himself at a barbecue grill.

With all his nervous energy he found it almost impossible to sit still throughout an entire meal, and between courses he would get up from the table and throw a rope—keeping up a steady flow of conversation all the while. If Fred Stone was there for dinner, the two men would leave the table and begin swinging lassos while they talked and joked—sometimes aiming at a chair, sometimes throwing a loop over another dinner guest. One friend, the artist Ed Borein, finally tired of being roped and presented Will with a stuffed calf on casters.

The big living room overflowed with the mementos he loved: over the stone fireplace was the head of a Texas steer; a light fixture in the ceiling was made from an old wagon wheel; there were spurs, riding quirts, and beautifully worked saddles from all over the world; Navaho blankets and rugs; Western paintings by his friends Charlie Russell and Ed Borein; skins of a tiger and a black leopard sent him by the sultan of Johore; the model of a covered wagon; a barrel full of his ropes; and, for a couch, a porch swing hanging from the exposed beams.

At one end of the living room was a big picture window, the gift of Florenz Ziegfeld. The producer had always admired the view from the house but didn't like having to go outside to see it, so one day when Will was not home he sent his chauffeur to take measurements, and the next thing the Rogers family knew, workmen were tearing out the wall and installing the window. At a table in front of it, Will ate breakfast, read the morning papers, and planned his daily article.

Now in his early fifties, Will had begun to experience some difficulty in reading; the old "Injun eyes" weren't quite as good as they had been. One day in The Lambs, a club in New York, an actor friend saw him holding a newspaper at arm's length and offered his glasses. Will put them on and left the club with them in his pocket. He never had his eyes tested; Betty simply had the friend's prescription duplicated and ordered a dozen pairs at a time, since Will was so hard on them. When talking to someone he would twirl them in his hand or chew on the earpieces until they were twisted and gnawed out of shape.

WHEN he was home Will was outdoors constantly. If he was not roping calves—a small bunch was always kept on the ranch for this purpose—or riding or playing polo, he was having new fences built, buildings altered, new roads or bridle paths cut into the hills. Several Mexicans were employed for this type of work, and to help around the house there was a butler named Emil Sandmeier, as well as a former cowboy, turned chauffeur, whose principal qualification in Will's eyes was that he could teach the children how to rope.

The two boys, Bill and Jim—and, for a time, Mary—played polo with Will, and since each rider needed five or six mounts for an afternoon's game, the stables and corrals were usually full. All this exercise kept Will in superb physical condition (he still did the Texas skip, jumping back and forth through a vertically spinning loop, every morning). And the result, his son Jim remembers, was that "he was *tough,* physically."

Active as he was, he also had the ability to relax completely. Coming into the house after roping or riding, he could sit down and be sound asleep within minutes; then he would wake up, restored, and start on another project. He was, Jim says, an extremely nervous person who always had to keep moving, "and like so many creative people, he had days when he was riding high, on the crest of the wave, and the next day he would hit bottom. Mother always knew when to jolly him along and how to play to his moods." She was also the calming influence, "the balance wheel," Will called her. As he wrote on their twenty-fifth wedding anniversary, "The day I roped Betty, I did the star performance of my life."

Disciplining the children was evidently Betty's job; she once told an interviewer that Will had never spanked them—she took care of that. Even so, Jim retains a vivid recollection of his father's quick temper—his "short fuse." Whatever tension may have flared up occasionally between parents and children, Will's feelings on the matter were expressed in a letter he wrote Mary on her nineteenth birthday: "Sometimes we old ones dont see eye to eye with you Kids. But its *us* that dont stop to see your modern viewpoint. Times change. But Human Nature dont."

THE PATTERN OF the Rogers' homelife was directly traceable to Betty's and Will's upbringing and background. "Our parents were wholesome country people," Betty once said, "and that's the kind of life we like. And the kind we want our children to like." All three children were given music and dancing lessons, but Will didn't want them in show business. He was content to have Mary play in summer stock, but he didn't want her career to go further than that.

His sons recall that their parents were away from home continually; there never seemed a time when their father, in particular, was not involved in something that took him away. While the children were young, Betty Rogers had had to make a choice: to be with her husband as much as possible or to stay at home with them, and she chose the former, after arranging for her unmarried sister, Theda Blake, or "Aunt Dick" as the children called her, to be with Bill, Mary, and Jim. For several years, while the family was in Beverly Hills, Will's niece Paula McSpadden also lived at the house, helping the youngsters with their lessons, riding with them, and taking them to plays, ball games, and picnics.

In the fall of 1931 both boys were away at school, and there must have been some discussions between their mother and father about their failure to write home. Will brought the matter to his readers' attention in his column on October 29, brightening the day for many an American parent: "Early in the autumn," he wrote, "Mrs. Rogers and I sent two sons away supposedly to school (we got tired trying to get 'em up in the morning). One went north here in this state, another to New Mexico. Since then we have received no word or letter. We have looked in every football team all over the country. Guess they couldn't make the teams, knew their education was a failure and kept right on going. Any news from any source will be welcome. I am flying to Mexico City today. The big one spoke Spanish so maybe he is there. The little one didn't even speak English but he loved chili and hot tamales so he may be there too."

In 1932 Bill accompanied his father to the Democratic convention and shared a hotel room with him in Chicago. He never got any sleep at night because Will was constantly on the telephone, and during the day it was Bill's job to keep people away from his father as much as possible, since everyone seemed to want to meet him. At one point a man dressed in an old sailor suit approached, and Bill dutifully began to fend him off. The sailor called out to Will, who hurried over, greeted him with open arms, and introduced him to his son as the poet Carl

Sandburg. One of Bill's colorful recollections was a late night in the hotel room when Will, Sandburg, and Groucho Marx sat together playing guitars and singing. Will had a high regard for Groucho, who "can play as good on the guitar as Harpo can on the harp, or Chico on the piano, but he never does. He is really what I call an ideal musician. He can play but don't."

Despite considerable evidence to the contrary, by his own account Will was not much of a reader of books. As he put it: "I just got started in wrong. All educated people started in reading good books. Well I didn't. I seem to have gone from Frank Merriwell and Nick Carter, at Kemper Military Academy, right to the Congressional Record, just one set of low fiction to another."

There are occasional glimpses of his pride in having succeeded without benefit of college or degree, but he regretted not having taken advantage of the opportunities to acquire a good education. In May 1931, hearing of plans to give him an honorary degree, he fired off a telegram:

WHAT ARE YOU TRYING TO DO, MAKE A JOKE OUT OF COLLEGE DEGREES? THEY ARE IN BAD ENOUGH REPUTE AS IT IS, WITHOUT HANDING 'EM AROUND TO COMEDIANS. THE WHOLE HONORARY DEGREE THING IS THE "HOOEY." I GOT TOO MUCH RESPECT FOR PEOPLE THAT WORK AND EARN 'EM TO SEE 'EM HANDED AROUND TO EVERY NOTORIOUS CHARACTER. I WILL LET OOLOGAH KINDERGARTEN GIVE ME ONE—D.A. (DOCTOR OF APPLESAUCE).

Although he belonged to no church and rarely attended services, he was a deeply religious man on his own terms. He had been raised a Methodist, he once told a clergyman, but having traveled so widely and seen so many types of people, "I don't know now just what I am. I know I have never been a nonbeliever. But I can honestly tell you that I don't think that any one religion is *the* religion. Which way you serve your God will never get one word of argument or condemnation out of me."

His whole outlook on living was relaxed and casual. He disliked plans intensely, Betty said, and "would not make an engagement two weeks ahead of time if he could possibly help it." His idea of heaven was to have a free day when he and Betty could get in the car and drive without any preconceived notion of where they were going, and she recalled those trips as some of their happiest times, when she had him all to herself.

"Come on, Blake, let's get going," he would say, and they would drive until it was time to file his daily article. He would pull off the road and sit on the running board with the typewriter on his knees while she worked at her knitting, and then they would drive to the nearest telegraph office. If they had no sandwiches with them, Will liked to stop at a small-town grocery store and wander from shelf to shelf, collecting cans and boxes of food for lunch; then he would chat for a while with the storekeeper before they went on.

He had a rule about clothes. "He dressed only once a day," Betty said. "After his bath in the morning he put on a clean shirt, and that bath and that shirt had to last him through the evening, no matter what came up." On the ranch he wore work clothes—blue jeans, boots, a cowboy shirt and sometimes a handkerchief around his neck, and a small, light-colored Stetson. For more formal occasions he had a reliable double-breasted blue serge suit which, with a white shirt and black bow tie, had to do also for evening wear. He did not dress up for anyone.

It occurred to Betty now and again that she had four children, not three, and that Will "was the greatest child of all." He was not unaware of this himself. Speaking to a radio audience he alluded to "the mother of our little group," saying that she "had been for twenty-two years trying to raise to maturity four children, three by birth and one by marriage. While she hasn't done a good job, the poor soul has done all that mortal human could do with the material she has had to work with."

DESPITE the Depression, there was little concern about the family fortunes in the Rogers household. If ever his father did feel the need of ready cash, Bill remembers, he used to say he could always make another lecture tour; there was more money in that than in anything else. Will's own attitude toward money was simple; he liked making it, he wanted to make a lot of it, but once he had it he disposed of it prodigally. Money was for trips, and he liked to travel in style; it was also something to be given away, and he was extroadinarily generous to relations less fortunate than he, to charities, and to friends.

Will was never comfortable in smart shops, but he liked to do his own Christmas shopping. Putting it off until the last possible moment, he would hurry out alone and buy a staggering number of presents for everyone. He never asked the price of anything, and when he had finished he would carry his bundles to the car, drive home, and spend the remaining hours of Christmas Eve wrapping his packages.

For Florenz Ziegfeld the country's economic plight had brought the golden days to an end. He was faced, in the early thirties, with failing health and mounting debts, but still he would come over to Will's ranch, immaculately attired in riding habit, looking for all the world as if nothing had changed. In 1932 Ziegfeld died, a bankrupt, and Will—after delivering a moving tribute to his old boss in a newspaper article—quietly paid his medical and funeral expenses.

IN SPITE of the immense amount of time Will Rogers devoted to his career, it was rarely discussed within the family circle. What success he had achieved he viewed largely as the result of luck or accident, and he suspected that the public would "catch onto" him sooner or later. When people did, he figured, he and Betty might go back to Claremore, Oklahoma, where he had purchased acreage on a hillside at the edge of town. That would be the site of their house.

When some people began giving serious thought to the possibility that Will might run for public office, he was both annoyed and embarrassed. He had gotten a kick out of having his name put in nomination at the 1924 Democratic convention; he had rejoiced in the Anti-Bunk candidacy of 1928. However, in 1931 matters took a different turn. A committee called on him to urge that he run for senator from California, and that overture was followed by talk of his running for President.

He dealt with this matter firmly. "I hereby and hereon want to go on record," he wrote, "as being the first Presidential, Vice-Presidential, Senator, or Justice of Peace candidate to withdraw. I not only 'Don't choose to run,' I won't run. . . . Who will be the next to do the public a favor and withdraw? . . . It's one year away but the candidates will be Hoover and Curtis versus Franklin D. Roosevelt and some Western or Southern Democratic Governor."

Roosevelt's running mate was a Southerner *and* a Westerner. He was the Speaker of the House of Representatives, John Nance Garner of Texas. The campaign—which came at the bottom of the Depression—was as bitterly contested as that of 1928.

Fifteen million people were out of work. In New York City alone, a hundred thousand meals were served each day to destitute people waiting in breadlines. Huey Long, the vulgar, self-styled "Kingfish," was promising the confiscation and redistribution of wealth to make "Every man a king, every girl a queen." A radio priest named Charles Coughlin was preaching about social justice to thousands of rapt listeners; and on the West Coast, Dr. Francis E. Townsend was giving elderly Americans a vision of a society in which anyone over sixty would receive two hundred dollars a month.

On Democrats: *"The Democrats are having a lot of fun exposing the Republican campaign corruptions, but they would have a lot more fun if they knew where they could lay hands on some of it themselves for next November."*

Not everyone took Franklin Roosevelt's candidacy seriously when it was announced in January 1932. The best that columnist Walter Lippmann could say was, "He is a pleasant man who, without any important qualifications for the office, would very much like to be President."

Will had regarded Roosevelt as the Democrats' likeliest candidate since 1930, when he wrote of his reelection as governor of New York, "The Democrats nominated their President yesterday, Franklin D. Roosevelt." But the presidential nomination was by no means a sure thing. The party split into factions supporting one candidate or another; it was divided along religious and sectional lines, by disparate views on Prohibition, and by a host of other ideological disputes. When Will arrived in Chicago late in June he was astonished to see so many smiling delegates; he wondered if they were going to "degenerate into a party of agreement and mutual admiration." But the next day "They fought, they fit, they split and adjourned in a dandy wave of dissension." That was the old party spirit he was accustomed to.

During those dead hours while the platform committee was meeting, Will was called upon to address the convention delegates. For a quarter of an hour he kept them laughing. Then he got to his point: "Now, you rascals . . . no matter who is nominated, go home and act like he was the man you came to see nominated. Don't say he can't win. You don't know what he can do until next November. I don't see how he could . . . not win. If he lives until November, he is in!" He left the rostrum to an enormous ovation, with the crowd standing and whooping in the aisles, begging for more.

On Republicans: *"You can't make the Republican Party pure by more contributions, because contributionns are what got it where it is today."*

When the nominations began, Will received Oklahoma's twenty-two votes as a favorite son on the first ballot, but as he said, "Politics ain't on the level. I was only in 'em for an hour but in that short space of time somebody stole 22 votes from me . . . didn't even leave me a vote to get breakfast on."

By the time the convention settled down to more serious business, Roosevelt had an almost certain majority, and by the fourth ballot it was all over. The band struck up "Happy Days Are Here Again," the tune that was to become the perennial anthem of the "Squire of Hyde Park."

WHAT Will Rogers called "the same old vaudeville team of Hoover and Curtis" had been renominated without opposition earlier in June, and Hoover was quick to announce that he perceived in Roosevelt's philosophy elements of the poison that had already spread through Europe and "the fume of the witch's caldron which boiled in Russia." Will took a fairly relaxed view of things: "This is not an election of parties or policies," he wrote. "It's an election where both sides really need the work." Midway into September, Roosevelt was scheduled to make a campaign speech in Los Angeles, but he learned that the city's Republican mayor would not welcome him. FDR's managers got in touch with Will, who assured them he would greet their candidate; as a former mayor of Beverly Hills, he thought he was entitled to welcome the man to southern California. On the night of September 24 he introduced the Democratic challenger to a huge crowd at the Hollywood Bowl. "Now, I don't want you to think that I am overawed by being asked to introduce you," Will told Roosevelt. "I'm not. I'm broad-minded that way and will introduce anybody." Apologizing for his lack of flower-iness, Will said, "Come back as President and I will do right by you. I'm wasting no oratory on a prospect." Roosevelt led the laughter.

The following Monday, Will commented on Roosevelt's obvi-ous cheerfulness. "That is one thing about Democrats," he said. "They take the whole thing as a joke. The Republicans take it serious but run it like a joke. There's not much difference."

His daily article of November 1, advocating a moratorium on speeches by the candidates, stirred up a first-class rhubarb. Stating that these two ordinarily fine men had been goaded by their political advisers to say things that "if they were in their right minds they wouldn't think of saying," he pointed to Hoo-ver's remark that any change of policies would bring disaster to every fireside in America. That was ridiculous: "This country is a thousand times bigger than any two men in it, or any two parties. . . . This country has gotten where it is in spite of politics, not by the aid of it." He advised both candidates to go fishing until the election the following Tuesday instead of call-ing each other names.

"You will be surprised," he told them, "but the old U.S. will keep right on running while you boys are sitting on the bank," adding that when they came back the day after the election, "we will let you know which one is the lesser of the two evils."

A few days later he was in a more philosophical mood. Even though the candidates had lost their tempers, he advised voters not to be too critical. Neither man was going to save the country; neither would ruin it. And if the Depression contin-ued, the loser was going to be the winner: "This President business is a pretty thankless job. Washington or Lincoln, either one, didn't get a statue until everybody was sure they was dead."

Will was attacked for his remarks by partisans of both sides. His reply took the form of a letter to the editor of the Los Angeles *Times,* which had been one of his severest critics. He was surprised, he wrote, that people were so exercised over his suggestion that the candidates go fishing. There was not a man in public life that he didn't like; most of them were his good friends—"but that's not going to keep me from taking a dig at him when he does something or says something foolish." Hoover knew better than to say grass was going to grow in the streets if Roosevelt's tariff proposals were adopted—"You can't get it to grow on your lawns." And it was foolish for Roosevelt to blame the Depression on Hoover because he knew it was not so. Will meant what he said about the United States being bigger than any two men or any two parties.

IN THE wake of the election he offered solace to Mr. Hoover. "It wasn't you, Mr. President, the people just wanted to buy something new, and they didn't have any money to buy it with. But they could go out and vote free and get something new for nothing." The people, he wrote, had simply lost their taste for the Republican Party, which proved only that "There is something about a Republican that you can only stand for him just so long. And on the other hand there is something about a Democrat that you can't stand for him quite that long."

Then he had some advice for the incoming chief executive. In a personal telegram he told Roosevelt that to see a smile in the White House again would be "like a meal to us." As for handling congressmen and senators, "don't scold 'em. They are just children that's never grown up. Don't send messages to 'em, send candy."

In the month following the election a number of daily telegrams voiced his thoughts on Europe's war debts to the United States—an old and favorite topic. "Don't ever lay the fault on Europe for not paying us," he advised. "They would start tomorrow if we would just loan 'em the money to do it on."

Perhaps the mood of the country was changing; perhaps Will's comments were slightly more acerb. Whatever the reason, he received an increasing amount of criticism from readers and editorial writers—notably in *The New York Times,* which published a spate of letters from readers who took him to task for what they considered his destructive criticism, lack of taste, and general mischief-making on the crucial issue of war debts. There were letters in his defense, but the *Times* took a hands-off posture, while harrumphing in an editorial about the importance of publishing views that differed from its own.

Will's response to that was to dish out some of the same medicine: "I would like to state to the readers of the *New York Times* that I am in no way responsible for the editorial or political policy of this paper. I allow them free rein as to their opinion, so long as it is within the bounds of good subscription gathering. . . . Every paper must have its various entertaining features, and their editorials are not always to be taken seriously, and never to be construed as policy."

On foreign relations:
"There's one thing no nation can ever accuse us of and that's Secret diplomacy. Our foreign dealings are an open book . . . generally a check book."

There were signs that incessant travel and the demands of his complicated life were beginning to tell on Will. Increasingly sensitive to criticism, he was now defending his opinions by replying to letters that he might have ignored in earlier years.

One tragic occurrence in 1932 had had a profound effect on him. On March 1 the twenty-month-old son of Charles and Anne Morrow Lindbergh was kidnapped from their home in Hopewell, New Jersey. Only two weeks earlier Will had visited them and watched in delight as the aviator played with the child, and in the days following the crime his columns reflected the nationwide feeling of horror and outrage. Deeply troubled by his friends' tragedy, he lashed out at the society that had somehow permitted it to occur. "120 million people cry one minute and swear vengeance the next. A Father who never did a thing that didn't make us proud of him. A Mother who though only the wife of a hero, has proven one herself. At home or abroad they have always been a credit to their country. Is their country going to be a credit to them? Will it make him still proud that he did it for them? Or in his loneliness will . . . a thought creep into his mind that it might have been different if he had flown the ocean under somebody's colors with a real obligation to law and order?"

In January of 1933 he bade farewell to an old friend. "Mr. Coolidge," he wrote, "you didn't have to die for me to throw flowers on your grave. I have told a million jokes about you but every one was based on some of your splendid qualities. . . . By golly, you little red-headed New Englander, I liked you." After a ceremony was held in the House of Representatives to honor the memory of the former President, Will's comment had a bite to it: "The lawmakers . . . can pay more homage to a President in death and deal him more misery in life than happens in any civilized nation."

As WINTER and the Depression deepened, America's banks faced a new crisis. Over the past three years, despite Hoover's reassurances that the credit system was sound, five thousand banks had closed, and despite the President's efforts to resuscitate them with aid from the Reconstruction Finance Corporation, in mid-February Michigan's banks began closing their doors. As Inauguration Day, then March 4, approached, the bank panic spread to other states.

When Roosevelt proclaimed in his inaugural address that "the only thing we have to fear is fear itself" and almost immediately declared a national bank holiday, many Americans felt there might now be an end to the uncertainty that had plagued the country. In an almost springtime mood, people made the most of a common plight, accepted scrip, and joked about it.

According to Will, "America hasn't been as happy in three years as they are today—no money, no banks, no work, no nothing." He was confident that the entire nation was behind the new President. "Even if what he does is wrong they are with him, just so he does something. If he burned down the capitol we would cheer and say, 'Well, we at least got a fire started, anyhow.'" The Republicans had never voluntarily closed a bank—"Their theory was to leave 'em open till they shut." It was astonishing, he thought, how little money people really needed to get by on; even if the banks never reopened, "it's such a novelty to find that somebody will trust you that it's changed our whole feeling toward human nature." He couldn't recall when the country had seemed more united, and suggested that "The worse off we get the louder we laugh, which is a great thing."

He admired the way the new occupant of the White House was dealing with Congress, making them act for the first time in their lives like U.S. citizens and not like senators or representatives. "Roosevelt just makes out a little list of things every morning that he wants them to do that day (kinder like a housewife's menu list)," and they were doing it. And Eleanor Roosevelt immediately endeared herself to Will by making it plain that she was air-minded—"no maid, no secretary, just the first lady of the land on a paid ticket on a regular passenger plane."

12

"I never met a man I didn't like."

THE public's regard for Will Rogers was never higher than in the spring of 1933. The twenties and early thirties had seen a succession of heroes flash like meteors across the national scene— polar explorers Richard Byrd and Roald Amundsen; aviators Charles Lindbergh, Amelia Earhart, and Wiley Post; athletes "Big Bill" Tilden, Jack Dempsey, Babe Ruth, and Red Grange; and a host of others—but none managed to retain such constant, unwavering affection as Will Rogers. He was the one man, people seemed to believe, who was above fame and success. His consuming interest and involvement in the nation's affairs were such that no man's importance was quite confirmed until he had been kidded by Will Rogers—and no event was complete unless it drew the gentle barb of his wit. His brief commentary was the first item to which millions of Americans turned in their daily newspaper. His motion pictures were so successful that he now ranked as the number two box-office attraction in Hollywood. And soon another string was added to his bow.

In May it was announced that he had signed a contract to make seven nationwide broadcasts for the Gulf Oil Company. He would be paid fifty thousand dollars for the series, and immediately said he would donate all the money to unemploy-

Will started in radio in 1933 and for three seasons was heard in millions of homes from coast to coast.

ment relief—half to be distributed by the American Red Cross, half by the Salvation Army.

SO MANY years later it is difficult to suggest the powerful hold radio had on Americans, when the voices of Amos 'n' Andy, Rudy Vallee, Kate Smith, Jack Benny, Fred Allen, Eddie Cantor, George Burns and Gracie Allen, Edgar Bergen and Charlie McCarthy, were as familiar in the nation's living rooms as those of old friends. During the Depression years listening to the radio became the public's greatest diversion—radio was one of the few mediums of entertainment that were free. On weekdays between 7:00 and 7:15 p.m., when thirty million people were listening to Amos 'n' Andy, the use of telephones regularly fell off by fifty percent. And listening to Will Rogers on Sunday nights at nine became a ritual that people still remember with a smile.

Will's success in show business, as he readily admitted, was the result of a happy coincidence of talent and timing. He had appeared on the scene with a highly original act when vaudeville and the *Ziegfeld Follies* were at the height of their popularity; his arrival in Hollywood coincided with the heyday of the silent films; his personality and manner were precisely right for the advent of talking pictures; and although he was never as comfortable in radio, his style was superbly suited to the format of the variety show, which offered a half hour of humorous comment sprinkled with light music.

His first broadcast for Gulf, in the spring of 1933, established a pattern for those that followed. After a medley by Al Goodman's orchestra and a song from the Revelers (the quartet that had accompanied him on many benefit performances), Will came on to deliver a monologue that ran about fifteen minutes. It was a variation on the familiar *Follies* routine, of which audiences never seemed to tire. He drew on the headlines and news of the day for his commentary, so it was no accident that Franklin D. Roosevelt dominated the programs. In the opening broadcast Will proclaimed it to be President's Day: "We have apple week, and potato week, and don't murder your wife week. . . . If prunes are worth a week, the President ought to be worth something anyhow."

Roosevelt had been in office for seven weeks, and "That bird has done more for us in seven weeks than we've done for ourselves in seven years. . . . He was inaugurated at noon in Washington, and they started the inaugural parade down Pennsylvania Avenue, and before it got halfway down there, he closed every bank in the United States." Jokes followed about Republicans, Mahatma Gandhi, Al Smith, the repeal of Prohibition, and presidential commissions.

Will's act, perfected over the years, involved rambling from one anecdote to another, with no real concern for the length of time he talked. But radio was geared to split-second timing; if a program was scheduled to end at 9:30, that was when it ended, even if the star performer was in midsentence. Characteristically he took advantage of the situation to extract a few additional laughs from the audience by bringing an alarm clock to the studio. "The hardest thing over this radio is to get me stopped," he announced during his second broadcast. "So tonight, I got me a clock here. . . . When that alarm goes off, I am going to stop, that is all there is to it. I don't care whether I am in the middle of reciting Gunga Din or the Declaration of Independence, I am going to stop right when that rings." And every Sunday night thereafter the alarm would ring when his time was up; he would quickly tell the listeners what was in store for them next week, and sign off.

When the Chicago World's Fair opened in 1933 Will asked his listeners if they agreed with its theme—a "Century of Progress." One hundred years earlier, he reminded them, we had had only thirty-six senators, "and the evil has grown now until we have ninety-six." We were on the gold standard in 1833; there was no golf except in Scotland; there were no chamber of commerce luncheon speakers; and you lived until you died and not until you were run over by an automobile.

On the final program of that series he discussed the pros and cons of working on radio. He admitted he did not like the microphone, which put him in mind of an automobile radiator cap; he had feared that the listeners weren't much interested in politics, but had discovered that they knew more about it than a congressman; and he had thought he might have to speak as well as an announcer did, but found that "you don't have to speak correctly at all, and you are understood by everybody." Having relieved his mind of those worries, he concluded that the only trouble with radio was that "you never know how good you are." The studio audience might applaud; but the real test was whether Gulf sold more gasoline.

Actually there was little risk that Will would give up radio once he had made a success of it. As with so many enterprises, he was filled with doubts at the beginning, and only after he realized that he was good at it did he regain his self-confidence. He signed up to make six additional broadcasts for Gulf in the fall of 1933; the next year he was on the radio every Sunday night for twenty-four weeks; and in 1935 for sixteen more.

NOR did this perceptibly tax his phenomenal store of energy. In the spring of 1934 he made three motion pictures while continuing to write his daily and weekly articles, and in July he and his family sailed from San Francisco for a trip around the world to celebrate Will's and Betty's recent silver anniversary. It was in the nature of a second honeymoon, with the boys, Bill and Jim, accompanying them. (Will had tried to interest Mary in going along, but she was playing in a summer theater in Maine and turned him down.)

The preliminaries to a family expedition, Will realized, were far more complicated than they were when he was traveling alone and carrying only the "old soft, flat red grip that packed itself." Betty packed and repacked. Will wanted to be outside roping calves, but Betty and the butler, Emil Sandmeier, insisted that he try on some white shoes and new Palm Beach suits. The last straw was to find that someone had packed his bathrobe: "You only wear them when you are getting well from an operation."

Their arrival in Honolulu coincided with Franklin Roosevelt's visit to the islands, and the President and the comedian were honored at a dinner in which Will was kept speaking by an enthusiastic crowd for two hours. He and the President had an opportunity to chat about something that was very much on FDR's mind; when he learned that the Rogerses were going to Japan, he said, "Will, don't jump on Japan, just keep them from jumping on us."

From Japan, Will and his family went to Korea and then to Siberia, where they boarded a trans-Siberian train after laying in a supply of food for the long trip, including a big basket of oranges, a canned-heat cooker, and plenty of beans for Will and the boys. They were cooped up in a tiny compartment, with their luggage and supplies stacked around them, for nearly eight days. The wild, unspoiled country made a deep impression on Will, reminding him of his youth in Oklahoma. "It's exactly like the Indian Territory when I grew up in it as a boy. And if you can find a finer one than that was before they plowed and ruined it, I don't know where." Siberia was ideal cow country: "Not a fence, all you would need would be one drift line between you and the Arctic Ocean."

Moscow, when they arrived at last, was something else—"a town on a boom," with buildings going up everywhere, a new subway being built, the excitement of a horse race, and stimulating talk with experts on Russia—Maurice Hindus, Walter Duranty, and Louis Fischer. From Moscow, Will and Betty went to Leningrad, leaving Bill to go to Germany and Jim to Paris. Before leaving the States, Will had announced his intention of "finding Finland." If Finland could go to the trouble of repaying its war debts, he said, "I can certainly take the time to try and find them," and he was happy to arrive in the land of "integrity's last stand." Then he and his wife toured the Scandinavian countries, Austria, and the Balkans before going to the British Isles.

In Will's first radio talk in the fall—broadcast while he was still in England—he gave listeners a report on what he had seen on his travels. He had learned that England, which he described as the first country to recover from the Depression, had "the highest income tax rate of anybody in the world; they are the nation that first give the dole to unemployed." Russia was getting along better than he had expected because "there is no Communists or Reds there"—no agitators, no one trying to start a strike. Each country, he concluded, had its own form of government peculiar to it— "Russia has her Soviet, Italy her dictator, England her king, Japan her Son of Heaven, China

On diplomats: *"A diplomat is one that says something that is equally misunderstood by both sides, and never clear to either."*

her various bandits, and us, we don't know what form of government it is. But whatever it is, it's ours. . . . And as bad off as we are we are better than anybody else I have seen."

Probably the statement most frequently associated with Will Rogers, and the one that endeared him most to the American public, was his remark, "I never met a man I didn't like." This was the attitude that characterized all his trips abroad; in Moscow, Dublin, Hong Kong, or Mexico City he talked to everyone with whom he could strike up a conversation—in the streets, in restaurants, wherever he went—and his inclination was to believe that the world was basically a family in which all would be well if man's native instincts were allowed to prevail instead of being gummed up by the politicians. This old-fashioned confidence in the virtues of the common man, seasoned with a benevolent tolerance for the human condition and mankind's frailties, was suspected by some critics of his day as being a pose. They refused to believe that anyone as successful or as wealthy as Will Rogers could possibly remain the eternal homespun cowboy.

WILL'S success as a humorist was constructed, as are all such successes, upon a formula. But the formula was concocted out of real elements and was an extension of a personality that had not altered substantially since he was a boy in Indian Territory. What had changed was not Will Rogers but the world, and something of what audiences responded to was the aura of nostalgia that his manner suggested—a trace of the days when life had seemed far less complex, confused, and phony. In a curious way, his radio broadcasts came closer to suggesting what Will was all about than did his stage or movie appearances, because what he said to an audience that could not see him was not obscured by gestures or mannerisms. No shuffling about, no pulling the forelock, no sheepish grins or sly winks or glances from under his eyebrows intruded on the talk. More original than what he said was the peculiar twist he gave it, with the result that the listener—hearing Will say pretty much what he himself had thought or known all along, but hearing it placed in an entirely different context—suddenly found himself thinking that Will had uttered some eternal truth. For example, in 1934 everyone knew about Austria's troubles with Hitler's Germany, but it was left to Will to say that "If ever a nation lived in the wrong place it seems to be them."

In much of what he said there was a strong element of compassion, as when he remarked that "we are the last civilized nation, if you can call us that, to do anything for old people. All we do is just watch them get older." Or, on the subject of government relief programs, "Now is this thing of havin' millions of people . . . workin' for the government—is that a good thing? Well, no, it's not a good thing, but it's better than starvin'."

When not discussing politics or the international scene he frequently dealt with God, family, mother, honesty, common sense, the underdog, just plain folks—contriving to do so in a way that was neither maudlin nor cloying. On Mother's Day in 1935 he reminded the audience that "it's a beautiful thought, but it's somebody with a hurting conscience that thought of the idea. It was someone who had neglected their mother for years and they figured out, I got to do something about mama, and then they says, 'Well, we'll give mama a day.'. . . You give her a day and then in return mother gives you the other 364."

BEFORE Will and the family left on their round-the-world trip he said he had hit on a formula for avoiding wars. Most friction between countries, he stated, was caused by proximity. "Now Germany and France, they fight every forty years, you know—just as true as history. Every forty years they just come around, and they look at the calendar and start fighting. Well, it isn't anyone's particular fault, but it just seems to be habit." So he had devised a scheme to move neighbors away from each other if they couldn't get along. "Take Germany, for instance, and place it where Mexico is." And once Mexico was transplanted to Germany's place, "France and Mexico would get along fine." Since England and Ireland were always fighting, he would swap Ireland and Canada, being careful not to let England know where the Irish were going.

The trip somehow convinced him, despite the ominous rumblings from Europe, that there would be no war. In his travels, he said, he had found one surefire thing to say when he arrived in a country: " 'Folks, I bring you no good will.' The whole world is fed up on somebody bringing good will in. . . . Nations don't want to have any good will, and all that. They want to be let alone, the same as we do. Let 'em alone and let 'em work out their own plans and their own salvation."

Unhappily events were getting out of hand, beyond the control of the ordinary man in whom Will had such faith. In March 1935 Hitler tore up the Versailles treaty, which, as Will said, "wasn't a good treaty, but it was the only one they had." Mussolini would soon pounce on Ethiopia, and civil war was about to erupt in Spain. Will, saddened by the course of events, could only mourn, "England's got a gun, France has got a gun, Italy's got a gun, Germany wants a gun, Austria wants a gun. All God's children want guns . . . going to buckle on the guns and smear up all of God's heaven."

The state of the world was not the only thing on his mind that spring, fortunately. He had three pictures to make, and when they were finished, he thought he might take another trip—maybe fly someplace he had never been before.

13

"This Alaska is a great country."

To WHAT extent chance plays a part in human affairs is beyond all knowing. Certain actions are taken on the basis of sudden whim; others result from a chain of interrelated factors that, like the pieces of an intricate Chinese puzzle, fall into place one by one. The latter seems to be the case with the trip Will made to Alaska in 1935.

The year before, while he was playing the lead in a stage production of Eugene O'Neill's *Ah, Wilderness!* in California, he received a letter from a clergyman who had taken his fourteen-year-old daughter to the show. After watching a scene in which Will lectured his "son" on the subject of immoral relations with a woman, the minister left the theater, taking his daughter with him, and in his letter told Will that he had not been able to look her in the face since.

Will was stunned. He had regarded the play as just an "old family affair," but if it struck even one person as improper, he wanted nothing further to do with it. He not only quit the play but decided he would not accept the role in the screen version. Because of a letter from an indignant clergyman, he would have the summer of 1935 open and would be free to travel.

Another factor in the equation was the state of Will's mind in the spring of 1935. At fifty-five, for the first time in his life, he was showing signs of weariness. In addition to the radio broadcasts, he had recently given speeches or played benefits all over the country. The daily and weekly articles consumed their usual share of his time. His contract with Fox obligated him to make three movies annually, and he crowded all three into the first half of the year in order to have the remaining six months to himself. The plain fact was that he was worn out and, Bill Rogers remembers, increasingly nervous, restless, and tense. He longed to be on the wing. He considered making a long trip, but his plans were vague. Then another piece of the puzzle dropped quickly into place with a visit from a famous aviator—a fellow Oklahoman who had started life with nothing and had gained a worldwide reputation.

WILEY POST was born in Texas, the son of an itinerant farmer, and had spent much of his boyhood in Oklahoma. He first saw an airplane in 1913, and from that day on he was determined to become a pilot. He took a job with a flying circus as a parachute jumper and acquired some flight training. He worked for a time in the oil fields, where an accident occurred that made it possible for him to purchase his first plane. An iron chip from a sledgehammer lodged in his left eye, which became infected and had to be removed. Wiley was awarded $1700 in compensation, with which he immediately bought a damaged aircraft. He worked for months on training his vision, learning how to calculate distances by guessing how far it was to a tree or building, then pacing it off to see how nearly right he was.

He married a Texas girl, became a barnstormer, took passengers on rides for $2.50, and gave flight lessions. He was a natural pilot, one of his students said. "He didn't just fly an airplane, he put it on." When barnstorming failed to provide enough income he landed a job as personal pilot for two Oklahoma oilmen, Powell Briscoe and F.C. Hall. Briscoe remembered vividly that Post didn't have a nerve in his body. "When other people were scared, Wiley just grinned."

On government: *"Lord, the money we do spend on Government and it's not one bit better than the government we got for one third the money twenty years ago."*

After some months of braving the wind in an open cockpit, Hall was ready for a novel craft developed by the Lockheed Aircraft Company that became available in 1928. It was a cabin ship called the Vega, with plywood fuselage and no exposed struts or braces. Hall bought one, named it the *Winnie Mae* for his daughter, and had Wiley fly it until the stock market crash of 1929 forced him to sell the plane.

For a year Wiley worked as a Lockheed test pilot; then Hall bought another Vega, to which he gave the same name, and in 1931 he decided to sponsor Post and an Australian navigator named Harold Gatty in a round-the-world flight. In one of those dramatic air exploits of which the twenties and thirties were so full, Post and Gatty flew around the globe in eight days, fifteen hours, and fifty-one minutes, arriving in New York to a wild heroes' welcome. "This Post and Gatty," Will commented, "are making this world of ours look like the size of a watermelon." (Later Will flew to Tulsa to participate in the celebration for the Oklahoma boy, and rode with the fliers in the *Winnie Mae* to Claremore.)

Two years later Wiley, flying solo, bettered his round-the-world record, making it in a little under eight days. Howard

Hughes, who made the same trip in 1938 in less time, but with a crew of five, called Post's feat the most remarkable flight in history. "What did I tell you about that little one-eyed Oklahoma boy?" Will crowed. "He is a hawk, isn't he? He holds the doubles and singles championship now."

IN 1935 WILEY acquired a new airplane. Because he was short of funds he had to settle for a hybrid craft assembled from the parts of two previously damaged ships. To a Lockheed Orion he added wings taken from a Lockheed Explorer and some flight instruments from the *Winnie Mae.* The Lockheed company did not encourage this amalgamation of parts, but Post applied for a restricted license to operate the ship for experimental cross-country flights and other special tests. Post discovered that he was going to have difficulties with the unconventional craft. When the plane was operated at low airspeeds and reduced power, it had a definite heaviness in the front end and a tendency to pitch forward.

At the time Post visited Will in California it was rumored that the aviator was about to make a flight to study the feasibility of an air route between Alaska and Russia. Will was thinking of going along. In August, when Post flew to Seattle to have a set of pontoons installed in place of landing wheels, Will asked that he telephone from there; at that time Will would let him know whether he was coming.

"There was nothing unusual about his vagueness," Betty recalled. "Our trips were nearly always made that way, and we didn't plan beyond the first stop." She had not fully reconciled herself to Will's departure, because she dreaded his flying across Siberia. Yet she could tell that "Will wanted me to want him to go. And so I tried to be happy about this."

BY AUGUST 3 WILL was fairly certain he would make the trip. That morning he and Betty went for a long ride over the ranch, discussing what he wanted done while he was away, and stopping to see a little log cabin that had just been completed in a canyon back in the Santa Monica Hills, away from the ranch house and its steady stream of visitors. When Betty suggested that he put off his trip for a few days so they could camp out there, Will said, "No, let's wait till I get back."

Early in the afternoon, while he was packing, Betty came into the room several times, and once he called her back, gave her a sheepish look, and said, "Say, Blake, you know what I just did? I flipped a coin."

Betty said she hoped it came out tails. Will laughed, held out his hand, and replied, "No, it's heads. See, I win."

That evening their son Bill had dinner with them, and then they went to a rodeo at Gilmore Stadium in Los Angeles. As usual, Will knew most of the performers, and a number rode over to shake hands. During the evening someone gave him a small wood-and-paper puzzle, and Betty watched him toy with it unconsciously while he watched the riders in the arena. "It was a mannerism I knew so well," she said. "His restless hands could never stay still. Then, when the show was over, I saw him stuff the puzzle in the pocket of his coat." In with it went the rodeo program. His pockets, Betty said, were always filled with trinkets, like those of a little boy.

Will had a reservation on the eleven-o'clock flight to San Francisco. They drove to the airport, and it was time to say good-by. Will, with an overcoat slung over a shoulder and a stack of newspapers clutched under an arm, climbed the steps and boarded the plane. Betty caught a last glimpse of him in the window, smiling, and she and Bill watched until the plane's green and red wing lights vanished in the night sky.

IN SEATTLE, Wiley Post was having his problems. He had ordered a set of Edo pontoons, similar to those used by Alaskan bush pilots, but they had not arrived by the time Will got there. Since Will was financing the trip and was impatient to be off, Wiley settled for what he could find: a pair of pontoons from a Fokker trimotor, much heavier than he required. When he took the hybrid plane up he discovered that the big pontoons accentuated the nose-heaviness; landing or takeoff would be quite hazardous unless the plane was operated under a good deal of power. Will asked about the pontoons, thinking they were "awful big looking things," but Wiley replied laconically, "None too big." The pilot, Will was learning, was "kinder a Calvin Coolidge on answers; none of 'em are going to bother you with being too long."

In 1935, at fifty-five, Will was overworked and tired out.
With the veteran flier Wiley Post (second from right)
he set out on a trip to Alaska. As they took off for
Barrow on August 15 the plane (inset), equipped
with oversized pontoons, seemed nose-heavy.

Post decided that if Will rode as far aft in the plane as possible, his weight would compensate slightly for the heaviness of the nose. It would have been possible to correct the condition more scientifically by installing a new stabilizer-elevator on the plane, but since the change would delay their departure further, it was not made. In the front of the plane was a single seat; Wiley had removed the other to provide as much room as possible for their baggage, a rubber boat and canoe paddle, some life vests, several coils of rope, sleeping bags, and Post's rifle and fishing tackle.

At 9:20 a.m. on August 6, after loading two precious cases of chili aboard the plane and dodging a reporter's question as to whether they planned to fly around the world, Wiley taxied out onto the waters of Lake Washington, made a short run, and "took off like a bird," in Will's phrase, pointing the ship's nose in the direction of Juneau, Alaska.

EN ROUTE Will's enthusiasm for the beauty of the scenery was equalled only by his admiration of Post's skill at navigating; the maze of channels and islands along the coast all looked alike to him, "but this old boy turns up the right alley all the time." In Juneau, where they were grounded for several days because of bad flying conditions, Will met the governor of the territory and spent a nostalgic evening with Rex Beach, who had written his first silent movie, *Laughing Bill Hyde.*

Before taking off the next morning Will bought a red-fox fur, took it to the post office in Juneau, and mailed it to Betty. As the plane made its way north he sat in the rear seat, typewriter in his lap, pounding out his columns, which were chatty, newsy observations on the scenery, on the vastness of Alaska, and on the Eskimos and their way of life.

Flying east into Canada, they traveled over the Yukon and the Klondike region, then headed north along the MacKenzie River to the Arctic Ocean, then west to Fairbanks. "Was you ever driving around in a car and not knowing or caring where you went?" Will wrote on August 12. "Well, that's what Wiley and I are doing. We sure are having a great time. If we hear of whales or polar bears in the Arctic, or a big herd of caribou or reindeer, we fly over and see it."

The next day, with nothing pressing to do, they went down to Anchorage in a different plane, piloted by two local fliers, one of whom, Joe Crosson, was known as Alaska's best bush pilot. They flew over Mount McKinley on a brilliant sunny day, and Will said it was the most beautiful sight he had ever seen. They also visited the Matanuska Valley, to which some seven or eight hundred pioneers from the States had recently migrated, hoping to find good farm country. The settlers swarmed out to see Will.

"Where you boys from?" he asked, surveying the group. "Anybody here from Claremore?"

At the end of an hour and a half's inspection, during which time Will had the crowd laughing, they were climbing into the plane when a construction-crew cook rushed up with half a dozen fat cookies. "They're good!" Will called, taking a bite. "But I'll toss 'em out if we can't get off the ground." And on a wave of laughter the plane taxied down the strip for takeoff.

One man Will wanted to see while he was in Alaska was Charles Brower, an old-timer known as the "King of the Arctic," who was U.S. Commissioner in Barrow, a little settlement three hundred miles north of the Arctic Circle. When Will spoke to Crosson about going there, the flier, who had observed the excessive nose-heaviness of Wiley's aircraft, advised against it until some alterations could be made to correct the problem. As an experienced bush pilot, he was concerned about the possibility of engine failure. He realized that if Post had to make a forced landing somewhere without power, he might not be able to prevent the plane from nosing over into a dive.

FROM FAIRBANKS, Post radioed the government weather station in Barrow for a report on conditions and was told that snow, sleet, and zero visibility made a landing impossible; but after waiting a day he decided they could make it. Crosson, who knew what the weather could be like five hundred miles to the north, didn't like the sound of this. But when he realized that Post was determined to leave, he advised him to fly directly north until he sighted the Arctic Ocean; then he should turn

On conferences: *"There is one line of bunk that this country falls for, and always has. 'We are looking to America for leadership during the conference: She has a great moral responsibility.' Why, they didn't discover us till 1492 and the world had had 1492 wars. 1492 peace and economic conferences, all before we was ever heard of."*

"A conference is a place where countries meet and find out each other's short comings and form new dislikes for the next conference."

west, hugging the coast until he reached Point Barrow, an easily identifiable peninsula that was the northernmost reach of the North American mainland.

About twelve miles south of Point Barrow lay the village of Barrow, a fishing community inhabited by about three hundred Eskimos and nine whites. Dr. Henry W. Greist and his wife, a nurse, were in charge of a Presbyterian mission and hospital there. The Signal Corps operated the weather station, and Commissioner Brower described his own work as recording births and deaths, performing marriages, and trying to play Solomon in settling disputes. The surrounding region was bleak, treeless tundra, one of the most desolate places imaginable.

Before leaving Fairbanks about eleven in the morning on August 15, Will handed his daily article to Joe Crosson and asked him to take it, with a telegram he had written to Mary, to the telegraph office. He wired her:

GREAT TRIP. WISH YOU WERE ALL ALONG. HOW'S YOUR ACTING? YOU AND MAMA WIRE ME ALL THE NEWS TO NOME. GOING TO POINT BARROW TODAY. FURTHEST POINT OF LAND ON WHOLE AMERICAN CONTINENT. LOTS OF LOVE. DON'T WORRY.   DAD

Mary was in Skowhegan, Maine, performing in summer stock. That week she had the lead in *Ceiling Zero,* a play in which her stage father was killed in an airplane crash.

POST decided not to take off with a full load of fuel from the narrow, winding Chena River in Fairbanks. He arranged for enough gasoline for the hop to Barrow, and headed north. The little red plane made its way through the notch in the mountain barrier, and somewhere beyond the north face ran into a bad storm. Ninety miles from the settlement some natives tending a herd of reindeer heard the sound of a plane overhead. A trader named Gus Masik heard it while he was crossing Smith's Bay; so did an Eskimo at Point Tangent; and from these reports it appeared that Post, flying blind after losing his way in the storm, had at some point turned due west. Providentially about three o'clock in the afternoon he spotted a break in the dense cloud cover and caught sight of land and a stream. Flying low along the stream, he came to a lagoon and went in for a landing.

The body of water was known as the Walakpa lagoon, and there was an Eskimo fishing camp on the shore. Wiley taxied over, cut the engine, and he and Will climbed out onto the pontoons and spoke to two of the natives—Claire Oakpeha and his wife, who knew English fairly well. Wiley asked how far Barrow was (it was no more than a ten-minute flight); Will inquired what the Eskimos were fishing for (they were after seals). Following a brief consultation, the two Americans climbed back into the plane, waved, and began their takeoff.

Watching from the lonely shoreline, the Eskimos saw the plane begin moving faster and faster across the water—the pontoons throwing twin sprays behind. It lifted off, started to climb, and banked to the right. Then suddenly the engine misfired, sputtered, and went dead. The red plane turned nose down, hurtling like a stone into the shallow lagoon, spewing a geyser of sand and gravel and water into the air as the fuselage split open on impact. One wing broke off, the plane flipped over on its back, and at the same instant there was a dull explosion and a quick flash of fire, which went out immediately. Then silence. There was only the soft lapping of waves on the shore as ripples from the shattered plane broke, ebbed, and finally died.

The terrified Eskimos' first instinct was to run away; then Claire Oakpeha took courage and went as close to the plane as he could and shouted, again and again. There was no answer.

He told his wife that he must get word to the Americans, and leaving the others behind to stare in disbelief at the spectral, broken hulk in the water, he started running toward Barrow.

14

"A smile has disappeared from the lips of America. . . ."—John McCormack

FIVE HOURS AFTER the crash Claire Oakpeha, having run for sixteen miles through the tundra grass, finally staggered into the store in Barrow. Gasping for breath, he told the owner, a man named Bert Panigeo, about the crash he had seen, and Panigeo called Frank Dougherty, the local schoolteacher, on the telephone. There was some immediate speculation that it might be a party of American hunters or possibly a Russian plane that had gone off course. It occurred to nobody that it might be Will Rogers and Wiley Post, since they were not expected for several days.

Dougherty sent Oakpeha to tell Commissioner Brower what had happened, while he phoned Sergeant Stanley Morgan, the man in charge of the Signal Corps weather station, got a launch into the water, and rounded up a rescue party. Dougherty, Morgan, and a group of Eskimos headed out at once. Brower, who had loaded a launch with blankets, sleeping bags, and medicine, sent it after them, with his son David in charge. Dave's boat also towed an umiak, a large, light, open boat made of hides stretched over a wooden frame, which could be portaged across the sandbar surrounding the lagoon.

On the long voyage through the fog and ice Oakpeha gave Sergeant Morgan some additional details about the catastrophe. "One mans big, have tall boots," he said. "Other mans short, have sore eye, rag over eye." And suddenly it dawned on Morgan who must be in the plane.

At the lagoon the Eskimos from the sealing camp had removed Will's broken body from an opening in the side of the fuselage, but Post was wedged between the engine and one of the big pontoons. After Dave Brower arrived with a block and tackle, they pulled off the pontoon and the remaining wing, and with great difficulty got his body out. They placed the two corpses in sleeping bags they found in the plane, loaded them into the umiak, and headed for open water and the long trip to Barrow.

It was three o'clock in the morning when Charles Brower and Dr. Greist, who had been detained at the hospital by an operation, heard the launches returning. They knew at once that the worst had happened: the doctor could hear the voices of the Eskimos, chanting the "plaintive song they sing when the headman in a village dies. . . . Once heard it is never forgotten."

Dave Brower came ashore and told his father, "Dad, it's Will Rogers and Wiley Post."

THE TWO BODIES were carried to the hospital, where the badly shaken Greist, his wife, and Brower removed the men's clothing and began to prepare the corpses for burial. When the contents of the pockets were examined, it was noted that Wiley Post's gold watch had stopped at 8:18 p.m., the time of the crash. (He was still carrying Oklahoma time, which meant that it was 3:18 at Barrow.) In Will's clothing Dr. Greist found cash and traveler's checks, a newspaper clipping with a picture of his daughter, a stub of a pencil, a pocketknife, a pair of eyeglasses, a magnifying glass, and a pocket watch that was still running. The doctor also noticed that there was a program from a rodeo in Los Angeles and a curious little puzzle made of paper and wood. To Charlie Brower the watch somehow symbolized "all that made Will the simple, beloved man of the people he was. It couldn't have cost over a dollar and a half. He wore it tied to the end of an old string."

In Will's badly smashed typewriter was the third page of his

latest weekly article. There was a description of their departure from Fairbanks only hours before and several stories about Alaskan dog teams. He had started to tell a yarn he had heard about Joe Crosson's partner, a Swede, and a wirehaired terrier who had the unfortunate habit of barking at bears. The article ended in the middle of a sentence; the last word he had typed was "death."

PRECISELY what had happened between the time the plane lifted off the lagoon and the moment, a few seconds later, when it banked and crashed will never be known for certain. Dr. Greist, who talked with Joe Crosson and others, had his own ideas about what had caused the engine to fail. The plane was equipped with two gas tanks, one in each wing, which meant

As the plane carrying Post and Rogers passed overhead, a party of Eskimo seal hunters heard the motor die, and as they watched in horror, the ship nose-dived into a shallow lagoon. Both passengers perished.

that when one tank ran low, the pilot had to turn a hand control to open the other. Perhaps, the doctor thought, Post heard the engine misfire, realized the tank was empty, and quickly turned the hand control. But he was too late; the plane was only about fifty feet off the ground, and before the gasoline could reach the engine the nose-heavy plane plunged into the lagoon.

Charles Brower was more positive than anyone about what had occurred. In a book describing his fifty years in Alaska he told what his son Dave had found that night on Walakpa lagoon after the bodies had been removed from the wreckage. "Before leaving, Dave examined the plane carefully to try and discover why it had crashed. That was easy. Not only did none of the tanks contain so much as a drop of gas but there was no sign of any on the surface of the landlocked lagoon. . . . It seems certain that the men were entirely out of gas. Perhaps they thought they had enough for a bare twelve miles or more. Perhaps they didn't even check their gauge. We shall never know."

As SOON as the bodies were brought to Barrow and positively identified, a radio message from Sergeant Morgan went out to Seattle. Communications between the northern outpost and the outside world were so tenuous that it took nearly two hours for news of the tragedy to reach the continental United States.

Betty Rogers was in Skowhegan, Maine, visiting Mary. The last word from Will was the telegram he had given Joe Crosson to send to Mary; it had gone out from Fairbanks on August 15— the day of the crash. What disturbed Betty was Will's reference to Nome, the point from which Wiley intended to fly to Siberia. She was still hoping that Will, after flying around Alaska for a week or two, would have had enough and would return to the States and join her in Maine.

Bill Rogers was working that summer as a wiper in the engine room of a tanker, and his brother Jim and a cousin were driving east from California. On August 16 Betty was talking with a friend outside her cottage when she saw a car coming up the road and recognized the driver as the manager of the theater where Mary was working. When he got out of the automobile and spoke to her sister, Theda, something about his manner alarmed her.

She ran to speak to him. "Has something happened to Jimmy? Tell me," she pleaded.

There was no answer from the theater manager, but Theda told her, "No, Betty, it's Will. Will has had an accident."

For an instant, Betty remembered, she felt only relief, knowing that nothing could possibly happen to Will—nothing more serious than mechanical trouble or a forced landing. Then she was told of Sergeant Morgan's message from Barrow.

On inflation: *"I have been accused of being worried over this 'inflation.' I wasn't worried. I was just confused. . . . When you are worried, you know what you are worried about, but when you are confused you don't know enough about a thing to be worried."*

PERHAPS NOT SINCE the death of Abraham Lincoln had a tragedy touched so many Americans as did the loss of Will Rogers and Wiley Post. It overshadowed everything that was going on in the world. Four full pages of *The New York Times* were devoted to the event on Saturday, August 17, and for a week the newspaper and radio coverage continued. From every city and hamlet across the land came stories of people shocked and heartbroken. In a grocery store in a small New Hampshire town, customers were waiting to be served when a little boy came in and told them Will Rogers was dead. People walked out silently, their errands forgotten. In Locust Grove, Oklahoma, half a dozen Cherokees were building a fence when they received the news. Again, there was only stunned silence—people could find no words to express themselves. After a time some of the Indians spoke of how they had known Will, or remembered a favor he had done for someone. Then one said, "I can't work any more today," and all of them stacked their tools and quietly walked away.

Some of the most poignant messages of sympathy came from countries Will had visited and helped in one way or another—from Ireland, where he had put on the benefit in 1926 for victims of a theater disaster; from Puerto Rico, where he had aided victims of the 1932 hurricane; from Nicaragua, whose president recalled how Will "made me cry one minute and laugh the next during the bitter days following the 1931 earthquake."

It was extraordinarily difficult then, as now, to describe the hold Will Rogers had on so many millions of Americans. "A peculiar sense of national loss will be stirred by the tragic death of Mr. Rogers," a *New York Times* editorial read. "He had a unique career, which we all like to think could have been run only in America. He came to hold such a place in the public mind that, of his passing from the stage it might be said, as it was by Dr. Johnson of Garrick's, that it will 'eclipse the gaiety of nations.' "

It was left for John McCormack, whom Betty and Will had heard sing at the St. Louis Exposition so many years earlier and who had become their friend over the years, to sum it up. "A smile has disappeared from the lips of America," he wrote, "and her eyes are now suffused with tears. He was a man, take this for all in all, we shall not look upon his like again."

SHORTLY after Betty Rogers learned of Will's death, Charles Lindbergh called to say that he would take charge of bringing the bodies home and that Pan American Airways, for which he worked as a consultant, would make its facilities available for this purpose. Joe Crosson flew to Barrow to pick up the bodies, and on August 17 Will and Wiley began their journey home. In Fairbanks the next morning hundreds of Alaskans saw Crosson off when he left for Vancouver. In Seattle people had waited all night for a glimpse of his airplane; flags were at half-mast, and planes overhead dipped their wings in salute.

On the nineteenth Crosson landed in Burbank, California, just as darkness was falling, and as the plane moved slowly through the twilight into the hangar, the throb of its idling motors reminded thousands of onlookers of muffled funeral drums.

While arrangements were being made for Will's funeral, Post's body was put aboard another plane bound for Oklahoma City. Without telling anyone, his elderly parents drove to the Oklahoma City airport, parked their car among the thousands of others, and waited, unrecognized by anyone, to see their son's body arrive. "We didn't want to create a stir," Wiley's father said.

On the day before Betty was due to reach the coast by train, a parcel arrived at the ranch. It was addressed in a familiar, rambling scrawl to Mrs. Will Rogers, and inside was Will's final gift to his wife—the small red-fox fur.

On August 22 the last rites for Will Rogers were held in Los Angeles. Prior to a simple service at the Wee Kirk o' the Heather, his casket lay in state in Forest Lawn Memorial Park, where fifty thousand people—many of whom had been standing in line since the previous night—filed by in silence under the scorching sun. Other memorial services were held in the Hollywood Bowl, in Beverly Hills, and in Claremore. In many towns the flags were at half-mast; the nation's motion-picture theaters were darkened; the CBS and NBC networks observed a half hour of silence; and in New York a squadron of planes, each towing a long black streamer, flew over the city in final tribute to the hero and the friend of aviation.

Across the nation Americans were pausing to take Will Rogers' measure and to think what a different place their world would be now that he was gone. None of the descriptive labels—cowboy-philosopher, humorist, star of stage, screen, and radio—suggested what was in the hearts of most Americans when they learned of his death. Damon Runyon hinted at it when he called Will "the closest approach to what we call the true American."

In the years following his death many memorials to Will Rogers were established. In 1944 Will's children gave the Santa Monica ranch to California for a state park. On a high cliff above the Walakpa lagoon, facing the Arctic Ocean, is a marker of Oklahoma stone in which these words are cut: "Will Rogers and Wiley Post ended life's flight here, August 15, 1935." Clem Rogers' old ranch in the Verdigris valley was flooded when the Oologah dam and reservoir were built by the Army Engineers; but not before the Rogers ranch house was moved to high ground about a mile west of its original location. In 1959 the family donated a hundred-acre tract to the state, with the understanding that the house be relocated.

In 1938 Betty Rogers gave twenty acres of land in Claremore to Oklahoma for a memorial to her husband. It was a hillside Will had purchased in 1911, with the thought that he would come back there to live one day. Here, in 1944, his remains were brought from California, and a month later, when Betty died, she was buried at his side. In the rambling limestone building are all his letters, his newspaper articles, films, broadcast transcriptions, and the personal memorabilia of fifty-five restless, energetic years.

This is the place to which more than half a million Americans journey each year to pay tribute to the man they have never forgotten. In the center of the towering hall is a bronze statue of Will that bears the epitaph he wrote for himself: "I never met a man I didn't like."

The statue, by Jo Davidson, is a deep brown color, except for two gleaming bright spots on the toes of the shoes. Nearly every one of those millions of Americans who have come here since the Will Rogers Memorial was dedicated in 1938 has paused before the statue, looked up at the face, and then, before moving away, silently reached out to touch the tip of one shoe in a gesture of love. As it did in life, a little of Will Rogers has rubbed off on each of them.

THE
ELEANOR
ROOSEVELT
STORY

A CONDENSATION OF

THE
ELEANOR
ROOSEVELT
STORY

by
ARCHIBALD
MacLEISH

ADAPTED FROM THE FILM
BY SIDNEY GLAZIER

Where is the dramatic light and shadow in Eleanor Roosevelt's life? Clearly in the contrast—the extraordinary disparity between beginning and end. She dies the object of the world's attention and is buried not only with the ceremonies reserved for the great but with something the greatest rarely achieve—the real grief of millions of human beings. But she was born at the farthest possible remove from all this. She suffered because she was not the "beauty" her mother's family was supposed to produce, or because she lacked the graces young girls of her class were supposed to have, or because her grandmother, when her grandmother took over her life, didn't approve of her. She was, in short, a child of her class and place and time, who asked for nothing better than to win its approval—and who failed.

And out of *that* comes *this*. Out of a rejected child in the most provincial city of a provincial age comes the most remarkable woman to appear in the twentieth century!

How? The answer might be found in the myth of the sleeping beauty. People aren't "made" by themselves or by anyone else: they are *released to be* what they always were but had never known they were—and what releases them is the touch of life. For thirty years of her life, the woman who was to change the world lay in a sound if not too comfortable sleep back of the thorns and thickets of the decaying castle of the dying age into which she was born. The time came when the realization came through to her—the burning sense of need, of human suffering—which is to say, of life. And the rest of her history was the playing out of that tremendous discovery.

—Archibald MacLeish

IN THE Rose Garden at Hyde Park beside the grave of her husband, the thirty-second President of the United States, Eleanor Roosevelt is buried. She was seventy-eight years old.

It was not her life, as her friend Adlai Stevenson put it, that the world had lost— "She had lived that out to the full. What we have lost," he said, "what we have to recall for ourselves—to remember—is what she was herself. And who can name it?"

Who can name it?

There are fairy tales in all the tongues of the world about children who live under the spell of sleep in a magic prison surrounded by thickets and thorns: a prison from which they are one day awakened by a touch, to turn into shining figures of life. No one knows how they become what they are at the end—only that they are.

What Eleanor Roosevelt remembered, looking back, was an unhappy little girl in a lost family in a vanished world—a child she never could have been, but was!

She said that her mother was always a little troubled
by her lack of beauty and that she knew it as a child senses
those things—and that her pretty young aunts, her mother's
sisters, told her so—in so many words.

MRS. ROOSEVELT: One of the aunts was to say to me,
"You are the ugly duckling of the family." It was an
unknown thing for a Hall girl not to be a belle at every party.
MRS. COLE (a niece of Theodore Roosevelt and Eleanor
Roosevelt's cousin and bridesmaid): And it was, too. They
were a pretty lot—her aunts and her mother . . . above all her
mother, whose clothes she loved to stroke. But her mother
preferred her little brothers and showed it, and called her
Granny because Eleanor was so old-fashioned.

With her father, however, things were different. He called
her Little Nell and she adored him.
But her relationship with him was brief. He began drinking

when she was small and he was sent off to a little town
in Virginia. Eleanor never knew why—only that she loved
him and he was gone.

A LETTER TO ELEANOR FROM HER FATHER: My darling
Little Nell . . . Because father is not with you is not because
he doesn't love you. For I love you tenderly and dearly—
and maybe soon I'll come back well and strong and we
will have such good times together, like we used to have.

MRS. COLE: When she was eight her mother died almost
overnight: diphtheria went very fast in those days.

And her brother Elliott also died of diphtheria. And
Eleanor and her baby brother went to live with her
grandmother Hall on Thirty-seventh Street and, in the
summers, at Tivoli on the Hudson.

I remember the Thirty-seventh Street home as the darkest,
most desolate house I have ever seen.

And Tivoli, too, was grim and lonely. There were no
children her age to play with and later, when her
uncle Vallie began drinking, none were allowed—no one
who did not know the family well enough to "understand."

One day Eleanor said to my mother, "Auntie, I have
no real home," and burst into tears.

And then, when she was not quite ten, her father died
as the result of a riding accident and she was really alone.

Alone with her grandmother Hall, who had been a great
belle in her youth, and who lived all her life as though
the entire world were "society." Eleanor belonged to that
world, of course, and she knew its customs.

But though she "belonged" she was never a part of it:
her sadness and loneliness set her apart.

And yet, for the rest of us, it was a lovely world to be
young in—to go dancing in—to do all the things that seemed
simpler and surer and pleasanter than they ever could have
been, we thought, in any other time or place.

MRS. ROOSEVELT: My grandmother was convinced that
the world she was brought up in was the world that was

always going to exist . . . it was never suggested to me that the world was going to be different.

MRS. COLE: Not that that world of ours was merely a pleasant world. Eleanor's and my grandfather, Theodore Roosevelt's father, had founded the Newsboys Club, now called the Children's Aid Society, and when we were quite small we used to be taken to help serve Christmas dinner.

MRS. ROOSEVELT: I had this horrible sense of obligation which was bred in me. I couldn't help it.

MRS. COLE: Her "horrible sense of obligation" and a deep and isolating sense of loneliness—of life in a dream—made life difficult for Eleanor.

After her father's death Eleanor was seldom allowed to visit her Roosevelt relatives . . . and when we did see her at Uncle Ted's she felt at a great disadvantage because she was not used to companions her own age.

And her education, too, had been neglected. When she was six her great-aunt discovered to her horror that Eleanor couldn't read.

MRS. ROOSEVELT: I had learned French before I learned English, from a French nurse who was bad for my character but good for my language.

My grandmother felt that she was doing the best she knew how. She was sending me to the most fashionable little class conducted by a pompous old gentleman named Mr. Rosa.

MRS. COLE: That wasn't the whole of her childhood education, of course.

Finally, when she was fifteen, it was decided to send her to a French school in England. Its headmistress, Mademoiselle Souvestre, was a remarkable woman, with strong ideas of her own.

The years at school with Mademoiselle Souvestre must have been like the opening of a window in Eleanor's life.

When she came back at the end of her three years it was to return to Tivoli.

Tivoli, that summer, was a grim, closed, miserable

world of its own—not a very good preparation for being a gay and joyous debutante.

Coming out in New York at the turn of the century was something of an ordeal for anyone; for Eleanor it was a nightmare.

"That first winter," she said, "when my sole object in life was society, nearly brought me to a state of nervous collapse."

She was a stranger in her own world and worse—almost an outcast. "There was absolutely nothing about me," she said, "to attract anybody's attention."

She was wrong, of course, and it was about this time she began seeing something of her cousin Franklin—fifth cousin once removed.

Many of Eleanor's friends thought she was too good for him. All they could see in Franklin Roosevelt was a handsome Harvard boy, whereas she with her unflinching

honesty and total lack of self-pity touched their hearts.

But then, he felt the same way. He had somehow the maturity and insight to recognize Eleanor for what she was under all that surface awkwardness and embarrassment.

In the fall of 1903, when she was nineteen and he twenty-one, he asked her to marry him. It seemed, she said, "an entirely natural thing"—the sort of thing you *did*.

But she also said, long afterward, that it was years before she understood "what being in love or what loving really meant."

As for Franklin, he too had his difficulties; he had his widowed mother, Sara Delano Roosevelt, a formidable and, in many ways, a remarkable woman.

A letter from Franklin Delano Roosevelt to his mother: Dearest Mama, I know what pain I must have caused you and you know I wouldn't do it if I really could have helped

it . . . you know that nothing can ever change what we have always been and always will be to each other—only now you have two children to love and to love you—and Eleanor as you know will always be a daughter to you in every true way. Your ever loving F.D.R.

MRS. COLE: The wedding was set for March 17, 1905, to allow Uncle Ted, now President Theodore Roosevelt, to give Eleanor away.

Franklin and Eleanor were married at 8 East Seventy-fifth Street by the Reverend Endicott Peabody. It was a most exciting affair, with the bridesmaids—I was one—in cream taffeta.

But when the reception began, the bride and groom found themselves deserted. Uncle Ted had gone into the library, where the refreshments were, and the wedding guests had followed the President in a body. Finally Eleanor and Franklin followed, too.

Eleanor thought of herself in those years as a curious mixture of extreme innocence and unworldliness, with a great deal of knowledge of some of the less attractive and less agreeable sides of life.

"I had painfully high ideals," she said, "and a tremendous sense of duty, entirely unrelieved by any sense of humor or any appreciation of the weaknesses of human nature."

The young Roosevelts took their honeymoon in Europe—London, where they were mistaken for the Theodore Roosevelts and given the royal suite in Brown's Hotel; Paris, where Franklin bought books on the Quais; then a motor trip through France, with the customary hazards of the time; and on to northern Italy and Venice, where they spent most of the hot nights in a gondola on the canals and Franklin refused to look at any more churches; Cortina and up through the Alps to Saint-Moritz—England again—Scotland . . .

AND SO HOME—to a little house on East Thirty-sixth Street three blocks from Franklin's mother's house, which she had rented for them and furnished and provided with servants.

Eleanor was beginning, she said, to be an "entirely dependent person," driving with her mother-in-law every afternoon, taking at least one meal with her every day, and generally doing whatever she was told.

It was a pleasant enough time in her life. Some of the shyness wore off. She began, as she put it, "to fit into the pattern of a fairly conventional, quiet, young society matron."

That was the pattern she continued to fit into for the next ten years and more. She was a dutiful wife, a docile daughter-in-law, and a constant mother, bearing child after child, living in houses her mother-in-law owned or built or rented, in cities her husband's law practice or political activities or government service took him to—New York, Albany, Washington.

When Franklin became Assistant Secretary of the Navy
in Woodrow Wilson's Cabinet in 1913, she accepted what
she called the slavery of the Washington social system
without question. *Her* job, Eleanor insisted, was "to do
exactly as the majority of women were doing—perhaps
to be a little more meticulous about it." And she was.

If the story of Eleanor Roosevelt had ended in 1917, there
would have been little enough to remember: a lonely and
dutiful little girl, a self-effacing young wife, a frequent
mother, a conventional woman of her place and time, who
nevertheless was not a part of her place and time . . . a shy
and lonely ghost wandering under the trees of a Hyde Park
she could never think of, she said, as home.

But the story did not end in 1917 . . . it began then.

BY 1917 that world of Eleanor's grandmother, that world
that "was always going to exist," had stopped existing—
stopped in a welter of meaningless and idiotic death and
destruction in the old Europe out of which it had come.
  The hidden flaw in the structure of modern history was
cracking open in one country after another around the world
and nothing would ever be the same again.
  Men died—millions of them—who had barely begun
to live. And men began to live—and women too—who had
had no lives before. Eleanor Roosevelt was one.

MRS. ROOSEVELT: I went into the canteen which served
in the railroad yard, and I suddenly began to understand
what some of the conditions were in our country. We were
sending men to fight who had no idea where they were
going or why.

She was face-to-face with something she had never guessed
or dared to guess before.
  Not the realization that the world outside was a tragic
world; she had always known that—she had learned that

by suffering herself. Rather the sudden perception that there
was something *she* could do about it—she herself—
Eleanor Roosevelt, dutiful and obedient child, and girl and
woman.

One can almost name the day of that realization. She had
driven over to Saint Elizabeth's, the federal insane asylum,
where her husband's department, the Navy, had taken over
a block of buildings for shell-shocked sailors and marines.

What she saw as she drove through the grounds horrified
her. "Poor demented creatures," she said, "with apparently
little attention being paid them, gazing from behind bars
or walking up and down on enclosed porches."

Before the war she would have kept her horror to herself,
acquiescing in the world the way it was. Now she acted.
She went to the Secretary of the Interior, whose department
was responsible for Saint Elizabeth's, told him he "had better
go over and see" for himself; kept after him until he had
persuaded the Congress to increase the hospital's appropria-

tions; got a charitable organization to contribute five hundred dollars for occupational therapy; hounded the Red Cross to build a recreation room.

A NEW FORCE had appeared in the world, although the world would not know it for some years to come; a woman who accepted personal responsibility for her country and her time—a citizen who took self-government personally and seriously and would not rest until she had done what she felt she had to do.

She had learned a lesson—a lesson she put for herself in nine words: "What one has to do usually can be done . . ." meaning that what her conscience demanded of her she would henceforth somehow accomplish.

There was another lesson that went with it: Hope is not enough.

In the fall of 1918, the "Great War," "The World War," ended in the brightest moment of hope in modern times— the hope for an end of war, for a parliament of mankind, a League of Nations.

It was a hope that came out of America in the proposal of an American President, and the people of Europe went mad with joy.

Eleanor Roosevelt, who was in Europe with her husband, was a witness of that hope. Returning home on the same ship as Woodrow Wilson, she was also a witness to his campaign across the United States on behalf of the League, and to the maneuvers of the enemies of the League of Nations, and to the final tragedy: the death of the hope— and the death of a man.

Nothing was left of all that suffering and aspiration but the grave of the Unknown Soldier in Arlington Cemetery— that, and the graves of all the others around the world.

America returned to what Warren Harding, the Republican candidate for the presidency in 1920, called "normalcy."

Her husband was the Democratic candidate for the vice-
presidency and she saw the whole campaign, beginning with
Franklin's notification at Hyde Park, through the long weeks
of train trips and speeches and parades . . . until their final
defeat in November.

"Normalcy" for the young Roosevelts meant a return
to domesticity, to the practice of the law and to what
Eleanor called a winter "with nothing but teas, luncheons,
and dinners to take up time"—"an impossible mode of
living" after the realities of the war.

Eleanor Roosevelt and her husband were caught with
the rest of that generation in a dead eddy of time, like the
suck of a bathtub running out—the circling, directionless
eddy we call the Twenties—a time when time existed to be
spent—lost—forgotten.
Except that Eleanor Roosevelt never wasted anything—

434

least of all time. She learned to write shorthand, to cook,
to type. And a winter passed and a spring . . . and suddenly
for Eleanor Roosevelt and her husband even that meaningless
clock stopped.

ONE DAY he was sailing his boat at Campobello, swimming
in the Bay of Fundy—a tall man, handsome, vigorous
as all the Roosevelts were vigorous . . . and the next he was
a helpless cripple—paralyzed, his legs useless. He was not
yet forty and he would never move again without awkwardness and difficulty.

His life, his political, public life, was over. His mother
knew that: he would return to Hyde Park as the invalid he
was and live there.

But there was one man who didn't know it—Louis Howe,
the little newspaperman from Albany.

And there was a woman who didn't know it either: Eleanor, his wife.

Why? You can answer for Louis Howe. He was a superb politician, a kingmaker, and he knew a king when he saw one. You can answer for Louis Howe, but why did Eleanor Roosevelt agree with him? Fight her mother-in-law for her husband's soul? Struggle through "the most trying winter," as she called it, of her entire life.

She knew it was kinder, gentler, to that suffering and uncomplaining husband of hers, to let him be, as his mother wanted to let him be, as most wives would have wanted to let him be.

She knew that pain and disappointment and public humiliation might well lie ahead. And yet she persisted, staked her womanhood on it, her husband's affection, her mother-in-law's goodwill, her family's happiness.

Why? Because she had learned that "what one has to do usually can be done"? Because she felt there was something her husband *had to do?*

All we know for certain is that she won her fight.

Eleanor Roosevelt entered politics herself, first through the Women's Trade Union League and then as a member of the Women's Division of the Democratic State Committee, to draw her husband's interest back to the political world.

By 1924 Franklin Roosevelt had made the difficult return. At the Democratic National Convention he nominated Al Smith for the presidency, likening him to "the Happy Warrior." But to those who listened, the Happy Warrior was the broken man with the confident, smiling face who stood there balanced precariously on his crutches, taking up his life again.

The great gamble had paid off. Franklin Roosevelt was back in the world again—so firmly back that four years later the state convention of his party nominated him for the governorship of New York—back so effectively that when the Democratic national ticket lost New York in 1928, he carried it.

The two Roosevelts, Franklin and Eleanor, had the future in their hands.

Looking around her from that triumphant moment, Eleanor Roosevelt could see what before she could only have guessed. There was indeed something "to be done."

Hitler was on the rise in Germany.

Corruption in the Harding Cabinet had shaken the faith of Americans in their government.

And the eight years of stock-market profits that had paid for the dizzy dance of the Twenties were about at an end. The market crashed, and the world came crumbling down into the Great Depression that the war had dug for it—the pit at the world's end—or at the end, at least, of *one* world.

Breadlines appeared in every city. Self-respecting men with shame in their faces sold pencils and apples in the streets and their children went hungry. Before Hoover's term was

out, veterans of the World War marched on Washington
to demand the immediate payment of a bonus.

Eleanor Roosevelt reacted as she always had to human
suffering—personally. She gave her card to the miserable
in Times Square, invited the hungry to her own table.

But by now it was obvious to others than Eleanor
Roosevelt that there were things to be done.

Only what?

And by whom?

THE ELECTION of 1932 answered the second half of that
question. A tall man, his legs braced in a metal contraption,
his face confident among frightened faces, arrived at the
White House in March of 1933. He drove up Pennsylvania
Avenue with the outgoing President, Herbert Hoover,
beside him. Took the oath of office on the Capitol steps
and said:

F.D.R.: . . . first of all let me assert my firm belief that the
only thing we have to fear is fear itself.

Our greatest primary task is to put people to work. This is
preeminently the time to speak the truth, the whole truth,
frankly and boldly. Nor need we shrink from honestly facing
conditions in our country today. This nation is asking for
action, and action now.

But what type of action? The first half of the question
remained: *What* should be done? What *could* be done? The
wreckage in the great Republic was *human* wreckage. *People*
had been hurt, frightened, bewildered. How did you deal
with *people?*

The new economists in the White House had their theories;
Eleanor Roosevelt had hers. Only hers were never theories, but
actions. That year, as the Depression deepened and the winter
came on, she began to speak her own mind in her own way.

MRS. ROOSEVELT: The needs are going to be great this coming
winter. There will be, I hope, more people employed, but

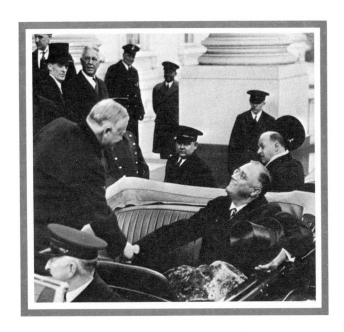

those who are not employed will need more than they have needed before. Their clothes have completely gone, their courage is not as high as it was a year ago. So there is no reason for letting up in our sense of responsibility.

Certainly *she* never let up: she went everywhere misery was to be found—and that was everywhere in those days— everywhere misery could be found and everywhere misery could be fought . . .

Up in the air on the sling of one of the great cranes building dams for the Tennessee Valley Authority . . .

Down to earth in one of the rural slums where the Resettlement Administration was building hospitals . . . teaching skills . . . feeding children . . . *Underground* in West Virginia or Pennsylvania or Illinois, where the mines were

dying, and men were out of work, and the equipment was idle.

Until she became an American legend of ubiquity, of ceaseless movement—an American myth of measureless energy . . .

Until she became something more—a center of controversy, the kind of controversy that conscience in action—personal conscience in personal action—always provokes.

Her own kind—her own class, as they called themselves—found it difficult to forgive talk as honest as hers: anyone who saw unpleasant things and mentioned them was palpably an enemy of the established order.

And journalists of a certain stripe agreed, with the result that the President's wife became the target of column after column of vituperation.

Some patriotic organizations disapproved and one, the Daughters of the American Revolution, expressed its dissent from her well-known views on racial discrimination by

refusing the use of its Washington auditorium to one of the finest of American singers because she sang in a dark skin.

Marian Anderson, needless to say, was not embarrassed by the refusal; she appeared instead at the Lincoln Memorial as a guest of the government of the United States.

And Eleanor Roosevelt was not embarrassed; she had more Revolutionary soldiers in her ancestry than many of her fellow members put together and needed the Daughters far less than the Daughters needed her.

But the President *was* concerned as the abuse became uglier, and eventually he put his wife's detractors in their proper places.

F.D.R.: These Republican leaders have not been content with attacks on me or on my wife or on my son.

No . . . not content with that, they now include my little dog, Fala. Well, of course *I* don't resent attacks and my *family* don't resent attacks . . . but *Fala* does resent them . . .

443

MRS. ROOSEVELT: You know, curiously enough, I never minded criticism much. I think I learned very young to know that everything passes and if you just live it through it comes to an end. If there is criticism and there is a foundation of right in it, well then it's their criticism and you have to take it. If there is no foundation in it, sooner or later people are going to find it out, and in the meantime it doesn't really matter much.

The only thing I would mind would be if it really affected the people I loved—people whose feeling of affection it really disturbed.

O F COURSE it never did affect the people she loved. People were everything to her; not only her own people but all the others everywhere. And it is largely for this reason that her understanding of her own time—of the tragic and violent events that made up her own time—seems sounder in retrospect than the understanding of many of her husband's best-informed advisers. They thought in terms of policies; she thought in terms of people.

Hitler to her was not a new political leader who might or might not change the balance of power in Europe: he was a perverter of humanity—including the humanity of the German people and particularly of the German young. Franco was not a general who had checked Russian ambitions in Spain: he was a Fascist who had overthrown the first hopeful Republican government Spain had ever had and turned the country back into a police state from which thousands of Spaniards escaped as best they could.

It is for this reason that she understood long before the majority of the American people that fascism and nazism were dangers not only in Europe but to our own continent and Republic as well.

The real question, she saw, was the human question. The issue everywhere—Russia, Germany, Italy, Spain—was the issue of human decency, human freedom. And the ultimate outcome would depend on human choice—particularly the choice and decision of the young.

Feeling as she did, Eleanor Roosevelt could hardly help expressing her feelings, President's wife or not.

MRS. ROOSEVELT: All of us have an equal responsibility in the one great country that is free . . . to the rest of the world wherever there may be people who are not free to become free again . . .

The dictatorships replied in kind. Goebbels called her a figure of fun, a silly woman talking of things that should be reserved for politicians. Mussolini attacked her as a nuisance who should be embargoed. And Franco added his bitter word from behind the skirts of his defenders. None of this, needless to say, interested Eleanor Roosevelt. But democracy was on trial even in the United States, where voices were already arguing for a change in American purposes toward the left or toward the right.

What mattered to Mrs. Roosevelt was not the speakers but the response—above all the response of the young. If young Americans decided, as some already had, that authoritarianism was "the wave of the future," then freedom and self-government in America would also disappear.

The young generation of those years had grown up in the universal disillusionment after the World War.

They believed the generation before them had been "had" by the imperialists of Germany and England and France. They were determined not to be "had" themselves.

They were persuaded, many of them, that the way not to be "had" was to support the Russian Revolution which had rejected the World War in 1917: to become Communists or to follow the Communist Party line.

Most of their elders in the Thirties reacted by denunciations and threats. Not so Mrs. Roosevelt. She could understand perfectly well why young people might call themselves Communists in the conditions of the Thirties. But she understood also how little chance communism had to hold the allegiance of the young if the young had a free chance to decide for themselves.

For this reason, and despite considerable criticism, Mrs.
Roosevelt had extended her hospitality and her friendship
to a number of leftward-looking youth organizations.
In the winter of 1939–40, the American Youth Congress,
largest and most vocal of these groups, held a meeting
in Washington and invited Mrs. Roosevelt to speak.

Already the issue between the young leftists and American
opinion in general was sharply drawn: the Nazi-Soviet pact
had been signed six months earlier, and World War II had
already begun with the German invasion of Poland.

When the Soviet Union attacked Finland the sympathy
of most Americans, Eleanor Roosevelt included, was with
the Finns—while the Youth Congress followed the Russian
line in calling Finland the aggressor.

But despite these differences, Mrs. Roosevelt agreed to
attend their meeting and answer their questions. Her husband,
at her request, had addressed the delegates first, forty-five
hundred of them, standing in the rain in the White House

garden while the President characterized their views on the Finnish war as "unadulterated twaddle." By the time Mrs. Roosevelt's turn came, the atmosphere was sullen and hostile. But she gave candid, uncompromising, and courteous answers to loaded and often insulting questions.

MRS. ROOSEVELT: I agree with you in your sympathy for Spain. I agree with you in your sympathy for China and Czechoslovakia; but I also have sympathy for Finland.

And when Mrs. Roosevelt walked out, she went to a standing ovation. The sight of an honest woman, respectful of the right of her listeners to differ but loyal also to her own beliefs, was a reminder of the strength and decency of the democratic tradition which shook all but the most doctrinaire.

It was a memorable occasion. And a few months later Mrs. Roosevelt's audience began to recollect it with a vivid comprehension.

WAR WAS no longer something to debate: war existed. England evacuated Dunkirk in the spring of 1940, France fell, and the writing was on the wall.

F.D.R.: December 7, 1941—a date which will live in infamy . . . the United States of America was suddenly and deliberately attacked by naval and air forces of the empire of Japan . . .

Hostilities exist. There is no blinking at the fact that our people, our territory, and our interests are in grave danger . . .

Guam fell on the tenth, Wake on the twenty-third.

Hong Kong surrendered on Christmas Day. Eight days later Manila fell and the Americans in the Philippines were cut off on the Bataan peninsula.

The British lost an army at Singapore, and naval units of Great Britain, the Netherlands, and the United States were beaten in the battle of the Java Sea.

Every news bulletin was a new disaster.

To most Americans in those terrible months the one task
was the prosecution of the war, the one end and aim the
survival of the country. But not to Eleanor Roosevelt.

Not even the greatest cataclysm in history could quiet her
conscience; what mattered to her was not survival only
but the *things* that survived.

When she discovered that the Japanese-Americans of
California and the Coast had been herded into American
detention camps in the panic that followed Pearl Harbor, she
protested. For one thing, the whole idea of such camps was
abhorrent to a free society. For another there was no proof—
and history bore her out—that Japanese-Americans were less
loyal than other Americans.

There could hardly have been a more unpopular cause
in that place and time, but she fought it out, and by fighting
it helped to fix her countrymen's attention on the real human
cause—the cause of human decency and self-respect. This,
throughout the war, was her continuing mission: to keep
the human perspective.

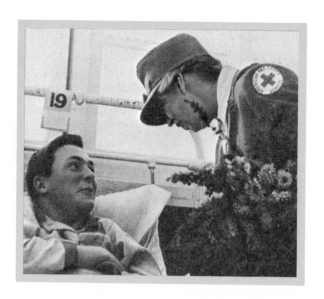

She traveled the country from one end to the other
to serve it.

In the fall of 1942 American troops in England were about
to leave, though she didn't know it at the time, for the
North African invasion. The President wanted her to visit
the camps, so she flew the Atlantic in a commercial amphibian
at her own expense; froze in the cold austerity of Buckingham
Palace; went from American camp to American camp;
talked to British women.

A year later she crossed the Pacific; traveled twenty-five
thousand miles through seventeen Pacific islands; visited
hospitals and bases, recreation centers and nurses' homes;
ate breakfast with enlisted men at unlikely hours; lost thirty
pounds; talked to enormous audiences; and came home
tireder than she had ever been in her life, to tell anyone
who would listen of the *feel* of her experience—"the horrible
consciousness of waste" which the hospitals left with her—
to try to prepare the families of wounded boys for their
return.

MRS. ROOSEVELT: The first thing is to write cheerful letters. The next thing, I believe, is to prepare yourselves for the return of your men. Some of them are coming back wounded, some of them are going to face handicaps all their lives; their feeling of confidence will depend on your being prepared to help them earn a living and enjoy life.

T WENTY months later her husband died at Warm Springs in Georgia.

When the news came she flew south at once, returning in the train with the President's body. All through the April night she kept the window shade open beside her berth so that she could see the faces of the crowds in the dimly lighted stations and at the country crossroads . . .

She thought, she said, about the ballad of the lonely train that carried Lincoln's body to Springfield.

And when morning came and the caisson with its flag-covered coffin had come down between silent, weeping crowds from the Union Station in Washington to the White House, she was waiting.

She walked slowly down the steps beneath the portico and touched the flag.

And she was waiting too at the funeral in the East Room of the White House: it seemed to her, she said, that everyone in the world was there "except three of my own sons"— two of them sailors, one a soldier.

And afterward, as the great of the world came to leave their wreaths on the grave of the dead President, she was still waiting . . . looking forward . . . looking back . . .

She said, once, that Franklin Roosevelt "might have been happier with a wife who was completely uncritical."

But she said, too, "I think I sometimes acted as a spur, even though the spurring was not always wanted or welcome.

"I was one of those," she said, "who served his purposes."

452

But she was also one of those who gave his purposes their meaning and their words.

On the sixth of June in 1944, when the whole mind of the Republic was fixed on the beaches of Normandy, Eleanor Roosevelt had spoken to the women of her own country, and beyond them to the women of the world.

"Every woman," she said, "will be praying that the victory may be speedy and that, this time, the sacrifices, whatever they are, will bring results that will justify, in the eyes of those who fight, whatever they have gone through."

And then she added, "It is not enough to win the fight. We must win *that for which we fight*—the triumph of all people who believe that the people of this world are worthy of freedom."

One can see what she was remembering. Her mind had gone back twenty-five years. "*This time*" the victory must be worthy of the suffering that bought it.

"This time" we must remember our purposes, our cause, not only in the hour of anguish but in the hour of happiness when the troops return.

All this was in her mind when she looked back from her husband's death, a few months before the war had ended. But when she looked the other way, into the future, she saw nothing.

She didn't matter anymore.

What had mattered was the President and he was dead—his work finished—"the glory left behind him for the others."

To the reporters who met her in the train shed of the Pennsylvania Station when she returned to New York on her way to anonymity, she said, "The story is over."

But, of course, the story wasn't over. In a sense it had just begun.

IN THE last fifteen years of her life, Eleanor Roosevelt, who had been the remarkable wife of a great President, became *herself*—became more than herself—something close to the conscience of her generation. And not in her own country alone but throughout the world: something close to the voice of a common humanity which had had no voice before.

It began when President Truman appointed her, eight months after her husband's death, to the American delegation to the first, the organizational, meeting of the General Assembly of the United Nations, to be convened in London in January of 1946.

No one, including Eleanor Roosevelt, was enthusiastic about the appointment. She thought she was not qualified— an opinion the rest of the delegation, particularly the Republicans, Dulles and Vandenberg, warmly endorsed. Mr. Truman, however, insisted, and the event proved him right.

Assigned by her colleagues to Committee Three, which was to deal with humanitarian and social and cultural matters and where, obviously, she could do the least harm, she soon found herself at the center of the hottest fight of the session—the fight over the Russian demand that all refugees be forced to return to their own countries regardless of what their countries had become in the interim—as, for example, Communist satellites.

Ultimately the debate reached the floor of the Assembly, where Andrei Vishinsky, head of the Russian delegation and the most formidable advocate in the Assembly, presented the Soviet case.

Who was to represent the United States?

Her fellow delegates, not eager themselves for the honor, appealed to their "unqualified" colleague.

MRS. ROOSEVELT: I gather that Mr. Vishinsky felt that anyone who did not wish to return under the present forms of government must of necessity be Fascist. I talked to a great many of these people: their country they feel no longer belongs to them. They did not strike me as Fascist.

And Eleanor Roosevelt scored a notable victory, carrying the Assembly with her against every one of the Soviet amendments.

It was a victory won without triumph, without leaving bitterness behind. And by the end of the session it was obvious to everyone in London—including the members of the American delegation itself—that the most effective American in the General Assembly was Eleanor Roosevelt.

It was a *personal* effectiveness. She was beginning to be treated, her critics complained, like a sovereign power—and sometimes they seemed to be right.

Yet Eleanor Roosevelt's greatest talent, as the world came more and more to see, was her ability to reduce the quarrels of doctrine and dogma to human differences which could be discussed in human terms.

Mrs. Roosevelt: We must be able to disagree with people and to consider new ideas and not to be afraid . . .

That she herself was not afraid was demonstrated in what has come to be called the McCarthy era, when the Junior Senator from Wisconsin had launched his inquisition into the opinions of his fellow citizens.

MRS. ROOSEVELT: The day I am afraid to sit down with people that I do not know because perhaps five years from now someone will say, "You sat in a room—five people were Communists —you are a Communist"—that will be a bad day. We must preserve our right to think and to differ in the United States.

"To think and to differ"—you could write a definition of America on that text, as well as the story of Eleanor Roosevelt's greatest achievement. It was because she believed— really believed—in the right of human beings to think and to differ that she became, toward the end of her life, a symbol of the American aspiration, and therefore of the belief in humanity for which the American aspiration has always stood.

And it was because the world thought of her in these terms that she became chairman of the United Nations commission appointed to draft a universal declaration of human rights. President Truman had named her as American representative on the commission, but it was the members of the commission themselves who elected her chairman.

MRS. ROOSEVELT: I don't know how other people feel but I always get a lift out of the fact that you can hear all the criticism and still have faith that the majority of the people will be right. I think it is always a very encouraging thing, and one which we in the Human Rights Commission must have tremendous faith in, because that's really the way that human rights will come to be a reality—only as the people really come to believe in human rights, and want to live for human rights.

It was largely because of her chairmanship that the commission was able, after two years of exhausting debate, to agree on a draft.

That draft of the Declaration of Human Rights was presented on December 10, 1948, to a meeting of the General Assembly under the presidency of Dr. Herbert Vere Evatt of Australia.

It was three o'clock in the morning; the room was half empty as the voting went on, clause by clause, until at last the draft had been approved.

DR. EVATT: . . . So that we reach the stage, gentlemen, in which, by an enormous vote and without any direct opposition, this Assembly has adopted this very important declaration. It is the first occasion on which the organized community of nations has made a declaration of human rights and fundamental freedoms, and it has the authority of the body of opinion of the U.N. as a whole. Millions of people, men, women, and children all over the world, many miles from Paris and New York, will turn for hope and guidance and inspiration to this document. It is particularly fitting that here tonight should be the person who has been the leader in this movement, assisted though she has been by many others—the person who has raised to even greater honor so great a name . . .

I refer, of course, to Mrs. Roosevelt, the delegate of the United States.

The figure that emerges in those last full years is a figure without likeness in our history. The lonely little girl in the dark parlor on Thirty-seventh Street who asked only to be left to her unhappiness had become a woman known by sight to millions of human beings and by repute to nearly all the world—a woman who stood for compassion and hope in every continent of the earth—for courage and for belief; a woman who met the great and the simple with the same simplicity, giving and taking what she had given and taken all her life; the sense of humanity, of human worth.

She was still "plain," if that is, or ever was, the right word for her candid, selfless face, but no one who looked at her now ever thought of her plainness, only of her eyes. She was old; but it was her youth you saw when you met her.

She was a "great lady," as everyone kept saying over and over—"the first lady of the world"—but what the world found in her was a woman—a warm, completely honest, fearless woman who lived a woman's life, accepted a woman's responsibilities, and changed the history of her time.

COLOR
FROM
A LIGHT
WITHIN

A vivid re-creation

of the life of the

immortal El Greco,

with twelve full-color

reproductions

of his paintings

COLOR
FROM A
LIGHT
WITHIN

A condensation of the book by

DONALD
BRAIDER

Illustrated by
William Hofmann

The Spaniards called him El Greco—the Greek—and so he has been known ever since. He was Cretan-born Domenikos Theotokopolous, a merchant's son who yearned to paint by the light he knew to be within him. His quest for instruction took him to Venice, then the bustling capital of an empire, whose great painters— Titian, Tintoretto, Veronese—were the public idols of their day. Incredibly, he persuaded the haughty Titian to accept him as a pupil, and when he had learned all the master could teach him, he blazed his own artistic trail, settling in Spain's "holy city" of Toledo and producing work of a power and intensity that makes a direct appeal to us today.

El Greco's life was shaped by private demons. Considering himself cursed by Heaven, he saw his family fortunes wiped out, his young bride, Maria, go mad, and the woman he loved doomed through him to spend her life in public sin. He came to fear happiness since it consumed those dearest to him while leaving him unscathed.

Against the colorful sixteenth-century background of the Counter-Reformation and the Inquisition, Donald Braider has brilliantly re-created the character of this tormented, deeply spiritual man whose entire career was a striving for a closeness to God.

PART I: CRETE (1541–1560)

CHAPTER 1

MASS WAS being chanted in the Metropolitan Church of Candia. Worshipers, dressed in Sunday black, knelt in prayer as the intonations echoed sonorously. Except for the hundred little ovals of candlelight that illuminated the altar, all was obscurity within the church. It was a November morning in 1546.

Suddenly, the rays of the autumnal sun pierced the banks of cloud and shone dazzlingly through the narrow windows of the nave, catching the twin icon paintings of St. Catherine and St. Titus, patrons of Crete, that adorned the iconostasis, the altar screen. The gold of the frames, the silver and encrusted jewels of the icons flashed brilliantly, startling a five-year-old boy who sat with his parents and his brother. He looked up from his prayers, the words of which he understood not at all; after nearly two hours of the long Eastern ritual, he was bored. But as he saw the icons blazing in the sunlight he stared. Never had he seen anything so beautiful. He had never even noticed these little pictures.

Throughout the remaining hour of the mass, Domenikos Theotokopoulos found it impossible to avert his eyes from the iconostasis. It was as if he were seeing through the icons, but seeing what? Something sublime. As the little family left the church, mother, father and older brother, Manusos, chat-

465

tered, but Domenikos was silent. As a rule, he babbled after mass, out of relief. Now he was still, seeing the two saints caught in the sunlight.

IT WAS spring, the first real spring day in the year 1552. Domenikos, now eleven, sat in his classroom in the Monastery of St. Catherine, wishing he were outside and only half listening as Brother Constantine began yet another class in drawing. Domenikos and his classmates had been taught to draw in charcoal, then in ink, slowly learning precision. But learning to draw precisely had been a simple matter for Domenikos, and he waited with growing impatience for the others to catch up.

"Who will volunteer," Brother Constantine suddenly said, "to go to the—" before he had finished, Domenikos had sprung up from his bench "—poultry house and find me three eggs?"

The boy nearly slipped on the terra-cotta floor, so abruptly did he bring himself to a halt before the tall figure of his master. He looked up in perplexity. "Eggs, Brother?"

"Eggs, Domenikos. We're going to make tempera."

"Do you mean that we're going to paint with eggs, Brother?" The boys all giggled at the preposterous idea.

The monk merely grinned. With a wave of his long, thin hand, he dispatched Domenikos, who speedily disappeared toward the court where the hens and other domestic beasts were confined.

Delighted to escape, the boy paused to caress the soft ears of a donkey. But curiosity about the strange process of converting eggs to color prevailed, and he ran on to the poultry house. He deftly plucked the eggs from the nests. Then, holding them carefully, he made for the classroom.

Brother Constantine began his demonstration. "Always employ an egg that is absolutely fresh," he said as he cracked one on the edge of a bowl. "Separate the yolk from the white carefully." He poured the clear albumen into one container, the yellow into a second to which he added a little water from a ewer. "Mix the yolk and the water very, very slowly." He poured a small quantity of the mixture into a shallow dish, then took a pinch of a dark powder. "Now, add your pigment. Remember, it must be fine or it will not blend with the yolk and water. So if it is lumpy, grind it in a mortar. Once your color is mixed, use it quickly, otherwise the egg yolk will dry and your paint will be wasted." He picked up a small rectangular panel. "This piece of wood has been prepared with gesso, a thin coating of plaster." With a narrow brush, he painted a few short strokes on the smooth surface.

"What a wonderful dark blue," Domenikos exclaimed.

The monk glanced at him. "Ah, yes, a very fine color. But tempera becomes paler and more transparent as it dries. Watch."

Domenikos observed, fascinated, as the deep blue faded to a faint, translucent film on the white of the panel. "But how do you get darker colors, Brother?"

"You keep adding layers of paint." He showed the boys how this was done, painting over the brushstroke he had just made, then turned to Domenikos. "Now you try it. Pour some of the egg and water into a clean dish and add a different pigment to it."

This was a great moment. The boy poured a little of the mixture into a dish, sprinkled in the pigment—vermilion—and began to blend it with a spatula. In his eagerness, he beat it into a froth.

"No, no," said the monk, his tone gentle. "No bubbles. Mix it slowly—you are not going to make a meal of it. Start again."

When the boy had finally concocted a satisfactory tempera, Brother Constantine told him to paint a few strokes on the panel. Domenikos was surprised by the slippery ease with which the color went on. He painted a straight line, a curve and an S shape.

At mass that evening, in the monastery chapel, Domenikos expressed his fervent thanks to God for having put color in his hands. Afterward, halfway down the slope to Candia, he began to run. He was bursting to tell his parents about the wonder of it.

WITH HIS wife, Cleo, and his older son, Manusos, Giorgio Theotokopoulos had just returned home from prayers in the town. They now gathered at the table to wait for Domenikos, while the servant girl made noisy preparations for supper in the kitchen.

Giorgio was a handsome man, squarish, with thick, wiry hair

that was going gray, as were his wide mustache and full beard. He was fifty, an age then thought advanced, but there was nothing ancient about the snapping black eyes or the vigorous gestures that accompanied his conversation. For Giorgio, everything was either yes or no, seldom maybe. He was impulsive and impatient. When he was hungry, as now, he wanted to eat at once. When he was happy, he wanted to celebrate. When he was sad, he wept. When frustrated, he became petulant.

He was a successful man, a merchant with warehouses overlooking the small, fortified harbor of Candia, and vineyards and olive groves at nearby Fodele, managed now by Manusos. His trade with Venice was so profitable that his younger brother, also named Manusos, was permanently installed there. And he was on good enough terms with the Venetian rulers of Crete to have been given the important post of tax collector. He contributed a tithe to his own Eastern Church and gave grudgingly to the Roman Church supported by the Venetians. He was proud of his island's heritage, as he was of his family and his position. And he was determined that his sons should follow in the family business. Manusos, tractable if not brilliant, was doing so.

But about Domenikos, Giorgio had severe misgivings. As he saw it, the boy was soft, and for this he blamed his wife's family. Two of her brothers were monks in the great monastic community of Mount Athos on the Greek mainland. The gentle lad with those intense, enormous eyes might be similarly inclined.

Thus he reflected as Cleo poured his wine. "I don't think Domenikos has any iron in his soul," he said fiercely. "Where's the Cretan in him? Answer me that. Where's the Greek?"

Cleo's small, sweet features broke into a smile. "Domenikos has all the will he needs. You'd be surprised how willful he can be."

"You know what I think? He's going to become one of those icon-painting monks!"

"If he has a true calling, surely you won't stand in his way?"

"No, no, of course not. But I'll not have these monks putting ideas into his head."

Cleo laughed. "But isn't that why you're sending him to the brothers in the first place, to have them put ideas into his head?"

Giorgio threw up his hands. "All anyone needs to learn in a

school is how to pray and how to count. Isn't that right, Manusos?"

The young man shrugged. "It's all *I* learned."

Cleo protested. "You learned to read, didn't you?"

"Yes, mama, but I never do."

"Manusos isn't interested in reading," Cleo said. "Domenikos is. You must give some consideration to *his* desires."

Giorgio pointed toward the monastery. "They say he's their best pupil. He can become my pupil and learn my business. I need him more than the Church does."

At that moment Domenikos entered, panting with exertion and excitement. His face, similar to his mother's, though longer and narrower, was streaked with dust and perspiration. His lay-pupil's cassock was dirty, his hands stained by red pigment. He planted a kiss on Giorgio's woolly cheek, kissed his mother, and exchanged a perfunctory embrace with his brother. He was about to seat himself when Cleo lifted her hand. "Go wash yourself."

He disappeared into the inner courtyard. The servant girl came in with bowls of soup and a basket containing chunks of dark bread. Domenikos returned, his hair smoothed down, wiping his hands on his filthy cassock. He took his place by his brother.

"And what made you late *this* evening?" his father inquired.

"We made colors by mixing them with eggs." The boy was still breathless. "And then we painted with them."

"And *that's* what you're all out of breath about?" Giorgio said incredulously. "Is *this* an education?"

"Brother Constantine is teaching us how to paint panels," Domenikos said carefully. "His own panels are perfect."

"How many icon panels have you ever seen?" Giorgio demanded.

"Every one in every church around Candia, I think. I've decided I'm going to be a painter of icons." He hadn't intended to say so much just now, but his desire had forced the words out.

Giorgio stared, then rose and departed in hostile silence.

"You want to be a monk, Domenikos?" Cleo said, at last.

"I don't think so, mama. Brother Constantine says that in Venice and Constantinople quite a few laymen paint icons."

469

"And that's what you want, to go away?"

The boy hesitated. "Well, it's been in my mind. But I wasn't certain until this afternoon, when I put some color on a panel."

If Giorgio could just *look* at the boy, Cleo thought, he would see how different he was from other children. You had only to watch him in his strange silences to notice his intensity.

Domenikos was wise enough to say no more to his father about his desire to paint. Giorgio also managed to keep silent. He did, however, arrange a meeting with Brother Constantine.

IT WAS a warm Sunday in April, just after mass. Giorgio walked slowly, perspiring, up the long hill to the monastery. As he stood before the white gates and looked into the exterior courtyard, he recalled with very little nostalgia his own years there as a pupil.

Brother Constantine was waiting in his classroom. On shelves and in niches were models of icons to be copied, and examples of the boys' work. All the subjects were religious, all based on the rigid style so long established: all the figures stylized, adhering to the divine prescriptions and proscriptions. As he approached the gaunt, aging monk whom his son so adored, Giorgio thought he looked as if he hadn't eaten a decent meal in years.

Brother Constantine extended his arms in welcome. "I am glad to meet the man who could produce such a boy. He is brilliant."

"Thank you, Brother. So my wife says. But what does this mean? Are you trying to tell me that he can't join my business?"

"You have it in your mind," the monk said, leading Giorgio to a hard bench, "that I'm interfering with your plans?"

Giorgio shook his head stubbornly. "I'm asking a question."

"I'm doing for Domenikos only what I do for all my pupils. I show him how to apply paints to a panel. He will soon be able to teach *me*. I have had talented boys; Domenikos is the first who seems touched with genius. I believe he will serve God as a painter of icons and be a true ornament to our Church. But I have never attempted to persuade him."

The monk's calm induced rage in Giorgio, but he controlled it. "Can't he serve God in my vineyards and warehouses?"

"Oh, yes. But aren't we taught that each of us best serves God by doing what we know and love best?"

"And how would you know, Brother, whether Domenikos isn't just as well suited for commerce as he is for art?"

"Only he can know that, and God, of course."

Giorgio flailed the air with his arms. "Do you mean to tell me that I have no right to my son's help during my old age?"

"You imagine your rights to Domenikos greater than God's?"

So gently had the monk put this question that Giorgio's rage dissolved. "What's he really like, this boy?" he asked helplessly.

"Exceptional. He has intelligence, grace of body and grace of speech. He has, I think, a beautiful soul. He is also *very* stubborn."

The father of this prodigy grinned. "*That* I know."

The monk went on. "Our Church owes a great deal to men and women who were obstinate. Our Lord Himself was a stubborn man." He walked to the window that overlooked a rugged landscape in which scrub-covered ridges, interrupted now and then by groves and vineyards, stretched southward to Mount Ida. "What disturbs me is that Domenikos is full of doubt. He never seems content with my answers." He faced Giorgio. "If he *were* to become a monk, he would have difficulty learning to accept authority. The experience might break his spirit, and I would not like that." He picked up a panel of St. George and the Dragon. "Domenikos asked me why the sky in this picture did not resemble the real sky." He pointed to a series of rippling lines, like no sky Giorgio had ever seen. "I told him the picture was inspired by God."

"And what did Domenikos say to that?"

"He said, 'Do you mean that God doesn't see the sky in the same way we do?' I said, 'You are not to bother your head about things like that. We copy icons with so much care because, originally, they came to us from God. They are the word of God in images, and are neither to be altered nor questioned.'"

"I hope he said no more to you about it after that, Brother."

Brother Constantine sighed. "For every answer you give him he has a question. He is very logical, and very hard to put off."

Giorgio, believing he saw light, said, "Then, if I understand you, he's very ill suited to becoming a monk."

"Oh, I can scarcely tell you that. But if he continues along his

16TH-CENTURY CRETAN ICON OF ST. GEORGE AND THE DRAGON

present path he would be a very unhappy one." Brother Constantine held the little picture at arm's length, smiling proudly. "He has it in him to be a great icon painter, though. And what a fine thing that would be."

It was all Giorgio could do not to laugh. Icon painters were monks and Domenikos, he had just been told, had not the temperament to be a monk.

THE SOCIAL, economic and religious structure of Crete at this time reflected the curious relations between the natives and their masters from Venice. The Venetians had governed Crete since the early thirteenth century, but had never quite succeeded in keeping ascendancy over their spirited subjects. Even a man as dependent for his prosperity on Venetian friendship as Giorgio frequently expressed contempt for Venetian rule. And he was permitted his scorn, as he was also permitted his observation of the Eastern Church ritual, the faith of the islanders.

In the matter of religion, Venice believed she could be generous because, in this epoch when most of western Europe was rocked by conflict, she was still a bastion of enlightenment, a product of the humanist revolution in thought and worship later called the Renaissance. Besides, the great doges who presided over the Venetian empire were primarily concerned with the maintenance of their vital commerce with Asia Minor, in which Crete was a major protective link. The Cretans' loyalty to the Most Serene Republic of Venice, the Serenissima, was therefore far more important than their loyalty to the Church of Rome.

So the Venetian bishops of Crete dealt softly with the separated brethren of the Eastern faith. The schism, after all, had taken place a long time ago, and the issues that divided the two great churches were questions more of practice than of doctrine. For example, the Latin Curia insisted on total clerical celibacy, while the Eastern hierarchy required only bishops to be unmarried; the priests of the Roman Church shaved their beards, while Eastern priests did not. And on the central issue of the schism, the Venetian bishops agreed with their Cretan subjects. Both resented the authority of the Pope. Why, the Venetians asked, as the Easterners had five hundred years ago, should the Bishop of Rome automatically be Pope? Surely others had equal claims.

The only severe limitation imposed by the Venetians was on the size of Cretan churches. This was intended to prevent more than a handful of islanders from congregating to plan a revolt. But as Giorgio put it, "Cretans have no need of churches to plot rebellions in. We can manage that in the open air."

Over the centuries, there had been many attempts to overthrow Venetian authority. All had failed; all had resulted in brutal reprisals. But revolt was always in the air. Now Cretans were saying with glee that Venice was slipping. Since the discovery of the New World, Genoa seemed to be supplanting the Serenissima as the great mercantile state of Italy. Spain was becoming more powerful than either. And in the east the Ottoman Empire had been systematically snapping up Venetian holdings. Many islanders would have welcomed a Turkish conquest, but the Ottoman invasion of Crete lay far in the future. For some time to come, the presence of Venice would permeate Cretan life.

Giorgio was obsessed with the niceties of dealing with his Venetian masters. The position was precarious, and few Cretans could walk on both sides of the fence as his business required him to do. He doubted, alas, that his son Manusos could take over this daily diplomacy. With plaintive frequency, he said to Cleo: "Only Domenikos will have the intelligence to take my place." Domenikos might continue to play with his paints but when he attained manhood, he must join his father.

WHEN Brother Constantine's pupils copied icon panels, the sole criterion was fidelity "to God's work," he would say, with a glance at Domenikos. The youth eventually became a brilliant copyist. And under the direction of another monk, he learned the application of color to wet plaster, the process of painting frescoes.

The adolescent was becoming a man, his long features filling out, his slender body stretching. How he longed to talk with Giorgio about his determination to paint. The gay, open child had become brooding, introspective, and as Brother Constantine observed with sorrow, he appeared to avoid his fellows.

In the summer evenings, he would walk up into the hills to the site of the ancient Roman ruins. Here he made sketches of the wind-bent trees, the sharply angled clumps of scrub, the endlessly rolling hills. And he drew the fragments of Roman columns and entablatures. He recognized that his efforts were inept. He knew nothing about perspective and proportion. His eye, which perceived what was wrong, couldn't direct his hand.

One day, after an especially tedious session of icon copying, Domenikos hung back after class and asked Brother Constantine: "What is the law that prevents me from going beyond what I've learned from you, from painting what I see in nature?"

The monk sighed. "You ask that as if you were a papist. Domenikos, I've told you: that is not for icon painters. You are questioning the will of God."

Domenikos had but the faintest idea what it was to be a papist; he had never set foot in a Roman church. "You mean it's a sin to apply what I've learned to a use that's secular? Then why is it, Brother, that I never feel any sense of sin when I look at beautiful landscapes, or at people or animals, or at churches and houses? They were made by God, or inspired by God, so why should we not paint them as we see them?"

"You see as a layman, not as a cleric, my son. It *is* evil to paint in this way within the framework of the Church."

"I realize that. So how am I to learn?"

"Not from me. *I* know no other way of painting." Tears came to Brother Constantine's eyes. "When February comes, Domenikos, you will have to leave the monastery. I should have urged you to go before, since I long ago taught you all I know. But your other teachers thought you might find a vocation in the Church." He shook his head. "You will not. Your spirit is too arrogant, confused by your intellect. You have genius in your mind and in your hands. God put it there, and you should be grateful."

"I am, Brother."

"Not sufficiently to do His work on earth."

Domenikos found it difficult to suppress his annoyance. "Are you telling me that God's work can only be done by monks?"

The old monk smiled. "Only you, and God, of course, can know in truth what you can do. I wish you well, Domenikos. No other pupil has given me the joy that you have. Nor the pain and anguish. Whatever you do with your life, my son, you must do by yourself. I hope it proves a happy existence, a rich one for you, a noble one. Because I am sure you will be lonely."

Domenikos went out into the bright cloister and could feel in advance the pain he would know when the moment of departure came. Virtually all the delight of his life was in some way associated with this monastery. "I'm alone," he muttered as he gazed about the cloister. And abruptly he was elated. If he was destined, like Ishmael, to be a wanderer all his life, then let it be so.

It was a Saturday afternoon. Domenikos was taking a desultory stroll along the quays. There were few ships moored at the wharves, so there was little activity to distract his eye from its inward focus. The yawping gulls had grown torpid in the heat of the day. They swooped lazily across the still, intensely blue water.

He reached an intersection, and turned aimlessly toward the main square with the principal buildings of the Venetian administration. Before him was the Cathedral of St. Titus, a Roman church. He approached the fine, classical facade with its sculptural adornments and its Corinthian pilasters. The great bronze doors stood open invitingly. He entered, and was surprised by the cheerful, open arrangement of this church, so much brighter than the one he attended. All was color and air and sunlight, the light transmitted through tall, broad windows. Slender columns supported the high, coffered ceiling. Small chapels lined both sides of the nave, each with its gilded altar and alabaster statuary. But it was the brilliant high altar that held his attention. The retable was a large triptych, framed in gold, depicting the Annunciation, the Baptism and, in the center, the Crucifixion of Christ.

He was electrified. The saints, the archangel of the Annunciation, the Virgin, Our Lord Himself, were portrayed in poses that were natural. They had a quality no painter of icons would have dared to attempt, or even known how to begin. The flesh of these figures was flesh. The clothing was draped realistically. And the colors—such richness of tones, such light!

A tap on the shoulder made Domenikos turn. A wizened

little priest was peering up at him, amused. "You're standing in the sanctuary, you know. I'm afraid you're not supposed to be here."

Domenikos flushed and backed away, muttering an apology. But the priest restrained him. "It's all right this time." He turned to the altarpiece. "Magnificent, isn't it? It's one of the treasures of Crete. It's by a pupil of Titian, Venice's greatest painter."

"It *is* magnificent, Father. I'm ashamed to confess that I've never heard of Titian. Is he still alive?"

The old priest laughed. "Oh, yes. He lives in a great house in Venice. Some say he's almost as rich as the Doge himself."

Domenikos grew excited. "Does he take pupils, Father?"

"As to that I really couldn't tell you." He looked curiously at Domenikos. "You speak Italian well, but you're a Cretan, aren't you?"

"I am, Father."

"And they let you enter our cathedral? How astonishing."

"I just wandered in. Is it wrong for me to be here?"

"Come as often as you like. Our doors are open to all God's children. You *are* one of His children, aren't you?"

"I suppose I am, Father, but my Church doesn't see it in the same light as you do."

"Well, we Venetians regard these differences as unimportant. Man's soul is our only concern. The Romans are lawyers, they enjoy splitting hairs." He smiled. "What is your name, my son?"

"Domenikos Theotokopoulos, Father."

"Giorgio's son? Well, Domenikos, you're very welcome. I know your father, in a business way, you might say. I'm Father Vincenzo. I shall always be glad to see you."

IT WOULD BE inaccurate to suggest that Domenikos' conversion to the Roman faith was the result of his enthusiasm for the paintings in the cathedral, or even of the generous outlook of Father Vincenzo. These were important elements, however, for they were evidence of a sort of faith that he realized he had been seeking: the recognition of man as more than the toy of a whimsical and frequently angry God.

The priest met frequently with Domenikos, after dark. He

instructed the youth in the Mysteries, the articles of faith, and the ritual of the Roman communion. He gave him volumes by the Fathers of the Church. And not long after Christmas he saw to it (quiet improperly) that Domenikos was admitted, in secret, as a communicant.

Domenikos' conversion and his exposure to Venetian art convinced him that he must go to Venice to study with the great Titian. However, this would be impossible without his father's consent and assistance, which never seemed less likely than it did in February of 1560, after Domenikos had said farewell to the Monastery of St. Catherine. For it was understood by Giorgio that his younger son would now join the family concern. Domenikos was disturbed to discover that he would use any means to gain his end; would even conceal his conversion, which was central to the person he had become. He saw, with shock, that he was as willful as his father—and probably more devious.

He took care to select an evening when Manusos was not dining at home. The servant girl had cleared away the dinner things, and Giorgio was about to leave the table when Domenikos spoke.

"There's something I have to say to you, papa." His heart seemed to stop as he watched his father sit down again. He blurted it out. "I want to go to Venice to study painting with Titian."

The silence that followed was broken by Cleo, her face contracted with anxiety. "You're sure about this, Domenikos?"

"Absolutely sure, mama. If I'm to learn more about painting, I have to go to Venice, and Titian is the greatest master there."

Giorgio's voice was unnaturally controlled. "Why isn't Cretan painting good enough for you?"

"It *is* good, papa, for its purposes. But I want to paint people who look like people, in settings that look like life."

Giorgio grunted. "I've seen such paintings in the Venetians' houses. What have they to do with God?"

Domenikos suppressed a smile; his father sounded like Brother Constantine. "In the Roman faith these pictures are acceptable. I've seen them in the cathedral and the churches."

"And what would you know about the Roman faith?"

"I've talked with their priests about the paintings."

"And that's as far as it went?"

"That's as far as it went." The lie came easily. "I may go, papa?"

Giorgio brought a heavy fist down on the table. "Yes, by God. Yes." He began to laugh, enjoying the astonished stare on his son's face. "I need you, Domenikos. I'll not pretend I don't. Manusos is a fine fellow, but he hasn't your intelligence. On the other hand, it seems that God has intended you to be a painter. I can't see why, but who am I to fly in His face?" He aimed a finger at his son. "But you have it in you to be the greatest merchant. I will not stand for your being second-rate at anything."

"No reason to fear, papa."

Giorgio leaned forward. "What makes you so sure?"

"I feel the thing I can do best with my life is to paint. I can feel it in my hands." He extended his arms, his slender fingers splayed. "Painting is all they'll let me do, all I've ever wanted to do."

Giorgio sighed and turned to his wife. "Why me? Why should such an unreasonable, irresponsible idea occur to a son of mine?"

"Perhaps it's something to do with my side of the family," she said with a mischievous smile.

He stiffened. "And why your side of the family? You think there's no quality, no intellectuality, on my side?"

She laughed gaily. "You imagine that I would have married you if I thought you without quality? You think my father could have forced me to do something so important against my will?"

He shook his head. "No, by God. The devil himself couldn't force you to do something against your will."

"You can *persuade* me to do almost anything, Giorgio."

Their eyes met and held. Giorgio said, "I knew you'd have your way. So I thought I'd try something different. Instead of saying no, I'd say yes." He chuckled. "I never had a chance, did I?"

"Never."

"And you—" He looked at Domenikos. "I used to think you had no will, but it takes a great strength to want the same thing at nineteen that you wanted at eleven. We're going to miss you. My God, how we'll miss you, Domenikos." He began to weep softly. "But go, and go with my blessing."

The old Giorgio returned as rapidly as he had vanished. Again he pointed at Domenikos. "You can't manage this expedition without money, and without making arrangements ahead of time. You'll stay with your uncle Manusos in Venice. And I'll provide you with enough money to live as a son of mine should."

Domenikos struggled up to embrace Cleo, then his father. Giorgio took the youthful face between his powerful hands and looked into the immense dark eyes. "I'm not sure that you're right in this, but you should have a chance at it. If anything goes wrong, it's easier to come home if you've not had to run away, isn't it?"

Domenikos nodded and grinned through his tears.

He slept badly that night. He had lied about his conversion, though Father Vincenzo had urged him to tell the truth. He rued it bitterly. But how could he imperil the trip to Venice?

PART II: VENICE (1560–1570)

CHAPTER 2

DOMENIKOS Theotokopoulos was reborn the morning of May 7, 1560. A Venetian galley had taken the barque in tow and was drawing her slowly toward her mooring by the quay called the Molo. As the craft glided through the still water of the lagoon, the only sound was of the galley's oarsmen rowing in time to the cries of the coxswain. The sun appeared as an orange ball through the morning mist. Domenikos stood at the bow with the other passengers, scarcely able to contain his excitement.

He was sure he would recognize the chief landmarks. Had he not studied, in the library of the archbishop in Candia, Jacopo de Barbari's wonderful plan of Venice? The mist parted to give him a brief glimpse of the green domes of San Marco, the tall shaft of the Campanile, and on the Molo itself, the elegant facade of the Doge's Palace. But Barbari's old woodcut hadn't shown the glitter of the spires and domes, the colored walls of the palace, the pale blue of the sky, the muddy waters of the canals. Nor could any picture convey the impression of bustle, of vitality.

A crowd was gathered about the foot of the gangway. In front were flocks of grubby boys begging for coins or sweets, and men with ill-kempt beards and torn clothing offering to unload cargo. Beyond were merchants with their clerks, the former dressed in garish silks that no self-respecting Cretan would dream of wearing. Domenikos searched their faces but saw none that looked familiar. He felt helpless and homesick. Then he gazed at the white stone arcade of the Doge's Palace. And there, leaning casually against a column, was his uncle Manusos, gaudily dressed but unmistakable in his resemblance to Giorgio. He was looking directly at Domenikos, smiling sardonically.

THE PHYSICAL likeness was deceptive. Manusos' interests and outlook were very different from Giorgio's. He had, since his arrival in Venice many years before, become almost wholly Italianized. He was preoccupied with the *appearance* of success, and he was ambitious politically as well as socially. He had achieved a high position in the Greek community, which numbered several thousand, and would have liked to be their leader, head of their Council of Forty. But most he dreamed of being elected to the Consiglio, the council that advised the Doge, even though he knew it to be impossible—one had to be of noble birth. He was, therefore, in a curious Italian fashion, extremely cautious in expressing his opinions, a policy that served him well in a commercial way, by not alienating powerful Venetians, but that made him enemies among the outspoken Greeks. His tendency to shilly-shally thus threatened his attainable ambitions, but it was by now as much a part of his nature as was his conspicuous generosity.

When Domenikos came down the gangway, Manusos embraced him warmly. He took him by the arm as he arranged for the transportation of Domenikos' effects to his house in the Rio dei Greci. Then, elbowing his way through the crowd, he guided the youth toward the Piazzetta. Between the columns that supported the celebrated Venetian winged lion and the warrior St. Theodore, he paused and smiled up at his tall young nephew. "Well, how do you like our magnificent Venice?"

Domenikos laughed. "It's so busy. It confuses me."

"Busy? Why, this is nothing. Wait until noon. Or wait until

the Feast of San Marco. Venice is the most beautiful and the greatest city in the world, my boy."

As they moved on toward the great Piazza and St. Mark's Cathedral, all the young man's senses were absorbed. His nose was assaulted with a noxious blending of dead fish, sewage, and the food that was cooked and vended in the streets. But no odor could distract his eye from the masterpieces of architecture, or from the color and vivacity of the pedestrians who darted across the great square in all directions. What a variety of people, from white to Chinese to darkest Nubian slave; even, astounding Domenikos, pairs of prostitutes patrolling in broad daylight.

In one corner of the Piazza rose the Campanile, the immense bell tower made of delicate marble and warm-toned brick. As Domenikos stared at it, the great bells began to chime, a wild sound that thrilled and startled him and sent the innumerable pigeons madly swooping about the square. And then he turned to face the Cathedral of San Marco itself. It was surely a wonder of the world. From the ship he had seen its five great copper domes, green with weathering. Here was its facade, a fantasy so extravagant that he was unable at first to comprehend the whole vision. His eyes seized on details, and he could not have said whether he was more struck by the mosaics, the first he had seen, or by the huge bronze horses above the central portal.

Manusos tugged at the youth's cape. "Come, Domenikos. You must be hungry, and your aunt Marica is waiting."

Domenikos nodded, taking a final look. "My God," he said.

"*Their* God, you mean," said Manusos, chuckling. "It's a Latin church. Actually, it's the Doge's private chapel."

Domenikos followed his uncle through narrow streets to a substantial stone house in the Rio dei Greci. "Here we are," Manusos said with pride, ushering him into a white-walled room with a high, beamed ceiling. "Sit down. I'll fetch your aunt."

The room was furnished with a heavy oak table and chairs, and a large cupboard full of pottery. A tapestry with a colorful geometric pattern hung opposite a large fireplace. Next to it were a pair of Cretan icons of St. George and St. Catherine. A pretty, dark-haired servant girl entered with a tray on which were bread and cheese, a pitcher of wine and a Venetian glass goblet. He thanked her as she placed the tray in front of him.

Manusos returned, preceded by his wife. Aunt Marica had a strong face, with black eyes and a ready smile that disclosed even white teeth. Domenikos stood up and she embraced his waist with her short, fleshy arms. Then she stood back, laughing wholeheartedly. "My goodness, Domenikos, you are really a big fellow."

The girl returned with two more trays and as they ate, his aunt talked. "How's your dear mother? Has she put on weight? No? I don't see how she manages it. And Giorgio, is he well? Good. Is your brother married yet? Too bad. A man ought to marry before he's twenty-five. That's what I say to my Anastos. Of course, he's only sixteen. He's studying at our monastery school. . . ."

Manusos listened, amused, and when at last Marica paused, he put his own question. "What would you like to do first?"

"Why," said Marica, "he wants to go to his room and rest."

"Oh, no," Domenikos said. "I'd like to see more of Venice. I've waited so long for this. I want to see the house of Maestro Tiziano. And I want to pray, of course, to thank God for my safe arrival."

Manusos cleared his throat. "Well, now, Domenikos, as I wrote your father, I'm afraid that you're going to have trouble finding a place in Titian's studio."

Domenikos nodded. "I read your letter. But you must know someone who can help me. Papa says you know every important man in Venice." He felt ashamed for thus preying on his uncle's vanity.

Manusos smiled smugly. "Well, perhaps most of them. But Tiziano Vecellio is one of the nobility, a count palatine. You'd be a lot easier in your mind if you were studying with someone who speaks our language, like Michele Damaskinos who's doing the frescoes in our new Greek church. I'm told he's a wonderful teacher. And he's had great success as an icon painter."

Domenikos was dismayed. He had no need of further training in icon painting, and he proposed to make himself clear. "But you see, I want to study with Titian. That's why I came to Venice."

Manusos sighed. "It will be very difficult. Damaskinos told me that Titian takes no more pupils."

A WEEK passed. Manusos scurried from acquaintance to acquaintance in a vain quest for an introduction to Titian. Domenikos explored Venice, visiting churches, the public portions of the Doge's Palace, the Library of San Marco, and the Procuratie, observing with amazement the gaudy panoply of daily life, its violence, its richness, and its appalling poverty.

Venice had been at the height of her power three centuries before, during the Crusades. She now sought to conceal her accelerating decline by building ever more wonderful monuments to her eternal greatness. Almost alone among Italian cities, she had been left unscarred by the Holy Roman Emperor Charles V's terrible sweep southward in 1527. She was still, in 1560, the Pearl of the Adriatic, a dream city floating off the coast, glittering with a hundred domes and spires. And her citizens, intelligent and adaptable, had offset declining trade revenues with increased banking activities. So for most Venetians the present seemed prosperous enough, and they did not peer too deeply into the future.

One wound, however, was obvious—the state of the Church—and fifteen years earlier Pope Paul III had convened the nineteenth Ecumenical Council to try to heal it. The Council was still sitting at the town of Trento in the mountains near Venice. Its debates were the subject of vehement discussion in the Piazza, to which Domenikos listened with interest. If his understanding of such things was limited, he could have taken solace from the fact that many churchmen were in ignorance of the issues.

In the early part of the century, the defection from the Church of the cleric Martin Luther had sparked the Protestant Reformation. Luther and his followers had denounced the ethics of the popes, had questioned their authority, and had protested the system by which kings and princes—with an eye on the vast wealth the Church collected in tithes—controlled the appointment of the bishops entrusted with the expenditure of that wealth. It was to conceal the blemishes caused by venal popes (notably Rodrigo Borgia, Alexander VI) and all-too-human kings, and to retard the spread of Protestantism and other heresies that the first Council of Trent was called. The philosophy it propounded came to be called the Counter-Reformation, a churchwide movement to clarify doctrine and purify the clergy.

The effort was proving futile, though the debates on doctrine did stimulate people to examine their beliefs. But Protestantism was not destroyed. Purification of the clergy seemed unlikely until an entire generation of priests, monks and nuns died off, and in her passion to stamp out venality, debauchery and heresy, the Church took overzealous measures. Books were banned. Rational discussion was inhibited. Ridiculous rules were laid down for religious art, for poetry and music.

To most intelligent Venetian churchmen, the debates at Trento were anathema. The Holy Inquisition, which had been successfully revived in Spain, was but grudgingly accepted in Venice and functioned timidly. Heresy was hard to identify in a city overrun with transients. Mass arrests and persecutions were deemed un-Italian. It was a popular Venetian view that the most dangerous heretics were those who supported the Inquisition.

Domenikos' wanderings took him daily, late or early, to the Biri Grande where, across the street from the house of Tiziano Vecellio, he waited for a glimpse of the great man. Each day when the door opened on a tantalizing view of gardens stretching down to the lagoon and of the master's immense studios, Domenikos held his breath in hope; each day, disappointed, he would go on to the Church of San Canciano and burn a candle in supplication.

One day, as he was leaving the church, he was startled by the voice of his uncle. "What are *you* doing here, Domenikos?"

"I was praying, uncle."

"There?" his uncle said. "You belong? You're a communicant?"

"I am." Too late he wished he had not spoken the truth.

"And how does your father feel about it?"

"He doesn't know. I couldn't tell him. I meant to—"

"Why did you do it? Why?"

It was so complicated. He had no reason to apologize for his religious convictions. Yet to offer no explanation might anger his uncle and cause him to communicate with Giorgio.

"It's their art," he said at last.

Manusos looked puzzled. Then his face cleared. "You mean, to succeed in *their* world you have to be one of them?"

This had never occurred to Domenikos, but he saw that his

uncle would accept it. With a conscience less than easy, he nodded. "Greeks won't buy the sort of painting I hope to do."

Manusos patted his shoulder. "You surprise me, Domenikos. I had the feeling you weren't much better than a spoiled monk, all conscience and regret. You're right. The only way for you to get ahead is to join them." He chuckled. "Very Italian. I'm proud of you. Say nothing to Giorgio, though. Nor to your aunt. She'd write to your mother, and then you'd be in trouble."

A few days later the family was seated at dinner, including young Anastos, Domenikos' cousin. The boy looked like his father, but he had inherited Marica's candid nature and common sense.

"I suppose you've made no progress with Domenikos' little problem?" Marica said to her husband.

"None," he responded curtly.

"Whom have you seen?" she asked.

Manusos slammed the flat of his hand loudly on the table. "Whom *haven't* I seen. And they all tell me the same thing. Maestro Tiziano takes no more pupils. He's a rich man, he's an old man, he doesn't want the trouble of teaching any more."

Anastos ventured boldly in. "Have you seen our bishop, papa?"

Manusos stared at him. "Gabriele Seviros? Now why in the name of God should I disturb *him* about a thing like this?"

"Because he knows Maestro Tiziano. There's a portrait of him by Tiziano in the monastery."

Marica clapped her hands with delight, then blew a kiss to her son. "You see? He has brains, this little one."

"You know," Manusos said to Domenikos, "he might just be right. We'll try to see His Excellency tomorrow. Now, I'm going to the taverna." It was his customary evening exit line.

THE RESIDENCE of the Eastern Church's patriarch in Venice was no luxurious episcopal palace. A modest town house, candlelit, somber, it evoked in Domenikos a memory of the Candia Metropolitan Church. Bishop Gabriele Seviros was seated on a black-lacquered throne, his pure white beard reaching the heavy jeweled cross on his ample breast. Manusos kneeled to kiss the episcopal ring, and Domenikos respectfully followed suit. They stood, and the bishop smiled, waiting for Manusos to speak.

"It's my nephew, Excellency, from Crete. He would like—"

The bishop lifted his right hand. "Let him speak for himself." He faced Domenikos. "You speak Italian?"

"I do, Excellency."

The old man was pleased. "A more civilized tongue than Greek. I would not want so dangerous an opinion to be generally known, but I can count on my good friend Manusos for discretion."

Manusos bowed deeply. "Discretion's very soul, Excellency."

"Exactly so." There was a hint of skepticism in the dry old voice. "Forgive me, young man. I interrupted you."

"I'm from Candia, Excellency. I studied icon painting for ten years with Brother Constantine at the Monastery of St. Catherine. I've come to Venice to learn painting." He took a deep breath. "I would like to study with Maestro Tiziano Vecellio."

"You show admirable taste." The bishop smiled.

"My uncle has very kindly given up most of his time during the past fortnight trying to arrange an introduction for me. . . ."

Seviros looked at Manusos. "Why didn't you ask me at once?"

"I hoped it wouldn't be necessary to disturb you, Excellency."

"What could be more important to me than to help a promising young man in a worthy ambition? I assume you are promising?"

The youth flushed. "I'm proficient, Excellency, in what I've learned, but there's so much I've not been able to learn."

"It is good and proper to understand one's worth, without illusion." The bishop turned to his clerk. "I wish to dictate a letter."

The clerk sat at a small table, holding a sharpened quill. The bishop's head sank back on the cushioned rest and he closed his eyes. "Maestro," he began, "the bearer of this letter is of a fine Cretan family with important connections in our city. He is said to be a painter of great ability in his native style of art, and he now wants to learn the craft as it is so wonderfully practiced by your noble self. You would do me honor by appraising his skill, and if you find him worthy, by taking him into your studio. I am informed that you no longer wish to teach. I would not, therefore, seek to impose on your time and energies were it not that I have reason to regard this young man so highly. It would seem a pity if your virtues were not passed on to someone of such

487

talents and eagerness." Gabriele Seviros broke off and fixed his bright little eyes on Domenikos. "Do you find this to your satisfaction?"

"It's far too generous, Excellency. It may be that I do not deserve such praise."

The old man smiled. "I respect the way you suggest the possibility of doubt without granting its certainty. But I do not exaggerate. You see, I've had a letter from Brother Constantine."

CHAPTER 3

TIZIANO VECELLIO was the kind of man who lied about his age. At different times during his life, he had allowed it to be believed that he had been born in 1472, in 1477, and even as recently as 1490. The fact was, however, that this greatest of all Venetian painters was, in 1560, not a day less than eighty and perhaps as much as eighty-eight. He was very rich, immensely admired, and covered with honors. And he was not a bit better behaved than was demanded of him by a society notorious for its looseness.

He was not, as some alleged, a peasant. He had been born in the town of Pieve di Cadore, in the Dolomites, where his forefathers had served with distinction as soldiers and lawyers. He had come to Venice as a young man and had studied with Gentile Bellini, then with his even more celebrated brother, Giovanni, working also for a while with the great Giorgione. His rise had been rapid. In Italy Titian's name was now rivaled only by Michelangelo's; but in Venice and elsewhere on the Continent, it was Titian who was known as Europe's master painter.

To achieve and retain this eminence, he had moved with the tastes and temper of his times, producing the sort of art demanded by those of Church or laity who could afford his prices. Since the Counter-Reformation had been launched, Titian, the master opportunist, had reverted from portraiture to theological themes. Not that he felt himself threatened, for he had important protectors. He had been a principal painter to the court of the emperor Charles V, and was now the favorite painter of Philip II of Spain.

Domenikos stood before Titian's house in the Biri Grande, armed this morning with the bishop's letter. The white light of midsummer blanched the two stories of pink brick, casting long shadows on the protruding cornice and window ledges. Resolutely, he approached the door and knocked. There were sounds of bolts being thrown and a liveried servant stared bleakly at him.

"For Maestro Tiziano." Domenikos offered his letter.

The man contemplated the scarlet wax of the episcopal seal. "Is there to be an answer at once?"

Domenikos nodded. The servant motioned him into the vaulted hallway, and left him to study the barrel arches and fluted pilasters while his mind thrashed between hope and despair. Absorbed in thoughts of his future, he was startled when the man's voice, now deferential, said, "Would you come with me, signore?"

Two immense doors gave access to the vast main studio, its walls hung with paintings on which craftsmen were working. In the center of the room stood Titian, short, heavily built, his back to Domenikos. He wore a dark red velvet tunic, his arms were encased in cream silk, his head was covered by a black cap. He turned to reveal a face at once fierce and curious, arrogant and humorous. The high forehead loomed over sharp, glittering eyes, a long nose, a voluptuous mouth. From his belligerent jaw a beard grew outward almost horizontally, giving him a diabolical air.

Titian glanced contemptuously at his visitor. "You had to have a letter from a bishop to give you courage to present yourself? You imagine that I'd be impressed by what the Doge himself told me about painters?" He looked at the letter in his hand. " '. . . a fine Cretan family . . .' There are no fine Cretan families. The Cretans are our slaves."

Domenikos couldn't decide whether the man was serious or simply attempting to provoke him. He smiled weakly. "If you were a Roman, master, I think you'd feel that there were only fine Roman families. I'm a Cretan. I know what *I* think."

Titian seemed about to smile, but he maintained his severity. " '. . . said to be a painter of great ability in his native style of art . . .' Said by *whom?*"

"My old teacher, Brother Constantine."

Titian laughed. "Oh, so now we have monks as authorities on art. I suppose this 'native style' is icon painting?"

Domenikos nodded. "But I recognize its limitations."

"Do you now? Well, congratulations. And why, may I ask, do you come to me, of all the painters in Europe?"

"Is there anyone else?"

The laughter this time was almost amiable. "There is not."

"That's why I came to you, master."

Titian tapped his cap more firmly down on his head. "Another talent, for God's sake. And a Greek, a savage. Do they wear shoes where you come from, boy?" He had turned his back to the youth, and suddenly he whirled. "Well," he snarled, "tell me what you know. Can you stretch a canvas? Of course not, they only use panels where you come from. Can you mix oils? No, you only know tempera. Can you paint the blue of the sky or the green of a leaf? No. Do you understand the delicacy of a flower or the beauty of a woman's breast? Of course not. Your mad coreligionists believe that God won't permit art to advance beyond the point when Christians were scrawling on the walls of the Catacombs."

Emboldened by anger, Domenikos said, "Most of us do wear shoes in Crete—that is, those who can grind the cost of them out of their Venetian masters—and some of us manage to be educated. I speak and write three languages. I can't stretch a canvas, nor can I mix oils. I can't paint a sky or a leaf or a tear in the eye. That's why I'm here, to learn. And I *can* learn, master."

Titian's expression grew milder. "Oh?"

"And I can learn *quickly*. I can be useful to you."

"Is that what they call Greek fire? Well, good for you." The master cast a half-despairing look at the men working at the canvases. Some were standing on the tiled floor; others were on scaffolding and ladders. "I have a dozen men working with me, and all of *them* are useful to me. One of them happens to be my son. But there's not a touch of genius in the lot." He lifted his gnarled, blunt, ringed hand in a gesture of entreaty to the heavens. "God preserve me from peasant boys who imagine they have a vocation for painting. No, whatever-you-call-your-self! Oh, no. I implore you. Go away. If you truly admire me, have mercy and leave me in peace. *You* I have no need of."

Domenikos grinned. "I know that, master. But I need you."

"Whatever energies I have left for teaching belong to my son. Who needs another Greek painter, anyhow? I've already tried to teach one, and in three years he learned nothing."

Domenikos refused to be intimidated. "But you've not seen my work, master."

"All right, then, where is it?"

"In my eyes."

The old man stared. "Who told you to say that to me?"

"No one. It's the truth. If I'd brought you the kind of thing I'm able to paint now, you would have laughed at me. If I were content with what I can paint now, I'd not be here."

Titian grunted. "Well, can you copy something? At present all I'm interested in is your skill, what you can make your hands do."

"I'll try, master."

Imperiously, Titian snapped his fingers, and a man at once descended from a scaffold. He was in early middle age and somewhat taller than Titian, whom he resembled but for a cowed demeanor. He gazed at Domenikos with obvious ill will.

"Orazio, get me the model of St. Francis and Brother Leo."

It was the custom of Titian and other painters to keep miniature studies of their important pictures so that duplicates, when ordered, could be made by assistants. Orazio went to a rank of vertical stacks and selected a small canvas. As he returned, Titian said, "This is Domenikos Theoto . . . Oh, it doesn't matter. This is my son." To Orazio he added, "Get some eggs and dry pigments, and a gessoed panel. I want to see what he can do."

"But I thought you said there were to be no more pupils."

"There may be an exception. That's what I want to find out."

Orazio set the miniature painting on an easel and disappeared in search of the materials. Titian studied the canvas. "You know, it's not bad, for something I did so long ago."

Domenikos examined the rendering of St. Francis receiving the Stigmata from the heavens while his old friend Brother Leo looked on. "It's wonderful, master." He paused. " 'Pondering what this vision might mean, he finally understood that by God's

THE MARTYRDOM OF ST. LAWRENCE — BY TITIAN

providence he would be made like the crucified Christ. . . .' "

Titian smiled appreciatively. "I know that. That's St. Bonaventura. And how would a Cretan know about St. Francis of Assisi? You belong to the Roman Church? Not that I care—"

"I do."

"I selected this picture only because it's simple. But if *you* like it, for you that's all that counts. To the devil with what anyone else thinks." He grinned. "Unless the someone else happens to be me."

Orazio returned with the eggs, some pigments, and a panel coated with plaster. An assistant followed with an easel.

Titian said, "I'm not asking for a replica. Use it as the basis of another painting, your own. Be as original as you like."

Appalled, Domenikos protested. "But copying is all I know."

The master shrugged. "All right, then, copy it."

DOMENIKOS STOOD BEFORE Titian's model. St. Francis was kneeling in ecstasy as he received the Stigmata on his upturned hands, his narrow, haggard face in profile, inclined toward the sky. Brother Leo, half reclining on the rock-strewn earth, shielded his face with one hand from the dazzling light of heaven. Nothing Domenikos had seen in Candia approached in immediacy the canvas before him. He memorized each detail— the contorted tree to the right of the saint, the little valley with its green meadows and tree-lined stream, the angry sky shot through with God's light.

"You haven't started yet?" Orazio had come to stand beside him.

The youth shook his head. "I have to understand it first."

Orazio laughed, though not unkindly, and swept the great room with his hand. "We have two years' work here. There's no time to understand. The only thing that should concern you, *if* my father takes you in, is how to do what you're told."

Domenikos bowed his head. If this man took a dislike to him, he could make life trying for Domenikos. He began to prepare his pigments while Orazio looked on with tolerant disdain.

"How the devil did you persuade my father to let you get this far?" he said. "I'd have sworn it was impossible. How is it that you call yourself again?"

"Domenikos Theotokopoulos, master."

Orazio laughed. "Papa will call you *il Greco*. I know him."

"But I'm not Greek, Maestro Orazio. I'm Cretan."

"It's all one, isn't it?"

"You'd make few friends in Candia if you said that there. The Cretans take those differences seriously."

"How seriously do *you* take them, Greco?"

"When I was younger, they mattered to me because they mattered to my father. But after I became a Roman communicant, my confessor said to me, 'We're all children of God.' "

Orazio touched Domenikos lightly on the shoulder. "Work now, Greco. Don't try to understand it. Just work."

Domenikos' task consumed four long June days. So absorbed was he that he was unaware of the banter of Titian's assistants echoing through the studio. Even summonses to meals failed to draw him from his work. The little rectangle of wood was his universe, all that mattered to him.

With tempera, the work proceeded slowly. Domenikos recalled Brother Constantine's observation: "It's slow. So many layers invisible to others, known only to you and God. Those are the layers of your soul, your genius, your love of God." Domenikos remained each evening in the studio until it was too dark to go on, until his eyes felt as if they stood out on sticks.

And then, incredibly, the copy was completed. Stroke for stroke, he compared it to the original. Yes, it was really done. He felt giddy, like one recovering consciousness. Slowly, he went to the scaffold on which Orazio was working. "Master," he croaked.

Orazio looked down. "So you're finished, young Greco?" He descended and carefully disposed of his palette and brushes, then he patted the young man's shoulder and walked to his easel.

Domenikos found suddenly that it was difficult not to weep. He watched Orazio's every movement. All was soon to be decided, and he cared—dear God, how he cared.

Orazio turned to him at last, his face a mask. "Go home, Greco, and rest. My father is at San Marco. There's no point in waiting."

"May I not stay, master?"

Continued on page 505

THE ART
OF
EL GRECO

A Portfolio of his Paintings

Introduction
by
John Canaday

ART CRITIC

It is easier, somehow, to think of El Greco as a modern artist than as an old master. And in a very definite way, the El Greco we know *is* a product of the twentieth century. All but forgotten outside Spain for more than two hundred years, and long regarded as a freak even by those who knew his work at all, El Greco was rediscovered as a great artist in the light of the aesthetic revolution called modern art. His distortion of form, his violent and unnatural color, the extreme personalism of his style and (as it seemed) his spontaneous, impulsive technique under the drive of an intense emotional force—all of this brings El Greco close to the expressionist painters who early in our century were in revolution against a decayed tradition.

In this light, El Greco is easiest for a modern audience to understand. We accept the distortions, the color and the sometimes violent technique without question, since contemporary painters have accustomed us to them in exaggerated form. But this kind of response often costs us a true appreciation of El Greco as an old master.

He stands in a most curious relationship to the art of his own time, an isolated figure who cannot quite be called a member of a school and certainly did not become the father of one, although he fused three seemingly incompatible influences into a perfectly unified style. Trained, as a Greek youth, in the formal, restrictive tradition of Byzantine icon painting, he managed after emigrating to Venice to marry this conventional, restrained style to the worldly opulence of the Venetian masters. But fulfillment came only after his transplantation to Spain, where this Greek-Italian became—so unpredictably— the Spanish artist of all Spanish artists who expressed most passionately the mystical agonies of the Spanish soul.

It must be said emphatically that while El Greco understood the nature of this Spanish emotionalism, and, possibly, experienced it as a Spaniard-by-adoption, he was first of all an intellectual artist. The convolutions of his style, even in works such as *The Agony in the Garden* (plate 10) that are easily imagined to have been painted in a mystical frenzy, were the inventions of a great creative artist who did not go into a creative trance, but applied theories that he developed in long discussions with his intellectual colleagues, the poets and philosophers of Toledo—men like Fray Hortensio Felix Paravicino, immortalized in one of El Greco's finest portraits (plate 2).

In the art of El Greco, passion and reason mutually support one another. This is the balanced tradition of the old masters, which we tend to forget when we see El Greco as virtually an artist of our time. But El Greco remains a great artist by either aesthetic standard—traditional or revolutionary. And that can be said of only a handful of the greatest artists who ever lived. ✍

1. This *Portrait of a Man*, painted about 1600, is assumed to be of El Greco himself.

2. *Fray Hortensio Felix Paravicino* (c. 1609). The brilliant poet
and monk whose friendship enriched El Greco's last years.
3. *Portrait of Cardinal Don Fernando Niño de Guevara.* This
portrait of the Grand Inquisitor was painted on the occasion
of Philip III's visit to Toledo in 1600. 4. *Giulio Clovio* (c. 1570).
The young painter's first patron and friend in Rome.

5

5. *Burial of Count Orgaz* (c. 1587). St. Stephen and St. Augustine
descend to bury the nobleman while Heaven opens up in glory.
The painting was commissioned by Don Andrés Núñez, parish priest
of Santo Tomé, Toledo, who appears on the far right as the
chaplain reading the lesson. Other prominent Toledans, portrayed
as chief mourners, possibly include two Castillas, the lawyer
Gregorio Angulo, the mayor, and Cervantes, author of *Don
Quixote*. El Greco himself is directly behind St. Stephen, and his son
Jorge is the black-clothed page on the left.

6. *Virgin of Charity* (c. 1605).
This painting is part of the altar on
which El Greco and Jorge collaborated
for the Hospital de la Caridad in Illescas.
Jorge (right) and the lawyer Angulo
are depicted as recipients of the
Virgin's charity; their pleated linen
ruffs, decreed as fashion by Philip III,
were considered "unseemly" by the
hospital's appraisers.

7. *St. Mary Magdalen* (c. 1589).
El Greco's Jerónima was the model
for this "penitent Magdalen."

8

8. *The Disrobing of Christ (El Espolio).* Painted about
1579, this was El Greco's first commission for the cathedral
chapter in Toledo, and established him as Spain's
foremost painter. It also occasioned his first prolonged dispute
over fees and brought accusations of "religious lapses."

9

9. *The Martyrdom of St. Mauritius* (c.1580). Philip II so admired the
Espolio (plate 8) that he commissioned this painting for the Escorial.
However, he found El Greco's new style grotesque and rejected the
picture. Philip appears in armor second from right, and the face of the
saint, who is repeated in the left foreground, is El Greco's own.

10

10. *The Agony in the Garden*
(c. 1590). The transformation
of El Greco's style that followed
his painting of Count Orgaz' burial
is nowhere more evident than in
this mystical and powerful work.

11. *The Visitation* (c. 1612).
The next to last painting of
El Greco's life — a scene of
"mystery and simplicity" — was
done for the Oballe Chapel of the
Church of San Vicente, Toledo.

11

12

12. *View of Toledo* (after 1600). El Greco's
beloved Toledo, built on a steep bluff almost
surrounded by the River Tajo, is crowned by the
Alcázar (citadel) with its four towers. The artist's
own house, the Casa Villena, is on the side
of the hill below the cathedral spire, inside the
city walls and overlooking the Bridge of San Martín.

Orazio smiled, compassionately now, and pointed to a low couch against a wall. "Wait there, if you like."

Domenikos lay down and was sleeping almost at once.

IT WAS after seven when Titian returned. It was his custom, one afternoon each week, to proceed to San Marco, accompanied by a pair of liveried servants, one of whom held a parasol over his head. "I do it to let people know I've not yet died," he would say. "Tintoretto and Veronese have been spreading hopeful rumors. But they'll not have done with me so easily. Not yet."

His procession took him to Sansovino's magnificent marble Logetta at the foot of the Campanile. Here, with a number of personages who were associated with the affairs of the Serenissima, Titian exchanged spicy bits of information and acquired knowledge that might prove useful. Today's excursion had been disappointing. No murders, no rapes, no earthshaking scandals.

Back in the studio, he unbuckled his heavy leather belt, letting his glittering ceremonial sword tumble with a clatter to the floor. The noise aroused Domenikos, but he did not stir.

The master glanced around the studio. Orazio knew he would find something to object to. He always did. "Who the devil is that?" he inquired sharply, pointing to the reclining Domenikos.

"Your little Greek, papa. He's finished his copy."

"If he's finished, why didn't he go home? This is no inn."

"He wouldn't go. He wanted to know what you'd think of it."

"You're too softhearted, Orazio, too much like your dear mother, God rest her soul."

Orazio shrugged. He recognized himself to be of no importance. All he demanded was that others make his life with Titian no more difficult than it was. "Papa, do look at what he's done."

The master walked to the corner where Domenikos, now fully awake, had been working. There was a pause. "It's incredible," Titian mumbled at last. "Do you see what he's done?"

"He's painted every one of your brushstrokes in proportion to the original. Is that what you mean?"

"Something more important. He's understood my painting from inside. He's understood me. What do you think of it?"

The son's reply was muted. "He seems able enough."

"Then you think we'd be wise to keep him?"

" 'Whatever I may tell you, Orazio,' you keep saying to me, 'don't let me accept any more pupils.' Your words, papa."

The old man chuckled. "So you want me to be consistent. But this boy has ability. And he has courage—he dared to put me down the first day he laid eyes on me. He hasn't an idea of how much he already knows. Just look what he's done with temperas. What fire he has. This boy is very important to us . . . to me."

"Do you suppose he has money to pay his expense with us?"

Titian laughed. "You're my son where money is concerned. I've already looked into it. His father has provided well. But I'd have taken him without a penny. He can work under you."

"Then I can tell you, papa, that I'm delighted. I was afraid that if *I* said I wanted him, *you'd* have found a reason for sending him away. You're a very perverse old man."

Titian grinned. "You may be right. I do hate to be agreed with. I don't much like being outwitted either, even by my son, but I'll overlook it in a higher interest."

Orazio sighed. "Should I wake him now?"

The master smiled. "You can go through the motions. But if I'd been in his position, I'd have listened to every word."

Domenikos promptly sat up. He had the grace to blush.

THERE MUST be limits to elation—but what were they? As he entered the dining room, where Marica and Anastos were conversing after dinner, Domenikos' face gave his feelings away. Marica rose and embraced him. "Titian has accepted you!"

He nodded and stood back from her, grinning broadly.

"But it's magnificent, Domenikos. You know, when your father wrote that you wanted to study with Titian, I said, 'But it's madness. The boy is dreaming.' " She threw back her head and laughed, embracing him again. "But it wasn't madness at all. The dream has come true." She turned to Anastos. "Isn't it magnificent? And it was your idea that papa see Gabriele Seviros."

"It's good," the boy said quietly.

"Have something to eat, Domenikos. And tell us everything."

Domenikos was delighted to recount the heady words. When he had finished, Marica said to her son, "You must take him to your father. How happy he'll be. How happy I am."

"Must I, mama? Domenikos knows the way to the taverna."

"You don't want to go with him?" She was astonished.

"I've heard the news, haven't I? It's *his* success, not mine."

Domenikos intervened. "I know how he feels. I'll go alone."

As he walked to the taverna, thinking of Anastos, Domenikos recalled the look in the eyes of his brother when he had told him that Giorgio was letting him come to Venice. It was the same look. Was it jealousy, reproach for his having prevailed against the gods? "Go," Manusos had said with asperity, "and I'll never see you again. You're lost to us already, a stranger." Their conversation had ended on this bleak note. And here Anastos echoed it. Domenikos shuddered, his joy stifled by dismay.

The lights and sounds of the taverna were welcome respite. It was still early in the evening, so the men—mostly Greeks, Cretans and Cypriots—were merely garrulous, not yet drunk. When Manusos saw Domenikos, he looked up, surprised. Then, from his nephew's face, he divined the news. He bounced to his feet and took Domenikos in his arms. "It's true? He's taken you?"

"It's marvelously true, thanks to you, uncle, and the bishop."

His uncle grew suddenly casual. "Oh, you can forget about the bishop. We needed no one but ourselves. You with your talents, and me with my connections." He turned to the men at his table. "This is the boy who wanted to study with Tiziano. Well, what do you think? Titian has accepted him!" He snorted. "And they say that Greeks can't get ahead in Venice!"

There was a wild outburst of applause, and the pounding of pewter mugs on the table. Hours later, uncle and nephew returned to the Rio dei Greci, arm in arm, singing songs of their native island. Not even Marica's icy reception could mar their joy.

CHAPTER 4

A BRILLIANT summer gave way to autumn and at last to the bone-chilling winds, rain and snow of the Adriatic winter. Domenikos made his daily pilgrimage to Titian's studio, but on Sundays and holidays he visited the city's many churches, frequently with Orazio. The master made it possible for him to explore the interior of the great basilica of San Marco and portions of the Doge's Palace not open to the public. He was chiefly interested in contemporary painting, by the brothers Bellini, by Giorgione and Raffaello, and by Titian's only serious rivals in Venice, Tintoretto and Veronese. But he also examined the sculpture and the architecture of Sansovino, Palladio and the brothers Bon, determined to master these arts as well as painting.

His friendship with Orazio grew, in spite of the disparity in their ages, or perhaps because of it. Orazio enjoyed extending protection; Domenikos welcomed it. He was grateful for Orazio's willingness to accept him both as a person and as a painter—the better painter of the two, in fact, as Orazio acknowledged, ruefully perhaps, but with a whole heart.

The gaps in Domenikos' skill were being filled rapidly. Even Titian congratulated him. "You were right, Greco. You *can* learn. But don't get puffed up. You have a long journey to travel, and you started it late. When I was nineteen, I'd been at it ten years."

As soon as he was thought proficient with oils, he began sharing the labors of the workshop, filling in sky, landscape and drapery. He was at first appalled at how much was not from the master's own hand, although Titian signed all the canvases. To Domenikos it seemed like forgery, and he vowed that when his career was launched he would use assistants as little as possible, never permitting them to touch a picture which he signed. However, by the end of a year, he saw how impossible it would be for one man alone to complete the number of paintings that Titian sold; and he conceded that what Titian did contribute transformed a routine canvas into a masterpiece. And he said so.

The old man was sly. "But of course, my boy. I'm the leader of an army. I've trained my forces to fight, and then I leave them to do the fighting. But once in a while I'm called in to do a bit of leading. I, as leader, accept the rewards."

Domenikos was then toiling on the master's version of the Purification of the Temple, a celebrated subject of the Counter-Reformation. Shortly after this exchange with Titian, he began drawing with charcoal his own conception of the Purification.

Orazio peered at it and laughed. "I see. You think the time has come for you to improve on papa."

Domenikos flushed. "No, no. It's just that I've been wondering if there isn't a different way of doing it."

"So what is it about papa's version that you don't like?"

"I know it's presumptuous, but—" he pointed to Titian's figure of Christ driving out the money changers "—he's nothing but a well-nourished Venetian merchant. It's not reverent."

"Here in Venice, Greco, we concern ourselves very little with such problems. Papa's paintings are in the Venetian style, colorful and dramatic; they don't strain for dogmatic accuracy. We make pictures that people like."

"That's almost blasphemy."

Orazio chuckled. "No danger of that. We respect the Church and believe its teaching, but we leave theology to the Curia in Rome. You're God-struck, Greco. Papa and I are not. Oh, I don't object to churchmen—" then, angrily "—except Franciscans and Dominicans. God deliver us from those thieves and scoundrels." This view of the mendicant orders was shared by most Venetians.

"I know, I know," Domenikos said. "But should the Purification theme be treated cynically because you think two monastic orders are money changers today? A Purification seems to me meaningless unless it's painted as pure."

"I'll enjoy seeing what *you* think pure." Orazio laughed.

Domenikos decided to make this painting in tempera, for he wasn't yet sure enough of oils. The task took him nearly three weeks. It was late one Saturday when the picture was completed, and he stood back to study it. "To be intelligently self-critical," Titian had told him, "is the first obligation the artist has. Unhappily it's almost always the skill he acquires last—if ever." Domenikos found he could not judge the painting.

Wiping tacky fingers on his smock, he approached Orazio and Titian, who were putting the final touches to an immense rendering of the Rape of Europa, a favorite mythological scene.

Orazio said, "Papa, I think your protégé has finished his latest effort. Shall we see how he thinks you should be painting?"

Titian followed Orazio to "Greco's Corner." He folded his stubby fingers over his modest paunch. "I see you've not spent *all* your time in my studio, Greco," he said dryly at last. "You've been looking at other Venetians, even a Roman or two."

"Oh, yes." Domenikos added quickly, "Was that wrong?"

"No, I simply mean that your sight-seeing reveals itself. For example, I detect Sansovino's style in the temple architecture and sculptures. The statues are Apollo and Athena?"

"Not Athena, master, but Hera."

"I see. Then this creature beside her is a peacock?"

Domenikos flushed. "It is. I'm not very good at birds."

"That is evident. And I'm happy to know you've been improving yourself with my prints too. Don't I find something familiar in the face of that old gentleman?"

Domenikos suddenly saw the resemblance. "Michelangelo," he conceded. "I honestly didn't intend it. I must have had the sketches you made of him in my mind."

"The 'divine Michelangelo.' " The master chuckled, but there was iron in the sound. "He told me I didn't know how to draw. If I could draw, he said, I'd be unmatched on this earth, by which he meant unmatched except for him. I told *him* he didn't know how to paint, and that, God knows, is true. He's dreadful as a colorist." The old man sighed. "I hope you'll forgive me for saying that there's no definition to *your* colors, Greco."

"I find them very difficult," Domenikos admitted quietly.

Titian grinned wickedly. "I'm pleased you like my Ariadne." He pointed to a voluptuous, semi-reclining woman. "But some of your women look like Veronese's. And in the way you've posed all these people, it appears you were thinking of my erstwhile friend Tintoretto. Look at the angles you placed them in. He makes this strangeness work, now and then, but *your* people look as if they're suspended by cords. If you want to paint like Tintoretto or Veronese, I'll send you to them. You're wasting your time here."

"Oh, master, what am I to do?"

"Orazio has taught you all he can. On Monday, you'll begin work in *my* studio." Without a further word, Titian stamped out.

Feeling perplexed and humiliated, Domenikos put away his brushes and set off through the dusky streets toward the Rio dei Greci. He had failed miserably, and yet Titian was now taking him into his own studio. He hoped the deserted Orazio would not become his enemy. He reflected on how fortunate he had been in having Orazio for a friend, sharing a love of literature and learning; and it was Orazio who had introduced him to a publisher and seller of books, commodities which were both dear and rare in the sixteenth century. Saddened by the possibility of losing that friendship, he determined to go and see Orazio immediately after mass in the morning.

ORAZIO OCCUPIED an extensive apartment in Titian's house. Domenikos found him seated in an arcade flanking the courtyard, a volume of Ariosto in his lap.

"Ah, it's you," he said when he saw Domenikos. "The maestro is away for the day, passing the time with the Doge."

Domenikos seated himself. "It's you I came to see."

His friend smiled regretfully. "As papa put it, Greco, there's nothing more I can do for you."

"That's why I came. I'm so sorry for what he said."

"What in God's name have *you* to be sorry about?"

"I feared it might mean the end of our friendship."

Orazio laughed, a bit forcedly, Domenikos thought. "I'm touched that my friendship means so much to you."

"You're the only person I've ever been able to speak with about things that are really important to me. And I'm grateful for everything I've learned from you."

"Handsomely said, Greco. But now you have the master to talk with, what further need do you have of me? Besides, you need friends your own age. You've been associating with old men here."

"You're mocking me, Orazio. You know what I mean— philosophy, poetry, as well as painting. I don't think you old, and besides I've never learned how to make friends."

"You've withdrawn like a hermit, Greco. Painting seems to consume you. There's a whole world out there, outside yourself. Give yourself some room, some air, some light. I warn you that if you don't, you'll always find you're alone, and miserable."

"Odd—Brother Constantine said much the same thing." Domenikos paused. "Does this mean that you'll cast me out?"

"What a fellow! I suggest only that you meet other people too."

Domenikos stood up, smiling, and offered Orazio a long, pale hand. "Thank you for that. But I'm truly sorry about yesterday."

The older man laughed. "That was just my esteemed father in one of his moments of candor." He became serious. "Only rarely is he intentionally cruel. He's never learned not to say what he thinks. But we live through it. He's the greatest man I know. And it's the regret of my life, and of his, that I'm not the son he wanted. I try to make up in affection what I lack in genius. The gap is a big one, Greco, and you help to fill it." He smiled warmly. "Together, you and I can be his son, his talented, loving son."

Domenikos shook his head. "But he scorned what I'd done."

"Nonsense. If he didn't think you had genius, he'd leave you with me." Orazio added softly, "You *know* that, Greco. That's what made you come. And *I* thank *you* for that consideration."

CHAPTER 5

It was the beginning of Domenikos' fourth year in Titian's studio, and Venice was preparing for the most important celebration in her calendar—the Sposolizio del Mare, Venice's marriage to the sea, which took place on Ascension Day. No one was more excited than the young Cretan, for he had just been invited to join Titian on his barge for the public festivities and to attend a private gathering later in the Biri Grande. He had witnessed the pageant before, but always with his uncle and aunt in a craft that followed the Doge's barge out into the lagoon at a distance. As Titian's guest, he would be much closer to that golden galley *Bucintoro*, so-called because of its figurehead, half man, half ox.

He rushed breathlessly to the Rio dei Greci to announce his good fortune. To his consternation, his aunt was indignant.

"But Ascension Day, the Feast of Bucintoro, is a family occasion," Marica protested. "You had no right to accept. I don't care how important Tiziano is." She turned angrily to her husband. "Isn't that the way you feel?"

"Well, my love, you're right in principle, but—"

"Oh, you!" Marica snorted. "Getting ahead. Getting ahead.

It's the only thing that matters to you *and* Domenikos."

"Well, you have to admit that getting ahead has its points. Suppose he refused the invitation and Titian took umbrage. How would you feel about that?"

"Suppose, suppose. My God. Suppose the plague struck us again?" She crossed herself hastily. "May God forgive me. But I know how I feel about it. Who cares what the old man feels?"

The young painter intervened. "I'd like to go with the master, aunt. His galley will be very close to *Bucintoro*."

"It's against religion. No good Greek should associate with a Roman Catholic on Ascension Day."

"But I—" Domenikos began, and stopped abruptly. This was scarcely the moment to disclose the secret of his conversion.

Marica studied him critically. "I don't like the life you've been leading, Domenikos. It's unnatural. All you do is read or work. You should begin looking for a wife."

Domenikos laughed. "Not until I'm able to support one."

"And how long will that be? A couple of years?"

"No less than ten. Oh, I'll get a few commissions before then, but it takes a long time for an artist to establish himself."

"Ten years!" breathed his uncle. "You'll be thirty-two."

"As I say, it's unnatural." Marica sighed. "But then, I suppose, there's nothing very natural about being a painter." She smiled, accepting defeat with grace. "You'll want me to arrange a costume for you, won't you, for the party after the festival?"

"I hadn't thought about that. Is it necessary?"

"It's a masked ball your master is giving, so I've been told. For the finest ladies and most expensive courtesans. There's not much to choose between them, from all I've heard."

"The ladies," said Manusos, "are worse than the courtesans."

WATCHING Titian work in his own studio, Domenikos was alternately excited and depressed by the master's boldness and nonchalance. Details over which the young man had been instructed by Orazio to slave were of no consequence to Titian. The day before the festival, Domenikos questioned him about a canvas that seemed overcasual in its treatment of background: all was concentrated on the sense of movement and drama.

Titian was disdainful. "When I was young, Greco, I cared too about your landscapes and your architecture. No longer. I'm seeking the essence of my image now. I haven't time for anything else." He wagged a finger at his pupil. "That doesn't mean *you* shouldn't learn to do these things. It's only after you've learned them that you can afford to forget them and decide for yourself what's important." He smeared a dark pigment onto his canvas with a palette knife and began with his blunt fingers to manipulate it on the picture. "In painting, color is the important thing, to shade it, to mold it, even to sculpture it, to give it a body and a life of its own—to make it conform to your own plan for it." The old man sighed. "It's my only remaining battle, Greco."

"But your sketchy backgrounds, master, make everything depend on the figure."

"Of course. Give the figure the importance it deserves."

"But I believe in details, in their symbolism. How else can you make someone believe the scenes you paint are real?"

Titian nodded. "That's what you think now. But it will change as you get older. The great painter is an illusionist." He looked at Domenikos. "You accept Dante's description of hell?"

"I do as I'm reading him, but when I've stopped, I say, 'But *he* didn't know any more about it than I do.' "

"He just sweeps you along, doesn't he? And does the illusion he creates depend on details? Would you perhaps call it magic?"

"I might."

"Good. Now observe the festival tomorrow, and tell me whether it's the details that give it its special flavor, or its magic—the atmosphere that you and I and all the people bring to it."

THE MORNING dawned clear. Soon after ten, the great flotilla of galleys, barges and gondolas began to form along both banks of the Canale Grande. Domenikos met Titian and his impressive entourage in the Piazza, and they proceeded to the Molo, where the Doge's *Bucintoro* glittered gold and red in the sunlight.

Titian's barge was richly decorated in scarlet, festooned with ribbons. When the old man had been lifted into his seat and the others had taken their places around him, it was propelled toward the middle of the canal to await the departure of *Bucin-*

toro. In the center of the barge were three musicians who sang bawdy songs while a servant made his way aft to the master with wine and fruit. Titian was on a sort of throne, his aspect one of resolute if somewhat baleful majesty, his legs wrapped in blankets.

Orazio laughed. "Papa resents the fact that the Doge is taking part in all this too. He hates to share glory."

Bucintoro left her mooring and, oars flashing in perfect unison, moved into the canal and led the long procession across to the Lido. There, the Doge preceded members of the Consiglio and other dignitaries, including Titian and his companions, into the Church of San Nicolo, where a solemn mass was offered by the Venetian patriarch. It was on the return journey that the Doge reconsecrated the Serenissima's mystic marriage with the sea, casting a jeweled ring into the lagoon and murmuring, "*Desponsamus te Mare, in signum veri perpetuique domini!*" ("We marry you, sea, as a sign of true and perpetual rule!") Then *Bucintoro* moved on toward the Molo. The rite was completed.

The remaining hours of daylight were given over to dancing in the streets, to ogling the performances of the mountebanks who had set up stages on the Piazzetta, to examining the merchandise of vendors, to drinking and eating. At dusk, Domenikos returned to the Rio dei Greci to dress for the masked ball.

At the Biri Grande, the noise of celebration could be heard from the street—singers and musicians, laughter and shouting. And entering the house was like walking into a solid wall of sound. Punctuating the music of the orchestra playing in the studio, the corridors echoed with the delighted giggles and outraged screams of the city's most esteemed ladies and cultivated courtesans. In a corner of the studio sat the master, his eyes glazed with drink, accepting the attentions of two pretty women. When Domenikos approached to pay his respects, Titian brushed him off. "Go away," he muttered thickly. "Get drunk. Find a woman. Do you good." He laughed uproariously.

Domenikos turned away, dismayed. He edged his way around the dancers, feeling awkward and out of place, wondering why he had come. As he neared the doors that led to the courtyard, a small hand suddenly appeared on his arm, the touch so light and feminine that without thinking Domenikos placed his hand over it. Only then did he turn to see a diminutive figure with fair hair and dark eyes that peered at him through a mask.

"You've just arrived," she said, her voice soft and warm.

"How did you deduce that?"

Laughing, she drew him into the courtyard where torches provided a flickering, golden light. "Because you haven't a glass."

"I might have left it somewhere."

She shook her head. "You're too timid to be drunk."

"You're very observant. What else do you know about me?"

They sat on the wall. "Many things. You're not from Venice. And probably not from Italy. You're Spanish?"

"A reasonable guess. I'm from Crete, but most foreigners in Venice *are* from Spain. I happen to be the exception."

Her reply was soft. "In more ways than one, I've no doubt." She took his right hand in both of hers and peered into it. "You use your hands in your work. They're very powerful."

"Yes."

"You're the most uncommunicative man I've ever met."

"It's a masked ball, identities secret. Tell me more of what you guess about me. It's amusing."

She brought her full lips into caressing contact with his hand. Then, laughing musically, she straightened. "You paint."

He laughed too. "I should have washed more carefully."

"I see great things in your future. You'll be successful."

"In Venice?"

"Not as a painter, I think, not here. Maybe in love."

"Love is so frivolous in Venice."

"You're speaking from hearsay, not from experience."

He blushed. "Well then, from what I've been told, men and women here fall in love for a matter of days, or even minutes."

"You have no faith in the eternity of each moment you live?"

"I have trouble enough with the larger concept of eternity."

"You're confusing love with marriage. They're not the same."

"They are to me. When I find myself in love, it will be with a woman who, I hope, will become my wife, and there'll be no other woman in my life after that."

She laughed. "What a ravishing idea. Is it that way in Crete?"

"It is. Do you mind if I ask how often you've been in love?"

"Hundreds of times. I'm almost always in love."

He thought of the softness of her touch and trembled with pleasure. "Are you married?" he inquired, almost in a whisper.

"No, of course not."

"Ah."

"You've finally recognized what I am, haven't you?"

"Yes." He was humiliated, even shocked by her directness.

"And this makes you unhappy?"

"I don't know. You're so intelligent, so gay, so beautiful."

Her laughter trilled. "Don't be offended if I say you're naïve."

"I think it would be very difficult for you to offend me."

"What a nice thing to say. But now that your surmise about me has been confirmed, you feel differently, don't you?"

"More drawn to you. You're less encumbered, in my terms."

She squeezed his arm. "Will you dance with me?"

"With delight, though I warn you I'm very inept."

In the studio they joined the couples who were dancing. As he followed the supple movements of her lithe body, he felt an almost overwhelming desire to crush her to him.

"It's enough," she murmured at last, "but you're not so awkward. With practice, you'd be an excellent dancer."

He laughed. "You must never tell me lies."

"But that wasn't a lie." She stared at him evenly. "I think that you and I should get on very well. We both try to speak the truth."

"For your eternal moment?"

"Oh, yes, only for that. I could promise no more. Except for ugly wives, there is no fidelity in Venice."

"You make me uneasy, not for myself but for you. What will happen to you when this beauty of yours has passed?"

"Am I beautiful?" She stood now in the moonlit courtyard.

He caressed her white throat. "That's a shameless question. You know the answer. I've never seen a woman who better understood how beautiful she was, and how far her beauty would take her." He paused, almost breathless, before going on. "Would you consider instructing a painter from Crete in the ways of the world?"

"I find him very attractive."

"I have to tell you, I have *some* money, but I'm not rich."

She laughed. "I know—and you spend your gold on books."

"You know that?"

517

She was indignant. "You don't imagine I'd choose just any-one, even a guest of Titian's, without knowing about him."

He grinned. "So all those deductions were a hoax." He held her face now with the tips of his fingers, gently but with the certainty of possession. "May I kiss you?"

Her mouth was cool and sweet. Domenikos started to lift the mask from her eyes. She restrained him. "No, no, my love. There are few enough rules. We must obey them. Come with me."

Her apartment overlooked the Canale della Giudecca, at a considerable distance from the Biri Grande. Her name was Veronica, and she became Domenikos' mistress.

NEWS OF HIS liaison was received enviously by his uncle, icily by Marica. He continued officially to live in the Rio dei Greci, but spent little time there. At twenty-two, he had begun a new life. He rejoiced in the change, despite its shocks.

He found to his horror that Veronica was utterly indiffer-ent to untidiness. "You're wasting time," she complained when he attempted to create order out of her chaos. "Leave that for the servants." "But you won't see that they do it," he protested.

An adjustment was soon made; what she didn't put away before his arrival, she hastily hid in cupboards. And when Domenikos discovered this he said with a grin, "I'm glad you're not my wife." "So am I," she answered, laughing.

He learned much from her. Not only did she educate him in the arts of love, but gave him as well an appreciation of food as a form of art. She took infinite care in preparing each meal they shared.

And she learned from him. She listened with attention when he spoke or read to her, and responded with perceptive ques-tions. But after an hour of seriousness, she would frown. "If I'm not careful, you'll ruin me for any other man. No man wants a woman who's better informed than he is."

Veronica appeared unstinting in her devotion, and Domenikos gained a self-confidence he had previously lacked, the security of a man who is attractive to a woman. Because he couldn't marry her, he wouldn't permit himself to love her completely. But she had brought a fullness to his life. He was less tense, less introspective. And one day Titian said to him, "Greco, you've at last begun to grow up."

MICHELANGELO died in February of 1564. Titian, as dean of Venetian artists, sent a letter of condolence to the great man's erstwhile patron, Duke Cosimo de' Medici, of Florence. To Domenikos he admitted that his letter was loftier than his thoughts. "I'll not miss him." He rubbed his hands in satisfaction. "I'm at least as old as he was and there's still plenty of life left in me."

Only a few months later, the Council of Trent published its edicts on art, and the Pope ordained that the nudes in Michelangelo's *Last Judgment*, the chief ornament of the Vatican's Sistine Chapel, be covered up. "Even if I didn't like Michelangelo," said Titian sorrowfully, "I respected him. It's tragic that his life should end on this note of defeat. The Church is denying artists a freedom they've enjoyed since Giotto and Dante opened the world to us. Next they'll be burning books and pictures."

He marched to a table and picked up a printed abstract of the Trent decree. " 'No superstition,' it says. There goes mythology. 'No false doctrine.' There goes the Apocrypha. 'No grave error.' Here comes the Holy Inquisition. 'All filthy quest for gain eliminated.' " He stared hotly at Domenikos. "What does that mean?"

Domenikos laughed. "That we paint for the love of God, not money."

"Precisely. You think that amusing? The Church takes her tithe from us, and we hope to receive our reward in heaven."

"I was joking, master. Surely, that passage only means that we're to introduce nothing into our paintings that's intended to make them more desirable than the subject would indicate. We're not to try to attract people to the Faith for the wrong reasons."

"I hope you're right, Greco, for *your* sake. I hardly sell pictures to churches anymore." Suddenly Titian grinned. "I wonder how His Most Catholic Majesty of Spain feels. He specially likes the lascivious touches I put in my paintings for him."

Domenikos studied the decree for a moment. "This seems

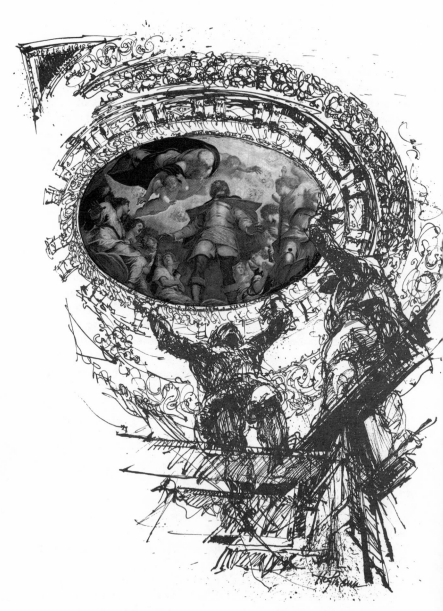

SAN ROCCO IN GLORY — BY TINTORETTO

only to apply to religious painting. If it's reasonably interpreted, I don't see that we have much to worry about."

Titian threw his hands in the air. "If you think I exaggerate the danger, talk to Tintoretto. Ask him what he thinks."

JACOPO ROBUSTI—called Tintoretto because his father was a dyer—had begun his studies with Titian at twenty-five. His association with the old master was brief, for their personalities and artistic tastes conflicted sharply. This did Tintoretto no harm. He soon established himself in Venice as second only to Titian.

Titian had made it clear to Domenikos that any overtures on his part toward Tintoretto would be considered treachery. But Domenikos had met him on many occasions in a taverna near the Piazza and been impressed by his vigor. He now seized eagerly on the old man's suggestion that he speak to Tintoretto.

He found him at his usual table in the taverna and accepted an invitation to visit his studio. Tintoretto was in a particularly cheerful mood, and when they entered his studio, the reason for it was disclosed. He pointed to an immense oval canvas, nearing completion, and said, "You know the story of this?"

"I don't. Should I?"

"I wondered how long the secret could be kept. In Venice you never know." He drew his guest into a sitting room and poured glasses of red wine. "Have you been in the Scuola de San Rocco, on the other side of the Canale Grande?" When Domenikos nodded, he said. "That's for the ceiling of the great hall."

"Congratulations, master."

"They're deserved, but I've not obtained the commission. The scuola is holding a competition for it. I thought Titian might have told you. He was invited to submit a design, of course."

Domenikos smiled. "He no longer competes."

"An enviable state. Well, I was asked too, as were Veronese and others, to submit sketches of a scene from San Rocco's life."

"But that's no sketch," Domenikos said.

Tintoretto laughed, delighted. "Exactly. That's the joke. Only you must promise to tell no one until it's settled. Since Titian's not involved, you won't hurt him."

Domenikos promised and Tintoretto continued. "It's a very rich commission, and whoever gets the great hall will almost certainly be asked to finish the whole building. I said to myself, 'This calls for ingenuity.' So I went to the scuola and persuaded the porter to measure the oval in the center of the ceiling. I made this painting to fit it. The other competitors will submit sketches, but I'll submit a finished work, all installed in the ceiling."

"Isn't that risky? The committee doesn't have to accept it."

Tintoretto's laughter all but overwhelmed him. "But they *do*. It's in their bylaws. They may reject no gifts."

"But they can move your picture and accept another design."

"They'll take mine. Come and look at it carefully, Greco."

The picture was *San Rocco in Glory*—a blaze of yellow, violet and ultramarine—transfixed as he observed the descent of God from heaven. Domenikos studied it. The distortion of the figures disturbed and intrigued him; and for Tintoretto's use of light he felt pure admiration. "I don't know," he said at last. "It's very daring. I hope they approve, but I'm not sure."

"You're seeing it from the wrong position. You have to imagine it directly above you—fifty feet."

"So the distortions will cease to be distortions?"

"Yes. The eye plays tricks."

"But it never occurred to me that a trick of proportion could overcome them." Domenikos grinned. "I'd like a hand in this adventure. Let me help with the installation."

Tintoretto slapped him on the shoulder. "But of course."

So Domenikos was present a few nights later when Tintoretto and his assistants transported the painting to the Scuola de San Rocco and, having bribed the porter to let them in, installed it in the ceiling of the great hall.

THE OFFICIALS of the scuola behaved precisely as Tintoretto had predicted. Some were outraged by his high-handedness, but even they conceded a grudging admiration for his audacity. The competitors accused Tintoretto of foul play. But their protests were unavailing. He was awarded the commission, and to Domenikos' astonishment he agreed to complete it within a year.

"It's not possible," Domenikos protested.

Tintoretto shrugged. "I work quickly. But I could use some assistance," he added. "If your master wouldn't disown you, would you work with me while he is in Vicenza this summer?"

"I'm honored, of course. But I'll have to ask him."

Titian's reaction to Domenikos' request was amusement. "So you want to play nearer the fire. I warn you, Greco, if you come back painting in his manner, I will have nothing more to do with you."

"There's no need to fear that, master."

The methods employed by Venice's two greatest painters differed markedly. Tintoretto himself painted most of the pictures intended for local installation, while those being sent abroad he left largely to his assistants, after first blocking out the basic elements. To this end, he had developed an ingenious device for demonstrating the spatial essentials of a painting. It was a shadow box fitted with tightly drawn cords, on which he suspended models of his figures so that they could be viewed in their relative positions. When Domenikos admired this invention, Tintoretto said, "I don't believe in letting my assistants think for themselves."

"In that at least you and Titian are agreed."

Tintoretto laughed harshly. "Do you know how long I was with Titian before he drove me out of his studio? Ten days. He said I was 'too formed,' by which he meant he didn't like my drawing; it was too like Michelangelo's. But he's a great painter, the best." He sighed. "I'd like to paint like Titian and draw like Michelangelo." He pointed to a work in progress. "Michelangelo is in everything I do. When I first visited the Sistine Chapel, it was like finding a new way of seeing. My God, Greco, how he could *see*, how he could *conceive* on a grand scale. Overwhelming."

"Until I see his work, I'll keep an open mind. Titian complains about his women; he says they're not feminine."

The older man laughed. "He means they're not like his voluptuous women. They have something else, though. They're superhuman, transcendent. Titian feared him as a competitor. You don't know how badly he wanted to be in Michelangelo's position. He wanted to be in Rome, not Venice. He wanted to make the earth tremble, as Michelangelo did, and he couldn't."

Domenikos disapproved of the turn in conversation. "You and Titian are so different, it's not possible for you to agree."

"Greco, Titian is great, I've just said so, but he has no convictions."

"I think his conception of art is much more profound than yours. I'm sorry to say that, but you've invited it. He's after a simplicity. You pursue the pageant. You're concerned with life. He's concerned with an aesthetic."

The artist stared at Domenikos. "That's right," he muttered. "I try to tell a story. That's what tempts me about this project. I can paint San Rocco's whole career—as you say, a pageant."

By the time Titian returned to Venice, Domenikos had mastered Tintoretto's principles of illuminating his canvases. And as he expressed his gratitude on his last day, Tintoretto said to him, "You really helped me, Greco. It was a true gesture of friendship. See that Titian doesn't keep you all to himself now."

The young man smiled. "He'll not keep me from a friend."

CHAPTER 6

IT WAS A perfect day in June of 1566. The noontime sun of Crete cast short, precise shadows on the parched ground. In the shabby little hilltop cemetery, clusters of black-clothed mourners gathered beside the grave of Giorgio Theotokopoulos.

The news of his father's illness had come as a shock to Domenikos. As he reflected on the unhappy events of recent months, he was moved to believe that God was seeking to redress an imbalance of good fortune and joy which He had accorded the young Cretan during his early years in the Serenissima.

First there had been his quarrel with Tintoretto after a second summer of working with him. The subject, inevitably, had been Titian. Tintoretto, slightly drunk, had disparaged the master once too often, and Domenikos had exploded. Superficially, the wound had healed, but the friendship had dwindled.

Barely a week later his aunt Marica had accidentally learned that Domenikos was a communicant of the Roman Church. Her rage was astonishing. She ordered him out of her house. "It's bad enough that you take a Catholic mistress, but that you should have betrayed me in *this* way is the last straw!"

Certain that his aunt would communicate with Candia, Domenikos had at once written to his mother, breaking the news of his conversion. The reaction was even worse than he had feared. Cleo wrote that she had kept his information from Giorgio. "But you have broken my heart, Domenikos, not only by what you have done, but because you only told us when you saw no alternative. As it happens, Marica has written nothing."

The next calamity came soon afterward, when Veronica announced that she had met a Venetian gentleman of wealth and influence to whom she intended to devote her favors. Her dismissal of Domenikos seemed to him cruelly airy. "You were beginning to bore me," she said. "It's not that I don't enjoy talking about serious things, but no woman likes being elevated all the time."

It was difficult for Domenikos to decide whether his heart or his pride had suffered more. Either way, the fabric of his life in Venice had been shredded. Save for Titian and Orazio, he was alone. He moved to lodgings convenient to the Biri Grande.

Then had come word of his father's desperate illness. Black in spirit, Domenikos had sailed at once for Candia, but Giorgio died the evening before the ship cleared the breakwater of Candia's little harbor. And now the handful of Cretan earth he cast into his father's grave seemed a trifling gesture to a man so beloved, so generous. Domenikos wept and turned away. He and his brother led the shrouded Cleo back toward the house.

The six years of Domenikos' absence had produced changes that stunned him. Death had taken Brother Constantine and Father Vincenzo. His mother was weary and frail. Of his boyhood here, only Manusos remained, and this tie was tenuous indeed.

As if guessing his thoughts, Cleo peered up at him through her veil. "When do you return to Venice, Domenikos?"

"I don't know, mama."

"Why don't you stay here?" Manusos asked eagerly.

"No," said Cleo. "It wouldn't be wise." She looked again at Domenikos. "There's nothing for you here, is there?"

It was true, but he had a feeling that he ought to stay. "You and Manusos are here." And he added gently, "I'll do what you want."

"I know you will," she replied tranquilly. "You must go. It's important for you to finish the thing you've started so well. And the sooner you leave, the easier the break will be."

"But we need him." Manusos' shrill tone surprised his brother.

Cleo shook her head. "No, Manusos. I'll help you with the business. I know most of what Giorgio knew." Manusos made no response. ·They finished the journey to the house in silence.

GIORGIO had done handsomely by his younger son, leaving him a sum that would assure his independence for years to come. The remainder of the estate—the house, the lands, the warehouses— passed to Manusos, who also inherited his father's post of tax collector. And it was understood that he would care for Cleo.

After the will had been witnessed and filed in Candia, Manusos grew expansive and relaxed. He sat with Domenikos in the dining room of what was now his own house, drinking retsina.

"Well, Domenikos, we both have what we want."

"And you'll carry on the business where papa left off."

"Oh, I'm going to do better than that. Papa was wise, but he was cautious. He never took chances."

Domenikos hid his apprehension. "You're going to take chances?"

"Well, not exactly chances. Risks. When you gamble, you're taking a chance. When you invest, you're taking a risk. But you have information, not just a hunch."

Domenikos nodded. "And what's the nature of this risk?"

"Piracy," was the cool response.

The younger man stared at him. "Piracy? You're joking!"

"I thought that might surprise you. But quite a few Cretans are doing it, and making handsome profits. It's legal, you know. All you need is a license from the Consiglio. The Serenissima will provide the ship in exchange for a share of the takings." He grinned. "It's understood that we raid only Turkish shipping, of course."

"It sounds dangerous. Have you told mama?"

"Not yet. There's some danger, but the gains can be enormous."

"And when will you start out on this remarkable venture?"

"Well, it's indefinite at the moment. You have to know your men. There are complications." His tone became confidential. "When the time comes, you and uncle Manusos could be very useful to us in Venice. You could petition the Consiglio for us."

"I don't like it, Manusos." Domenikos sighed. "If you become a pirate, I assume you've given up any thought of marriage."

"Marriage has never interested me much. And now I have mama to look after."

"What about the family name?"

"You'll carry it on. When you get married, I'll come and visit you in Venice."

"If I'm there. I'm not going to work for Titian forever."

"Why do you stay with him? You have enough to be on your own now."

"I'm not ready. I have more to learn from him."

"After six years? How will you know when you *are* ready?"

"When I want to paint everything differently from Titian."

On the day Domenikos left, Cleo stood beside him in the courtyard. Below, in the harbor, the ship was being prepared for departure. "I'll say good-by to you here," she said. "Manusos will go down to the quay with you." She smiled sadly and took his hand. "Go with God."

"And you too, mama. Take care of yourself until I see you."

She shook her gray head. "I don't think we'll see each other again in this world. You'll never come back to Candia."

"You make it very painful. I *would* return, if you sent for me."

She looked down at the ground. "I'd never send for you. I have Manusos. He's a bit reckless, but good and kind." She sighed. "Distance is a harsh thing. It makes us forget."

"I should have written more often." In the ensuing silence, only the soft rustling of the leaves of an olive tree could be heard. "I'll write a letter for every ship that leaves for Candia."

"Don't say that. It would be cruel to let me hope."

He looked away, down toward the ships in the harbor. "You seem determined to make me feel even guiltier than I do already."

"I was only speaking the truth. There are such changes in you . . . I hope it matters that you've become the kind of man I'd like, a man I'd admire if I had a chance to know him." Cleo looked into her son's eyes and wept. Then she forced a smile. "Your father would have been pleased too. He was proud of you."

Domenikos took a deep breath. "You've said nothing about my conversion. Don't you want to chastise me?"

She laughed softly, sardonically. "*That's* what you want, isn't it? Oh, no, Domenikos. I've given you what you deserve, silence. Isn't that what you gave us?"

"Yes."

"All right. But perhaps you'll realize that it's wrong to pretend or to lie to people who love you. Giorgio would have understood if you'd told us sooner. He wouldn't have liked it, but he would have known that your motives were pure. By waiting so long, you'd have hurt him mortally. That's why I didn't let him know."

"Uncle Manusos persuaded me to say nothing; he was afraid of what aunt Marica would do. Not that that alters anything, but he was right about her." Domenikos smiled. "If she lets me enter her house again, she'll try to marry me off to a girl of her church."

"And you have other ideas?"

"Not yet, mama."

"Marry well, Domenikos. I'm not thinking in terms of a dowry. Marry a real person."

Manusos appeared in the doorway. Behind him, two laborers were struggling with Domenikos' belongings.

"Is it time?" Cleo asked plaintively. The older son nodded.

"Well," said Domenikos, embracing her closely.

She pressed a finger to his lips, her eyes filled with tears. "God be with us all," she whispered. "Your God and ours."

FOR THE Roman Catholic world, the year 1566 was agonizing. The Turks were applying such pressure against the Serenissima's bases in the eastern Mediterranean that the Consiglio was considering the Pope's suggestion for the formation of a Holy League against them, an alliance of the Papal States, Venice and the Holy Roman Empire (which consisted of Spain, Naples, Austria and the Low Countries). But Venice would not throw in her lot with the detested King Philip of Spain, not for another four years, not until Cyprus fell to the Turks.

Meanwhile, Queen Elizabeth had reestablished the Protestant Church of England. With her aid, the Huguenots in France were threatening the Church of Rome, and the enfeebled French monarchy. The Low Countries, long dominated by the Holy Roman Empire, now mocked their masters and their masters' Roman Church. Only Spain appeared unaffected by the Reformation.

"Do NOT mourn, Greco," said Titian. He laid a heavy hand on the young man's sleeve, seemingly embarrassed. "I'm never sure how to show sympathy. You've lost someone precious, and that makes *me* sad. I remember the day I lost my beautiful Cecilia." The black, fierce old eyes filled. "I was certain God had gone mad."

Domenikos looked away, moved more by Titian than by the sense of his own loss, and the old man went on. "Have you come to an understanding with your uncle and his good woman?"

"Yes, master. She speaks of nothing but finding me a wife."

"She's right, you know. It's time you thought of marriage. What would you think of *my* finding you a wife?"

"I'd entertain the notion favorably."

Titian chuckled. "I'll see what I can do. I've not tried anything like this since I arranged things for Orazio. Must she be rich?"

"No, but if she's extravagant, she should have a dowry."

"Very reasonable. And what attributes do you look for? Loyalty? Virtue? Intelligence? Appearance? Breeding? Piety? Good temper?"

"I admire all those qualities."

Titian snorted. "So do we all. Well, I'll see what I can arrange. And now, let's see if your travels among the savages harmed your craft. Paint me a picture, any subject you like."

The theme of Christ Healing the Blind had long appealed to Domenikos. "According to your faith be it unto you," Jesus had said. The idea of the picture came to him as a revelation, like the act of faith it depicted.

He worked swiftly, reverting to tempera, which he now used only for studies. He felt restored, at peace, because he was painting again. The setting was a paved square with a Venetian gondola stage in the right foreground, the arcaded facade of a palazzo on the left. The Saviour stood in front of the palazzo, His left hand holding that of a kneeling man, the right touching his eyes. Bent over the blind man and giving him support was a young man with dark, curly hair. Behind this group, three men and a youth were engaged in conversation. A larger group balanced the picture on the right. On the landing platform, a crouching dog protected a sack and a gourd.

"It's cleaner," said Titian with pleasure. "There are awkward things. Whose hand is that, for instance?" He pointed to the group behind the Saviour. "But it's really quite good and the dog is superb. You still have trouble capturing the human being in motion, but it will come." He slapped Domenikos affectionately on the back. "Now perhaps you'll give *me* some help."

He turned and pointed to a new rendering of *The Martyrdom of St. Lawrence*, a subject he had painted before. "King Philip is snapping at my heels for this." He grunted angrily. "My informants in Rome tell me that the Spanish ambassador there has been saying I'm past my prime. Painters can't afford important enemies." He laughed. "But I forget that you've no interest in money."

Domenikos was exasperated. "You keep teasing me about that, master. I do want to sell pictures, I do want commissions but—"

Titian interrupted him. "But you think it undignified to display your wares." Then he went on. "Your friend Tintoretto showed his under the arcade of the Piazzetta. It's how he got his first commission. How long do you think you can afford such pride? If you intend to play the role of a fish, my young friend, you'll have to learn to breathe water."

"When I find that I must become a fish, I'll learn to live in water, but not before. I have time, fortunately, and patience."

Titian's laughter was edged with anger. "What an important fellow! Don't imagine yourself an established artist because I praise one picture or that people will beg you to accept commissions. You'll have to struggle to find work. You'll have to lie, to cheat. It's a dirty business, Greco, getting a major reputation."

"I've never seen you do anything of the sort."

"I don't have to any longer, thank God. People come to *me* now. I command my own prices. But it wasn't always so. And you'll find things harder than I did. There are more painters and they're more skilled. The competition is very unattractive."

Domenikos listened politely but skeptically. "I understand," he said. "But when I'm ready, I know what I'll have to do."

Titian sighed. "Your arrogance makes me tremble. Don't swim with your eyes closed, I beg you."

Her matchless person every charm combined.

Ariosto's line came to Domenikos' mind when Titian presented him to Maria, the only daughter of a widowed Venetian merchant, Mario da Verona. She stood by the high double doors of her father's drawing room, her pale, slightly angular face held high, her deep-set brown eyes clear and bright, her smile conveying self-assurance. A gown of deep green silk delineated a form that was lithe and youthful.

Titian's introduction was characteristic. "This is Domenikos Theotoko . . . Oh Lord, I've never learned to say it. He's called Il Greco."

Maria inclined her dark head, extending a small, soft hand. Domenikos kissed it, inhaling her musky perfume. "My name, signorina, is Domenikos Theotokopoulos," he said.

She laughed. "Surely you can't expect me to call you by so long a name, beautiful though it sounds."

Domenikos smiled. "You may call me what you like."

With a delicate gesture of head and hand she invited Domenikos to follow her to a broad couch in the center of the elegantly furnished room. Titian withdrew.

The young man's eyes were drawn at once to a large tapestry that covered one wall. He stared at it, oblivious to the beautiful young woman. Surprised, she studied this intense, darkly handsome artist whom her father and Titian were so anxious for her to marry. His style of dress was not fashionable—if they married, he should wear bolder, more cheerful colors. But otherwise he seemed endowed with manliness and manners. He spoke well too, with a trace of an accent that she found not unattractive.

Not that her views made much difference. Her father had made it clear that if this young man approved of her, she had no choice. Poor papa, deeply in Titian's debt, would thus be released from his obligations. For so great an amount of gold, the master must indeed think highly of Domenikos.

"You admire the tapestry?" she said at last.

"It's magnificent. It must be Raffaello's design. May I sit down?"

"Oh, yes. Forgive me, I should have asked you."

"I should have waited for you to ask me. After six years in Venice, there are many things that I haven't learned."

"Surely not, signore."

Was she mocking him? Domenikos sat beside her. "Does your father choose the decorations?"

"Papa selects, but I must express my approval."

"What happens if you and your father disagree?"

She laughed. "You give me the feeling that I'm being tested."

"Perhaps. This is a rather painful situation for us, isn't it?"

She shrugged. "Is it? I'm rather enjoying it." It had dawned on her that Domenikos was more than attractive; he was desirable.

He became severe. "It's no game we're playing, signorina. We're considering the idea that if we don't find each other too objectionable we shall spend the rest of our lives together." He went on, "I enjoy your company. I mean I think I would enjoy it. You're young and beautiful. You seem intelligent. You have humor and grace. But this is difficult for me, and it's fateful for you."

"Thank you," she said softly, "for conceding me that."

He blushed. "I suppose that the only thing that commends me to you is that Titian is your father's creditor."

"It *is* a factor," she murmured. "But since you mean to test me, there must be more that you need to know. Let me see. I eat a great deal, but I'm not too heavy for my age. As far as I know, I'm capable of bearing children. I play the lute well, but I sing badly. I despise Latin. I can sew, but I don't like to. I cook indifferently. I shall expect servants to do everything in my house."

Domenikos smiled ironically. "Forgive me for thinking you might be a serious person. It should have been obvious that—"

"The daughter of a man so deeply in debt couldn't be serious?"

"That anyone so young and beautiful—"

"Oh, signore, those words sound cheap."

"Completely honest, nevertheless."

Her fine eyes held his fiercely. "You mean it, truly?"

"Truly."

She smiled, half gay, half mocking. "A truce, then? I can be serious. But not for too long, please. You do know that when we leave this room an answer is expected of you?"

"Is an answer expected only of me, signorina? What is yours?"

"My hands are tied. You know that."

He was, he knew, immensely drawn to this girl. "I couldn't live with you if you'd married me against your will."

Maria became alarmed. "You'll not accept me, then?"

"I *do* accept you." He smiled. "I'm beginning to think that in this case an arranged marriage has its advantages."

She shook her head. "That's flattery."

"You'll never hear flattery from me, signorina."

"Good. You'll not hear it from me either. I detest it."

"You see? We agree about something important already."

She seemed shy as she turned to him. "There's an important question I'd like to ask you, signore. *Must* you paint?"

"Yes, I must paint. It's the true imperative of my life."

Maria nodded. "I'm not a very profound person. I'm possessed by nothing, obsessed by nothing."

Domenikos looked intently into her brilliant eyes. "We might balance each other nicely—you so cool, me so hot."

"Is that a proposal of marriage, signore?"

He laughed. "You never doubted the outcome, did you? I'm hoping your enthusiasm is half as great as mine. Have you any?"

She smiled, and reached for his hands. "Let me say that if I *had* a choice, I would accept your proposal with eagerness."

MARIA and Domenikos were married after Easter, 1567, in the Church of San Canciano. The wedding breakfast was one of the most elaborate in many seasons, with every kind of entertainment, and a lavish banquet. It was attended "by all the people of Venice who were obligated to Titian," Tintoretto told Domenikos. The bridegroom's aunt, uncle and cousin were also present. Marica noted with approval the comparative brevity of the Latin nuptials, and partook eagerly of the refreshments. At last Maria and Domenikos were permitted to escape by gondola to the mainland, where they were borne by carriage to Titian's villa near Vicenza.

There, in the warm days and cool nights, they came to discover and understand each other. As Maria's knowledge of the rites of love grew deeper, she proved a more demanding partner than the languid Veronica had been. Domenikos responded happily, caught up in a passion reborn after each moment of satiety.

Though spoiled, Maria was never petulant. Her convent up-bringing had taught her obedience; her husband's gentleness made obedience a pleasure. He read to her—from Dante, from Aristotle, and from Catullus. "I like it best when you read in Greek," she said to him. "Then I can just listen to the music of your voice."

Domenikos laughed. "I'm going to teach you Greek, *cara*. Then you can be bored in three languages."

He made her pose for him, clothed at first, then in the nude. She sat for him patiently, moving only when her muscles grew stiff. For all the discomfort of posing, she enjoyed being the object of his total attention. And she loved the finished sketches of herself.

They returned to Venice and installed themselves in apart-ments generously provided by Maria's father in a wing of his imposing house, which, like Titian's, overlooked the lagoon and the bleak Isola de San Michele. Maria's dowry had included some furniture, but much remained to be acquired. Making these purchases, Maria rejoiced in exploring strange corners of the city, until, distressed at the scenes of poverty they encoun-tered, she one day protested. "With so much wealth in Venice, how can so many be so wretched? Oh, please don't take me back there, Domenikos."

He chided her gently. "Our not going back isn't going to alter things, you know. Those poor people aren't going to go away, *carissima*. And what you've learned, you can't unlearn."

"When I don't want to see something, I don't want to *have* to see it. I just want to crawl into my burrow and hide."

In June, Maria announced that she was pregnant. Domenikos was overjoyed; he would have a son. His pleasure was gratifying to her, but she confessed herself apprehensive about this adven-ture on which her body was about to take her. The young painter therefore gratefully accepted Titian's invitation to join him in Vicenza for the summer. There he could also continue his work with the master on *The Martyrdom of St. Lawrence.*

Pregnancy gave Maria a radiance that made Domenikos want to paint her as the Virgin Mary with Child. The project disturbed her. "You don't think it might be better to wait until after the baby is born? It might be tempting fate."

He responded with wonder. "You're superstitious?"

"Not normally. But when it concerns a first baby . . ."

But when he insisted, Maria sat for him willingly. She wore a pale blue cloak with a cowl that cast shadows on her features, creating an air of somberness and mystery. As she stood before the finished painting with Orazio and Titian, she clapped her hands and embraced her husband. "Do I really look like that?"

"Of course not," Titian answered tartly. "You haven't had the baby yet. Don't you see what your young man has done for you?"

"You mean this is how I'll look *after* I've had my baby?"

"I'm sure of it," said the old man. "Why not use her in an Annunciation, Greco, or a Nativity or one of the Adorations?"

Domenikos decided on the *Adoration of the Shepherds*, his conception of which was different from Titian's. He would experiment with exaggerations of light and shadow, chiaroscuro, a technique of Tintoretto's that interested him. He worked on this, the first of his studies in oils, into the winter of 1567.

When the painting was completed, Titian looked at it for a long time. "Well," he said at last, "you've finally decided that you're somebody else, no longer Titian's man. I see other painters here, but the plan seems mostly your own. It's original."

"Thanks for that word."

Titian shuffled over to a disordered writing table and picked up two sheets of paper. "I've written to King Philip. Listen." The letter explained the delay in completing *The Martyrdom of St. Lawrence*, and went on, "In this great picture I have been aided by a most gifted pupil . . ." He handed it to Domenikos, smiling affectionately. "That's what I think of you. If *I* were a young man, Spain is where I'd go. It's the seat of Europe's power. And there's money; people pay respectable fees for paintings. I'm told it will take Philip twenty years to finish this fantastic Escorial he's building. Just think of the commissions you could have."

Domenikos shrugged. "Perhaps. I'd prefer to stay here."

"I'm ninety years old, Greco. After I'm gone, I don't think Venice will be the place for you. If not Spain, Rome perhaps—"

"I'm going nowhere now. I have to wait for the birth of my son."

DOMENIKOS' son was born in February of 1568. There could have been no more radiant parents for a newly baptized child— named, naturally, Tiziano. The young painter continued working during the infant's first months, but it was soon evident that his work had become routine. It seemed that all his creative energies were expended in his delight, and in projecting a noble future for the little boy. Titian accused him of neglecting not only his painting but his wife in his obsession with the continuation of his line.

Then, as spring yielded to summer, the tiny Tiziano's health started to falter. Slowly, inexorably, his strength waned. The end came in the first days of September, just after their return from Vicenza. A numbed Maria and Domenikos could merely stare at one another, able to communicate their misery only through their eyes. *My God, why hast Thou forsaken me?* These words of Christ's echoed in the painter's mind. And at first only God could have said which of the bereaved young parents was the more stricken. Soon, however, it became plain to everyone.

The deterioration in Maria's health had seemed a temporary reaction, a depression that would pass. Domenikos told himself, and her, that infant mortality, so common a thing, was a condition with which every parent had to cope. "We'll try again," he said.

Lying in bed, she shook her head. "You don't understand. It's in my blood. My mother died after my baby brother died."

"But *her* dying has nothing to do with you, my love."

"She'd failed. I've failed. It's the same thing."

"Not at all. We'll hope that God lets the next child survive."

"No, Domenikos. The spirit isn't in me." She rolled away from him, the first sign of rejection she had ever shown.

Domenikos consulted his father-in-law. "She speaks of her mother's dying after losing a son. Maria expects the same fate."

The father pursed his lips. "I have to tell you. My little Maria doesn't know, but her mother is alive. When the baby died, she became depressed, and then she went mad."

"My God. Where is she now?"

"In a convent for the mad. It's not a bad place; the nuns are very gentle. Poor Alicia recognizes no one."

"And was she once as gay and bright and calm as Maria?"

"Much the same. But it won't happen to Maria. She has *my* blood in her. She'll be all right, Greco. You'll see."

MARIA remained in bed most of each day, dressing only in anticipation of her husband's return from Titian's studio. But within three months of the baby's death, as the cold air from the Dolomites swept across the Venetian plain, even this pretense of participation in his life was abandoned. She could no longer abide the daylight. Through each short winter's day the curtains of the bedchamber remained drawn. Through each long winter's night, she would barely stir in response to a despairing husband's words of tenderness. The fine dark eyes stared vacantly, the sleek black hair went lank. She appeared to be disintegrating before his eyes.

Domenikos turned for aid to Pietro Fiorentino, said to be one of the wisest physicians in Venice. He pontificated on the subject of melancholia, and prescribed unguents, inhalations and infusions. But as if the body throve on the mind's decay, she grew physically stronger while her mental condition steadily deteriorated.

From Father Jacopo, the intelligent new parish priest of San Canciano, he drew a small measure of solace. The curate laid a hand on the painter's shoulder. "God understands, Greco. We must pray for a miraculous healing."

"Father, it's becoming very difficult for me to believe in God. Prayer seems hopeless."

"To God, nothing is hopeless. Don't lose your faith."

"But I'm not God. I want action. I want to know what I can do to help my poor Maria, to bring her back to me."

"God understands that, Greco."

"That's not good enough for me now."

"Don't you see that you're fighting Him? What we're not meant to understand, Greco, we must accept as the will of God.

And you must find peace of soul. If you don't you'll follow Maria."

"I can't believe her illness can be God's will. And the little Tiziano, was his death God's will too?"

"Has it occurred to you that God might not be striking at Maria, or at the child, but at you?"

"Would God strike at one person for the sins of another?"

"Perhaps."

Domenikos bowed his head. "I can accept that idea, but I wonder if I've sinned in proportion to such a terrible punishment. I feel myself the accursed of God."

In his despair, Domenikos was driven to seek companionship. He called frequently on his aunt and uncle and was touched by their concern. He haunted the taverna where he had first met Tintoretto, drank more wine than he could sustain, and found relief in saying to casual acquaintances what he recognized to be the fact: Maria was lost to him forever.

For a time he continued his nightly vigils at her bedside, searching her ravaged features for some sign of recognition. There was none. He felt he had expended all his tears, that he would never weep again. Gradually the vigils shortened, and finally ceased. The shape huddled in the bed seemed no longer a person.

Now Domenikos took to reading voraciously, grasping at every available printed word. And he painted as furiously as he read, until the brush fell from his fingers. He found in this recklessness a sense of freedom, of adventure, and he discovered new elements in his skill. Repeating themes he had painted earlier, he made modifications that Titian noted with gratified astonishment.

Months passed. Mario da Verona at last approached his son-in-law. "We must put her in a hospital, Greco. The doctor says she might live for years like this. It's too much for the servants, for me, for you above all."

"How could I live with the thought of her in a madhouse?"

Mario gently touched his son-in-law's cheek. "Greco, I've been through this, I understand what you're feeling. We all know you love her. But there's a difference between love and self-destruction. Everything that could possibly be done for her has been done."

"Maria locked up—no, I'd be haunted. Those places on the Isola del Desole—how could you have done that to your wife?"

"Alicia doesn't understand, and neither will Maria. Would I let my daughter suffer, Greco? You think me heartless?"

Domenikos embraced the old man. "Forgive me."

"I have your consent, then?" Mario was weeping.

"Reluctantly. But I'll have to leave. I couldn't abide it."

"I AGREE," said Titian. "But where will you go?"

"To Rome, master, as you suggested. If I fail, then Spain."

"Will you listen to some advice, Greco? Not that I expect you to follow it. But I think you're destroying yourself."

"Over Maria?"

"No, your books, your constant brooding, your religion. Books aren't for painters. Thinking isn't for painters. Stop thinking. Painters must feel, enjoy themselves, laugh and cry, shout, rage, bellow, scream. You've never learned to unwind. How long is it since you came to one of my evening parties?"

"A long time, master. Since before my father died, I think."

"Why? You think them sinful? You think our senses should be inspired by the head, not the heart?"

"The head isn't always the worst guide, master."

"For a painter, the head is always the wrong guide. To us, the needs of the flesh have to be the guide. You've got to learn to let yourself feel."

"It's the soul that shows me the way. And I have no choice but to follow. If people behaved as you suggest, we'd be no better than animals."

Titian grunted. "Well, what's so wrong with being an animal? Most people are, you know. I'm ninety-three and I'm in a better position than most men to know what people are like. We may have souls, as the Church says, but our instincts tell us how we ought to behave. You're fighting nature."

"The more I improve my intellect, master, the more I improve my soul. The more I improve my soul, the better I am as a painter. I can see more plainly with my soul than with my eyes. And forgive me for saying so, but it's the same for you."

"That's the remark of a prig." The old man folded his hands. "The subject is closed. Rome may be just the place for you. It's filled with God-struck people. Most of them are Spaniards." Suddenly the old man's eyes filled with tears and he sniffed mightily. "I'll not pretend your going doesn't pain me. I suppose that's why I spoke so sharply."

Domenikos' preparations for departure were feverish. After each day of packing, his sleep was tormented by fearful dreams about the future and his loneliness, about his poor Maria and his beloved Titian. Maria was now confined to a convent. Her father promised to visit her weekly and to report to Rome. But Domenikos was unable to dismiss a feeling that he was deserting her.

It was hardly easier to say good-by to Titian. The old man made considerable fuss about Domenikos' letters of introduction to important persons along the route to Rome and the sights he must on no account overlook. But in the end, there were tears. "We'll not meet again," said Titian softly and sighed. "Now, for God's sake, go."

PART III: ROME (1570–1575)

CHAPTER 7

DOMENIKOS reached Rome in November 1570, after an arduous journey on horseback. Although he had taken only those articles he thought indispensable, no less than eight donkeys were required for each stage of the trip, plus the beasts' drivers, and a pair of mounted guards to protect the caravan from brigands on the mountain roads. Fortunately, there were no untoward events.

The nine months since his departure from Venice had been almost too exhilarating. His eyes were weary, his senses dulled by the great paintings he had seen. Giotto's in Padua, Mantegna's in Mantua, Correggio's in Parma, Piero della Francesca's in Ferrara, the mosaics of Ravenna. And in Florence, where he had spent two months and celebrated his twenty-ninth birthday, he had at last appreciated the near-idolatry of Michelangelo.

Because Rome had for so many centuries dominated the culture of the western world, Domenikos had imagined it as a flawless diamond, different from all other cities. It was the stronghold of Christianity, the symbol of his faith, the place where his talent was to be tested, his genius made manifest. But the Rome of his image was not the Rome he found. At the time of his arrival, the capital of Christendom lay in spiritual and physical ruins. The decrees of Trent and the installation of the austere Pope Pius V had combined to create a dispiriting effect on the once gay city, while physically she was recovering from the terrible sacking by Charles V's army in 1527. Much had been done by Michelangelo and others toward the completion of the new Basilica of St. Peter's, but more remained to be done. Meanwhile Vignola, whose real name was Barocchio, was supervising the construction of the mother church for the Society of Jesus, the famous Church of the Gesù that was to revolutionize architectural taste with the style that would come to be known as baroque.

Domenikos made his entry into Rome through the Porta del Popolo and the Piazza del Popolo, a large unpaved square, its muddy surface rutted by wheels of cart and carriage. Flanking it were low, shambling houses, shops, a few inns, and the Church of Santa Maria del Popolo. In the Piazza de Spagna, under the glowing fifteenth-century Church of Trinità dei Monti, he found lodgings at a noisy inn. It was all less elegant than he would have liked. "Rome is not Venice," he wrote Titian.

Within a week of his arrival, Domenikos sought out Don Giulio Clovio, the painter of miniatures, to whom Titian had recommended him. Clovio was in the employ of Cardinal Farnese, and received Domenikos in the library of the magnificent Palazzo Farnese, which Michelangelo had helped to design—a room, Domenikos thought with pleasure, which gave the impression of true prodigality. By the end of the interview Don Giulio was proposing to write to the cardinal, recommending that Domenikos be given quarters in the Palazzo.

"I'm sure he'll let you stay here until you find something more suitable than that stinking inn you chose for yourself. If your potential patrons knew you were living in a place like that, they'd not be impressed. In Rome you have to impress people. You must have important connections, important protectors—"

"Like the cardinal?" Domenikos smiled. "I'm grateful to you for writing His Excellency."

Clovio leaned back in his cross-legged chair and folded his arms. "You needn't imagine, Greco, that I'm going to let you off with a word of thanks. I want you to paint my portrait."

Now in his seventies, Giulio Clovio was no longer at the height of his modest powers as an artist, though he was enjoying his period of greatest success, his reputation resting on miniature copies of Titian, Raffaello, Michelangelo, which were little masterpieces of delicacy. A Croatian, he had sought refuge in Rome from the depredations of the Turks upon his native land, only to find himself caught in the 1527 sack of Rome. In this most atrocious of massacres, made the more terrible by the participation of Italians in the ravaging of their greatest city, Clovio was beaten and tortured, then left with both legs broken to starve in prison. After the sated pillagers had left, he escaped and became a lay brother in an order of penitents. There Cardinal Grimani had discovered him, and thinking his talents would be of greater use to God outside monastery walls, invited him to join the service of Alessandro Farnese.

As Don Giulio had predicted, Cardinal Farnese responded to his letter with instructions to his majordomo to provide the young painter with two rooms on the top floor of the Palazzo Farnese, one of which overlooked the broad, muddy, winding Tiber, with a glimpse of the crenellated Castel Sant' Angelo, the Pope's fortress. Domenikos asked that one room be stripped of its furnishings for a studio, and here he went to work on the portrait of Don Giulio.

He was both pleased and discontented with this painting. It was his most carefully executed, but it lacked something. Conviction? Understanding of his subject? He found it superficial.

Clovio, however, had no reservations. "It's superb, Greco. Titian himself couldn't have done better. I congratulate you."

Domenikos' expression of thanks for Farnese's hospitality had been acknowledged by the cardinal in the annoyingly offhand way of the benevolent rich. The palazzo was crawling with artists and scholars to whom he gave shelter. The two remained distant until Farnese was shown the portrait of Clovio.

Domenikos was working in his room when he was summoned

by a page. "His Excellency requires your presence at once." Hastily he changed into a fresh blouse. The page then led him to the gallery where the cardinal stood before the portrait, conversing with Clovio and his librarian, Don Fulvio Orsini.

As Domenikos entered, bowing, Farnese pointed to the picture with an eloquent hand. "I want you to paint my portrait," he said.

Domenikos bowed again. "Of course, Excellency."

"I shall be interested to see whether you can do today what your master did twenty-five years ago. You've seen that portrait?"

"I have, Excellency. You ask more than is quite fair."

"Not if you can paint Don Giulio as you have. It's a wonderful likeness, and Orsini here tells me it's a fine picture too."

Domenikos turned quickly to smile at the stocky librarian, then shifted his eyes once again to the cardinal. "I shall do my best, Excellency. When would it be convenient for you to begin?"

"At once." And the cardinal moved through the adjoining library and mounted the stairs, followed by the astonished painter.

In the Rome of 1571, Alessandro Farnese was an anachronism. He reflected an age, a spirit, a taste and exuberance that placed less emphasis on inward than on outward manifestations of style, grace and religious conviction. He was a High-Renaissance man, a breed that was losing fashion in the Catholic world of the Counter-Reformation. His background explained a lot. Immorality had been common among many earlier masters of the Church, and Farnese could point out that his grandfather had been Pope Paul III; his great-aunt Julia mistress of another pope. Fifty now, he had himself been a cardinal since the age of fourteen.

He brought to the office charm, wit and a passion for art and scholarship; his palace was a center of culture for all Italy. In his view, the arts were quite as consonant with the works of God as were the gestures of purification and penitence demanded by the present rulers of the Church—and they were a good deal more pleasant. He therefore felt little sympathy for the edicts of Trent, and ignored the rulings on books and the index of forbidden literature promulgated by the Holy Office. The proscription of such writers as Boccaccio, Machiavelli and Ariosto was repugnant to him, a fact that endeared him to Domenikos, whose growing library contained a number of banned volumes.

Farnese's portrait seemed to Domenikos to suffer from the same defect as Clovio's: its elegance was cold, distant, austere. It proved, however, even more gratifying to its subject, who ordered its permanent display in his library—a most auspicious augury.

Hardly less vital to Domenikos than the cardinal's patronage, of which he now had hope, was the friendship of the cardinal's librarian. Fulvio Orsini had joined the Farnese entourage while a youth and had become his master's principal adviser on all things cultural and scholarly. As enthusiastic about Farnese's portrait as he had been about Clovio's, he at once commissioned one of himself. During the sittings, he discovered that this new artist was a brilliant young man who had ideas and expressed them. He offered to introduce him to what he called "internal Rome."

A better guide would have been impossible to find than this small, cheerful, bouncy man; and as they scudded from palace to ruin to church, they also explored each other's minds, discussing all the things that mattered to them both. Domenikos found in Orsini the first person to whom he could confide the whole of his experience without need for explanation or defense. And Orsini, watching the artist at work, thought that for the first time he could comprehend not only the concentration and discipline demanded, but the creative process itself. The contradictions in the young man's mind intrigued him—the intellectual and the passionate, the disciple of Aristotle and the religious mystic. He frequently complained that Domenikos would enjoy martyrdom.

He complained more bitterly about his friend's maddening refusal to cultivate those members of Roman society who might become patrons. At the end of a year, important commissions had not materialized, only portraits. "I'm not yet anxious," Domenikos wrote Titian, "but it would be pleasant to report that at least one of the studies I have made for altarpieces had been accepted."

He had, however, succeeded in organizing his living arrangements. He had rented a house close to the Palazzo Farnese, with a large room facing north which he could use as a studio. So far he had resisted Orsini's plea that he employ a manservant.

One of the most prophetic discussions that Orsini had with Domenikos about his future took place on the day all Rome was buzzing with news of the great naval victory of Lepanto. An immense fleet under Don John of Austria, the illegitimate son of Emperor Charles V, had sailed with the blessing of the Pope to meet a substantial force of Ottoman vessels bound for another Mediterranean island invasion. Don John's ships came from Spain, Genoa and Venice, the Holy League the Pope had proposed some years before. At Lepanto, near the Gulf of Corinth, on October 7, this fleet had inflicted a sharp defeat on the Turks. It was said that the Holy League would now begin to drive the infidel Turk from the Greek mainland and from his island holdings.

This optimism was not shared by the politically astute Orsini. "If the Holy League could stay together," he told Domenikos, "the wishful thinkers might be right. But it will come apart."

"I wish I had your clarity of thought, Fulvio, but I haven't."

The librarian agreed heartily. "No, you haven't! And you wish the world would go away and leave you alone. You're not even interested, are you?"

The painter laughed. "I can't afford to waste my passion."

"What is it you seek, apart from glorifying God in paint?"

"Peace. Is there any place in the world that's safe and peaceful? Not Rome, not Venice, and certainly not Crete."

"If it's remoteness from the world you're looking for, Greco, I suppose Spain would be the place for you. Spain is secure. The Turks won't invade her." He paused, musing. "They're a curious lot, the Spaniards, the most joyless people I've ever encountered." He grinned maliciously. "Unless, as *you* seem to, one regards suffering as joy, and is in love with death."

"You're wrong. I accept death, but I certainly don't love it. And I have my joys, joys that are not painful."

"You take me too literally. I do recognize your moments of gaiety! But Greco, you know, you should have a woman."

The young man grimaced, embarrassed. He knew his reply

would invite Orsini's scorn. "I vowed before I married Maria never to be unfaithful to her."

"But surely, Greco, with your wife mad—forgive me—but surely the situation is different now."

"That doesn't alter the vow." He smiled dolefully. "But there have been temptations—"

"Thank God for that at least." A warm smile spread over Orsini's face. "We'll have to do something about this, Greco. Nothing tawdry, but no complicated love affair either. Just a nice strapping girl from the country. How does that strike you?"

Domenikos was shaken. He couldn't look at Orsini, because at his friend's words he had felt the sudden stinging of desire, so long kept dormant. At last he raised his eyes, defeated. "You're a disgrace to your cardinal. *Lead us not into temptation.*"

Orsini laughed jubilantly. "We shall make a normal man of you. A sainthood for Greco no more."

THE GIRL'S name was Catarina de Preboste. She was from the hills of the Abruzzi, the younger sister of a woman who worked in the kitchens of the Palazzo Farnese. She was a strongly built child of seventeen, full of peasant laughter, tender, and expressing a gay gentleness for his early embarrassment in her presence. She was passionate too, and touchingly concerned for his pleasure with her. Orsini had been right: no sainthood for Il Greco, after their first lovemaking. Domenikos felt relieved, restored.

The girl said as they lay quiet, side by side, "It's too late for me to go back to my sister's room in the palazzo. May I spend the night here, signore?"

Laughing softly, he said, "Of course, Catarina. You didn't think I'd let you leave so soon anyhow, did you?"

"I didn't know." She gazed wistfully about the bedchamber with its pale shadows dancing in the faltering light. "This must be a very large house. Do you live here all alone?"

"There's a woman who comes in to clean for me."

"You need a manservant, signore, to live here and cook for you." She ran a finger over the corrugations of his rib cage. "You don't eat enough. He could clean for you too, and run your errands."

"You're thinking of someone, aren't you, Catarina?"

She nodded, smiling. "My brother Francesco. He's my twin. You'll like him. He's fine and strong. He's pleasant too."

"Naturally, if he's your brother."

"He needs work," she said. "Will you see him tomorrow?"

The painter felt vaguely alarmed, lest Catarina complicate his life. But he was committing himself to nothing. "Yes, tomorrow."

She nuzzled his ear. "You'll not be sorry, signore."

THE FIRST thing Domenikos liked about Francesco was that he came to present himself alone. Above a stocky, muscular body he had a fine head, with observant, intelligent eyes and a ready, broad smile revealing white teeth.

"Catarina tells me you might like to work for me."

"I would, signore."

"If I won't employ you, what will you do?"

"Go back to our village. I work with my father and my older brother Filippo. Papa owns a small farm with sheep and vines, but when he dies, the farm will belong to Filippo."

"You read and write, Francesco?"

"My brother does, signore. Papa thought one son who could read was enough."

"Your father sounds like a hard man. How does he feel about Catarina being with me?"

" 'One less appetite is always a blessing,' he told us when we left, 'and two would be a papal benediction.' " The boy uttered this monstrous phrase without reproach. "It was God's will."

"And you can cook and clean and run errands for me?"

"I can, signore."

"Look, Francesco. I'll teach you to read and write. I'll give you your bed and your food and your clothes. And I'll pay you one ducat a month. Does my proposal satisfy you?"

"It's very generous. When would you like me to begin?"

"Today, if you want."

The presence of other lives beneath his roof proved an unmitigated pleasure to Domenikos. Not since the early days of his marriage had he felt so content. As a gift for Orsini to whom he owed this state of mind, he began a new rendition of Christ Healing the Blind. It amused him to include in the painting the features of the librarian, of Catarina and her brother, and of himself. As he was completing this canvas, he was suddenly aware that Francesco was watching him. "Oh, master," the boy said, fascinated, "if you taught me to paint, I'd ask for no money at all."

The painter gave Francesco a long, intense look. At last he smiled. "No need to give up your pay. I'll teach you what I can."

Francesco seemed about to explode. He jumped up and down. He embraced Domenikos, then broke away to dance in tight circles about the floor. "Oh, master, what a wonderful thing!" As simply as that, Domenikos acquired a pupil.

The painting was finished in 1572. The artist recognized it as the finest work he had ever done, yet realized it owed more to his Venetian training than to his own conception. He was not yet wholly himself. Sighing, he added his signature in Greek.

Orsini's approval was gratifying. He flatly refused to accept it as a gift, however. "This is for the cardinal. I'll be surprised if it doesn't lead to another commission." He was right. Farnese purchased the painting for seventy-five ducats, and commanded a large canvas of the Purification of the Temple for the palazzo.

A Roman lawyer, Lancilotti, who visited the palazzo, insisted that the *Christ Healing the Blind* should be seen by the Pope, with whom he was acquainted. So, with Orsini, the cardinal and Lancilotti in close attendance, Domenikos appeared before His Holiness. He had hardly begun to reply to the Pope's first question when Pius interrupted accusingly, "But you're not Italian. We must first take care of our own." Domenikos was dismissed, furious that he had been scorned because of his nationality and aware that he had no hope of a commission from the Holy See.

But soon, and unexpectedly, Pius V died, and a fortnight later, on May thirteenth, the College of Cardinals elected Ugo Buoncompagni to be Pope Gregory XIII. Though not the zealot his predecessor had been, Gregory was quite as dedicated to suppressing the Protestant rebellion. Whether this Pope also would reject his art for the wrong reasons was a question that caused Domenikos some apprehension.

Meanwhile Domenikos had other matters to occupy him. A letter arrived from his brother, Manusos, sent from Venice where Manusos and his partners had gone to get the Consiglio's permission to operate four pirate vessels. The ships and their equipment, armament and crews were all to be financed by the Republic, secured by a bond which the partners were to post. In exchange, they were to turn over to the Consiglio all captured captains and one-fourth of all prisoners, selling the remaining captives as slaves. There remained, Manusos wrote, one small but thorny problem. The Venetian authorities insisted that the partners pay for all repairs to the ships.

"It is impossible," he wrote, "to estimate what repairs might cost or when they might be necessary. They might be required before we'd had any contact with an enemy vessel, and we'd be ruined. I beg you to write to your friend Tiziano, and ask him to intercede with the Consiglio. Call it your wedding present to me, for I am to be married. Katina is the daughter of one of my partners and sweet enough, although mama thinks her ordinary. The truth is he wouldn't join me unless I married her."

Domenikos didn't know whether to laugh or cry. He thought the plan foolhardy beyond belief, but he knew he would accede to his brother's request. Never before had his family asked anything of him, and his guilt at his neglect of them outweighed his knowledge that he would be doing Manusos a favor by refusing.

Less than a month later he learned from Titian that the Consiglio had granted the petition.

CHAPTER 8

THE PAINTING of the Purification so pleased the cardinal that he promised to arrange an audience for Domenikos with Pope Gregory. Meanwhile, Orsini introduced him to a number of clerics, mostly Jesuits, who might prove helpful. One was Don Pedro Chacón, a frail, middle-aged Spanish scholar, who was at the Pope's request helping prepare a new calendar to replace the inaccurate one then in use.

Chacón's appreciation of Domenikos' painting was profound, and he kept urging his new friend to go to Spain where, he assured him, his talents would find far greater acceptance than

KING PEPIN RETURNING RAVENNA TO THE ROMAN CHURCH — BY SICCIOLANTE

they had met in Rome. When he heard that the painter had also had some training in architecture and sculpture, he was even more emphatic. But Domenikos was now sure that he could eventually prevail here, the more so because of the cardinal's offer to introduce him to the Pope. Chacón then graciously volunteered to join his influence with Farnese's. He had known Pope Gregory when he was a legate to Chacón's beloved native city of Toledo.

The cardinal, however, had had differences with the Pope. "I opposed his election," he told Domenikos. "He's not forgotten."

He had not. The audience went badly from the beginning. "I have seen your work," Gregory said, after Domenikos had kissed the pontifical ring. "I like it well enough. What is it you want?"

"I would be most grateful, Holiness, if my work were considered when another altarpiece is to be commissioned."

The Pontiff closed his eyes as if bored. "I am not much interested in such things. I leave the selection of artists to the Jesuits."

Cardinal Farnese said, "He's considered by many to be the finest painter in Rome, Holiness."

"So you have already told me, Farnese. But why should I extend favors to a protégé of yours?" He cleared his throat. "In any event, Maestro Il Greco, I have taken the trouble of looking into your career. You have failed to impress the Jesuits favorably . . ."

Farnese said, "The objection of the Jesuits, Holiness, is that he is foreign. They prefer Italians."

The Pope said, "So do I. The reason, however, is unimportant to me. The Jesuits seem perfectly satisfied with Zuccaro and Sicciolante, the painters we have at present."

Domenikos sighed. "Their work is familiar to me, Holiness."

"You think it inferior?"

"Timid might be a better word."

The Pope stared at Domenikos, and now he spoke with all the authority of his great office. "We shall not permit our artists to be too venturesome at a time in our history when there are so many dangers. The audience is ended."

Numb in mind and body, Domenikos took leave of the cardinal and Chacón as they left the Vatican, and walked off alone in the bright fall air. Look at reality. Stare it down. He could have a pleasant, remunerative career under the Farnese patronage. He was already Rome's greatest portraitist. But he would *not* be Il Greco, Rome's new Michelangelo, not so long as the present Pope reigned.

He saw suddenly that, at thirty-one, he was still not completely formed, as a painter or as a person. At thirty-seven, the great Raffaello had died, his legacy vast, his identity established since adolescence. But he, Il Greco, had stood still for five years.

Going back to Venice was out of the question. It would be an acknowledgment of failure. What had his father said? "I will not stand for your being second-rate at anything." Spain, Titian had said. It sounded attractive. Orsini had suggested it; Chacón kept urging it. But there must be a plan. He would learn Spanish, get Chacón to introduce him to Spaniards in Rome. He would ask Titian to help him solicit Philip II's patronage.

TITIAN replied, "I shall communicate with His Majesty directly. I am glad that at last you plan to do the reasonable thing."

Cleo wrote from Crete, "So far away?" But she consoled herself. "I shall soon have a grandchild to divert my last hours. The girl is plain but honest, and devoted to your brother. . . ."

Catarina and Francesco were eager to accompany him. Although the girl's role as mistress-housekeeper might be viewed differently in Spain, the joyful affection between her and Domenikos made leaving her behind unthinkable. But early in 1573, Catarina became pregnant. The journey would have to be postponed until the infant was strong enough to endure it.

One afternoon, Domenikos went to the Palazzo Farnese to meet one more Spanish dignitary. There had been many, none of whom attracted him especially. He found Chacón in the gallery with Orsini and a tall young cleric with steeply arched brows, clear dark eyes bright with gaiety, a flaring mustache, and a pointed beard. "Greco, this is Don Luis de Castilla," Orsini said.

Castilla smiled, bowed and offered his hand in a strong grip.

"Don Luis," said Chacón, "has come to Rome on an important mission to the Holy Office."

"No, no. Merely routine diplomacy. To learn the Holy Father's attitude toward literature and the arts, as well as other heresies."

Chacón was alarmed at a tone of veiled mockery. "Heresy is not to be joked about, Don Luis."

Castilla gazed at his compatriot. "Was I joking, Don Pedro?"

"You're connected with the Inquisition?" Domenikos asked.

"In Spain, maestro, every cleric is connected with the Inquisition." Castilla's expression was unmistakably sardonic.

"I've been told that nowhere else has it been so effective."

The priest bowed. "The Inquisition is intended to suppress heresies among the people and in *this* we've met with a gratifying success. But never would we jeopardize the investigations of the true scholar. Our university in Toledo is a source of great pride. To suppress certain studies would be painful."

"Painful," said Chacón primly, "but necessary. You agree?"

"But of course, Don Pedro. Can you imagine our archbishop setting himself against the will of the Holy Father?"

Domenikos noted little sincerity in this reply. "But surely you've suppressed undesirable literature wherever you've discovered it!"

Castilla regarded him curiously. "We feel knowledge should not be repressed until it proves in contravention of holy ordinance."

Orsini interposed. "Greco's question was not wholly abstract, Don Luis. His library contains a number of proscribed volumes."

"How dare you say a thing like that to me, Don Fulvio?" Don Luis said angrily. "You don't know who I am. Suppose I were sent precisely to find out what you've just volunteered?"

Orsini reddened. "I simply assumed—"

Castilla relaxed. "You assumed correctly, but it was reckless."

"You're right, Don Luis. But since my spies described you as worldly and broad-minded, and since Greco is thinking of going to Spain, it seemed an appropriate remark."

"If the maestro comes to Toledo, he will have no trouble."

Chacón was scandalized. "Then the Inquisition has lost its true meaning. If it can be manipulated for personal ends—"

"Not at all, Don Pedro. In Toledo the Inquisition has *found* its true meaning. We've learned how to distinguish between the man who seeks truth and the man whose mind is depraved."

"And who makes these fine distinctions?" Orsini asked.

Before Castilla could reply a cold-voiced Chacón interrupted. "I suspect it would be Don Luis' brother, the dean of Toledo."

"Ah?" said the librarian his eyes bright with pleasure. "In Toledo as in Rome, connections matter more than virtue."

If Spain had required a further advocate, Domenikos could have discovered none more convincing than Don Luis, as acquaintance ripened to friendship. To Spain Domenikos would proceed when he could, unless some word from King Philip changed the idea, to Toledo where the elder Castilla, as dean of the chapter and an authority on art, could assure a flow of commissions.

THE BABY was born in October, a splendid jet-eyed girl whom her parents called Francesca, to the pleasure of her young uncle. "Next time, *caro*, I'll give you a son," Catarina said. She assumed maternity with a grace that profoundly moved Domenikos. So in spite of his impatience to leave Rome, he found life sweet.

Francesca was robust and passed into her second year without giving her parents any cause for alarm. As 1574 drew to a close, they began to make travel arrangements. Since there had been no word from King Philip, Domenikos had decided to settle in Toledo. By the summer of 1575, the family should be on its way.

"*Plague!*" The word cried out by shrouded figures from street to street had for centuries evoked panic throughout every city of western Europe. During the fourteenth century the Black Death, bubonic and pneumonic plagues, had carried off twenty-five million souls, about a quarter of the Continent's population.

The cause of the disease was unknown, treatment nonexistent, survival all but unheard of. The afflicted were hustled into the isolation of what were virtually charnel houses, to perish in agony and squalor. No one was spared this fate. The house believed to harbor a victim of the plague was usually set afire.

The plague struck Rome that spring of 1575. The city shriveled. The streets were all but emptied. Even the cats and dogs retreated, as if they too were frightened by the rats that died by thousands in the gutters. Only the churches continued to attract people, for only prayer could prevail against pestilence. Friends looked at one another, helpless and terrorized, and wondered, Are you next? Am I next?

Neither Catarina nor Francesco would leave the house, and it was Domenikos who did the marketing. He couldn't share this craven fear: as Orsini complained, he accepted the idea of death as calmly as he did life. That so many people should give themselves up to despair dismayed him. And the panic of those beneath his roof imposed on him a pressure that was almost palpable.

Painting became impossible to him. With curtains drawn against the incongruous sunlight, he sat brooding in his studio. No one came to visit him. The creaking tumbrels rolling past his window reminded him how meaningless his plans were. At any moment one of his household might catch the dreaded fever and be carted away to die. He contemplated an emptiness unlit by the light he had described to Don Luis as the one by which he would make his paintings—the light within.

This torpor was abruptly and cruelly shattered. First Francesca and then Catarina contracted the plague. Domenikos refused to believe it, would not summon the cart to have them taken away. It was not panic he felt but numbing anguish. And the frightened Francesco met the crisis. "They have to be taken, master."

The artist could barely nod. And when the masked attendants came to the bedchamber he and Catarina had shared, he couldn't bring himself to help them carry the swollen bodies. Francesco returned to find him standing in the center of the room, sobbing.

The youth touched his arm. "Let me give you wine, master."

He watched mutely as Francesco filled his goblet from a flagon.

"Drink with me, Francesco. What are we to drink to?"

"The safety of the souls that have left, master."

"Never have there been two purer souls." He hurled the goblet against the wall. "God hates me," he roared. "And I hate God."

PART IV: TOLEDO (1575–1589)

CHAPTER 9

THEY WENT by way of Venice. The bitterness of the last days in Rome had been somewhat dissipated by travel with the resilient Francesco, but Domenikos accepted his father-in-laws's invitation to be his guest with mixed feelings. Conversation with Mario could not be cheering. They talked after dinner in the salon, on the same couch, where he had met Maria eight years before.

"Tell me of Maria," Domenikos said. "Is there any change?"

His father-in-law shook his head. "She's comfortable, not violent. But barring a miracle, no change."

Domenikos was surprised by the pain this expected response evoked, surprised that he still felt the separation so deeply.

They discussed his trip to Spain. "If you plan a permanent move," Mario said, "take your things with you, and Maria's. We've not used your apartments. I can't bear to open the door."

"I understand." Domenikos laid a hand on his shoulder. "But I'll not take Maria's gold. Use it to keep her comfortable, and when she dies, see that it goes to the nuns taking care of her."

"How good of you, Greco. You're staying long?"

"Only long enough to arrange transport to Genoa, and from there to Barcelona. And I must see my aunt and uncle, and Tiziano."

Older and frailer the master was, but he had lost little of his vigor. Orazio, however, seemed to have become even more inconsequential, his identity now quite lost in his father's.

"So Rome didn't suit you." Titian seemed pleased.

"Worse than that." Domenikos described his private tragedy.

"And did you learn anything?" Titian asked finally.

"As a painter, you mean? That I was making no progress. That I can't paint any longer as I have been."

"Well, that's a first step. How *can* you paint?"

"I'm still thinking." Before the old man could interrupt, Domenikos continued with a chuckle, "I know. I shouldn't be thinking. I meant I've been experimenting, sketching, making studies."

"And what did you learn as a man, Greco?"

"Perhaps—how to get along in the world. And I made

friends, real friends, a Roman and a Spaniard. The only pain I felt in leaving Rome was that I had to say farewell to Orsini."

"Well," said Titian, "*that* never grows easier. You've grown up a bit. High time, at thirty-four. When you're ninety-eight, you'll realize that everything I've ever said to you was true."

Orazio was delighted. "The old devil hasn't changed, Greco!"

"You've heard nothing from the King of Spain?" Titian said.

"No."

Titian grunted. "Nor have I. Who do these kings think they are?"

Domenikos explained about his connections in Toledo.

"I have only one reservation about Toledo, Greco. It's the heart of the Spanish Inquisition, and you've already had trouble with two Popes. What a fire-eater!"

Domenikos laughed. "It's always calm in the center of a storm."

Arrangements for his journey took longer than Domenikos had anticipated. He stayed with his aunt and uncle and was still in Venice when, in the late spring of 1576, he was again caught by plague. Though the epidemic was milder than Rome's, panic reigned. Travel to and from the city was cut off. And in the final week of August, Titian was struck down.

In the great house in the Biri Grande, Domenikos found Orazio standing bewildered by his father's empty chair. "I believed he'd never die. God knows, he suffocated me. But working with him, in spite of everything, was enough. And he *was* my father."

"And mine too," said Domenikos.

Plague or no, Titian's funeral was celebrated on a scale comparable in grandeur only to Michelangelo's a dozen years before. A fortnight later, Domenikos and Francesco left for Genoa, where they boarded a ship for Barcelona. Throughout the long days, Domenikos tutored his assistant in Spanish which he himself had learned in Rome. But it was the nights that proved difficult, as his sense of loss came to him then like a physical pain. Maria, Catarina, Titian. Their faces filled his anguished sleep.

"THERE'S MADNESS even in being born in a country like this," Francesco said, as they made the slow difficult journey from

Barcelona to Madrid. But to Domenikos the desolate landscape with its sparse, dry vegetation and empty stream beds gouged in the sullen hills seemed to cry out a grim, bitter welcome. The black-clothed inhabitants could belong only to the grudging earth from which they scratched their livelihood—creatures of sadness, anger, anxiety, suspicion; creatures, too, he felt, of ecstasy and rapture. There was a profound spirituality in their sun-coarsened faces. Domenikos was certain that at last he had found his home.

The Spain of Philip II should have been Europe's richest nation, with gold and silver from the New World overflowing its coffers. But Philip himself was extravagant, and the expenditures on foreign wars, on the subjugation of the Moors in the south, and on buildings in the new capital of Madrid, including the massive Escorial—palace, church, monastery and mausoleum in one—had brought the country to virtual bankruptcy.

Philip's problems outside Spain were complicated by the Protestant Reformation. Apart from his perpetual quarrel with Portugal, his northern provinces were constantly menaced by religious wars in France. In the Low Countries, the grip of the Reformation was so strong that it was increasingly difficult to impose Spanish, and therefore Catholic, rule. And the Protestant Queen Elizabeth of England was giving financial help both to the Huguenots in France and the rebels in the Low Countries, while her ships marauded Philip's treasure vessels from the New World.

Within Spain there were other expensive problems. Considered Europe's most piously Catholic country, she had been struggling for a hundred years to rid herself of heresy. The Moors, who had lived there for nine centuries, had been offered the choice of expulsion or conversion. Most had chosen the latter, but since few churchmen could speak their dialect, they had in fact remained Moslem, and it was left to the army to "convert" by force, and the Inquisition by terror. The Jews, offered the same choice, had mostly opted for exile, but had taken with them their gold, and more significantly, their knowledge of commerce and banking, thus depriving the country of the backbone of her middle class.

The Inquisition's persecution of Moriscos and Marranos, as

the converted Moors and Jews were called, was as much political as religious: opposition to the power of the Crown was to be eliminated. Though an ardent Catholic, Philip didn't hesitate to use the Church as an instrument of policy; and he controlled the Church by his appointment of bishops. At least he could govern his country from the newly completed portion of the Escorial and find his authority virtually unquestioned.

Madrid was a disappointment to Domenikos and Francesco. Since Philip's decision, in 1560, to transfer the seat of power from Toledo, little had been done to transform Madrid into a city worthy of the monarchy. They spent one night there and then set out for Toledo, arriving before sunset the following day.

Crowning the summit of a broad butte which was all but encircled by the River Tajo, the walled and ramparted city seemed suspended in the cold, clear air. Its high bluffs descended precipitously to the murky, swift stream. The four towers of the massive Alcázar, or palace-fortress, and the high Gothic spire of the cathedral reached toward the fast-darkening sky.

Passing through the Puerta Nueva de Bisagra, they climbed up steep, narrow alleys to the principal square of the city, the Zocodovér. As elsewhere in Spain, everyone was in black, but here the crowd was different, so many were of the Church: priests, nuns, monks, clerks. Monasteries, convents, seminaries and hospitals abounded in Toledo. The strange silence of this city, its austerity, reached out to Domenikos and took possession of him. "We're home," he announced triumphantly. Francesco shivered.

One legend held that Toledo was the earth's first city, founded by Adam himself. It certainly existed before the Roman conquest of Spain in the second Christian century. For five hundred years, it had been not only the capital city but the seat of Spain's principal cardinal. It was still a center of religion and learning, and renowned for its manufacture of swords—the famous Toledo blade—and of high-quality silks and woolens.

The hot Christian spirits of two future saints—Teresa de Ávila and Juan de la Cruz—typified this city which they often visited. Their complex natures combined pure devotion with a superb ability to organize. The Church found their ideas very

nearly heretical, yet they were more often heckled than persecuted. For Toledo was worldly as well as holy, committed to the
suppression of heresy yet tolerant of deviations. It was, as Luis
de Castilla had assured the painter, a very sophisticated city.

Diego de Castilla occupied quarters in the Archbishop's Palace. When Domenikos was ushered into his presence, he saw an
elegant man in his sixties, shorter than his brother, Luis, and
very thin, with fine black eyes, a ready smile, and a composure
that left no doubt of his authority, which was second only to that
of the cardinal. The dean rose to greet him and for some
minutes they chatted in Italian of the journey from Venice, of
Titian's death, of Rome. Domenikos was impressed with his
graciousness.

"I've detained you too long, Maestro El Greco," the cleric
said at last, the El sound in place of the Italian Il surprising the
painter. "You'll be anxious to see Luis. Did you know he's been
made dean of Cuenca? Fortunately, he's in Toledo today,
though on an unhappy mission. We must discipline a priest,
Don Juan de la Cruz, who's been creating difficulties among the
Barefoot Carmelites. A good Christian, but too enthusiastic. He
takes matters into his own hands." He opened the door. "Let me
take you to Luis."

They walked through corridors to the great tribunal hall.
Here Domenikos saw his friend in conversation with several
richly gowned dignitaries, one of whom was the archbishop. As
they entered, Luis hastened toward him, embracing him warmly.

Domenikos said, "Am I taking you from something important?"

"I'm relieved to have an excuse. It's a sorry business."

They emerged from the palace into the cold Plazuela del
Ayuntamiento, drawing their cloaks about them against the
sharp north wind. Castilla laughed. "I told you the climate was
vile. Come on, I want to show you something."

At the end of an interminable series of winding alleys, they
arrived in a small square before a church under construction.
"Santo Domingo el Antiguo," Luis said. "Shall we go in?"

Despite the scaffolding, it was possible to make out the
design of the interior which was, to Domenikos, gratifying in its
simplicity. "It will be handsome," he said, "but what—"

Don Luis held up a hand. "It's being built with funds left for the purpose by a lady named Doña María da Silva. My esteemed brother is executor of her estate. Just before she died, she asked the cathedral's master of work, Nicolás de Vergára, to make plans. Diego was unhappy with them, so he asked Juan de Herrera, who designed the Escorial, to take over. These plans are Herrera's."

"It's a good piece of work. Who's doing the altarpieces?"

Castilla laughed. "A design was made by Hernando de Ávila. I told Diego you could do a much better one. That's the story. If you want it, he'll give you the commission."

Domenikos was incredulous. "You're not serious!"

Castilla became brisk. "You and Diego can work out the details. You'll have at least two years before the church is finished. You would do the whole of the main altar and two side altars—everything, frames, paintings and sculptures."

"But what about the other man, Hernando?"

"What about him? Diego paid him. That's the end of it."

Domenikos felt like dancing. "But are you sure I'm your man, Luis? All you know of my sculpture are the little figures I had in Rome. And of my architecture—nothing."

"I saw your sketches."

The painter stared at the great space of the apse that he must fill, then at the sites on either side of the crossing where the smaller altars would be. "Thank you, Luis," he said simply.

"Thank Diego. Now let's arrange for your living quarters."

THE QUARTERS they found were spacious enough for both living and working. Domenikos was daily more grateful for Frances-co's cheerful efficiency, which left him free to plan for the Santo Domingo commission. By comparison with anything he had previously attempted, this commission was enormous. For two full months, he drew and redrew his sketches. In mid-April he was sufficiently satisfied to present the plans for Don Diego's approval.

He felt sanguine as the dean began to study them. He had seen enough Toledan art to be sure he was the finest craftsman ever to practice here. But when an hour had gone by and Don Diego was still examining every detail, a wave of anger swept over him. Who did this clergyman think he was? He said nothing however; and at last the dean had finished. "It's going to be a masterpiece," he said, "the finest Toledo has ever seen."

Domenikos sighed with relief. "I'm happy you find it so."

"We must draft an agreement, Maestro El Greco."

A clerk was summoned and the details of the contract were agreed on. Then the dean laid a hand on Domenikos' shoulder. "I'd like you to join me, maestro, at supper at the palace of the Conde de Fuensalidas. He presides over a group of intellectuals, a true academy, that I think you'd enjoy. But tonight is purely a social occasion. There will even be ladies present."

THE SURROUNDINGS were luxurious. The count, a man of considerable charm, invited Domenikos to take part in the weekly discussions of "our academy," twenty or so clerics and nobles. "We need an artist," he said, "and Castilla says you're a scholar too."

Domenikos found it difficult to catch names in the hail of swiftly spoken Spanish. When his host and Castilla had moved on, he stood aside and contemplated the other guests. Their dress was more somber than Romans' or Venetians', their gestures less grandiloquent, he was thinking, when a woman passed before him. She was a few inches shorter than he, her body lithe beneath her black gown, her profile soft but forceful, with a long, delicately fashioned nose. Above a high forehead rose a mass of black hair held by a crisp white lace headdress. She turned to look up at him, and Domenikos was blinded by her eyes, wide and long as almonds, a clear gray-blue. Her self-possession was absolute; her generous mouth showed the beginning of a smile.

She paused, like the rest in a bar of music. Domenikos was confused. What was the proper thing to do? He bowed. She curtsied with grace. He reached for her hand, raising it awkwardly to his lips. He saw a small ruby ring on her right hand.

"Señorita," he said, smiling, "I am Domenikos Theotokopoulos."

"But in Toledo you're called Maestro El Greco," she said. "I've heard much of you. You're a friend of Don Diego de Castilla."

"Yes, señorita. And of Don Luis whom I met in Rome."

Her smile dazzled him. "To have one Castilla for a friend is a good thing. To be a friend of both is ingenious. They don't make friends easily. I am Doña Jerónima de las Cuevas."

Domenikos bowed once more. "I am enchanted, Doña Jerónima. In a single moment, you've made me happy. You're beautiful and you've said something pleasant."

She laughed. "Your tongue is Italian in its flattery, señor."

"I'm Cretan. And I speak only the truth."

"You amuse yourself in Toledo?"

"This is my first moment of diversion since I arrived. I'm making some altarpieces for Santo Domingo. Perhaps when I'm done I shall speak your language correctly. I read it but it's hard to bring words from the eyes to the lips."

She spoke so softly that Domenikos had to lean forward to hear her. "Your lips do well enough, señor. They need no instruction."

Don Diego reappeared. He greeted Doña Jerónima, then said, "I must take Maestro El Greco. There are others he must meet."

The remainder of the evening passed pleasantly, but was pallid compared with the delicious moments with Doña Jerónima. In the days that followed, Domenikos found it difficult to work. Her tranquil, slightly mocking features clouded all other images. It wasn't merely that he needed a woman; he needed her.

"Who is she?" he asked Don Luis eagerly when his friend next came to Toledo.

"You admire her and want to see her again?"

"I do. Both. Unless she's betrothed."

"That she is not." He paused. "Doña Jerónima has a past."

"Which you propose to tell me?"

"Not unless she declines to tell you herself. But almost everything about Doña Jerónima is in her favor."

A few evenings later, Don Luis accompanied the painter to another gathering at Fuensalidas' mansion, expressly to see Doña Jerónima. They found her in a small reception room. Domenikos kissed her hand. "Señorita, good evening."

Castilla grinned. "Greco, let me formally introduce Doña Jerónima de las Cuevas." He closed the doors, then went to sit in a corner of the room. "Please ignore me. It must be one of the few times when a dean has performed the role of dueña."

"Shall we sit down, maestro?" Doña Jerónima said. He nodded and they sat in silence until, unable to control her amusement, she laughed. "Forgive me. Your expression was so comical." She collected herself. "You look thunderstruck."

"At seeing you again, señorita. So often our hopes are beyond attainment."

"It's unwise to hope for the impossible."

"Yet the Spanish have a reputation—"

"Maestro." She hesitated. "My reputation . . ."

Domenikos coughed and looked away. "You need say nothing."

"No, maestro, you have a right to know before . . ."

"Before we become friends?" he inquired gently.

"Yes." She took a deep breath. "My family is of the poor nobility. My grandfather was deprived of his lands for rebelling against Charles the Fifth. So my father, his only son, was forced to become an officer in the army. God rest his soul, he was killed in the battle of Saint-Quentin. Because of this my mother receives a small pension from the King. So all we have, my mother, my brother and I, is our ancient name—and our pride."

Domenikos shifted uneasily. "Since you've been so frank, Doña Jerónima, I hope you won't think me impertinent if I ask you how you've been able to exist in such circumstances."

"You're wondering why, at my age, I'm neither married nor in a convent. I was unable to marry because I had no dowry."

"But there must be men who would accept you without one."

"I daresay. A man might accept *me*, but my mother wouldn't have accepted *him*. If I married well, the family's position would improve. But only a small merchant or an artisan would take me without a dowry. This mama refused to permit."

"I'm desolate for you, señorita. You need say no more."

"You must hear me out, maestro. Since a suitable marriage was impossible, mama sent me to a convent when I was sixteen. It was a failure. I wasn't intended to be a nun."

"You're too direct."

She smiled. "Mother Teresa of Ávila is very direct, too, and she's an abbess. It was simply that I was a woman. I enjoyed the company of men. I *enjoy* their company still."

It was almost unbearable not to reach out and touch the soft arm. "And as you must feel, you're attractive to me. If I were free to marry, I'd accept you without a ducat. Would you accept me?"

"I might, maestro. But you're *not* free."

"My wife, in Venice, is ill in her mind. She'll never recover."

"I'm sorry. She's very dear to you?"

"She *was*. I suppose what I love now is my memory of her."

"So, in a way, you and I are in the same position." She paused. "But I have more to say. When I left the convent, only one course seemed open, that I become the mistress of someone rich and influential. It was the only way I could help mama."

So matter-of-fact was this statement that Domenikos, who supposed he should be shocked, found himself agreeing with her logic. "How old were you then?"

"Eighteen."

"And your mother accepted this?"

"She was unhappy about it, but she's a *Toledana*, very devout, very practical, reasonable. So a marqués was found. I was taken to see him." She became unexpectedly demure. "He liked me."

Domenikos shuddered. "Did you like *him?*"

"Well enough. He was very generous to mama."

"You were his mistress for a long time?"

"Nine years. He died a year ago, and I returned to Toledo."

"And you found no other protector?"

"There are few men who'd be interested in a woman of twenty-nine who's been another man's mistress."

"*I'm* interested, Doña Jerónima," he said quietly.

"You'd think of becoming my protector?"

"Your lover."

Her smile was grave. "I think that's the nicest thing that's ever been said to me. But consider it carefully, discuss it with Don Luis and Don Diego. And you'll have to see mama."

"But you yourself, señorita? Can you love?"

The responding smile was soft. "I think so. And you?"

"I loved my wife. But it's not what I feel for you."

"You're confusing love with passion."

"I think not. Where I was born, Doña Jerónima, we never question the wisdom of the heart."

"Nor in Spain, either." She smiled. "I should be honored to be loved by you."

"I don't presume that you'll return my love."

"I might surprise you, maestro," she said.

CHAPTER 10

Doña Ana de las Cuevas received Domenikos in a modest drawing room. She was a well-made woman in her fifties, her face sad and lined. With a candor that charmed him, she said she had heard that artists were notoriously poor and irresponsible. He explained his circumstances, his father's generosity. She wished also to be assured that El Greco would not desert her daughter.

"If we separate, Doña Ana, I can promise the decision will be Doña Jerónima's. I shall regard her as my wife."

Doña Ana stood up and offered him her hand. "I count on you to treat my daughter gently, maestro."

"I hope you can't believe otherwise, Doña Ana."

She studied his face. "No, I can't, she said finally. "I shall bring her to you."

Standing there, waiting for Doña Jerónima, Domenikos found himself trembling with joy. So the thing was settled. It was fantastic. Passion he had felt before, and tenderness. But this was different. He knew now that he was in love.

Jerónima appeared in a close-fitting gown of black wool, her loose hair falling below her shoulders. "Mama says you're a good, kind man, and that I'm to cherish you," she said, smiling. Still stunned by what was happening, Domenikos embraced her.

Doña Ana's farewell was formal, yet she smiled as she saw Domenikos take Jerónima's arm, leading her from the doorway.

"I don't want to take you directly to my house," he said, and guided her through contorted alleys to the small Church of Santo Tomé. He stopped and looked down at her. "Shall we go in?"

"If you want to. But I'll not take communion. I'm no hypocrite. I repent nothing."

"But you regret, don't you?"

She smiled wisely. "You reason like a Jesuit. I suppose I do, but not very much. Since I left the convent, it's seemed I could find no alternatives that were as acceptable to God as to me."

"I've had the same feelings," he responded.

"And you take communion?"

"Regularly, and with dispensation from a cardinal."

She laughed. "And you propose to obtain one for me?"

"If you want one."

She reflected. "It would please you, wouldn't it?"

"Yes." He took her slender arm. "Let's go in. I want us to be seen together first in God's house, not mine."

She stared at him in astonishment. "You mean that?"

"Of course I do. In my heart, I'm marrying you. If we can't have the Church's blessing, we can have its presence."

JERÓNIMA'S possessions were few. Domenikos' two serving women, aided by Francesco and Juanita, the peasant girl who was Jerónima's maid, had no trouble transporting them to his apartments.

Within a few days, Domenikos was painting Jerónima's portrait. She was a superb model. He posed her with a fur about her shoulders and a translucent white scarf over her black hair, her body angled, her face looking forward.

He felt that it was his finest portrait. Jerónima examined it critically, her elusive smile playing across her features. "You've made me an *hidalga*, a noblewoman."

"God did that for you, *amada*. I've just shown you as you are."

Diego de Castilla was a regular visitor to the artist's studio. He greatly admired the portrait, but expressed concern about the progress of the plans for Santo Domingo. Nevertheless he proposed another commission, a painting of the rending of Christ's garments for the vestry of the Toledo Cathedral.

Domenikos soon found himself with almost more work than he could manage, even with Francesco's help. In addition to the dean's two commissions, patrons referred by both Castillas were requesting copies of pictures he had made in Rome. Far from being fatigued by all this, the artist discovered unexpected sources of energy within himself. He liked to think that Jerónima's presence was responsible for his excitement and joy. He was restored, even optimistic.

When the working drawings for Santo Domingo were completed, in late June, Domenikos took them to the builder-architect whom Don Diego recommended. Juan Bautista Monegro, a solid figure with angry eyes and a temperament to match, glanced disdainfully at the plans. "You're a painter. Why did they ask you to do architecture and sculpture? I'd have done a better design."

The artist looked calmly at this hot-eyed man. "But they *asked* me. If you prefer, I'll have the work done somewhere else."

Monegro grunted. "No, we'll do it. Then we'll at least know it's properly made, won't we?" He laughed harshly.

Though vaguely alarmed by Monegro's hostility, Domenikos had too much work to do to give it any further thought. It would be some months before Monegro had the altars constructed, but studies for the eight paintings to be framed by the altar retables had to be done; and at Don Diego's urging he was completing a small tempera version of the Spoliation of Christ, *El Espolio*, which the cathedral chapter was proposing to commission.

This study of the mob tearing off Christ's garments was submitted to a group of canons of the cathedral in July. Only one, the bursar, García de Loysa, showed more than a passing interest in it. The dean had described him as a formidable character, brilliant, hardheaded, and reluctant to part with the chapter's money. After prolonged study, the bursar turned to the artist. "Do you mind my asking the basis of your iconography?"

Domenikos was pleased, for the derivation of the picture was interesting. "Not at all. The theme is very unusual. When I was in Italy, I saw only two pictures of the subject, one by Duccio and a Dürer." He produced a small woodcut of the Dürer Spoliation. "I took a few ideas from this."

"But they're hardly alike, maestro," the bursar said.

The artist tapped his forehead. "The difference is here."

García de Loysa nodded appreciatively. "Where it should be. Don Diego was right. You are our man." He took some golden ducats from his purse. "A token of our intentions, maestro. You understand our method in Spain of determining your fee? You designate an appraiser, the chapter another, and agreement is reached by discussion."

"It sounds potentially very dangerous."

The bursar nodded affably. "It is, maestro, for you."

IN EARLY August, Jerónima told him she was pregnant.

"You're certain?" he murmured as he embraced her gently. She nodded. "You're angry?"

"No, no, *querida*. Only apprehensive and delighted."

"Apprehensive? But you want a child?"

"Yes. I want a son. But thinking of Maria, I was fearful for you."

"There's nothing to fear. I'm a healthy woman."

He looked at her earnestly. "I feel myself cursed. Four lives are on my head—the little Tiziano, Maria, Catarina, Francesca. It's the will of God."

He consulted Don Rodrigo de La Fuente, Toledo's leading physician. His opinion of medicine had not risen since Maria's illness, but La Fuente, who was also a poet, had a first-rate intelligence and was better informed than anyone else he knew.

"Relax, maestro," La Fuente observed. "See that she eats well, sleeps well, and isn't bedeviled by an overanxious progenitor." And he amusedly consented to be present at the birth to instruct the midwife.

The baby was not due until April, and the waiting grew no more bearable as time passed. Not even when painting was he able to drive the worry from his mind. He attended evensong regularly, offering fervent prayers for Jerónima's safety and the health of their unborn child. This frantic concern was deeply moving to Jerónima. She finally could say in the darkness of their bedchamber, "I love you. I'm sure of it now."

Just after Christmas, he received from his brother the news that his mother had died after a long illness. He replied at once. "I weep as I write. I have never known anyone who accepted life with such grace. She permitted herself not a moment of self-pity for the limitations it imposed on her. I think she had ultimate wisdom." He expressed delight at news of his brother's three daughters. "I could wish," he added, "that you were more specific about your prosperity."

Late in March, Jerónima began to feel pain. La Fuente summoned the midwife. "Take that mad painter to a tavern and get him drunk," he told Francesco. But Domenikos had other ideas.

"If anything happens you can find me at Santo Tomé, Francesco." And before the altar of a chapel dedicated to St. Francis, he knelt in prayer, lighting candle after candle.

When he could bear the suspense no longer, he returned home, to find the situation unchanged. "I will have something to drink now, Antonia," he said wearily to his cook.

"It's no good worrying, master," she said, putting a flagon in front of him. He drank steadily for an hour, and then he slept.

Francesco awakened him with difficulty. "Master, master," he said. "The baby is born. You have a son."

"A son?" he muttered drowsily. "And Doña Jerónima?"

"She's well, master. The doctor has just left."

Domenikos embraced Francesco, laughing maniacally. "By God, my friend, what a wonderful thing," and he made for the chamber where this great event had taken place.

Feeling at once awkward, grateful and bewildered, he went to Jerónima's bedside and stared down at the mother and the child beside her. Jerónima's eyes were bright with pleasure, her face drawn. "You see, Domenikos?" she said. "There was nothing to worry about."

The infant was baptized Jorge Manuel, after the parents' fathers, with an honored Don Luis de Castilla standing as godfather.

THE BROWN-HAIRED, brown-eyed child prospered, and his doting father again found concentration difficult. However, by the end of July, he was able to show Don Diego the paintings of the Assumption and the Trinity destined for Santo Domingo, and to report progress by the sullen Monegro on the construction of the altarpieces. The dean expressed his rapture by offering to pay Domenikos the entire sum agreed on for the finished work.

The artist, whose materials had been alarmingly expensive, consented. "But I'll accept only a thousand ducats, Don Diego."

Castilla was perplexed. "But why, Greco?"

"A gesture of gratitude to Toledo—and to you and Luis. For the first time in my life, I'm a completely happy man."

Domenikos had by now begun a full-scale rendering of the

Espolio. To give it the right qualities of light and shadow, he followed a practice learned from Tintoretto and visited the vestry at different hours of the day to evaluate the light admitted by the narrow windows. Toledo's fourteenth-century cathedral was his first exposure to the French and Spanish Gothic styles combined with Moorish influence. Most striking to him were the stained-glass windows, unknown in Crete and rare in Italy, which cast wonderful colors on the columns and floor.

On one of these visits to the vestry, he met Pompeo Leoni, an Italian sculptor with whom he was casually friendly. Some artists in Toledo had shown themselves jealous of Domenikos, but Leoni, who was in the service of the King, could scarcely think him a rival, and Domenikos would have welcomed a closer bond.

The sculptor muttered a brusque greeting and followed Domenikos to the altar. "Gloating over the space you're to fill?"

The painter laughed and told him of Tintoretto's study of light.

Leoni listened with interest. "Ingenious," he said. "But at least a painter doesn't have to bother about a third dimension."

"But he does, Leoni. The painter's third dimension is all the more difficult because it's illusory."

The sculptor considered this, plainly impressed. "I'd not thought of that. You plan to stay in Toledo?" he asked curiously.

"Indefinitely. It suits me. And you?"

Leoni shook his head. "I prefer a growing city, like Madrid."

"What are you working on?"

"A bust of the King and a sarcophagus for the nave here."

"I'd like to see them," Domenikos said, and Leoni, obviously pleased, took him to his studio. The two pieces were a disappointment, products of an excellent craftsman but without inspiration. Yet Domenikos was drawn to the man. Behind a mannered arrogance there was something else. Bitterness? Disappointment?

Leoni was astounded that Domenikos had made no effort to establish contact with the King. "You should get a commission from him. He pays when he promises to and he never dickers over price, which is more than you can say for these church people."

"I've no time for another commission. And I've had no trouble with the church people." He described his dealings with the dean.

Leoni wasn't impressed. "Just wait, Greco."

Leoni was an entertaining friend, though there was none of the intimacy of Domenikos' relationship with Orsini or with Luis de Castilla. He was prevailed on to paint Leoni's portrait.

Leoni arrived for a sitting one October morning, breathless and excited. "Don Juan of Austria died of fever in Namur."

"Oh?" said the painter, without interest.

"Greco. This is the King's half brother, commander of the fleet at the battle of Lepanto. Ruler of the Low Countries. And he's dead. You must paint a picture to commemorate his death."

"For whom?"

"For Philip, of course. He despised Don Juan, but is now treating him as a hero. His remains are to be brought to the Escorial."

"I don't paint occasional pictures."

The sculptor sighed. "It would help to establish you."

Domenikos dropped the discussion, but he did mention it to Jerónima. She agreed with Leoni. "You can't be considered the greatest painter in Spain if you do no work for the King." Added to this unanswerable point, with which both Castillas concurred, was the announcement that King Philip would make a state visit to Toledo the following June.

Accordingly, Domenikos began work on an allegorical scene based on the battle of Lepanto, a fantasy that would appeal to a patron reportedly enamored of the work of Hieronymus Bosch. It incorporated portraits of the King as well as his brother, of Pius V, the Doge and other major figures in the Holy League's great victory over the Turks. He called it *The Dream of Philip II*.

In the meantime, Domenikos had continued to press Monegro to finish assembling the altars for the Church of Santo Domingo. Just before his son's first birthday, he heard that it had been done, and hastened to the architect's workshop. The three works were propped against a wall. After one look at them, he turned, enraged, to Monegro. "You've ruined them, you fool. They're wider than they should be, all three of them, and two feet too high."

Monegro nodded. "Your proportions were wrong."

Domenikos gasped. "Wrong? Who told you so?"

"I could see it for myself," the architect said sullenly. "I *told* you the commission should have been mine. You're no builder."

"This is the most arrogant thing I've ever known, Monegro. I'm not even sure the thing will fit when the sculpture is attached."

"It will fit. I've measured. I'm a craftsman. Those altars are better than you designed them." He grinned. "If they don't fit, you can have me scourged in the Zocodóver."

"If they don't, it will give me pleasure to scourge you myself."

The dean of Toledo offered cold comfort. "If we insist that Monegro correct the altars, we'll have to wait a year or even two. I have an idea he wouldn't rush the work."

The painter sighed. "So we yield?"

"We yield."

TOLEDO's population lined the battlements to observe the approach of Philip II and his entourage across the plain. The King, magnificent in his ritual armor, rode directly behind the banners of the vanguard, his black stallion prancing. Amid great rejoicing the procession wound up through the gates, to draw up in ceremonial order in the Plazuela del Ayuntamiento.

The royal party was quartered in Toledo's Alcázar. The palace-fortress had been refurbished for the occasion by Herrera, the King's favorite architect. Official functions had been planned for each day and evening of the visit. The King was in Toledo to insist that the Church contribute more money to the Crown. The cardinal was sympathetic, but adamant. The Church, he said, was not as rich as the King imagined. Discussion was necessary. Committees must be formed.

Diego de Castilla had thought it unlikely that Philip would have time to visit Domenikos' studio. On the afternoon of the fourth day, however, a perspiring young clerk from the Archbishop's Palace ran panting to tell the painter that the King would be there within the hour. Domenikos summoned Francesco. Together they carried the painting of the *Espolio* into the studio and leaned it against a high white wall. On an easel beside it, they set the study for the Allegory of the Holy League.

For the first time in his experience Jerónima appeared flustered when Domenikos told her that the King was coming. She jumped up from where she had sat watching Jorge toddle. "Heavens! I've got to change, and so should you. You're a fright."

Domenikos laughed nervously. "I'm all right. I'm in working clothes." He hurried back to his studio and was desperately surveying the unprepossessing scene when a young courtier loomed in the doorway. The man gazed about the room, his face a study in distaste. "But surely, you don't expect His Majesty to stand."

Domenikos couldn't restrain his laughter. "I'm sorry, I didn't know His Majesty was coming."

"Well, fetch him a chair, a clean chair, if one's to be found in such a filthy loft."

With difficulty Domenikos swallowed a rude retort. Francesco disappeared and came back carrying, with Jerónima's help, a leather armchair. The young man sniffed and withdrew. In a moment he was back, standing very erect against the doorjamb.

The King was suddenly standing in the studio. Smaller than the painter had imagined, and dressed in the modest black he affected for modest occasions, he suggested regality in his bearing. Domenikos knelt as Jerónima curtsied gracefully.

Philip acknowledged the gestures with a little bow. "You are Maestro El Greco." His eyes turned to Jerónima. "And the lady?"

Doña Jerónima de las Cuevas, sire."

The King reached for her hand and raised it to his lips. "Doña Jerónima. Your father was in my service, wasn't he?"

"He fell at Saint-Quentin, sire."

Philip's expression divulged no sympathy. "In our great cause. You're fortunate, maestro, in your companion." He looked at Jerónima. "What is it about artists that attracts lovely women?"

She laughed. "I can't answer, sire, in general terms. But for my own part it's that El Greco keeps all his anger for his painting and all his gentleness for our son and me."

The King smiled, something it seemed clear he didn't do often. "Guard her well, maestro." His voice hardened. "You have persuasive friends in Toledo. Your name is on every tongue. I have seen your portrait of Pompeo Leoni. It is admirable."

"Thank you, sire."

He pointed at the *Espolio*. "This is a new work?"

"Yes, sire, for the vestry of the cathedral."

Philip settled himself in the chair and considered the painting. "Magnificent," he said at last, "and quite appropriate for a vestry. Otherwise I'd have it for myself."

"I could make you a replica, sire."

"No, maestro. The work I commission must be unique." He looked at Domenikos, his expression curious. It's daring, very advanced. Your friends didn't prepare me for that in your work."

"They haven't your breadth of experience with art, sire. You must be the world's greatest collector."

"I *am* acquisitive. Spendthrift, say my enemies."

"When I was a pupil of Titian, sire, I had the honor of helping with several paintings you'd commissioned from him."

"He was a great master. I miss his presence in this life." A frown corrugated the royal brow. "Didn't he write me once about you?"

"Twice, I think, sire."

Philip hesitated, then went on. "Don Diego tells me you've made a study of a subject connected with my late brother."

"This small panel on the easel, sire."

Domenikos detected the trace of a smile as Philip's eyes rested on his own portrait in the painting. And as he stared into the jaws of hell in the lower right-hand corner, he seemed, for an instant, in a sort of ecstasy. "What do you call this?" he said. "It has power."

"It's an allegory, sire, of the Holy League."

"I'd like a full-size rendering. How long will it take?"

"A few months, I should think."

"Good. When it's finished, bring it to me yourself at the Escorial. We can discuss another commission." He became wary. "I promise nothing, you understand." Philip rose, acknowledged the painter's bow and Jerónima curtsy, and disappeared.

DOMENIKOS had looked forward with trepidation to the evaluation of the *Espolio* that García de Loysa had described to him. He had asked Leoni to act as one of his appraisers, but Leoni refused because of their friendship and suggested instead a Toledan sculptor, Martínez de Casteñada, and a painter from Murcia, Baltasar de Castro Cimbrón. The chapter selected Luis de Velasco, a local painter, and Nicolás de Vergára, the cathedral's master of work. This choice alarmed Domenikos. Vergára not only resented the fact that he had himself lost the commission to build Santo Domingo, but also that his friend Ávila had been replaced by El Greco as designer of the altarpieces.

The evaluation took place on the day after the King's visit. The result might have amused Domenikos if it had concerned someone else's work. Vergára and Velasco, after expressing vast admiration for the painting, declared that the chapter should pay 227 ducats. Domenikos' own appraisers set a figure of 900. Domenikos angrily demanded a second evaluation. "I'll burn the painting," he told García de Loysa, "before I'll accept so derisory an amount." The bursar finally consented to a second appraisal, on condition that it would be made by one mutually acceptable expert whose figure would be binding. The artist reluctantly concurred.

A month later, Alejo de Montoya, Toledo's most highly regarded goldsmith, came to look at the painting, lavished praise on it and set the price at 317 ducats.

As soon as Montoya had left, the painter descended to his strong room. He counted out two hundred gold ducats, the amount the chapter had so far advanced him for the *Espolio*, and hastened to the Archbishop's Palace.

García de Loysa received him coolly and expressed little surprise when Domenikos placed a velvet purse on his table. "This is all you've paid me," Domenikos said. "I'm retaining the picture. It's the finest thing I've painted. I'll not see it treated as a joke."

The bursar pushed the purse away. "There is one thing you should bear in mind, maestro. We were not going to bring it up until the price was settled. Changes must be made in the picture, masterpiece though it may be."

Domenikos sat down heavily and stared as the bursar went on.

"As it stands it's heretical. It violates the decree of the Council of Trent. There's not a shred of canonical or scriptural evidence to justify the presence of the three Marys."

"But the Scriptures don't say they were not present."

"You are instructing the Church on Holy Writ? Then perhaps you'll explain something even more damaging. Every person in the painting except for the three Marys and the peasant is either taller or posed at a higher level than Our Lord."

In spite of his anger, Domenikos could only laugh. "You're not suggesting that I've not made Our Lord the dominant figure?"

"I'm discussing your iconography. You well know the decree that Christ shall not be shown as inferior to mortals."

The painter's expression was grim. "You've completely misunderstood my *Espolio*. I'll make no changes."

A BRIEF respite from this prolonged dispute was provided by the consecration of the Church of Santo Domingo. Monegro's alterations had in fact not seriously affected Domenikos' conception. He was pleased to note that when Don Diego's attention could be diverted from his role in the mass, his eyes flitted to the painting of the Resurrection in which he was represented as St. Ildefonso. And it was quickly evident that Toledo was responding to Domenikos' first major commission with enthusiasm.

The relief, however, was only temporary. Both the Castillas deplored his obstinacy over the *Espolio* and urged him to seek legal advice. He therefore consulted Dr. Gregorio Angulo, whom he knew from the meetings of the academy in the Palacio Fuensalidas. This clever, cheerful member of the city's governing council listened to his story with sympathy, then asked, "Which is more important to you, the money or the painting?"

"The painting."

"Then why not suggest a settlement? You accept the evaluation, but refuse to change the picture."

"What's the alternative, Angulo?"

"A hearing in the town hall. The mayor will support the chapter. You'd have almost no chance at all."

"Would the canons agree to the compromise you suggest?" Angulo chuckled. "Probably not."

"What do you propose, then?"

"Agree to their terms. Get on with your work."

"No," Domenikos said defiantly. "I'll fight."

All concerned in this miserable affair therefore appeared before the mayor in the magnificent Renaissance town hall. The canons and the appraisers repeated their views on the painting's religious lapses and its monetary value, the goldsmith adding, "My figure was based on prices normally paid for paintings of this size by a master. Its true value, no one could pay."

Angulo's interrogation of Domenikos was designed to elicit sympathy for the painter, drawing attention to his refusal to accept full payment for the picture, to his reputation abroad, to his audience with the King in his own house, and the offer of royal patronage.

Then counsel for the chapter rose to question him. "Would you tell us in precisely what manner you live in Toledo?"

The painter, agitated, shook his head sharply. "I see no reason to answer. My personal life has no bearing on the matter at issue."

"Do you own property in Toledo?"

"I don't see that this question bears on the case either."

The lawyer turned to the mayor, who nodded. "It's germane," he said to Domenikos, "because the painting is in your possession. It would be possible for you to leave the city at any moment if you do not own property here, thus depriving the chapter of a work for which you've already been paid two hundred ducats."

"Are you suggesting I'd steal a picture after attempting to return the amount advanced me for it? You've heard Maestro Alejo. No one could afford this painting at its true worth. But the price that's proposed is unacceptable."

"Nor is your painting acceptable to the chapter. It appears," the lawyer cited, "to take intolerable liberties with Scripture."

Domenikos hesitated. How plainly should he speak? Then he shrugged. If he were doomed, let the record show he had stated his views unequivocally. "Our Lord stands out in my painting triumphant. This is a painting within the traditions of Christian art. It seems to me that these questions of iconography—raised only after I'd refused to accept the second appraisal—are intended to distract attention from the central point. I resent any suggestion that I am a heretic or have misinterpreted Holy Writ."

Hardly had Domenikos returned to his place beside an alarmed Jerónima than the mayor delivered his judgment. "I direct that Maestro El Greco accept payment of three hundred seventeen gold ducats; that he make such changes in the painting as the chapter deems necessary; and that he surrender the painting at once."

Domenikos bowed. In the plaza, he turned sadly to Angulo. "You did what you could. I wrecked it."

To his surprise, the lawyer disagreed. "You did take chances, but you won all your points. You certainly established the right of a painter to speak his mind. I was astonished. And then the mayor ordered you to deliver the painting to the vestry *at once*— that means *unchanged*. What he was trying to tell you was that once it's hanging, the canons may feel differently."

Domenikos began to laugh. "Good Lord, of course."

THE ACCLAIM THAT FOLLOWED the consecration of Santo Domingo was modest compared with that accorded the *Espolio*—a public triumph over the chapter which gave Domenikos some satisfaction, as did the responses of Antonio de Covarrubias, renowned jurist and theologian: "The finest picture ever painted in Spain," and of Luis de Castilla: "If you paint nothing else, your coming here will have been justified by this," and of Don Diego: "Now you're a true son of Spain, Greco." But the comment he most treasured came from García de Loysa, who praised both the painting and the painter's courage, adding, "I'd like to be your friend."

In the wake of his elation came depression. His first great projects were completed; there was no comparable work to replace them. He became restless, unable to concentrate. He roamed the apartments in so withdrawn a state that he failed even to notice little Jorge's delighted cries of greeting to him. Only when the small boy rushed to clutch his leg would he pause to pat the curly head. He slept badly, which disturbed

THE DREAM OF PHILIP II — BY EL GRECO

Jerónima. He could tell her nothing of the fantastic and fearful images which haunted his nights and days.

Desperate, he applied his distracted forces to the completion of the painting of the Holy League that the King had commanded him to deliver in person, and then wrote inquiring whether it would be convenient if he and Francesco began the trip. Even if he were not appointed master painter at the Escorial, as he half expected, the journey might give him the change he needed.

As soon as an affirmative reply was received, the canvas was rolled and wrapped and the two men set out on horseback as a snowy northwest wind drove relentlessly down from the Sierra de Guadarrama. The very discomfort of the trip invigorated Domenikos. Just before dark, on the third day, they found themselves face-to-face with the brooding, chill splendor of Philip's monastery to the memory of St. Lawrence, San Lorenzo del Escorial.

The guards at the imposing entrance eyed with suspicion the rolled canvas Francesco carried, and demanded to know their business. Then they were led to the entrance hall of the palace and instructed to wait. Francesco, though plumper than his master, trembled with the cold and clutched the painting to him as if he hoped to derive warmth from it.

A dour monk in black cape and cowl appeared. "You are Maestro El Greco? Follow me." And he led them through the vast complex of buildings and courtyards, finally opening a door to a small, bleak cell. It was roughly furnished, and unheated.

"Brother," said Francesco, "how are we to stay warm?"

A sly grin flashed across the gaunt features. "The suffering of the flesh is good for the soul." He added that they would be summoned for meals and prayers, and that the King would see them when it pleased him. Domenikos asked if Pompeo Leoni could be informed of their presence. The brother promised to see to it.

Three nights and two days elapsed without further official communication. The visitors ate in silence with the monks in a lofty, cold refectory, the fare as Spartan as their cells.

Then they were summoned to the King. Philip was seated at a desk at the end of a large hall, a great fire blazing cheerfully behind him. He looked up at Domenikos and permitted a flicker of pleasure to cross his cold features. "You're welcome to the Escorial, maestro. Almost any face is welcome that has no connection with Portugal or Flanders or England."

The painter knelt, then arose smiling. "You're harassed, sire?"

"It's the lot of a king to be harassed."

Francesco set the canvas before Philip. The monarch looked at it for a moment, then nodded sharply. "Excellent. I was right. It's much better in this size. What price to you place on it?"

"No price, sire. I mean it as a gift."

Philip smiled wryly. "You wouldn't try to bribe a king, maestro."

"One is not often in a position to give a king something."

"I accept your gift with thanks, though I'd have been happy— No, not even kings part happily with money. And I have the feeling that my association with you is going to be extravagant."

"I could hope for nothing better, sire."

"You know the story of the martyrdom of St. Mauritius?"

"I do, sire. It's a third-century tale. The Emperor Maximinian ordered the execution of one-tenth of a legion because the men refused to sacrifice to the Roman gods before battling against the Gauls. When they refused a second time, the legion was decimated again. On their third refusal, the rest of the men were executed, including St. Mauritius and others who were later canonized."

"Greco, you're exceptionally well informed."

"The subject interests me, sire."

"Martyrdom interests you?"

"Martyrs interest me."

"There we differ. I suppose what they say is true: I have a streak of cruelty in me. Have you seen my church?"

"I've seen nothing, sire. I awaited your pleasure."

"Your friend Pompeo Leoni can show it to you. We've recently acquired a precious relic of St. Mauritius. We need a painting of his martyrdom. Leoni will show the space it's to fill. I shall have a contract drawn. Since it will be a large painting, I shall pay you eight hundred ducats. Does that suit you?"

"Eminently, sire," Domenikos said, recalling Leoni's description of the King's probity in matters of money.

"When it's finished, we'll discuss the post of master painter."

IN FEBRUARY of 1580, shortly after Domenikos' return from the Escorial, the Academy of the Conde de Fuensalidas could talk of nothing but the death of the King of Portugal. There seemed only one serious contender for the Portuguese throne and that was King Philip, who had long wanted to add it to his peninsular holdings.

But his most potent enemy, Elizabeth of England, vigorously opposed any Spanish move toward Portugal. Philip therefore took his time. It was not until summer that the Duke of Alba began his military expedition, so brilliantly executed that the war was over within months. The Portuguese crown now awaited. But Philip's arrival in Lisbon was delayed by the most serious epidemic of influenza ever to occur in Europe. It killed the Queen and left the King with health permanently impaired. Not until April 1581 did he mount the Portuguese throne.

Domenikos, in deep concern for the health of Jerónima and Jorge during the terrible epidemic, attended evensong each day, praying with fervor that they be spared. His own vitality, rekindled by the King's commission and by the hope of becoming the King's master painter, was such that he could accept the orders—for portraits, paintings of saints, and scenes from the life of Christ—that poured in from all over Spain as his fame spread.

But during 1580 and for most of the next two years, it was *The Martyrdom of St. Mauritius* that chiefly occupied him. The painting was the largest he had ever made, measuring fourteen feet by ten. In the right foreground the great Christian soldier was in conversation with the Roman captain. Behind him were other Romans, one in armor who looked like Philip II. St. Mauritius, who figured twice in the canvas, resembled a bearded Domenikos. In a vignette in the left foreground one of the legionnaires had just been beheaded, and the saint prayed for his soul. The remaining soldiers, all nude, calmly awaited their fate. A gloria of angels and cherubs was in a sky of clouds and intense blue.

As he worked Domenikos became aware of a change not merely in his view of the painting in hand but in his artistic vision. The mixture of fantasy and reality seemed to him to characterize what he must now think of as his mysticism, his private notion of faith and of God. He realized fully how much he risked in painting all this into the King's picture.

So did Luis de Castilla when he saw the painting. "Beware, my friend," he said. "The King wants a painting with an idiom he's familiar with, and you are presenting him with a revolution."

LITTLE JORGE Manuel often watched his father at work. On his fifth birthday he found himself alone in Domenikos' studio and decided to improve an incomplete canvas of the Crucifixion, making additions with brush, palette knife and fingers.

When Francesco caught him at it, Jorge responded to the Italian's yelp of dismay with a gap-tooth smile. "See, Franco? See?"

The noises of this encounter drew the parents to the studio. Jerónima was outraged. Domenikos, however, said, "Marvelous! You see, querida? He means to be a painter like his papa."

Jerónima had begged Domenikos to let the boy develop as he chose, for the painter had told her about his dispute with his own father, a point she used against him whenever he encouraged Jorge to draw. "You're trying to influence him. Let him be."

Today Domenikos said, "He did it on his own this time."

IN MAY of 1583, the painter and Francesco made their second trip to the Escorial, this time with a cart to carry the huge rolled canvas of *The Martyrdom of St. Mauritius*. Though unable at once to see Philip, Domenikos found his friend Leoni, who helped them stretch the canvas and hang it in the space it was to fill. When it was in place, Leoni said, "You're no longer Titian's man. I see Michelangelo and Tintoretto in it. But most of all it's yourself, Greco. It's pure wizardry, all motion and mystery." But the painter kept his hopes from rising. It was for the King to judge.

Two days later, Philip made his appearance in the church. Time and influenza and bitter grief had taken a toll. His face was deeply lined, his hair and beard white, his speech thick, his pace slow. For several minutes he contemplated the work, then looked up at the artist. "You had a scriptural quotation in mind for this?"

"Yes, sire, from St. Matthew. 'Be ye therefore wise as serpents and sinless as doves.' "

"I take it you had the ambiguity of that phrase in mind."

"I did, sire. I find it hard to draw a distinction between the glory of the martyr and his sheer folly."

"Explain that in terms of this," said the King, pointing.

Domenikos spoke slowly, pensively. "I was thinking initially of the Emperor, sire. He seems to have regarded the legionnaires as traitors because they refused to sacrifice to pagan gods, not because they refused to fight the Gauls. We see this as folly, but in his eyes the decision was justified. The gods that were spurned were the gods of the state, and he believed that if they weren't propitiated, Rome might fall."

"Are you suggesting a parallel with our present Church?"

Domenikos recognized the trap, but said, "Yes, sire."

"You see the Counter-Reformation movement as folly?"

"Not at all, sire."

The King pointed to the representation of himself. "Do I appear here as the foolish Maximinian protecting the empire?"

"No, sire, as the wise leader protecting the Church."

"And you appear not once but twice. Whom do you represent, maestro, the sinless saint or the misguided heretic?"

"Both, sire."

"Then surely my role is as ambiguous as yours. I'm disappointed. I hoped for something as straightforward as your *Espolio*, and you've given me a paradox. I wanted a masterpiece."

"I'm sorry to have displeased you, sire, but you're mistaken. This is my finest painting."

"Kings are never mistaken," Philip snapped. He turned to the men with him. "Leoni, is it a masterpiece?"

Leoni nervously wiped his hands on his smock. "It's interesting, sire, but not a masterpiece." The painter gasped as Leoni went on. "I object to these distorted bodies. They're grotesque."

"I agree. Whom should I ask to paint it properly?"

"There's a friend of mine in Madrid, sire, Romulo Cincinato."

Philip nodded. "Arrange it." Leoni bowed and disappeared.

Domenikos was uncertain whether he was more distressed by the King's rejection of his painting or by his friend's perfidy.

Other disasters were to follow. On his return to Toledo, Domenikos learned that his brother was under house arrest in

Candia. Manusos' pirate ships had been captured by Turks, and the Serenissima had compelled the partners to forfeit their bond of twenty thousand ducats. To pay his debts, Manusos had sold all holdings in Crete except the family house, and borrowed from the tax money he had collected. Until he could reimburse the amount embezzled, he would remain in custody. "I am not asking you for the money," he wrote. "Better that one of us remain solvent."

Domenikos arranged for some money to be transferred to Crete. A few hundred ducats at regular intervals would at least permit his brother to keep his head up. Jerónima was appalled. "But if the authorities won't release him until he's paid what he owes . . . ?" The painter was certain that Manusos would think of some solution. "He's like papa, very crafty."

Early the next year, Diego de Castilla died suddenly. To the dean's brother, Domenikos said, "Don Diego was my beginning in Toledo. And now my beginning has ended."

IN THE years that followed, Domenikos found it necessary to take in apprentices and assistants. By 1586 he had eight. But he kept to his resolve never to sign a painting made by his workshop.

His reputation continued to grow, and the market for replicas of his paintings spread as far as the New World. In Toledo his position was unchallenged. He wore his laurels gracefully and became almost convivial. He even visited the Academy of the Conde de More, rival of the Conde de Fuensalidas, where he found a somewhat raffish gathering of writers, including Cervantes.

Persuaded by García de Loysa to construct an altar for his *Espolio*, he was forced to move his burgeoning workshop to more spacious quarters. The only place he found to suit him was a section of a palace in the parish of Santo Tomé that overlooked the churning Tajo and the ancient bridge, Puente de San Martín. He signed a lease in September 1585. As he and Jerónima went to sleep on their first night in their new home, he sighed contentedly. "After forty-four years, El Greco lives where he belongs. Let's have a great reception. We'll invite everyone we know, mix them together and see what happens."

Preparations for the reception were frantic. The palace was cleaned inside and out. Cooks from the Archbishop's Palace prepared a mountainous collation, and Domenikos laid in a stock of wines that would, he hoped, cause his guests' normal hostilities to subside into amiability. In the cavernous ground-floor room an orchestra would play for the stately dances permissible in the Spanish City of God, and musicians would sing keening Morisco songs.

Music and food and drink did indeed prevail over social distinctions. Merchant, nobleman, cleric, and the ladies who accompanied them, soon fell into the Italianate mood of the festivities. Several bishops were heard to laugh; a lady-in-waiting to the late Queen resisted the advances of a handsome canon; Jerónima reported that Domenikos' apothecary had pinched her. Juan Bautista Monegro became so enamored of Jerónima's maid, Juanita, that Francesco, now her husband, threatened "measures." Luis de Castilla summed up the evening. "Toledo, Greco, will never be the same again."

PADRE ANDRÉS Núñez, parish priest of Santo Tomé, who was Domenikos' confessor and a close friend, had for several years been proposing that his most famous parishioner do a painting for his church based on a miracle of 1323. The tale concerned Don Gonzalo Ruiz de Toledo, the first Count Orgaz, who had financed the rebuilding of Santo Tomé. When he died, it was said that St. Augustine, whose monks served the church, and St. Stephen had appeared at his funeral to lay him to eternal rest.

Domenikos warned the priest that his prices were high. But the padre had access to funds left by a later count of Orgaz, and he continued his siege. Domenikos at last signed a contract in which Núñez, "in the unlikely event that we should one day find ourselves in disagreement," stated his precise requirements for the picture.

"There must be a procession showing how the vicar and other priests read mass for the interment of Don Gonzalo Ruiz de Toledo, lord of Orgaz, and how St. Stephen and St. Augustine descended to bury the body of this nobleman, the one holding him by the head, and the other by the feet, whilst many people should be represented around it watching, and above all this must appear Heaven opened up in glory."

Domenikos added a suggestion that delighted Núñez. "Since we can't know who watched the burial in 1323, Andrés, I'll portray some of our better-known citizens."

Because of Núñez' specifications, the *Burial of Count Orgaz* could not be the imaginative work that *The Martyrdom of St. Mauritius* had been. But when it was completed in March of 1587, Domenikos thought it the best of El Greco to date. And it did, as he had promised, portray the most highly regarded of his Toledan friends, including Don Andrés Núñez himself.

"How soon can we have it in Santo Tomé? When will the evaluation be made?" Núñez came daily to contemplate this great painting. But when the appraisers set a figure of twelve hundred ducats, the priest refused to accept it. The impasse lasted for nearly a year before a second appraisal was agreed on. Domenikos even permitted the priest to select both evaluators this time. "But no arguments, or I'll take the matter before the mayor."

These experts declared the painting to be the most magnificent in all of Spain and called for sixteen hundred ducats. Núñez was apoplectic and again rejected the appraisal. He was now, however, willing to pay the twelve hundred ducats he had earlier declined.

Domenikos lost his temper. "What a charlatan you are, masquerading as a man of God, a man of honor! Twice you've made a bargain, and twice broken your word."

"You can insult me all you please, Greco, but this is just a little parish church. We can't afford to pay sixteen hundred ducats."

The lawyer Angulo advised Domenikos to settle. "Even if you won before the mayor, Greco, you'd lose. Nothing is to be gained by setting yourself against the Church."

"You acknowledge the Church's right to play extortionist?"

The lawyer shrugged. "That's the reality. If you win in a secular tribunal, you might find yourself dragged before the Inquisition."

So in June of 1588, the Orgaz Burial, bought for twelve hundred ducats, was unveiled in Santo Tomé. It was the wonder of Toledo, exceeding in popularity even the *Espolio* in the cathedral. El Greco was acknowledged as the greatest painter in the history of Spain. Luis de Castilla said, "It's your apotheosis, Greco."

PART V: TOLEDO, THE LAST YEARS (1588–1614)

CHAPTER 11

IN THE summer of 1588, the defeat of the Spanish Armada by the English fleet occupied the men who met at the Academy of the Conde de Fuensalidas. The extent of the defeat and its causes were not yet fully known; but it was clear that Philip's grand design to retard the Reformation by conquering Britain, its principal source of financial support, had been forever lost.

Domenikos was too disturbed in spirit to take much interest in these discussions. It was ironic that acclaim should bring so powerful a sense of despair. *Was* the Orgaz Burial his "apotheosis?" If so, he was lost. It wasn't enough to be Spain's greatest painter, to stand out among dwarfs. He must be unique for all time. He must escape the bounds that held other painters.

But escape into what? Into the unexplored recesses of his soul. To seek what? The vision within himself, what he had once described as "the light within." This new way of painting could not be achieved by reason. In this, Titian had been right. It was to be found by exploration of the spirit. He tried to explain to Jerónima. "I want the painting of a saint to *be* a saint."

Castilla warned him against this new interiorness. "You mustn't jeopardize your future." But Domenikos knew that only by being reborn could he succeed in his own terms.

The first painting in which his preoccupations revealed themselves was a Mary Magdalen for whom Jerónima served as model. "But you've made me look so harrowed," she protested.

"Bereaved," he said. "She's alone, desolate, empty of life and of hope, full only of memory and God."

Castilla was disturbed. "You've stripped the picture of everything except Our Lord's skull and the crucifix and the rocks."

"What's left is the essential, Luis."

"And how is the one who commissioned it going to feel?"

Domenikos laughed. "That's the advantage of an established reputation. The patron doesn't question. If a client wants an original El Greco, he'll accept what I offer."

"Don't go too far too quickly, Greco," Castilla warned.

"I won't. But you know, Luis, I'm beginning to feel young again, like Jorge."

THOUGHTS of Jorge's future, always near the surface of his father's mind, came into the open on the boy's fourteenth birthday. Slender, fastidious and handsome, Jorge was a loving child with good manners, who got on easily with everyone. He was responsive and quick to learn; the abbot in the monastery school thought him a likely candidate for the university if he elected to take orders. But what alarmed his father was that nothing really seemed to interest him. Domenikos said to Jerónima, "When I was fourteen I'd known for three years what I was going to be."

"You were an exception," Jerónima said. "He'll find something. I'll not have you try to persuade him."

Domenikos embraced her gently. "As you like, querida. No persuading. But I think we should discuss things."

As soon as he entered the room that evening the boy was aware that something concerning him was to be brought up. "Sit down, Jorge," said Domenikos, carefully. "I want to ask you a serious question. Have you considered your future, what you plan to be?"

Jorge looked from father to mother. "A painter, like papa?"

"Are you asking us?" Jerónima said.

The boy's expressive face looked puzzled. "Is this a game?"

"Not a game," said his father sharply.

"I want to paint, like papa, and build things."

"You realize," said his mother, "it means leaving school. You'd not be able to play in the afternoons with your friends."

Jorge grinned. "Most of my friends are leaving school, mama. Most boys do what their fathers do, unless they become priests."

"You're serious, Jorge? You're sure it's what you want?"

"Yes, mama," he replied softly.

Jerónima turned to Domenikos, smiling. "So be it."

At the end of school in June, therefore, Jorge moved into the studio and began to learn the rudiments of his craft. He seemed happy; and Domenikos found him apt and intelligent.

THE GATHERING mystery and exaltation of the new El Greco style was nowhere more evident than in a painting of Christ's Agony in Gethsemane. Its power lay in his conception of the moment when Jesus, visiting with His disciples in the garden, paused in the ominous moonlit setting and knelt to pray. All the force and the drama came from the colors; drawing, as such, had all but disappeared. The first of Domenikos' friends to see *The Agony in the Garden* was the poet-cleric Luis de Argote y Góngora. His voice husky with sharp pain, he said, "It's a religious *experience*, Greco."

Domenikos was grave. "Painting it was a religious experience."

Castilla's anxiety proved groundless. El Greco's fame grew. As his painting became more emotionally charged, his colors more dramatic, his figures more strangely elongated, abstract, eerie and mystical, he seemed to have his patrons increasingly hypnotized.

Domenikos was now entering his fifties. As his importance as a public figure grew, so did his need to escape into his work, and into the Bible; The Book of Revelation inspired him most. When he was creating he was alone, and this isolation assumed the character of mystical experience: God and he, together and alone.

This frenzied withdrawal drained Jerónima. She recognized that only when he was working at the edge of his physical limits was he content. Her fear was that he was exceeding them, so exhausted was he at the end of each day. He insisted however that he needed more work, not less. And more work he soon found in abundance.

At the end of 1596 his old friend and adversary, García de Loysa, in his capacity as a member of the Council of Castile, asked him to construct the altar for the collegiate Church of Nuestra Señora de la Encarnación, recently finished in Madrid. It would be an enormous commission, a large single altar to frame three paintings; and Domenikos felt it was time for his work to be represented in Madrid. But the funds for the work were controlled by the council, which was presided over by the

King. Domenikos would not consider the proposal without knowing that Philip approved. He therefore took Jorge and set off for the capital.

Philip received them in his bedchamber. "You're looking at a dead man, Greco," he said. Then, knowing what Domenikos was there for, he gave his approval. "I still fail to respond to your painting, but you've become the vogue—our greatest master, they call you. Why can't you paint like Titian? I'd have made you a duke."

Domenikos was never to see the King again. Philip died in September of 1598. His son, Philip III, was to be the puppet of his chosen adviser, the Duke of Lerma. The resulting uncertainties in policy left Domenikos most apprehensive about his Madrid contract, and another imposing commission he had in Toledo.

These two contracts alone taxed the artist's workshop to capacity. But there was still other work to be done. More painters and apprentices were added, more carpenters and gilders.

Domenikos hoped that Jorge, after training so long, would prove a useful assistant, but it had become plain that his son, as a painter, had limitations. He complained to Jerónima, "He doesn't understand what he's doing, he doesn't understand what *I'm* trying to do. He listens to everything I say, answers, 'Yes, papa,' and goes back to doing what I just finished criticizing."

"I warned you."

"I didn't force him to become a painter. He might be an architect, though. He's a first-rate draftsman."

"Then, in Heaven's name, let him be an architect. Painting is your escape. When reality distresses you, you run to it. Now you're running from the reality of your own son! The world of El Greco, the painter, is the world poor Jorge can never enter. Let his world be architecture."

"That's why I agreed to take the Chapel of St. Joseph altar here in Toledo. With the collegiate church in Madrid, it will give him an opportunity to see how altars are designed and put together."

Since Jorge was not to be his successor in painting, Domenikos directed the boy tactfully toward this other aspect of his craft, and found him a proficient and enthusiastic student. The work for the Chapel of St. Joseph was finished just after Jorge's twenty-first birthday, and the son shared in the success of the father.

But El Greco's mind was all on the other, larger work, the one for Madrid. To the central painting of the three in the collegiate church altar, an Annunciation, Domenikos brought all his zeal and fire. This first of the great Christian Mysteries was painted ethereally, for in its very essence it was an event that had nothing to do with reality as the world understood it.

"Now," he told Castilla, "I *am* approaching my apotheosis."

In July of 1600 Domenikos, Jorge and Francesco supervised the loading of the delicate elements of this great altarpiece and accompanied them to the capital where it was at once installed in the church. But the negotiations were even more trying than Domenikos had feared. An appraisal was finally made; the sum of 5920 ducats was agreed to; but payment was not made until six years later, after bitter litigation.

In the meantime, with further commissions looming, and his workshop already overcrowded, the painter reluctantly decided that the Casa Villena quarters were no longer adequate. It was in a mood of sorrow over leaving the palace that he determined to paint a view of Toledo that would include the Casa Villena.

He followed the familiar cobbled alleys to the River Tajo, and stopped a few hundred yards north of the Alcántara Bridge. Here, as he sketched, the sky grew stormy, full of the angry turbulence so typical of Toledo's summer weather. Lightning and thunder snapped, whiplike, clawing furiously at the spire of the cathedral. The rain came, then passed. He walked rapidly homeward, drenched but contented. Now he could paint his picture.

It was a miracle of greens, grays and browns beneath a sky that signaled the approaching storm. In no other picture was weather so controlling a factor; the city was bathed in a weird bluish light, a sort of halo. He beautified his beloved Toledo, transfigured it.

THE HOUSEHOLD'S removal to new quarters had barely been accomplished before the young King and his Queen made a long-heralded visit to Toledo. Philip III was more brilliantly attired than his father had ever been. His face, fat, shrewd and ordinary—a pig's face, said his enemies—like that of his Hapsburg Queen, bespoke a minimum of intelligence and a maximum of indolence. He was, however, rigid in his piety, and the highlight of the celebrations was therefore an auto-da-fé in the Zocodovér, in which a pathetic group of Moriscos was handed over by the Inquisition to the civil authority to be burned. As the odor of roasting flesh wafted across the square, God and the Faith were well served.

It was on this occasion, and with distaste for the project, that Domenikos painted a portrait of the Grand Inquisitor, Cardinal Niño de Guevara. El Greco had long been spared the necessity of courting favor, but Castilla insisted that a portrait of Guevara might give Jorge access to the King and put Jorge in the way of royal architectural commissions. Domenikos painted Guevara precisely as he saw him, dour, with sharp eyes wary behind black spectacles, yet with the elegance that was in all his portraits. Guevara was satisfied. But the audience with the King never materialized.

Whatever disappointment this meant for Jorge, however, was quickly erased by his betrothal to the beautiful Doña Alfonsa de los Morales, the daughter of a merchant. In honor of this, Domenikos named his son a full partner in all future commissions.

And then, suddenly, Domenikos was assailed by his past. A letter from his aunt in Venice told of the death of his uncle Manusos. Almost as an afterthought, she added: "I assume you have heard from the convent that your poor Maria has died."

Stunned, he went into the studio, closing the door and leaning against it as memories railed at him like assassins. At last he crossed the room to a mirror on the opposite wall. He studied the reflection. "I'm an old man," he bellowed. The texture of the flesh was rough, the beard and hair sketchy. It was a worldly face. But in the dark, deep-set eyes was the spirituality that emanated from his paintings. The eyes looked not through the beholder but beyond him. For these eyes, life held no more surprises. And through the sorrow in them, he saw a ferocity that startled him.

Domenikos painted the face he saw in the mirror that day—a portrait of the artist, old, but in full possession of his forces.

JERÓNIMA refused to marry him. "Call it superstition. Life has been so good to me for twenty-two years that I'm afraid to change its terms." She declined even to discuss it further.

One chilly morning, about a year after Jorge and Alfonsa were married, Domenikos was working alone in his studio when there was a knock on the door. Annoyed, he got to his feet and opened it. Before him stood an old man, his features begrimed, his cloak brown with dust and age. The old eyes, red and watery, stared at him balefully. The right hand, holding a stick, trembled.

For a long moment, Domenikos contemplated with hostility this pathetic ruin, then reached into his purse for a coin. But the intruder shook his shaggy head and began to weep, staggering in Domenikos' direction. The artist reluctantly helped him to a chair.

"What is it?" he asked irritably. "I'm occupied just now."

The wretched old man continued to sob, his frame shaking. At last, he found words—in Greek. "You don't know me, Domenikos?"

The artist sat down heavily. "Manusos? Oh, God in heaven!"

The brother drew a filthy sleeve over his nose. "Is there a God in heaven?"

Domenikos went to the door and summoned Jerónima.

"Oh, God, Manusos," he cried. "What have they done to you?"

"Better ask what I've done to myself," the thick voice said.

Jerónima appeared at the door, then stopped, her face full of alarm. Domenikos put his arm around her and drew her in. "This is my brother, amada," he said. "I'm afraid he hasn't any Spanish."

She looked with fear at the pitiful figure. Then, with a gesture Domenikos would always remember, she bent over and gently embraced Manusos, holding the grimy, tear-streaked face between her hands, smiling compassionately. The old man looked into the clear eyes and wrenched his face into a toothless smile.

Jerónima straightened. "Come," she said.

Domenikos helped him to his feet. "Ask one of the men to help him bathe," he said, "and put him to bed. I'll send for the doctor."

The physician reported that apart from gout Manusos was not in bad health, that rest and food would restore him. Two days later Domenikos found him sufficiently recovered to converse, propped against his pillows, contemplating the remains of breakfast.

"You look better," Domenikos said. "You're safe now. You're home. You'll be all right."

"I know." Tears came. "Such kindness for a sack of old flesh."

"You're my brother. You'd do the same for me. But what happened, Manusos? It's been so long since I heard from you."

"A chronicle of catastrophe. That's been my life for twenty years. My own fault, of course. You warned me. I was a fool."

"Why did you leave Candia?"

"My Katina died, a year ago."

"And your daughters?"

"Two are nuns. Two are married. They left me to die."

"You're exaggerating. Where are they?"

"One is in Venice. Little Katina is in Candia."

"She never came to see you?"

"Oh, I can't reproach her. I wasn't much of a father. Only you were loyal. Your ducats saved my life, literally."

"And your debt?"

Manusos sighed. "That, ostensibly, is my reason for being here. The Serenissima gave me leave to come and beg you for three thousand ducats. Of course, I have no intention of doing so. I don't believe they have any illusions about it. It probably seemed a fair gamble. They knew they'd get nothing from me as things stood."

"But it's a debt of honor."

"Honor is for those who can afford it. I can't."

"I'll see to it. Don't be concerned about it anymore."

"I'm not concerned, Domenikos. It doesn't matter to me."

"It matters to me," Domenikos answered with a softness that failed to conceal the iron of his undertone. "I want nothing to affect papa's name, either in Venice or in Candia. That's important to me."

MANUSOS SOON regained strength. Seventy-three now, he established himself in the household, which now included Jerónima's mother, Doña Ana, as well as Jorge's lovely Alfonsa. With the air of one accustomed to luxuries, he took childish delight in the richness of his new clothes and the quality of the wine served at table. From Jerónima and Alfonsa he garnered enough Spanish to recount his adventures as sponsor of four ill-fated pirate ships. Jorge treated him as a figure of fun, a role that Manusos accepted with good humor, glad to spend his last years in comfort, even as court jester.

He hobbled frequently to the Moorish section of Toledo where he found transient Greeks, many of whom were in dire need. Domenikos gave him gold with which to make himself a missionary to these people, knowing this would restore Manusos' self-respect. And in the winter afternoons, Manusos would sit with Doña Ana, he looking much the older though she was more than eighty now.

Her sole remaining ambition was to live to hold her great-grandchild in her arms. If Alfonsa's casual assertion could be relied on, the infant should be arriving in March. The girl treated her pregnancy as a matter of no great moment. Gently, she declined Jerónima's offers of assistance. "I've always done things for myself. I wouldn't be happy otherwise." The thought of Alfonsa unhappy stayed all hands.

A son was born in the last week of March 1604. Domenikos thought himself even more delighted than Jorge, who had another reason for rejoicing. He had been asked to make plans for the refurbishing of the Casa de Comedias, the theater where Toledo's poet-playwrights presented their pageants of manners and morals.

Four months later, Domenikos was informed that larger apartments in the Casa Villena were available. It was a godsend. The family returned "home," as Domenikos felt it to be, occupying all but a few of the palace's twenty-four rooms. But his contentment was dashed in December when Manusos succumbed to his gout after much agony. Soon afterward Doña Ana also died.

CHAPTER 12

THE EARLY months of 1605 were tranquil. Domenikos and Jorge were working together on a high altar for the Church of the Hospital de la Caridad, in Illescas. Several years before, Domenikos had done a painting for this new church, hoping for Jorge's sake to get the altar commission. Francesco, who now handled most of the business, had accepted a commission for another painting—a Coronation of the Virgin—but had warned against undertaking any major work in Illescas. He had been disturbed by the attitude of the authorities there. Domenikos usually took Francesco's advice. This time he had shrugged it off; he wanted the contract for Jorge.

When in August of 1605 the altar was installed, Domenikos was pleased because so much of the work was Jorge's. As an architect, the young man's abilities now seemed to his father beyond dispute.

The three men returned to Toledo. A week passed and then came the first indication of difficulties that would make the *Espolio* dispute look amiable. Without a word to the painter, the hospital administrators named a sculptor and painter from Madrid to appraise the altar. They proposed 2200 ducats, which didn't even cover the cost of materials and labor; and they alleged that the principal painting, a large *Virgin of Charity*, was "unseemly" because Domenikos had included among the recipients of the Madonna's charity portraits of Angulo and Jorge wearing *lechuguillas*, the current fashion of lettuce-leaf ruffs prescribed by the King.

Narbona, the Madrid advocate who now undertook the artist's case, advised him against appearing before the authorities. So Domenikos wrote a statement complaining that the administrators had carried out the appraisal "like thieves in the night," and deploring the derisory price. He defended the portraits as necessary to the theme of the painting: the Virgin must be surrounded by three mortals, not by saints. He demanded a new appraisal.

Francesco's warnings had been all too well-founded. The next two years were Domenikos' Gethsemane. The Council of Toledo, to whom the hospital first appealed, sided with the artist on every issue. The council twice ordered new appraisals, both of which named a sum more than double that offered by the hospital. But each time the Illescas authorities found grounds for rejecting the appraisal. They finally took the case to the nunciature in Madrid, threatening to go to Rome to His Holiness himself.

Domenikos had one triumph during the long ordeal, when he was summoned by the Royal Council of Castile in Illescas to show cause why he should not pay taxes on the thousand ducats advanced by the hospital. Spanish custom had treated the artist as a craftsman, like a carpenter or a cobbler. Any piece he sold was therefore subject to taxation. The accepted way out would have been for Domenikos to state that his intention was not to sell the altarpiece to the hospital, but to place it in perpetual pawn. This, however, he refused to do.

He rose in the great council chamber and spoke slowly, his agile hands fluttering, clenching. "In what respect," he asked, "does the artist differ from the scholar or the lawyer or the physician? Is the work he does less demanding of spirit and intellect? Does art have a practical value that makes it comparable to a chair or a loaf of bread? The artist glorifies God quite as much as the theologian or the priest. He contributes to our spiritual needs. Therefore his work should be regarded not as craft, but on a par with the contribution of scholars and others who practice the liberal arts."

Domenikos made legal history. The tribunal agreed with him. From April 1606 on, the artist was no longer thought a craftsman.

It was a year later that the deadlock with the hospital was broken by the Council of Toledo's insisting on a final appraisal, binding to both sides. The result had for Domenikos a double bitterness. The "monsters of Illescas," as he now called them, brought in as their expert Pompeo Leoni, the erstwhile friend who had betrayed him over *The Martyrdom of St. Mauritius*. And from the final sum—2093 ducats—there was no appeal. To Jerónima, Domenikos said in despair: "Not even Judas Iscariot was given the opportunity to betray Our Lord twice."

That evening he walked alone in the aromatic gardens overlooking the Tajo. He was sixty-six. His breath came shorter than before. He was, if possible, more inward-seeking, more determined that the painting of his last years be his supreme work, the image of his soul laid bare.

IF THE Illescas disaster hadn't broken Domenikos it had affected his capacity to produce. But, in time, the friendship that was lavished on him, added to the always exhilarating pressure of work, gradually restored his morale. And the frequent and welcome intrusions of his babbling grandson, Gabriel, reminded him that life perpetuated itself, that though his years were numbered he would leave his work as a testament to his love of beauty and of God.

With this return of creative vitality, he felt he was soaring as never before. Immersed in The Book of Revelation and the poetry of Dante, he planned more and more visionary paintings— "an apocalyptic painter," he was called by his friend Fray Hortensio Felix Paravicino, a brilliant young monk and poet who, early in 1609, was sitting for his portrait in the Casa Villena.

Paravicino's respect for El Greco was nearly idolatrous; and Domenikos greatly enjoyed him. Never successful in attracting a pupil who could grasp the principles of his art, he had now found someone capable of understanding the philosophy that underlay it.

His inclination to the mystical was at least partly induced by a desire to flee the Spanish reality. Though never the political animal his friends were, he could see that conditions which might not affect him would intrude on the lives of Jorge, Alfonsa and little Gabriel—for Spain was in decline. The first eleven years of Philip III's reign had been nearly total calamity, both at home and abroad. The war with the Low Countries dragged miserably on, though all hope of victory had perished with Philip II.

By April of 1609 it was evident that Spain had neither the funds nor the stomach to carry on the hostilities. A twelve-year truce, tantamount to surrender, was signed. Spain was near bankruptcy. Except in Toledo and one or two coastal cities, there was little industry or commerce. Only in the service of the court, the great families or the Church was survival possible. Food prices soared. The poor starved, and the rich looked on them with indifference.

To divert public attention from the defeat, an appalling proclamation was issued on the day the armistice was signed: all Moriscos—three hundred thousand Christianized Moors— were to be expelled from the country forthwith.

No external event in his lifetime had ever so stirred and alarmed Domenikos. To anyone who would listen, he protested it as mad and monstrous. Even those who agreed with him at the Fuensalidas Academy urged discretion. One was his old friend

Don Pedro Salazat de Mendoza, for whose Hospital de San Juan Bautista he was painting three altarpieces. "I don't care how important you are in Toledo," Mendoza said. "You can't risk alienating the court or the Church. They can break you."

"It's unspeakable, Pedro. These Moriscos are being driven from a country where they've lived for eight centuries." He laughed angrily. "It would be easier to make a case for driving the Spaniards out. The monarchy is Austrian. And in many ways the Moors have formed this country. Look at what they've done for our music, our art and architecture. This decree stinks of depravity."

Mendoza stared at his friend, astonished. "Does this mean that you plan to set yourself in public against the King?"

But there was no answer. The painter didn't hear him.

FIRST THERE was a rustling, the abrasion of cloth against cloth, or a breath taken in quickly. Then there was a trace of light, barely detectable through eyes scarcely opened; and at last, as vision cleared, there was the subdued illumination of a room. Was it evening? He couldn't be certain. He opened his mouth to speak, but found his lips, his palate, dry. He tried to shift his position and discovered that his right leg refused to respond. Once more he attempted to speak.

"What's happened?" He twisted his head and peered into the anxious eyes of Jerónima, who sat holding his chilled hand.

"You've been ill, my poor Domenikos. Very, very ill."

With a difficulty that frightened him, he raised his free hand to his brow, noting a peculiar thickness in his perceptions. "Have I received the sacraments?"

She nodded. "But now, if you're careful, the doctor thinks you'll stay with us for a long time, may it please God." She gently kissed his hand. "How do you feel?"

He put his hand over his heart. "Dull pain."

"You had an apoplexy. What's your last recollection?"

He considered. "I think I was arguing with Mendoza." He hesitated. "About the expulsion of the Moriscos? Was that it?"

"Oh, good. You do remember. Your mind's undamaged. Pedro said he'd never seen you so upset." She snorted. "And you say you don't care about politics!"

He grinned. "I promise not to, ever again."

Her mood changed, her tone became husky. "You called for me and for Jorge and Gabriel and Alfonsa. You tore the heart right out of me. Over and over again, like a litany, you called our names." Tears welled up, and she leaned over to kiss him. "I knew then that you had affection for me, in your own way."

"What's the matter with you?" he said shrilly. "Did you think I'd call for paint? Don't you know I love you?"

As he gained strength, Domenikos discovered that far from having lost his powers, he had attained a new fluency. He was ecstatic. He began a number of canvases, devoting himself now to one, now to another. Cadaverous, emaciated, but possessed by the conviction that his survival depended on work, he drove himself feverishly. And he seemed to flourish beneath this terrible pressure. Only Paravicino knew that he had embarked upon his painting of *The Opening of the Fifth Seal*, the fruit of long brooding on the Apocalypse. So awed and frightened was even Domenikos by what he was now creating that he could not talk about it to his own family.

THE SECOND attack devastated the household, but it was not nearly so severe as the first. Domenikos promised that, after recovery, he would curtail his schedule. At first he contented himself with watching Jorge's architectural successes and the efficiency with which he presided over the workshops. But after a while he became gloomy on his own account. "I'm not allowed to work, that's what's killing me," he said to Angulo. "I'm perishing, as plants do in the autumn. The frost of age is creeping over my leaves. Two hours a day. That's all they'll give me in my studio."

The lawyer was amused. "What self-pity. You ought to be ashamed. You'll be around as long as Titian was, and then, no doubt, you'll be run down in the street by an ass and cart."

"My friend, I'm dying. Every day I feel more of life's force seeping from me. I think I should do something about a burial place in Santo Domingo. My altarpieces there are the first work I did in Toledo. I'd like to lie in the place where I began."

The lawyer nodded. "Jorge and I will see to it."

"A chapel near the transept. I'll make a painting for it."

"We'll arrange it. Stop fretting, Greco. You're not dead yet."

"But soon." His voice grew almost inaudible. "Soon now."

It seemed paradoxical that the occasion for a revival of Domenikos' spirits should be Angulo's announcement that a funerary chapel in Santo Domingo had been placed at his disposal. He at once began to design the painting for his ultimate resting place, an *Adoration of the Shepherds*, the theme of the first freely painted work he had ever done for Titian, more than half a century earlier. But this version would compare in intensity, in luminosity, in exaggeration of form with only one of his other pictures, an *Immaculate Conception* on which he was then still working.

This was one of several paintings he had undertaken, before his first seizure, for the new Oballe Chapel of the Church of San Vicente in Toledo. In contrast to its dramatic treatment was a tranquil, intimate painting of *The Visitation*, everything about which suggested mystery, secrecy and, above all, simplicity. For he had chosen to depict the moment after Mary and Elisabeth had spoken, and could only look at each other in silent astonishment, in awe. What was happening in their wombs was miraculous. They had been touched by the hand of God. Thus did Domenikos explain it to his oldest and dearest friend, Luis de Castilla.

ONE DECEMBER afternoon in 1612, Paravicino, now a prior, was chatting with Domenikos and Jorge in the spacious salon of the Casa Villena. Suddenly an odd urgency came into his tone and he turned to the painter. "When will you show me the *Fifth Seal?*"

Domenikos fell back against the couch, as if he had been struck. In the gathering darkness of the afternoon, he looked at the ceiling, at last speaking thickly. "It was only this morning that I felt I'd opened it completely." Still giddy, he struggled to his feet. "We'll have to bring candles, but I think you'd better see it now."

Paravicino rose quickly to take the master's arm, and protested, "It can wait until there's full light."

The painter stubbornly shook his head. "I don't think so."

Aided by the monk and a puzzled Jorge, he shuffled slowly through the long series of rooms, the broad doorways, the lofty, narrow corridors that separated the salon from his studio. Servants were summoned to bring all the candelabra in the house.

Aware of the oddness of the request, these domestics called

THE ASSUMPTION OF THE VIRGIN — BY EL GRECO

the other members of the household—the painters, the carpenters, the gilders and, lastly, Jerónima, Alfonsa and nine-year-old Gabriel. All hastened to the master's studio. Silent, all stood against the wall, watching with fascination as his bent figure, flanked by Jorge and Paravicino, stood in the brilliant amber of the candlelight before the picture the prior had asked about.

The Opening of the Fifth Seal of the Apocalypse wasn't a very big painting. Nor was it brilliant in range of tone or color. There was no evidence of landscape. Indeed, it lacked everything—except people, all nude save for a blue-robed figure in the left foreground. And beyond the strange, straining, tormented souls, there was a sky, muddy and morose, pierced with a light one could only imagine to be apocalyptic. As he stared at this painting in silence, Domenikos perceived that he could press his art no further.

Solemnly, Paravicino recited the scriptural words: " 'And when he had opened the fifth seal, I saw under the altar the souls of them that were slain for the word of God, and for the testimony which they held: And they cried with a loud voice, saying, How long, O Lord . . . dost thou not judge and avenge our blood on them that dwell on the earth? And white robes were given unto every one of them; and it was said unto them, that they should rest yet for a little season, until their fellow-servants also and their brethren, that should be killed as they were, should be fulfilled.' "

The final phrase hung portentously in the great room. Domenikos slowly revolved on the arms of his son and young friend and, in the dancing light of the candles, saw that the entire household was gathered. He lifted a tired arm in greeting. "I thank you from my heart for this gesture of affection. I hope I shall rest with you yet for a little season." He turned, looking first at the weeping Jorge, then at his painting. He smiled. "But I am fulfilled."

IT WAS a very little season. On April 7, 1614, Domenikos Theotokopoulos, at peace with man and God, died in his sleep.

ACKNOWLEDGMENTS

The condensations in this volume have been created by The Reader's Digest
Association, Inc., and are used by permission of and special arrangement with
the publishers and the holders of the respective copyrights.
THE AUTOBIOGRAPHY OF BENJAMIN FRANKLIN, copyright © 1964 by Yale
University, is reprinted by permission of Yale University Press.
MARY QUEEN OF SCOTS, original full-length version copyright © 1969 by Antonia
Fraser, abridged edition copyright © 1978 by Antonia Fraser, is reprinted by permission of
Delacorte Press and George Weidenfeld & Nicolson Limited.
WILL ROGERS: HIS LIFE AND TIMES, copyright © 1973 by American Heritage, a
division of Forbes Inc., is reprinted by permission of American Heritage, a division of
Forbes Inc.
THE ELEANOR ROOSEVELT STORY, copyright © 1965 by Archibald MacLeish, is
reprinted by permission of Houghton Mifflin Company and The Estate of Archibald
MacLeish.
COLOR FROM A LIGHT WITHIN, copyright © 1967 by Donald Braider, is reprinted
by permission of John Hawkins & Associates, Inc.

ILLUSTRATION CREDITS

COVER: Will Rogers, photo Brown Brothers; El Greco, The Granger Collection, New York; Ben
Franklin, from *Handbook of Early Advertising Art* by Clarence P. Hornung, Dover Publications,
Inc.; Mary Stuart, Bibliothèque Nationale, Paris; Eleanor Roosevelt, courtesy of James Roosevelt.
INSERT: The Palace of Holyrood, Royal Commission on Ancient Monuments, Edinburgh,
Scotland.
THE AUTOBIOGRAPHY OF BENJAMIN FRANKLIN: *Page 6:* portrait engraved after painting
by Alonzo Chappel, The Granger Collection, New York. *12, 76, 81:* from *The Autobiography*,
reproduced by permission of The Huntington Library, San Marino, California. *13:* Culver Pictures,
Inc. *18, 20, 70, 89:* The Bettmann Archive. *25:* American Philosophical Society Library,
Philadelphia. *26:* Massachusetts Historical Society, Boston. *33, 35, 49, 51, 123:* The Granger
Collection, New York. *36:* drawing by Victor Mays. *41, 57, 92:* engravings by Wm. Birch & Son, The
Granger Collection, New York. *44, 58:* drawings by Thomas Beecham. *65, 66, 98:* Benjamin
Franklin Papers, Yale University Library. *68:* National Museum of American History, Smithsonian
Institution. *74:* engraving by Wm. Birch & Son, American Philosophical Society Library,
Philadelphia. *84:* title page from only existing copy of the *Almanack*, Rosenbach Museum & Library,
Philadelphia. *86:* illustration by O. Pelton, Benjamin Franklin Papers, Yale University Library. *100:*
engraving by J. W. Steel, The Historical Society of Pennsylvania. *105:* detail of engraving by J.
Hulett, The Granger Collection, New York. *107:* engraving from painting by Joseph B. Smith, Old
John Street United Methodist Church, New York. *108:* cartoon from the *Pennsylvania Gazette*,
American Philosophical Society Library, Philadelphia. *116:* engraving by A. Anderson, The
Historical Society of Pennsylvania.